P9-BBP-415

Merriam-Webster's

Pocket Thesaurus

Merriam-Webster's

Pocket Thesaurus

Merriam-Webster, Incorporated
Springfield, Massachusetts

A GENUINE MERRIAM-WEBSTER

The name *Webster* alone is no guarantee of excellence. It is used by a number of publishers and may serve mainly to mislead an unwary buyer.

Merriam-Webster™ is the registered trademark you should look for when you consider the purchase of dictionaries or other fine reference books. It carries the reputation of a company that has been publishing since 1831 and is your assurance of quality and authority.

Library of Congress Cataloging-in-Publication Data

Merriam-Webster's pocket thesaurus.
p. cm.
ISBN 0-87779-524-X
1. English language—Synonyms and antonyms.
I. Merriam-Webster, Inc.
PE1591.M479 2002
423'.1—dc21

2002006751

Made in the United States of America

7 8 9 10 DF:NFWP 07060504

Preface

Merriam-Webster's Pocket Thesaurus is an extremely concise guide for the understanding and selection of synonyms, near synonyms, and antonyms. This thesaurus is the smallest of the family of thesauruses published by Merriam-Webster. It is intended to serve as a quick reference for those who want a compact and handy thesaurus. *As is the case with any thesaurus, it is essential that this book be used in conjunction with an adequate dictionary.*

This thesaurus shares many details of presentation with the more comprehensive members of the Merriam-Webster family, such as *Merriam-Webster's Collegiate Thesaurus*. Like other Merriam-Webster thesauruses, it includes lists of related words (near synonyms) and antonyms at most entries to provide users with additional significant and pertinent assistance. It also provides at each main entry a concise statement of the meaning shared by the listed synonyms, and it includes an entry at its own alphabetical place for every synonym that appears at a main entry.

However, conciseness of presentation necessarily requires special treatment of entries, and this book has a number of special features uniquely its own. Users need to be familiar with the following major features of this thesaurus.

Entry Order The body of the book consists of main and secondary entries introduced by alphabetically ordered boldface headwords.

Homographs (words spelled the same but having different meanings) are given separate entries and are identified with an italic part-of-speech label, as at **fair** *adj* and **fair** *n* for the adjective *fair* and the noun *fair*.

Headwords that are synonyms and alphabetically close to each other are sometimes listed together, as **finicky, finicking, finical.**

Headwords ordinarily conform to normal dictionary practice: nouns are styled as singulars; verbs as infinitives. Special situations, such as plural usage, are signaled by the use of boldface, as at the entry **wage, wages**, or at sense 2 of **game**, where **games** is shown as the alternate form of the headword synonymous with *athletics*.

Main Entry and Its Basic Elements Each main entry consists of a headword followed by a part-of-speech label when needed, a sense number when needed, a meaning core, and a list of synonyms. Lists of related words (near synonyms) and antonyms follow the synonym list.

The meaning core is marked by a small bullet and indicates the area of meaning shared by the synonyms.

Two or more meanings (or senses) of a headword are separated and numbered with a boldface numeral (as **1**).

The italic abbreviation *syn* introduces a synonym list; the italic abbreviation *rel* introduces a list of related words (near synonyms); the italic abbreviation *ant* introduces a list of antonyms. More information about *rel* and *ant* lists is provided in the section on Main and Secondary Entries: Elements Common to Both, which appears below.

Secondary Entry and Its Basic Elements A secondary entry consists of a boldface headword followed by a part-of-speech label when needed, a sense number when needed, and a list of synonyms. The first synonym in the list appear in small capitals and serves as a cross-reference to the main entry at which the meaning core appears. Lists of related words and antonyms may be included as well.

Main and Secondary Entries: Elements Common to Both Lists of related words and antonyms may appear at both main entries and secondary entries.

The italic abbreviation *rel* introduces a list of related words. The related words—words that are almost but not quite synonymous with the headword—are included in the entry after the synonym list. A *rel* list is often composed of words separated into subgroups that each share a common likeness or relation with the headword and its synonyms. Subgroups within *rel* lists are separated by semicolons (see also the section on Punctuation, below).

Related words are chosen because they are distinctly related to the headword, and the list of related words will be slightly different at the entries for each word in the synonym list. Therefore, the user should check the list of related words at the entries for each synonym in the list for the most complete listing of related words.

The italic abbreviation *ant* introduces an antonym or list of antonyms. Within *ant* lists, commas are used between words that are synonyms of one another; semicolons are used to separate words that do not have such a relationship (see also the section on Punctuation, below).

In lists of antonyms, italic notations in parentheses indicate the limited use or application in which the word serves as an antonym to the headword (see the section on Punctuation, below).

At some entries users are directed to another entry at which the appropriate *rel* or *ant* list can be found, as at **mistreat,** where the user is directed to the entry for *ill-treat* to find related words, or at **hefty**, where the user is directed to the entry for *heavy* to find antonyms. When the user is being directed to a multisense entry, the cross-reference includes the number of the sense that includes the relevant *syn* and/or *rel* list, as **resort** *n,* where users are directed to sense 2 at the entry for *resource*.

Punctuation A comma links items (as synonyms or members of a single group or subgroup of related words or antonyms) that are alike in their relation to the headword. A semicolon signals a break in the continuity and is used in *rel* and *ant* lists to separate subgroups of words which differ in their relation to the headword, as in the *rel* list at **fabulous** and the *ant* list at **facile.**

Parentheses enclose a particle or particles usually associated with a word. They may accompany a headword, as **rely** (on *or* upon), or a word in a list, as *fail (in)* in the *ant* list at **fulfill** and *fall short (of)* at another *ant* list in the same entry.

Parentheses also enclose material indicating a typical or, occasionally, a sole object of reference, as in the meaning core at **money** or the *ant* list at **gaudy**, where the antonym *quiet* carries the parenthetical note *(in taste or style)*.

A

abaft · toward or at the stern (of a vessel) *syn* aft, astern *rel* after, rear, back, posterior, hind, hinder *ant* afore

abandon *vb* **1** · to quit absolutely *syn* desert, forsake *rel* discard, cast, scrap, junk; reject, repudiate, decline *ant* reclaim **2** *syn* RELINQUISH, surrender, yield, resign, leave *ant* cherish (*hopes, opinions*); restrain (*oneself*)

abandon *n*, *syn* UNCONSTRAINT, spontaneity *rel* license, freedom, liberty; relaxation, laxity, laxness, looseness *ant* self-restraint

abandoned · utterly depraved *syn* reprobate, profligate, dissolute *rel* depraved, debauched, perverted, debased; degenerate, corrupt, vicious; wanton, lewd, lascivious, libidinous, lecherous, licentious *ant* redeemed, regenerate

abase · to lower in one's own estimation or in that of others *syn* demean, debase, degrade, humble, humiliate *rel* cringe, truckle, cower, fawn, toady; grovel, wallow; abash, discomfit, disconcert, embarrass; mortify *ant* exalt; extol (*especially oneself*)

abash *syn* EMBARRASS, discomfit, disconcert, faze, rattle *rel* fluster, flurry, discompose, perturb, disturb, agitate; chagrin, mortify; confound, dumbfound, nonplus, puzzle *ant* embolden; reassure

abate **1** *syn* ABOLISH, extinguish, annihilate *rel* end, terminate, close; annul, void, abrogate; cancel, obliterate, erase; nullify, invalidate *ant* perpetuate **2** *syn* DECREASE, reduce, diminish, lessen *rel* retard, slow, slacken, delay; moderate, temper; mitigate, lighten, alleviate; relieve *ant* augment; accelerate (*pace, speed*); intensify (*hopes, fears, a fever*) **3** · to die down in force or intensity *syn* subside, wane, ebb *rel* dwindle, diminish, decrease *ant* rise; revive

abatement *syn* DEDUCTION, rebate, discount *ant* addition

abbey *syn* CLOISTER, convent, nunnery, monastery, priory

abbreviate *syn* SHORTEN, abridge, curtail *rel* reduce, decrease, lessen; contract, compress, shrink, condense; attenuate, extenuate, thin *ant* elongate, lengthen

abdicate · to give up formally or definitely a position of trust, honor, or glory *syn* renounce, resign *rel* relinquish, surrender, abandon, leave *ant* assume; usurp

abdomen · the part of the body between the chest and the pelvis *syn* belly, stomach, paunch, gut

abduct · to carry off (a person) surreptitiously for an illegal purpose *syn* kidnap *rel* seduce, entice, lure, inveigle

aberrant *syn* ABNORMAL, atypical *rel* divergent, different, disparate; irregular, anomalous, unnatural; exceptional; singular, peculiar, odd, strange, eccentric *ant* true (*to a type*)

aberration **1** *syn* DEVIATION, deflection *rel* abnormality, aberrancy; error, blunder, mistake, slip, lapse; fault, failing; anomaly *ant* conformity; regularity **2** · mental disorder *syn* derangement, alienation *rel* insanity, lunacy, dementia; delusion, hallucination, illusion; mania, delirium, hysteria, frenzy *ant* soundness (*of mind*)

abet *syn* INCITE, foment, instigate *rel* aid, assist, help; back, support, uphold; cooperate, concur; forward, further, promote, advance *ant* deter (*with a personal subject*)

abettor *syn* CONFEDERATE, accessory, accomplice, conspirator

abeyant *syn* LATENT, dormant, quiescent, potential *rel* deferred, suspended, postponed, stayed, intermitted; suppressed, repressed *ant* operative; active; revived

abhor *syn* HATE, abominate, loathe, detest *rel* despise, contemn, scorn; shun, avoid, eschew *ant* admire

abhorrence • a feeling of extreme disgust or dislike *syn* detestation, loathing, abomination, hatred, hate *rel* distaste, repugnance, repellency; horror, dismay *ant* admiration; enjoyment

abhorrent **1** *syn* HATEFUL, abominable, detestable, odious *rel* contemptible, despicable, scurvy; execrable, damnable *ant* admirable; enjoyable **2** *syn* REPUGNANT, repellent, obnoxious, distasteful, invidious *rel* antipathetic; uncongenial, unsympathetic; foreign, alien *ant* congenial

abide **1** *syn* STAY, wait, remain, tarry, linger *rel* dwell, reside, live, sojourn, lodge; stick, cleave, cling, adhere *ant* depart **2** *syn* CONTINUE, endure, last, persist *rel* stay, remain, linger; subsist, exist, live *ant* pass **3** *syn* BEAR, endure, suffer, tolerate, stand, brook *rel* submit, yield, bow, defer; acquiesce, accede, consent, assent; accept, receive, take

ability • physical, mental, or legal power to perform *syn* capacity, capability *rel* power, strength, might, force, energy; proficiency, skill, adeptness; aptitude, talent, genius, faculty, gift; competence, qualification *ant* inability, incapacity

abject *syn* MEAN, ignoble, sordid *rel* servile, slavish, menial, subservient; miserable, wretched; cringing, truckling, cowering; groveling; abased, demeaned, humbled, humiliated *ant* exalted (*in rank, state, condition, mood, behavior*); imperious (*in manner, speech, attitude*)

abjure • to abandon irrevocably and, usu., with solemnity or publicity *syn* renounce, forswear, recant, retract *rel* forgo, forbear, eschew; abstain, refrain; reject, repudiate, spurn, decline; abandon, relinquish *ant* pledge (*allegiance, a vow*); elect (*a way of life, a means to an end, an end*)

able • having marked power or fitness for work *syn* capable, competent, qualified *rel* skilled, skillful, proficient, expert; efficient, effective; clever, brilliant, intelligent, smart *ant* inept; unable

abnegate *syn* FORGO, sacrifice, eschew, forbear *rel* renounce, abdicate; surrender, abandon, relinquish, waive; abstain, refrain *ant* indulge (in)

abnegation *syn* RENUNCIATION, self-abnegation, self-denial *rel* forgoing, forbearance, eschewal; abstinence, abstemiousness, continence, temperance; restraining, curbing, bridling *ant* indulgence, self-indulgence

abnormal • deviating markedly from the rule or standard of its kind *syn* atypical, aberrant *rel* irregular, unnatural, anomalous; unusual, unwonted, uncustomary, unaccustomed; monstrous, prodigious *ant* normal

abode *syn* HABITATION, dwelling, residence, domicile, home, house

abolish • to make nonexistent *syn* annihilate, extinguish, abate *rel* extirpate, eradicate, wipe, exterminate; obliterate, efface, blot out, expunge, erase; negate, nullify, annul, abrogate *ant* establish

abominable *syn* HATEFUL, detestable, odious, abhorrent *rel* execrable, damnable, accursed, cursed; scurvy, despicable, contemptible, sorry; loathsome, repulsive, revolting, repugnant, offensive; horrid, horrible *ant* laudable; enjoyable, delightful

abominate *syn* HATE, loathe, detest, abhor *rel* despise, contemn, scorn, disdain; execrate, objurgate, curse, damn *ant* esteem; enjoy

abomination **1** *syn* ABHORRENCE, detestation, loathing, hatred, hate *rel* scorn, despite, contempt, disdain; execration, objurgation *ant* esteem; enjoyment **2** · a person or thing from which one shrinks with intense dislike *syn* anathema, bugbear, bête noire *rel* plague, pest, annoyance; aversion, antipathy *ant* joy

aboriginal *syn* NATIVE, indigenous, autochthonous *rel* primitive, primordial, primeval, pristine; savage, barbaric, barbarian, barbarous

abortive *syn* FUTILE, fruitless, vain, bootless *rel* immature, unmatured, unripe; unformed, formless; ineffectual, ineffective, inefficacious; unfortunate, unlucky *ant* consummated

abound *syn* TEEM, overflow, swarm *rel* predominate, preponderate *ant* fail, fall short

about · in reference to *syn* concerning, regarding, respecting

above · at a higher level *syn* over *ant* below

aboveboard *syn* STRAIGHFORWARD, forthright *rel* open, frank, candid; honest, upright, scrupulous; fair, impartial, just; ingenuous, unsophisticated, artless, natural *ant* underhand, underhanded

abracadabra *syn* GIBBERISH, hocus-pocus, mummery *rel* magic, sorcery, thaumaturgy; amulet, charm, fetish

abrade · to affect a surface by rubbing, scraping, or wearing away *syn* excoriate, chafe, fret, gall *rel* scrape, scratch, grate, grind, rasp; injure, damage, impair, mar; irritate, exasperate

abridge *syn* SHORTEN, curtail, abbreviate, retrench *rel* condense, contract, compress, shrink; cut, slash; limit, restrict; reduce, diminish, decrease *ant* expand; extend

abridgment · a condensation of a larger work *syn* abstract, epitome, brief, synopsis, conspectus *rel* digest, précis, compendium, sketch, syllabus *ant* expansion

abrogate **1** *syn* ANNUL, vacate, quash, void *rel* abolish, extinguish, abate *ant* institute (*by enacting, decreeing*) **2** *syn* NULLIFY, annul, negate, invalidate *rel* abolish, annihilate, extinguish; destroy, demolish; ruin, wreck; cancel, obliterate, blot out, erase *ant* establish, fix (*a right, a character, a quality, a custom*)

abrupt **1** *syn* STEEP, precipitous, sheer *rel* perpendicular, vertical, plumb *ant* sloping **2** *syn* PRECIPITATE, sudden, headlong, impetuous, hasty *rel* quick, speedy, fast; hurried, hastened; unceremonious; curt, brusque, bluff *ant* deliberate, leisurely

abscess · a localized swollen area of infection containing pus *syn* boil, furuncle, carbuncle, pimple, pustule

abscond *syn* ESCAPE, decamp, flee, fly *rel* depart, leave, quit, go *ant* give (*oneself*) up

absence *syn* LACK, want, dearth, defect, privation *rel* need, necessity, exigency; deficiency; destitution; void, vacuum, *ant* presence

absent *syn* ABSTRACTED, preoccupied, absentminded, distraught *rel* engrossed, absorbed, intent, rapt; heedless, inadvertent; careless; oblivious, unmindful, forgetful *ant* attentive

absentminded *syn* ABSTRACTED, absent, preoccupied, distraught *rel* inattentive, thoughtless, inconsiderate; heedless, inadvertent, careless; unobserving, unseeing, unperceiving, unnoticing *ant* wide-awake

absolute **1** *syn* PURE, simple, sheer *rel* perfect, whole, entire; real, true; abstract, ideal; consummate, finished *ant* mixed, qualified **2** · exercising power or authority without external restraint *syn* autocratic, arbitrary, despotic, tyrannical, tyrannous *rel* totalitarian, authoritarian; dictatorial, magisterial; domineering, imperious, masterful *ant* restrained; limited **3** *syn* ULTIMATE, categorical *rel* ideal, transcendent, transcendental, abstract; independent, autonomous, free, sovereign; infinite, eternal, boundless *ant* conditioned

absolution *syn* PARDON, amnesty *rel* forgiveness, remission *ant* condemnation

absolve *syn* EXCULPATE, exonerate, acquit, vindicate *rel* pardon, forgive, remit, excuse; release, free, discharge *ant* hold (*to a promise, an obligation*); charge (*with a sin, the blame, the responsibility*)

absorb **1** · to take (something) in so as to become imbued with it or to make it a part of one's being *syn* imbibe, assimilate *rel* soak, saturate, impregnate; receive, take; incorporate, embody, identify *ant* exude, give out **2** *syn* MONOPOLIZE, engross, consume *rel* fix, fasten; rivet, secure; immerse, submerge *ant* dissipate (*time, attention, energies*)

absorbed *syn* INTENT, engrossed, rapt *rel* immersed; riveted; fixed, fastened *ant* distracted

absorbing *syn* INTERESTING, engrossing, intriguing *ant* irksome

abstain *syn* REFRAIN, forbear *rel* forgo, eschew, abnegate; decline, refuse, spurn, reject; desist, stop *ant* indulge

abstemiousness *syn* TEMPERANCE, abstinence, sobriety, continence *rel* self-denial, self-abnegation, renunciation; asceticism, austerity *ant* gluttony

abstinence *syn* TEMPERANCE, continence, abstemiousness, sobriety *rel* forbearance, refrainment; forgoing, eschewal, abnegation; renunciation, self-denial, self-abnegation *ant* self-indulgence

abstract *adj* · having conceptual rather than concrete existence *syn* ideal, transcendent, transcendental *rel* universal, general, generic; ultimate, absolute, categorical *ant* concrete

abstract *n, syn* ABRIDGMENT, brief, synopsis, epitome, conspectus *rel* sketch, précis, aperçu, compendium, digest *ant* amplification

abstract *vb, syn* DETACH, disengage *rel* separate, part, divorce, divide; purloin, filch, steal *ant* insert, introduce

abstracted · inattentive to what presently claims or demands consideration *syn* preoccupied, absent, absentminded, distraught *rel* intent, engrossed; oblivious, unmindful, forgetful; ignoring, overlooking, disregarding *ant* alert

abstruse *syn* RECONDITE, occult, esoteric *rel* complex, complicated, intricate, knotty; abstract, ideal; enigmatic, cryptic, dark, obscure *ant* obvious, plain

absurd *syn* FOOLISH, silly, preposterous *rel* ludicrous, ridiculous, laughable, droll, funny, comic; irrational, unreasonable; asinine, silly, fatuous, simple *ant* rational, sensible

abundant *syn* PLENTIFUL, copious, ample, plenteous *rel* abounding, teeming, overflowing; profuse, lavish, luxuriant, lush, exuberant *ant* scarce

abuse *vb* · to use or treat a person or thing improperly or wrongfully *syn* misuse, mistreat, maltreat, ill-treat, outrage *rel* hurt, injure, harm, damage, impair, mar, spoil; wrong, persecute, oppress; pervert, corrupt, debase, debauch, vitiate *ant* respect, honor

abuse *n* • vehemently expressed condemnation or disapproval *syn* vituperation, invective, obloquy, scurrility, billingsgate *rel* aspersion, reflection, stricture, animadversion; reviling, railing, rating, berating, scold; vilification, malignment *ant* adulation

abusive • coarse, insulting, and contemptuous in character or utterance *syn* opprobrious, vituperative, contumelious, scurrilous *rel* insulting, affronting, offending, outraging; aspersing, maligning, vilifying *ant* complementary; respectful

abutment *syn* BUTTRESS, pier

abutting *syn* ADJACENT, contiguous, adjoining, tangent, conterminous, juxtaposed *rel* close, near, nigh, nearby; joining, connecting; nearest, next; impinging

abysm *syn* GULF, chasm, abyss

abysmal *syn* DEEP, profound *rel* illimitable, infinite

abyss *syn* GULF, chasm, abysm

academic 1 *syn* PEDANTIC, scholastic, bookish *rel* dry, arid; erudite, scholarly, learned 2 *syn* THEORETICAL, speculative

accede *syn* ASSENT, acquiesce, consent, agree, subscribe *rel* concur, cooperate; yield, submit, defer, relent; allow, permit, let *ant* demur

accelerate *syn* SPEED, quicken, hurry, hasten, precipitate *rel* forward, further, advance, promote; drive, impel, move *ant* decelerate; retard

accent 1 *syn* EMPHASIS, stress, accentuation *rel* beat, pulse, throb, pulsation; rhythm, cadence, meter 2 *syn* INFLECTION, intonation *rel* pronunciation, enunciation, articulation

accentuation *syn* EMPHASIS, accent, stress *rel* rhythm, cadence, meter; pronunciation, enunciation, articulation *ant* inaccentuation

accept *syn* RECEIVE, admit, take *rel* adopt, embrace, espouse; acquiesce, assent, agree, subscribe *ant* reject

acceptance • the act or fact of accepting or the state of being accepted *syn* acceptation

acceptation 1 *syn* MEANING, sense, signification, significance, import 2 *syn* ACCEPTANCE

access 1 *syn* ENTRANCE, ingress, entrée, entry *rel* approaching, approach, nearing; admittance, admission; way, route, passage; door, portal, gate, gateway *ant* outlet 2 *syn* FIT, accession, attack, paroxysm, spasm, convulsion *rel* onset, onslaught, assault; seizure, clutch, taking; twinge, pain, stitch, pang, throe

accession 1 *syn* ADDITION, accretion, increment *ant* discard 2 *syn* FIT, access, attack, paroxysm, spasm, convulsion *rel* see ACCESS 2

accessory *n* 1 *syn* APPENDAGE, appurtenance, adjunct *rel* concomitant, accompaniment; addition, accretion, increment 2 *syn* CONFEDERATE, accomplice, abettor, conspirator *ant* principal

accessory *adj, syn* AUXILIARY, contributory, subsidiary, adjuvant, ancillary, subservient *rel* secondary, collateral, tributary, subordinate; concomitant, concurrent, coincident; incidental, adventitious, accidental *ant* constituent, integral; principal (*in law*)

accident 1 *syn* QUALITY, character, attribute, property *rel* mark; sign, note, badge, token, symptom; characteristic, peculiarity *ant* substance (*in philosophy*) 2 *syn* CHANCE, hazard, luck, fortune, hap *rel* contingency, fortuity, adventitiousness *ant* design, intent 3 · chance or a chance event bringing injury or loss *syn* casualty, mishap *rel* disaster, catastrophe; mischance, misfortune, mishap

accidental · not amenable to planning or prediction *syn* casual, fortuitous, contingent, incidental *rel* haphazard, random, hit-or-miss, chance; unintended, undesigned, unpurposed; contingent, dependent, conditional *ant* planned; essential

acclaim *vb, syn* PRAISE, extol, laud, eulogize *rel* applaud, cheer, root; exalt, magnify; glorify, honor *ant* vituperate

acclaim *n, syn* APPLAUSE, acclamation, plaudits *rel* homage, honor, reverence; renown, glory, éclat, fame; cheer *ant* vituperation

acclamation *syn* APPLAUSE, acclaim, plaudits *rel, ant* see ACCLAIM

acclimate *syn* HARDEN, acclimatize, season *rel* accustom, habituate; adapt, adjust, conform

acclimatize *syn* HARDEN, acclimate, season *rel* see ACCLIMATE

accommodate 1 *syn* ADAPT, adjust, conform, reconcile *rel* yield, submit, bow, defer; modify, change, alter, vary; temper, moderate, qualify *ant* constrain 2 *syn* OBLIGE, favor *rel* help, aid, assist; gratify, gladden, please; indulge, humor *ant* incommode 3 *syn* CONTAIN, hold *rel* lodge, house, board, shelter, harbor, entertain; take (in), receive, admit

accompaniment · something attendant upon or found in association with another thing *syn* concomitant

accompany · to go or be together with *syn* attend, conduct, escort, convoy, chaperon *rel* associate, link, combine, join; guide, lead, pilot

accomplice *syn* CONFEDERATE, accessory, abettor, conspirator

accomplish *syn* PERFORM, achieve, effect, fulfill, discharge, execute *rel* complete, finish, conclude, close; consummate; implement, enforce *ant* undo

accomplished *syn* CONSUMMATE, finished *rel* proficient, skillful, skilled, adept, expert, masterly; versatile, many-sided, all-around

accomplishment *syn* ACQUIREMENT, attainment, acquisition *rel* art, skill, craft; proficiency, adeptness, expertness

accord *vb* 1 *syn* AGREE, harmonize, correspond, tally, conform, square, jibe *rel* concur, coincide, agree; blend, fuse, merge, coalesce, mix; cohere, adhere, stick *ant* conflict 2 *syn* GRANT, vouchsafe, concede, award *rel* deign, condescend, stoop; bestow, present, confer, give *ant* withhold

accord *n* 1 *syn* HARMONY, concord, consonance *rel* agreement, acquiescence, consent; union, solidarity, unity; sympathy, affinity, attraction *ant* dissension, strife; antagonism 2 *syn* AGREEMENT, understanding *rel* pact, compact, treaty, entente, concordat, contract

accordingly *syn* THEREFORE, so, consequently, hence, then

accost *syn* ADDRESS, greet, hail, salute *rel* speak, talk, converse; affront, offend, insult

account *n* 1 *syn* USE, service, advantage, profit, avail *rel* benefit; usefulness, utility; worth, value 2 · a statement of actual events or conditions or of purported occurrences or conditions *syn* report, chronicle, version, story

account *vb* 1 *syn* CONSIDER, deem, regard, reckon *rel* regard, esteem; rate, appraise, evaluate, assess, estimate 2 *syn* EXPLAIN, justify, rationalize *rel* answer; expound, elucidate, interpret

accountable *syn* RESPONSIBLE, answerable, amenable, liable *rel* unaccountable

accouter *syn* FURNISH, equip, arm, outfit, appoint *rel* array, attire, clothe, dress; deck, adorn, embellish, decorate

accredit **1** *syn* APPROVE, certify, endorse, sanction *rel* recommend, commend; vouch, attest **2** *syn* AUTHORIZE, commission, license **3** *syn* ASCRIBE, credit, charge, assign, attribute, impute *rel* attach, fasten; connect, link, associate, join

accretion *syn* ADDITION, increment, accession *rel* adjunct, appendage; adhesion, cohesion; increase, augmentation, enlargement

accumulate • to bring together so as to make a store or great quantity *syn* amass, hoard *rel* gather, collect; heap, pile, stack *ant* dissipate

accumulative *syn* CUMULATIVE, summative, additive *rel* aggregative, conglomerative; multiplicative, augmentative

accurate *syn* CORRECT, exact, precise, nice, right *rel* true, veracious, truthful; impeccable, errorless, flawless, faultless; punctilious, meticulous, careful *ant* inaccurate

accursed *syn* EXECRABLE, damnable, cursed *rel* abominable, odious, hateful, abhorrent, detestable; revolting, repulsive, loathsome, offensive, repugnant *ant* blessed

accuse • to declare a person guilty of a fault or offense *syn* charge, incriminate, indict, impeach, arraign *rel* denounce, blame, reprobate, censure, criticize *ant* exculpate

accustom *syn* HABITUATE, addict, inure *rel* adapt, accommodate, adjust; harden, season, acclimatize *ant* disaccustom

accustomed *syn* USUAL, wonted, customary, habitual *rel* natural, normal, regular, typical; common, ordinary, familiar *ant* unaccustomed

acerbity *syn* ACRIMONY, asperity *rel* sourness, acidity, tartness; crabbedness, surliness, dourness, saturninity, sullenness; bitterness, acridity; harshness, roughness *ant* mellowness

ache *syn* PAIN, pang, throe, twinge, stitch *rel* distress, suffering, agony, misery; anguish, heartache, heartbreak, sorrow; hurt, injury; torment, torture, rack

achieve **1** *syn* PERFORM, accomplish, effect, fulfill, execute, discharge *rel* complete, finish, conclude, close; surmount, overcome, conquer *ant* fail **2** *syn* REACH, attain, gain, compass *rel* win, secure, obtain, acquire, get; realize, actualize; come, arrive *ant* miss (*getting or attaining*)

achievement *syn* FEAT, exploit *rel* deed, act, action; victory, conquest, triumph; consummation, accomplishment *ant* failure

achromatic *syn* COLORLESS, uncolored *rel* neutral, negative *ant* chromatic

acid *syn* SOUR, acidulous, tart, dry *rel* acrid, bitter; sharp *ant* bland; sweet; alkaline

acidulous *syn* SOUR, acid, tart, dry *rel* sharp; pungent, piquant; biting, cutting, incisive *ant* saccharine

acknowledge **1** • to disclose something against one's will or inclination *syn* admit, own, avow, confess *rel* disclose, divulge, reveal; grant, concede, allow; publish, declare, proclaim *ant* deny **2** • to take cognizance of in some way, usually in a way dictated by custom or convention and implying acceptance or assent *syn* recognize *rel* accept, receive; notice, note, remark; respond, reply, answer *ant* ignore

acme *syn* SUMMIT, apex, zenith, culmination, climax, peak, apogee, pinnacle, meridian

acoustic, acoustical *syn* AUDITORY

acquaint *syn* INFORM, apprise, advise, notify *rel* tell, reveal, disclose, divulge; teach, instruct, educate, school; accustom, habituate

acquaintance *syn* FRIEND, intimate, confidant *rel* associate, companion, comrade, crony

acquiesce *syn* ASSENT, consent, agree, accede, subscribe *rel* accept, receive; conform, adapt, adject, accommodate, reconcile (*oneself*); yield, submit, bow; concur, coincide *ant* object

acquiescence *syn* compliance, resignation *rel* deference, obeisance, honor; submissiveness *ant* rebelliousness, rebellion

acquiescent *syn* COMPLIANT, resigned *rel* submissive, tame; yielding, submitting, deferring, bowing, relenting *ant* rebellious

acquire *syn* GET, obtain, gain, win, secure, procure *rel* attain, achieve, compass, reach; annex, add, superadd; buy, purchase; take, seize, snatch, grab *ant* forfeit

acquirement · a power or skill that is the fruit of exertion or effort *syn* acquisition, attainment, accomplishment *rel* achievement, feat; addition, accretion

acquisition *syn* ACQUIREMENT, attainment, accomplishment *rel* addition, accession, accretion, increment; possessions, belongings, means, assets; gift, genius, talent, aptitude; art, skill, cunning

acquisitive *syn* COVETOUS, grasping, avaricious, greedy *rel* avid, eager, keen, athirst; possessing, possessive, owning, enjoying *ant* sacrificing, abnegating

acquit **1** *syn* EXCULPATE, absolve, exonerate, vindicate *rel* discharge, free, release, liberate; excuse, pardon, forgive, remit *ant* convict **2** *syn* BEHAVE, quit, conduct, demean, deport, comport *rel* act, behave, work, operate, react

acrid **1** *syn* BITTER *rel* pungent, piquant; biting, incisive; offensive, repugnant, loathsome *ant* savory **2** *syn* CAUSTIC, mordant, scathing *rel* sharp, keen; surly, crabbed, morose, sullen; malevolent, malign, spiteful, malicious; virulent, venomous, poisonous *ant* benign, kindly

acrimonious *syn* ANGRY, irate, indignant, wrathful, wroth, mad *rel* testy, splenetic, choleric, irascible, cranky, cross; rancorous, hostile, antagonistic; quarrelsome, contentious, belligerent *ant* irenic, peaceable

acrimony · temper or language marked by irritation or some degree of anger or resentment *syn* acerbity, asperity *rel* bitterness; ill will, malignity, malignancy, spite, spleen, malice, malevolence; rancor, animus, animosity, antipathy, enmity *ant* suavity

across · so as to intersect the length of something *syn* crosswise, crossways, athwart

act *n, syn* ACTION, deed *rel* performance, accomplishment, achievement; feat, exploit

act *vb* **1** · to perform esp. in an indicated way *syn* behave, work, operate, function, react **2** · to assume the appearance or role of another person or character *syn* play, impersonate

acting *syn* TEMPORARY, ad interim, provisional

action **1** · something done or effected *syn* act, deed *rel* process, proceeding, procedure; performance, execution, fulfillment; activity, operation, work, behavior, reaction **2** *syn* SUIT, cause, case, lawsuit **3** *syn* BATTLE, engagement *rel* combat, conflict, fight, fray, affray, contest; encounter, skirmish, brush

activate *syn* VITALIZE, energize *rel* animate, vivify, quicken, enliven; stir, rouse, arouse, rally, awaken *ant* arrest

active · at work or in effective action *syn* operative, dynamic, live *rel* agile, nimble, brisk; alert, wide-awake, watchful; busy, industrious, assiduous, diligent; energetic, strenuous, vigorous *ant* inactive

actor · one who, for the entertainment or edification of an audience, takes part in an exhibition simulating happenings in real life *syn* player, performer, mummer, mime, mimic, thespian, impersonator, trouper

actual *syn* REAL, true *rel* material, physical, phenomenal, objective; particular *ant* ideal; imaginary

actuality *syn* EXISTENCE, being *rel* realization, actualization, materialization, externalization, incarnation; attainment, achievement *ant* potentiality, possibility

actualize *syn* REALIZE, embody, incarnate, externalize, objectify, materialize, hypostatize, reify

actuate 1 *syn* MOVE, drive, impel *rel* stimulate, provoke, excite, galvanize, quicken; stir, rouse, arouse; energize, activate, vitalize 2 *syn* ACTIVATE, motivate *rel* influence, affect, sway; incline, dispose, predispose; induce, prevail *ant* deter

acumen *syn* DISCERNMENT, penetration, insight, perception, discrimination *rel* shrewdness, sagacity, perspicacity, astuteness; sharpness, keenness, acuteness *ant* obtuseness

acute 1 *syn* SHARP, keen *rel* incisive, trenchant, cutting; penetrating, piercing *ant* obtuse 2 · of uncertain outcome *syn* critical, crucial *rel* culminating, climactic; dangerous, hazardous, precarious, perilous; menacing, threatening; intensified, aggravated

adage *syn* SAYING, saw, proverb, maxim, motto, epigram, aphorism, apothegm

adamant, adamantine *syn* INFLEXIBLE, obdurate, inexorable *rel* unyielding, unsubmitting; immovable, immobile; grim, implacable, unrelenting *ant* yielding

adapt 1 · to bring into correspondence *syn* adjust, accommodate, conform, reconcile *rel* temper, qualify, moderate; acclimatize, acclimate, harden *ant* unfit 2 *syn* EDIT, rewrite, revise, redact, compile *rel* fit, prepare, condition, qualify

adaptable *syn* PLASTIC, pliant, ductile, pliable, malleable *rel* tractable, amenable, obedient; supple, flexible, resilient, elastic *ant* inadaptable, unadaptable

add 1 · to find or represent the amount reached by putting together arithmetically a series of numbers of quantities *syn* sum, total, tot, cast, figure, foot 2 · to bring in or join on something more so as to form a larger or more inclusive whole *syn* append, annex, subjoin, superadd *rel* fasten, attach, affix; augment, enlarge, increase *ant* subtract, deduct

addendum *syn* APPENDIX, supplement

addict *vb, syn* HABITUATE, accustom, inure *rel* incline, dispose, predispose, bias; devote, apply, address, direct *ant* wean

addict *n* · a person who by habit and strong inclination indulges in something or the pursuit of something *syn* votary, devotee, habitué

addition · a thing that serves to increase another in size, amount or content *syn* accretion, increment, accession

additive *syn* CUMULATIVE, summative, accumulative *rel* aggregative, conglomerative, agglomerative; constituent, component, elemental

addle *syn* CONFUSE, muddle, fuddle, befuddle *rel* confound, dumbfound, nonplus, bewilder, puzzle; amaze, flabbergast, astound, surprise; fluster, flurry, agitate, upset, discompose *ant* refresh (*mentally*)

address *vb* **1** *syn* DIRECT, devote, apply *rel* bend; appeal, pray, sue, plead; aim, point, level **2** • to speak to or less often to write or make a sign to a person in recognition or in order to obtain recognition *syn* accost, greet, salute, hail *rel* speak, talk, converse; court, woo

address *n* **1** *syn* TACT, savoir faire, poise *rel* dexterity, facility, ease, readiness; adroitness, cleverness; graciousness, affability; suavity, urbanity, diplomacy *ant* maladroitness, gaucherie **2** *syn* SPEECH, oration, harangue, lecture, talk, sermon, homily

adduce • to bring forward by way of explanation, proof, illustration, or demonstration *syn* advance, allege, cite *rel* exemplify, illustrate; remark, comment, commentate, animadvert

adept *n, syn* EXPERT, wizard, artiste, artist, virtuoso *ant* bungler

adept *adj, syn* PROFICIENT, skilled, skillful, expert, masterly *rel* conversant, versed; efficient, effective; dexterous, adroit, deft; competent, able, capable, qualified *ant* inadept, inept; bungling

adequate *syn* SUFFICIENT, enough, competent

adhere *syn* STICK, cohere, cling, cleave *rel* fasten, attach, affix; unite, link, combine, join

adherence • a physical adhering *syn* adhesion *ant* inadherence, nonadherence

adherent *syn* FOLLOWER, disciple, partisan, satellite, henchman, sectary *rel* supporter, upholder, backer, champion *ant* renegade

adhesion *syn* ADHERENCE *ant* nonadhesion, inadhesion

ad interim *syn* TEMPORARY, provisional, acting *ant* permanent

adjacent • in close proximity *syn* adjoining, contiguous, abutting, tangent, conterminous, juxtaposed *rel* nearest, next; successive, consecutive; joining, connecting *ant* nonadjacent

adjoining *syn* ADJACENT, contiguous, abutting, tangent, conterminous, juxtaposed *rel* joined, connected; attached *ant* detached, disjoined

adjudge *syn* JUDGE, adjudicate, arbitrate *rel* rule, decide, determine, settle; award, accord, grant; allot, assign

adjudicate *syn* JUDGE, adjudge, arbitrate *rel* determine, settle, rule, decide

adjunct *syn* APPENDAGE, appurtenance, accessory *rel* addition, accretion; appanage, right; attachment, affix, fixture

adjure *syn* BEG, entreat, beseech, implore, importune, supplicate *rel* pray, plead, appeal; request, ask; bid, enjoin, charge, command

adjust **1** • to set right or to rights *syn* regulate, fix *rel* rectify, correct; trim, steady, stabilize, balance; order, arrange; align, line, line up, range *ant* derange **2** *syn* ADAPT, accommodate, conform, reconcile *rel* harmonize, attune; correspond, conform, accord, square, agree

adjuvant *syn* AUXILIARY, contributory, ancillary, accessory, subsidiary, subservient *rel* aiding, helping, assisting; supporting, upholding, backing; effective, efficient, efficacious, effectual *ant* counteractive

administer • to act on the behalf of another in or as if in the capacity of a steward *syn* dispense

admiration 1 *syn* WONDER, wonderment, amazement *rel* astonishment, surprise; awe, fear, reverence; rapture, transport, ecstasy 2 *syn* REGARD, esteem, respect *rel* appreciation; liking, loving, enjoying; adoration, veneration, reverence, worship *ant* abhorrence

admire *syn* REGARD, esteem, respect *rel* appreciate, value, prize, cherish; revere, reverence, venerate, adore, worship *ant* abhor

admission *syn* ADMITTANCE

admit 1 *syn* RECEIVE, accept, take *rel* allow, permit, suffer, let; harbor, entertain, shelter, lodge, house *ant* eject, expel 2 *syn* ACKNOWLEDGE, own, confess, avow *rel* concede, grant, allow; assent, acquiesce, agree, subscribe; divulge, disclose, reveal *ant* gainsay; disdain 3 *syn* ENTER, introduce *rel* induct, initiate, install; introduce, insert, interject, interpose *ant* exclude

admittance · permitted entrance *syn* admission

admixture 1 *syn* MIXTURE, composite, blend, compound, amalgam 2 · an added ingredient that destroys the purity or genuineness of a substance *syn* alloy, adulterant *rel* addition, accretion; touch, suggestion, streak, dash, spice, tinge, smack, shade; infusion, suffusion, leaven

admonish *syn* REPROVE, chide, reproach, rebuke, reprimand *rel* warn, forewarn, caution; counsel, advise; criticize, reprehend, reprobate *ant* commend

ado *syn* STIR, fuss, pother, flurry, bustle *rel* trouble, pains, exertion, effort

adolescence *syn* YOUTH, puberty, pubescence *ant* senescence

adopt · to make one's own what in some fashion one owes to another *syn* embrace, espouse *rel* appropriate, arrogate, usurp; assume, affect *ant* repudiate; discard

adoration *syn* REVERENCE, worship, veneration *rel* honor, homage, obeisance; praise, laud, extolling *ant* blasphemy

adore 1 *syn* REVERE, worship, venerate, reverence *rel* laud, praise, extol; exalt, magnify *ant* blaspheme 2 · to love or admire excessively *syn* worship, idolize *rel* love, dote, like; admire, esteem *ant* detest

adorn · to add something unessential in order to enhance the appearance *syn* decorate, ornament, embellish, beautify, deck, bedeck, garnish *rel* enhance, heighten, intensify *ant* disfigure

adroit 1 *syn* DEXTEROUS, deft, handy *rel* agile, nimble; expert, masterly, adept, skillful, skilled, proficient; effortless, smooth, facile, easy *ant* maladroit 2 *syn* CLEVER, cunning, ingenious *rel* shrewd, astute, perspicacious; intelligent, quick-witted, smart; artful, crafty, sly *ant* stolid

adulation *syn* COMPLIMENT, flattery *rel* praise, laud; applause, acclaim; fulsomeness, unctuousness *ant* abuse

adult *syn* MATURE, grown-up, matured, ripe, mellow *rel* developed, ripened, aged *ant* juvenile; puerile

adulterant *syn* ADMIXTURE, alloy

adulterate · to alter fraudulently esp. for profit *syn* sophisticate, load, weight, doctor *rel* debase, vitiate, corrupt; pollute, defile, taint, contaminate *ant* refine

adumbrate *syn* SUGGEST, shadow *rel* symbolize, typify, emblematize; signify, denote, mean

adumbration *syn* SHADE, shadow, umbra, penumbra, umbrage *rel* symbol, type, emblem; sign, token, symptom, note; hint, suggestion, intimation *ant* revelation

advance *vb* 1 · to move or put ahead *syn* promote, forward, further *rel* help, aid, assist; hasten, accelerate, quicken, speed; elevate, raise, lift *ant* retard; check **2** · to move forward in space, in time, or in approach to a material or ideal objective *syn* progress *rel* develop, mature; intensify, heighten *ant* recede **3** *syn* ADDUCE, allege, cite *rel* offer, present, proffer; propose; broach, express, air

advance *n* **1** · movement forward in space, in time, or in approach to a material or ideal objective *syn* progress *rel* development, evolution; improvement, betterment *ant* recession, retrogression **2** *syn* OVERTURE, approach, tender, bid *rel* proposal, proposition; offer, proffer

advanced **1** *syn* PREMATURE, forward, precocious, untimely *ant* backward **2** *syn* LIBERAL, radical, progressive *rel* daring, venturesome, adventurous *ant* conservative

advancement · the act of raising a person in grade, rank, or dignity, or the honor that comes to one who is so raised *syn* preferment, promotion, elevation *ant* degradation; reduction (*in rank or status*)

advantage **1** · a factor or set of factors in a competition or rivalry giving one person or side a position of superiority over the other *syn* handicap, allowance, odds, edge *rel* preeminence, superlativeness; supremacy, ascendancy *ant* disadvantage; handicap **2** *syn* USE, service, account, profit, avail *rel* improvement, betterment; enhancement, heightening; benefit *ant* detriment

advantageous *syn* BENEFICIAL, profitable *rel* expedient, advisable; useful, utilitarian *ant* disadvantageous

advent *syn* ARRIVAL *rel* coming, arriving; approaching, nearing; appearing, emerging *ant* leaving, passing

adventure · an undertaking, an exploit, or an experience involving hazards and requiring boldness *syn* enterprise, quest *rel* exploit, feat, achievement; hazard, peril, risk, danger

adventurous · courting danger or exposing oneself to danger in a greater degree than is required for courage *syn* venturesome, daring, daredevil, rash, reckless, foolhardy *rel* audacious, bold, intrepid, doughty, brave; aspiring, panting; ambitious, emulous *ant* unadventurous; cautious

adversary *syn* OPPONENT, antagonist *rel* assailant, attacker, assaulter; enemy, foe; competitor, rival *ant* ally

adverse · so opposed as to cause interference, often harmful or fatal interference *syn* antagonistic, counter, counteractive *rel* harmful, hurtful, injurious; hindering, impeding, obstructing; detrimental, deleterious, pernicious; fatal, deadly *ant* propitious

adversity *syn* MISFORTUNE, mischance, mishap *rel* trial, tribulation, affliction; distress, misery, suffering; poverty, privation, indigence, destitution *ant* prosperity

advert *syn* REFER, allude *rel* remark, notice, note, observe

advertise *syn* DECLARE, publish, announce, proclaim, broadcast, promulgate *rel* report, recount, relate; communicate, impart

advertisement *syn* DECLARATION, publication, announcement, broadcasting, proclamation, promulgation *rel* publicity, ballyhoo, promotion, propaganda

advice **1** · a recommendation as to a decision or a course of conduct *syn* counsel *rel* admonition; warning, forewarning, cautioning; instruction, teaching **2** *syn* NEWS, intelligence, tidings

advisable *syn* EXPEDIENT, politic *rel* prudent, wise, sensible; beneficial, advantageous, profitable; practical, practicable *ant* inadvisable

advise **1** • to make a recommendation as to a decision or a course of conduct *syn* counsel *rel* admonish, reprove; warn, forewarn, caution; induce, persuade **2** *syn* CONFER, consult, commune, parley, treat, negotiate *rel* discuss, debate, argue; converse, talk, speak; deliberate, think **3** *syn* INFORM, notify, apprise, acquaint *rel* tell, disclose, reveal; communicate (with), impart (to)

advised *syn* DELIBERATE, considered, premeditated, designed, studied

advocate *n, syn* LAWYER, counselor, barrister, counsel, attorney, solicitor

advocate *vb, syn* SUPPORT, uphold, champion, back *rel* defend, justify, vindicate, maintain; espouse, adopt; promote, forward, advance *ant* impugn

aeon *syn* PERIOD, age, era, epoch

aerial *syn* AIRY, ethereal *rel* immaterial, incorporeal; impalpable, imperceptible, imponderable

aesthete • a person conspicuous for his enjoyment and appreciation of the beautiful, the exquisite, or the choice *syn* dilettante, connoisseur

affable *syn* GRACIOUS, cordial, genial, sociable *rel* courteous, polite, civil; open, candid, frank; amiable, obliging, complaisant; talkative, loquacious; suave, urbane *ant* reserved

affair **1** • something done or dealth with *syn* business, concern, matter, thing **2** *syn* AMOUR, intrigue, liaison

affect *syn* ASSUME, simulate, pretend, feign, counterfeit, sham

affect • to produce or to have an effect upon a person or upon a thing capable of a reaction *syn* influence, touch, impress, strike, sway *rel* move, actuate, drive, impel; pierce, penetrate; thrill, electrify

affectation *syn* POSE, air, mannerism *rel* pretense, pretension; pretentiousness, ostentation *ant* artlessness

affecting *syn* MOVING, touching, pathetic, poignant, impressive *rel* stirring, rousing, rallying; distressing, troubling; pitiful, piteous, pitiable

affection **1** *syn* FEELING, emotion, passion, sentiment *rel* propensity, leaning, penchant; predilection, bias; inclination, disposition *ant* antipathy **2** *syn* ATTACHMENT, love *rel* devotion, piety, fidelity; liking, doting, enjoying; tenderness, warmth, sympathy *ant* coldness **3** *syn* DISEASE, disorder, condition, ailment, malady, complaint, distemper, syndrome *rel* attack, access, paroxysm, fit; disorder, derangement

affectionate *syn* LOVING, devoted, fond, doting *rel* ardent, fervent, passionate, impassioned; tender, sympathetic, warm *ant* cold; undemonstrative

affiliated *syn* RELATED, allied, kindred, cognate *rel* dependent, subordinate *ant* unaffiliated

affinity **1** *syn* ATTRACTION, sympathy **2** *syn* LIKENESS, resemblance, similarity, similitude, analogy *rel* agreement, conformity, correspondence, accord

affirm *syn* ASSERT, profess, aver, avow, protest, avouch, declare, warrant, predicate *rel* attest, certify, couch, witness; state, relate *ant* deny

affix *syn* FASTEN, attach, fix *rel* append, add, subjoin, annex; stick, adhere *ant* detach

afflatus *syn* INSPIRATION, fury, frenzy

afflict • to inflict upon a person

something which he finds hard to endure *syn* try, torment, torture, rack *rel* worry, annoy, harass, harry, plague, pester; vex, bother, irk, annoy; distress, trouble, ail *ant* comfort

affliction *syn* TRIAL, visitation, tribulation, cross *rel* adversity, misfortune, mischance, mishap; distress, suffering, misery, agony; anguish, sorrow, grief, woe, heartbreak *ant* solace, consolation

affluent *syn* RICH, wealthy, opulent *rel* possessing, owning, holding, having, enjoying; acquisitive, covetous *ant* impecunious; straitened

afford *syn* GIVE, confer, bestow, present, donate *rel* offer, proffer; furnish; grant, accord *ant* deny (*something one wants*)

affray *n, syn* CONTEST, fray, fight, combat, conflict *rel* brawl, row, fracas, melee, rumpus; encounter, skirmish, brush; dispute, argument, controversy

affray *vb, syn* FRIGHTEN, fright, affright, scare, alarm, terrify, terrorize, startle *rel, ant* see AFFRIGHT

affright *vb, syn* FRIGHTEN, fright, affray, scare, alarm, terrify, terrorize, startle *rel* daunt, horrify, appall, dismay; cow, intimidate, bulldoze; confound, bewilder, puzzle *ant* nerve, embolden

affront *vb, syn* OFFEND, outrage, insult *rel* slight, ignore, neglect; nettle, peeve, provoke, irritate *ant* gratify (*by an attention*)

affront *n* • a speech or an action having for its intention or effect the dishonoring of something or someone *syn* insult, indignity *rel* slighting, ignoring, overlooking, neglecting; offending, outraging; impudence, brazenness, shamelessness *ant* gratification

afraid *syn* FEARFUL, apprehensive *rel* alarmed, scared, frightened; timorous, timid *ant* unafraid; sanguine

aft *syn* ABAFT, astern *rel* after, behind; rear, back, posterior, hind *ant* fore

after *prep, adj, adv* • following upon, especially in place or in time *syn* behind *rel* abaft, aft, astern *ant* before

after *adj, syn* POSTERIOR, hinder, hind, rear, back

aftereffect, aftermath *syn* EFFECT, result, consequence, upshot, sequel, issue, outcome, event

age *n* **1** • the period in one's life when one is old in years and declining in body or mind or both *syn* senility, senescence, dotage *ant* youth **2** *syn* PERIOD, era, epoch, aeon

age *vb, syn* MATURE, ripen, develop

aged • far advanced in years *syn* old, elderly, superannuated *rel* infirm, feeble, decrepit, weak *ant* youthful

agency *syn* MEAN, agent, instrumentality, instrument, medium, vehicle, channel, organ *rel* cause, determinant, antecedent; operation, action, working; activity; machinery, apparatus, gear, equipment

agenda *syn* PROGRAM, schedule, timetable

agent **1** *syn* MEAN, instrument, agency, instrumentality, medium, vehicle, organ, channel *rel* actor, operator, worker; activator, energizer; performer, executor, executive *ant* patient **2** • one who performs the duties of or transacts business for another *syn* factor, attorney, deputy, proxy *ant* principal

agglomerate, agglomeration *syn* AGGREGATE, conglomerate, conglomeration, aggregation *rel* combination, association; accumulation; heap, pile, mass

aggrandize *syn* EXALT, magnify *rel* heighten, enhance, aggravate, intensify; elevate, raise, lift, boost *ant* belittle

aggravate 1 *syn* INTENSIFY, heighten, enhance *rel* magnify, aggrandize, exalt; augment, increase, multiply, enlarge *ant* alleviate 2 *syn* IRRITATE, exasperate, provoke, rile, peeve, nettle *rel* perturb, upset, disturb, discompose; vex, irk, annoy; anger, incense, infuriate *ant* appease

aggregate 1 *syn* SUM, total, whole, number, amount, quantity *ant* individual, particular 2 • a mass formed by parts or particles that are not merged into each other *syn* aggregation, conglomerate, conglomeration, agglomerate, agglomeration *rel* union, unity, integrity; unification, consolidation; complex, system, organism, network *ant* constituent

aggregation *syn* AGGREGATE, conglomerate, conglomeration, agglomerate, agglomeration *rel, ant* see AGGREGATE 2

aggression *syn* ATTACK, offense, offensive *rel* invasion, incursion, raid, inroad *ant* resistance

aggressive 1 *syn* attacking, offensive *rel* invading, encroaching, trespassing *ant* resisting; repelling 2 • conspicuously or obtrusively active or energetic *syn* militant, assertive, self-assertive, pushing, pushy *rel* energetic, strenuous, vigorous; masterful, domineering, imperious; fighting, combating, combative

aggrieve *syn* WRONG, oppress, persecute *rel* afflict, try, torment; harass, harry, plague, annoy, worry; injure, hurt, harm *ant* rejoice

agile • acting or moving with quickness and alacrity *syn* nimble, brisk, spry *rel* dexterous, adroit, deft; quick, fleet, speedy, fast; limber, lithesome, supple; lively, sprightly *ant* torpid

agitate 1 *syn* SHAKE, rock, convulse *rel* stir, rouse, arouse; move, actuate, drive, impel *ant* quiet, lull, still 2 *syn* DISCOMPOSE, perturb, upset, fluster, flurry, disturb, disquiet *rel* irritate, provoke, rile, exasperate, peeve; worry, harass, plague; annoy, vex, irk, bother *ant* calm, tranquilize 3 *syn* DISCUSS, argue, dispute, debate *rel* controvert, disprove; assail, attack; consider; air, ventilate, broach, express

agitation *syn* COMMOTION, tumult, turmoil, turbulence, confusion, convulsion, upheaval *rel* motion, movement; stir, bustle, ado; disturbance, perturbation, disquiet *ant* tranquillity

agnostic *syn* ATHEIST, deist, freethinker, unbeliever, infidel

agog *syn* EAGER, keen, anxious, avid, athirst *rel* excited, galvanized, stimulated; roused, aroused, stirred; impatient, restive *ant* aloof

agonize *syn* WRITHE, squirm *rel* suffer, endure, bear; torment, rack, torture, afflict

agonizing *syn* EXCRUCIATING, racking *rel* torturing, tormenting, racking; intense, vehement, fierce, exquisite, violent

agony *syn* DISTRESS, suffering, passion, misery, dolor *rel* pang, throe, ache, pain, twinge; trial, tribulation, affliction, visitation

agrarian *syn* agricultural

agree 1 *syn* ASSENT, accede, consent, acquiesce, subscribe *rel* grant, concede, allow; accept, receive; admit, acknowledge *ant* protest (*against*); differ (*with*) 2 • to come into or to be in harmony regarding a matter of opinion or a policy *syn* concur, coincide *rel* unite, cooperate *ant* differ; disagree 3 • to exist or go together without conflict or incongruity *syn* square, conform, accord, harmonize, correspond, tally, jibe *ant* differ (*from*)

agreeable *syn* PLEASANT, grateful, pleasing, gratifying, welcome *rel* comfortable, easy, restful; delightful, delectable; attractive, charming, alluring *ant* disagreeable

agreement · a reconciliation of differences as to what should be done or not done *syn* accord, understanding *rel* pact, entente, concordat, convention, cartel, contract

agriculture · the science or the business of raising useful plants and animals *syn* farming, husbandry

ahead *syn* BEFORE, forward *ant* behind

aid *vb, syn* HELP, assist *rel* support, uphold, back; relieve, lighten, alleviate, mitigate; abet, incite *ant* injure

aid *n* **1** *syn* help, assistance *rel* relief, assuagement, alleviation, mitigation; remedy, cure, medicine; support, backing *ant* impediment **2** *syn* ASSISTANT, helper, coadjutor, aide, aide-de-camp

aide *syn* ASSISTANT, aide-de-camp, coadjutor, helper, aid

aide-de-camp *syn* ASSISTANT, aide, aid

ail *syn* TROUBLE, distress *rel* afflict, try; annoy, vex, irk, bother

ailment *syn* DISEASE, disorder, condition, affection, malady, complaint, distemper, syndrome

aim *vb* **1** *syn* DIRECT, point, level, train, lay *rel* bend, curve, twist **2** · to have as a controlling desire something beyond one's present power of attainment *syn* aspire, pant *rel* intend, purpose, propose, design; attempt, essay, endeavor, try

aim *n, syn* INTENTION, end, goal, objective, purpose, object, intent, design *rel* aspiration, ambition; effort, exertion, pains, trouble

air *n* **1** *syn* POSE, affectation, mannerism *rel* mien, bearing, port, presence; ostentation, pretentiousness, show; art, artifice, craft **2** *syn* MELODY, air, tune

air *vb, syn* EXPRESS, ventilate, vent, utter, voice, broach *rel* reveal, disclose, divulge, tell, discover; publish, proclaim, broadcast, declare

airport · a place where airplanes take off and land *syn* airdrome, airfield, airstrip, landing strip, flying field, landing field

airy · as light and insubstantial as air *syn* aerial, ethereal *rel* tenuous, rare, thin; delicate, dainty, exquisite, choice; light, volatile, frivolous *ant* substantial

aisle *syn* PASSAGE, passageway, ambulatory, corridor, gallery, hall, hallway, cloister, arcade

akin *syn* LIKE, alike, similar, analogous, comparable, parallel, uniform, identical *rel* related, kindred, cognate, allied; corresponding, agreeing, harmonizing, according, conforming *ant* alien

alacrity *syn* CELERITY, legerity *rel* eagerness, avidity, anxiety; quickness, promptness, readiness; agility, nimbleness, briskness; expedition, dispatch, haste *ant* languor

alarm *n* **1** · a signal that serves as a call to action or to be on guard especially in a time of imminent danger *syn* tocsin, alert **2** *syn* FEAR, fright, panic, terror, horror, dismay, dread, consternation, trepidation *rel* frightening, scaring, startling; agitation, perturbation, upset *ant* assurance; composure

alarm *vb, syn* FRIGHTEN, fright, scare, startle, terrify, affright, terrorize, affray *rel* appall, daunt, horrify, dismay; surprise, astound, amaze, astonish *ant* assure; relieve

albeit *syn* THOUGH, although

alchemy *syn* MAGIC, thaumaturgy, wizardry, sorcery, witchery, witchcraft

alcoholic *syn* DRUNKARD, inebriate, dipsomaniac, sot, soak, toper, tosspot, tippler

alert *adj* **1** *syn* WATCHFUL, wide=

awake, vigilant *rel* agile, nimble, brisk; wary, circumspect, cautious **2** *syn* INTELLIGENT, clever, smart, bright, quick-witted, brilliant, knowing *rel* sharp, keen, acute; quick, ready, prompt, apt; shrewd, perspicacious

alert *n, syn* ALARM, tocsin

alias *syn* PSEUDONYM, nom de guerre, incognito, nom de plume, pen name

alibi *syn* APOLOGY, excuse, pretext, plea, apologia *rel* explanation, justification, rationalization

alien *adj, syn* EXTRINSIC, foreign, extraneous *rel* external, exterior, outside; adventitious, incidental, accidental; repugnant, repellent, abhorrent; incompatible, incongruous, inconsonant *ant* akin; assimilable

alien *n, syn* STRANGER, foreigner, outlander, outsider, immigrant, émigré *ant* citizen

alienate **1** *syn* TRANSFER, convey, deed **2** *syn* ESTRANGE, disaffect, wean *rel* convert, proselyte, proselytize; separate, part, sever, sunder, divorce *ant* unite; reunite

alienation **1** *syn* ABERRATION, derangement *rel* insanity, lunacy, mania, dementia; imbecility, idiocy, moronity **2** *syn* SOLITUDE, isolation, seclusion

alight **1** *syn* DESCEND, dismount **2** • to come to rest after or as if after a flight, a descent, or a fall *syn* light, land, perch, roost

align *syn* LINE, line up, range, array *rel* order, arrange, marshal; regulate, fix, adjust

alike *syn* LIKE, similar, analogous, comparable, akin, parallel, uniform, identical *rel* same, selfsame, equivalent, identical *ant* different

aliment *syn* FOOD, pabulum, nutriment, nourishment, sustenance, pap

alive **1** *syn* LIVING, animated, animate, vital *rel* active, dynamic, live, operative; lively, vivacious, sprightly; being, existing *ant* dead, defunct **2** *syn* AWARE, awake, sensible, cognizant, conscious *rel* alert, wide-awake, vigilant, watchful; intelligent, knowing, quick-witted *ant* blind (*to*); anesthetic (*to*)

alkaline • being a compound that reacts with an acid to form a salt *syn* basic

all **1** *syn* WHOLE, entire, total, gross *rel* complete, plenary, full **2** • including the entire membership of a group with no exceptions *syn* every, each *ant* no

all-round *syn* VERSATILE, many-sided *rel* complete, full; apt, ready, quick

allay *syn* RELIEVE, alleviate, lighten, assuage, mitigate *rel* abate, lessen, decrease, diminish; mollify, pacify, appease; moderate, temper *ant* intensify

allege *syn* ADDUCE, cite, advance *rel* affirm, assert, declare, profess, avouch, avow; recite, recount, rehearse, state, relate *ant* contravene; (*in law*) traverse

allegiance *syn* FIDELITY, fealty, loyalty, devotion, piety *rel* faithfulness, steadfastness, constancy, staunchness; obeisance, deference, homage, honor; obedience; obligation, duty *ant* treachery; treason

allegory **1** • a concrete representation in art of something that is abstract or for some other reason not directly representable *syn* symbolism **2** • a literary form that typically tells a story for the sake of presenting a truth or of enforcing a moral *syn* parable, myth, fable

alleviate *syn* RELIEVE, lighten, assuage, mitigate, allay *rel* moderate, temper; lessen, reduce, diminish, decrease; remedy, cure *ant* aggravate

alliance • a chiefly political combination for a common object *syn* league, coalition, fusion, confederacy, confederation, federation

allied *syn* RELATED, cognate, kindred, affiliated *rel* akin, parallel, similar, like; linked, associated, united, connected; cooperating, uniting, conjoining *ant* unallied

allocate *syn* ALLOT, assign, apportion *rel* distribute, dispense, divide, deal, dole; grant, accord, award

allot · to give as one's share, portion, role, or place *syn* assign, apportion, allocate *rel* divide, dispense, distribute, deal, dole; give, bestow

allow 1 *syn* LET, permit, suffer, leave *rel* tolerate, endure, stand, brook, bear; accede, acquiesce, assent; yield, submit, defer *ant* inhibit 2 *syn* GRANT, concede *rel* admit, acknowledge, confess; acquiesce, accede, assent *ant* disallow

allowance 1 *syn* RATION, dole, pittance *rel* allotment, apportionment, assignment; share; grant, appropriation, subsidy 2 · a change made by way of compromise or adjustment *syn* concession *rel* adjustment, accommodation, adaptation; modification, variation 3 *syn* ADVANTAGE, handicap, odds, edge

alloy *syn* ADMIXTURE, adulterant

allude *syn* REFER, advert *rel* suggest, imply, hint, intimate

allure *syn* ATTRACT, captivate, charm, fascinate, enchant, bewitch *rel* lure, entice, seduce; invite, solicit, woo, court; beguile, delude, deceive *ant* repel

alluring *syn* ATTRACTIVE, charming, fascinating, bewitching, enchanting, captivating *rel* lovely, fair, beautiful, pretty, bonny; seductive, enticing, tempting, luring; beguiling, delusive *ant* repulsive

ally *syn* PARTNER, colleague, copartner, confederate *rel* associate, comrade, companion, supporter, upholder, backer; cooperator *ant* adversary

almost *syn* NEARLY, approximately, well-nigh

alms *syn* DONATION, benefaction, contribution *rel* charity, philanthropy; dole, pittance, allowance, ration

alone *adj* 1 · isolated from others *syn* solitary, lonely, lonesome, lone, lorn, forlorn, desolate *rel* single, sole, lone, unique; deserted, abandoned, forsaken; isolated, secluded *ant* accompanied 2 *syn* ONLY

alone *adv, syn* ONLY

aloof *syn* INDIFFERENT, detached, uninterested, disinterested, unconcerned, incurious *rel* disdainful, haughty, arrogant, proud; cool, cold; reserved, reticent, silent *ant* familiar, close

alp *syn* MOUNTAIN, peak, mount

also *syn* too, likewise, besides, moreover, furthermore

alter 1 *syn* CHANGE, vary, modify *rel* adjust, accommodate, adapt; qualify, temper, moderate; transform, metamorphose, convert *ant* fix 2 *syn* STERILIZE, castrate, spay, emasculate, mutilate, geld

alteration *syn* CHANGE, variation, modification *rel* adjustment, adaptation, accommodation; transformation, metamorphosis, conversion *ant* fixation; fixity

altercate *vb, syn* QUARREL, wrangle, squabble, bicker, spat, tiff *rel* fight, contend, battle, war; dispute, debate, agitate, discuss *ant* concur

altercation *syn* QUARREL, wrangle, squabble, bickering, spat, tiff *rel* fight, conflict, combat, contest; discord, dissension, contention, difference, variance, strife; controversy, dispute, argument *ant* concurrence; accord

alternate *adj, syn* INTERMITTENT,

recurrent, periodic *rel* alternating, rotating; reciprocal, corresponding, complementary *ant* consecutive

alternate *vb, syn* ROTATE *rel* recur, return, revert; oscillate, fluctuate, sway, waver, swing

alternate *n, syn* SUBSTITUTE, supply, understudy, double, stand-in, pinch hitter, locum tenens

alternation *syn* CHANGE, vicissitude, mutation, permutation *rel* rotation; oscillation, fluctuation, wavering; turning, revolving, rotating, wheeling; recurrence, return, reversion

alternative *syn* CHOICE, option, preference, selection, election

although *syn* THOUGH, albeit

altitude *syn* HEIGHT, elevation *rel* highness, tallness, loftiness; summit, peak, apex

altruistic *syn* CHARITABLE, benevolent, humanitarian, philanthropic, eleemosynary *rel* self-abnegating, self-denying; generous, bountiful, bounteous, openhanded, liberal *ant* egoistic

amalgam *syn* MIXTURE, admixture, compound, blend, composite

amalgamate *syn* MIX, blend, commingle, merge, coalesce, fuse, mingle *rel* combine, unite, link, associate, join; consolidate, unify, compact

amalgamation *syn* CONSOLIDATION, merger

amass *syn* ACCUMULATE, hoard *rel* collect, gather, assemble; heap, pile, mass, stack *ant* distribute

amateur • a person who follows a pursuit without attaining proficiency or a professional status *syn* dilettante, dabbler, tyro *rel* novice, apprentice, probationer *ant* professional; expert

amative *syn* EROTIC, amorous, amatory

amatory *syn* EROTIC, aphrodisiac, amative, amorous

amaze *syn* SURPRISE, astound, flabbergast, astonish *rel* dumbfound, bewilder, confound, nonplus, puzzle; impress, touch, strike, affect

amazement *syn* WONDER, wonderment, admiration

amazon *syn* VIRAGO, termagant

ambassador • a diplomatic agent serving his or her sovereign or government in a foreign country *syn* legate, nuncio, minister, envoy, internuncio, chargé d'affaires

ambiguity • expression or, more often, an expression, capable of more than one interpretation *syn* equivocation, tergiversation, double entendre *ant* lucidity; explicitness

ambiguous *syn* OBSCURE, equivocal, cryptic, enigmatic, vague, dark *rel* dubious, doubtful, questionable *ant* explicit

ambition • strong desire for advancement *syn* aspiration, pretension *rel* urge, lust, desire; eagerness, avidity, keenness, anxiety; spur, goad, incentive, motive

ambitious **1** • extremely desirous of something that will give one power, fame, success, or riches *syn* emulous *rel* eager, avid, anxious, keen; aspiring, panting, aiming; daring, venturesome, adventurous *ant* unambitious **2** • straining or exceeding the capacity of their authors or executants *syn* pretentious, utopian *rel* audacious, bold, brave; daring, adventurous; ostentatious, showy *ant* modest

amble *syn* SAUNTER, stroll *rel* loiter, dawdle, delay; meander, ramble, roam, wander

ambulant *syn* ITINERANT, ambulatory, peripatetic, nomadic, vagrant *ant* bedridden

ambulatory *adj, syn* ITINERANT, ambulant, peripatetic, nomadic, vagrant

ambulatory *n, syn* PASSAGE, passageway, aisle, gallery, cloister, arcade, hall, hallway, corridor

ambuscade *syn* AMBUSH

ambush *vb, syn* SURPRISE, waylay *rel* attack, assault, assail; trap, entrap, snare, ensnare, capture, catch

ambush *n* · a device to entrap an enemy by lying in wait under cover for an opportune moment to make a surprise attack *syn* ambuscade *rel* trap, snare, lure; attack, onset, onslaught, assault

ameliorate *syn* IMPROVE, better, help *rel* amend, remedy, reform, rectify, correct; mitigate, alleviate, relieve, lighten *ant* worsen; deteriorate

amenable 1 *syn* RESPONSIBLE, answerable, liable, accountable *rel* open, subject, liable; subordinate, dependent *ant* independent (*of*); autonomous 2 *syn* OBEDIENT, tractable, docile, biddable *rel* pliant, adaptable, pliable, plastic; responsive, tender; sensitive, open, liable; submissive, tame, subdued *ant* recalcitrant, refractory

amend *syn* CORRECT, reform, rectify, revise, emend, remedy, redress *rel* improve, better, ameliorate; mend, repair; elevate, raise, lift *ant* debase; impair

amends *syn* REPARATION, redress, indemnity, restitution *rel* compensation, recompense, payment; atonement, expiation

amenity 1 · something that gives refined or exquisite pleasure or is exceedingly pleasing to the mind or senses *syn* luxury *rel* pleasure, delight, joy, enjoyment; ease, comfort, relaxation, rest; mildness, softness, blandness, lenity, leniency, gentleness *ant* rigor 2 *syn* COURTESY, attention, gallantry *rel* civility, politeness, courteousness; graciousness, affability, cordiality, geniality, sociability; form, convention, convenance; ceremony, formality, form *ant* acerbity, asperity; rudeness

amerce *syn* PENALIZE, fine, mulct

amercement *syn* FINE

amiable · having or manifesting the desire or disposition to please *syn* good-natured, obliging, complaisant *rel* gracious, cordial, affable, genial; warmhearted, warm, responsive, tender; kindly, kind, benignant, benign *ant* unamiable; surly

amicable · marked by or exhibiting goodwill or absence of antagonism *syn* neighborly, friendly *rel* peaceful, pacific, peaceable; harmonious, concordant, accordant; social, gregarious, cooperative, hospitable *ant* antagonistic

amiss · otherwise than intended *syn* astray *rel* wrong, wrongly, bad, badly *ant* aright, right

amity *syn* FRIENDSHIP, comity, goodwill *rel* harmony, concord, accord; amicableness, neighborliness, friendliness *ant* enmity

amnesty *syn* PARDON, absolution

among *syn* BETWEEN

amorous *syn* EROTIC, amative, amatory *rel* passionate, fervid, ardent, impassioned; enamored, infatuated; lustful, lascivious, licentious *ant* frigid

amount *syn* SUM, total, quantity, number, aggregate, whole

amour · an instance of illicit sexual relationship *syn* liaison, intrigue, affair

amour propre *syn* CONCEIT, self=esteem, self-love, egoism, egotism *rel* pride, vanity, vainglory; complacency, self-complacency, smugness, self-satisfaction

ample 1 *syn* SPACIOUS, capacious, commodious *rel* expanded, distended, swelled, swollen, inflated; large, big, great *ant* meager; circumscribed 2 *syn* PLENTIFUL, abundant, plenteous, copious *rel* liberal, generous, handsome, bountiful, bounteous; profuse, lavish, prodigal *ant* scant, meager

amplify *syn* EXPAND, swell, distend, dilate, inflate *rel* develop, mature; enlarge, augment, increase *ant* abridge, condense

amplitude *syn* EXPANSE, spread, stretch *rel* largeness, bigness, greatness; spaciousness, commodiousness, capaciousness; magnitude, extent, size; bulk, mass, volume *ant* straitness; limitation

amulet *syn* FETISH, charm, talisman

amuse • to cause or enable one to pass one's time in pleasant or agreeable activity *syn* divert, entertain, recreate *rel* engross, absorb; beguile, while, wile; enliven, quicken, animate; thrill, electrify *ant* bore

amusement • an agreeable activity or its effect *syn* diversion, entertainment, recreation *rel* engrossment, absorption; play, sport, fun, jest; disporting, frolicking, rollicking, romping; jollity, mirth *ant* boredom

anagogic *syn* MYSTICAL, mystic, cabalistic *rel* allegorical, symbolical; occult, esoteric, recondite

analgesic *syn* ANODYNE, anesthetic *ant* irritant

analogous *syn* LIKE, alike, similar, comparable, akin, parallel, uniform, identical *rel* corresponding, convertible, reciprocal; kindred, related, allied, cognate

analogue *syn* PARALLEL, counterpart, correlate

analogy **1** *syn* LIKENESS, similitude, resemblance, similarity, affinity **2** • a comparison between things essentially or generically different but strikingly alike in one or more pertinent aspects *syn* simile, metaphor

analysis • separation of a whole into its fundamental elements or constituent parts *syn* resolution, dissection, breakdown *rel* separation, division; disintegration, decomposition *ant* synthesis

analytical *syn* LOGICAL, subtle *rel* acute, keen, sharp; profound, deep; penetrating, piercing; organizing, ordering, marshaling *ant* creative, inventive, constructive

analyze • to divide a complex whole or unit into its component parts or constituent elements *syn* resolve, dissect, break down *rel* separate, divide, part; classify, pigeonhole, assort *ant* compose, compound; construct

anarchy • absence, suspension, breakdown, or widespread defiance of government, law, and order *syn* chaos, lawlessness *ant* order; discipline

anathema **1** *syn* ABOMINATION, bête noire, bugbear **2** *syn* CURSE, malediction, imprecation *rel* denunciation, condemnation, reprobation, censure, criticism

anathematize *syn* EXECRATE, curse, damn, objurgate *rel* denounce, condemn, censure, reprobate, criticize; proscribe, sentence

anatomy *syn* STRUCTURE, skeleton, framework

ancestor • a person from whom one is descended *syn* progenitor, forefather, forebear *ant* descendant

ancestry • one's progenitors or their character or quality as a whole *syn* lineage, pedigree *ant* descendants; posterity

anchor *syn* SECURE, rivet *rel* fasten, attach, fix, affix

anchorite *syn* RECLUSE, hermit, eremite, cenobite *rel* ascetic, mystic; religious, monk, friar

ancient *syn* OLD, venerable, antediluvian, antique, antiquated, archaic, obsolete *rel* primeval, pristine, primal, primordial *ant* modern

ancillary *syn* AUXILIARY, contributory, subsidiary, adjuvant, subservient, accessory *rel* assisting, aiding, helping; secondary, subordinate; supplementary, complementary

androgynous *syn* BISEXUAL, hermaphroditic, hermaphrodite, epicene

anecdote *syn* STORY, tale, yarn, narrative *rel* incident, episode, event, occurrence; narration, relation, recital

anemic *syn* PALE, bloodless *ant* fullblooded; florid

anesthetic *adj, syn* INSENSIBLE, insensitive, impassible *rel* dull, obtuse; impassive, apathetic, stolid; impervious, impermeable, impenetrable, impassable *ant* alive

anesthetic *n, syn* ANODYNE, analgesic *ant* stimulant

angel *syn* SPONSOR, backer, patron, surety, guarantor

anger *n* • emotional excitement induced by intense displeasure *syn* ire, rage, fury, indignation, wrath *rel* acrimony, asperity; exasperation, irritation, provocation *ant* pleasure, gratification; forbearance

anger *vb* • to make angry *syn* incense, enrage, infuriate, madden *rel* offend, outrage, affront; exasperate, provoke, irritate, nettle, rile; vex, annoy, irk *ant* please, gratify; pacify

angle *n* **1** *syn* POINT OF VIEW, viewpoint, standpoint, slant *rel* attitude, position, stand **2** *syn* PHASE, aspect, facet, side *rel* item, detail, particular

angry • feeling or showing strong displeasure or bad temper *syn* irate, indignant, wrathful, wroth, acrimonious, mad *rel* impassioned, passionate; angered, incensed, enraged, infuriated, maddened

anguish *syn* SORROW, woe, heartache, heartbreak, grief, regret *rel* distress, suffering, dolor, misery, agony; worry, anxiety, care; pain, pang, throe, ache; torture, torment, affliction *ant* relief

angular *syn* LEAN, gaunt, rawboned, lank, lanky, spare, scrawny, skinny *rel* thin, slender, slim; awkward, clumsy; cadaverous, haggard *ant* rotund

animadversion • a remark or statement that is an adverse criticism *syn* stricture, aspersion, reflection *rel* criticism, reprehension, censure; observation, comment, remark; captiousness, faultfinding, caviling, carping, censoriousness *ant* commendation

animadvert *syn* REMARK, comment, commentate *rel* criticize, reprehend, censure, reprobate; deprecate, disapprove; depreciate, disparage, decry

animal *syn* CARNAL, fleshly, sensual *rel* physical, corporeal, bodily; bestial, brutal *ant* rational

animalism *syn* ANIMALITY *rel* sensualism, voluptuousness; lustfulness, lasciviousness, lecherousness

animality • the animal aspect or quality of human beings or human nature *syn* animalism *rel* virility, maleness, masculinity

animate *adj, syn* LIVING, alive, animated, vital *rel* physical, corporeal, bodily; animal, carnal, fleshly *ant* inanimate

animate *vb* **1** *syn* QUICKEN, vivify, enliven *rel* vitalize, activate, energize **2** *syn* INFORM, inspire, fire *rel* motivate, actuate, activate; move, drive, impel, actuate; stir, rouse, arouse *ant* inhibit

animated **1** *syn* LIVING, alive, animate, vital *rel* active, live, dynamic; vitalized, energized, activated *ant* inert **2** *syn* LIVELY, vivacious, sprightly, gay *rel* buoyant, volatile, effervescent; agile, brisk, spry, nimble; spirited, high-spirited *ant* depressed, dejected

animosity *syn* ENMITY, animus, rancor, hostility, antipathy, antagonism *rel* hatred, hate, detestation, abhorrence; vindictiveness, revengefulness, vengefulness; malice, ill will, malevolence, spite *ant* goodwill

animus *syn* ENMITY, animosity, rancor, hostility, antipathy, antagonism *rel* ill will, spite, spleen, grudge, malice; prejudice, bias *ant* favor

annals *syn* HISTORY, chronicle

annex *vb, syn* ADD, append, subjoin, superadd *rel* join, unite, connect, link, associate; attach, affix, fasten

annex *n* • an addition to a main (and, often, the original) building *syn* extension, wing, ell *rel* addition, increment, accretion

annihilate *syn* ABOLISH, extinguish, abate *rel* obliterate, efface, expunge, blot out, cancel, erase; extirpate, exterminate, eradicate, wipe

annotate • to add or append comment *syn* gloss *rel* elucidate, interpret, construe, explain, expound; comment, commentate, remark

annotation • added or appended comment intended to be helpful in interpreting a passage or text *syn* gloss *rel* commentary, comment, observation, note, remark

announce *syn* DECLARE, publish, proclaim, promulgate, advertise, broadcast *rel* disclose, reveal, divulge, tell; communicate, impart

announcement *syn* DECLARATION, publication, proclamation, promulgation, advertisement, broadcasting

annoy **1** • to disturb and nervously upset a person *syn* vex, irk, bother *rel* irritate, nettle, aggravate, exasperate, rile; perturb, disturb, upset, agitate, discompose *ant* soothe **2** *syn* WORRY, pester, plague, tantalize, tease, harass, harry *rel* fret, chafe, abrade; badger, hector, heckle, chivy, bait; trouble, inconvenience

annul **1** *syn* NULLIFY, negate, invalidate, abrogate *rel* neutralize, negative, counteract; cancel, efface, obliterate, blot out, erase; annihilate, abolish, extinguish **2** • to deprive of legal validity, force, or authority *syn* abrogate, void, vacate, quash

anodyne **1** • something used to relieve or prevent pain *syn* analgesic, anesthetic **2** • something used to dull or deaden one's senses or one's sensibility *syn* opiate, narcotic, nepenthe *ant* stimulant; irritant

anoint *syn* OIL, cream, grease, lubricate

anomalous *syn* IRREGULAR, unnatural *rel* abnormal, aberrant, atypical; monstrous, prodigious; singular, unique, peculiar, strange

anomaly *syn* PARADOX, antinomy

answer *n* • something spoken or written by way of return to a question or demand *syn* reply, response, rejoinder, retort *rel* defense, vindication, justification refutation, rebuttal

answer *vb* **1** • to say, write, or do something in response *syn* respond, reply, rejoin, retort *rel* acknowledge, recognize; disprove, refute, rebut; defend, justify, vindicate, maintain **2** *syn* SATISFY, meet, fulfill

answerable *syn* RESPONSIBLE, accountable, amenable, liable *rel* obliged, constrained, compelled; subject, subordinate

antagonism *syn* ENMITY, antipathy, hostility, animosity, rancor, animus *rel* opposition, resistance, withstanding, contesting, fighting, combating, conflict; strife, difference, variance, dissension, contention, discord *ant* accord; comity

antagonist *syn* OPPONENT, adversary *rel* foe, enemy; rival, competitor; assailant, attacker *ant* supporter

antagonistic *syn* ADVERSE, counteractive, counter *rel* opposing, resisting, withstanding, contesting, fighting, combating, conflicting; incompatible, discordant, inconsonant; hostile; antipathetic, averse *ant* favoring, favorable

antagonize *syn* RESIST, withstand, contest, oppose, fight, combat, conflict *rel* attack, assail, assault; offend, outrage, affront, insult; incite, foment, instigate *ant* conciliate

ante *syn* BET, stake, pot, wager

antecedent *n, syn* CAUSE, determinant, reason, occasion *rel* precursor, forerunner; progenitor, forebear, ancestor *ant* consequence

antecedent *adj, syn* PRECEDING, precedent, foregoing, previous, prior, former, anterior *ant* subsequent; consequent

antediluvian *syn* OLD, ancient, antiquated, obsolete, antique, venerable, archaic *rel* primordial, primeval, primal, pristine, primary; early

anterior *syn* PRECEDING, precedent, previous, prior, foregoing, antecedent, former *ant* posterior

anthropoid · resembling man *syn* anthropomorphic, anthropomorphous

anthropomorphic, anthropomorphous *syn* ANTHROPOID

antic *n, syn* PRANK, monkeyshine, caper, dido *rel* trick, wile, artifice; caprice, freak, vagary, whim; gambol, frolic, romp

antic *adj, syn* FANTASTIC, grotesque, bizarre *rel* preposterous, absurd, foolish; ludicrous, ridiculous, comic, comical, farcical, laughable

anticipate 1 *syn* PREVENT, forestall *rel* introduce, enter; foretell, forecast, presage; frustrate, thwart, balk *ant* consummate 2 *syn* FORESEE, apprehend, foreknow, divine *rel* foretell, forecast, prognosticate; foretaste; await, expect

anticipation *syn* PROSPECT, foretaste, outlook *rel* foreseeing, foreknowing; presentiment, foreboding, apprehension; forecast, prophecy, prediction, presage; conceiving, envisioning, imagining *ant* retrospect

antidote *syn* CORRECTIVE, check, control *rel* counteractive, neutralizer; nullifier, negator, annuller; remedy, medicine, physic

antinomy *syn* PARADOX, anomaly *rel* opposite, contradictory, contrary, antithesis; contradiction, denial; conflict, variance, discord

antipathetic · arousing marked aversion or dislike *syn* unsympathetic *rel* repellent, repugnant, distasteful, abhorrent, obnoxious; offensive, loathsome, repulsive, revolting *ant* congenial

antipathy 1 *syn* ENMITY, antagonism, hostility, animosity, rancor, animus *rel* repugnance, abhorrence, repellency, distaste; avoidance, evasion, eschewal, escape *ant* taste (*for*); affection (*for*) 2 · the state of mind created by what is antipathetic *syn* aversion *rel, ant* see ANTIPATHY 1

antipodal, antipodean *syn* OPPOSITE, antithetical, contrary, contradictory, antonymous

antipode *syn* OPPOSITE, antithesis, contrary, opposite, contradictory, antonym *rel* converse, counter, reverse

antiquated *syn* OLD, archaic, obsolete, antediluvian, antique, ancient, venerable *rel* superannuated, aged *ant* modernistic; modish

antique *syn* OLD, ancient, venerable, antiquated, antediluvian, obsolete, archaic *ant* modern; current

antisocial *syn* UNSOCIAL, asocial, nonsocial *rel* anarchic, anarchistic, anarchist; misanthropic, pessimistic, cynical *ant* social

antithesis 1 *syn* COMPARISON, contrast, parallel, collation 2 *syn*

OPPOSITE, antipode, contradictory, contrary, antonym *rel* converse, counter, reverse

antithetical *syn* OPPOSITE, contrary, contradictory, antonymous, antipodal, antipodean

antonym *syn* OPPOSITE, contradictory, contrary, antithesis, antipode *rel* converse, counter, reverse

antonymous *syn* OPPOSITE, contradictory, contrary, antithetical, antipodal, antipodean

anxiety *syn* CARE, worry, concern, solicitude *rel* distress, suffering, misery; fear, dread, alarm, panic; apprehension, foreboding, misgiving; doubt, uncertainty, mistrust *ant* security

anxious **1** *syn* WORRIED, concerned, solicitous *rel* fearful, apprehensive, afraid; uneasy, jittery, impatient; perturbed, agitated, upset *ant* composed **2** *syn* EAGER, keen, agog, avid *rel* desiring, desirous, wishing, wishful, craving; yearning, longing, pining *ant* loath

apartment *syn* ROOM, chamber

apathetic *syn* IMPASSIVE, phlegmatic, stolid, stoic *rel* insensitive, impassible, insensible, anesthetic; callous, hardened; unaffected, untouched, unimpressed; listless, spiritless, languid *ant* alert; aghast

apathy *syn* IMPASSIVITY, impassiveness, phlegm, stolidity, stoicism *rel* inertness, inactivity, passiveness, supineness; indifference, unconcern, aloofness, detachment; lethargy, torpidity, torpor *ant* zeal; enthusiasm

ape *syn* COPY, imitate, mimic, mock *rel* caricature, burlesque; emulate, rival

aperçu *syn* COMPENDIUM, sketch, précis, survey, digest, pandect, syllabus *rel* epitome, brief, abstract, abridgment

aperitif *syn* APPETIZER

aperture · an opening allowing passage through or in and out *syn* interstice, orifice *rel* perforation, puncture, bore, prick; hole, hollow, cavity; slit, slash, cut

apex *syn* SUMMIT, peak, culmination, pinnacle, climax, acme, meridian, zenith, apogee

aphorism *syn* SAYING, apothegm, epigram, saw, maxim, adage, proverb, motto

aphrodisiac *syn* EROTIC, amatory, amorous *ant* anaphrodisiac

apiece *syn* EACH, severally, individually, respectively

aplomb *syn* CONFIDENCE, assurance, self-assurance, self-possession, self-confidence *rel* coolness, collectedness, nonchalance, imperturbability; equanimity, composure, sangfroid; poise, savoir faire, tact *ant* shyness

apocalypse *syn* REVELATION, vision, prophecy

apocryphal *syn* FICTITIOUS, mythical, legendary, fabulous *rel* questionable, dubious, doubtful

apogee *syn* SUMMIT, climax, peak, culmination, apex, acme, meridian, zenith, pinnacle *ant* perigee

apologia *syn* APOLOGY, excuse, plea, alibi, pretext *rel* defense, justification, vindication; interpretation, elucidation, explanation

apology · the reason or reasons offered in explanation or defense of something (as an act, a policy, or a view) *syn* apologia, excuse, plea, pretext, alibi *rel* defense, justification, vindication; extenuation, palliation, glozing, whitewashing; amends, reparation

apostasy *syn* DEFECTION, desertion

apostate *syn* RENEGADE, turncoat, recreant, backslider *rel* deserter, forsaker, abandoner; heretic, schismatic, dissenter, nonconformist

apothecary *syn* DRUGGIST, pharmacist, chemist

apothegm *syn* SAYING, aphorism,

epigram, saw, maxim, adage, proverb, motto

apotheosis *syn* PARAGON, nonpareil, nonesuch

appall *syn* DISMAY, horrify, daunt *rel* terrify, affright, frighten; confound, dumbfound, bewilder, puzzle *ant* nerve, embolden

appalling *syn* FEARFUL, dreadful, terrible, horrible, frightful, shocking, awful, terrific, horrific *rel* dismaying, horrifying, daunting; bewildering, dumbfounding, confounding *ant* reassuring

appanage *syn* RIGHT, prerogative, privilege, perquisite, birthright

apparatus **1** *syn* EQUIPMENT, gear, tackle, outfit, paraphernalia, machinery, matériel *rel* tool, implement, utensil, instrument; network, system, scheme **2** *syn* MACHINE, mechanism, machinery, engine, motor *rel* device, contrivance, contraption, gadget

apparel *vb, syn* CLOTHE, attire, dress, array, robe *rel* outfit, accouter, appoint, equip, furnish *ant* divest

apparel *n, syn* CLOTHES, clothing, dress, attire, raiment

apparent **1** *syn* EVIDENT, manifest, patent, distinct, obvious, palpable, plain, clear *rel* discernible, noticeable; perceptible, ponderable, tangible, appreciable *ant* unintelligible **2** • not actually being what appearance indicates *syn* illusory, seeming, ostensible *rel* false, wrong; deceptive, delusory, delusive, misleading; specious, credible, plausible *ant* real

apparition • a visible but immaterial appearance of a person or thing, esp. a likeness of a dead person or of a person or thing that is not physically present *syn* phantasm, phantom, wraith, ghost, spirit, specter, shade, revenant *rel* illusion, delusion, hallucination

appeal *n, syn* PRAYER, plea, petition, suit *rel* entreating, entreaty, beseeching, supplicating, supplication, imploring; soliciting, solicitation, requesting, request, asking

appeal *vb, syn* PRAY, plead, sue, petition *rel* implore, beg, beseech, entreat, supplicate; solicit, request, ask

appear **1** • to come out into view *syn* loom, emerge *rel* come, arrive; issue, emanate, rise, arise, spring *ant* disappear; vanish **2** *syn* SEEM, look

appearance • the outward show presented by a person or thing *syn* look, aspect, semblance

appease *syn* PACIFY, placate, mollify, propitiate, conciliate *rel* assuage, alleviate, mitigate, lighten, relieve; palliate, extenuate; satisfy, content *ant* exasperate, aggravate

appellation *syn* NAME, title, designation, denomination, style

append *syn* ADD, subjoin, annex, superadd *rel* affix, attach, fasten

appendage • something regarded as additional and at the same time as subsidiary to another object *syn* appurtenance, accessory, adjunct

appendix • additional matter subjoined to a book *syn* addendum, supplement

apperception *syn* RECOGNITION, assimilation, identification

appertain *syn* BEAR, pertain, belong, relate, apply

appetite *syn* DESIRE, lust, passion, urge *rel* hungering, hunger, thirsting, thirst, yearning, longing; craving, wishing, coveting impulse, spring, motive; cupidity, greed

appetizer *syn* hors d'oeuvre, aperitif

appetizing *syn* PALATABLE, relishing, tasty, toothsome, flavorsome, savory, sapid *ant* nauseating

applaud **1** • to demonstrate one's feeling, esp. one's approbation or joy, audibly and enthusiastically *syn* cheer, root *rel* acclaim, extol, praise *ant* hiss; boo **2** *syn* COMMEND, compliment, recommend *rel* praise, eulogize, laud; approve, endorse, sanction *ant* disparage; criticize

applause • public expression of approbation *syn* acclamation, acclaim, plaudits *rel* cheering, cheers, rooting *ant* hisses; boos

appliance *syn* IMPLEMENT, tool, instrument, utensil *rel* accessory, adjunct; device, contrivance, gadget

applicable *syn* RELEVANT, pertinent, apposite, apropos, germane, material *rel* fit, suitable, appropriate, apt, felicitous, happy, meet, fitting, proper *ant* inapplicable

applicant *syn* CANDIDATE, aspirant

application *syn* ATTENTION, concentration, study *rel* intentness, engrossment, absorption; toil, grind, drudgery, work; sedulousness, assiduousness, industriousness, industry, diligence *ant* indolence

appliqué *syn* OVERLAY, superpose, superimpose *rel* ornament, adorn, decorate; affix, attach, fasten

apply **1** *syn* USE, employ, utilize, avail **2** *syn* DIRECT, devote, address *rel* attend, mind, tend; addict, accustom, habituate; toil, labor, work, grind **3** *syn* RESORT, go, turn, refer *rel* appeal, petition; beg, beseech, implore, supplicate **4** *syn* BEAR, relate, pertain, appertain

appoint **1** *syn* DESIGNATE, name, nominate, elect *rel* choose, select, pick, single; commission, authorize, accredit **2** *syn* FURNISH, equip, accouter, outfit, arm *rel* garnish, beautify, embellish, bedeck, deck, adorn; array, clothe

appointment *syn* ENGAGEMENT, rendezvous, tryst, assignation, date

apportion **1** *syn* ALLOT, allocate, assign *rel* distribute, divide, dispense, deal, dole; share, participate, partake **2** • to divide something carefully and distribute it among a number *syn* portion, parcel, ration, prorate *rel* grant, accord, award; give, bestow; separate, divide, part

apposite *syn* RELEVANT, pertinent, germane, apropos, applicable, material *rel* felicitous, happy, apt, appropriate, suitable, fit, fitting; pat, timely, opportune, seasonable *ant* inapposite, inapt

appraise *syn* ESTIMATE, value, evaluate, assay, rate, assess *rel* judge, adjudge; determine, ascertain, discover; inspect, examine, scrutinize, audit

appreciable *syn* PERCEPTIBLE, sensible, ponderable, palpable, tangible *rel* apparent, evident; discernible, noticeable *ant* inappreciable

appreciate **1** *syn* UNDERSTAND, comprehend *rel* appraise, value, rate, estimate, evaluate; judge, adjudge; apprehend, comprehend *ant* depreciate **2** • to hold in high estimation *syn* value, prize, treasure, cherish *rel* admire, esteem, respect, regard; enjoy, like, relish *ant* despise

apprehend **1** *syn* ARREST, detain, attach *rel* seize, take; capture, catch **2** • to lay hold of something with the mind so as to know it *syn* comprehend *rel* understand, appreciate; grasp, take; perceive, observe, notice, note, see **3** *syn* FORESEE, divine, anticipate, foreknow *rel* fear, dread forecast, predict, forebode, foretell

apprehension **1** *syn* ARREST, detention, attachment *rel* seizing, seizure, taking; capturing, capture, catching **2** • something that is known *syn* comprehension *rel* understanding, appreciation; perceiving, perception, observing, observation, noticing, notice, noting **3** • fear (or an instance of it) that something is going wrong or will go wrong *syn* foreboding, misgiving, presentiment *rel* fear, dread, alarm, panic; worry, anxiety, care *ant* confidence

apprehensive *syn* FEARFUL, afraid *rel* anxious, worried, solicitous; nervous, uneasy, jittery *ant* confident

apprentice *syn* NOVICE, novitiate, probationer, postulant, neophyte *rel* beginner, starter; tyro, amateur

apprise *syn* INFORM, advise, notify, acquaint *rel* tell, reveal, disclose, divulge, discover, betray; publish, proclaim, declare, announce

approach *vb* **1** · to come or draw close (to) *syn* near, approximate *rel* accost, address; begin, commence, initiate; consult, confer, advise, negotiate **2** *syn* MATCH, touch, equal, rival

approach *n, syn* OVERTURE, advance, tender, bid *rel* attempt, endeavor, essay, try *ant* repulse

approbation · warmly commending acceptance or agreement *syn* approval *rel* admiration, esteem, respect, regard; applause, acclaim, acclamation, plaudits *ant* disapprobation

appropriate *vb, syn* ARROGATE, preempt, confiscate, usurp *rel* take, seize, grab; annex, add

appropriate *adj, syn* FIT, fitting, proper, suitable, apt, meet, happy, felicitous *rel* apposite, pertinent, germane, relevant; pat, timely, seasonable, opportune *ant* inappropriate

appropriation · money or property given or set apart by an authorized body for a predetermined use by others *syn* grant, subvention, subsidy

approval *syn* APPROBATION *rel* commending, commendation, applauding, applause, compliment; endorsing, endorsement, sanction *ant* disapproval

approve · to have or to express a favorable opinion of *syn* endorse, sanction, accredit, certify *rel* commend, applaud, compliment; ratify, confirm *ant* disapprove

approximate *syn* APPROACH, near

approximately *syn* NEARLY, almost, well-nigh *ant* precisely, exactly

appurtenance *syn* APPENDAGE, accessory, adjunct *rel* furnishing, furniture, equipment, appointment

apropos *syn* RELEVANT, apposite, pertinent, germane, applicable, material *rel* pat, timely, opportune, seasonable; appropriate, fitting, fit, suitable, apt, proper, meet, happy *ant* unapropos

apt **1** *syn* FIT, happy, felicitous, appropriate, fitting, suitable, meet, proper *rel* apposite, pertinent, relevant, apropos; pat, timely, opportune, seasonable; telling, convincing, compelling, valid; right, nice, precise, exact, correct *ant* inapt, inept **2** *syn* likely, liable *rel* inclined, disposed, predisposed; prone **3** *syn* QUICK, prompt, ready *rel* clever, smart, bright, intelligent, quick-witted, alert; gifted, talented

aptitude *syn* GIFT, bent, turn, talent, faculty, knack, genius *rel* taste, gusto, zest; propensity, leaning, penchant, flair *ant* inaptitude

aqueduct *syn* CHANNEL, canal, conduit, duct

arbiter *syn* JUDGE, arbitrator, umpire, referee

arbitrary *syn* ABSOLUTE, autocratic, despotic, tyrannical, tyrannous *rel* dictatorial, authoritarian, magisterial, oracular; domineering, masterful, imperious, peremptory, imperative *ant* legitimate

arbitrate *syn* JUDGE, adjudicate, adjudge *rel* mediate, intervene, interpose; decide, determine, settle; conciliate, placate, appease, pacify

arbitrator *syn* JUDGE, referee, arbiter, umpire

arc *syn* CURVE, arch, bow

arcade *syn* PASSAGE, gallery, cloister, ambulatory, passageway, corridor, hall, hallway, aisle

arcane *syn* MYSTERIOUS, inscrutable *rel* occult, esoteric, recondite; cabalistic, anagogic, mystic, mystical

arch *n, syn* CURVE, bow, arc

arch *adj, syn* SAUCY, pert *rel* roguish, waggish, impish, mischievous, playful; mocking, deriding, derisive, twitting

archaic *syn* OLD, obsolete, antiquated, antique, ancient, antediluvian, venerable *ant* up-to-date

architect *syn* ARTIST, artificer, artisan

archive *syn* DOCUMENT, record, monument

arctic *syn* COLD, frigid, freezing, frosty, icy, gelid, glacial, chilly, cool *ant* torrid

ardent *syn* IMPASSIONED, passionate, fervid, perfervid, fervent *rel* intense, fierce; enthusiastic, zealous; eager, avid, keen; glowing, flaming, blazing *ant* cool

ardor *syn* PASSION, fervor, enthusiasm, zeal *rel* excitement, stimulation, quickening, galvanizing; eagerness, avidity; zest, gusto *ant* coolness; indifference

arduous *syn* HARD, difficult *rel* laborious, toilsome; exhausting, wearying, wearisome, tiring, fatiguing; onerous, exacting, oppressive *ant* light, facile

area 1 · a distinguishable extent of surface and esp. of the earth's surface *syn* tract, region, zone, belt *rel* locality, district; expanse, stretch 2 *syn* SIZE, extent, dimensions, magnitude, volume

argot *syn* DIALECT, cant, jargon, slang, lingo, vernacular, patois

argue 1 *syn* DISCUSS, debate, dispute, agitate *rel* prove, demonstrate; disprove, refute, rebut, controvert; expostulate, protest, object, remonstrate 2 *syn* INDICATE, bespeak, prove, attest, betoken *rel* show, manifest, evidence, demonstrate, evince; imply, suggest, intimate

argument 1 *syn* REASON, proof, ground *rel* proving, demonstrating, demonstration; disproving, disproof, refuting, refutation, rebutting, rebuttal 2 · a vigorous and often heated discussion of a moot question *syn* dispute, controversy *rel* argumentation, disputation, debate; controverting, refuting, rebutting; contention, dissension, discord 3 *syn* SUBJECT, theme, matter, subject matter, topic, text, motive, motif, leitmotiv

argumentation · the act or art of argument or an exercise of one's powers of argument *syn* disputation, debate, forensic, dialectic *rel* argument, dispute, controversy

arid *syn* DRY *rel* barren, infertile, sterile, unfruitful; bare, bald, barren; desiccated, dehydrated, parched *ant* moist; verdant

arise 1 *syn* RISE, ascend, mount, soar, levitate, surge, tower, rocket *rel* lift, raise, elevate, rear *ant* recline; slump 2 *syn* SPRING, rise, originate, derive, flow, issue, emanate, proceed, stem *rel* emerge, appear, loom; begin, commence, start; ensue, succeed, follow

aristocracy 1 *syn* OLIGARCHY, plutocracy 2 · a body of persons who constitute a socially superior caste *syn* nobility, gentry, county, elite, society *ant* people, proletariat

aristocrat *syn* GENTLEMAN, patrician *ant* commoner

arm *syn* FURNISH, accouter, outfit, equip, appoint *ant* disarm

armistice *syn* TRUCE, cease-fire, peace

army *syn* MULTITUDE, host, legion *rel* throng, press, crush, crowd, mob, rout, horde

aroma *syn* SMELL, odor, scent *rel* fragrance, perfume, redolence, incense, bouquet; savor, taste *ant* stink, stench

aromatic *syn* ODOROUS, balmy, redolent, fragrant *rel* spicy, pungent, piquant; savory, palatable *ant* acrid (*of odors*)

arouse *syn* STIR, rouse, awaken, waken, rally *rel* stimulate, quicken, galvanize, excite, provoke; electrify, thrill; kindle, fire, light; move, drive, impel *ant* quiet, calm

arraign *syn* ACCUSE, charge, impeach, indict, incriminate *rel* summon, cite; try, test

arrange **1** *syn* ORDER, marshal, organize, systematize, methodize *rel* dispose; line, line up, range, array, align; assort, classify, pigeonhole, sort *ant* derange, disarrange **2** *syn* NEGOTIATE, concert *rel* plan, design, scheme, project

arrant *syn* OUTRIGHT, out-and-out, unmitigated

array *vb* **1** *syn* LINE, line up, range, align *rel* marshal, arrange, order *ant* disarray **2** *syn* CLOTHE, apparel, attire, robe, dress

array *n, syn* DISPLAY, parade, pomp *rel* showing, show, exhibiting, exhibition, exposing, exposition; arranging, arrangement, marshaling; disposition

arrear *syn* DEBT, indebtedness, debit, obligation, liability

arrest *vb* **1** · to stop in midcourse *syn* check, interrupt *rel* interpose, intervene, interfere; delay, detain, retard; frustrate, thwart, balk *ant* activate; quicken **2** · to seize and hold under restraint or in custody by authority of the law *syn* apprehend, attach, detain *rel* seize, take; catch, capture; imprison, incarcerate, jail

arrest *n* · seizing and holding under restraint or in custody by authority of the law *syn* apprehension, detention, attachment *rel* seizing, seizure, taking; capturing, capture, catching

arresting *syn* NOTICEABLE, striking, remarkable, outstanding, salient, signal, prominent, conspicuous *rel* impressive, moving, touching, affecting, poignant; fascinating, attractive, enchanting

arrival · the reaching of a destination *syn* advent *rel* coming; appearing, appearance, emerging, emergence *ant* departure

arrive *syn* COME *ant* depart

arrogant *syn* PROUD, haughty, lordly, insolent, overbearing, supercilious, disdainful *rel* imperious, domineering, masterful, peremptory, imperative; pretentious, ostentatious, showy *ant* meek; unassuming

arrogate · to seize or take over in a high-handed manner *syn* usurp, preempt, appropriate, confiscate *rel* seize, take, grab *ant* renounce; yield

art **1** · the faculty of performing or executing expertly what is planned or devised *syn* skill, cunning, artifice, craft **2** *syn* TRADE, craft, handicraft, profession

artery *syn* WAY, route, course, passage, pass

artful *syn* SLY, wily, guileful, crafty, cunning, tricky, foxy, insidious *rel* adroit, dexterous; politic, diplomatic, smooth, suave *ant* artless

article **1** *syn* PARAGRAPH, clause, plank, count, verse **2** *syn* THING, object *rel* item, detail, particular **3** *syn* ESSAY, paper, theme, composition

articled *syn* BOUND, indentured, bond

articulate *adj* **1** *syn* VOCAL, oral *rel* distinct, clear, evident; uttered, voiced *ant* inarticulate, dumb **2** *syn* VOCAL, fluent, eloquent, voluble, glib *rel* expressing, voicing, uttering, venting; expressive, meaningful, significant; voluble, glib, talkative *ant* inarticulate, dumb

articulate *vb* **1** *syn* INTEGRATE, concatenate *rel* unite, join, connect, link, relate; organize, systematize, methodize, order **2** • to form speech sounds *syn* pronounce, enunciate

articulation **1** *syn* INTEGRATION, concatenation *rel* organization, systematizing, methodizing; system, organism, economy, scheme, complex **2** *syn* JOINT, suture

artifact *syn* WORK, product, production, opus

artifice **1** *syn* ART, cunning, craft, skill *rel* ingeniousness, ingenuity, cleverness, adroitness; adeptness, proficiency, expertness **2** *syn* TRICK, ruse, wile, stratagem, maneuver, gambit, ploy, feint *rel* deception, chicanery, chicane, trickery; deceit, guile, duplicity, dissimulation

artificer *syn* ARTIST, artisan, architect *rel* craftsman, handicraftsman, mechanic, workman, worker

artificial • not brought into being by nature but by human art or effort or by some process of manufacture *syn* factitious, synthetic, ersatz *rel* fabricated, manufactured, fashioned; simulated, feigned, counterfeited, counterfeit *ant* natural

artisan **1** *syn* ARTIST, artificer, architect **2** *syn* WORKER, mechanic, workman, workingman, operative, craftsman, handicraftsman, hand, laborer, roustabout

artist **1** • one who makes something beautiful or useful or both *syn* artificer, artisan, architect *rel* craftsman, workman, worker; creator, maker; writer, composer, author **2** *syn* EXPERT, artiste, virtuoso, adept, wizard

artiste *syn* EXPERT, artist, virtuoso, adept, wizard

artless *syn* NATURAL, simple, ingenuous, naïve, unsophisticated, unaffected *rel* spontaneous, impulsive; candid, open, plain, frank; straightforward, aboveboard, forthright *ant* artful; affected

as *syn* BECAUSE, since, for, inasmuch as

ascend **1** *syn* RISE, arise, mount, soar, tower, rocket, levitate, surge *rel* elevate, raise, rear, lift; advance, progress *ant* descend **2** • to move upward to or toward a summit *syn* mount, climb, scale *ant* descend

ascendancy *syn* SUPREMACY *rel* dominance, predominance, command, sway, dominion, control, power, authority; sovereignty

ascension • the act of moving upward or the movement upward *syn* ascent

ascent *syn* ASCENSION

ascertain *syn* DISCOVER, determine, unearth, learn *rel* inquire, query, interrogate, ask; study, contemplate, weigh, consider; observe, survey, see

ascetic *syn* SEVERE, austere, stern *rel* disciplined, trained, schooled; self-denying, self-abnegating; abstaining, abstinent, forbearing; abstemious *ant* luxurious, voluptuous, sensuous

ascribe • to lay something (creditable, discreditable, or neutral) to the account of a person or thing *syn* attribute, impute, assign, refer, credit, accredit, charge *rel* attach, fasten, affix; conjecture, surmise, guess; allege, advance, adduce, cite

ash • the remains of combustible material after it has been destroyed by fire *syn* cinders, clinkers, embers

ashamed • acutely or manifestly conscious of embarrassment and humiliation *syn* mortified, chagrined *rel* embarrassed, discomfited, abashed; humiliated, humbled, abased; abject, mean; contrite, penitent, repentant *ant* proud

ashen *syn* PALE, ashy, livid, pallid, wan *rel* ghastly, grim, macabre; blanched, bleached, decolorized, whitened

ashy *syn* PALE, ashen, livid, pallid, wan *rel* see ASHEN

asinine *syn* SIMPLE, fatuous, silly, foolish *rel* stupid, crass, dumb, dense, dull, slow; puerile, youthful; irrational, unreasonable *ant* sensible, judicious

ask 1 · to address a person in an attempt to elicit information *syn* question, interrogate, query, inquire, catechize, quiz, examine 2 · to seek to obtain by making one's wants or desires known *syn* request, solicit *rel* appeal, petition, plead, pray, sue; address, accost

askance *syn* AWRY, askew *rel* mistrustfully, distrustfully; enviously, jealously *ant* straightforwardly, directly

askew *syn* AWRY, askance *rel* crookedly, obliquely *ant* straight

asocial *syn* UNSOCIAL, antisocial, nonsocial *ant* social

aspect 1 *syn* APPEARANCE, look, semblance *rel* face, countenance, visage; bearing, mien, port, presence 2 *syn* PHASE, side, facet, angle *rel* slant, point of view, viewpoint, standpoint

asperity *syn* ACRIMONY, acerbity *rel* sharpness, keenness; causticity, mordancy; snappishness, waspishness, irritability *ant* amenity

asperse *syn* MALIGN, vilify, traduce, calumniate, slander, defame, libel *rel* disparage, depreciate, derogate, detract, decry; revile, vituperate, scold; defile

aspersion *syn* ANIMADVERSION, reflection, stricture *rel* libel, lampoon, pasquinade, squib, skit; abuse, vituperation, invective, obloquy; detraction, backbiting, calumny, slander, scandal

asphyxiate *syn* SUFFOCATE, stifle, smother, choke, strangle, throttle

aspirant *syn* CANDIDATE, applicant, nominee

aspiration *syn* AMBITION, pretension *rel* aim, goal, objective, intention; desire, passion, lust

aspire *syn* AIM, pant *rel* crave, covet, desire; long, yearn, hunger, thirst, pine

assail *syn* ATTACK, bombard, assault, storm *rel* beset, infest; belabor, pummel, buffet, pound, beat

assassin · one who can be hired to murder *syn* cutthroat, gunman, bravo *rel* murderer, slayer, killer

assassinate *syn* KILL, murder, slay, dispatch, execute

assault *n, syn* ATTACK, onslaught, onset *rel* assailing, bombarding, bombardment, storming, storm; invasion, incursion, raid

assault *vb, syn* ATTACK, storm, bombard, assail *rel* smite, slug, strike; beat, pound, buffet, pummel

assay *syn* ESTIMATE, assess, evaluate, appraise, value, rate *rel* analyze, resolve; calculate, compute, reckon; prove, test, try, demonstrate

assemblage *syn* GATHERING, assembly, collection, congregation *rel* aggregate, aggregation; crowd, throng, horde, crush, press

assemble *syn* GATHER, congregate, collect *rel* convene, convoke, muster, summon; combine, associate, unite, join *ant* disperse

assembly *syn* GATHERING, assemblage, congregation, collection *rel* company, party, troop, band; crowd, throng, crush, press

assent · concurrence with what someone else has stated or proposed *syn* consent, accede, acquiesce, agree, subscribe *rel* accept, receive; adopt, embrace, espouse; believe, credit *ant* dissent

assert 1 • to state positively usu. either in anticipation of denial or objection or in the face of it *syn* declare, profess, affirm, aver, protest, avouch, avow, predicate, warrant *rel* allege, advance, cite, adduce *ant* deny; controvert 2 *syn* MAINTAIN, vindicate, justify, defend *rel* proclaim, declare, publish, advertise; express, voice, utter

assertive *syn* AGGRESSIVE, self-assertive, pushing, pushy, militant *rel* positive, affirmative; blatant, clamorous, vociferous; cocksure, certain, sure, positive; confident, assured, sanguine, presumptuous *ant* retiring; acquiescent

assess *syn* ESTIMATE, assay, appraise, value, evaluate, rate *rel* calculate, compute, reckon

asset 1 **assets** *pl, syn* POSSESSIONS, resources, means, effects, belongings *ant* liabilities 2 *syn* CREDIT *ant* handicap

assiduous *syn* BUSY, sedulous, diligent, industrious *rel* indefatigable, tireless, untiring, unwearied *ant* desultory

assign 1 *syn* ALLOT, allocate, apportion *rel* fix, set, establish, settle; distribute, deal, dole, dispense 2 *syn* ASCRIBE, refer, attribute, impute, credit, accredit, charge *rel* attach, fasten, affix; relate, link, associate, join; pigeonhole, classify, assort 3 *syn* PRESCRIBE, define *rel* determine, settle, decide; consign, relegate, commit, entrust

assignation *syn* ENGAGEMENT, rendezvous, tryst, date, appointment

assignment *syn* TASK, duty, job, stint, chore

assimilate 1 *syn* IDENTIFY, incorporate, embody *rel* change, alter, modify, vary; transform, metamorphose, transmute; blend, fuse, merge, commingle, mix 2 *syn* ABSORB, imbibe *rel* engross, absorb, monopolize; adopt, embrace, espouse; infuse, imbue, ingrain, suffuse, inoculate, leaven

assimilation *syn* RECOGNITION, apperception, identification

assist *syn* HELP, aid *rel* support, uphold, back, champion; profit, avail, benefit; attend, accompany, escort, cooperate, concur, unite *ant* hamper; impede

assistance *syn* HELP, aid *rel* service, advantage, profit, avail, use; supporting, upholding, backing; subsidy, grant, subvention, appropriation; cooperation, concurrence *ant* impediment; obstruction

assistant *n* • a person who takes over part of the duties of another, esp. in a subordinate capacity *syn* helper, coadjutor, aid, aide, aide-de-camp

associate *vb, syn* JOIN, connect, relate, link, conjoin, combine, unite *rel* merge, mingle, mix, blend, amalgamate, coalesce; organize

associate *n* • mean a person frequently found in the company of another *syn* companion, comrade, crony *rel* partner, colleague, ally, confederate; accomplice, abettor, accessory, confederate; assistant, helper, coadjutor, aide

association • a body of persons who unite in the pursuit of a common aim or object *syn* society, club, order

assort • to arrange in systematic order or according to some definite method of arrangement or distribution *syn* sort, classify, pigeonhole *rel* arrange, methodize, systematize, order

assorted *syn* MISCELLANEOUS, heterogeneous, motley, promiscuous *rel* diverse, different, various, disparate, divergent; selected, picked, chosen, preferred; mixed, mingled *ant* jumbled

assuage *syn* RELIEVE, alleviate, mitigate, lighten, allay *rel* temper, moderate; comfort, solace, console; mollify, placate, appease, pacify *ant* exacerbate; intensify

assume **1** • to put on a false or deceptive appearance *syn* affect, pretend, simulate, feign, counterfeit, sham *rel* dissemble, disguise, cloak, mask, camouflage **2** *syn* PRESUPPOSE, postulate, presume, premise, posit *rel* conjecture, surmise; grant, concede, allow; assert, affirm, aver, predicate, profess

assumption • something that is taken for granted or advanced as fact *syn* presupposition, postulate, posit, presumption, premise *rel* hypothesis, theory; principle, fundamental, axiom, theorem; conjecture, surmise

assurance **1** *syn* CERTAINTY, certitude, conviction *rel* belief, faith, credence, credit; trust, confidence, reliance, dependence; positiveness, sureness, cocksureness *ant* mistrust; dubiousness **2** *syn* CONFIDENCE, self-assurance, self-confidence, self-possession, aplomb *rel* sangfroid, composure, equanimity; sureness, sanguineness; mettle, resolution, spirit, courage, tenacity; effrontery, temerity, nerve *ant* diffidence; alarm

assure *syn* ENSURE, insure, secure *ant* alarm

assured *syn* CONFIDENT, sanguine, sure, presumptuous *rel* fearless, unapprehensive, unafraid; cool, composed, unruffled, imperturbable, unflappable, collected *ant* abashed; timorous

astern *syn* ABAFT, aft *rel* after, hind, rear, back *ant* ahead

astonish *syn* SURPRISE, astound, amaze, flabbergast *rel* nonplus, dumbfound, bewilder, confound, puzzle; impress, strike, touch, affect

astound *syn* SURPRISE, astonish, amaze, flabbergast *rel* dumbfound, confound, nonplus, bewilder, puzzle; startle, affright, alarm, terrify, frighten

astral *syn* STARRY, stellar, sidereal

astray *syn* AMISS

astute *syn* SHREWD, perspicacious, sagacious *rel* sharp, keen, acute; discreet, prudent, foresighted; knowing, intelligent, clever, smart; wily, crafty, cunning, sly *ant* gullible

asylum *syn* SHELTER, refuge, retreat, sanctuary, cover

atavism *syn* REVERSION, throwback

atavistic *syn* REVERSIONARY

atheist • a person who rejects some or all of the essential doctrines of religion and particularly the existence of God *syn* agnostic, deist, freethinker, unbeliever, infidel *ant* theist

athirst *syn* EAGER, avid, keen, anxious, agog *rel* thirsting, hungering, pining, yearning, longing; craving, coveting, covetous, desiring, desirous

athletic *syn* MUSCULAR, husky, sinewy, brawny, burly *rel* strong, stalwart, sturdy; lusty, vigorous, strenuous, energetic

athletics • physical activities engaged in for exercise or play *syn* sports, games

athwart *syn* ACROSS, crosswise, crossways

atmosphere • an intangible and usually unanalyzable quality or aggregate of qualities which gives something an individual and distinctly recognizable character *syn* feeling, feel, aura *rel* quality, character, property; peculiarity, individuality, characteristic; impression, impress

atom *syn* PARTICLE, bit, mite, smidgen, jot, tittle, iota, whit *rel* smack, spice, dash, suspicion, soupçon, touch, suggestion, tincture, tinge, shade

atone *syn* EXPIATE *rel* compensate, pay; propitiate, conciliate, appease, pacify

atonement *syn* EXPIATION *rel* compensating, compensation, offsetting; conciliation, propitiation, appeasement; reparation, amends

atrabilious *syn* MELANCHOLIC, hypochondriac, melancholy *rel* morose, glum, saturnine, crabbed, sullen; despondent, hopeless, forlorn; depressed, dejected, gloomy, sad *ant* blithe

atrocious *syn* OUTRAGEOUS, heinous, monstrous *rel* flagrant, gross, rank, glaring; nefarious, flagitious, infamous, iniquitous, vicious; barbaric, savage, barbarous, barbarian *ant* humane; noble, moral

attach **1** *syn* ARREST, apprehend, detain *rel* seize, take, grab; capture, catch **2** *syn* FASTEN, affix, fix *rel* join, link, unite, connect; annex, add, append; tie, bind *ant* detach

attachment **1** *syn* ARREST, apprehension, detention **2** • the feeling which animates a person who is genuinely fond of someone or something *syn* affection, love *rel* fondness, devotedness; devotion, piety, fealty, fidelity, allegiance *ant* aversion

attack *vb* • to make an onslaught upon *syn* assail, assault, bombard, storm *rel* fight, contend, battle, war; beset, overrun, infest; surprise, waylay, ambush

attack *n* **1** • an attempt made on another or on others to injure, destroy, or defame *syn* assault, onslaught, onset *rel* action, battle; striking, hitting, smiting, slugging; criticism, condemnation, denouncing, denunciation **2** • action in a struggle for supremacy which must be met with defense or by means of defenses *syn* aggression, offense, offensive **3** *syn* FIT, access, accession, paroxysm, spasm, convulsion

attacking • initiating hostile action in a struggle for supremacy *syn* aggressive, offensive

attain *syn* REACH, compass, gain, achieve *rel* come, arrive; win, acquire, secure, obtain, get; accomplish, effect

attainment *syn* ACQUIREMENT, accomplishment, acquisition

attaint *syn* CONTAMINATE, taint, pollute, defile

attempt *vb* • to make an effort to do something that may or may not be successful *syn* try, endeavor, essay, strive, struggle *rel* begin, commence, start, initiate, inaugurate *ant* succeed

attempt *n* • an effort made to do or accomplish something *syn* endeavor, essay, try, striving, struggle *rel* trial, test; beginning, commencement, starting, start, initiation

attend **1** *syn* TEND, mind, watch *rel* nurse, foster, nurture, cherish; supervise, oversee **2** *syn* ACCOMPANY, escort, chaperon, convoy

attention **1** • the direct focusing of the mind esp. on something to be learned, worked out, or dealt with *syn* study, concentration, application *rel* diligence, assiduity, sedulousness, industriousness *ant* inattention **2** *syn* COURTESY, gallantry, amenity *rel* courting, court, wooing; deference, homage, honor, reverence; solicitude, care

attentive *syn* THOUGHTFUL, considerate *rel* courteous, polite, gallant, chivalrous, civil; solicitous, concerned, careful *ant* inattentive; neglectful

attenuate *syn* THIN, rarefy, dilute, extenuate *rel* weaken, sap; reduce, lessen, decrease; dissipate, scatter; contract, shrink, constrict, deflate *ant* enlarge; dilate; enrich

attest 1 *syn* CERTIFY, witness, vouch *rel* confirm, corroborate, substantiate, verify 2 *syn* INDICATE, argue, prove, bespeak, betoken *rel* demonstrate, test, prove; confirm, authenticate, substantiate *ant* belie

attire *vb, syn* CLOTHE, apparel, array, dress, robe *rel* accouter, appoint, equip, outfit, arm, furnish *ant* divest

attire *n, syn* CLOTHES, clothing, apparel, raiment, dress

attitude 1 *syn* POSTURE, pose *rel* mien, bearing, port, presence, demeanor 2 *syn* POSITION, stand *rel* point of view, angle, slant, viewpoint, standpoint; bias, prepossession, prejudice, predilection

attorney 1 *syn* AGENT, deputy, proxy, factor *rel* substitute, supply, alternate 2 *syn* LAWYER, solicitor, counselor, barrister, counsel, advocate

attract • to draw another by exerting an irresistible or compelling influence *syn* allure, charm, fascinate, bewitch, enchant, captivate *rel* invite, solicit, court; entice, lure, tempt, seduce; catch, capture *ant* repel

attraction • the relationship between persons or things that are involuntarily or naturally drawn together *syn* affinity, sympathy

attractive • drawing another by exerting a compelling influence *syn* alluring, charming, fascinating, bewitching, enchanting, captivating *rel* lovely, fair, beautiful, bonny, pretty, comely; luring, enticing, tempting, seductive *ant* repellent; forbidding

attribute *n* 1 *syn* QUALITY, property, character, accident 2 *syn* SYMBOL, emblem, type *rel* sign, mark, token, badge, note; character, symbol, sign

attribute *vb, syn* ASCRIBE, impute, assign, credit, accredit, refer, charge *rel* fasten, attach, fix; predicate, assert; blame, criticize; accuse, charge

attrition *syn* PENITENCE, contrition, repentance, remorse, compunction *rel* regret, sorrow, grief, anguish

attune *syn* HARMONIZE, tune *rel* adapt, adjust, accommodate, reconcile, conform; accord, agree, harmonize; temper, moderate; balance, counterbalance, compensate

atypical *syn* ABNORMAL, aberrant *rel* irregular, anomalous, unnatural; divergent, different; deviating, departing; exceptional *ant* typical; representative

audacious *syn* BRAVE, courageous, unafraid, fearless, intrepid, valiant, valorous, dauntless, undaunted, doughty, bold *rel* daring, daredevil, reckless, venturesome, adventurous, rash, foolhardy; brazen, brash, shameless *ant* circumspect

audacity *syn* TEMERITY, hardihood, effrontery, nerve, cheek, gall *rel* intrepidity, boldness, courageousness, bravery; daring, daredeviltry, recklessness, rashness, foolhardiness, adventurousness; courage, mettle, spirit; brazenness, brass, shamelessness *ant* circumspection

audience 1 *syn* HEARING, audition 2 *syn* FOLLOWING, public, clientele *rel* devotees, votaries

audit *n, syn* SCRUTINY, examination, inspection, scrutiny, scanning *rel* check, corrective, control; investigation, probe, inquiry

audit *vb, syn* SCRUTINIZE, examine, inspect, scan

audition *syn* HEARING, audience

auditory • of or relating to the hearing of sounds *syn* acoustic, acoustical

augment *syn* INCREASE, enlarge,

multiply *rel* intensify, aggravate, enhance, heighten; swell, expand, amplify, dilate *ant* abate

augur *syn* FORETELL, prognosticate, presage, portend, forebode, prophesy, forecast, predict *rel* betoken, indicate, bespeak, argue; apprehend, anticipate, divine, foreknow, foresee

augury *syn* FORETOKEN, omen, portent, presage, prognostic *rel* sign, symptom, token, note, badge, mark; precursor, forerunner, harbinger, herald

august *syn* GRAND, majestic, imposing, stately, noble, grandiose, magnificent *rel* impressive, moving; splendid, sublime, superb; awful, fearful *ant* unimpressive; unimposing

aura *syn* ATMOSPHERE, feeling, feel

aureate *syn* RHETORICAL, euphuistic, flowery, grandiloquent, magniloquent, bombastic *rel* ornate, florid, flamboyant, rococo, baroque *ant* austere (*in style*)

auspicious *syn* FAVORABLE, propitious, benign *rel* lucky, fortunate, happy, providential; hopeful, roseate; indicating, indicative, betokening *ant* inauspicious; ill-omened

austere *syn* SEVERE, stern, ascetic *rel* bald, bare; unembellished, unadorned, unornamented, undecorated; dispassionate, fair; rigorous, strict, rigid; grave, somber, serious, sober, earnest *ant* luscious (*of fruits*); warm, ardent (*of persons, feelings*); exuberant (*of style, quality*)

autarchic *syn* FREE, autarkic, autonomous, independent, sovereign

autarchy *syn* FREEDOM, autarky, autonomy, independence, sovereignty

autarkic *syn* FREE, autarchic, autonomous, independent, sovereign

autarky *syn* FREEDOM, autarchy, autonomy, independence, sovereignty

authentic • being exactly as appears or is claimed *syn* genuine, veritable, bona fide *rel* authoritarian, oracular, dictatorial; reliable, trustworthy, dependable; correct, right, exact; true, real, actual *ant* spurious

authenticate *syn* CONFIRM, validate, verify, substantiate, corroborate *rel* certify, accredit, endorse, approve; prove, try, test, demonstrate; avouch, warrant, assert *ant* impugn

author *syn* MAKER, creator

authoritarian *syn* DICTATORIAL, dogmatic, magisterial, doctrinaire, oracular *rel* despotic, autocratic, arbitrary, tyrannical, tyrannous, absolute; domineering, imperious, masterful *ant* liberal, libertarian; anarchistic, anarchic

authority **1** *syn* POWER, jurisdiction, command, control, dominion, sway *rel* ascendancy, supremacy; government, ruling, rule **2** *syn* INFLUENCE, weight, credit, prestige *rel* exemplar, ideal, standard, pattern, model, example; expert, adept, artist; connoisseur, aesthete

authorize • to invest with power or the right to act *syn* commission, accredit, license *rel* empower, enable; permit, allow, let

autobiography *syn* BIOGRAPHY, memoir, life, confessions

autochthonous *syn* NATIVE, indigenous, aboriginal, endemic *ant* naturalized

autocratic *syn* ABSOLUTE, arbitrary, despotic, tyrannical, tyrannous *rel* dictatorial, magisterial; authoritarian, totalitarian; masterful, domineering, imperious; overbearing, arrogant, proud

automatic *syn* SPONTANEOUS, mechanical, instinctive, impulsive *rel* trained, disciplined, schooled, instructed; prompt, quick, ready

autonomous *syn* FREE, independent, sovereign, autarchic, autarkic

autonomy *syn* FREEDOM, independence, sovereignty, autarchy, autarky

auxiliary • supplying aid or support *syn* subsidiary, accessory, contributory, subservient, ancillary, adjuvant *rel* subordinate, secondary, tributary; supporting, upholding, backing; helping, aiding, assisting; supplementary, complementary

avail *vb* **1** *syn* BENEFIT, profit *rel* meet, answer, satisfy, fulfill; help, aid **2** *syn* USE, utilize, employ, apply

avail *n, syn* USE, service, account, advantage, profit

avarice *syn* CUPIDITY, greed, rapacity *rel* avariciousness, covetousness, acquisitiveness; stinginess, niggardliness, miserliness, parsimoniousness *ant* prodigality

avaricious *syn* COVETOUS, acquisitive, grasping, greedy *rel* miserly, close, closefisted, parsimonious, stingy *ant* generous

avenge • to inflict punishment by way of repayment for *syn* revenge *rel* requite, recompense, compensate, pay; vindicate, defend, justify, maintain; punish, chasten, chastise

aver *syn* ASSERT, declare, avouch, avow, profess, affirm, protest *rel* maintain, defend, justify *ant* deny

average *n* • something (as a number, quantity, or condition) that represents a middle point between extremes *syn* mean, median, norm, par *ant* maximum; minimum

average *adj, syn* MEDIUM, middling, indifferent, fair, moderate, mediocre, second-rate *rel* common, ordinary, familiar; usual, customary *ant* exceptional; extraordinary

averse *syn* DISINCLINED, indisposed, loath, reluctant, hesitant *rel* recoiling, shrinking, flinching, quailing; uncongenial, unsympathetic, inconsonant; balky, contrary, perverse *ant* avid (*of* or *for*); athirst (*for*)

aversion **1** *syn* DISLIKE, distaste, disfavor *rel* antipathy, hostility, antagonism, enmity; horror, dread, fear *ant* predilection **2** *syn* ANTIPATHY *rel* repugnance, repellency, abhorrence, distaste, distastefulness; horror, dread, fear *ant* attachment, predilection

avert **1** *syn* TURN, deflect, sheer, divert *rel* bend, twist, curve; shift, remove, transfer, move **2** *syn* PREVENT, ward, obviate, preclude *rel* escape, avoid, shun, eschew, evade, elude; forestall, anticipate, prevent; frustrate, balk, thwart, foil

avid *syn* EAGER, keen, anxious, agog, athirst *rel* desiring, desirous, craving, coveting, covetous; longing, yearning, pining, hankering, hungering, thirsting *ant* indifferent; averse

avoid *syn* ESCAPE, shun, eschew, evade, elude *rel* avert, ward, prevent, obviate; forestall, anticipate, prevent; flee, fly, escape *ant* face; meet

avouch *syn* ASSERT, aver, affirm, avow, profess, declare, protest, warrant, predicate *rel* confirm, corroborate

avow **1** *syn* ASSERT, affirm, profess, declare, aver, avouch, warrant, protest, predicate *rel* maintain, defend, vindicate **2** *syn* ACKNOWLEDGE, own, confess, admit *rel* proclaim, declare, publish, announce; reveal, discover, disclose, divulge, tell *ant* disavow

await *syn* EXPECT, hope, look *rel* wait, abide, stay *ant* despair

awake *syn* AWARE, alive, cognizant, conscious, sensible *rel* alert, vigilant, watchful; roused, aroused, stirred up, awakened

awaken *syn* STIR, waken, rouse, arouse, rally *rel* excite, galvanize, quicken, stimulate, provoke; kindle, fire, light; elicit, evoke, educe *ant* subdue

award *vb, syn* GRANT, accord, vouchsafe, concede *rel* bestow, confer, present, give; assign, allot, apportion, allocate; adjudicate, adjudge, judge, arbitrate

award *n, syn* PREMIUM, prize, reward, guerdon, meed, bonus, bounty

aware · having knowledge of something *syn* cognizant, conscious, sensible, alive, awake *rel* sure, certain, positive; informed, acquainted, apprised *ant* unaware

awe *syn* REVERENCE, fear *rel* respect, esteem, regard; wonder, wonderment, admiration, amazement

awful *syn* FEARFUL, dreadful, frightful, terrible, horrible, shocking, appalling, terrific, horrific *rel* impressive, moving; solemn, serious, grave; imposing, august, majestic; sublime, superb, splendid; ominous, portentous

awkward · not marked by ease (as of performance, movement, or social conduct) *syn* clumsy, maladroit, inept, gauche *rel* stiff, wooden, rigid; embarrassing, discomfiting, disconcerting *ant* handy, deft; graceful

awry · deviating from a straight line or direction *syn* askew, askance

axiom *syn* PRINCIPLE, fundamental, law, theorem

B

babble *syn* CHAT, gabble, jabber, prattle, chatter, patter, prate, gibber, gab *rel* gossip, blab, tattle; converse, talk, speak

babel *syn* DIN, hubbub, clamor, racket, uproar, hullabaloo, pandemonium *rel* clamorousness, clamor, vociferousness; confusion, disorder

baby *syn* INDULGE, mollycoddle, humor, pamper, spoil

back *n, syn* SPINE, backbone, vertebrae, chine

back *adj, syn* POSTERIOR, rear, hind, hinder, after *ant* front

back *vb* **1** *syn* SUPPORT, uphold, champion, advocate *rel* assist, aid, help; favor, accommodate, oblige; abet, incite **2** *syn* RECEDE, retrograde, retreat, retract

backbiting *syn* DETRACTION, slander, scandal, calumny *rel* aspersion, animadversion, reflection, stricture; abuse, invective, obloquy, vituperation; vilifying, vilification, defaming, defamation *ant* vindication

backbone **1** *syn* SPINE, back, vertebrae, chine **2** *syn* FORTITUDE, grit, guts, sand, pluck *rel* courage, resolution, tenacity, mettle, spirit; courageousness, intrepidity, dauntlessness, valiancy; nerve, temerity, hardihood *ant* spinelessness

backdrop *syn* BACKGROUND, setting, milieu, mise-en-scène, environment

backer *syn* SPONSOR, surety, guarantor, patron, angel

background · the place, time, and circumstances in which something occurs *syn* setting, environment, milieu, mise-en-scène, backdrop

backslide *syn* LAPSE, relapse *rel* revert, return; deteriorate, degenerate, decline; recede, retreat, retrograde

backslider *syn* RENEGADE, apostate, recreant, turncoat

backsliding *syn* LAPSE, relapse *rel* retrogressiveness, retrogression, retrogradation; abandoning, deserting, forsaking

backward • not moving or going ahead *syn* retrograde, retrogressive, regressive *rel* laggard, dilatory, slow; stupid, dull, dense; lethargic, sluggish; abnormal, atypical *ant* advanced

bad 1 • deviating from the dictates of moral law *syn* evil, ill, wicked, naughty *rel* iniquitous, vicious, villainous; base, low, vile; immoral, unmoral, amoral *ant* good 2 • not measuring up to a standard of what is satisfactory *syn* poor, wrong *ant* good

badge *syn* SIGN, token, mark, note, symptom

badger *syn* BAIT, hound, chivy, hector, ride, heckle *rel* annoy, vex, bother, irk; harass, harry, worry, pester, plague, tease

badinage • animated back-and-forth exchange of remarks *syn* persiflage, raillery *rel* bantering, banter, chaffing, kidding, joshing, jollying; fun, game, jest, sport

badlands *syn* WASTE, desert, wilderness

baffle *syn* FRUSTRATE, balk, circumvent, outwit, foil, thwart *rel* puzzle, mystify, confound, dumbfound; discomfit, rattle, faze, embarrass, disconcert; confuse, addle, muddle; hamper, fetter, hog-tie; hinder, impede, obstruct, block

bag *n* • a container made of a flexible material and open or opening at the top *syn* sack, pouch

bag *vb, syn* CATCH, capture, trap, snare, entrap, ensnare

bail *n, syn* GUARANTEE, bond, surety, security, guaranty

bail *vb, syn* DIP, ladle, scoop, spoon, dish

bailiwick *syn* FIELD, province, domain, territory, sphere

bait *vb* • to persist in tormenting or harassing another *syn* badger, heckle, hector, chivy, hound, ride *rel* worry, annoy, harass, harry; torment, rack, torture, try, afflict

bait *n, syn* LURE, snare, trap, decoy *rel* allurement, attraction; enticement, temptation

bake *syn* DRY, parch, desiccate, dehydrate

balance *n* 1 • the stability or efficiency resulting from the equalization or exact adjustment of opposing forces *syn* equilibrium, equipoise, poise, tension 2 *syn* SYMMETRY, proportion, harmony 3 *syn* REMAINDER, rest, residue, residuum, leavings, remnant, remains

balance *vb* 1 *syn* COMPENSATE, counterpoise, counterbalance, countervail, offset *rel* attune, harmonize, tune; correspond, accord, square, agree 2 *syn* STABILIZE, poise, ballast, trim, steady *rel* settle, set; waver, sway, oscillate, fluctuate

bald *syn* BARE, barren, naked, nude *rel* austere, severe; unembellished, unadorned, unornamented; colorless, uncolored

balderdash *syn* NONSENSE, twaddle, drivel, bunk, poppycock, gobbledygook, trash, rot, bull

bale *syn* BUNDLE, package, pack, parcel, bunch, packet

baleful *syn* SINISTER, maleficent, malefic, malign *rel* threatening, menacing; ominous, portentous, fateful; hellish, infernal; diabolical, fiendish, devilish *ant* beneficent

balk 1 *syn* FRUSTRATE, thwart,

foil, baffle, circumvent, outwit *rel* defeat, beat, lick, conquer, overcome; block, obstruct, impede, hinder; prevent, forestall *ant* forward **2** *syn* DEMUR, jib, shy, boggle, stickle, scruple, strain, stick *rel* hesitate, falter, waver; refuse, decline; shrink, flinch, quail, recoil

balky *syn* CONTRARY, restive, perverse, froward, wayward *rel* hesitant, reluctant, averse, loath, disinclined, indisposed; obstinate, stubborn, mulish; refractory, recalcitrant, unruly

ballast *syn* STABILIZE, steady, balance, trim, poise

ballot *syn* SUFFRAGE, vote, franchise

ballyhoo *syn* PUBLICITY, promotion, propaganda *rel* advertisement, broadcasting

balmy **1** *syn* ODOROUS, aromatic, fragrant, redolent *rel* refreshing, restoring, rejuvenating; pleasing, grateful, welcome, pleasant *ant* rank, noisome **2** *syn* SOFT, gentle, smooth, bland, mild, lenient *rel* agreeable, pleasant, gratifying, grateful; gladdening, delighting, rejoicing, regaling; assuaging, allaying, lightening, relieving; salubrious, salutary, healthful

bamboozle *syn* DUPE, trick, hoodwink, gull, hoax, befool *rel* delude, deceive, beguile, mislead; outwit, circumvent, frustrate; defraud, cozen, overreach, cheat, swindle

ban *syn* FORBID, prohibit, interdict, inhibit, enjoin *rel* bar, block, hinder; prevent, preclude; exclude, debar, rule out

banal *syn* INSIPID, flat, jejune, inane, vapid, wishy-washy *rel* trite, hackneyed; simple, fatuous, silly, asinine; commonplace, platitudinous, bromidic *ant* original; recherché

band **1** *syn* BOND, tie *rel* connection, link, joining; joint, articulation, suture **2** *syn* STRIP, stripe, ribbon, fillet **3** *syn* COMPANY, troop, troupe, party *rel* coterie, clique, set, circle; horde, mob, crowd; society, club, association, order

bandy *syn* EXCHANGE, interchange

bane *syn* POISON, venom, virus, toxin

baneful *syn* PERNICIOUS, noxious, deleterious, detrimental *rel* harmful, injurious, mischievous, hurtful; malign, sinister, baleful; poisonous, venomous, toxic *ant* beneficial

banish · to remove by authority or force from a country, state, or sovereignty *syn* exile, expatriate, ostracize, deport, transport, extradite *rel* eject, expel, oust; exclude, debar, eliminate, shut out

bank *n* **1** *syn* SHOAL, bar, reef **2** *syn* SHORE, strand, coast, beach, foreshore, littoral **3** *syn* HEAP, mass, pile, stack, shock, cock *rel* aggregate, aggregation, conglomerate, conglomeration; assemblage, assembly, collection, gathering

bank *vb, syn* HEAP, mass, pile, stack, shock, cock *rel* collect, assemble, gather

bank *vb, syn* RELY, count, reckon, trust, depend

bankrupt *syn* DEPLETE, impoverish, exhaust, drain *rel* denude, strip, bare; sap, cripple, disable, undermine, weaken

banner *syn* FLAG, standard, ensign, color, streamer, pennant, pendant, pennon, jack

banquet *syn* DINNER, feast

banter · to make fun of good-naturedly *syn* chaff, kid, rag, rib, josh, jolly *rel* twit, rally, deride, ridicule

baptize · to administer the rite of baptism *syn* christen

bar *n* **1** · something which hinders or obstructs *syn* barrier, barricade **2** *syn* OBSTACLE, obstruction, impediment, snag *rel* hindrance, block, dam; difficulty, hardship, vicissitude *ant* advantage **3** *syn* SHOAL, bank, reef

bar *vb, syn* HINDER, obstruct, block, dam, impede *rel* shut out, debar, exclude; prevent, preclude, obviate; forbid, prohibit, interdict; close, shut *ant* admit; open

barbarian · of, relating to, or characteristic of people that are not fully civilized *syn* barbaric, barbarous, savage *ant* civilized

barbaric *syn* BARBARIAN, savage, barbarous *rel* showy, ostentatious; florid, ornate, flamboyant; gaudy, garish, flashy, meretricious *ant* restrained; refined; subdued

barbarism · a word or expression which offends against standards of correctness *syn* corruption, impropriety, solecism, vernacularism, vulgarism

barbarous **1** *syn* BARBARIAN, savage, barbaric *rel* rough, harsh; untutored, untaught, uneducated, illiterate, ignorant; rude, rough, crude *ant* civilized; humane **2** *syn* FIERCE, savage, inhuman, ferocious, cruel, fell, truculent *rel* pitiless, ruthless, uncompassionate; atrocious, monstrous, outrageous *ant* clement

bard *syn* POET, minstrel, troubadour, rhymer, rhymester, versifier, poetaster

bare *adj* **1** · lacking naturally or conventionally appropriate covering or clothing *syn* naked, nude, bald, barren *rel* stripped, divested, denuded; unclothed, undressed, unrobed *ant* covered **2** *syn* MERE, very

bare *vb, syn* STRIP, denude, divest, dismantle *ant* cover

barefaced *syn* SHAMELESS, brazen, brash, impudent *rel* open, plain, frank, candid; indecent, unseemly, indecorous *ant* furtive

bargain *syn* CONTRACT, compact, pact

bark *vb* · to make the sound of or a sound suggestive of a dog *syn* bay, howl, growl, snarl, yelp, yap *rel* bellow, vociferate, bawl, roar; yell, shout, scream, shriek

bark *n, syn* SKIN, rind, peel, hide, pelt

baroque *syn* ORNATE, florid, rococo, flamboyant

barren **1** *syn* STERILE, unfruitful, infertile, impotent *ant* fecund **2** *syn* BARE, bald, naked, nude *rel* arid, dry; desolate, forlorn, alone; impoverished, exhausted, depleted; austere, severe, stern

barricade *syn* BAR, barrier

barrier *syn* BAR, barricade

barrister *syn* LAWYER, counselor, counsel, advocate, attorney, solicitor

basal **1** *syn* FUNDAMENTAL, basic, underlying, radical **2** *syn* ELEMENTARY, beginning, elemental, rudimentary

base *n* · something on which another thing is reared or built or by which it is supported or fixed in place *syn* basis, foundation, ground, groundwork *ant* top

base *vb* · to supply or to serve as a basis *syn* found, ground, bottom, stay, rest *rel* support, sustain; set, establish, fix, settle

base *adj* · deserving of contempt because of the absence of higher values *syn* low, vile *rel* mean, ignoble, abject, sordid; bad, evil, ill, wicked; ignominious, infamous, disgraceful *ant* noble

baseless · not justified or justifiable in any way *syn* groundless, unfounded, unwarranted *rel* false, wrong; unsupported, unsustained

bashful *syn* SHY, diffident, modest, coy *rel* shrinking, recoiling; timorous, timid; embarrassed, abashed *ant* forward; brazen

basic **1** *syn* FUNDAMENTAL, basal, underlying, radical *rel* principal, capital, chief, main; primordial, primary *ant* top; peak **2** *syn* ALKALINE *syn* ELEMENTAL, elementary, essential, fundamental, primitive, underlying

basis *syn* BASE, foundation, ground, groundwork *rel* principle, fundamental, axiom, law, theorem; premise, postulate, presupposition, presumption, assumption

baste *syn* BEAT, pummel, thrash, buffet, pound, belabor *rel* chastise, castigate, punish, discipline

bastion *syn* BULWARK, breastwork, parapet, rampart

bathos *syn* PATHOS, poignancy *rel* mawkishness, maudlinism, soppiness, mushiness

batter *syn* MAIM, mangle, mutilate, cripple *rel* beat, pound, pummel, thrash, buffet, belabor, baste

battle *n* • a hostile meeting between opposing military forces *syn* engagement, action *rel* encounter, skirmish, brush; attack, assault, onslaught, onset; combat, conflict, fight, contest

battle *vb, syn* CONTEND, war, fight *rel* combat, oppose, resist, withstand, fight; attack, assail, assault, bombard; kick, protest, object

bawl *vb* **1** *syn* ROAR, bellow, bluster, vociferate, clamor, howl, ululate *rel* yell, shout, scream, shriek; bay, bark, growl, yelp; cry, wail **2** *syn* SCOLD, rate, berate, tongue-lash, upbraid, chew out, wig, rail, revile, vituperate *rel* reprimand, rebuke, reproach, reprove, chide; censure, denounce, condemn, reprehend, reprobate, criticize

bawl *n, syn* ROAR, bellow, bluster, vociferation, ululation

bay *syn* BARK, howl, growl, snarl, yelp, yap *rel* bellow, vociferate, clamor, roar; yell, holler, shout

be • to have actuality or reality *syn* exist, live, subsist

beach *syn* SHORE, strand, coast, foreshore, bank, littoral

beak *syn* BILL, neb, nib

beam *syn* RAY *rel* flash, gleam, glint, scintillation, coruscation

beaming *syn* BRIGHT, radiant, refulgent, effulgent, brilliant, luminous, lustrous, lambent, lucent, incandescent *rel* flashing, gleaming, glittering, glistening, glinting, sparkling, coruscating, scintillating; glowing, flaming

bear **1** *syn* CARRY, convey, transport, transmit *rel* move, remove, shift, transfer, hold, contain **2** • to bring forth as products *syn* produce, yield, turn out *rel* reproduce, propagate, breed, generate **3** • to sustain something trying or painful *syn* suffer, endure, abide, tolerate, stand, brook *rel* accept, receive; afflict, try, torment, torture **4** *syn* PRESS, bear down, squeeze, crowd, jam *rel* weigh, oppress, depress; burden, encumber, load, saddle **5** • to have a connection especially logically *syn* relate, pertain, appertain, belong, apply *rel* concern, affect; touch, influence, affect; weigh

beard *syn* FACE, brave, challenge, dare, defy *rel* confront, meet, encounter

bear down *syn* PRESS, bear, squeeze, crowd, jam

bearing • the way in which or the quality by which a person outwardly manifests personality *syn* deportment, demeanor, mien, port, presence *rel* posture, attitude, pose; behavior, conduct; attitude, stand, position; poise, address, tact

beastly *syn* BRUTAL, bestial, brute, brutish, feral *rel* abominable, detestable, hateful; loathsome, repulsive, revolting, offensive; disgusting, sickening, nauseating

beat *vb* **1** • to strike repeatedly *syn* pound, pummel, thrash, buffet, baste, belabor *rel* slug, clout, swat, punch, strike, hit, smite, slap, box, cuff **2** *syn* CONQUER, defeat, lick, vanquish, subdue, subjugate, reduce, overcome, surmount, overthrow, rout *rel* surpass, excel, outstrip, exceed; confound, nonplus, puzzle **3** *syn* PULSATE, throb, pulse, palpitate *rel* quiver, quaver, quake, shake; vibrate, oscillate, fluctuate, pendulate, swing

beat *n, syn* PULSATION, pulse, throb, palpitation *rel* accent, accentuation, stress, emphasis; rhythm, cadence

beatitude *syn* HAPPINESS, blessedness, bliss, felicity *rel* rapture, ecstasy, transport; joy, fruition, enjoyment, pleasure *ant* despair; dolor

beau *syn* FOP, exquisite, dandy, coxcomb, dude, buck

beau ideal *syn* MODEL, ideal, exemplar, pattern, example, mirror, standard

beauteous *syn* BEAUTIFUL, pulchritudinous, fair, good-looking, handsome, pretty, comely, bonny, lovely *rel* alluring, attractive, fascinating, charming

beautiful · very pleasing or delightful to look at *syn* lovely, handsome, pretty, bonny, comely, fair, beauteous, pulchritudinous, good-looking *rel* splendid, resplendent, glorious, sublime, superb; exquisite, elegant, choice *ant* ugly

beautify *syn* ADORN, embellish, deck, bedeck, ornament, decorate, garnish *rel* enhance, heighten, intensify *ant* uglify

because · for the reason that *syn* for, since, as, inasmuch as

becloud *syn* OBSCURE, cloud, eclipse, fog, befog, dim, bedim, darken, obfuscate *rel* confuse, muddle, addle, befuddle; puzzle, perplex, distract

bedeck *syn* ADORN, deck, garnish, embellish, beautify, decorate, ornament

bedim *syn* OBSCURE, dim, eclipse, cloud, becloud, fog, befog, obfuscate, darken *rel* cloak, mask, disguise; conceal, hide, screen

beetle *syn* BULGE, overhang, jut, project, protrude, stick out *rel* menace, threaten

befall *syn* HAPPEN, betide, occur, chance, transpire

befog *syn* OBSCURE, fog, cloud, becloud, eclipse, darken, dim, bedim, obfuscate *rel* puzzle, perplex, distract, bewilder, dumbfound; confuse, muddle, addle

befool *syn* DUPE, trick, hoax, hoodwink, gull, bamboozle *rel* cheat, cozen, overreach; deceive, delude, beguile, mislead; blandish, cajole, wheedle, coax

before · in advance, especially in place or in time *syn* ahead, forward *ant* after

beforehand *syn* EARLY, betimes, soon *ant* behindhand

befoul *syn* SOIL, foul, dirty, sully, smirch, besmirch, grime, begrime, tarnish *rel* spot, spatter, sprinkle

befuddle *syn* CONFUSE, fuddle, addle, muddle *rel* bewilder, distract, confound, perplex, puzzle; intoxicate, inebriate *ant* clarify, clear

beg · to ask or request urgently *syn* entreat, beseech, implore, supplicate, adjure, importune *rel* solicit, request, ask; plead, pray, petition, sue; demand, exact

beget *syn* GENERATE, get, sire, procreate, engender, breed, propagate, reproduce *rel* bear, produce, yield

beggarly *syn* CONTEMPTIBLE, cheap, scurvy, shabby, sorry, despicable, pitiable *rel* paltry, measly, petty, trifling; mean, abject, sordid

begin · to take the first step in a course, process, or operation *syn* commence, start, initiate, inaugurate *rel* found, institute, establish, organize; introduce, admit, enter;

originate, derive, spring, arise, rise *ant* end

beginning *n* • the first part or stage of a process or development *syn* genesis, rise, initiation *rel* origin, source, inception, root; rise, derivation, emanation; emergence, appearance

beginning *adj, syn* ELEMENTARY, basal, elemental, rudimentary

begrime *syn* SOIL, grime, smirch, besmirch, dirty, sully, foul, befoul, tarnish *rel* spot, spatter, sprinkle

begrudge *syn* COVET, envy, grudge

beguile **1** *syn* DECEIVE, delude, mislead, betray, double-cross *rel* dupe, gull, befool, trick, hoax, hoodwink, bamboozle; cajole, wheedle, blandish, coax; cheat, cozen; lure, entice, seduce **2** *syn* WHILE, wile, beguile, fleet *rel* divert, amuse, entertain; comfort, solace; speed, hasten, hurry

behave **1** • to act or to cause oneself to do something in a certain way *syn* conduct, comport, demean, deport, acquit, quit *rel* bear, carry; manage, control, direct *ant* misbehave **2** *syn* ACT, react, operate, work, function

behavior • one's actions in general or on a particular occasion *syn* conduct, deportment *rel* demeanor, mien, bearing; action, act, deed

behest *syn* COMMAND, bidding, dictate, injunction, order, mandate *rel* precept, rule, law; request, solicitation

behind *syn* AFTER *ant* ahead

behindhand *syn* TARDY, late, overdue *rel* dilatory, laggard, slow; delayed, retarded, detained *ant* beforehand

behold *syn* SEE, view, survey, observe, descry, espy, notice, perceive, discern, remark, note, contemplate *rel* watch, look, see; regard, consider

beholder *syn* SPECTATOR, onlooker, looker-on, observer, witness, eyewitness, bystander, kibitzer

being **1** *syn* EXISTENCE, actuality *rel* personality, individuality, character, disposition *ant* becoming; nonbeing **2** *syn* ENTITY, creature, individual, person *rel* thing, object, article; idea, concept, thought

belabor *syn* BEAT, pound, pummel, thrash, buffet, baste *rel* strike, hit, smite, slug, clout, swat, punch, box, cuff, slap

belch • to eject (gas) from the stomach by way of the mouth or matter from a containing cavity by way of an opening *syn* burp, vomit, disgorge, regurgitate, spew, throw up *rel* eject, expel

beleaguer *syn* BESIEGE, invest, blockade *rel* surround, environ, encircle, encompass, hem, gird; enclose, envelop; harass, pester, worry, annoy

belie *syn* MISREPRESENT, falsify, garble *rel* contradict, contravene, negative, deny; controvert, disprove *ant* attest

belief **1** • the act of one who assents intellectually to something proposed or offered for acceptance as true or the state of mind of one who so assents *syn* faith, credence, credit *rel* certitude, assurance, certainty, conviction; assenting, assent, acquiescing, acquiescence *ant* unbelief, disbelief **2** *syn* OPINION, conviction, persuasion, view, sentiment *rel* doctrine, dogma, tenet; principle, fundamental; conclusion, judgment

believable *syn* PLAUSIBLE, credible, colorable, specious *rel* probable, possible, likely *ant* unbelievable

belittle *syn* DECRY, depreciate, disparage, derogate, detract, minimize *rel* underestimate, undervalue, underrate; diminish, reduce, lessen, decrease *ant* aggrandize, magnify

bellicose *syn* BELLIGERENT, pugnacious, combative, contentious, quarrelsome *rel* militant, aggressive, assertive; antagonizing, antagonistic, combating, combative; fighting, warring, battling, contending; rebellious, factious, seditious, mutinous, insubordinate *ant* pacific; amicable

belligerent • having or taking an aggressive or fighting attitude *syn* bellicose, pugnacious, combative, quarrelsome, contentious *rel* hostile, antagonistic; fighting, warring, battling, contending; warlike, martial *ant* friendly

bellow *vb, syn* ROAR, bluster, bawl, vociferate, clamor, howl, ululate *rel* yell, shout, scream, shriek; bay, bark, yelp; cry, wail, keen

bellow *n, syn* ROAR, bluster, bawl, vociferation, ululation

belly *syn* ABDOMEN, stomach, paunch, gut

belong *syn* BEAR, pertain, appertain, relate, apply

belongings *syn* POSSESSIONS, effects, means, resources, assets

below • in a lower position relative to some other object or place *syn* under, beneath, underneath *ant* above

belt *syn* AREA, zone, tract, region

bemoan *syn* DEPLORE, bewail, lament *rel* grieve, mourn, sorrow *ant* exult

bemuse *syn* DAZE, stun, stupefy, benumb, paralyze, petrify *rel* confuse, muddle, addle, fuddle, befuddle

bend *syn* CURVE, twist *rel* contort, deform; deflect, divert, turn *ant* straighten

beneath *syn* BELOW, underneath, under *ant* above, over

benefaction *syn* DONATION, contribution, alms *rel* gift, present, largess, boon; endowment; grant, subvention, appropriation; charity, philanthropy

beneficial • bringing good or gain *syn* advantageous, profitable *rel* salutary, healthful, wholesome; favorable, benign, propitious *ant* harmful; detrimental

benefit • to do good or to be of advantage to someone *syn* profit, avail *rel* better, improve, ameliorate; help, assist, aid *ant* harm

benevolent *syn* CHARITABLE, philanthropic, eleemosynary, humanitarian, humane, altruistic *rel* benign, benignant, kindly, kind; generous, liberal, bountiful, bounteous, openhanded; obliging, complaisant, amiable *ant* malevolent

benign **1** *syn* KIND, benignant, kindly *rel* gracious, genial, cordial, affable; sympathetic, tender, compassionate; suave, urbane, bland *ant* malign **2** *syn* FAVORABLE, auspicious, propitious *rel* fortunate, happy, providential, lucky; gentle, mild, soft; benevolent, humane, charitable; merciful, clement, forbearing *ant* malign

benignant *syn* KIND, benign, kindly *rel* benevolent, humane, charitable, humanitarian, philanthropic, eleemosynary; gracious, affable; compassionate, tender, sympathetic *ant* malignant

bent *syn* GIFT, turn, talent, aptitude, knack, faculty, genius *rel* propensity, penchant, leaning, proclivity, flair; predilection, bias, prepossession, prejudice, partiality; capacity, ability, capability

benumb *syn* DAZE, stun, bemuse, stupefy, paralyze, petrify *rel* chill, freeze; congeal, coagulate; dumbfound, confound, nonplus, bewilder, puzzle

bequeath *syn* WILL, devise, leave, legate *rel* give, present, bestow; distribute, dispense

berate *syn* SCOLD, rate, tongue-lash, upbraid, jaw, bawl, chew out, wig, rail, revile, vituperate *rel* censure, denounce, condemn, reprehend, reprobate, criticize; rebuke, reprimand, reproach, reprove, chide

berth 1 *syn* ROOM, play, elbowroom, leeway, margin, clearance 2 *syn* WHARF, dock, pier, quay, slip, jetty, levee

beseech *syn* BEG, entreat, implore, supplicate, importune, adjure *rel* pray, petition, sue, plead, appeal

beset *syn* INFEST, overrun *rel* worry, annoy, harass, harry, pester, plague; assail, attack, assault

besides *adv, syn* ALSO, moreover, furthermore, too, likewise

besiege • to surround an enemy in a fortified or strong position so as to prevent ingress or egress *syn* beleaguer, invest, blockade *rel* enclose, envelop, pen; surround, environ, encircle, encompass, hem; beset, infest; assail, attack, assault

besmirch *syn* SOIL, smirch, dirty, sully, foul, befoul, grime, begrime, tarnish *rel* spot, spatter, sprinkle *ant* cleanse

besotted *syn* FOND, infatuated, insensate *rel* fatuous, asinine, foolish, silly, simple; drunk, drunken, intoxicated, inebriated; stupid, slow, dull, dense, crass

bespangle *syn* SPOT, spangle, spatter, sprinkle, mottle, fleck, stipple, marble, speckle *rel* illuminate, illumine, lighten, light; glow, blaze, flame; flash, gleam, sparkle, scintillate, twinkle

bespangled *syn* SPOTTED, spangled, spattered, sprinkled, mottled, flecked, stippled, marbled, speckled *rel* bright, brilliant, radiant, luminous; illuminated, illumined, lighted

bespeak *syn* INDICATE, betoken, attest, argue, prove *rel* manifest, evidence, show, evince, demonstrate; imply, hint, suggest

bestial *syn* BRUTAL, brutish, brute, feral, beastly *rel* debased, depraved, corrupted, corrupt; degenerate, vicious; degraded; sensual, fleshly, carnal

bestow *syn* GIVE, confer, present, donate, afford *rel* distribute, dispense, divide; grant, award

bet • something (as money) staked on a winner-take-all basis on the outcome of an uncertainty *syn* wager, stake, pot, ante

bête noire *syn* ABOMINATION, bugbear, anathema

bethink *syn* REMEMBER, recollect, remind, recall, reminisce, mind

betide *syn* HAPPEN, befall, chance, occur, transpire

betimes *syn* EARLY, soon, beforehand *ant* unseasonably, inopportunely

betoken *syn* INDICATE, bespeak, attest, argue, prove *rel* presage, augur, portend, forebode, foretell; import, signify, denote, mean; evidence, manifest, show, evince, demonstrate

betray 1 *syn* DECEIVE, mislead, delude, beguile, double-cross *rel* trap, entrap, snare, ensnare, catch; dupe, trick, befool, hoodwink, gull 2 *syn* REVEAL, discover, disclose, divulge, tell *rel* manifest, evidence, evince, show, demonstrate; attest, betoken, bespeak, argue, indicate

better *adj* • more worthy or more pleasing than another or others *syn* superior, preferable *rel* choice, delicate, dainty; selected, culled, picked, preferred

better *vb, syn* IMPROVE, ameliorate, help *rel* correct, amend, reform, rectify, remedy, redress; enhance, intensify *ant* worsen

between • in common to (as in position, in a distribution, or in participation) *syn* among

bewail *syn* DEPLORE, lament, bemoan *rel* sorrow, grieve, mourn; wail, weep, cry *ant* rejoice

bewilder *syn* PUZZLE, mystify, perplex, distract, confound, nonplus, dumbfound *rel* confuse, addle, fuddle, muddle; fluster, flurry, perturb, agitate, upset, discompose; baffle, foil, frustrate

bewitch *syn* ATTRACT, enchant, captivate, fascinate, charm, allure *rel* thrill, electrify; delight, please; infatuate, enamor

bewitching *syn* ATTRACTIVE, enchanting, captivating, fascinating, charming, alluring

beyond *syn* FARTHER further

bias *n, syn* PREDILECTION, prejudice, prepossession, partiality *rel* slant, standpoint, point of view, viewpoint, angle; leaning, propensity; inclining, inclination, predisposition, disposition

bias *vb, syn* INCLINE, dispose, predispose *rel* sway, influence, affect, impress

bicker *syn* QUARREL, squabble, spat, tiff, wrangle, altercate *rel* contend, fight, battle, war

bickering *syn* QUARREL, spat, tiff, squabble, wrangle, altercation *rel* discord, contention, dissension, strife, conflict

bid *vb* **1** *syn* COMMAND, order, enjoin, direct, instruct, charge *rel* summon, summons, call, cite *ant* forbid **2** *syn* INVITE, solicit, court, woo *rel* ask, request

bid *n, syn* OVERTURE, tender, advance, approach *rel* offering, offer, proffering, proffer; proposal, proposition; inviting, invitation, soliciting, solicitation

biddable *syn* OBEDIENT, docile, amenable, tractable *rel* compliant, acquiescent; obliging, complaisant, good-natured, amiable; submissive, tame *ant* willful

bidding *syn* COMMAND, behest, order, injunction, mandate, dictate *rel* direction, instruction; summoning, summons, calling, call, citing, citation

big *syn* LARGE, great *rel* grand, magnificent, imposing, grandiose, majestic, august; huge, immense, enormous, gigantic, colossal *ant* little

bigot *syn* ENTHUSIAST, fanatic, zealot

bigoted *syn* ILLIBERAL, narrow-minded, narrow, intolerant, hidebound

bill • the jaws of a bird together with their horny covering *syn* beak, neb, nib

billingsgate *syn* ABUSE, scurrility, vituperation, invective, obloquy

bind *syn* TIE *rel* fasten, attach; join, link, unite, connect *ant* loose; unbind

biography • an account of the events and circumstances of a person's life *syn* life, memoir, autobiography, confessions

biologic *syn* DRUG, simple, medicinal, pharmaceutical

biotope *syn* HABITAT, range, station

birthright **1** *syn* RIGHT, appanage, prerogative, privilege, perquisite **2** *syn* HERITAGE, patrimony, inheritance

bisexual • combining male and female qualities *syn* hermaphroditic, hermaphrodite, androgynous, epicene

bit *syn* PARTICLE, mite, smidgen, whit, atom, iota, jot, tittle *rel* piece, fragment, detail, fraction, part, portion

bite • to attack with or as if with the teeth *syn* gnaw, champ, gnash *rel* eat, consume, devour

biting *syn* INCISIVE, cutting, crisp, trenchant, clear-cut *rel* caustic, mordant, acrid; pungent, poignant, piquant, racy

bitter • having or being an unusually unpleasant flavor or odor *syn* acrid *rel* sour, acid, acidulous, tart; pungent, piquant *ant* delicious

bizarre *syn* FANTASTIC, grotesque, antic *rel* outlandish, erratic, eccentric, strange, singular, odd, queer, curious; extravagant, extreme, excessive *ant* chaste; subdued

blab *syn* GOSSIP, tattle *rel* babble, gabble, chatter, prate, chat; divulge, disclose, betray, reveal

blackball *syn* EXCLUDE, debar, shut out, eliminate, rule out, disbar, suspend

blackguard *syn* VILLAIN, scoundrel, knave, rascal, rogue, scamp, rapscallion, miscreant

blame *vb, syn* CRITICIZE, reprehend, reprobate, condemn, denounce, censure *rel* accuse, charge, indict, impeach; impute, attribute; ascribe; implicate, involve

blame *n* • responsibility for misdeed or delinquency *syn* culpability, guilt, fault *rel* responsibility, accountability, answerability; censure, condemnation, denunciation, reprehension

blameworthy • deserving reproach and punishment for a wrong, sinful, or criminal act, practice, or condition *syn* guilty, culpable *ant* blameless

blanch *syn* WHITEN, bleach, decolorize, etiolate

bland **1** *syn* SUAVE, smooth, urbane, diplomatic, politic *rel* benign, benignant, kind, kindly; amiable, complaisant, obliging, good-natured; slick, unctuous, fulsome *ant* brusque **2** *syn* SOFT, mild, gentle, smooth, balmy, lenient *rel* neutral, indifferent; temperate, moderate; insipid, flat, vapid, wishy-washy *ant* pungent, piquant; savory, tasty, palatable

blandish *syn* COAX, wheedle, cajole *rel* allure, charm, bewitch, captivate, attract; lure, entice, seduce; beguile, delude, deceive

blank *syn* EMPTY, void, vacant, vacuous *rel* bare, barren; clean

blasé *syn* SOPHISTICATED, worldly-wise, worldly, disillusioned *rel* indifferent, unconcerned, incurious; nonchalant, imperturbable, unruffled, cool

blasphemous *syn* IMPIOUS, profane, sacrilegious *rel* cursing, damning, execrating, anathematizing, objurgating; irreligious, ungodly, godless *ant* reverent

blasphemy **1** • impious or irreverent speech *syn* profanity, swearing, cursing *rel* insult, affront, indignity; scurrility, vituperation, abuse *ant* adoration **2** *syn* PROFANATION, desecration, sacrilege *rel* debasement, corruption, perversion; misrepresentation, falsehood, untruth, lie

blast *n* • severe, sudden, or surprising ruin or injury *syn* blight, nip *rel* destruction; extermination, extirpation, wiping out; ruin, wreck

blast *vb* • to ruin or to injure severely, suddenly, or surprisingly *syn* blight, nip *rel* destroy; ruin, wreck; exterminate, extirpate, wipe; injure, damage, spoil

blatant *syn* VOCIFEROUS, clamorous, strident, boisterous, obstreperous *rel* assertive, self-assertive, pushing, aggressive, militant; vocal, articulate, voluble, glib; vulgar, coarse, gross *ant* decorous; reserved

blaze *n* • brightly burning light or fire *syn* flare, flame, glare, glow *rel* firing, fire, kindling, igniting, ignition; effulgence, refulgence, radiance, brilliance, brilliancy

blaze *vb* • to burn or appear to burn brightly *syn* flame, flare, glare, glow *rel* illuminate, illumine, light; burn; flash, gleam, glance

bleach *syn* WHITEN, etiolate, decolorize, blanch *ant* dye

bleak *syn* DISMAL, cheerless, dispiriting, dreary, desolate *rel* cold, chilly, frigid, freezing; barren, bare, bald; stripped, denuded

blemish • an imperfection (as a spot or crack) *syn* defect, flaw *rel* blot, stain, stigma; tainting, taint, pollution, defilement; fault, failing, frailty; lack, want, privation *ant* immaculateness

blench *syn* RECOIL, quail, shrink, flinch, wince *rel* evade, elude, avoid, shun, eschew, escape; tremble, quiver, shudder, quake, shake

blend *vb, syn* MIX, fuse, merge, coalesce, mingle, commingle, amalgamate *rel* combine, unite, conjoin, join; integrate; consolidate, unify, compact *ant* resolve

blend *n, syn* MIXTURE, admixture, compound, composite, amalgam

blessed *syn* HOLY, sacred, divine, spiritual, religious *ant* accursed

blessedness *syn* HAPPINESS, beatitude, bliss, felicity *rel* enjoyment, fruition, joy, pleasure *ant* misery, dolor

blight *n, syn* BLAST, nip *rel* injury, damage, hurt, harm; frustration, thwarting

blight *vb, syn* BLAST, nip *rel* injure, damage, hurt, harm, spoil; maim, cripple, batter; frustrate, thwart

blind *adj* · lacking or deficient in the power to see or to discriminate objects *syn* sightless, purblind

blind *n* · a device that serves as a screen for a window *syn* shade, shutter

blink *syn* WINK *rel* ignore, disregard, overlook, slight, neglect; evade, elude, avoid, shun, escape

bliss *syn* HAPPINESS, beatitude, blessedness, felicity *rel* enjoyment, joy, delectation, fruition, pleasure; rapture, ecstasy, transport *ant* anguish; bale

blithe *syn* MERRY, jocund, jovial, jolly *rel* gay, lively, animated, vivacious, sprightly; joyful, joyous, lighthearted, glad, happy, cheerful; buoyant, effervescent, volatile *ant* morose; atrabilious

bloc *syn* COMBINATION, party, faction, ring, combine

block *syn* HINDER, obstruct, bar, dam, impede *rel* check, arrest, interrupt; hamper, clog, trammel; prohibit, forbid, inhibit; frustrate, thwart, foil; prevent, forestall

blockade *n* · the isolation of an enemy area by a belligerent force to prevent the passage of persons or supplies *syn* siege

blockade *vb, syn* BESIEGE, beleaguer, invest *rel* close, shut; block, impede, obstruct, hinder; enclose; surround, environ, encircle

bloodless *syn* PALE, anemic *rel* colorless, uncolored; wishy-washy, vapid, inane, insipid *ant* sanguine; plethoric

bloody · affected by or involving the shedding of blood *syn* sanguinary, sanguine, sanguineous, gory

bloom *n, syn* BLOSSOM, flower, blow

bloom *vb, syn* BLOSSOM, flower, blow *rel* flourish, thrive, succeed

blossom *n* · the period or state of florescence of a seed plant *syn* flower, bloom, blow

blossom *vb* · to become florescent *syn* bloom, flower, blow

blot *syn* STIGMA, brand, stain *rel* taint, defilement, pollution; blemish, flaw, defect; shame, disgrace, ignominy, obloquy

blot out *syn* ERASE, delete, obliterate, expunge, cancel, efface *rel* abolish, annihilate, extinguish; wipe, exterminate, extirpate

blow *vb, syn* BLOSSOM, bloom, flower *rel* expand, swell; enlarge, augment, increase

blow *n, syn* BLOSSOM, bloom, flower

blowsy *syn* SLATTERNLY, frowzy, dowdy *rel* flashy, tawdry, gaudy, garish; slovenly, sloppy, disheveled, unkempt, slipshod; florid, flamboyant, ornate; vulgar, coarse *ant* smart, spruce; dainty

blubber *syn* CRY, weep, wail, keen, whimper

bluejacket *syn* MARINER, sailor, seaman, tar, gob

blueprint *n, syn* SKETCH, draft, tracing, plot, diagram, delineation, outline

blueprint *vb, syn* SKETCH, draft, trace, plot, diagram, delineate, outline

blues *syn* SADNESS, dejection, depression, melancholy, gloom, dumps

bluff • abrupt and unceremonious in speech or manner *syn* blunt, brusque, curt, crusty, gruff *rel* hearty, sincere; plain, open, frank, candid; abrupt, precipitate *ant* suave, smooth

blunder *syn* STUMBLE, lurch, flounder, trip, lumber, galumph, lollop, bumble *rel* stagger, reel, totter; wallow, welter

blunder *syn* ERROR, mistake, bull, howler, boner, slip, lapse, faux pas *rel* fault, failing, frailty, vice; anachronism, solecism; aberration, deviation; transgression, violation, breach

blunt **1** *syn* DULL, obtuse *ant* keen, sharp **2** *syn* BLUFF, brusque, curt, gruff, crusty *rel* plain, candid, frank; rude, discourteous, ungracious, uncivil, impolite; forthright, downright *ant* tactful; subtle

blurb *syn* CRITICISM, puff, review, critique

blush *vb* • to turn or grow red in the face *syn* flush *rel* color, tint, tinge

blush *n* • reddening of the face *syn* flush *rel* color, tint, tinge, hue

bluster *vb, syn* ROAR, bellow, bawl, vociferate, clamor, howl, ululate *rel* boast, brag, vaunt, crow; threaten, menace

bluster *n, syn* ROAR, bellow, bawl, vociferation, ululation *rel* boast, brag, vaunt, crow; threaten, menace

board *syn* HARBOR, house, lodge, shelter, entertain *rel* feed, nourish

boast • to give vent in speech to one's pride in oneself or something intimately connected with oneself *syn* brag, vaunt, crow, gasconade *rel* flaunt, parade, show; pride, plume, pique, preen; exalt, magnify, aggrandize *ant* depreciate (*oneself, one's accomplishments*)

boat • a floating structure designed to carry persons or goods over water *syn* vessel, ship, craft

bodily • of or relating to the human body *syn* physical, corporeal, corporal, somatic *rel* carnal, fleshly, animal, sensual

body • the dead physical substance of a human being or animal *syn* corpse, carcass, cadaver

boggle *syn* DEMUR, stickle, stick, strain, scruple, balk, jib, shy *rel* object, protest, kick, remonstrate, expostulate; recoil, shrink, flinch, wince, blench, quail *ant* subscribe (*to*)

bogus *syn* COUNTERFEIT, spurious, fake, sham, pseudo, pinchbeck, phony *rel* fraudulent, deceitful, deceptive; duping, hoaxing, gulling, hoodwinking

boil *n, syn* ABSCESS, furuncle, carbuncle, pimple, pustule

boil *vb* • to prepare (as food) in a liquid heated to the point where it emits considerable steam *syn* seethe, simmer, parboil, stew

boisterous *syn* VOCIFEROUS, obstreperous, clamorous, blatant, strident *rel* sporting, disporting, rollicking, frolicking, gamboling; unruly, ungovernable; indecorous, unseemly

bold *syn* BRAVE, courageous, unafraid, fearless, intrepid, valiant, valorous, dauntless, undaunted, doughty, audacious *rel* daring, reckless, venturesome, adventurous, daredevil, rash, foolhardy; mettlesome, spirited; fearless, unapprehensive, unafraid *ant* cowardly

bolster *syn* SUPPORT, prop, sustain, buttress, brace *rel* strengthen, reinforce, fortify; uphold, champion

bombard *syn* ATTACK, assail, storm, assault

bombast · speech or writing characterized by high-flown pomposity or pretentiousness of language disproportionate to the thought or subject matter *syn* rhapsody, rant, fustian, rodomontade *rel* grandiloquence, magniloquence, rhetoric; inflatedness, turgidity, tumidity, flatulence

bombastic *syn* RHETORICAL, grandiloquent, magniloquent, aureate, flowery, euphuistic *rel* inflated, turgid, tumid; verbose, diffuse, wordy; eloquent, voluble, fluent, articulate, vocal

bona fide *syn* AUTHENTIC, genuine, veritable *rel* true, real, actual; reliable, dependable, trustworthy; pure, absolute, simple, sheer *ant* counterfeit, bogus

bond *adj, syn* BOUND, indentured, articled *ant* free

bond *n* **1** · something which serves to bind or bring two or more things firmly together *syn* band, tie **2** *syn* GUARANTEE, surety, security, bail, guaranty

bondage *syn* SERVITUDE, slavery

boner *syn* ERROR, blunder, mistake, howler, bull, slip, lapse, faux pas

bonny *syn* BEAUTIFUL, comely, pretty, good-looking, fair, lovely, handsome, beauteous, pulchritudinous *rel* pleasing, agreeable, pleasant; attractive, charming, captivating *ant* homely

bonus *syn* PREMIUM, bounty, reward, guerdon, award, prize, meed

bon vivant *syn* EPICURE, gastronome, gourmet, gourmand, glutton *ant* ascetic

bookish *syn* PEDANTIC, academic, scholastic

boon *syn* GIFT, favor, present, gratuity, largess *rel* benefaction, donation, contribution *ant* calamity

boor · an uncouth ungainly person *syn* churl, lout, clown, clodhopper, bumpkin, hick, yokel, rube *ant* gentleman

boorish · uncouth in manners, or appearance *syn* loutish, clownish, churlish *rel* awkward, clumsy, maladroit, inept; rude, discourteous, ungracious, uncivil, impolite, ill-mannered *ant* gentlemanly

boost *syn* LIFT, raise, elevate, hoist, rear, heave *rel* exalt, aggrandize; heighten, enhance, intensify; mount, soar, levitate, surge, ascend, rise

bootleg *syn* SMUGGLED, contraband

bootless *syn* FUTILE, fruitless, vain, abortive *rel* idle, empty, hollow, nugatory, vain, otiose

bootlicker *syn* PARASITE, sycophant, toady, lickspittle, hanger-on, favorite, leech, sponge, sponger

booty *syn* SPOIL, loot, plunder, prize, swag

border · the line or relatively narrow space which marks the limit or outermost bound of something *syn* margin, verge, edge, rim, brim, brink *rel* limit, bound, confine, end

bore *syn* PERFORATE, drill, puncture, punch, prick *rel* penetrate, pierce, enter

boredom *syn* TEDIUM, ennui, doldrums *rel* amusement

boring *syn* IRKSOME, tiresome, wearisome, tedious *rel* dull, humdrum, monotonous, dreary, stodgy, pedestrian

botch · to handle or treat awkwardly or unskillfully *syn* bungle, fumble, muff, cobble *rel* patch, mend, repair; treat, handle; mutilate; wreck, ruin

bother *syn* ANNOY, vex, irk *rel* worry, harass, harry, pester, tease, tantalize; interfere, meddle, tamper; puzzle, perplex, distract; trouble, inconvenience, incommode, discommode *ant* comfort

bottom *syn* BASE, found, ground, stay, rest *rel* support, sustain; set, fix, establish

bough *syn* SHOOT, branch, limb

bounce *syn* DISMISS, drop, sack, fire, discharge, cashier

bound *n, syn* LIMIT, confine, end, term *rel* border, verge, edge

bound *adj* • obliged to serve a master or in a clearly defined capacity for a certain number of years by the terms of a contract or mutual agreement *syn* bond, indentured, articled

bound *n, syn* JUMP, leap, spring, vault *rel* advance, progress; haste, hurry, speed, expedition

bound *vb* **1** *syn* JUMP, leap, spring, vault *rel* advance, progress; speed, precipitate, hasten, hurry **2** *syn* SKIP, ricochet, hop, curve, lope, lollop *rel* dart, skim, skud, fly; rebound, recoil, resile

bounder *syn* CAD, rotter

boundless *syn* INFINITE, uncircumscribed, illimitable, eternal, sempiternal *rel* vast, immense, enormous, huge; monstrous, prodigious, tremendous, stupendous

bountiful, bounteous *syn* LIBERAL, generous, openhanded, munificent, handsome *rel* charitable, philanthropic, benevolent; prodigal, lavish, profuse *ant* niggardly

bounty *syn* PREMIUM, award, reward, meed, guerdon, prize, bonus *rel* gratuity, largess, gift, boon; grant, subvention, subsidy, appropriation

bouquet *syn* FRAGRANCE, perfume, redolence, incense *rel* odor, aroma, smell, scent

bout *syn* SPELL, stint, turn, trick, tour, shift, go

bow *vb, syn* YIELD, defer, submit, capitulate, succumb, relent, cave

bow *n, syn* CURVE, arc, arch

bow *vb, syn* FLEX, crook, buckle *rel* bend, curve, twist

box *syn* STRIKE, hit, smite, punch, slug, slog, swat, clout, slap, cuff

boyish *syn* YOUTHFUL, juvenile, puerile, maiden, virgin, virginal

brace *n, syn* COUPLE, pair, yoke

brace *vb, syn* SUPPORT, sustain, buttress, prop, bolster *rel* strengthen, reinforce, fortify, energize, invigorate

brag *syn* BOAST, vaunt, crow, gasconade *rel* plume, pique, pride, preen; flaunt, parade *ant* apologize

braid *syn* WEAVE, plait, knit, crochet, tat

brain *syn* MIND, intellect, intelligence, wit, psyche, soul

branch *syn* SHOOT, limb, bough

brand *n* **1** *syn* MARK, stamp, label, tag, ticket *rel* impression, impress, imprint, print **2** *syn* STIGMA, blot, stain *rel* sear, scorch, burn; tainting, taint, defilement; blemish, defect, flaw

brand *vb, syn* MARK, stamp, label, tag, ticket

brandish *syn* SWING, flourish, shake, wave, trash *rel* wield, swing, handle, manipulate, ply; flaunt, parade, display, exhibit, show

brash *syn* SHAMELESS, brazen, barefaced, impudent *rel* bold, audacious, brave; rash, reckless, adventurous; impetuous, headlong, abrupt, precipitate; intrusive, officious, impertinent *ant* wary

brave *adj* • having or showing no fear when faced with something dangerous, difficult, or unknown *syn* courageous, unafraid, fearless, intrepid, valiant, valorous, dauntless, undaunted, doughty, bold, audacious *rel* daring, venturesome, daredevil, adventurous; heroic, gallant; plucky, gritty *ant* craven

brave *vb, syn* FACE, dare, defy, beard, challenge *rel* confront, meet, encounter; oppose, combat, resist, fight

bravo *syn* ASSASSIN, cutthroat, gunman

brawl · a noisy fight or quarrel *syn* broil, fracas, melee, row, rumpus, scrap *rel* conflict, fight, fray, affray, contest; contention, dissension, strife, discord; wrangle, altercation, quarrel, squabble; uproar, racket, din, hubbub, clamor

brawny *syn* MUSCULAR, burly, husky, sinewy, athletic *rel* stalwart, strong, sturdy, stout, tough; fleshy *ant* scrawny

brazen *syn* SHAMELESS, brash, impudent *rel* callous, hardened, indurated; insolent, arrogant, proud; rash, reckless, adventurous; bold, audacious, brave *ant* bashful

breach **1** · the act or the offense of failing to keep the law or to do what the law, duty, or obligation requires *syn* infraction, violation, transgression, trespass, infringement, contravention *ant* observance **2** · a pulling apart in relations or in connections *syn* break, split, schism, rent, rupture, rift *rel* division, severance, separation; dissension, discord, difference, variance, strife; estrangement, alienation

bread, bread and butter *syn* LIVING, sustenance, livelihood, subsistence, maintenance, support, keep

break *vb* · to come apart or cause to come apart *syn* crack, burst, bust, snap, shatter, shiver *rel* disintegrate, crumble, decay; detach, disengage; demolish, destroy *ant* cleave (*together*); keep (*of laws*)

break *n* **1** · a lapse in continuity *syn* gap, interruption, interval, interim, hiatus, lacuna *rel* division, separation, severance; falling, sinking, dropping; respite, lull, intermission, recess, pause **2** *syn* BREACH, split, schism, rent, rupture, rift *rel* see BREACH 2 **3** *syn* OPPORTUNITY, chance, occasion, time

break down *syn* ANALYZE, resolve, dissect

breakdown *n, syn* ANALYSIS, resolution, dissection

breastwork *syn* BULWARK, bastion, parapet, rampart

breed *vb, syn* GENERATE, engender, propagate, reproduce, procreate, beget, sire, get

breed *n, syn* VARIETY, subspecies, race, cultivar, strain, clone, stock

breeding *syn* CULTURE, cultivation, refinement *rel* tact, address, poise, savoir faire; courtesy, amenity, gallantry; grace, dignity, elegance *ant* vulgarity

breeze *syn* WIND, gale, hurricane, zephyr

bridle **1** *syn* RESTRAIN, check, curb, inhibit *rel* repress, suppress; govern, rule; control, direct, manage, conduct *ant* vent **2** *syn* STRUT, bristle, swagger *rel* plume, preen, pique, pride

brief *adj* · not long *syn* short *rel* transient, fleeting, passing, momentary, short-lived; concise, terse, succinct, laconic, pithy; compacted, compact, concentrated; shortened, abbreviated, abridged, curtailed *ant* prolonged, protracted

brief *n, syn* ABRIDGMENT, abstract, epitome, synopsis, conspectus

bright **1** · actually or seemingly shining or glowing with light *syn* brilliant, radiant, luminous, lustrous, effulgent, refulgent, beaming, lambent, lucent, incandescent *rel* illuminated, illumined, lighted, lightened, enlightened; flashing, gleaming, glistening, sparkling; glowing, flaming *ant* dull; dim **2** *syn* INTELLIGENT, smart, quick-witted, brilliant, clever, knowing, alert *rel* sharp, keen, acute; quick, ready, prompt, apt; precocious, advanced *ant* dense, dull

brilliant 1 *syn* BRIGHT, radiant, luminous, effulgent, lustrous, refulgent, beaming, lambent, lucent, incandescent *rel* flashing, scintillating, sparkling, gleaming, glittering, coruscating; blazing, flaming, flaring, glowing *ant* subdued (*of light, color*) 2 *syn* INTELLIGENT, clever, bright, smart, alert, quick-witted, knowing *rel* erudite, learned, scholarly; sage, sapient, wise *ant* crass

brim *syn* BORDER, rim, edge, brink, verge, margin

bring · to convey from one place to another *syn* take, fetch *rel* bear, carry, convey; obtain, procure, get *ant* withdraw, remove

brink *syn* BORDER, rim, brim, verge, edge, margin *rel* limit, bound, end, confine; shore, strand, coast

brisk *syn* AGILE, nimble, spry *rel* fast, quick, rapid, fleet, swift, speedy; ready, prompt, quick; dynamic, live, active *ant* sluggish

bristle *syn* STRUT, bridle, swagger *rel* preen, plume, pride, pique; evince, manifest, show, evidence; flaunt, parade, display, exhibit

brittle *syn* FRAGILE, crisp, frangible, short, friable *rel* hardened, indurated *ant* supple

broach *syn* EXPRESS, voice, utter, vent, air, ventilate *rel* reveal, disclose, divulge; introduce, interject, interpose

broad · having horizontal extent *syn* wide, deep *rel* extended, extensive; spacious, capacious, commodious, ample; vast, immense, huge; expanded, dilated *ant* narrow

broadcast 1 *syn* STREW, straw, scatter, sow *rel* spread, circulate, disseminate, propagate 2 *syn* DECLARE, promulgate, publish, advertise, announce, proclaim

broadcasting *syn* DECLARATION, promulgation, publication, advertisement, announcement, proclamation

Brobdingnagian *syn* HUGE, vast, immense, enormous, elephantine, mammoth, giant, gigantic, gigantean, colossal, gargantuan, Herculean, cyclopean, titanic *ant* lilliputian

broil *syn* BRAWL, fracas, melee, row, rumpus, scrap *rel* fray, affray, fight, conflict, combat, contest; altercation, wrangle, quarrel; contention, strife, dissension, conflict, discord

bromide *syn* COMMONPLACE, cliché, platitude, truism

brook *syn* BEAR, stand, abide, tolerate, suffer, endure

browbeat *syn* INTIMIDATE, bulldoze, bully, cow *rel* terrorize, terrify, frighten, scare

bruise *vb*, *syn* CRUSH, mash, smash, squash, macerate *rel* batter, mangle, maim; press, squeeze

bruise *n*, *syn* WOUND, contusion, trauma, traumatism, lesion

brush *vb* · to touch lightly in passing *syn* graze, glance, shave, skim *rel* touch, contact; scatter, disperse, dispel; slide, slip, glide

brush *n*, *syn* ENCOUNTER, skirmish *rel* contest, conflict, combat, fight, fray; engagement, action, battle; attack, assault, onset, onslaught

brusque *syn* BLUFF, curt, blunt, gruff, crusty *rel* ungracious, rude, impolite, uncivil, discourteous; rough, harsh *ant* unctuous; bland

brutal · characteristic of an animal in nature, action, or instinct *syn* brute, brutish, bestial, beastly, feral *rel* sensual, animal, fleshly, carnal; coarse, gross, vulgar; stupid, dull, dense, crass; barbarous, savage, barbarian

brute *syn* BRUTAL, brutish, bestial, beastly, feral *rel* inanimate, lifeless, dead; inert, supine, inactive; impotent, powerless

brutish *syn* BRUTAL, brute, bestial, beastly, feral *rel* dull, dense, crass, stupid; sluggish, comatose, lethargic; stolid, impassive, apathetic

buccaneer *syn* PIRATE, freebooter, privateer, corsair

buck *syn* FOP, dude, dandy, beau, coxcomb, exquisite

buckle *syn* FLEX, crook, bow *rel* break, crack, snap, burst; bend, twist, curve

bucolic *syn* RURAL, pastoral, rustic *rel* boorish, loutish, clownish, churlish; natural, simple, naïve, ingenuous *ant* urbane

buffet *syn* BEAT, baste, pummel, pound, belabor, thrash *rel* strike, smite, hit, slap, slug; batter

bugbear *syn* ABOMINATION, bête noire, anathema

build *vb* · to form or fashion a structure or something comparable to a structure *syn* construct, erect, frame, raise, rear *rel* fabricate, fashion, manufacture, make; produce, turn out, yield, bear *ant* unbuild, destroy

build *n*, *syn* PHYSIQUE, habit, constitution *rel* form, figure, shape, conformation, configuration; structure, framework; contour, outline; style, fashion

building · a construction (as of wood, brick, or stone) intended to house a family, a business, or an institution *syn* edifice, structure, pile

bulge *vb* · to extend outward beyond the usual and normal line *syn* jut, stick out, protrude, project, overhang, beetle *rel* swell, distend, dilate, expand

bulge *n*, *syn* PROJECTION, protuberance, protrusion

bulk *n* · a body of usually material substance that constitutes a thing or unit *syn* mass, volume *rel* form, figure, shape

bulky *syn* MASSIVE, massy, monumental, substantial *rel* huge, gigantic, colossal, mammoth, elephantine, enormous; corpulent, obese, portly, fleshy; burly, husky, muscular

bull **1** *syn* ERROR, blunder, howler, boner, mistake, slip, lapse, faux pas **2** *syn* NONSENSE, twaddle, drivel, bunk, balderdash, poppycock, gobbledygook, trash, rot

bulldoze *syn* INTIMIDATE, bully, browbeat, cow *rel* threaten, menace; terrorize, terrify, frighten; worry, harass, harry

bullheaded *syn* OBSTINATE, pigheaded, stiff-necked, stubborn, mulish, dogged, pertinacious

bully *syn* INTIMIDATE, bulldoze, browbeat, cow *rel* torment, rack, torture, afflict; threaten, menace; terrorize, terrify, frighten, scare *ant* coax

bulwark · an aboveground defensive structure that forms part of a fortification *syn* breastwork, rampart, parapet, bastion *rel* stronghold, fortress, fort, citadel

bum *syn* VAGABOND, vagrant, tramp, hobo, truant

bumble *syn* STUMBLE, trip, blunder, lurch, flounder, lumber, galumph, lollop

bump · to come or cause to come into violent contact or close or direct opposition *syn* clash, collide, conflict *rel* hit, strike, smite; impinge, jolt, jar, impact

bumpkin *syn* BOOR, hick, yokel, rube, clodhopper, clown, lout, churl

bunch **1** *syn* GROUP, cluster, parcel, lot *rel* see BUNCH 2 **2** *syn* BUNDLE, bale, parcel, pack, package, packet *rel* collection, assemblage, gathering; quantity, number, aggregate, sum

bundle · things done up for storage, sale, or carriage *syn* bunch, bale, parcel, pack, package, packet *rel* collection, assemblage, gathering; bag, sack

bungle *syn* BOTCH, fumble, muff,

cobble *rel* confuse, muddle, addle, befuddle; confuse, confound, mistake; disorder, disarrange, disorganize, derange; entangle, enmesh

bunk *syn* NONSENSE, twaddle, drivel, balderdash, poppycock, gobbledygook, trash, rot, bull

buoyant *syn* ELASTIC, volatile, expansive, resilient, effervescent *rel* spirited, high-spirited, mettlesome, gingery; lively, vivacious, animated, sprightly; jocund, blithe, merry; optimistic, hopeful *ant* depressed, dejected

burden *n, syn* LOAD, cargo, freight, lading

burden *vb* • to lay a heavy load upon or to lie like a heavy load upon a person or thing *syn* encumber, cumber, weigh, weight, load, lade, tax, charge, saddle *rel* oppress, depress, weigh; crush, mash

burden *n, syn* SUBSTANCE, purport, gist, core, pith *rel* subject, matter, subject matter, theme, text, topic

burdensome *syn* ONEROUS, oppressive, exacting *rel* heavy, ponderous, cumbersome, cumbrous, weighty; irksome, wearisome; fatiguing, exhausting, fagging, tiring; arduous, hard, difficult *ant* light

burglar *syn* THIEF, robber, larcener, larcenist *rel* stealer, pilferer, filcher, purloiner; plunderer, looter, rifler

burglarize *syn* ROB, plunder, rifle, loot *rel* steal, pilfer, filch, purloin, lift, pinch, snitch, cop, swipe; sack, pillage, ravage, despoil

burglary *syn* THEFT, larceny, robbery

burlesque *n, syn* CARICATURE, parody, travesty *rel* mimicry, mockery, imitation; fun, jest, sport, game; satire, sarcasm, humor, wit; derision, ridicule

burlesque *vb, syn* CARICATURE, parody, travesty *rel* mimic, ape, mock, imitate, copy; ridicule, deride

burly *syn* MUSCULAR, husky, brawny, athletic, sinewy *rel* corpulent, fleshy, portly; bulky, substantial, massive; vigorous, lusty; powerful, forceful, potent *ant* lanky, lank

burn • to injure by exposure to fire or intense heat *syn* scorch, char, sear, singe *rel* kindle, fire, ignite, light; blaze, flame, glow

burp *syn* BELCH, vomit, disgorge, regurgitate, spew, throw up

burst *syn* BREAK, crack, bust, snap, shatter, shiver *rel* distend, swell, expand; push, shove, thrust, propel

bury *syn* HIDE, secrete, cache, conceal, screen, ensconce

business **1** *syn* WORK, occupation, pursuit, calling, employment *rel* trade, craft, handicraft, art, profession **2** *syn* AFFAIR, concern, matter, thing *rel* function, office, duty, province; task, job, assignment, chore, stint **3** • one of the forms or branches of human endeavor which have for their objective the supplying of commodities *syn* commerce, trade, industry, traffic

bust *syn* BREAK, crack, burst, snap, shatter, shiver *rel* see BURST

bustle *syn* STIR, flurry, ado, fuss, pother *rel* business, commerce, trade, industry, traffic; movement, motion; hubbub, clamor, racket, babel, din

busy • actively engaged or occupied in work or in accomplishing a purpose or intention *syn* industrious, diligent, assiduous, sedulous *rel* engrossed, absorbed, intent; working, toiling, laboring, travailing *ant* idle; unoccupied

butchery *syn* MASSACRE, slaughter, carnage, pogrom *rel* murdering, murder, slaying, killing

butt in *syn* INTRUDE, obtrude, interlope *rel* interfere, meddle, intermeddle; interpose, intervene, interfere, mediate, intercede

buttress *n* · auxiliary structures designed to serve as a prop, shore, or support for a wall (as of a building) *syn* pier, abutment

buttress *vb, syn* SUPPORT, sustain, prop, bolster, brace *rel* uphold, back, champion; strengthen, reinforce, fortify; defend, protect, shield, guard

buy · to acquire something for money or an equivalent *syn* purchase *rel* obtain, acquire, procure, get; pay, compensate, remunerate

by · using as a means of approach or action *syn* through, with

bystander *syn* SPECTATOR, onlooker, looker-on, witness, eyewitness, observer, beholder

byword *syn* CATCHWORD, shibboleth, slogan *rel* proverb, saying, saw, motto; abuse, invective; legend, caption, inscription

C

cabal *syn* PLOT, intrigue, conspiracy, machination

cabalistic *syn* MYSTICAL, anagogic, mystic *rel* occult, esoteric, recondite, abstruse; cryptic, enigmatic, obscure; arcane, mysterious

cache *syn* HIDE, secrete, bury, conceal, ensconce, screen

cad · one who shows himself to be no gentleman *syn* bounder, rotter

cadaver *syn* BODY, corpse, carcass

cadaverous *syn* HAGGARD, wasted, pinched, worn, careworn *rel* gaunt, skinny, scrawny, angular, rawboned, lank, lanky, lean, spare *ant* plump, stout

cadence *syn* RHYTHM, meter *rel* accentuation, accent, stress, emphasis; beat, pulse, throb, pulsation

cage *syn* ENCLOSE, envelop, fence, pen, coop, corral, wall *rel* confine, circumscribe, limit; imprison, incarcerate, jail; surround, environ, encompass, hem

cajole *syn* COAX, wheedle, blandish *rel* entice, inveigle, seduce, decoy, lure; beguile, delude, deceive; tease, tantalize, worry

cake *syn* HARDEN, solidify, indurate, petrify *rel* compact, consolidate; contract, compress, condense, shrink

calamitous *syn* UNLUCKY, disastrous, ill-starred, ill-fated, unfortunate, luckless, hapless

calamity *syn* DISASTER, catastrophe, cataclysm *rel* accident, casualty, mishap; misfortune, mischance, adversity, mishap; tribulation, visitation, affliction, trial, cross; ruin, wreck *ant* boon

calculate · to determine something (as cost, speed, or quantity) by mathematical processes *syn* compute, estimate, reckon *rel* weigh, study, consider; ponder, ruminate; determine, ascertain, discover

calculating *syn* CAUTIOUS, circumspect, wary, chary *rel* deliberate, designed, considered, studied, premeditated; designing, scheming, plotting; wily, guileful, crafty, artful, cunning, sly *ant* reckless, rash

calculation *syn* CAUTION, circumspection, wariness, chariness *rel* prudence, forethought, foresight, providence, discretion; care, concern, solicitude; astuteness, perspicacity, sagacity, shrewdness *ant* recklessness, rashness

caliber *syn* QUALITY, stature *rel* capability, capacity, ability; force, power

call *vb, syn* SUMMON, summons, cite, convoke, convene, muster *rel* assemble, gather, collect; invite, bid

call *n, syn* VISIT, visitation

caller *syn* VISITOR, visitant, guest

calling *syn* WORK, occupation, pursuit, business, employment *rel* profession, trade, craft, art, handicraft

callous *syn* HARDENED, indurated *rel* tough, tenacious, stout, strong; firm, solid, hard; inflexible, adamant, obdurate, inexorable; insensitive, impassible, insensible, anesthetic *ant* tender

callow *syn* RUDE, green, crude, raw, rough, uncouth *rel* puerile, boyish, juvenile, youthful; naïve, ingenuous, simple, unsophisticated, artless, natural; adolescent, pubescent *ant* full-fledged, grown-up

calm *adj* • quiet and free from all that disturbs or excites *syn* tranquil, serene, placid, peaceful, halcyon *rel* still, quiet, stilly, noiseless; pacific, peaceable; impassive, stoic; unruffled, composed, collected, imperturbable, unflappable, cool *ant* stormy; agitated

calm *vb* • to relieve or to bring to an end whatever distresses, agitates, or disturbs *syn* compose, quiet, quieten, still, lull, soothe, settle, tranquilize *rel* allay, assuage, mitigate, alleviate, relieve; mollify, placate, appease, pacify *ant* agitate, arouse

calumniate *syn* MALIGN, defame, slander, asperse, traduce, vilify, libel *rel* revile, vituperate, scold; decry, derogate, detract, belittle, disparage *ant* eulogize; vindicate

calumny *syn* DETRACTION, slander, backbiting, scandal *rel* aspersion, reflection, animadversion, stricture; defaming, defamation, maligning, traducing, vilifying, vilification, libeling, libel *ant* eulogy; vindication

camouflage *syn* DISGUISE, cloak, mask, dissemble

canal *syn* CHANNEL, conduit, duct, aqueduct

cancel *syn* ERASE, efface, obliterate, expunge, delete, blot out *rel* invalidate, annul, nullify; void, abrogate; deface, disfigure; neutralize, counteract, negative

candid *syn* FRANK, open, plain *rel* truthful, veracious; fair, dispassionate, impartial, unbiased, just; sincere; honest, scrupulous, upright *ant* evasive

candidate • one who seeks an office, honor, position, or award *syn* aspirant, nominee, applicant

canon *syn* LAW, precept, regulation, rule, statute, ordinance *rel* principle, fundamental, axiom; criterion, standard, yardstick, touchstone, gauge

cant **1** *syn* DIALECT, jargon, argot, lingo, vernacular, slang, patois *rel* phraseology, vocabulary, diction, language; idiom, speech **2** *syn* HYPOCRISY, sanctimony, pharisaism

canting *syn* HYPOCRITICAL, sanctimonious, pharisaical

capability *syn* ABILITY, capacity *rel* competence, qualification, qualifications; proficiency, adeptness, expertness, skillfulness; art, skill, cunning *ant* incapability, incompetence

capable *syn* ABLE, competent, qualified *rel* efficient, effective, effectual, efficacious *ant* incapable

capacious *syn* SPACIOUS, commodious, ample *rel* broad, wide; extended, extensive; expanded, expansive *ant* exiguous

capacity *syn* ABILITY, capability *rel* amplitude, expanse, spread; extent, magnitude, size, volume; aptitude, gift, faculty, talent, bent, turn, knack *ant* incapacity

caper *syn* PRANK, monkeyshine, antic, dido *rel* gamboling, gambol, rollicking, rollick, romping, romp, frolicking, frolic; skipping, skip, hopping, hop, bounding, bound

capital *syn* CHIEF, principal, main, leading, foremost *rel* primary, primordial, primal; fundamental, basic, radical, underlying; cardinal, vital, essential

capitulate *syn* YIELD, submit, succumb, relent, defer, bow, cave *rel* surrender, abandon, waive, cede, relinquish

capitulation *syn* SURRENDER, submission *rel* yielding, relenting, succumbing, caving in; truce, cease-fire, armistice, peace

caprice • an arbitrary notion that usually lacks a logical basis and therefore may be unsound, impractical, or even irrational *syn* freak, fancy, whim, whimsy, conceit, vagary, crotchet *rel* humor, mood, temper, vein; notion, idea; impulse, motive; irrationality, unreasonableness; perverseness, contrariness

capricious *syn* INCONSTANT, mercurial, unstable, fickle *rel* changeable, changeful, protean, variable; moody, humorsome; volatile, effervescent *ant* steadfast

capsize *syn* OVERTURN, upset, overthrow, subvert

caption *syn* INSCRIPTION, legend

captious *syn* CRITICAL, caviling, carping, hypercritical, faultfinding, censorious *rel* contrary, perverse; exacting, demanding; peevish, petulant, snappish, irritable; testy, choleric, irascible *ant* appreciative

captivate *syn* ATTRACT, fascinate, bewitch, enchant, charm, allure *rel* delight, please, gratify; win, gain, get *ant* repulse

captivating *syn* ATTRACTIVE, fascinating, bewitching, enchanting, charming, alluring *rel* pleasing, pleasant, agreeable, grateful; delightful, delectable; lovely, bonny, fair, beautiful *ant* repulsive

captive *syn* PRISONER

capture *syn* CATCH, trap, snare, entrap, ensnare, bag *rel* seize, take, grasp, clutch, snatch; arrest, apprehend

carbon copy *syn* REPRODUCTION, copy, duplicate, transcript, facsimile, replica

carbuncle *syn* ABSCESS, boil, furuncle, pimple, pustule

carcass *syn* BODY, corpse, cadaver

cardinal *adj, syn* ESSENTIAL, vital, fundamental *rel* requisite, necessary, indispensable, needful; radical, fundamental, basic; capital, principal, chief, main, leading; important, significant, momentous *ant* negligible

care • a troubled or engrossed state of mind or the thing that causes this *syn* concern, solicitude, anxiety, worry *rel* trouble, pains, effort, exertion; disquieting, disquiet, perturbing, perturbation, discomposing, discomposure; vigilance, watchfulness, alertness

careful • marked by close attention to details or care in execution or performance *syn* meticulous, scrupulous, punctilious, punctual *rel* cautious, circumspect, wary; provident, foresighted, prudent; accurate, precise, nice, exact, correct; studied, deliberate *ant* careless

careless • showing lack of concern or attention *syn* heedless, thoughtless, inadvertent *rel* negligent, neglectful, lax, slack, remiss; casual, desultory, haphazard, random, hit-or-miss, happy-go-lucky *ant* careful

caress • to show affection or love by touching or handling *syn* fondle, pet, cosset, cuddle, dandle *rel* trifle, toy, dally, flirt, coquet; cherish, nurse

careworn *syn* HAGGARD, worn, pinched, wasted, cadaverous *rel* troubled, distressed; lean, gaunt, scrawny, skinny; exhausted, fagged, jaded, tuckered *ant* carefree

cargo *syn* LOAD, burden, freight, lading

caricature *n* • a grotesque or bizarre imitation of something *syn* burlesque, parody, travesty *rel* satire, humor, sarcasm, wit; grotesqueness, fantasticality, bizarreness; lampoon, libel, skit, squib, pasquinade

caricature *vb* • to make a grotesque or bizarre imitation of something *syn* burlesque, parody, travesty *rel* mimic, mock, ape, imitate, copy; distort, deform; simulate, counterfeit, assume; ridicule, deride

carnage *syn* MASSACRE, slaughter, butchery, pogrom

carnal • characterized by physical rather than intellectual or spiritual orientation *syn* fleshly, sensual, animal *rel* physical, bodily, corporeal, corporal, somatic; sensuous; gross, coarse, vulgar, obscene; earthly, earthy, worldly, mundane; lustful, lewd, wanton, lascivious, licentious *ant* spiritual; intellectual

carol *syn* SING, toll, descant, warble, trill, hymn, chant, intone

carping *syn* CRITICAL, caviling, faultfinding, captious, hypercritical, censorious *rel* blaming, reprehending, reprobating, criticizing; upbraiding, jawing, railing; depreciating, depreciative, disparaging, decrying *ant* fulsome

carry • to be the agent or the means whereby something or someone is moved from one place to another *syn* bear, convey, transport, transmit *rel* take, bring, fetch; move, remove, shift, transfer; drive, ride

cartel **1** *syn* CONTRACT, compact, pact, convention, bargain, concordat, treaty, entente **2** *syn* MONOPOLY, pool, syndicate, corner, trust *rel* combine, combination; consolidation, merger, amalgamation

carve **1** *syn* CUT, slit, hew, chop, slash *rel* shape, fashion, form, make; separate, divide, part **2** • to cut an outline or a shape out of or into some substance *syn* incise, engrave, etch, chisel, sculpture, sculpt, sculp *rel* shape, fashion, form, make; produce, turn out

case **1** *syn* INSTANCE, illustration, example, specimen, sample *rel* occurrence, event, incident, episode, circumstance; situation, condition, state **2** *syn* SUIT, cause, action, lawsuit

casement *syn* WINDOW, dormer, oriel

cash *syn* MONEY, currency, legal tender, specie, coin, coinage

cashier *syn* DISMISS, discharge, drop, fire, sack, bounce *rel* eject, expel, oust; eliminate, disbar, exclude, suspend

cast **1** *syn* THROW, fling, hurl, pitch, toss, sling *rel* direct, aim, point, level, train, lay; scatter, disperse **2** *syn* DISCARD, shed, molt, slough, scrap, junk *rel* relinquish, abandon, yield, surrender, leave; repudiate, reject, decline; dismiss, drop **3** *syn* ADD, figure, foot, sum, total, tot *rel* compute, calculate, reckon

castaway *syn* OUTCAST, derelict, reprobate, pariah, untouchable

castigate *syn* PUNISH, chastise, chasten, discipline, correct *rel* beat, baste, thrash, pummel, belabor; berate, tongue-lash, rate, upbraid, wig, rail, scold; penalize, fine, amerce, mulct

castrate *syn* STERILIZE, spay, emasculate, alter, mutilate, geld

casual **1** *syn* ACCIDENTAL, incidental, contingent, fortuitous *rel* unpremeditated, extemporaneous; indifferent, unconcerned, incurious; negligent, slack, lax, remiss; inadvertent, careless, heedless **2** *syn* RANDOM, desultory, haphazard, chancy, hit-or-miss, happy-go-lucky *rel* offhand, impromptu, improvised, extemporaneous, extempore; spontaneous, impulsive; unmethodical, unsystematic *ant* deliberate

casualty *syn* ACCIDENT, mishap *rel* disaster, calamity, catastrophe, cataclysm; misfortune, mischance, mishap

casuistical *syn* FALLACIOUS, sophistical *rel* plausible, specious; tortuous, winding; oblique, devious, crooked; misleading, delusive, deceptive, delusory

casuistry *syn* FALLACY, sophistry, sophism

cataclysm *syn* DISASTER, catastrophe, calamity *rel* convulsing, convulsion, rocking, shaking, agitation; revolution, rebellion; misfortune, mischance, mishap

catalog *n, syn* LIST, inventory, table, schedule, register, roll, roster

catalog *vb, syn* RECORD, register, list, enroll *rel* enumerate, number, count; enter, admit

cataract *syn* FLOOD, deluge, inundation, torrent, spate

catastrophe *syn* DISASTER, calamity, cataclysm *rel* trial, tribulation, visitation; defeating, defeat, overthrowing, overthrow, routing, rout

catch **1** · to come to possess or control by or as if by seizing *syn* capture, trap, snare, entrap, ensnare, bag *rel* seize, take, grasp, grab, clutch, snatch; apprehend, arrest *ant* miss **2** *syn* INCUR, contract

catching *syn* INFECTIOUS, contagious, communicable

catchword · a phrase that catches the eye or the ear and is repeated so often that it becomes a formula *syn* byword, shibboleth, slogan *rel* caption, legend, inscription; phrase, expression, idiom; commonplace, platitude, truism, bromide, cliché

catechize *syn* ASK, interrogate, quiz, examine, question, query, inquire

categorical **1** *syn* ULTIMATE, absolute **2** *syn* EXPLICIT, express, definite, specific *rel* positive, certain, sure; forthright, downright

category *syn* CLASS, *rel* genus, species, denomination, genre; division, section, part; classification

cater · to furnish with what satisfies the appetite or desires *syn* purvey, pander *rel* furnish, equip, appoint, accouter; pamper, indulge, humor; satisfy, content

catholic *syn* UNIVERSAL, cosmic, ecumenical, cosmopolitan *rel* whole, entire, total; all-around, many-sided, versatile; prevalent, prevailing, current *ant* parochial; provincial

catnap *syn* SLEEP, nap, snooze, slumber, drowse, doze

cause · that (as a person, fact, or condition) which is responsible for an effect *syn* determinant, antecedent, reason, occasion *rel* motive, spring, incentive, inducement, spur, goad, impulse; motivation, activation, actuation; agent, agency; origin, root, source, prime mover **2** *syn* SUIT, lawsuit, action, cause, case

caustic · stingingly incisive *syn* mordant, acrid, scathing *rel* biting, cutting, incisive, trenchant; bitter; sharp, keen, acute; sarcastic, satiric, ironic *ant* genial

caution *n* · careful prudence esp. in reducing or avoiding risk or danger *syn* circumspection, wariness, chariness, calculation *rel* watchfulness, vigilance, alertness; prudence, providence, foresight, forethought, discretion *ant* temerity; adventurousness

caution *vb, syn* WARN, forewarn *rel* admonish, reprove; counsel, advise

cautious · prudently watchful and discreet in the face of danger or risk *syn* circumspect, wary, chary, calculating *rel* watchful, vigilant, alert; prudent, provident, foresighted, forethoughtful, discreet; heedful, careful *ant* adventurous, temerarious

cavalcade *syn* PROCESSION, parade, cortege, motorcade *rel* succession, progression, chain, train; array, display

cave *syn* YIELD, succumb, submit, capitulate, relent, defer, bow

caviling *syn* CRITICAL, captious, faultfinding, censorious, carping, hypercritical *rel* exacting, demanding; contrary, perverse; objecting, protesting, expostulating, kicking

cavity *syn* HOLE, hollow, pocket, void, vacuum

cease *syn* STOP, quit, discontinue, desist *rel* end, terminate, close, conclude, finish; stay, suspend, intermit, defer

cease-fire *syn* TRUCE, armistice, peace

cede *syn* RELINQUISH, surrender, abandon, waive, resign, yield, leave *rel* grant, concede, award, accord, vouchsafe

celebrate *syn* KEEP, commemorate, solemnize, observe

celebrated *syn* FAMOUS, renowned, famed, eminent, illustrious *rel* prominent, conspicuous, outstanding, signal, noticeable *ant* obscure

celebrity *syn* FAME, renown, glory, honor, éclat, reputation, repute, notoriety *rel* prominence, conspicuousness *ant* obscurity

celerity · quickness in movement or action *syn* alacrity, legerity *rel* expedition, dispatch, speed, hurry, haste; quickness, rapidity, swiftness, fleetness; velocity, speed; agility, briskness, nimbleness *ant* leisureliness

celestial · of, relating to, or fit for heaven or the heavens *syn* heavenly, empyrean, empyreal *rel* ethereal, aerial, airy; divine, spiritual, holy *ant* terrestrial

celibate *syn* UNMARRIED, single, virgin, maiden

cenobite *syn* RECLUSE, eremite, hermit, anchorite *rel* monk, friar, religious, nun

censorious *syn* CRITICAL, faultfinding, hypercritical, captious, carping, caviling *rel* reproaching, reproachful, chiding; condemning, condemnatory, denouncing, denunciatory, reprehending *ant* eulogistic

censure *syn* CRITICIZE, reprehend, blame, condemn, denounce, reprobate *rel* reprimand, rebuke, reproach, reprove; upbraid, berate, tongue-lash, scold *ant* commend

center *n* · the point, spot, or portion of a thing which is comparable to a point around which a circle is described *syn* middle, midst, core, hub, focus, nucleus, heart

center *vb* · to draw to or fix upon a center *syn* focus, centralize, concentrate *rel* depend, hinge, hang, turn; rest, base, ground

central · dominant or most important *syn* focal, pivotal *rel* dominant, paramount, predominant, preponderant; outstanding, salient, signal, noticeable; important, significant

centralize *syn* CENTER, focus, concentrate *rel* gather, collect, assemble; accumulate, amass; compact, consolidate, unify

cerebral *syn* MENTAL, intellectual, psychic, intelligent

ceremonial *adj* · characterized or marked by attention to the forms, procedures, and details prescribed as right, proper, or requisite *syn* ceremonious, formal, conventional, solemn *rel* liturgical, ritualistic

ceremonial *n, syn* FORM, ceremony, ritual, rite, liturgy, formality

ceremonious *syn* CEREMONIAL, formal, solemn, conventional *rel* impressive, moving; decorous, seemly, proper; stately, imposing, majestic, grandiose, grand *ant* unceremonious, informal

ceremony *syn* FORM, ceremonial, ritual, liturgy, rite, formality

certain **1** *syn* SURE, positive, cocksure *rel* confident, assured, sanguine *ant* uncertain **2** • bound to follow in obedience to the laws of nature or of thought *syn* inevitable, necessary *ant* probable; supposed

certainty • a state of mind in which one is free from doubt *syn* certitude, assurance, conviction *rel* belief, faith, credence; proof, demonstration *ant* uncertainty

certify **1** • to testify to the truth or genuineness of something *syn* attest, witness, vouch *rel* avouch, avow, aver, assert, profess **2** *syn* APPROVE, endorse, accredit, sanction *rel* vouch; authorize, commission, license

certitude *syn* CERTAINTY, assurance, conviction *rel* belief, faith, credence, credit; sureness, positiveness, cocksureness *ant* doubt

chafe *syn* ABRADE, excoriate, fret, gall *rel* injure, hurt, damage, impair; flay, skin, peel; abuse, maltreat, outrage; irritate, exasperate

chaff *syn* BANTER, kid, rag, jolly, rib, josh *rel* tease, tantalize, worry; ridicule, deride, twit, taunt

chagrined *syn* ASHAMED, mortified *rel* discomfited, abashed, embarrassed, disconcerted; humiliated; discomposed, perturbed, upset

chain *syn* SUCCESSION, series, train, string, sequence, progression

challenge *syn* FACE, brave, dare, defy, beard *rel* question, ask; dispute, discuss; claim; demand, require; invite, solicit

chamber *syn* ROOM, apartment

champ *syn* BITE, gnaw, gnash *rel* crush, smash, mash, macerate

champion *n, syn* VICTOR, vanquisher, winner, conqueror

champion *vb, syn* SUPPORT, back, advocate, uphold *rel* contend, fight, battle; espouse, adopt; defend, justify, vindicate, maintain; aid, assist, help *ant* combat

chance *n* **1** • something that happens without an apparent or determinable cause or as a result of unpredictable forces *syn* accident, fortune, luck, hap, hazard *rel* contingency, emergency, pass, juncture, exigency *ant* law, principle **2** *syn* OPPORTUNITY, occasion, break, time *rel* possibility, likelihood, probability; prospect, outlook, foretaste, anticipation

chance *vb* **1** *syn* HAPPEN, befall, betide, occur, transpire **2** *syn* VENTURE, hazard, risk, jeopardize, endanger, imperil *rel* dare, beard, face; meet, encounter, confront

chance *adj, syn* RANDOM, haphazard, chancy, casual, desultory, hit-or-miss, happy-go-lucky

chancy *syn* RANDOM, haphazard, chance, hit-or-miss, happy-go-lucky, casual, desultory

change *vb* • to make or become different *syn* alter, vary, modify *rel* transform, metamorphose, transmute, convert, transmogrify; exchange, interchange; fluctuate, oscillate, swing

change *n* **1** • a making different *syn* alteration, variation, modification *rel* variety, diversity; divergence, deviation, aberration *ant* uniformity; monotony **2** • a result of a making different *syn* mutation, permutation, vicissitude, alternation *rel* metamorphosis, transformation, conversion, transmutation, transmogrification; substitute, surrogate, shift

changeable · having or showing a marked capacity for changes or a marked tendency to alter under slight provocation *syn* changeful, variable, mutable, protean *rel* unstable, inconstant, mercurial, capricious, fickle; mobile, movable *ant* stable; unchangeable

changeful *syn* CHANGEABLE, variable, protean, mutable *rel* fluid, liquid; active, dynamic, live; progressing, advancing; declining, deteriorating, degenerating *ant* changeless; stereotyped

channel **1** *syn* STRAIT, passage, narrows, sound **2** · something through which a fluid (as water) is led or flows *syn* canal, conduit, duct, aqueduct *rel* passage, pass, way **3** *syn* MEAN, vehicle, instrument, instrumentality, organ, agency, agent, medium

chant *syn* SING, troll, carol, descant, warble, trill, hymn, intone

chaos **1** *syn* CONFUSION, disorder, disarray, jumble, clutter, snarl, muddle *ant* system **2** *syn* ANARCHY, lawlessness

chaperon *syn* ACCOMPANY, attend, escort, convoy, conduct *rel* protect, shield, guard, safeguard, defend

char *syn* BURN, scorch, sear, singe

character *n* **1** · an arbitrary or conventional device that is used in writing and in printing, but is neither a word nor a phrase nor a picture *syn* symbol, sign, mark **2** *syn* QUALITY, property, attribute, accident *rel* characteristic, peculiarity, distinctiveness, distinction, individuality **3** *syn* DISPOSITION, individuality, personality, complexion, temperament, temper *rel* mind, intellect, soul, intelligence; soul, spirit; courage, mettle, spirit, resolution **4** *syn* TYPE, nature, description, kind, ilk, sort, stripe, kidney **5** *syn* CREDENTIAL, reference, recommendation, testimonial

characteristic *adj* · being or revealing a quality specific or identifying to an individual or group *syn* individual, peculiar, distinctive *rel* special, especial, specific, particular; typical, natural, normal, regular

characteristic *n* · something that marks or sets apart a person or thing *syn* trait, feature *rel* quality, property, character; peculiarity, individuality

characterize · to be a peculiar or significant quality or feature of something *syn* distinguish, mark, qualify *rel* distinguish, differentiate, demarcate; individualize, peculiarize

charge *vb* **1** *syn* BURDEN, encumber, cumber, weigh, weight, load, lade, tax, saddle **2** *syn* COMMAND, direct, instruct, bid, enjoin, order *rel* request, solicit, ask; adjure, beg **3** *syn* ACCUSE, incriminate, indict, impeach, arraign *rel* denounce, blame, censure, condemn, criticize *ant* absolve **4** *syn* ASCRIBE, attribute, impute, assign, refer, credit, accredit *rel* fasten, attach, fix, affix; join, connect, link **5** *syn* RUSH, dash, tear, shoot *rel* impel, drive, move; fly, dart, scud

charge *n, syn* PRICE, cost, expense

chargé d'affaires *syn* AMBASSADOR, legate, nuncio, minister, envoy, internuncio

chariness *syn* CAUTION, circumspection, wariness, calculation *rel* prudence, providence, discretion, foresight, forethought

charitable · having or showing interest in or being concerned with the welfare of others *syn* benevolent, humane, humanitarian, philanthropic, eleemosynary, altruistic *rel* generous, liberal, bountiful, bounteous, openhanded, munificent; merciful, forbearing, lenient, clement, tolerant; tender, compassionate, warmhearted, sympathetic *ant* uncharitable

charity **1** *syn* MERCY, clemency, grace, lenity *rel* love, affection, attachment; benevolence, humaneness, altruism; benignity, benignancy, kindness, kindliness; generousness, generosity, liberalness, liberality, bountifulness, bounty, openhandedness; goodwill, amity, friendship *ant* malice, ill will **2** • love for one's fellowmen and a disposition to help those who are in need *syn* philanthropy

charlatan *syn* IMPOSTOR, mountebank, quack, faker *rel* humbug, fraud, cheat, fake, pretender, feigner, counterfeiter

charm *n, syn* FETISH, talisman, amulet

charm *vb, syn* ATTRACT, fascinate, allure, captivate, enchant, bewitch *rel* delight, rejoice, please, gratify *ant* disgust

charming *syn* ATTRACTIVE, fascinating, alluring, captivating, enchanting, bewitching *rel* delightful, delectable, delicious; pleasing, agreeable, grateful, pleasant *ant* forbidding

chart *n* • a stylized or symbolic depiction of something incapable of direct verbal or pictorial representation *syn* map, graph *rel* plan, plot, scheme, design, project

chart *vb* • to make a representation of something with a chart *syn* map, graph *rel* see CHART *n*

charter *vb, syn* HIRE, let, lease, rent

chary *syn* CAUTIOUS, circumspect, wary, calculating *rel* prudent, discreet, provident; sparing, economical, frugal, thrifty; reluctant, hesitant, loath, disinclined

chase *syn* FOLLOW, pursue, trail, tag, tail

chasm *syn* GULF, abyss, abysm

chaste • free from all taint of what is lewd or salacious *syn* pure, modest, decent *rel* virtuous, moral, righteous, ethical; faithful, true, constant, loyal; austere, severe *ant* lewd, wanton, immoral; bizarre (*of style, effect*)

chasten *syn* PUNISH, discipline, correct, chastise, castigate *rel* humble, humiliate, abase; afflict; test, try, prove *ant* pamper, mollycoddle

chastise *syn* PUNISH, discipline, correct, castigate, chasten *rel* beat, thrash, pummel, baste, belabor

chat • to emit a loose and ready flow of inconsequential talk *syn* gab, chatter, patter, prate, prattle, babble, gabble, jabber, gibber *rel* converse, talk, speak; gossip

chatter *syn* CHAT, gab, patter, prate, babble, gabble, jabber, gibber *rel* see CHAT

cheap *syn* CONTEMPTIBLE, beggarly, shabby, pitiable, sorry, despicable, scurvy *rel* mean, ignoble, sordid, abject; paltry, petty, measly, trifling; meretricious, tawdry, gaudy; low, base, vile; poor, bad, wrong *ant* noble

cheat *n, syn* IMPOSTURE, fraud, fake, deceit, deception, counterfeit, sham, humbug *rel* hoaxing, hoax, bamboozling, bamboozlement; deception, trickery, chicanery, chicane; charlatan, quack, mountebank, faker, impostor; swindler, defrauder, cozener

cheat *vb* • to obtain something and esp. money or valuables from or an advantage over another by dishonesty and trickery *syn* cozen, defraud, swindle, overreach *rel* dupe, gull, hoax, hoodwink, bamboozle, trick, befool; deceive, delude, beguile, double-cross, mislead

check *n, syn* CORRECTIVE, control,

antidote *rel* oversight, supervision, surveillance

check *vb* **1** *syn* ARREST, interrupt *rel* stay, suspend; stop, cease, discontinue, desist; repress, suppress; frustrate, thwart, foil, circumvent **2** *syn* RESTRAIN, bridle, curb, inhibit *rel* hinder, impede, obstruct, block; prevent, preclude, obviate; baffle, balk, frustrate; control, manage, conduct *ant* accelerate (*of speed*); advance (*of movements, plans, hopes*); release (*of feelings, energies*)

checked, checkered *syn* VARIEGATED, parti-colored, motley, pied, piebald, skewbald, dappled, freaked

cheek *syn* TEMERITY, nerve, effrontery, hardihood, gall, audacity *rel* boldness, intrepidity; impudence, brazenness, shamelessness, brashness *ant* diffidence

cheep *vb, syn* CHIRP, chirrup, peep, tweet, twitter, chitter

cheep *n, syn* CHIRP, chirrup, peep, tweet, twitter, chitter

cheer **1** *syn* ENCOURAGE, inspirit, hearten, embolden, nerve, steel *rel* comfort, console, solace; gladden, gratify, please; stimulate, excite, quicken, provoke *ant* deject; dismay **2** *syn* APPLAUD, root *rel* acclaim, laud, praise

cheerful *syn* GLAD, lighthearted, joyful, joyous, happy *rel* jolly, jovial, merry, blithe, jocund; mirthful, gleeful; gay, vivacious, lively, animated *ant* glum, gloomy

cheerless *syn* DISMAL, dreary, dispiriting, bleak, desolate *rel* discouraging, disheartening, dejecting *ant* cheerful

cheeseparing *syn* STINGY, close, closefisted, tight, tightfisted, niggardly, penny-pinching, parsimonious, penurious, miserly

chemist *syn* DRUGGIST, apothecary, pharmacist

cherish **1** *syn* APPRECIATE, prize, treasure, value *rel* love, enjoy, like; esteem, respect, regard; revere, venerate, reverence; protect, defend, shield, safeguard, guard *ant* neglect **2** *syn* NURSE, foster, nurture, cultivate *rel* preserve, conserve, save; harbor, shelter, entertain *ant* abandon

chew out *syn* SCOLD, upbraid, rate, berate, tongue-lash, jaw, bawl, wig, rail, revile, vituperate

chic *syn* STYLISH, smart, fashionable, modish, dashing

chicane, chicanery *syn* DECEPTION, trickery, double-dealing, fraud *rel* artifice, stratagem, maneuver, ruse, feint, trick, wile, gambit, ploy; intrigue, machination, plot; underhandedness, furtiveness, surreptitiousness

chide *syn* REPROVE, reproach, rebuke, reprimand, admonish *rel* criticize, reprehend, censure, blame, condemn, denounce; scold, upbraid, rate, berate *ant* commend

chief *n* · the person in whom resides authority or ruling power *syn* chieftain, head, headman, leader, master *rel* governor, ruler

chief *adj* · first in importance or in standing *syn* principal, main, leading, foremost, capital *rel* dominant, paramount, sovereign, predominant, preponderant, preponderating; primary, prime; supreme, preeminent *ant* subordinate

chiefly *syn* LARGELY, greatly, mostly, mainly, principally, generally

chieftain *syn* CHIEF, head, leader, master

childish *syn* CHILDLIKE *rel* puerile, boyish, youthful; simple, foolish, silly, fatuous, asinine *ant* mature, grown-up

childlike · having or showing the manner, spirit, or disposition of a child *syn* childish *rel* naïve, unsophisticated, ingenuous, artless, natural; docile, obedient, tractable, biddable

chilly *syn* COLD, cool, frigid, freezing, frosty, gelid, icy, glacial, arctic *ant* balmy

chimerical *syn* IMAGINARY, fantastic, fanciful, visionary, quixotic *rel* utopian, ambitious, pretentious; illusory, apparent; delusive, delusory, misleading, deceptive; fabulous, mythical, fictitious; preposterous, absurd, foolish *ant* feasible

chine *syn* SPINE, backbone, back, vertebrae

chink *syn* CRACK, cleft, fissure, crevasse, crevice, cranny *rel* break, gap, interruption; split, rift, breach

chirp *vb* • to make a short, sharp, and usu. repetitive sound *syn* chirrup, cheep, peep, tweet, twitter, chitter

chirp *n* • the little sounds characteristic of small animals or sounds that suggest such small animal sounds *syn* chirrup, cheep, peep, tweet, twitter, chitter

chirrup *vb, syn* CHIRP, cheep, peep, tweet, twitter, chitter

chirrup *n, syn* CHIRP, cheep, peep, tweet, twitter, chitter

chisel *syn* CARVE, sculpture, sculpt, sculp, incise, engrave, etch *rel* cut, chop; produce, turn out; shape, fashion, form, make

chitter *vb, syn* CHIRP, chirrup, cheep, peep, tweet, twitter

chitter *n, syn* CHIRP, chirrup, cheep, peep, tweet, twitter

chivalrous *syn* CIVIL, gallant, courtly, courteous, polite *rel* spirited, mettlesome, high-spirited *ant* churlish

chivy *syn* BAIT, badger, heckle, hector, hound, ride *rel* worry, annoy, harry, harass, tease; chase, pursue, trail, follow; torment, try, afflict

choice *n* • the act or opportunity of choosing or the thing chosen *syn* option, alternative, preference, selection, election

choice *adj* • having qualities that appeal to a fine or highly refined taste *syn* exquisite, elegant, recherché, rare, dainty, delicate *rel* preeminent, surpassing, peerless, incomparable, supreme, superlative; picked, selected, culled, chosen *ant* indifferent, medium

choke *syn* SUFFOCATE, asphyxiate, stifle, smother, strangle, throttle

choleric *syn* IRASCIBLE, splenetic, testy, touchy, cranky, cross *rel* irritable, fractious, huffy, querulous, petulant, peevish; angry, acrimonious, wrathful, wroth, indignant, mad, irate; fiery, peppery, spunky, spirited; captious, carping, faultfinding, critical *ant* placid; imperturbable

choose • to fix upon one of a number of things as the one to be taken, accepted, or adopted *syn* select, elect, opt, pick, cull, prefer, single *rel* adopt, espouse, embrace; desire, wish, crave *ant* reject; eschew

chop *syn* CUT, hew, slit, slash, carve *rel* split, cleave, rive, tear

chore *syn* TASK, duty, assignment, job, stint *rel* work, occupation, employment, business

christen *syn* BAPTIZE

chronic *syn* INVETERATE, confirmed, deep-seated, deep-rooted *rel* established, fixed, settled, set; hardened, indurated, callous *ant* acute (*of illness*)

chronicle **1** *syn* HISTORY, annals **2** *syn* ACCOUNT, story, report, version *rel* narration, recital, recountal

chthonic, chthonian *syn* INFERNAL, Hadean, stygian, hellish, Tartarean

chubby *syn* FLESHY, rotund, plump, fat, stout, portly, corpulent, obese *rel* chunky, stubby, dumpy, squat, stocky *ant* slim

chummy *syn* FAMILIAR, intimate, close, thick, confidential

chunky *syn* STOCKY, thickset,

thick, stubby, squat, dumpy *rel* rotund, chubby, fleshy

church *syn* RELIGION, denomination, sect, communion, creed, faith, cult, persuasion

churl *syn* BOOR, lout, clown, clodhopper, bumpkin, hick, yokel, rube *rel* gentleman, aristocrat

churlish *syn* BOORISH, loutish, clownish *rel* ungracious, ill-mannered, discourteous, rude, uncivil, impolite; curt, blunt, brusque, gruff, crusty, bluff; surly, dour, sullen *ant* courtly

cinders *syn* ASH, clinkers, embers

circadian *syn* DAILY, diurnal, quotidian

circle *n, syn* SET, coterie, clique *rel* friends, acquaintances, intimates; associates, companions, comrades

circle *vb* **1** *syn* SURROUND, environ, encircle, encompass, compass, hem, gird, girdle, ring *rel* enclose, envelop; circumscribe, restrict, limit **2** *syn* TURN, revolve, rotate, gyrate, wheel, spin, twirl, whirl, eddy, swirl, pirouette

circuit *syn* CIRCUMFERENCE, compass, perimeter, periphery *rel* route, course, way; tour, journey

circuitous *syn* INDIRECT, roundabout *rel* winding, serpentine, sinuous, tortuous, flexuous *ant* straight

circulate *syn* SPREAD, disseminate, diffuse, propagate, radiate *rel* revolve, rotate, turn; interchange, exchange

circumference • a continuous line enclosing an area or space *syn* perimeter, periphery, circuit, compass *rel* outline, contour

circumlocution *syn* VERBIAGE, periphrasis, pleonasm, redundancy, tautology *rel* prolixity, diffuseness, wordiness, verbosity

circumscribe *syn* LIMIT, confine, restrict *rel* restrain, inhibit, curb, check; hamper, trammel, fetter *ant* expand, dilate

circumspect *syn* CAUTIOUS, wary, calculating, chary *rel* careful, punctilious, punctual, meticulous, scrupulous; vigilant, watchful, alert *ant* audacious

circumspection *syn* CAUTION, wariness, calculation, chariness *rel* carefulness, care, punctiliousness, punctuality, meticulosity, scrupulousness; discretion, forethought, foresight, providence, prudence *ant* audacity

circumstance *syn* OCCURRENCE, event, incident, episode *rel* item, detail, particular; factor, constituent, component, element

circumstantial • dealing with a matter fully and usu. point by point *syn* minute, particular, particularized, detailed, itemized *rel* precise, nice, exact, accurate, correct; full, complete, replete *ant* abridged; summary

circumvent *syn* FRUSTRATE, outwit, baffle, balk, thwart, foil *rel* forestall, anticipate, prevent; evade, escape, elude, avoid; trick, befool, hoodwink, dupe *ant* conform (to *laws, orders*); cooperate (with *persons*)

citadel *syn* FORT, stronghold, fortress, fastness

citation *syn* ENCOMIUM, eulogy, tribute, panegyric *rel* commendation, recommendation, complimenting, compliment; award, guerdon, reward, premium

cite **1** *syn* SUMMON, summons, call, convoke, convene, muster *rel* bid, invite; arrest, detain, apprehend; praise, extol, eulogize, laud, acclaim; award, accord, grant **2** *syn* QUOTE, repeat **3** *syn* ADDUCE, advance, allege *rel* enumerate, tell, count, number; recount, recite, narrate, rehearse, relate

citizen **1** *syn* INHABITANT, resident, denizen **2** • a person who is regarded as a member of a sovereign state, entitled to its protection, and subject to its laws *syn* subject, national *ant* alien

civil · observant of the forms required by good breeding *syn* polite, courteous, courtly, gallant, chivalrous *rel* complaisant, obliging, amiable; gracious, affable, cordial; politic, diplomatic, bland, urbane, suave *ant* uncivil, rude

claim *vb, syn* DEMAND, exact, require *rel* maintain, assert, defend, vindicate, justify; allege, adduce, advance *ant* disclaim; renounce

claim *n* · an actual or alleged right to demand something as one's possession, quality, power, or prerogative *syn* title, pretension, pretense *rel* assertion, affirmation, protestation, declaration right, prerogative, birthright, privilege

clamor *n, syn* DIN, uproar, pandemonium, hullabaloo, babel, hubbub, racket

clamor *vb, syn* ROAR, bellow, bluster, bawl, vociferate, howl, ululate *rel* shout, yell, scream, shriek, screech, holler; agitate, dispute, debate, discuss; demand, claim

clamorous *syn* VOCIFEROUS, blatant, strident, boisterous, obstreperous *rel* importuning, importunate, begging, imploring, adjuring; vocal, articulate, voluble, eloquent; protesting, expostulating, remonstrating *ant* taciturn

clandestine *syn* SECRET, covert, surreptitious, furtive, underhand, underhanded, stealthy *rel* concealed, hidden; sly, artful, foxy; illicit, illegitimate *ant* open

clash *vb, syn* BUMP, collide, conflict *rel* contend, fight, battle, war; compete, vie, rival; resist, combat, withstand, oppose; disagree, differ *ant* blend

clash *n, syn* IMPACT, collision, impingement, shock, concussion, percussion, jar, jolt *rel* conflict, strife, discord; noise, sound; incompatibility, incongruousness, discordance

class *n* · a group including all individuals with a common characteristic *syn* category *rel* genus, species, denomination, genre; division, section, part; classification; grade, rank, gradation, rating

class *vb* · to order a number of things according to a scale or to place a thing in its due order *syn* grade, rank, rate, graduate, gradate *rel* divide, separate, part; assign, allot; distribute

classify *syn* ASSORT, pigeonhole, sort *rel* order, arrange, systematize, methodize, marshal

clause *syn* PARAGRAPH, verse, article, plank, count

clean · to remove whatever soils, stains, or contaminates *syn* cleanse *ant* soil

cleanse *syn* CLEAN *rel* sterilize, disinfect, sanitize *ant* defile, besmirch

clear *adj* **1** · having the property of being literally or figuratively seen through *syn* transparent, translucent, lucid, pellucid, diaphanous, limpid *rel* bright, luminous; liquid; pure, sheer *ant* turbid; confused **2** · quickly and easily understood *syn* perspicuous, lucid *rel* express, explicit, definite; graphic, vivid; clear-cut, incisive, trenchant *ant* unintelligible; abstruse **3** *syn* EVIDENT, manifest, obvious, distinct, apparent, patent, palpable, plain

clear *vb, syn* RID, unburden, disabuse, purge *rel* free, release, liberate, deliver; clean, cleanse; eliminate, rule out, exclude

clearance *syn* ROOM, berth, play, elbowroom, leeway, margin

clear-cut *syn* INCISIVE, trenchant, cutting, biting, crisp *rel* distinct, plain, clear, manifest, evident; definite, explicit, express; precise, exact, nice, correct

cleave *vb, syn* STICK, cling, adhere, cohere *rel* fasten, attach, fix, affix; unite, join, associate, link, combine, conjoin *ant* part

cleave *vb, syn* TEAR, split, rive, rend, rip *rel* separate, divide, sever, sunder, part, divorce; cut, hew, chop, slit

cleft *syn* CRACK, fissure, crevasse, crevice, cranny, chink *rel* split, rift, breach; gap, break, interruption

clemency **1** *syn* MERCY, lenity, charity, grace *rel* compassion, pity, commiseration, sympathy, ruth; gentleness, mildness; fairness, equitableness, justness *ant* harshness **2** *syn* FORBEARANCE, mercifulness, leniency, indulgence, tolerance *rel, ant* see CLEMENCY 1

clement *syn* FORBEARING, merciful, lenient, indulgent, tolerant *rel* compassionate, tender, sympathetic; benign, benignant, kindly, kind; humane, benevolent, charitable *ant* harsh; barbarous

clemently *syn* FORBEARINGLY, tolerantly, mercifully, leniently, indulgently

clever **1** *syn* INTELLIGENT, quick-witted, brilliant, bright, smart, alert, knowing *rel* quick, apt, ready, prompt; versatile, all-around, many-sided; capable, competent, able; sharp, keen, acute *ant* dull **2** · having or showing a high degree of practical intelligence or skill in contrivance *syn* adroit, cunning, ingenious *rel* dexterous, deft, handy; nimble, agile; proficient, skillful, skilled, adept, expert, masterly

cliché *syn* COMMONPLACE, platitude, truism, bromide

clientele *syn* FOLLOWING, public, audience

climax *syn* SUMMIT, culmination, peak, apex, acme, zenith, apogee, pinnacle, meridian

climb *syn* ASCEND, mount, scale *ant* descend

cling *syn* STICK, cleave, adhere, cohere *rel* depend, RELY, trust, count, bank, reckon; attach, affix, fasten; hang, dangle, suspend

clinkers *syn* ASH, cinders, embers

clip *syn* SHEAR, poll, trim, prune, lop, snip, crop *rel* cut, chop, slash, slit; curtail, shorten; sever, separate

clique *syn* SET, circle, coterie *rel* party, faction, bloc, ring, combine, combination

cloak *syn* DISGUISE, mask, dissemble, camouflage *rel* conceal, hide, screen *ant* uncloak

clodhopper *syn* BOOR, bumpkin, hick, yokel, rube, lout, clown, churl

clog *syn* HAMPER, fetter, hog-tie, shackle, manacle, trammel *rel* impede, obstruct, hinder, block; balk, baffle, frustrate; check, curb, restrain *ant* expedite, facilitate

cloister **1** · a place of retirement from the world for members of a religious community *syn* convent, monastery, nunnery, abbey, priory **2** *syn* PASSAGE, arcade, passageway, ambulatory, gallery, corridor, aisle, hall, hallway

clone *syn* VARIETY, subspecies, race, breed, cultivar, strain, stock

close *vb* **1** · to stop or fill in an opening by means of a closure *syn* shut *rel* exclude, debar; block, bar, dam, hinder *ant* open **2** · to bring or come to a limit or a natural or appropriate stopping point *syn* end, conclude, finish, complete, terminate *rel* stop, cease, quit, desist

close *adj* **1** · not far (as in place, time, or relationship) from the point, position, or relation that is indicated or understood *syn* near, nigh, nearby *rel* adjoining, adjacent, contiguous, abutting; related, kindred *ant* remote, remotely **2** • having constituent parts that are massed tightly together *syn* dense, compact, thick *rel* compressed, condensed, constricted; concentrated, compacted *ant* open **3** *syn* SILENT, close-lipped, closemouthed, tight-lipped, secretive, reserved, taciturn, reticent, uncommunicative *ant* open, frank **4** *syn* FAMILIAR, intimate, confidential, chummy, thick *ant* aloof **5** *syn* STINGY, closefisted, tight, tightfisted, niggardly, parsimonious, penurious, cheeseparing, penny-pinching *rel* sparing, economical, frugal, thrifty *ant* liberal

closefisted *syn* STINGY, close, tight, tightfisted, niggardly, parsimonious, penurious, miserly, cheeseparing, penny-pinching *rel, ant* see CLOSE *adj*, 5

close-lipped *syn* SILENT, close, closemouthed, uncommunicative, taciturn, reserved, reticent, secretive, tight-lipped *rel, ant* see CLOSE *adj*, 3

closemouthed *syn* SILENT, close, close-lipped, tight-lipped, reticent, reserved, uncommunicative, taciturn, secretive *rel, ant* see CLOSE *adj* 3

clot *syn* COAGULATE, congeal, curdle, set, jelly, jell

clothe • to cover with or as if with garments *syn* attire, dress, apparel, array, robe *ant* unclothe

clothes • a person's garments considered collectively *syn* clothing, dress, attire, apparel, raiment

clothing *syn* CLOTHES, dress, attire, apparel, raiment

cloud *syn* OBSCURE, dim, bedim, darken, eclipse, becloud, fog, befog, obfuscate *rel* confuse, muddle, addle, befuddle; puzzle, perplex, distract

clout *syn* STRIKE, hit, smite, punch, slug, slog, swat, slap, cuff, box *rel* beat, pummel, thrash, baste, belabor

clown *syn* BOOR, clodhopper, lout, bumpkin, hick, yokel, rube, churl *rel* simpleton, natural, fool

clownish *syn* BOORISH, loutish, churlish *rel* awkward, clumsy, gauche; rude, rough, raw, green, uncouth *ant* urbane

cloy *syn* SATIATE, sate, surfeit, pall, glut, gorge *rel* whet

club *syn* ASSOCIATION, society, order

clumsy *syn* AWKWARD, gauche, maladroit, inept *rel* rude, rough, green, callow, uncouth; loutish, clownish, boorish; stiff, wooden, tense, rigid *ant* dexterous, adroit; facile

cluster *syn* GROUP, bunch, parcel, lot *rel* collection, assemblage; aggregate, number, quantity, sum

clutch *vb, syn* TAKE, grasp, grab, seize, snatch *rel* capture, catch; hold, have, possess, own

clutch *n, syn* HOLD, grip, grasp *rel* seizing, grabbing, taking

clutter *syn* CONFUSION, disorder, disarray, jumble, chaos, muddle, snarl

coadjutor *syn* ASSISTANT, helper, aid, aide, aide-de-camp

coagulate • to alter by chemical reaction from a liquid to a more or less firm jelly *syn* congeal, set, curdle, clot, jelly, jell *rel* solidify, harden; cohere, stick; coalesce, fuse, blend, mix; concentrate, consolidate, compact

coalesce *syn* MIX, merge, fuse, blend, mingle, commingle, amalgamate *rel* compact, consolidate, concentrate, unify; contract, condense, compress; cohere, adhere, stick, cleave, cling; mass, heap

coalition *syn* ALLIANCE, fusion, confederacy, confederation, federation, league

coarse • offensive to good taste or morals *syn* vulgar, gross, obscene, ribald *rel* rough, crude, rude, raw, green, callow, uncouth; rank, rampant; boorish, loutish, clownish *ant* fine; refined

coast *n, syn* SHORE, strand, beach, bank, foreshore, littoral

coast *vb, syn* SLIDE, toboggan, glide, slip, skid, glissade, slither

coax • to use ingratiating art in persuading or attempting to persuade *syn* cajole, wheedle, blandish *rel* induce, persuade, prevail, get; tease, pester, worry; inveigle, entice, tempt, lure *ant* bully

cobble *syn* BOTCH, bungle, fumble, muff *rel* patch, mend, repair; fabricate, forge, manufacture, make; impair, mar, spoil, injure

cock *syn* HEAP, stack, shock, pile, mass, bank *rel* gather, collect, assemble

cock *n, syn* HEAP, stack, shock, pile, mass, bank

cocksure *syn* SURE, positive, certain *rel* confident, assured, sanguine, presumptuous; pretentious, showy; decided, decisive *ant* dubious, doubtful

coerce *syn* FORCE, compel, constrain, oblige *rel* intimidate, bulldoze, bully, browbeat, cow; threaten, menace; drive, impel, move; terrorize, frighten

coercion *syn* FORCE, compulsion, violence, duress, constraint, restraint *rel* power, might, puissance, strength; intimidation, bulldozing, bullying, browbeating; threatening, threat, menacing, menace

coetaneous *syn* CONTEMPORARY, coeval, contemporaneous, synchronous, simultaneous, coincident, concomitant, concurrent

coeval *syn* CONTEMPORARY, coetaneous, synchronous, concurrent, simultaneous, coincident, concomitant, contemporaneous

cogent *syn* VALID, convincing, compelling, telling, sound *rel* forceful, forcible, potent, powerful, puissant; compelling, constraining; inducing, persuading, persuasive; proving, demonstrating; effective, effectual

cogitate *syn* THINK, reflect, deliberate, reason, speculate *rel* ponder, ruminate, meditate, muse; consider, excogitate, weigh, contemplate, study; think, conceive, imagine, envisage, envision

cognate *syn* RELATED, allied, kindred, affiliated *rel* akin, alike, identical, similar, like; common, generic, general, universal

cognizant *syn* AWARE, conscious, sensible, alive, awake *rel* conversant, versed; informed, acquainted, apprised *ant* ignorant

cohere *syn* STICK, adhere, cleave, cling *rel* coalesce, fuse, merge, blend, mix; fasten, attach, affix; join, combine, unite, connect, associate

coherence • the quality or character of a whole all of whose parts cohere or stick together *syn* cohesion *rel* unity, integrity, solidarity, union; clearness, perspicuousness, lucidity *ant* incoherence

cohesion *syn* COHERENCE *rel* unification, consolidation, concentration, compacting; coalescence, fusing, fusion, blending, blend, merging

coil *syn* WIND, curl, twist, twine, wreathe, entwine *rel* turn, revolve, rotate, circle

coin *syn* MONEY, coinage, currency, specie, legal tender, cash

coinage *syn* MONEY, coin, currency, cash, specie, legal tender

coincide *syn* AGREE, concur *rel* accord, correspond, jibe, harmonize, tally; match, equal *ant* differ

coincident *syn* CONTEMPORARY, synchronous, simultaneous, concurrent, concomitant, coeval, coetaneous, contemporaneous

cold • having a temperature below that which is normal or comfortable *syn* cool, chilly, frigid, freezing, frosty, gelid, icy, glacial, arctic *ant* hot

collate *syn* COMPARE, contrast

collateral *syn* SUBORDINATE, secondary, dependent, subject, tributary *rel* related, allied, kindred, cognate; correlative, complementary, corresponding, reciprocal

collation *syn* COMPARISON, parallel, contrast, antithesis *rel* corroboration, verification, confirmation, authentication; emending, emendation, revising, revision, correcting, correction

colleague *syn* PARTNER, copartner, ally, confederate *rel* associate, companion, comrade

collect *syn* GATHER, assemble, congregate *rel* mass, heap, pile; accumulate, amass, hoard; consolidate, concentrate, compact *ant* disperse; distribute

collected *syn* COOL, composed, unruffled, imperturbable, unflappable, nonchalant *rel* calm, placid, tranquil, serene; quiet, still; assured, confident, sure, sanguine; complacent, smug, self-satisfied *ant* distracted, distraught

collection *syn* GATHERING, assemblage, assembly, congregation *rel* heap, pile, mass, stack; accumulation, hording, hoard

collide *syn* BUMP, clash, conflict *rel* hit, strike; impinge, impact; dash, charge, rush

collision *syn* IMPACT, impingement, clash, shock, concussion, percussion, jar, jolt *rel* striking, hitting; wrecking, wreck, ruining, ruin, dilapidation; demolishment, destruction

color **1** • a property or attribute of a visible thing recognizable only when rays of light fall upon it and serving to distinguish things otherwise visually identical (as shape or size) *syn* hue, shade, tint, tinge, tone **2** *usu pl* **colors** *syn* FLAG, ensign, standard, banner, streamer, pennant, pendant, pennon, jack

colorable *syn* PLAUSIBLE, credible, believable, specious *rel* convincing, compelling, telling, cogent, sound, valid

colorless • without color *syn* uncolored, achromatic *rel* pale, pallid, ashen, wan; whitened, blanched, bleached, decolorized *ant* colorful

colossal *syn* HUGE, vast, immense, enormous, elephantine, mammoth, giant, gigantic, gigantean, gargantuan, Herculean, cyclopean, titanic, Brobdingnagian *rel* monumental, stupendous, tremendous, prodigious, monstrous

column *syn* PILLAR, pilaster

comatose *syn* LETHARGIC, torpid, sluggish *rel* languid, languorous, listless, languishing; phlegmatic, impassive; insensible, anesthetic, impassible; inert, passive, supine, inactive *ant* awake

comb *syn* SEEK, search, scour, hunt, ferret out, ransack, rummage *rel* scrutinize, inspect, examine; investigate, probe

combat *vb, syn* RESIST, withstand, contest, oppose, fight, conflict, antagonize *rel* fight, contend, battle, war; attack, assail, assault, bombard, storm *ant* champion; defend

combat *n, syn* CONTEST, conflict, fight, affray, fray *rel* battle, engagement, action; encounter, skirmish, brush; controversy, dispute, argument; contention, strife, conflict, discord

combative *syn* BELLIGERENT, bellicose, pugnacious, quarrelsome, contentious *rel* aggressive, militant; strenuous, energetic, vigorous; virile, manly, manful *ant* pacifistic

combination • a union, either of individuals or of organized interests, for mutual support in obtaining common political or private ends *syn* combine, party, bloc, faction, ring *rel* monopoly, corner, pool, cartel, syndicate, trust

combine *vb* **1** *syn* JOIN, unite, associate, link, conjoin, connect, relate *rel* mix, mingle, commingle, blend, fuse, amalgamate; consolidate, unify, compact *ant* separate **2** *syn* UNITE, cooperate, concur, conjoin *rel* coalesce, merge, mix, coincide, agree, concur

combine *n, syn* COMBINATION, party, bloc, faction, ring *rel* see COMBINATION

combustible · showing a tendency to catch or be set on fire *syn* inflammable, flammable, incendiary, inflammatory *rel* burnable; kindling, firing, igniting

come · to get to one point from another more or less distant in space, time, relation, or development *syn* arrive *rel* approach, near; rise, arise, spring, proceed, emanate, issue, stem *ant* go

comely *syn* BEAUTIFUL, fair, pretty, bonny, handsome, lovely, good-looking, beauteous, pulchritudinous *ant* homely

comestibles *syn* FOOD, provisions, viands, victuals, feed, provender, fodder, forage

comfort *n, syn* REST, ease, repose, relaxation, leisure *rel* contentedness, content, satisfaction; enjoyment, joy, fruition, pleasure; relief, assuagement, alleviation *ant* discomfort

comfort *vb* · to give or offer a person help or assistance in relieving his suffering or sorrow *syn* console, solace *rel* delight, gladden, rejoice, please; relieve, assuage, mitigate, alleviate; refresh, restore, renew *ant* afflict; bother

comfortable · enjoying or providing condition or circumstances which make for one's contentment and security *syn* cozy, snug, easy, restful *rel* comforting, consoling, solacing; content, contented, satisfied, grateful, welcome, agreeable, gratifying, pleasant *ant* uncomfortable; miserable

comic *syn* LAUGHABLE, comical, farcical, funny, droll, risible, ludicrous, ridiculous *rel* diverting, amusing, entertaining; witty, humorous, facetious; grotesque, antic, fantastic *ant* tragic

comical *syn* LAUGHABLE, comic, farcical, ludicrous, ridiculous, risible, droll, funny *rel* absurd, silly, foolish; jocular, jocose, humorous, witty; waggish, impish, roguish, sportive, playful; deriding, derisive, ridiculing, mocking *ant* pathetic

comity *syn* FRIENDSHIP, amity, goodwill *rel* association, society; companionship, comradeship; concord, accord, harmony

command *vb* · to issue orders to someone to give, get, or do something *syn* order, bid, enjoin, direct, instruct, charge *rel* control, manage, conduct, direct; exact, demand, require; force, compel, coerce, constrain, oblige *ant* comply, obey

command *n* **1** · a direction that must or should be obeyed *syn* order, injunction, bidding, behest, mandate, dictate *rel* direction, instruction, charging, charge; precept, ordinance, law, statute, canon, rule **2** *syn* POWER, control, authority, jurisdiction, sway, dominion *rel* ascendancy, supremacy; sovereignty

commemorate *syn* KEEP, celebrate, observe, solemnize

commence *syn* BEGIN, start, initiate, inaugurate *rel* institute, found, organize, establish

commend · to voice or otherwise manifest to others one's warm approval *syn* recommend, applaud, compliment *rel* praise, laud, extol, eulogize, acclaim *ant* censure; admonish

commensurable *syn* PROPORTIONAL, commensurate, proportionate *rel* equivalent, equal, identical, tantamount, same; reciprocal, corresponding *ant* incommensurable

commensurate *syn* PROPORTIONAL, commensurable, proportionate *rel* corresponding, correspondent, according, accordant, squaring, conforming; balancing, counterbalancing, compensating, offsetting *ant* incommensurate

comment *n, syn* REMARK, commentary, observation, note, obiter dictum *rel* interpreting, interpretation, elucidation, explication, expounding, exposition, explaining, explanation; annotation, gloss

comment *vb, syn* REMARK, commentate, animadvert *rel* interpret, elucidate, expound, explain, construe, explicate; annotate, gloss; criticize; illustrate, exemplify

commentary *syn* REMARK, comment, observation, note, obiter dictum *rel* see COMMENT *n*

commentate *syn* REMARK, comment, animadvert *rel* see COMMENT *vb*

commerce 1 *syn* BUSINESS, trade, industry, traffic 2 *syn* INTERCOURSE, traffic, dealings, communication, communion, conversation, converse, correspondence

commercial · of, relating to, or dealing with the supplying of commodities *syn* mercantile

commingle *syn* MIX, mingle, blend, merge, coalesce, fuse, amalgamate *rel* combine, unite, conjoin, associate, join, integrate

commiseration *syn* SYMPATHY, compassion, pity, condolence, ruth, empathy *rel* compassionateness, tenderness, warmheartedness; mercifulness, clemency; lamenting, lamentation, bewailing, bemoaning; pitifulness, piteousness, pitiableness *ant* ruthlessness, pitilessness

commission *syn* AUTHORIZE, accredit, license *rel* appoint, designate, name, nominate; empower, enable; instruct, enjoin, charge, bid, order, command

commit 1 · to assign to a person or place for some definite end or purpose (as custody or safekeeping) *syn* entrust, confide, consign, relegate *rel* transfer, shift, remove, move; assign, allot 2 · to be responsible for or to be guilty of some offense or mistake *syn* perpetrate *rel* offend, sin, scandalize; transgress, trespass, violate, contravene

commodious *syn* SPACIOUS, capacious, ample *rel* comfortable; large, big, great; broad, wide, deep

common 1 *syn* UNIVERSAL, general, generic *rel* shared, partaken, participated; joined, joint, united, conjoined, connected, associated; merged, blended, amalgamated *ant* individual 2 *syn* RECIPROCAL, mutual *rel, ant* see COMMON 1 3 · generally met with and not in any way special, strange, or unusual *syn* ordinary, familiar, popular, vulgar *rel* prevalent, prevailing, rife, current; usual, customary; plentiful, abundant, ample *ant* uncommon; exceptional

commonplace · an idea or expression lacking in originality or freshness *syn* platitude, truism, bromide, cliché *rel* expression, phrase, idiom, locution; banality, jejuneness, inanity, wishy-washiness; triteness, threadbareness

common sense *syn* see SENSE 2

commotion · great physical, mental, or emotional excitement *syn* agitation, tumult, turmoil, turbulence, confusion, convulsion, upheaval *rel* hubbub, racket, din, uproar, pandemonium; motion, movement; stir, bustle, flurry, ado

commune *syn* CONFER, consult, advise, parley, treat, negotiate *rel* converse, talk, speak; discuss, debate, argue

communicable *syn* INFECTIOUS, contagious, catching

communicate • to convey or transfer something (as information, feelings, or qualities) neither tangible nor concrete *syn* impart *rel* acquaint, apprise, inform, advise, notify; tell, disclose, reveal, divulge, discover; convey, transfer

communication *syn* INTERCOURSE, commerce, traffic, dealings, conversation, converse, correspondence, communion *rel* exchanging, exchange, interchanging, interchange; conversing, talking; news, tidings, advice, intelligence

communion **1** *syn* INTERCOURSE, commerce, traffic, converse, dealings, communication, conversation, correspondence *rel* empathy, sympathy; mysticism; contemplation; ecstasy, rapture, transport **2** *syn* RELIGION, denomination, faith, church, creed, sect, cult, persuasion

compact *adj, syn* CLOSE, dense, thick *rel* compressed, condensed, contracted; concentrated, consolidated, compacted; solid, firm, hard; tight

compact *vb* • to bring or gather together the parts, particles, elements, or units of a thing so as to form a close mass or an integral whole *syn* consolidate, unify, concentrate *rel* compress, condense, contract; bind, tie; unite, combine, join; knit, weave

compact *n, syn* CONTRACT, pact, entente, convention, concordat, treat, cartel, bargain

companion *n, syn* ASSOCIATE, comrade, crony *rel* friend, confidant, intimate, acquaintance; partner, colleague; attendant, escort, chaperon

companionable *syn* SOCIAL, cooperative, convivial, gregarious, hospitable *rel* friendly, neighborly, amicable; amiable, obliging, complaisant, good-natured; sociable, affable, gracious, cordial

company • a group of persons who are associated in a joint endeavor or who are assembled for a common end *syn* party, band, troop, troupe *rel* set, circle, coterie, clique; association, society, club, order; crowd, throng, mob, horde

comparable *syn* LIKE, alike, similar, analogous, akin, parallel, uniform, identical *ant* disparate

compare • to set two or more things side by side in order to show likenesses and differences *syn* contrast, collate *rel* match, equal, approach, touch, rival

comparison • a setting of things side by side so as to discover or exhibit their likenesses and differences *syn* contrast, antithesis, collation, parallel *rel* likeness, similarity, resemblance, analogy, similitude, affinity; parallel, counterpart, analogue, correlate

compass *vb* **1** *syn* SURROUND, environ, encircle, circle, encompass, hem, gird, girdle, ring *rel* enclose, envelop; confine, circumscribe, restrict, limit **2** *syn* REACH, gain, attain, achieve *rel* effect, fulfill, accomplish, perform; complete, finish, close

compass *n* **1** *syn* CIRCUMFERENCE, perimeter, periphery, circuit *rel* area, extent, magnitude, size; field, sphere, domain **2** *syn* RANGE, gamut, reach, radius, sweep, scope, orbit, horizon, ken, purview *rel* circumscription, limitation, restriction; limits, bounds, confines

compassion *syn* SYMPATHY, pity,

commiseration, ruth, empathy, condolence *rel* tenderness, compassionateness, responsiveness, warmheartedness; mercy, charity, grace, lenity, clemency

compassionate *syn* TENDER, sympathetic, warmhearted, warm, responsive *rel* pitiful, piteous; merciful, forbearing, clement, lenient; humane, benevolent, charitable

compatible *syn* CONSONANT, congruous, consistent, congenial, sympathetic *rel* suitable, appropriate, proper, meet, fitting, fit; harmonizing, corresponding, correspondent, according, accordant; harmonious *ant* incompatible

compel *syn* FORCE, coerce, constrain, oblige *rel* impel, drive, move; command, order, enjoin

compelling *syn* VALID, telling, convincing, cogent, sound

compendious *syn* CONCISE, summary, pithy, succinct, terse, laconic *rel* compact, close; condensed, contracted; abridged, abbreviated, shortened

compendium · a condensed treatment of a subject *syn* syllabus, digest, pandect, survey, sketch, précis, aperçu *rel* conspectus, epitome, brief, abstract, abridgement

compensate **1** · to make up for or to undo the effects of *syn* countervail, balance, offset, counterbalance, counterpoise *rel* counteract, neutralize, negative; nullify, negate, annul, abrogate, invalidate; complement, supplement; correspond, square, tally, jibe, agree **2** *syn* PAY, remunerate, recompense, repay, reimburse, satisfy, indemnify

compete **1** · to strive to gain the mastery or upper hand *syn* contend, contest *rel* battle, fight; rival, vie; oppose, combat, withstand, resist **2** *syn* RIVAL, vie, emulate *rel* contend, fight; match, rival, approach, equal, touch

competent **1** *syn* ABLE, capable, qualified *rel* proficient, skillful, skilled, adept, expert, masterly; efficient, effective *ant* incompetent **2** *syn* sufficient, enough, adequate

compile *syn* EDIT, revise, redact, rewrite, adapt

complacent · feeling or showing an often excessive or unjustified satisfaction in one's possessions, attainments, accomplishments, or virtues *syn* self-complacent, self-satisfied, smug, priggish *rel* self-assured, self-confident, self-possessed, assured, confident; conceited, egotistic, egoistic; proud, vain, vainglorious

complaint *syn* DISEASE, ailment, disorder, condition, affection, malady, distemper, syndrome

complaisant *syn* AMIABLE, obliging, good-natured *rel* affable, genial, cordial, gracious; courteous, courtly, gallant, polite, civil; suave, urbane, politic, diplomatic, smooth, bland; agreeable, pleasant, pleasing *ant* contrary, perverse

complement *n* · something that makes up for a want or deficiency in another thing *syn* supplement *rel* counterpart, correlate, parallel

complement *vb* · to supply what is needed to make up for a want or deficiency *syn* supplement *rel* complete, finish, close

complementary, complemental *syn* RECIPROCAL, correlative, corresponding, convertible *rel* complementing, supplementing; completing, finishing; related, associated

complete *adj, syn* FULL, plenary, replete *rel* entire, whole, total, all; perfect, intact, whole, entire *ant* incomplete

complete *vb, syn* CLOSE, finish,

conclude, end, terminate *rel* effect, fulfill, achieve, execute, accomplish, perform, discharge

complex *adj* · having parts or elements that are more or less confusingly interrelated *syn* complicated, intricate, involved, knotty *rel* mixed, mingled, blended, merged, fused, amalgamated; composite, compound *ant* simple

complex *n, syn* SYSTEM, network, organism, scheme *ant* component

complexion *syn* DISPOSITION, temperament, temper, character, personality, individuality *rel* humor; mood, vein, temper; nature, kind, type, sort

compliance · passive or weak agreement to what is asked or demanded *syn* acquiescence, resignation *rel* obedience, docility, amenableness, tractableness; submitting, submission, yielding, deferring, deference *ant* forwardness

compliant · manifesting acceptance (as of another's will or something disagreeable) *syn* acquiescent, resigned *rel* obedient, amenable, tractable, docile; submissive, tame, subdued; accommodating, conforming, adapting, adaptable *ant* forward

complicated *syn* COMPLEX, intricate, involved, knotty *rel* difficult, arduous, hard; abstruse, recondite; perplexing, puzzling, mystifying *ant* simple

compliment *n* · praise addressed directly to a person *syn* flattery, adulation *rel* encomium, tribute, panegyric, eulogy; praise, lauding, laudation, extolling, extollation *ant* taunt

compliment *vb, syn* COMMEND, applaud, recommend *rel* praise, laud, extol, eulogize, acclaim

comply *syn* OBEY, mind *rel* accede, consent, agree, acquiesce, assent; yield, submit, defer, bow *ant* command, enjoin

component *syn* ELEMENT, constituent, ingredient, factor *rel* member, part, detail, portion, piece; item, particular *ant* composite; complex

comport *syn* BEHAVE, acquit, quit, demean, conduct, deport

compose *syn* CALM, quiet, quieten, still, lull, soothe, settle, tranquilize *rel* pacify, mollify, propitiate, conciliate; moderate, temper *ant* discompose

composed *syn* COOL, collected, unruffled, imperturbable, unflappable, nonchalant *rel* quiet, still; serene, placid, tranquil, calm; sedate, staid, serious; repressed, suppressed *ant* discomposed; anxious

composite *syn* MIXTURE, admixture, blend, compound, amalgam *rel* combining, combination, uniting, union

composition *syn* ESSAY, theme, paper, article

composure *syn* EQUANIMITY, sangfroid, phlegm *rel* coolness, collectedness, imperturbability, nonchalance; self-possession, aplomb, confidence; placidity, serenity, calmness *ant* discomposure, perturbation

compound *syn* MIXTURE, amalgam, composite, admixture, blend *rel* combining, combination, uniting, union, coalescence, fusing, fusion, merging, merger *ant* element

comprehend **1** *syn* UNDERSTAND, appreciate *rel* seize, grasp, take; conceive, envisage, envision, think **2** *syn* APPREHEND *rel* see COMPREHEND 1 **3** *syn* INCLUDE, embrace, involve, imply, subsume *rel* contain, hold; classify, pigeonhole, assort

comprehension *syn* APPREHENSION, *rel* understanding, appreciating, appreciation; knowledge, science, learning, erudition

compress *syn* CONTRACT, constrict, deflate, condense, shrink *rel* compact, concentrate, consolidate; bind, tie *ant* stretch; spread

compulsion *syn* FORCE, coercion, constraint, duress, violence, restraint *rel* impelling, impulsion, driving, drive; pressure, stress; necessity, exigency, need

compunction 1 *syn* PENITENCE, remorse, repentance, contrition, attrition *rel* regret, sorrow; conscientiousness, scrupulousness, scrupulosity 2 *syn* QUALM, scruple, demur *rel* hesitation, hesitancy; reluctance, disinclination

compute *syn* CALCULATE, reckon, estimate *rel* count, enumerate, number; sum, total, tot, figure, cast, add

comrade *syn* ASSOCIATE, companion, crony *rel* friend, intimate, confidant; colleague, partner, confederate, ally

conation *syn* WILL, volition *rel* effort, exertion; action, act; choice, selection, option

concatenate *syn* INTEGRATE, articulate *rel* link, connect, relate, unite, combine, join, associate; fuse, blend, merge, coalesce, mix; organize, systematize, order

concatenation *syn* INTEGRATION, articulation *rel* sequence, succession, chain, train

conceal *syn* HIDE, screen, secrete, bury, cache, ensconce *rel* cloak, mask, disguise, dissemble, camouflage *ant* reveal

concede 1 *syn* GRANT, allow *rel* admit, acknowledge; waive, cede, relinquish *ant* dispute 2 *syn* GRANT, vouchsafe, accord, award *rel* yield, submit; surrender, resign, cede, relinquish *ant* deny (*something to somebody*)

conceit 1 • an attitude of regarding oneself with favor *syn* egotism, egoism, self-esteem, self-love, amour propre *rel* pride, vanity, vainglory; arrogance, superciliousness, insolence; complacency, smugness, priggishness *ant* humility 2 *syn* CAPRICE, freak, fancy, whim, whimsy, vagary, crotchet

conceive *syn* THINK, imagine, fancy, realize, envisage, envision *rel* consider, excogitate; speculate, cogitate, think; ponder, ruminate, meditate

concentrate 1 *syn* CENTER, focus, centralize *rel* fix, set, settle, establish; muster, convoke, convene, summon 2 *syn* COMPACT, consolidate, unify *rel* gather, collect, assemble; mass, heap, pile; fix, fasten, attach; engross, monopolize, absorb *ant* dissipate

concentration *syn* ATTENTION, application, study *rel* intentness, raptness, engrossment, absorption *ant* distraction

concept *syn* IDEA, conception, notion, thought, impression

conception *syn* IDEA, concept, thought, notion, impression *rel* opinion, view, belief, conviction, persuasion, sentiment; theory, hypothesis

concern 1 *syn* AFFAIR, business, matter, thing 2 *syn* CARE, solicitude, anxiety, worry *rel* thoughtfulness, considerateness, consideration, attentiveness, attention *ant* unconcern

concerned *syn* WORRIED, solicitous, anxious *rel* engrossed, absorbed, intent; impressed, affected, influenced, touched; troubled, distressed *ant* unconcerned

concerning *syn* ABOUT, regarding, respecting

concert *syn* NEGOTIATE, arrange *rel* discuss, debate, argue; concur, cooperate, unite, conjoin, combine

concession *syn* ALLOWANCE *rel* favor, boon, gift; indulgence, leniency, tolerance, forbearance

conciliate *syn* PACIFY, appease, placate, propitiate, mollify *rel* arbitrate, adjudicate, judge; mediate, intervene, interpose; persuade, prevail, induce; calm, tranquilize; adjust, accommodate, reconcile, adapt *ant* antagonize

concise • presented with or given to brevity of expression *syn* terse, succinct, laconic, summary, pithy, compendious *rel* condensed, compressed; compacted, concentrated; abridged, abbreviated, shortened; brief, short *ant* redundant

conclude 1 *syn* CLOSE, finish, terminate, end, complete *ant* open 2 *syn* INFER, judge, gather, deduce *rel* reason, speculate, think; conjecture, surmise, guess

concluding *syn* LAST, final, terminal, latest, ultimate *rel* closing, terminating, ending, finishing, completing *ant* opening

conclusion *syn* INFERENCE, judgment, deduction

conclusive • having or manifesting qualities that bring something to a finish or end *syn* decisive, determinative, definitive *rel* convincing, compelling, telling, cogent, valid; certain, inevitable, necessary *ant* inconclusive

concoct *syn* CONTRIVE, devise, invent, frame *rel* make, fabricate, fashion, manufacture; create, discover, invent; conceive, envisage, envision, think

concomitant *adj, syn* CONTEMPORARY, coincident, concurrent, synchronous, simultaneous, contemporaneous, coeval, coetaneous *rel* attending, attendant, accompanying; associated, connected, related, linked

concomitant *n, syn* ACCOMPANIMENT

concord *syn* HARMONY, consonance, accord *rel* agreement, concurrence, coincidence; peacefulness, peace, tranquillity, serenity, placidity, calmness; amity, comity, goodwill, friendship *ant* discord

concordat *syn* CONTRACT, compact, pact, treaty, entente, convention, cartel, bargain

concourse *syn* JUNCTION, confluence

concur 1 *syn* UNITE, conjoin, combine, cooperate *rel* accord, harmonize, agree, jibe 2 *syn* AGREE, coincide *rel* consent, assent, accede, acquiesce, agree *ant* contend; altercate

concurrent *syn* CONTEMPORARY, coincident, simultaneous, synchronous, concomitant, contemporaneous, coeval, coetaneous

concussion *syn* IMPACT, shock, percussion, impingement, collision, clash, jar, jolt *rel* beating, pounding, buffeting; striking, smiting, swatting, slapping

condemn 1 *syn* CRITICIZE, denounce, censure, blame, reprobate, reprehend *rel* judge, adjudge; decry, belittle, depreciate, disparage; disapprove, deprecate 2 *syn* SENTENCE, doom, damn, proscribe

condense *syn* CONTRACT, shrink, compress, constrict, deflate *rel* abridge, abbreviate, shorten, curtail; reduce, diminish, decrease; compact, concentrate, consolidate *ant* amplify

condescend *syn* STOOP, deign *rel* favor, accommodate, oblige; vouchsafe, concede, grant *ant* presume

condign *syn* DUE, rightful *rel* just, equitable, fair; merited, deserved

condition *n* 1 • something that limits or qualifies an agreement or offer *syn* stipulation, terms, provision, proviso, reservation, strings *rel* prerequisite, requisite, requirement 2 *syn* STATE, situation, mode, posture, status *rel* circumstance, occurrence, event; occasion, antecedent, cause; phase, aspect, side, facet, angle 3 *syn* DISEASE, disorder, affection, ailment, malady, complaint, distemper, syndrome

condition *vb, syn* PREPARE, fit, qualify, ready

conditional *syn* DEPENDENT, contingent, relative *rel* problematic, questionable, doubtful; provisional, tentative; subject, prone, liable, open; accidental, fortuitous, incidental *ant* unconditional

condolence *syn* SYMPATHY, pity, commiseration, compassion, ruth, empathy *rel* consoling, consolation, solacing, solace, comforting

condone *syn* EXCUSE, forgive, pardon, remit *rel* disregard, overlook, forget, ignore, neglect; exculpate, absolve, acquit

conduct *n, syn* BEHAVIOR, deportment *rel* act, deed, action; demeanor, mien, deportment, bearing

conduct *vb* **1** *syn* ACCOMPANY, escort, convoy, attend, chaperon *rel* guide, lead; convey, transmit, carry **2** • to use one's skill, authority, or other powers in order to lead, guide, command, or dominate persons or things *syn* manage, control, direct *rel* supervise, oversee; govern, rule; engineer, pilot, steer, lead, guide; operate, work, function **3** *syn* BEHAVE, demean, deport, comport, acquit, quit

conduit *syn* CHANNEL, canal, duct, aqueduct

confederacy, confederation *syn* ALLIANCE, federation, coalition, fusion, league

confederate **1** *syn* PARTNER, copartner, colleague, ally *rel, ant* see ALLY **2** • one associated with another or others in a wrong or unlawful act *syn* conspirator, accessory, abettor, accomplice

confer **1** *syn* GIVE, bestow, present, donate, afford *rel* accord, award, vouchsafe, grant **2** • to carry on a conversation or discussion esp. in order to reach a decision or settlement *syn* commune, consult, advise, parley, treat, negotiate *rel* converse, talk, speak; discuss, debate, argue

confess *syn* ACKNOWLEDGE, avow, admit, own *rel* grant, concede, allow; disclose, divulge, reveal, discover; declare, proclaim, publish *ant* renounce (*one's beliefs, principles*)

confessions *syn* BIOGRAPHY, life, memoir, autobiography

confidant *syn* FRIEND, intimate, acquaintance *rel* comrade, crony, companion, associate

confide *syn* COMMIT, entrust, consign, relegate *rel* bestow, present, give; grant, vouchsafe, accord, award

confidence **1** *syn* TRUST, reliance, dependence, faith *rel* certitude, assurance, conviction, certainty; credence, credit, belief, faith *ant* doubt; apprehension **2** • a feeling or showing of adequacy or reliance on oneself and one's powers *syn* self-confidence, assurance, self-assurance, self-possession, aplomb *rel* courage, resolution, mettle, spirit, tenacity *ant* diffidence

confident • not inhibited by doubts, fears, or a sense of inferiority *syn* assured, sanguine, sure, presumptuous *rel* courageous, intrepid, brave, bold, dauntless, undaunted, valiant, fearless, unafraid; positive, certain, sure *ant* apprehensive; diffident

confidential *syn* FAMILIAR, close, intimate, chummy, thick *rel* secret; trusty, tried, trustworthy, reliable

configuration *syn* FORM, conformation, figure, shape *rel* outline, contour, silhouette, profile, skyline

confine *vb, syn* LIMIT, circumscribe, restrict *rel* bind, tie; restrain, curb, inhibit, check; hamper, trammel, fetter, shackle, hog-tie, manacle; imprison, incarcerate, immure, intern, jail

confine *n, syn* LIMIT, bound, end, term *rel* verge, edge, border; circumference, periphery, compass

confirm 1 *syn* RATIFY *rel* assent, consent, acquiesce accede, subscribe; validate; sanction, approve, endorse 2 • to attest to the truth, genuineness, accuracy, or validity of something *syn* corroborate, substantiate, verify, authenticate, validate *rel* support, uphold, back; vouch, attest, certify *ant* deny; contradict

confirmed *syn* INVETERATE, chronic, deep-seated, deep-rooted *rel* established, fixed, set, settled; hardened, indurated, callous

confiscate *syn* ARROGATE, appropriate, usurp, preempt *rel* seize, take, grab; condemn, proscribe, sentence

conflagration *syn* FIRE, holocaust

conflict *n* 1 *syn* CONTEST, combat, fight, affray, fray *rel* engagement, battle, action; encounter, skirmish, brush; controversy, dispute, argument 2 *syn* DISCORD, strife, contention, dissension, difference, variance *rel* clash, collision, impingement, impact; antagonism, hostility, enmity; incompatibility, incongruousness, inconsistency, inconsonance, discordance *ant* harmony

conflict *vb* 1 *syn* RESIST, withstand, contest, oppose, fight, combat, antagonize 2 *syn* BUMP, clash, collide *rel* contend, fight; differ, vary, disagree *ant* accord

confluence *syn* JUNCTION, concourse

conform 1 *syn* ADAPT, adjust, accommodate, reconcile *rel* harmonize, tune, attune; assent, accede, acquiesce; accept, receive 2 *syn* AGREE, accord, harmonize, correspond, square, tally, jibe *ant* diverge

conformation *syn* FORM, configuration, shape, figure *rel* structure, anatomy, framework, skeleton

confound 1 *syn* PUZZLE, dumbfound, nonplus, bewilder, mystify, perplex, distract *rel* flabbergast, amaze, astound, astonish, surprise; discomfit, faze, rattle, abash, embarrass, disconcert 2 *syn* MISTAKE, confuse *rel* muddle, addle, confuse; mix, mingle *ant* distinguish, discriminate

confront *syn* MEET, face, encounter *rel* defy, beard, challenge, brave, dare; oppose, withstand, resist *ant* recoil

confuse 1 • to make unclear in mind or purpose *syn* muddle, addle, fuddle, befuddle *rel* confound, bewilder, mystify, perplex, puzzle; discomfit, disconcert, faze, rattle, embarrass; fluster, flurry, discompose *ant* enlighten 2 *syn* MISTAKE, confound *ant* differentiate

confusion 1 • a condition in which things are not in their normal or proper places or relationships *syn* disorder, chaos, disarray, jumble, clutter, snarl, muddle *rel* derangement, disarrangement, disorganization, disturbance; din, babel, pandemonium, hullabaloo; anarchy, lawlessness 2 *syn* COMMOTION, agitation, tumult, turmoil, turbulence, convulsion, upheaval *rel* disorder, disorganization, disturbance; perturbation, agitation, disquiet, upset, discomposure; discomfiture, embarrassment

confute *syn* DISPROVE, controvert, refute, rebut

congeal *syn* COAGULATE, set, curdle, clot, jelly, jell *rel* solidify, harden; compact, concentrate, consolidate; cool, chill, freeze

congenial *syn* CONSONANT, consistent, compatible, congruous, sympathetic *rel* companionable, cooperative, social; sociable, genial, cordial, gracious, affable; pleasing, pleasant, agreeable *ant* uncongenial; antipathetic (*of persons*); abhorrent (*of tasks, duties*)

congenital *syn* INNATE, inborn, hereditary, inherited, inbred *rel* inherent, constitutional, ingrained; native

conglomerate, conglomeration *syn* AGGREGATE, agglomerate, agglomeration, aggregation *rel* mass, heap, pile, stack; accumulation, amassment, hoarding, hoard

congratulate *syn* FELICITATE

congregate *syn* GATHER, assemble, collect *rel* swarm, teem *ant* disperse

congregation *syn* GATHERING, assembly, assemblage, collection *rel* audience, following, public; crowd, throng, press, crush

congruous *syn* CONSONANT, compatible, congenial, sympathetic, consistent *rel* harmonizing, harmonious, according, accordant, corresponding, correspondent, agreeing, agreeable; seemly, proper, decorous; meet, appropriate, fitting fit *ant* incongruous

conjectural *syn* SUPPOSED, hypothetical, supposititious, reputed, putative, purported *rel* presumed, assumed, postulated; theoretical, speculative; alleged

conjecture *vb* • to draw an inference from slight evidence *syn* surmise, guess *rel* infer, gather, conclude, judge, deduce; speculate, reason; imagine, fancy, conceive, think

conjecture *n* • an inference based on slight evidence *syn* surmise, guess *rel* theory, hypothesis; opinion, view, belief, sentiment; inference, deduction, conclusion, judgment *ant* fact

conjoin 1 *syn* JOIN, combine, unite, connect, link, associate, relate 2 *syn* UNITE, combine, concur, cooperate

conjugal *syn* MATRIMONIAL, marital, connubial, nuptial, hymeneal *ant* single

connect *syn* JOIN, link, associate, relate, unite, conjoin, combine *rel* attach, fasten, affix; articulate, concatenate, integrate *ant* disconnect

connoisseur *syn* AESTHETE, dilettante *rel* epicure, gourmet, bon vivant; expert, adept

connubial *syn* MATRIMONIAL, conjugal, marital, nuptial, hymeneal

conquer • to get the better of or to bring into subjection by force or strategy *syn* defeat, vanquish, overcome, surmount, subdue, subjugate, reduce, overthrow, rout, beat, lick *rel* frustrate, thwart, foil, circumvent, outwit, baffle, balk

conqueror *syn* VICTOR, vanquisher, winner, champion

conquest *syn* VICTORY, triumph *rel* subjugation, subdual, defeating, defeat, overthrowing, overthrow, routing, rout

conscientious *syn* UPRIGHT, scrupulous, honorable, honest, just *rel* righteous, virtuous, ethical, moral; strict, rigid; particular, fastidious, finicky, nice; meticulous, punctilious, careful *ant* unconscientious, unscrupulous

conscious *syn* AWARE, sensible, cognizant, alive, awake *rel* attending, attentive, minding, mindful, watching; watchful, alert, vigilant; perceiving, noticing, noting, remarking, observing *ant* unconscious

consecrate *syn* DEVOTE, hallow, dedicate

consecutive • following one after the other in order *syn* successive, sequent, sequential, serial *rel* following, succeeding, ensuing; continuous, continual, incessant; coherent; logical *ant* inconsecutive

consent *syn* ASSENT, accede, acquiesce, agree, subscribe *rel* yield, submit, defer, relent; permit, allow, let; approve, sanction; concur *ant* dissent

consequence **1** *syn* EFFECT, result, upshot, aftereffect, aftermath, sequel, issue, outcome, event *ant* antecedent **2** *syn* IMPORTANCE, moment, weight, significance, import *rel* necessity, need, exigency; worth, value; renown, honor, reputation, repute, fame; eminence, illustriousness

consequently *syn* THEREFORE, hence, then, accordingly, so

conserve *syn* SAVE, preserve *rel* protect, shield, safeguard, guard, defend *ant* waste, squander

consider **1** · to give serious thought to *syn* study, contemplate, weigh, excogitate *rel* ponder, meditate, ruminate, muse; reflect, cogitate, think, reason, speculate; inspect, examine, scrutinize, scan **2** · to come to view, judge, or classify *syn* regard, account, reckon, deem *rel* think, conceive, imagine, fancy; judge, gather, infer, conclude

considerate *syn* THOUGHTFUL, attentive *rel* kindly, kind; tender, sympathetic, warmhearted, compassionate; obliging, complaisant, amiable *ant* inconsiderate

considered *syn* DELIBERATE, premeditated, advised, designed, studied *rel* intentional, voluntary, willful; planned, projected, schemed *ant* unconsidered

consign *syn* COMMIT, entrust, confide, relegate *rel* transfer, move, remove, shift; assign, allocate, allot; resign, surrender, yield, relinquish

consistent *syn* CONSONANT, congruous, compatible, congenial, sympathetic *rel* conforming, conformable, tallying, jibing, squaring; matching, equaling; identical, alike, similar, like *ant* inconsistent

console *syn* COMFORT, solace *rel* assuage, alleviate, mitigate, relieve, allay; calm, tranquilize; satisfy, content

consolidate *syn* COMPACT, unify, concentrate *rel* integrate, articulate, concatenate; amalgamate, merge, fuse, blend, mix; condense, compress, contract; weave, knit

consolidation · a union of two or more business corporations *syn* merger, amalgamation *ant* dissolution

consonance *syn* HARMONY, concord, accord *rel* agreement, conformity, correspondence; concurrence, coincidence; compatibility, congruity *ant* dissonance (*in music*); discord

consonant *adj* · conforming (as to a pattern, standard, or relationship) without discord or difficulty *syn* consistent, compatible, congruous, congenial, sympathetic *rel* conforming, conformable, harmonizing, harmonious, agreeing, agreeable, according, accordant; concurring, concurrent, coinciding, coincident *ant* inconstant; dissonant (*in music*)

conspectus *syn* ABRIDGMENT, synopsis, epitome, abstract, brief *rel* compendium, syllabus, digest, survey, sketch, précis, aperçu

conspicuous *syn* NOTICEABLE, prominent, salient, signal, remarkable, striking, arresting, outstanding *rel* patent, manifest, evident, distinct, obvious; eminent, celebrated, illustrious, famous *ant* inconspicuous

conspiracy *syn* PLOT, cabal, intrigue, machination *rel* sedition, treason; treacherousness, treachery, perfidiousness, perfidy, disloyalty, faithlessness, falseness, falsity

conspirator *syn* CONFEDERATE, accessory, accomplice, abettor

constant **1** *syn* FAITHFUL, true, loyal, staunch, steadfast, resolute *rel* abiding, enduring, persisting, persistent, lasting; dependable, trustworthy, reliable, trusty, tried *ant* inconstant, fickle **2** *syn* STEADY, uniform, even, equable *rel* established, settled, set, fixed; invariable, immutable, unchangeable; regular, normal, typical, natural *ant* variable **3** *syn* CONTINUAL, incessant, unremitting, continuous, perpetual, perennial *rel* persisting, persistent, persevering; pertinacious, dogged, obstinate, stubborn; chronic, confirmed, inveterate *ant* fitful

consternation *syn* FEAR, panic, terror, alarm, fright, dread, dismay, horror, trepidation *rel* confusion, muddlement, muddle; bewilderment, distraction, perplexity agitation, perturbation

constituent *syn* ELEMENT, component, ingredient, factor *rel* part, portion, piece, detail, member; item, particular *ant* whole, aggregate

constitution *syn* PHYSIQUE, build, habit *rel* temperament, temper, personality, disposition; organism, system; structure, framework, anatomy

constitutional *syn* INHERENT, intrinsic, essential, ingrained *rel* congenital, innate, inborn; native; natural, normal, regular; characteristic, individual, peculiar

constrain *syn* FORCE, oblige, coerce, compel *rel* impel, drive, move, actuate; require, exact, demand

constraint *syn* FORCE, compulsion, coercion, duress, restraint, violence *rel* suppression, repression; impelling, impulsion, driving, drive; goad, spur, motive, spring; obligation, duty

constrict *syn* CONTRACT, compress, shrink, condense, deflate *rel* tie, bind; restrict, confine, circumscribe, limit; restrain, curb

construct *syn* BUILD, erect, frame, raise, rear *rel* fabricate, manufacture, fashion, make; produce, turn out, yield, bear *ant* demolish; analyze

constructive *syn* IMPLICIT, virtual *rel* inferential, ratiocinative; implied, involved *ant* manifest

construe *syn* EXPLAIN, explicate, elucidate, interpret, expound *rel* analyze, resolve, break down, dissect; understand, comprehend, appreciate

consult *syn* CONFER, advise, parley, commune, treat, negotiate *rel* discuss, debate; deliberate, cogitate, think; counsel, advise

consume **1** *syn* WASTE, squander, dissipate, fritter *rel* exhaust, deplete, drain; dispel, disperse, scatter **2** *syn* EAT, swallow, ingest, devour **3** *syn* MONOPOLIZE, engross, absorb

consummate · brought to completion or perfection *syn* finished, accomplished *rel* perfect, whole, entire, intact; complete, full; flawless, impeccable, faultless; supreme, superlative, transcendent, peerless, surpassing *ant* crude

contact · the state of coming into direct connection or close association *syn* touch *rel* impingement, impact; connection, association, relation; union, unity; closeness, nearness

contagious *syn* INFECTIOUS, communicable, catching *rel* toxic, pestilential, pestilent, virulent, mephitic, miasmic, poisonous

contain · to have or be capable of having within *syn* hold, accommodate *rel* receive, admit, take; harbor, shelter, lodge, house

contaminate · to debase by making impure or unclean *syn* taint, attaint, pollute, defile *rel* debase, vitiate, corrupt, deprave; impair, spoil, injure, harm

contemn *syn* DESPISE, disdain, scorn, scout *rel* repudiate, reject, decline; slight, neglect, disregard; flout, scoff, jeer

contemplate 1 *syn* CONSIDER, study, weigh, excogitate *rel* ponder, meditate, muse, ruminate; reflect, cogitate, speculate, think 2 *syn* SEE, observe, survey, notice, remark, note, perceive, discern, view, behold, decry, espy *rel* scrutinize, inspect, examine, scan

contemplative *syn* THOUGHTFUL, meditative, reflective, speculative, pensive *rel* intent, rapt, engrossed, absorbed; musing, ruminating, pondering; reflecting, cogitating, reasoning, thinking

contemporaneous *syn* CONTEMPORARY, coeval, coetaneous, synchronous, simultaneous, coincident, concomitant, concurrent

contemporary · existing, living, or occurring at the same time *syn* contemporaneous, coeval, coetaneous, synchronous, simultaneous, coincident, concomitant, concurrent *rel* living, existing, subsisting

contempt *syn* DESPITE, disdain, scorn *rel* abhorrence, detestation, loathing, hatred, hate; aversion, antipathy; repugnance, distaste *ant* respect

contemptible · arousing or deserving scorn or disdain *syn* despicable, pitiable, sorry, scurvy, cheap, beggarly, shabby *rel* detestable, abominable, abhorrent, odious, hateful; vile, low, base; abject, mean, sordid, ignoble *ant* admirable, estimable; formidable

contend 1 · to strive in opposition to someone or something *syn* fight, battle, war *rel* quarrel, wrangle, altercate, squabble; resist, combat, withstand, oppose, fight; compete, vie, rival 2 *syn* COMPETE, contest *rel* battle, war; oppose, resist, withstand, combat, fight

content, contented *adj, syn* SATISFIED, *rel* gratified, pleased; sated, satiated, cloyed, surfeited; replete, full

content *vb, syn* SATISFY *rel* gratify, please; sate, satiate, surfeit, cloy

contention *syn* DISCORD, dissension, difference, variance, strife, conflict *rel* quarrel, wrangle, altercation, squabble; controversy, dispute, argument; contending, fighting, warring

contentious *syn* BELLIGERENT, quarrelsome, bellicose, pugnacious, combative *rel* contrary, perverse, froward; captious, faultfinding, caviling, carping, critical; aggressive, militant *ant* peaceable

conterminous *syn* ADJACENT, contiguous, abutting, adjoining, tangent, juxtaposed

contest *vb* 1 *syn* COMPETE, contend *rel* struggle, strive, endeavor, attempt; fight, battle, contend 2 *syn* RESIST, withstand, oppose, fight, combat, conflict, antagonize

contest *n* · a battle between opposing forces for supremacy, for power, or for possessions *syn* conflict, combat, fight, affray, fray *rel* encounter, skirmish, brush; competition, emulation, rivalry; battle, engagement, action

contiguous *syn* ADJACENT, adjoining, abutting, conterminous, tangent, juxtaposed *rel* nearest, next; close, near, nigh, nearby

continence *syn* TEMPERANCE, abstemiousness, sobriety, abstinence *rel* chasteness, chastity, purity; moderateness, moderation, temperateness *ant* incontinence

continent *syn* SOBER, temperate, unimpassioned *rel* restrained, bridled, curbed, inhibited; decent, chaste, pure; self-denying, self-abnegating *ant* incontinent

contingency *syn* JUNCTURE, emergency, exigency, pinch, pass, strait, crisis *rel* chance, break, opportunity, occasion, time

contingent 1 *syn* ACCIDENTAL, fortuitous, casual, incidental *rel* possible, probable, likely; unforeseen, unforeseeable, unanticipated 2 *syn* DEPENDENT, conditional, relative *rel* subject, liable, open, exposed

continual · characterized by continued occurrence or recurrence over a relatively long period of time *syn* continuous, constant, incessant, unremitting, perpetual, perennial *rel* unceasing, endless, interminable, everlasting; eternal, infinite; lasting, permanent, perdurable *ant* intermittent

continuance *syn* CONTINUATION, continuity *rel* endurance, persistence, lasting; perseverance, persistence; remaining, staying, tarrying

continuation · the quality, the act, or the state of continuing or of being continued *syn* continuance, continuity *rel* extending, extension, prolonging, prolongation, protracting, protraction *ant* cessation

continue · to remain indefinitely in existence or in a given condition or course *syn* last, endure, abide, persist *rel* remain, stay; survive, outlive, outlast

continuity *syn* CONTINUATION, continuance *rel* succession, sequence, chain, train, progression

continuous *syn* CONTINUAL, constant, perpetual, perennial, incessant, unremitting *rel* connected, related, linked, joined; successive, consecutive, sequent, serial; steady, constant, uniform *ant* interrupted

contort *syn* DEFORM, distort, warp *rel* twist, bend, curve

contour *syn* OUTLINE, silhouette, skyline, profile *rel* configuration, shape, form, conformation, figure

contraband *syn* SMUGGLED, bootleg

contract *n* · an agreement reached after negotiation and ending in an exchange of promises between the parties concerned *syn* bargain, compact, pact, treaty, entente, convention, cartel, concordat

contract *vb* 1 *syn* PROMISE, pledge, covenant, engage, plight 2 *syn* INCUR, catch 3 · to decrease in bulk, volume, or content *syn* shrink, condense, compress, constrict, deflate *rel* dwindle, diminish, decrease, reduce *ant* expand

contradict *syn* DENY, gainsay, negative, contravene, traverse, impugn *rel* dispute, discuss; controvert, disprove, refute, confute; belie, falsify, garble, misrepresent *ant* corroborate

contradictory *n, syn* OPPOSITE, contrary, antithesis, antonym, antipode *rel* converse, reverse

contradictory *adj, syn* OPPOSITE, contrary, antithetical, antonymous, antipodal, antipodean, converse, counter, reverse *rel* negating, nullifying; counteractive, antagonistic, adverse

contraption *syn* DEVICE, gadget, contrivance *rel* appliance, tool, instrument, implement, utensil; machine, mechanism, apparatus; expedient, makeshift, resource

contrary *n, syn* OPPOSITE, antithesis, contradictory, antonym, antipode *rel* converse, reverse

contrary *adj* 1 *syn* OPPOSITE, antithetical, contradictory, antonymous, antipodal, antipodean, converse, counter, reverse *rel* divergent, disparate, different; counter, antagonistic, adverse; negating, nullifying 2 · given to opposing or resisting wishes, commands, conditions, or circumstances *syn* perverse, restive, balky, froward, wayward *rel* refractory, recalcitrant, intractable, headstrong, unruly; contumacious, rebellious, insubordinate *ant* good-natured, complaisant

contrast *n, syn* COMPARISON, collation, parallel, antithesis *rel* distinction, difference, divergence, divergency, dissimilarity, unlikeness; conflict, discord

contrast *vb, syn* COMPARE, collate

contravene *syn* DENY, contradict, traverse, impugn, negative *rel* oppose, combat, resist, fight; controvert, disprove; trespass, encroach, infringe *ant* uphold (*law, principle*); allege (*right, claim, privilege*)

contravention *syn* BREACH, trespass, transgression, violation, infringement, infraction *rel* offense, vice, sin, crime

contribution *syn* DONATION, benefaction, alms *rel* grant, subvention, subsidy, appropriation; gift, present, largess, boon

contributory *syn* AUXILIARY, ancillary, adjuvant, subservient, accessory *rel* concurring, cooperating; helping, helpful, aiding, assisting, assistant

contrition *syn* PENITENCE, attrition, repentance, compunction, remorse *rel* sorrow, grief, regret

contrivance *syn* DEVICE, gadget, contraption *rel* invention, creation, discovery; implement, tool, instrument, appliance, utensil; machine, mechanism, apparatus

contrive • to find a way of making or doing something or of achieving an end by the exercise of one's mind *syn* devise, invent, frame, concoct *rel* plan, scheme, project; manipulate, ply, swing, handle

control *vb, syn* CONDUCT, direct, manage *rel* govern, rule; regulate, adjust; guide, lead, pilot, engineer, steer; restrain, curb, check

control *n* **1** *syn* POWER, command, dominion, authority, jurisdiction, sway *rel* ascendancy, supremacy; might, puissance, power, force; management, direction **2** *syn* CORRECTIVE, check, antidote *rel* regulation, law, ordinance, rule, precept, statute, canon

controversy *syn* ARGUMENT, dispute *rel* contention, dissension, discord; disputation, argumentation, forensic, debate

controvert *syn* DISPROVE, rebut, refute, confute *rel* contravene, traverse, impugn, deny, gainsay; oppose, combat, fight, resist; dispute, debate, agitate, argue, discuss *ant* assert

contumacious *syn* INSUBORDINATE, rebellious, mutinous, seditious, factious *rel* contrary, perverse, froward; refractory, recalcitrant, intractable, ungovernable, unruly, headstrong *ant* obedient

contumelious *syn* ABUSIVE, opprobrious, vituperative, scurrilous *rel* insolent, overbearing, arrogant, disdainful, proud; humiliating, demeaning, debasing, abasing; flouting, scoffing, jeering, sneering *ant* obsequious

contusion *syn* WOUND, bruise, trauma, traumatism, lesion

conundrum *syn* MYSTERY, puzzle, riddle, enigma, problem

convalesce *syn* IMPROVE, recover, recuperate, gain *rel* progress, advance; strengthen, invigorate; cure, heal, remedy

convenance *syn* FORM, convention, usage

convene *syn* SUMMON, convoke, muster, summons, call, cite *rel* gather, congregate, assemble, collect *ant* adjourn

convent *syn* CLOISTER, nunnery, monastery, abbey, priory

convention **1** *syn* CONTRACT, entente, compact, pact, treaty, cartel, concordat, bargain *rel* agreement, accord, understanding **2** *syn* FORM, convenance, usage *rel* custom, practice, habit; canon, precept, rule, law; etiquette, propriety, decorum

conventional *syn* CEREMONIAL, formal, ceremonious, solemn *rel* decorous, proper, seemly, decent;

correct, right, precise *ant* unconventional

conversant · familiar with something *syn* versed *rel* intimate, familiar; informed, acquainted; learned, erudite; adept, proficient, skilled, expert, skillful, masterly *ant* ignorant

conversation, converse *n, syn* INTERCOURSE, communion, communication, commerce, traffic, dealings, correspondence *rel* conversing, talking, talk, speaking, speech

converse *vb, syn* SPEAK, talk *rel* express, voice, broach, air, ventilate, vent, utter; chat, chatter, gabble; gossip, tattle; discourse, descant, expatiate, dilate

converse *n, syn* OPPOSITE, contrary, antithesis, contradictory, antipode, antonym, counter, reverse

conversion *syn* TRANSFORMATION, metamorphosis, transmutation, transmogrification, transfiguration

convert *vb, syn* TRANSFORM, metamorphose, transmute, transmogrify, transfigure *rel* manufacture, fabricate, forge, make; apply, utilize, employ, use

convert *n* · a person who has embraced another creed, opinion, or doctrine than the one he or she has previously accepted or adhered to *syn* proselyte *rel* neophyte, novice

convertible *syn* RECIPROCAL, corresponding, correlative, complementary, complemental *rel* interchangeable, exchangeable

convey 1 *syn* CARRY, transport, transmit, bear *rel* move, remove, shift, transfer; take, fetch, bring 2 *syn* TRANSFER, deed, alienate *rel* consign, commit, relegate

convict *syn* CRIMINAL, felon, malefactor, culprit, delinquent *rel* miscreant, blackguard, scoundrel, villain; offender, sinner

conviction 1 *syn* CERTAINTY, assurance, certitude *rel* faith, belief, credence, credit 2 *syn* OPINION, belief, persuasion, view, sentiment *rel* tenet, dogma, doctrine; judgment, conclusion

convincing *syn* VALID, compelling, telling, cogent, sound *rel* proving, demonstrating; persuading, persuasive, inducing; forceful, forcible, potent, powerful

convivial *syn* SOCIAL, companionable, gregarious, hospitable, cooperative *rel* sociable, genial, cordial, affable, gracious; gay, lively, vivacious; merry, jocund, jolly, jovial; hilarious, mirthful *ant* taciturn; staid

convoke *syn* SUMMON, convene, muster, summons, call, cite *rel* assemble, gather, congregate, collect; invite, bid *ant* prorogue, dissolve

convoy *syn* ACCOMPANY, escort, conduct, attend, chaperon *rel* protect, shield, guard, safeguard, defend; guide, lead, pilot

convulse *syn* SHAKE, rock, agitate *rel* discompose, disturb, disquiet, perturb

convulsion 1 *syn* FIT, spasm, paroxysm, attack, access, accession 2 *syn* COMMOTION, agitation, tumult, turmoil, turbulence, confusion, upheaval *rel* shaking, rocking; quaking, trembling, tottering; revolution, revolt, rebellion; cataclysm, disaster

convulsive *syn* FITFUL, spasmodic

cool 1 *syn* COLD, chilly, frigid, freezing, frosty, gelid, icy, glacial, arctic *ant* warm 2 · showing or seeming to show freedom from agitation or excitement *syn* composed, collected, unruffled, imperturbable, unflappable, nonchalant *rel* calm, tranquil, serene, placid; detached, aloof, indifferent; impassive, stoic, phlegmatic *ant* ardent; agitated

coop *syn* ENCLOSE, envelop, fence,

pen, corral, cage, wall *rel* confine, circumscribe, limit, restrict; hinder, impede, obstruct, block, bar

cooperate *syn* UNITE, conjoin, combine *rel* coincide, agree, concur *ant* counteract

cooperative *syn* SOCIAL, companionable, gregarious, convivial, hospitable *rel* sociable, cordial, genial, affable, gracious; helping, helpful, aiding, assisting *ant* uncooperative

cop *syn* STEAL, filch, pinch, snitch, swipe, lift, pilfer, purloin

copartner *syn* PARTNER, colleague, ally, confederate *rel* associate, companion, comrade

copious *syn* PLENTIFUL, abundant, ample, plenteous *rel* profuse, lavish, exuberant, prodigal, luxuriant, lush *ant* meager

copy *n, syn* REPRODUCTION, duplicate, carbon, carbon copy, transcript, facsimile, replica *rel* counterpart, parallel; imprint, print, impression, impress; image, effigy *ant* original

copy *vb* · to make something like an already existing thing in form, appearance, or obvious or salient characteristics *syn* imitate, mimic, ape, mock *ant* originate

coquet *syn* TRIFLE, flirt, dally, toy

cordial *syn* GRACIOUS, genial, affable, sociable *rel* warm, warmhearted, responsive, sympathetic, tender; sincere, heartfelt, hearty, wholehearted

core 1 *syn* CENTER, middle, midst, hub, focus, nucleus, heart 2 *syn* SUBSTANCE, purport, gist, burden, pith *rel* import, significance, importance, consequence; center, heart, nucleus

corner *syn* MONOPOLY, pool, syndicate, trust, cartel

corporal *syn* BODILY, corporeal, physical, somatic *rel* fleshly, carnal, animal, sensual

corporeal 1 *syn* MATERIAL, physical, sensible, phenomenal, objective *rel* actual, real; tangible, palpable, ponderable, perceptible *ant* incorporeal 2 *syn* BODILY, physical, corporal, somatic *rel* see CORPORAL

corpse *syn* BODY, carcass, cadaver *rel* remains, remainder

corpulent *syn* FLESHY, portly, fat, stout, obese, rotund, plump, chubby *rel* burly, husky, brawny, muscular; thickset, chunky, stubby, dumpy, stocky *ant* spare

corral *syn* ENCLOSE, envelop, fence, pen, coop, cage, wall

correct *vb* 1 · to set or make right something which is wrong *syn* rectify, emend, remedy, redress, amend, reform, revise *rel* improve, better, ameliorate; offset, compensate, countervail, counterbalance, balance; neutralize, counteract; adjust, regulate, fix; reprove, reprimand, admonish, chide 2 *syn* PUNISH, discipline, chastise, chasten, castigate

correct *adj* · conforming to standard, fact, or truth *syn* accurate, exact, precise, nice, right *rel* impeccable, faultless, flawless; punctilious, punctual, scrupulous, meticulous, careful *ant* incorrect

corrective *adj, syn* CURATIVE, remedial, restorative, sanative *rel* helping, aiding, assisting; salutary, hygienic, healthful

corrective *n* · something which serves to keep another thing in its desired place or condition *syn* control, check, antidote

correlate *syn* PARALLEL, analogue, counterpart

correlative *syn* RECIPROCAL, corresponding, complementary, complemental, convertible

correspond *syn* AGREE, square, accord, tally, jibe, harmonize, conform *rel* approach, touch, match, rival, equal

correspondence *syn* INTERCOURSE, communication, conversation, converse, communion, commerce, traffic, dealings

corresponding *syn* RECIPROCAL, correlative, complementary, complemental, convertible *rel* similar, analogous, like, parallel, comparable

corridor *syn* PASSAGE, passageway, hall, hallway, gallery, arcade, cloister, aisle, ambulatory

corroborate *syn* CONFIRM, substantiate, verify, authenticate, validate *rel* attest, vouch, certify; support, uphold, back *ant* contradict

corrupt *vb, syn* DEBASE, deprave, debauch, pervert *rel* degrade, debase, abase; ruin, wreck; pollute, defile, contaminate

corrupt *adj, syn* VICIOUS, iniquitous, nefarious, flagitious, infamous, villainous, degenerate *rel* crooked, devious, oblique; venal, mercenary; base, low, vile; pernicious, noxious, deleterious, detrimental, baneful; degraded, abased

corrupted *syn* DEBASED, corrupt, vitiated, depraved, debauched, perverted

corruption *syn* BARBARISM, impropriety, solecism, vulgarism, vernacular

corsair *syn* PIRATE, freebooter, buccaneer, privateer

cortege *syn* PROCESSION, cavalcade, parade, motorcade *rel* train, string, succession; followers, satellites, disciples, partisans, henchmen

coruscate *syn* FLASH, gleam, scintillate, glance, glint, sparkle, glitter, glisten, twinkle

cosmic *syn* UNIVERSAL, catholic, ecumenical, cosmopolitan

cosmopolitan *syn* UNIVERSAL, catholic, ecumenical, cosmic *rel* liberal, progressive; all-around, many-sided, versatile *ant* provincial; insular; parochial

cosset *syn* CARESS, fondle, pet, cuddle, dandle

cost *syn* PRICE, expense, charge

costly · having a high value or valuation, esp. in terms of money *syn* expensive, dear, valuable, precious, invaluable, priceless *rel* exorbitant, extravagant, excessive; sumptuous, luxurious, opulent *ant* cheap

coterie *syn* SET, circle, clique

couchant *syn* PRONE, recumbent, dormant, supine, prostrate

counsel *n* **1** *syn* ADVICE *rel* admonishing, admonition, chiding, reproaching, reproach; warning, forewarning, cautioning, caution; precept, rule, law **2** *syn* LAWYER, counselor, barrister, advocate, attorney, solicitor

counsel *vb, syn* ADVISE, *rel* admonish, chide, reprove; warn, forewarn, caution; remonstrate, expostulate, object; instruct, direct, command

counselor *syn* LAWYER, barrister, counsel, advocate, attorney, solicitor

count *vb* **1** · to ascertain the total of units in a collection by noting one after another *syn* tell, enumerate, number *rel* calculate, compute, reckon, estimate; add, sum, figure, total, tot, cast, foot **2** *syn* RELY, depend, bank, trust, reckon

count *n, syn* PARAGRAPH, verse, article, clause, plank

countenance *n, syn* FACE, visage, physiognomy, mug, puss

countenance *vb, syn* FAVOR, encourage *rel* approve, sanction, endorse; commend, applaud; support, uphold, champion, back

counter *adj, syn* ADVERSE, antagonistic, counteractive *rel* contrary, opposite, antithetical, antipodal, antipodean, antonymous, contradictory; hostile, inimical

counter *n, syn* OPPOSITE, contradictory, contrary, antithesis, antipode, antonym, converse, reverse

counteract *syn* NEUTRALIZE, negative *rel* correct, rectify; offset, counterbalance, countervail, counterpoise, balance, compensate *ant* cooperate

counteractive *syn* ADVERSE, counter, antagonistic *rel* countervailing, counterbalancing, counterpoising, compensating, offsetting, balancing; correcting; neutralizing

counterbalance *syn* COMPENSATE, offset, countervail, balance, counterpoise *rel* stabilize, steady, poise; correct

counterfeit *vb, syn* ASSUME, feign, sham, simulate, pretend, affect *rel* copy, imitate, mimic, ape; dissemble, disguise

counterfeit *adj* • being an imitation intended to mislead or deceive *syn* spurious, bogus, fake, sham, pseudo, pinchbeck, phony *rel* simulated, feigned, pretended; fraudulent; deceptive, misleading, delusive, delusory *ant* bona fide, genuine

counterfeit *n, syn* IMPOSTURE, fraud, sham, fake, cheat, humbug, deceit, deception *rel* reproduction, copy, facsimile

counterpart *syn* PARALLEL, correlate, analogue *rel* complement, supplement; duplicate, copy, facsimile, replica, reproduction

counterpoise *syn* COMPENSATE, balance, countervail, counterbalance, offset *rel* poise, stabilize, steady, balance, ballast, trim

countervail *syn* COMPENSATE, offset, balance, counterbalance, counterpoise *rel* correct; counteract, neutralize, negative; overcome, surmount, conquer; foil, thwart, frustrate

county *syn* ARISTOCRACY, gentry, elite, nobility, society

coup, coup d'etat *syn* REBELLION, revolution, uprising, revolt, insurrection, mutiny, putsch

couple • two things of the same kind *syn* pair, brace, yoke

courage • a quality of mind or temperament that enables one to stand fast in the face of opposition, danger, or hardship *syn* mettle, spirit, resolution, tenacity *rel* bravery, boldness, audacity, dauntlessness, intrepidity, doughtiness, fearlessness; valor, heroism, gallantry; fortitude, grit, pluck, guts, backbone, sand *ant* cowardice

courageous *syn* BRAVE, unafraid, fearless, intrepid, valiant, valorous, dauntless, undaunted, doughty, bold, audacious *rel* mettlesome, spirited, high-spirited, fiery; resolute, staunch, faithful; stout, tenacious, strong *ant* pusillanimous

course *n, syn* WAY, route, passage, pass, artery *rel* circuit, circumference; orbit, scope, range; drift, trend, tendency; procedure, process

court *syn* INVITE, woo, bid, solicit *rel* allure, attract, captivate, charm; toady, truckle, fawn, cringe

courteous *syn* CIVIL, polite, courtly, gallant, chivalrous *rel* gracious, affable, cordial; suave, urbane, politic, diplomatic; considerate, thoughtful, attentive; obliging, complaisant, amiable *ant* discourteous

courtesy • a manner or an act which promotes agreeable or pleasant social relations *syn* amenity, attention, gallantry *rel* graciousness, cordiality, affability, geniality; politeness, courteousness, courtliness, chivalrousness, chivalry, civility; considerateness, consideration, attentiveness, thoughtfulness *ant* discourtesy

courtly *syn* CIVIL, courteous, gallant, chivalrous, polite *rel* ceremonious, formal, conventional, ceremonial; elegant, dignified, graceful; finished, consummate *ant* churlish

covenant *syn* PROMISE, pledge, engage, plight, contract *rel* agree, concur, coincide; unite, combine, conjoin, cooperate

cover *vb* · to put or place or to be put or placed over or around *syn* overspread, envelop, wrap, shroud, veil *rel* hide, conceal, screen; close, shut; enclose, envelop; shield, protect, defend *ant* bare

cover *n, syn* SHELTER, retreat, refuge, asylum, sanctuary *rel* hiding, hiding place, concealment, screening, screen; safety, security *ant* exposure

covert *syn* SECRET, clandestine, surreptitious, underhand, underhanded, stealthy, furtive *rel* hidden, concealed, screened; disguised, dissembled, masked, cloaked, camouflaged *ant* overt

covet 1 · to desire selfishly to have something for one's own *syn* envy, grudge, begrudge 2 *syn* DESIRE, crave, wish, want *rel* yearn, long, pine, hanker, thirst, hunger; pant, aspire, aim *ant* renounce (*something desirable*)

covetous · having or manifesting a strong desire for esp. material possessions *syn* greedy, acquisitive, grasping, avaricious *rel* envious, jealous; desirous, lustful; avid, athirst, eager; rapacious, ravening, gluttonous, ravenous, voracious

cow *syn* INTIMIDATE, browbeat, bulldoze, bully *rel* frighten, terrorize, terrify; daunt, dismay, appall; abash, discomfit, rattle, faze, disconcert, embarrass

cower *syn* FAWN, cringe, truckle, toady *rel* shrink, quail, flinch, blench, wince, recoil

coxcomb *syn* FOP, dandy, beau, exquisite, dude, buck

coy *syn* SHY, bashful, diffident, modest *rel* nice, proper, seemly, decorous, decent; aloof, detached, indifferent; cautious, wary, chary *ant* pert

cozen *syn* CHEAT, defraud, swindle, overreach *rel* dupe, bamboozle, gull, trick, hoax, hoodwink, befool; delude, beguile, deceive, mislead

cozy *syn* COMFORTABLE, snug, easy, restful *rel* sheltering, harboring, housing, lodging; safe, secure; contenting, satisfying

crabbed *syn* SULLEN, surly, glum, morose, gloomy, sulky, saturnine, dour *rel* crusty, gruff, brusque, blunt, bluff; testy, choleric, cranky, cross, splenetic, irascible; snappish, huffy, irritable

crack *vb, syn* BREAK, burst, bust, snap, shatter, shiver *rel* split, rend, cleave, rive, tear

crack *n* 1 · an opening, break, or discontinuity made by or as if by splitting or rupture *syn* cleft, fissure, crevasse, crevice, cranny, chink *rel* split, rent, rift, breach 2 *syn* JOKE, wisecrack, witticism, jest, jape, quip, gag

craft 1 *syn* ART, skill, cunning, artifice *rel* adeptness, expertness, proficiency; ingeniousness, ingenuity, cleverness; competence, capability; efficiency 2 *syn* TRADE, handicraft, art, profession *rel* occupation, employment, pursuit, work 3 *syn* BOAT, ship, vessel

craftsman *syn* WORKER, handicraftsman, mechanic, artisan, workman, workingman, laborer, hand, operative, roustabout

crafty *syn* SLY, tricky, cunning, insidious, foxy, guileful, wily, artful *rel* adroit, clever, cunning; shrewd, astute; sharp, keen, acute

cram *syn* PACK, crowd, stuff, ram, tamp *rel* press, squeeze, jam; compress, contract; compact, consolidate; force, compel

cranky *syn* IRASCIBLE, cross, choleric, splenetic, testy, touchy *rel* irritable, fractious, peevish, petulant, snappish; contrary, perverse, froward; impatient, nervous, jittery

cranny *syn* CRACK, cleft, fissure, crevasse, crevice, chink *rel* hole, cavity, pocket, hollow; perforation, puncture, bore; interstice, aperture

crass *syn* STUPID, dense, slow, dull, dumb *rel* obtuse, dull; crude, raw, rude, rough, uncouth *ant* brilliant

crave *syn* DESIRE, covet, wish, want *rel* long, hanker, yearn, pine, hunger, thirst *ant* spurn

crawl *syn* CREEP

craze *syn* FASHION, vogue, fad, rage, style, mode, dernier cri, cry

crazy, crazed *syn* INSANE, mad, demented, lunatic, maniac, deranged, non compos mentis

cream *syn* OIL, grease, lubricate, anoint

create *syn* ESTABLISH, institute, organize *rel* make, form, fashion, shape, forge; design, plan, scheme; generate, engender

creator *syn* MAKER, author *rel* artist, architect, artificer; composer, writer, author

creature *syn* ENTITY, being, individual, person

credence *syn* BELIEF, credit, faith *rel* conviction, assurance, certitude, certainty; accepting, acceptance, admitting, admission, receiving, reception; assenting, assent, acquiescing, acquiescence; reliance, confidence, trust, faith

credential · something presented by one person to another in proof that he is what or who he claims to be *syn* testimonial, recommendation, character, reference *rel* certification, accreditation, endorsement, sanction

credible *syn* PLAUSIBLE, believable, colorable, specious *rel* probable, likely, possible; reasonable, rational; trustworthy, reliable, dependable *ant* incredible

credit *n* **1** *syn* BELIEF, faith, credence *rel* reliance, trust, confidence, faith; assurance, certitude, conviction, certainty **2** *syn* INFLUENCE, prestige, authority, weight *rel* reputation, repute, fame, renown; authority, power, sway *ant* discredit **3** · a person or thing that enhances another *syn* asset

credit *vb*, *syn* ASCRIBE, accredit, assign, attribute, impute, refer, charge

credulity · undue trust or confidence *syn* gullibility *rel* credence, credit, belief *ant* incredulity; skepticism

credulous · unduly trusting or confiding *syn* gullible *rel* assenting, acquiescing, acquiescent, agreeing, subscribing; believing, crediting *ant* incredulous; skeptical

creed *syn* RELIGION, faith, persuasion, denomination, sect, cult, communion, church

creep · to move slowly along a surface in a prone or crouching position *syn* crawl

crevasse *syn* CRACK, cleft, fissure, crevice, cranny, chink *rel* chasm, gulf; breach, split, rent, rift

crevice *syn* CRACK, cleft, fissure, crevasse, cranny, chink *rel* breach, split, rift, rent; break, gap

crime *syn* OFFENSE, vice, sin, scandal *rel* fault, failing, frailty, foible, vice

criminal · one who has committed a usu. serious offense esp. against the law *syn* felon, convict, malefactor, culprit, delinquent *rel* offender, sinner; transgressor, trespasser, violator

cringe *syn* FAWN, cower, truckle, toady *rel* recoil, quail, flinch, blench, wince; bow, cave, yield, submit, defer

cripple **1** *syn* MAIM, mutilate, batter, mangle *rel* injure, hurt **2** *syn* WEAKEN, disable, enfeeble, debilitate, undermine, sap *rel* damage, harm, impair, mar, injure

crisis *syn* JUNCTURE, exigency, emergency, pinch, pass, contingency, strait

crisp **1** *syn* FRAGILE, brittle, short, friable, frangible **2** *syn* INCISIVE, clear-cut, cutting, trenchant, biting *rel* terse, pithy, laconic, succinct, concise; piquing, stimulating, provoking, provocative

criterion *syn* STANDARD, touchstone, yardstick, gauge *rel* test, proof, trial, demonstration; principle, axiom, law; judging, judgment, adjudgment, adjudication

critical **1** · exhibiting the spirit of one who detects and points out faults or defects *syn* hypercritical, faultfinding, captious, caviling, carping, censorious *rel* judicious; wise; judicial; fastidious, finicky, particular, nice, fussy, squeamish; discriminating, discerning, penetrating; understanding, comprehending, appreciating *ant* uncritical **2** *syn* ACUTE, crucial *rel* decisive, determinative, conclusive; momentous, consequential, weighty, significant, important

criticism · a discourse presenting one's conclusions after examining a work of art and esp. of literature *syn* critique, review, blurb, puff

criticize · to find fault with someone or something openly, often publicly, and with varying degrees of severity *syn* reprehend, blame, censure, reprobate, condemn, denounce *rel* inspect, examine, scrutinize, scan; judge, adjudge; appraise, evaluate, assess, estimate

critique *syn* CRITICISM, review, blurb, puff

crochet *syn* WEAVE, knit, plait, braid, tat

crony *syn* ASSOCIATE, comrade, companion *rel* intimate, friend, confidant

crook *syn* FLEX, bow, buckle *rel* curve, bend, twist; contort, deform

crooked · not straight or straightforward *syn* devious, oblique *rel* awry, askew; twisted, bended, bent; distorted, contorted, deformed, warped; tortuous, winding; corrupt, nefarious, iniquitous, vicious; stealthy, furtive, underhand, secret *ant* straight

crop *syn* SHEAR, poll, clip, trim, prune, lop, snip *rel* cut, chop, hew, slash; detach, disengage

cross *n, syn* TRIAL, tribulation, affliction, visitation

cross *adj, syn* IRASCIBLE, cranky, testy, touchy, choleric, splenetic *rel* captious, carping, caviling, faultfinding, critical; irritable, fractious, peevish, petulant, snappish, waspish, querulous

crosswise, crossways *syn* ACROSS, athwart

crotchet *syn* CAPRICE, freak, fancy, whim, whimsy, conceit, vagary

crow *syn* BOAST, brag, vaunt, gasconade

crowd *vb* **1** *syn* PRESS, bear, bear down, squeeze, jam *rel* push, shove, thrust, propel; force, compel, constrain **2** *syn* PACK, cram, stuff, ram, tamp *rel* compress, contract; compact, consolidate, concentrate

crowd *n* · a more or less closely assembled multitude usually of persons *syn* throng, press, crush, mob, rout, horde *rel* multitude, army, host, legion

crucial *syn* ACUTE, critical *rel* threatening, menacing; trying, afflicting, torturing, torturous

crude *syn* RUDE, rough, uncouth, raw, callow, green *rel* primitive, primeval, primary; immature, unmatured; coarse, vulgar, gross *ant* consummate, finished

cruel *syn* FIERCE, inhuman, fell, truculent, ferocious, barbarous, savage *rel* atrocious, outrageous, monstrous, heinous; brutal, bestial; merciless, relentless, implacable, grim *ant* pitiful

cruise *syn* JOURNEY, voyage, tour, trip, jaunt, excursion, expedition, pilgrimage

crumble *syn* DECAY, disintegrate, decompose, rot, putrefy, spoil

crush *vb* **1** • to reduce or be reduced to a pulpy or broken mass *syn* mash, smash, bruise, squash, macerate *rel* press, squeeze, crowd, jam; batter, mangle, maim; beat, pound **2** • to bring to an end by destroying or defeating *syn* quell, extinguish, suppress, quench, quash *rel* destroy, demolish; ruin, wreck; annihilate, abolish; obliterate, blot out, efface, erase

crush *n, syn* CROWD, press, throng, horde, mob, rout *rel* multitude, army, legion, host

crusty *syn* BLUFF, brusque, gruff, blunt, curt *rel* snappish, waspish, irritable; choleric, splenetic, cranky, testy, irascible; crabbed, surly, saturnine, dour, sullen

cry *vb* • to show grief, pain, or distress by tears and usu. inarticulate utterances *syn* weep, wail, keen, whimper, blubber *rel* lament, bewail, bemoan, deplore; sob, moan, sigh, groan

cry *syn* FASHION, vogue, rage, style, mode, fad, craze, dernier cri

crying *syn* PRESSING, urgent, imperative, importunate, insistent, exigent, instant *rel* outstanding, conspicuous, noticeable; compelling, constraining

cryptic *syn* OBSCURE, enigmatic, dark, vague, ambiguous, equivocal *rel* puzzling, perplexing, mystifying; occult, esoteric, recondite; mysterious, arcane

cuddle *syn* CARESS, fondle, dandle, pet, cosset

cuff *syn* STRIKE, hit, smite, punch, slug, slog, swat, clout, slap, box

cull *syn* CHOOSE, pick, single, select, elect, opt, prefer

culmination *syn* SUMMIT, peak, climax, apex, acme, pinnacle, meridian, zenith, apogee

culpability *syn* BLAME, guilt, fault *rel* responsibility, accountability

culpable *syn* BLAMEWORTHY, guilty *rel* responsible, accountable, answerable, amenable, liable

culprit *syn* CRIMINAL, felon, convict, malefactor, delinquent *rel* prisoner; offender, sinner; scoundrel, blackguard, miscreant, rogue, rascal, villain

cult *syn* RELIGION, sect, denomination, communion, faith, creed, persuasion, church

cultivar *syn* VARIETY, subspecies, race, breed, strain, clone, stock

cultivate *syn* NURSE, nurture, foster, cherish *rel* develop, mature, ripen; raise, rear; educate, train, instruct, teach; improve, better, ameliorate

cultivation *syn* CULTURE, breeding, refinement

culture • enlightenment and excellence of taste acquired by intellectual and aesthetic training *syn* cultivation, breeding, refinement

cumber *syn* BURDEN, encumber, weigh, weight, load, lade, tax, charge, saddle *rel* see ENCUMBER

cumbersome, cumbrous *syn* HEAVY, ponderous, weighty, hefty *rel* burdensome, onerous; awkward, clumsy; irksome, wearisome, tiresome

cumulative • increasing or produced by the addition of like or assimilable things *syn* accumulative, additive, summative *rel* accumulated, amassed; multiplying, increasing, augmenting

cunning *adj* **1** *syn* CLEVER, ingenious, adroit *rel* skillful, skilled, adept, proficient, expert, masterly **2** *syn* SLY, crafty, tricky, artful, foxy, insidious, wily, guileful *rel* devious, oblique, crooked;

sharp, acute, keen; shrewd, astute; knowing, smart, intelligent *ant* ingenuous

cunning *n* **1** *syn* ART, skill, craft, artifice *rel* dexterousness, dexterity, adroitness, deftness; proficiency, adeptness, expertness; ingeniousness, ingenuity, cleverness **2** *syn* DECEIT, guile, duplicity, dissimulation *rel* craftiness, insidiousness, wiliness, guilefulness, trickiness, trickery, artfulness, slyness; stratagem, ruse, maneuver, feint, trick, wile, gambit, ploy *ant* ingenuousness

cupidity · intense desire for wealth or possessions *syn* greed, rapacity, avarice *rel* covetousness, avariciousness, greediness, acquisitiveness; avidity, eagerness; lust, desire

curative · returning or tending to return to a state of normalcy or health *syn* sanative, restorative, remedial, corrective *rel* healing, curing, remedying

curb *syn* RESTRAIN, check, bridle, inhibit *rel* repress, suppress; shackle, manacle, fetter, hamper, hog-tie; thwart, foil, balk, frustrate *ant* spur

curdle *syn* COAGULATE, congeal, set, clot, jelly, jell

cure *n, syn* REMEDY, medicine, medicament, medication, specific, physic

cure *vb* · to rectify an unhealthy or undesirable condition especially by some specific treatment *syn* heal, remedy

curious **1** · interested in what is not one's personal or proper concern *syn* inquisitive, prying, snoopy, nosy *rel* meddling, intermeddling, interfering, tampering; scrutinizing, inspecting, examining; intrusive, meddlesome, impertinent *ant* incurious; uninterested **2** *syn* STRANGE, singular, peculiar, unique, odd, queer, quaint, outlandish, eccentric, erratic

curl *syn* WIND, coil, twist, twine, wreathe, entwine *rel* curve, bend; flex, crook

currency *syn* MONEY, cash, legal tender, specie, coin, coinage

current *adj, syn* PREVAILING, prevalent, rife *rel* general, universal, common; popular, ordinary, familiar, common; usual, customary *ant* antique, antiquated; obsolete

current *n, syn* FLOW, stream, flood, tide, flux

curse *n* · a denunciation that conveys a wish or threat of evil *syn* imprecation, malediction, anathema *rel* execration, objurgation; profanity, blasphemy, swearing *ant* blessing

curse *vb, syn* EXECRATE, damn, anathematize, objurgate *rel* condemn, denounce, reprobate, criticize; blaspheme, swear *ant* bless

cursed *syn* EXECRABLE, accursed, damnable *rel, ant* see ACCURSED

cursing *syn* BLASPHEMY, profanity, swearing *rel* curse, imprecation, malediction, anathema; execration, objurgation

cursory *syn* SUPERFICIAL, shallow, uncritical *rel* hasty, speedy, quick, rapid, swift, fast; brief, short; casual, desultory, random, haphazard *ant* painstaking

curt *syn* BLUFF, brusque, blunt, crusty, gruff *rel* laconic, terse, summary, concise; brief, short; snappish, waspish, irritable; peremptory, imperious, masterful *ant* voluble

curtail *syn* SHORTEN, abbreviate, abridge, retrench *rel* reduce, decrease, lessen; cut, slash *ant* protract, prolong

curve *vb* · to swerve or cause to swerve from a straight line or course *syn* bend, twist *rel* deflect, divert, turn; swerve, veer, deviate

curve *n* · a line or something which follows a line that is neither straight nor angular but rounded *syn* arc, bow, arch *rel* circuit, compass, circumference

curvet *syn* SKIP, bound, hop, lope, lollop, ricochet

custom *syn* HABIT, usage, habitude, practice, use, wont *rel* convention, form, usage, convenance; rule, precept, canon, law

customary *syn* USUAL, wonted, accustomed, habitual *rel* regular, normal, typical, natural; prevailing, prevalent, current; familiar, ordinary, common; general, universal *ant* occasional

cut • to penetrate and divide something with a sharp-bladed tool or instrument *syn* hew, chop, carve, slit, slash *rel* split, cleave, rive, tear; sever, sunder, separate; curtail, shorten

cutthroat *syn* ASSASSIN, gunman, bravo

cutting *syn* INCISIVE, trenchant, clear-cut, biting, crisp *rel* sharp, keen, acute; piercing, penetrating, probing

cyclone *syn* TORNADO, twister *rel* whirlwind, whirly; hurricane, tropical storm, typhoon

cyclopean *syn* HUGE, vast, immense, enormous, elephantine, mammoth, giant, gigantic, gigantean, colossal, gargantuan, Herculean, titanic, Brobdingnagian

cynical • deeply and often contemptuously distrustful *syn* misanthropic, pessimistic *rel* sneering, girding, flouting, scoffing; captious, caviling, carping, censorious, critical; disbelieving, unbelieving

D

dabbler *syn* AMATEUR, tyro, dilettante

daily • of each or every day *syn* diurnal, quotidian, circadian

dainty **1** *syn* CHOICE, delicate, exquisite, elegant, recherché, rare *rel* petite, diminutive, little, small; pretty, bonny, fair, lovely, beautiful; delightful, delectable, delicious *ant* gross **2** *syn* NICE, fastidious, finicky, finicking, finical, particular, fussy, squeamish, persnickety, pernickety *rel* careful, meticulous, punctilious, scrupulous; discriminating, discerning

dally *syn* TRIFLE, flirt, coquet, toy *rel* play, sport, frolic, gambol; caress, fondle, pet

dam *syn* HINDER, bar, block, obstruct, impede *rel* clog, hamper, trammel, shackle, fetter, hog-tie; suppress, repress

damage *n, syn* INJURY, harm, hurt, mischief *rel* impairment, marring; ruining, dilapidation, wrecking; detriment, deleteriousness

damage *vb, syn* INJURE, harm, impair, mar, hurt, spoil *rel* ruin, dilapidate, wreck; deface, disfigure; abuse, misuse, mistreat, ill-treat, maltreat, outrage

damn **1** *syn* SENTENCE, doom, condemn, proscribe *rel* judge, adjudge; punish, castigate, discipline *ant* save (*from eternal punishment*) **2** *syn* EXECRATE, curse, anathematize, objurgate *rel* denounce, condemn, criticize; revile, vituperate, scold

damnable *syn* EXECRABLE, accursed, cursed *rel* atrocious, outrageous, monstrous, heinous; hateful, abominable, detestable, odious, abhorrent

damp *syn* WET, moist, dank, humid

dandle *syn* CARESS, cuddle, pet, cosset, fondle *rel* trifle, toy, dally; play, sport, disport; handle, swing

dandy *syn* FOP, beau, coxcomb, exquisite, dude, buck *ant* sloven

danger · the state of being exposed to injury, pain, or loss *syn* peril, jeopardy, hazard, risk *rel* threatening, threat, menacing, menace; precariousness; emergency, exigency, pass *ant* security

dangerous · attended by or involving the possibility of loss, evil, injury, or harm *syn* hazardous, precarious, perilous, risky *rel* unsafe, insecure; chancy, chance, haphazard, random, hit-or-miss *ant* safe, secure

dangle *syn* HANG, suspend, sling *rel* oscillate, sway, pendulate, fluctuate; swing, wave

dank *syn* WET, damp, humid, moist *rel* soaked, saturated, sopped, soppy, drenched

dappled *syn* VARIEGATED, parti-colored, motley, checkered, checked, pied, piebald, skewbald, freaked

dare *syn* FACE, brave, challenge, defy, beard *rel* venture, risk, chance, hazard

daredevil *syn* ADVENTUROUS, daring, rash, reckless, foolhardy, venturesome *rel* see DARING

daring *syn* ADVENTUROUS, rash, reckless, daredevil, foolhardy, venturesome *rel* bold, intrepid, audacious, brave

dark **1** · deficient in light *syn* dim, dusky, obscure, murky, gloomy *ant* light **2** *syn* OBSCURE, vague, enigmatic, cryptic, ambiguous, equivocal *rel* abstruse, occult, recondite, esoteric; mystical, mystic, anagogic, cabalistic; intricate, complicated, knotty, complex *ant* lucid

darken *syn* OBSCURE, dim, bedim, eclipse, cloud, becloud, fog, befog, obfuscate *ant* illuminate

dart *syn* FLY, scud, skim, float, shoot, sail *rel* speed, precipitate, hasten, hurry

dash *vb, syn* RUSH, tear, shoot, charge *rel* dart, fly, scud

dash *n* **1** *syn* VIGOR, vim, spirit, esprit, verve, punch, élan, drive *rel* force, energy, might, power; vehemence, intensity; impressiveness **2** *syn* TOUCH, suggestion, suspicion, soupçon, tincture, tinge, shade, smack, spice, vein, strain, streak

dashing *syn* STYLISH, smart, fashionable, modish, chic

date *syn* ENGAGEMENT, rendezvous, tryst, appointment, assignation

daunt *syn* DISMAY, appall, horrify *rel* cow, intimidate, browbeat; discomfit, disconcert, faze, embarrass; foil, thwart, baffle, frustrate; frighten, alarm, scare, terrify

dauntless *syn* BRAVE, courageous, unafraid, fearless, intrepid, valiant, valorous, undaunted, doughty, bold, audacious *rel* indomitable, unconquerable, invincible; heroic, gallant *ant* poltroon

dawdle *syn* DELAY, procrastinate, loiter, lag *rel* linger, tarry, wait, stay; trifle, toy, dally; play, sport, disport

daydream *syn* FANCY, dream, fantasy, phantasy, phantasm, vision, nightmare *rel* imagining, imagination, conceiving, conception, fancying; illusion, delusion, hallucination

daze · to dull or deaden the powers of the mind through some disturbing experience or influence *syn* stun, bemuse, stupefy, benumb, paralyze, petrify *rel* confound, bewilder, mystify, puzzle; confuse, muddle, befuddle; dazzle, dizzy

dazzled *syn* GIDDY, dizzy, vertiginous, swimming *rel* confused, addled, befuddled, muddled; confounded, bewildered, puzzled, perplexed

dead · devoid of life *syn* defunct, deceased, departed, late, lifeless, inanimate *rel* alive

deadlock *syn* DRAW, tie, stalemate, standoff *rel* situation, condition, state, posture; predicament, plight, dilemma, quandary

deadly · causing or causative of death *syn* mortal, fatal, lethal *rel* destroying, destructive, malignant, malign; baneful, pernicious; toxic, virulent, poisonous, pestilential, pestilant; ruinous

deal 1 *syn* DISTRIBUTE, divide, dispense, dole *rel* apportion, allot, assign, allocate; share, participate, partake 2 *syn* TREAT, handle *rel* manage, control, conduct, direct; rid, clear, unburden

dealings *syn* INTERCOURSE, commerce, traffic, communication, communion, conversation, converse, correspondence

dear *syn* COSTLY, expensive, precious, valuable, invaluable, priceless *rel* exorbitant, excessive, extravagant, inordinate *ant* cheap

dearth *syn* LACK, want, absence, defect, privation *rel* scarcity, infrequency, rareness, uncommonness; scantiness, meagerness, scantness *ant* excess

death · the end or the ending of life *syn* decease, demise, passing *ant* life

deathless *syn* IMMORTAL, undying, unfading *rel* everlasting, endless; eternal, infinite; enduring, abiding, persisting

debar *syn* EXCLUDE, blackball, disbar, suspend, shut out, eliminate, rule out *rel* preclude, obviate, prevent; forbid, prohibit, ban, interdict

debase 1 · to cause a person or thing to become impaired and lowered in quality or character *syn* vitiate, deprave, corrupt, debauch, pervert *rel* defile, pollute, taint, contaminate; adulterate, sophisticate, load, weight, doctor; impair, spoil, mar, damage, harm, injure *ant* elevate (*taste, character*); amend (*morals, way of life*) 2 *syn* ABASE, degrade, demean, humble, humiliate *rel* weaken, undermine, sap, enfeeble, debilitate, cripple, disable

debased · being lowered in quality or character *syn* vitiated, depraved, corrupted, debauched, perverted *rel* deteriorated, degenerated, degenerate, decadent

debate *n, syn* ARGUMENTATION, disputation, forensic, dialectic *rel* controversy, argument, dispute; contention, dissension, discord

debate *vb, syn* DISCUSS, dispute, argue, agitate *rel* contend, fight, battle, war; wrangle, altercate, quarrel; controvert, refute, confute, rebut, disprove; prove, demonstrate

debauch *syn* DEBASE, corrupt, deprave, pervert, vitiate *rel* injure, harm, damage, spoil, mar; seduce, inveigle, decoy, tempt, lure; pollute, defile, taint, contaminate

debauched *syn* DEBASED, corrupted, depraved, perverted, vitiated *rel* dissolute, reprobate, abandoned, profligate; licentious, libertine, lascivious, libidinous, lecherous, lewd, wanton

debilitate *syn* WEAKEN, enfeeble, undermine, sap, cripple, disable *rel* impair, injure, damage, harm, hurt, mar, spoil *ant* invigorate

debit *syn* DEBT, indebtedness, liability, obligation, arrear *ant* credit

debris *syn* REFUSE, waste, rubbish, trash, garbage, offal

debt · something, and esp. a sum of money, that is owed *syn* indebtedness, obligation, liability, debit, arrear

decadence *syn* DETERIORATION, decline, declension, degeneration, devolution *rel* retrogressiveness, retrogression, regressiveness, regression, regress, retrograding, retrogradation *ant* rise; flourishing

decamp *syn* ESCAPE, flee, fly, abscond *rel* depart, quit, leave, go; elude, evade, escape, shun, avoid

decay • to undergo or to cause to undergo destructive changes *syn* decompose, rot, putrefy, spoil, disintegrate, crumble *rel* weaken, undermine, sap, debilitate, enfeeble; taint, contaminate, defile, pollute; dilapidate, ruin, wreck

decease *syn* DEATH, demise, passing

deceased *syn* DEAD, departed, late, defunct, lifeless, inanimate

deceit **1** • the act or practice of imposing upon the credulity of others by dishonesty, fraud, or trickery *syn* duplicity, dissimulation, cunning, guile *rel* deception, fraud, trickery, double-dealing, chicane, chicanery; craft, artifice; cheating, cozening, defrauding, overreaching **2** *syn* IMPOSTURE, cheat, fraud, sham, fake, deception, counterfeit, humbug *rel* ruse, wile, trick, feint, stratagem, maneuver, artifice, gambit, ploy

deceitful *syn* DISHONEST, mendacious, lying, untruthful *rel* crafty, tricky, wily, guileful, foxy, insidious, cunning, sly, artful; underhand, underhanded, stealthy, furtive, clandestine, secret; crooked, devious, oblique; delusory, deceptive, delusive, misleading *ant* trustworthy

deceive • to lead astray or into evil or to frustrate by underhandedness or craft *syn* mislead, delude, beguile, betray, double-cross *rel* cheat, cozen, defraud, overreach; outwit, circumvent; dupe, gull, befool, trick, hoax, hoodwink, bamboozle *ant* undeceive; enlighten

decency *syn* DECORUM, propriety, dignity, etiquette *rel* seemliness, decorousness; fitness, suitability, fittingness, appropriateness

decent **1** *syn* DECOROUS, seemly, proper, nice *rel* fitting, fit, appropriate, suitable, meet; conventional, formal, ceremonious, ceremonial **2** *syn* CHASTE, modest, pure *rel* virtuous, moral, ethical, noble; pleasing, grateful, welcome, agreeable, pleasant *ant* indecent; obscene

deception **1** • the act or practice of deliberately deceiving *syn* fraud, double-dealing, trickery, chicane, chicanery *rel* deceit, duplicity, dissimulation, cunning, guile; cheating, cozening, defrauding, overreaching; duping, gulling, hoaxing, hoodwinking, bamboozling, befooling **2** *syn* IMPOSTURE, cheat, fraud, sham, fake, humbug, counterfeit, deceit *rel* illusion, delusion, hallucination, mirage

deceptive *syn* MISLEADING, delusory, delusive *rel* specious, plausible, colorable; false, wrong

decide • to come or to cause to come to a conclusion *syn* determine, settle, rule, resolve *rel* conclude, judge, gather; judge, adjudge, adjudicate

decided • free from any doubt, wavering, or ambiguity *syn* decisive, determined, resolved *rel* definite, definitive; positive, cocksure, certain, sure; categorical, explicit, express

decipher *syn* SOLVE, resolve, unfold, unravel *rel* interpret, construe, elucidate; translate, paraphrase

decisive **1** *syn* CONCLUSIVE, determinative, definitive *rel* critical, crucial, acute; momentous, significant, consequential, important *ant* indecisive **2** *syn* DECIDED, determined, resolved *rel* peremptory, imperative, masterful, imperious; certain, sure, positive, cocksure; resolute, steadfast *ant* irresolute

deck *syn* ADORN, bedeck, decorate, ornament, garnish, embellish, beautify *rel* array, apparel, attire, dress, clothe

declaration • the act of making known openly or publicly *syn* announcement, publication, advertisement, proclamation, promulgation, broadcasting

declare **1** • to make known explicitly or plainly *syn* announce, publish, advertise, proclaim, promulgate, broadcast *rel* inform, apprise, acquaint, advise, notify; impart, communicate; reveal, disclose, discover, divulge **2** *syn* ASSERT, profess, affirm, aver, avouch, avow, protest, predicate, warrant *rel* express, voice, utter, vent, broach, air, ventilate

declass *syn* DEGRADE, demote, reduce, disrate

declension *syn* DETERIORATION, decline, decadence, degeneration, devolution *rel* decaying, decay, disintegration, crumbling; retrogressiveness, retrogression, regressiveness, regression

decline *vb* • to turn away by not accepting, receiving, or considering *syn* refuse, reject, repudiate, spurn *rel* demur, balk, shy, boggle, jib, stick, stickle, scruple *ant* accept

decline *n, syn* DETERIORATION, declension, decadence, degeneration, devolution

decolorize *syn* WHITEN, blanch, bleach, etiolate

decompose *syn* DECAY, rot, putrefy, spoil, disintegrate, crumble *rel* deliquesce, liquefy, melt

decorate *syn* ADORN, ornament, embellish, beautify, deck, bedeck, garnish *rel* enhance, heighten, intensify

decorous • conforming to an accepted standard of what is right or fitting or is regarded as good form *syn* decent, seemly, proper, nice *rel* formal, conventional, ceremonious, ceremonial; dignified, elegant *ant* indecorous; blatant

decorticate *syn* SKIN, peel, pare, flay

decorum • the quality or character of rightness, fitness, or honorableness in behavior or conduct *syn* decency, propriety, dignity, etiquette *rel* formality, conventionality, ceremoniousness; form, convention, convenance, usage *ant* indecorum; license

decoy *n, syn* LURE, bait, snare, trap

decoy *vb, syn* LURE, entice, inveigle, tempt, seduce *rel* snare, ensnare, trap, entrap, capture, catch, bag; beguile, delude, deceive, mislead

decrease • to make or grow less esp. gradually *syn* lessen, diminish, reduce, abate, dwindle *rel* curtail, shorten, retrench, abridge, abbreviate; contract, shrink *ant* increase

decree *syn* DICTATE, prescribe, ordain, impose *rel* command, order, enjoin, charge, direct; constrain, oblige, compel, force

decrepit *syn* WEAK, infirm, feeble, frail, fragile *rel* worn, wasted, haggard; aged, superannuated, old; tottering, quavering, shaking *ant* sturdy

decry • to indicate one's low opinion of something *syn* deprecate, disparage, derogate, detract, belittle, minimize *rel* disapprove; criticize, denounce, reprehend, censure, reprobate, condemn *ant* extol

dedicate *syn* DEVOTE, consecrate, hallow *rel* direct, address, apply

deduce *syn* INFER, gather, conclude, judge *rel* reason, cogitate, think, speculate

deduct • to take away one quantity from another *syn* subtract *ant* add

deduction **1** • an amount subtracted from a gross sum *syn* abatement, rebate, discount **2** *syn* INFERENCE, conclusion, judgment

deed *n, syn* ACTION, act *rel* exploit, feat, achievement

deed *vb, syn* TRANSFER, convey, alienate

deem *syn* CONSIDER, regard, account, reckon *rel* conclude, gather, infer

deep **1** · having great extension downward or inward *syn* profound, abysmal **2** *syn* BROAD, wide

deep-rooted *syn* INVETERATE, deep-seated, chronic, confirmed *rel* established, fixed, set, settled

deep-seated *syn* INVETERATE, chronic, deep-rooted, confirmed *rel* ingrained, constitutional, inherent; profound, deep

deface · to mar the appearance of *syn* disfigure *rel* injure, damage, mar; deform, distort, contort; mutilate, batter, mangle, maim

defame *syn* MALIGN, vilify, calumniate, traduce, asperse, slander, libel *rel* vituperate, revile; decry, disparage, detract, derogate

default *syn* FAILURE, neglect, miscarriage, dereliction *rel* absence, lack, want, privation; imperfection, deficiency, shortcoming, fault

defeat *syn* CONQUER, beat, vanquish, lick, subdue, subjugate, reduce, overcome, surmount, overthrow, rout *rel* frustrate, thwart, foil, baffle, balk, circumvent, outwit

defect **1** *syn* LACK, want, dearth, absence, privation *rel* deficiency, defectiveness; need, necessity, exigency **2** *syn* BLEMISH, flaw *rel* fault, failing, frailty, foible

defection · conscious abandonment of allegiance or duty *syn* desertion, apostasy *rel* disaffection, alienation, estrangement; abandonment, forsaking

defective *syn* DEFICIENT *rel* impaired, damaged, injured, marred; vitiated, corrupted, debased; deranged, disordered *ant* intact

defend **1** · to keep secure from danger or against attack *syn* protect, shield, guard, safeguard *rel* ward, avert, prevent; oppose, resist, withstand; fight, battle, war, contend *ant* combat; attack **2** *syn* MAINTAIN, assert, vindicate *rel* voice, vent, utter, express, air; explain, account, rationalize; support, champion, uphold, back

defer *vb* · to a delay an action, activity, or proceeding *syn* postpone, intermit, suspend, stay *rel* delay, retard, slow

defer *vb, syn* YIELD, bow, submit, cave, capitulate, succumb, relent *rel* accede, acquiesce, assent, agree; conform, accommodate, adapt, adjust; truckle, fawn, cringe

deference *syn* HONOR, reverence, homage, obeisance *rel* veneration, worship, adoration; respect, esteem, admiration, regard *ant* disrespect

deficiency *syn* IMPERFECTION, shortcoming, fault *rel* lack, want, dearth, defect; flaw, blemish; failure, neglect, default, miscarriage, dereliction *ant* excess

deficient · showing lack of something necessary *syn* defective *rel* meager, scanty, scant, sparse, exiguous; scarce, rare, infrequent, uncommon *ant* sufficient, adequate; excessive

defile *syn* CONTAMINATE, pollute, taint, attaint *rel* debase, vitiate, deprave, corrupt, pervert, debauch; profane, desecrate *ant* cleanse; purify

define *syn* PRESCRIBE, assign *rel* limit, circumscribe; fix, set, establish

definite *syn* EXPLICIT, express, specific, categorical *rel* clear, plain, distinct; full, complete; downright, forthright; precise, exact; clear-cut, incisive *ant* indefinite; equivocal

definitive *syn* CONCLUSIVE, determinative, decisive *rel* settling, deciding, determining; final, concluding, last, terminal, ultimate *ant* tentative, provisional

deflate *syn* CONTRACT, compress, shrink, condense, constrict *rel* reduce, decrease, lessen; exhaust, deplete, drain; puncture, prick, perforate; attenuate, extenuate *ant* inflate

deflect *syn* TURN, divert, avert, sheer *rel* deviate, depart, diverge, swerve, veer, digress; bend, curve, twist

deflection *syn* DEVIATION, aberration, divergence *rel* bending, curving, twisting; swerving, swerve, veering, veer, departing, departure

deform • to mar or spoil by or as if by twisting *syn* distort, contort, warp *rel* maim, cripple, mutilate, mangle, batter; disfigure, deface; injure, mar, damage, impair

defraud *syn* CHEAT, swindle, overreach, cozen *rel* trick, bamboozle, hoax, gull, dupe, befool; outwit, circumvent, foil

deft *syn* DEXTEROUS, adroit, handy *rel* nimble, agile, brisk; quick, ready, apt, prompt; skillful, skilled, adept, proficient; sure, assured, confident *ant* awkward

defunct *syn* DEAD, deceased, departed, late, lifeless, inanimate *ant* alive; live

defy *syn* FACE, brave, challenge, dare, beard *rel* mock, deride, ridicule; flout, scoff; withstand, resist, oppose, fight; confront, encounter, meet *ant* recoil

degenerate *syn* VICIOUS, corrupt, infamous, villainous, iniquitous, nefarious, flagitious *rel* degraded, demeaned; debased, depraved, debauched, perverted; dissolute, abandoned, reprobate, profligate

degeneration *syn* DETERIORATION, devolution, decadence, decline, declension *rel* retrogressiveness, retrogression, regressiveness, regression; debasement, degradation

degrade **1** • to lower in station, rank, or grade *syn* demote, reduce, declass, disrate *rel* humble, humiliate, abase, debase; disbar, rule out, exclude *ant* elevate **2** *syn* ABASE, debase, demean, humble, humiliate *rel* deprave, debauch, pervert, corrupt, vitiate *ant* uplift

dehydrate *syn* DRY, desiccate, parch, bake

deign *syn* STOOP, condescend *rel* vouchsafe, accord, concede, grant, award

deject *syn* DISCOURAGE, dishearten, dispirit *rel* depress, weigh, oppress; distress, trouble *ant* exhilarate; cheer

dejected *syn* DOWNCAST, depressed, dispirited, disconsolate, woebegone *rel* weighed down, oppressed; despondent, forlorn, hopeless; morose, glum, gloomy, sullen

dejection *syn* SADNESS, depression, melancholy, melancholia, gloom, blues, dumps *rel* despondency, hopelessness, forlornness, despair, desperation *ant* exhilaration

delay **1** • to cause to be late or behind in movement or progress *syn* retard, slow, slacken, detain *rel* impede, obstruct, hinder, block; defer, postpone, stay, suspend, intermit *ant* expedite; hasten **2** • to move or act slowly so that progress is hindered or work remains undone or unfinished *syn* procrastinate, lag, loiter, dawdle *rel* linger, tarry, wait, stay; hesitate, falter, vacillate, waver *ant* hasten, hurry

delectable *syn* DELIGHTFUL, delicious, luscious *rel* gratifying, grateful, agreeable, pleasing, welcome, pleasant; exquisite, rare, delicate, dainty, choice; palatable, savory, sapid, toothsome

delectation *syn* PLEASURE, enjoyment, delight, joy, fruition *rel* amusement, diversion, entertainment; gratifying, gratification, regaling, regalement

delegate • a person who stands in place of another or others *syn* deputy, representative

delete *syn* ERASE, cancel, efface, obliterate, blot out, expunge *rel* eliminate, exclude, rule out; omit, neglect

deleterious *syn* PERNICIOUS, detrimental, baneful, noxious *rel* injuring, injurious, harming, harmful, hurting, hurtful; destroying, destructive; ruining, ruinous *ant* salutary

deliberate *adj* **1** *syn* VOLUNTARY, willful, intentional, willing *rel* purposed, intended; conscious, cognizant, aware; mortal, deadly *ant* impulsive **2** • arrived at after due thought *syn* considered, advised, premeditated, designed, studied *rel* planned, schemed, projected; calculated; careful, meticulous, scrupulous *ant* casual **3** *syn* SLOW, leisurely, dilatory, laggard *rel* cautious, circumspect, wary, chary, calculating; cool, collected, composed, imperturbable *ant* precipitate, abrupt

deliberate *vb, syn* THINK, reflect, cogitate, reason, speculate *rel* ponder, meditate, ruminate, muse

delicate *syn* CHOICE, exquisite, dainty, rare, recherché, elegant *rel* delectable, delightful, delicious; soft, gentle, mild, lenient, balmy; ethereal, airy, aerial *ant* gross

delicious *syn* DELIGHTFUL, delectable, luscious *rel* palatable, sapid, savory, toothsome, appetizing; delicate, dainty, exquisite, choice, rare

delight *n, syn* PLEASURE, delectation, enjoyment, joy, fruition *rel* glee, mirth, jollity, hilarity; rapture, transport, ecstasy; satisfaction, contentment *ant* disappointment; discontent

delight *vb, syn* PLEASE, gratify, rejoice, gladden, tickle, regale *rel* satisfy, content; divert, amuse, entertain; charm, enchant, fascinate, allure, attract *ant* distress; bore

delightful • highly pleasing to the senses or to aesthetic taste *syn* delicious, delectable, luscious *rel* enchanting, charming, fascinating, alluring, attractive; lovely, fair, beautiful; ineffable *ant* distressing; boring; horrid

delineate **1** *syn* SKETCH, trace, outline, diagram, draft, plot, blueprint *rel* describe, relate; design, plan **2** *syn* REPRESENT, depict, portray, picture, limn

delineation *syn* SKETCH, tracing, outline, sketch, diagram, plot, blueprint *rel* map, chart, graph; design, plan

delinquent *syn* CRIMINAL, felon, convict, malefactor, culprit

deliquesce *syn* LIQUEFY, melt, fuse, thaw *rel* decay, decompose, disintegrate

delirious *syn* FURIOUS, frantic, frenzied, wild, frenetic, rabid *rel* excited, stimulated; enthusiastic, fanatic; ecstatic, rapturous, transported

delirium *syn* MANIA, frenzy, hysteria

deliver *syn* RESCUE, redeem, save, ransom, reclaim

delude *syn* DECEIVE, beguile, mislead, betray, double-cross *rel* dupe, gull, hoodwink, befool, bamboozle, hoax, trick; cheat, cozen, overreach *ant* enlighten

deluge *syn* FLOOD, inundation, torrent, spate, cataract *rel* flow, stream, current, flux, tide

delusion • something which is believed to be or is accepted as being true or real but which is actually false or unreal *syn* illusion, hallucination, mirage *rel* deception, trickery, chicane, chicanery; imposture, counterfeit, cheat, fraud, sham, fake, humbug, deceit; fantasy, vision, dream, daydream, fancy

delusive, delusory *syn* MISLEADING, deceptive *rel* fantastic, chimerical, visionary, imaginary, fanciful, quixotic; fallacious, sophistical, casuistical; illusory, seeming, ostensible, apparent

delve *syn* DIG, spade, grub, excavate

demand • to ask or call for something as due or as necessary or as strongly desired *syn* claim, require, exact *rel* request, ask, solicit; order, command, charge, enjoin, direct, bid; call, summon, summons, cite

demarcate *syn* DISTINGUISH, differentiate, discriminate *rel* limit, restrict, circumscribe, confine; define, assign, prescribe

demean *vb, syn* BEHAVE, deport, comport, conduct, acquit, quit *rel* carry, bear (*as reflexive verbs*)

demean *vb, syn* ABASE, degrade, debase, humble, humiliate

demeanor *syn* BEARING, deportment, mien, port, presence *rel* behavior, conduct; posture, attitude, pose; air, mannerism, affectation

demented *syn* INSANE, mad, crazy, crazed, deranged, lunatic, maniac, non compos mentis *rel* irrational, unreasonable; delirious, hysterical, frenzied *ant* rational

dementia *syn* INSANITY, lunacy, mania, psychosis *rel* delirium, hysteria, frenzy

demise *syn* DEATH, decease, passing

demolish *syn* DESTROY, raze *rel* wreck, ruin, dilapidate; devastate, ravage, waste, sack *ant* construct

demoniac, demonic *syn* FIENDISH, diabolic, diabolical, devilish *rel* hellish, infernal; crazed, crazy, maniac, insane; inspired, fired

demonstrate **1** *syn* SHOW, manifest, evince, evidence *rel* reveal, disclose, discover, betray; display, exhibit, parade, flaunt, expose, show **2** *syn* PROVE, try, test *rel* argue, debate; substantiate, verify, authenticate, confirm, corroborate, validate

demonstration *syn* PROOF, trial, test *rel* substantiation, confirming, confirmation, corroboration, verification

demote *syn* DEGRADE, reduce, declass, disrate *ant* promote (*in rank, grade*)

demur *vb* • to hesitate or show reluctance because of difficulties in the way *syn* scruple, balk, jib, shy, boggle, stick, stickle, strain *rel* hesitate, falter, vacillate, waver; oppose, resist, combat, fight; object, remonstrate; disapprove, deprecate *ant* accede

demur *n, syn* QUALM, compunction, scruple *rel* hesitation, hesitancy; reluctance, loathness, aversion, disinclination; objection, remonstrance

denizen *syn* INHABITANT, resident, citizen

denomination **1** *syn* NAME, designation, appellation, title, style **2** *syn* RELIGION, sect, communion, faith, creed, cult, persuasion, church

denote *syn* MEAN, signify, import *rel* betoken, bespeak, indicate, attest, argue, prove; intend, mean; suggest, imply, hint, intimate, insinuate

denounce *syn* CRITICIZE, condemn, censure, reprobate, reprehend, blame *rel* accuse, charge, arraign, impeach, incriminate, indict; decry, disparage, depreciate; revile, vituperate, scold *ant* eulogize

dense **1** *syn* CLOSE, compact, thick

rel consolidated, concentrated, compacted; compressed, condensed; massed, heaped, piled, stacked *ant* sparse (*of population, forests*); tenuous (*of clouds, air, masses*) **2** *syn* STUPID, crass, slow, dull, dumb *rel* obtuse; stolid, phlegmatic, impassive *ant* subtle; bright

denude *syn* STRIP, bare, divest, dismantle *ant* clothe

deny · to refuse to accept as true or valid *syn* gainsay, contradict, negative, traverse, impugn, contravene *rel* decline, refuse, reject, repudiate; controvert, refute, rebut, confute, disprove *ant* confirm; concede

depart **1** *syn* GO, leave, withdraw, retire, quit *ant* arrive; remain, abide **2** *syn* SWERVE, digress, deviate, diverge, veer *rel* forsake, abandon, desert; reject, repudiate, decline; discard, cast

departed *syn* DEAD, deceased, late, defunct, lifeless, inanimate

depend **1** · (on *or* upon) *syn* RELY, trust, count, reckon, bank *rel* lean, incline **2** · to rest or to be contingent upon something uncertain, variable, or indeterminable *syn* hinge, hang, turn

dependable *syn* RELIABLE, trustworthy, trusty, tried *rel* sure, assured, confident; responsible; staunch, steadfast, constant, faithful

dependence *syn* TRUST, reliance, confidence, faith

dependent **1** · determined or conditioned by another *syn* contingent, conditional, relative *rel* subject, liable, open, exposed, susceptible *ant* absolute; infinite; original **2** *syn* SUBORDINATE, subject, tributary, secondary, collateral *rel* relying, depending, trusting, reckoning, counting; subsidiary, subservient, auxiliary; abased, humbled, debased *ant* independent

depict *syn* REPRESENT, portray, delineate, picture, limn *rel* describe, narrate, relate; sketch, draft, outline, trace

deplete · to bring to a low estate by depriving of something essential *syn* drain, exhaust, impoverish, bankrupt *rel* undermine, sap, debilitate, weaken, enfeeble, cripple, disable; reduce, diminish, decrease, lessen

deplore · to manifest grief or sorrow for something *syn* lament, bewail, bemoan *rel* deprecate, disapprove; grieve, mourn, sorrow; weep, wail, cry

deport **1** *syn* BEHAVE, demean, comport, conduct, acquit, quit *rel* see DEMEAN **2** *syn* BANISH, transport, exile, expatriate, ostracize, extradite

deportment **1** *syn* BEHAVIOR, conduct *rel* see BEHAVIOR **2** *syn* BEARING, demeanor, mien, port, presence *rel* form, formality, ceremony, ceremonial, ritual; culture, cultivation, breeding, refinement; dignity, grace, elegance

deposit · matter which settles to the bottom of a liquid *syn* precipitate, sediment, dregs, lees, grounds

deprave *syn* DEBASE, vitiate, corrupt, debauch, pervert *rel* defile, pollute, taint, contaminate; injure, impair, damage, spoil

depraved *syn* DEBASED, vitiated, corrupted, debauched, perverted *rel* dissolute, abandoned, reprobate, profligate; degenerate, infamous, villainous, vicious; degraded

deprecate *syn* DISAPPROVE *rel* deplore, lament, bewail, bemoan; reprobate, reprehend, condemn, criticize *ant* endorse

depreciate *syn* DECRY, disparage, derogate, detract, belittle, minimize *rel* underestimate, undervalue, underrate; asperse, malign *ant* appreciate

depreciative, depreciatory *syn* DEROGATORY, disparaging, slighting, pejorative *rel* decrying, belittling, minimizing; aspersing, maligning; underrating, underestimating, undervaluing

depress • to lower in spirit or mood *syn* weigh, oppress *rel* distress, trouble, ail; afflict, try, torment; tire, weary, fatigue, exhaust, fag, jade, tucker *ant* elate; cheer

depressed *syn* DOWNCAST, dejected, dispirited, disconsolate, woebegone *rel* gloomy, glum, morose, sullen; discouraged, disheartened; melancholy, lugubrious

depression *syn* SADNESS, dejection, gloom, blues, dumps, melancholy, melancholia *rel* despondency, forlornness, hopelessness, despair, desperation; doldrums, boredom, ennui, tedium *ant* buoyancy

deputy **1** *syn* AGENT, attorney, factor, proxy *rel* substitute, surrogate **2** *syn* DELEGATE, representative

deracinate *syn* EXTERMINATE, uproot, eradicate, extirpate, wipe *rel* abolish, extinguish, annihilate, abate; destroy, demolish

derange *syn* DISORDER, disarrange, unsettle, disturb, disorganize *rel* upset, discompose, perturb; discommode, incommode, inconvenience *ant* arrange; adjust

deranged *syn* INSANE, demented, non compos mentis, crazed, crazy, mad, lunatic, maniac

derangement *syn* ABERRATION, alienation

derelict *syn* OUTCAST, castaway, reprobate, pariah, untouchable *rel* vagabond, vagrant, tramp, hobo

dereliction *syn* FAILURE, neglect, default, miscarriage *rel* abuse, misuse, outrage

deride *syn* RIDICULE, mock, taunt, twit, rally *rel* scoff, jeer, gibe, flout, sneer, gird, fleer; chaff, banter, kid, rag, jolly, rib

derive *syn* SPRING, originate, arise, rise, emanate, issue, stem, flow, proceed

dernier cri *syn* FASHION, style, mode, vogue, fad, rage, craze, cry

derogate *syn* DECRY, disparage, detract, belittle, minimize, depreciate *rel* reduce, lessen, decrease, diminish

derogatory • designed or tending to belittle *syn* depreciatory, depreciative, disparaging, slighting, pejorative *rel* belittling, minimizing, decrying; aspersing, maligning

descant **1** *syn* SING, troll, carol, warble, trill, hymn, chant, intone **2** *syn* DISCOURSE, expatiate, dilate

descend • to get or come down from a height *syn* dismount, alight *ant* ascend, climb

descendant *syn* OFFSPRING, young, progeny, issue, posterity

describe *syn* RELATE, narrate, state, report, rehearse, recite, recount *rel* delineate, sketch, outline

description *syn* TYPE, kind, sort, character, nature, stripe, kidney, ilk

descry *syn* SEE, espy, behold, observe, notice, remark, note, perceive, discern, view, survey, contemplate

desecration *syn* PROFANATION, sacrilege, blasphemy *rel* defilement, pollution

desert *n, syn* WASTE, badlands, wilderness

desert *n, syn* DUE, merit *rel* meed, guerdon; punishment, chastisement, chastening, disciplining, discipline

desert *vb, syn* ABANDON, forsake *rel* leave, quit, depart *ant* stick to, cleave to

desertion *syn* DEFECTION, apostasy *rel* perfidiousness, perfidy, treacherousness, treachery, disloyalty, faithlessness

deserve · to be or become worthy of *syn* merit, earn, rate *rel* gain, win, get; evaluate, value, estimate; claim, demand

desiccate *syn* DRY, dehydrate, parch, bake

design *vb* **1** *syn* INTEND, mean, propose, purpose *rel* aim, aspire **2** *syn* PLAN, plot, scheme, project *rel* sketch, outline, diagram, delineate, blueprint, draft; invent, create

design *n* **1** *syn* PLAN, plot, scheme, project *rel* delineation, sketch, draft, outline, tracing, diagram; conception, idea **2** *syn* INTENTION, intent, purpose, aim, end, object, objective, goal *rel* will, volition, conation; deliberation, reflection, thinking, thought; intrigue, machination *ant* accident **3** *syn* FIGURE, pattern, motif, device

designate · to declare a person one's choice *syn* name, nominate, elect, appoint *rel* choose, select, single, opt, pick

designation *syn* NAME, denomination, appellation, title, style *rel* identification, recognition; classification, pigeonholing, pigeonhole

designed *syn* DELIBERATE, premeditated, considered, advised, studied *rel* intentional, voluntary, willful, deliberate, willing; purposed, intended; resolved, determined, decided *ant* accidental

desire *vb* · to have a longing for something *syn* wish, want, crave, covet *rel* long, yearn, hanker, pine, hunger, thirst; aspire, pant, aim

desire *n* · a longing for something that promises enjoyment or satisfaction *syn* appetite, lust, passion, urge *rel* longing, yearning, hankering, pining, hungering, hunger, thirsting, thirst; cupidity, greed, avarice, rapacity *ant* distaste

desist *syn* STOP, discontinue, cease, quit *rel* refrain, abstain, forbear; relinquish, yield, abandon, resign *ant* persist

desolate **1** *syn* ALONE, forlorn, lorn, lonesome, lone, solitary, lonely *rel* deserted, forsaken, abandoned; miserable, wretched **2** *syn* DISMAL, dreary, cheerless, dispiriting, bleak *rel* bare, barren, bald; destitute, poverty-stricken, poor

despair *syn* DESPONDENCY, hopelessness, desperation, forlornness *rel* dejection, melancholy, sadness, gloom, depression *ant* hope; optimism; beatitude

despairing *syn* DESPONDENT, hopeless, desperate, forlorn *rel* melancholy, melancholic, atrabilious; pessimistic, misanthropic, cynical; depressed, weighed down *ant* hopeful

desperate *syn* DESPONDENT, hopeless, despairing, forlorn *rel* reckless, rash, foolhardy, venturesome; precipitate, headlong; thwarted, foiled, frustrated, outwitted, circumvented, baffled, balked

desperation *syn* DESPONDENCY, hopelessness, despair, forlornness *rel* fury, frenzy; grit, pluck, guts, sand, fortitude; recklessness, rashness, foolhardiness; temerity, audacity

despicable *syn* CONTEMPTIBLE, pitiable, sorry, scurvy, cheap, beggarly, shabby *rel* base, low, vile; ignominious, infamous, disgraceful; ignoble, mean, abject, sordid *ant* praiseworthy, laudable

despise · to regard as beneath one's notice and as unworthy of attention or interest *syn* contemn, scorn, disdain, scout *rel* abominate, loathe, abhor, detest, hate; spurn, repduiate *ant* appreciate

despite *n* **1** *syn* MALICE, spite, ill will, malevolence, spleen, grudge, malignity, malignancy *rel* contempt, scorn, disdain; abhorrence, loathing, detestation, abomination, hatred, hate *ant* appreciation; regard **2** · the feeling or attitude of despising *syn* contempt, scorn, disdain

despite *prep, syn* NOTWITHSTANDING, in spite of

despoil *syn* RAVAGE, devastate, waste, sack, pillage, spoliate *rel* plunder, rob, rifle, loot; strip, bare, denude

despondency · the state or feeling of having lost hope *syn* despair, desperation, hopelessness, forlornness *rel* dejection, depression, melancholy, melancholia, sadness, blues, dumps *ant* lightheartedness

despondent · having lost all or nearly all hope *syn* despairing, desperate, hopeless, forlorn *rel* grieving, mourning, sorrowing; depressed, dejected, melancholy, sad *ant* lighthearted

despotic *syn* ABSOLUTE, tyrannical, tyrannous, arbitrary, autocratic *rel* domineering, imperious, masterful, imperative; dictatorial, authoritarian, magisterial

destiny *syn* FATE, lot, doom, portion *rel* end, termination, terminus, ending; goal, objective

destitute **1** *syn* DEVOID, void *rel* lacking, wanting; empty; barren, bare; depleted, drained, exhausted, bankrupted, bankrupt **2** *syn* POOR, indigent, needy, penniless, impecunious, poverty-stricken, necessitous *ant* opulent

destitution *syn* POVERTY, want, indigence, penury, privation *rel* need, necessity, exigency; lack, absence, want, privation, dearth; adversity, misfortune; strait *ant* opulence

destroy · to bring to ruin *syn* demolish, raze *rel* ruin, wreck, dilapidate; abolish, extinguish, annihilate; ravage, devastate, sack

destruction *syn* RUIN, havoc, devastation *rel* demolishing, demolition, razing; annihilation, extinction

desultory *syn* RANDOM, casual, hit or miss, haphazard, happy-go-lucky, chance, chancy *rel* fitful, spasmodic; unsystematic, unmethodical, disorderly; capricious, mercurial; inconstant, fickle *ant* assiduous; methodical

detach · to remove one thing from another with which it is in union or association *syn* disengage, abstract *rel* separate, part, sever, sunder, divorce; disjoin, disconnect, disunite *ant* attach, affix

detached *syn* INDIFFERENT, aloof, uninterested, disinterested, unconcerned, incurious *rel* impartial, dispassionate, objective, unbiased, fair; altruistic *ant* interested; selfish

detail **1** *syn* ITEM, particular **2** *syn* PART, portion, piece, parcel, member, division, segment, sector, fraction, fragment

detailed *syn* CIRCUMSTANTIAL, itemized, particularized, minute, particular *rel* full, complete, replete; copious, abundant; exhausting, exhaustive

detain **1** *syn* ARREST, apprehend, attach *rel* catch, capture; seize, take; imprison, incarcerate, intern, jail **2** *syn* KEEP, withhold, hold, hold back, keep back, keep out, retain, reserve **3** *syn* DELAY, retard, slow, slacken *rel* curb, check, restrain, inhibit; arrest, interrupt; defer, suspend, stay

detention *syn* ARREST, apprehension, attachment *rel* imprisonment, internment, incarceration

deter *syn* DISSUADE, discourage, divert *rel* prevent; hinder, impede, obstruct, block; debar, shut out, exclude; frighten, scare; restrain, inhibit *ant* abet; actuate, motivate

deterioration · a falling from a higher to a lower level in quality, character, or vitality *syn* degeneration, devolution, decadence, decline, declension *rel* impairment, spoiling; decaying, decay, decomposition, disintegration, rotting, crumbling; debasement, degradation *ant* improvement, amelioration

determinant *syn* CAUSE, antecedent, reason, occasion *rel* factor, element; influence, weight, authority

determinative *syn* CONCLUSIVE, decisive, definitive *rel* determining, deciding, settling; influencing, affecting; shaping, fashioning, forming, formative

determine **1** *syn* DECIDE, settle, rule, resolve *rel* fix, set, establish; dispose, predispose, incline, bias; drive, impel, move, actuate; induce, persuade **2** *syn* DISCOVER, ascertain, unearth, learn

determined *syn* DECIDED, decisive, resolved

detest *syn* HATE, abhor, abominate, loathe *rel* despise, contemn, scorn, disdain; spurn, repudiate, reject *ant* adore

detestable *syn* HATEFUL, odious, abominable, abhorrent *rel* contemptible, despicable, sorry, scurvy; atrocious, outrageous, monstrous, heinous; execrable, damnable, accursed

detestation *syn* ABHORRENCE, hate, hatred, abomination, loathing *rel* antipathy, aversion; despite, contempt, scorn, disdain

detract *syn* DECRY, belittle, minimize, disparage, derogate, depreciate *rel* asperse, malign, traduce, defame, vilify, calumniate, slander, libel; reduce, lessen, diminish, decrease

detraction • the expression of damaging or malicious opinions *syn* backbiting, calumny, slander, scandal *rel* injury, damage, harm, hurt; injustice, injury, wrong; defaming, defamation, aspersion, maligning, traducing, slandering, calumniation, vilification, libeling, libel

detriment *syn* DISADVANTAGE, handicap, drawback *rel* damage, injury, harm, hurt; impairment, spoiling, marring *ant* advantage, benefit

detrimental *syn* PERNICIOUS, deleterious, noxious, baneful *rel* harming, harmful, hurting, hurtful, injuring, injurious, damaging, impairing *ant* beneficial

devastate *syn* RAVAGE, waste, sack, pillage, despoil, spoliate *rel* destroy, demolish, raze; ruin, wreck; plunder, loot, rob, rifle

devastation *syn* RUIN, havoc, destruction *rel* demolishment, razing; ravaging, sacking, pillaging, despoliation

develop **1** *syn* UNFOLD, evolve, elaborate, perfect *rel* actualize, realize, materialize; attain, achieve, compass, reach **2** *syn* MATURE, ripen, age *rel* advance, progress; expand, dilate

development • advance from a lower to a higher form *syn* evolution

deviate *syn* SWERVE, digress, diverge, veer, depart *rel* deflect, turn, divert, avert, sheer; stray, wander, rove

deviation • departure from a straight course or procedure or from a norm or standard *syn* aberration, divergence, deflection

device **1** • something usu. of a mechanical character that performs a function or effects a desired end *syn* contrivance, gadget, contraption *rel* instrument, tool, implement, appliance, utensil; apparatus, machine, mechanism; expedient, resource, shift, makeshift, resort; invention, creation; artifice, ruse, trick, gambit, ploy **2** *syn* FIGURE, design, motif, pattern *rel* symbol, emblem, attribute, type

devilish *syn* FIENDISH, diabolical, diabolic, demoniac, demonic *rel* infernal, hellish; nefarious, iniquitous, villainous, vicious *ant* angelic

devious *syn* CROOKED, oblique *rel* deviating, diverging, digressing; aberrant, abnormal; tricky, crafty, artful, cunning, foxy, insidious, sly *ant* straightforward

devise 1 *syn* CONTRIVE, invent, frame, concoct *rel* create, discover, invent; fashion, forge, fabricate, shape, form, make; design, plan, scheme, plot 2 *syn* WILL, bequeath, leave, legate

devoid • showing a want or lack *syn* void, destitute *rel* barren, bare; lacking, wanting; empty

devolution *syn* DETERIORATION, decadence, decline, declension, degeneration *rel* retrogressiveness, retrogression, regressiveness, regression; receding, recession, retrograding, retrogradation *ant* evolution

devote 1 • to set apart for a particular and often a better or higher use or end *syn* dedicate, consecrate, hallow *rel* commit, consign, confide, entrust; assign, allot; sentence, doom 2 *syn* DIRECT, apply, address *rel* endeavor, strive, struggle, try, attempt

devoted *syn* LOVING, affectionate, fond, doting *rel* faithful, loyal, true, constant; attentive, considerate, thoughtful

devotee *syn* ADDICT, votary, habitué *rel* enthusiast, zealot, fanatic

devotion *syn* FIDELITY, loyalty, fealty, piety, allegiance *rel* fervor, ardor, zeal, enthusiasm, passion; love, affection, attachment; dedication, consecration

devour *syn* EAT, swallow, ingest, consume *rel* waste, squander, dissipate; destroy, demolish; wreck, ruin

devout • showing fervor and reverence in the practice of religion *syn* pious, religious, pietistic, sanctimonious *rel* fervent, fervid, ardent, impassioned; worshiping, adoring, venerating

dexterity *syn* READINESS, facility, ease *rel* dexterousness, adroitness, deftness; expertness, adeptness, skillfulness, proficiency *ant* clumsiness

dexterous • ready and skilled in physical movements *syn* adroit, deft, handy *rel* nimble, agile; skilled, skillful, expert, masterly, adept, proficient; easy, effortless, smooth, facile *ant* clumsy

diabolical, diabolic *syn* FIENDISH, demonic, devilish, demoniac *rel, ant* see DEVILISH

diagram *n, syn* SKETCH, outline, draft, tracing, delineation, plot, blueprint *rel* design, plan, plot, scheme

diagram *vb, syn* SKETCH, outline, plot, blueprint, draft, trace, delineate *rel* design, plan, plot, scheme

dialect 1 • a form of language that is not recognized as standard *syn* vernacular, patois, lingo, jargon, cant, argot, slang 2 *syn* LANGUAGE, tongue, speech, idiom

dialectic *syn* ARGUMENTATION, disputation, debate, forensic

diaphanous *syn* CLEAR, limpid, pellucid, transparent, translucent, lucid

diatribe *syn* TIRADE, jeremiad, philippic *rel* invective, vituperation, obloquy, abuse

dictate *vb* • to lay down expressly something to be followed, observed, obeyed, or accepted *syn* prescribe, ordain, decree, impose *rel* direct, control, manage; guide, lead; govern, rule; tell, utter, say

dictate *n, syn* COMMAND, behest, bidding, injunction, order, mandate *rel* law, rule, precept, canon, ordinance, statute, regulation

dictatorial • imposing one's will or opinions on others *syn* magisterial, authoritarian, dogmatic, doctrinaire, oracular *rel* masterful, domineering, imperative, imperious, peremptory; despotic, tyrannical, arbitrary, autocratic, absolute

diction *syn* LANGUAGE, vocabulary, phraseology, phrasing, style *rel* speech, tongue, idiom; enunciation, pronunciation, articulation

dido *syn* PRANK, caper, antic, monkeyshine

differ • to be unlike or out of harmony *syn* vary, disagree, dissent *rel* diverge, deviate, depart *ant* agree

difference **1** *syn* DISSIMILARITY, unlikeness, divergence, divergency, distinction *rel* discrepancy, inconsistency, inconsonance, discordance; variation, modification; disparity, diversity *ant* resemblance **2** *syn* DISCORD, strife, conflict, contention, dissension, variance

different • unlike in kind or character *syn* diverse, divergent, disparate, various *rel* distinct, separate, several; single, particular; sundry, divers, many *ant* identical, alike, same

differentiate *syn* DISTINGUISH, discriminate, demarcate *rel* separate, divide, part; detach, disengage *ant* confuse

difficult *syn* HARD, arduous *rel* perplexing, puzzling, mystifying; intricate, involved, complicated, complex, knotty; obscure, enigmatic, cryptic; exacting, onerous, burdensome *ant* simple

difficulty • something which demands effort and endurance if it is to be overcome or one's end achieved *syn* hardship, rigor, vicissitude *rel* obstacle, impediment, snag, obstruction; predicament, dilemma, quandary, plight, scrape, fix, jam, pickle; pinch, strait, emergency, exigency, pass

diffident *syn* SHY, modest, bashful, coy *rel* shrinking, flinching, blenching; hesitant, reluctant, disinclined; timorous, timid *ant* confident

diffuse *adj, syn* WORDY, prolix, redundant, verbose *rel* profuse, lavish, exuberant; desultory, casual, random; copious; loose, relaxed, slack, lax *ant* succinct

diffuse *vb, syn* SPREAD, circulate, disseminate, propagate, radiate *rel* disperse, dissipate, scatter; extend; expand *ant* concentrate

dig • to loosen and turn over or remove (as soil) with or as if with a spade *syn* delve, spade, grub, excavate *rel* pierce, penetrate, probe, enter

digest *syn* COMPENDIUM, syllabus, pandect, survey, sketch, précis, aperçu *rel* collection, assemblage, gathering; abridgment, conspectus, abstract, brief, synopsis, epitome

digit *syn* NUMBER, numeral, figure, integer

dignify • to enhance the status of or raise in human estimation *syn* ennoble, honor, glorify *rel* elevate, raise, lift; exalt, magnify, aggrandize; heighten, enhance, intensify

dignity **1** *syn* DECORUM, decency, propriety, etiquette *rel* excellence, virtue, merit, perfection; nobleness, nobility, morality, ethicalness, ethics **2** *syn* ELEGANCE, grace *rel* worth, value; beautifulness, beauty, loveliness, comeliness; grandness, grandeur, magnificence, stateliness, majesty, augustness

digress *syn* SWERVE, deviate, diverge, depart, veer *rel* wander, stray

digression • a departure from a subject or theme *syn* episode, excursus, divagation

dilapidate *syn* RUIN, wreck *rel* decay, disintegrate, crumble, decompose; neglect, ignore, disregard, forget, slight, overlook

dilapidated *syn* SHABBY, dingy, faded, seedy, threadbare *rel* damaged, injured, impaired, marred; ruined, wrecked

dilate 1 *syn* DISCOURSE, expatiate, descant *rel* relate, recount, rehearse, recite, narrate, describe; expound, explain; discuss, argue **2** *syn* EXPAND, distend, swell, amplify, inflate *rel* enlarge, increase, augment; extend, protract, prolong, lengthen; widen, broaden *ant* constrict; circumscribe; attenuate

dilatory *syn* SLOW, laggard, deliberate, leisurely *rel* procrastinating, delaying, dawdling; negligent, neglectful, lax, slack, remiss *ant* diligent

dilemma *syn* PREDICAMENT, quandary, plight, scrape, fix, jam, pickle *rel* perplexity, bewilderment, mystification; difficulty, vicissitude

dilettante 1 *syn* AMATEUR, dabbler, tyro **2** *syn* AESTHETE, connoisseur

diligent *syn* BUSY, assiduous, sedulous, industrious *rel* persevering, persisting, persistent; indefatigable, tireless, untiring, unwearied, unflagging *ant* dilatory

dilute *syn* THIN, attenuate, rarefy *rel* temper, moderate, qualify; weaken, enfeeble; liquefy, deliquesce; adulterate, sophisticate *ant* condense; concentrate

dim *adj, syn* DARK, dusky, obscure, murky, gloomy *ant* bright; distinct

dim *vb, syn* OBSCURE, bedim, darken, eclipse, cloud, becloud, fog, befog, obfuscate *rel* screen, conceal, hide; cloak, mask, camouflage, disguise *ant* illustrate

dimensions *syn* SIZE, extent, area, magnitude, volume

diminish *syn* DECREASE, reduce, lessen, abate, dwindle *rel* wane, ebb, subside; moderate, temper; lighten, alleviate, mitigate; attenuate, extenuate

diminutive *syn* SMALL, little, wee, tiny, minute, miniature

din · a disturbing or confusing welter of sounds *syn* uproar, pandemonium, hullabaloo, babel, hubbub, clamor, racket *rel* clamorousness, stridency, boisterousness, blatancy; clash, percussion *ant* quiet

dingy *syn* SHABBY, dilapidated, faded, seedy, threadbare *rel* soiled, grimed, sullied, smirched, tarnished; dull; dusky, murky, gloomy, dark

dinner · a usu. elaborate meal served to guests or to a group often to mark an occasion or honor an individual *syn* banquet, feast

dip 1 · to plunge a person or thing into or as if into liquid *syn* immerse, submerge, duck, souse, dunk **2** · to remove a liquid or a loose or soft substance from a container by means of an implement shaped to hold liquid *syn* bail, scoop, ladle, spoon, dish

diplomatic *syn* SUAVE, politic, smooth, bland, urbane *rel* astute, shrewd; courteous, courtly, polite, civil; artful, wily, guileful, crafty; tactful, poised

dipsomaniac *syn* DRUNKARD, alcoholic, inebriate, sot, soak, toper, tosspot, tippler

direct *vb* 1 · to turn or bend one's attention or efforts toward a certain object or objective *syn* address, devote, apply *rel* bend; set, fix, settle; endeavor, strive, try, attempt **2** · to turn something toward its appointed or intended mark or goal *syn* aim, point, level, train, lay *rel* steer, pilot, guide, lead, engineer *ant* misdirect **3** *syn* CONDUCT, manage, control *rel* govern, rule **4** *syn* COMMAND, order, bid, enjoin, instruct, charge *rel* prescribe, assign, define

direct *adj* · marked by the absence of interruption (as between the cause and the effect, the source and the issue, or the beginning and the end) *syn* immediate

directly *syn* PRESENTLY, shortly, soon

dirty *adj* · conspicuously unclean or impure *syn* filthy, foul, nasty, squalid *ant* clean

dirty *vb, syn* SOIL, sully, tarnish, foul, befoul, smirch, besmirch, grime, begrime *rel* pollute, defile, contaminate; spot, spatter

disable *syn* WEAKEN, cripple, undermine, enfeeble, debilitate, sap *rel* injure, damage, harm, hurt, impair, mar, spoil; maim, mutilate, mangle, batter; ruin, wreck *ant* rehabilitate

disabuse *syn* RID, clear, unburden, purge *rel* free, liberate, release; enlighten, illuminate

disadvantage · something which interferes with the success or well-being of a person or thing *syn* detriment, handicap, drawback *rel* obstacle, impediment, bar; barrier; hindrance, blocking *ant* advantage

disaffect *syn* ESTRANGE, alienate, wean *rel* upset, agitate, discompose, disquiet, disturb; sever, sunder, divorce, separate *ant* win over

disagree *syn* DIFFER, vary, dissent *rel* object, protest; demur, balk, jib; disapprove, deprecate; conflict, clash *ant* agree

disallow *syn* DISCLAIM, disavow, repudiate, disown *rel* reject, refuse, spurn, decline; deny, gainsay, traverse; debar, shut out, exclude *ant* allow

disappear *syn* VANISH, evanesce, evaporate, fade *rel* depart, leave, go *ant* appear

disapprove · to feel or to express an objection to or condemnation of *syn* deprecate *rel* reprehend, reprobate, censure, criticize; decry, disparage *ant* approve

disarrange *syn* DISORDER, derange, disorganize, unsettle, disturb *rel* misplace, mislay; displace, replace; upset, overturn *ant* arrange

disarray *syn* CONFUSION, disorder, chaos, jumble, clutter, snarl, muddle

disaster · an event bringing great damage, loss, or destruction *syn* calamity, catastrophe, cataclysm *rel* mishap, accident, casualty; adversity, misfortune, mischance

disastrous *syn* UNLUCKY, ill-starred, ill-fated, unfortunate, calamitous, luckless, hapless *rel* malign, sinister, baleful; unpropitious, inauspicious, ominous, portentous, fateful

disavow *syn* DISCLAIM, repudiate, disown, disallow *rel* deny, gainsay, traverse; disapprove, deprecate; reject, refuse, decline *ant* avow

disbar *syn* EXCLUDE, shut out, eliminate, rule out, suspend, debar, blackball

disbelief *syn* UNBELIEF, incredulity *rel* atheism, deism; rejection, repudiation, spurning *ant* belief

disburse *syn* SPEND, expend *rel* distribute, dispense; apportion, allot, allocate; pay

discard · to get rid of *syn* cast, shed, molt, slough, scrap, junk *rel* abandon, forsake, desert; reject, repudiate, spurn; dismiss, eject, oust

discern *syn* SEE, perceive, descry, observe, notice, remark, note, espy, behold, view, survey, contemplate *rel* discover, ascertain; divine, apprehend, anticipate, foresee; pierce, penetrate, probe

discernment · a power to see what is not evident to the average mind *syn* discrimination, perception, penetration, insight, acumen *rel* intuition, understanding, reason;

perspicaciousness, perspicacity, sagaciousness, sagacity, shrewdness, astuteness

discharge **1** *syn* FREE, release, liberate, emancipate, manumit *rel* eject, expel, oust; eliminate, exclude; deliver, enfranchise **2** *syn* DISMISS, cashier, drop, sack, fire, bounce *rel* displace, supplant, supersede, replace **3** *syn* PERFORM, execute, accomplish, achieve, effect, fulfill *rel* finish, complete, close, end, terminate

disciple *syn* FOLLOWER, adherent, henchman, satellite, sectary, partisan *rel* votary, devotee; enthusiast, zealot, fanatic

discipline *n, syn* MORALE, esprit de corps *rel* self-control, self-command; self-confidence, self-possession; nerving, steeling *ant* anarchy, lawlessness

discipline *vb* **1** *syn* TEACH, train, educate, instruct, school *rel* lead, guide; control, manage, direct, conduct; drill, exercise, practice **2** *syn* PUNISH, chastise, castigate, chasten, correct *rel* subdue, overcome, reduce, subjugate; restrain, curb, bridle, check, inhibit

disclaim · to refuse to admit, accept, or approve *syn* disavow, repudiate, disown, disallow *rel* deny, gainsay, traverse, contradict; reject, refuse, spurn; deprecate, disapprove; belittle, minimize, disparage, decry *ant* claim

disclose *syn* REVEAL, divulge, tell, discover, betray *rel* confess, admit, own, acknowledge, avow; declare, proclaim, announce, publish, broadcast, advertise

discomfit *syn* EMBARRASS, disconcert, faze, abash, rattle *rel* annoy, vex, irk, bother; perturb, discompose, agitate, upset, disturb; check, arrest, interrupt

discommode *syn* INCONVENIENCE, incommode, trouble *rel* disturb, perturb, upset, fluster, flurry, discompose; vex, irk, bother, annoy

discompose · to excite one so as to destroy one's capacity for clear or collected thought or prompt action *syn* disquiet, disturb, perturb, agitate, upset, fluster, flurry *rel* discomfit, disconcert, rattle, faze, embarrass; vex, irk, bother, annoy; worry, harass, plague, pester

disconcert *syn* EMBARRASS, rattle, faze, discomfit, abash *rel* bewilder, nonplus, perplex, puzzle; discompose, fluster, flurry, disturb, perturb

disconsolate *syn* DOWNCAST, woebegone, dejected, depressed, dispirited *rel* inconsolable, comfortless; sorrowful, woeful; melancholy, doleful

discontinue *syn* STOP, desist, cease, quit *rel* suspend, intermit, stay, defer; arrest, check, interrupt *ant* continue

discord · a state or condition marked by disagreement and lack of harmony *syn* strife, conflict, contention, dissension, difference, variance *rel* incompatibility, incongruity, inconsonance, inconsistency, uncongeniality, discrepancy; antagonism, hostility, enmity, rancor, animosity, antipathy

discordant *syn* INCONSONANT, incongruous, uncongenial, unsympathetic, incompatible, inconsistent, discrepant

discount *syn* DEDUCTION, rebate, abatement

discourage **1** · to weaken the stamina, interest, or zeal of *syn* dishearten, dispirit, deject *rel* depress, weigh; try, afflict; vex, bother, irk *ant* encourage **2** *syn* DISSUADE, deter, divert *rel* restrain, inhibit; prevent; frighten, scare

discourse *n* · a systematic, serious, and often learned exposition of a subject or topic *syn* treatise, disquisition, dissertation, thesis, monograph *rel* paper, article, essay; speech, lecture, talk, sermon

discourse *vb* • to talk or sometimes write esp. formally and at length upon a subject *syn* expatiate, dilate, descant *rel* discuss, argue, dispute; converse, talk, speak; lecture, harangue, orate, sermonize

discourteous *syn* RUDE, impolite, uncivil, ungracious, ill-mannered *rel* brusque, curt, crusty, gruff, blunt, bluff; boorish, churlish *ant* courteous

discover **1** *syn* REVEAL, disclose, divulge, tell, betray *rel* impart, communicate; declare, announce, publish, advertise, proclaim **2** • to find out something not previously known *syn* ascertain, determine, unearth, learn *rel* discern, observe, perceive, espy

discreet *syn* PRUDENT, forethoughtful, foresighted, provident *rel* cautious, circumspect, wary; politic, diplomatic, suave *ant* indiscreet

discrepant *syn* INCONSONANT, inconsistent, discordant, incompatible, incongruous, uncongenial, unsympathetic *rel* divergent, disparate, different, diverse *ant* identical (*as accounts, explanations*)

discrete *syn* DISTINCT, separate, several *rel* individual, distinctive, peculiar

discretion *syn* PRUDENCE, forethought, foresight, providence *rel* caution, circumspection, wariness; judgment, sense, wisdom, gumption *ant* indiscretion

discriminate *syn* DISTINGUISH, differentiate, demarcate *rel* compare, contrast, collate, separate, divide, part; detach, disengage *ant* confound

discrimination *syn* DISCERNMENT, penetration, insight, perception, acumen *rel* wisdom, judgment, sense; subtlety, logicalness, logic

discuss • to exchange views about something in order to arrive at the truth or to convince others *syn* argue, debate, dispute, agitate *rel* explain, expound, interpret, elucidate, explicate; discourse, expatiate, dilate, descant

disdain *n, syn* DESPITE, scorn, contempt *rel* aversion, antipathy; insolence, superciliousness, arrogance

disdain *vb, syn* DESPISE, scorn, scout, contemn *rel* spurn, repudiate, reject *ant* favor; admit

disdainful *syn* PROUD, supercilious, overbearing, insolent, arrogant, lordly, haughty *rel* spurning, repudiating, rejecting; scorning, despising, contemning, scouting; averse, antipathetic, unsympathetic

disease • an impairment of the normal state of the living body that interferes with normal bodily functions *syn* disorder, condition, affection, ailment, malady, complaint, distemper, syndrome

diseased *syn* UNWHOLESOME, morbid, sickly, pathological

disembarrass *syn* EXTRICATE, disencumber, disentangle, untangle *rel* release, free, liberate; relieve; disengage, detach

disencumber *syn* EXTRICATE, disembarrass, disentangle, untangle *rel* relieve, alleviate, lighten; disengage, detach; liberate, release, free

disengage *syn* DETACH, abstract *rel* disembarrass, disencumber, disentangle, untangle, extricate; release, liberate, free; disconnect, disjoin, dissociate, disunite *ant* engage

disentangle *syn* EXTRICATE, untangle, disembarrass, disencumber *rel* disengage, detach; separate, part, sever, sunder; free, release, liberate *ant* entangle

disfavor *syn* DISLIKE, distaste, aversion *rel* disapproval, deprecation; distrust, mistrust

disfigure *syn* DEFACE, *rel* mangle, batter, maim, mutilate; deform, distort, contort, warp; injure, damage, mar, impair *ant* adorn

disgorge *syn* BELCH, burp, vomit, regurgitate, spew, throw up

disgrace • the state of suffering loss of esteem and of enduring reproach *syn* dishonor, disrepute, shame, infamy, ignominy, opprobrium, obloquy, odium *rel* degradation, debasement, abasement, humbling, humiliation; stigma, brand, blot, stain *ant* respect, esteem

disguise • to alter so as to hide the true appearance or character of *syn* cloak, mask, dissemble, camouflage *rel* conceal, hide; misrepresent, belie, falsify, garble; assume, pretend, feign, counterfeit, sham, simulate, affect

disgust • to arouse an extreme distaste in *syn* sicken, nauseate *rel* revolt, repulse, offend *ant* charm

dish *syn* DIP, ladle, spoon, bail, scoop

dishearten *syn* DISCOURAGE, dispirit, deject *rel* depress, weigh; despair, despond *ant* hearten

disheveled *syn* SLIPSHOD, unkempt, sloppy, slovenly *rel* negligent, neglectful, lax, slack, remiss; slatternly, blowsy, frowzy, dowdy

dishonest • unworthy of trust or belief *syn* DECEITFUL, mendacious, lying, untruthful *rel* crooked, devious, oblique; false, faithless, perfidious; cheating, cozening, defrauding, swindling *ant* honest

dishonor *syn* DISGRACE, disrepute, shame, infamy, ignominy, opprobrium, obloquy, odium *rel* humiliation, humbling, debasement, degradation, abasement; stigma, brand, blot, stain *ant* honor

disillusioned *syn* SOPHISTICATED, worldly-wise, worldly, blasé *rel* undeceived; disenchanted

disinclined • lacking the will or the desire to do something *syn* indisposed, hesitant, reluctant, loath, averse *rel* antipathetic, unsympathetic; opposing, resisting; balking, shying, boggling, sticking, stickling; objecting, protesting

disinfect *syn* STERILIZE, sanitize, fumigate *ant* infect

disintegrate *syn* DECAY, crumble, decompose, rot, putrefy, spoil *rel* deliquesce; scatter, disperse, dissipate; break down, resolve, analyze, dissect *ant* integrate

disinterested *syn* INDIFFERENT, uninterested, detached, aloof, unconcerned, incurious *rel* dispassionate, unbiased, impartial, fair, just; neutral, negative *ant* interested; prejudiced, biased

dislike • a feeling of aversion or disapproval *syn* distaste, aversion, disfavor *rel* hate, hatred, detestation; disapproval, deprecation *ant* liking

disloyal *syn* FAITHLESS, false, perfidious, traitorous, treacherous *rel* disaffected, estranged, alienated; inconstant, fickle, unstable *ant* loyal

dismal • devoid of all that makes for cheer or comfort *syn* dreary, cheerless, dispiriting, bleak, desolate *rel* murky, gloomy, dark; forlorn, hopeless; barren, bare

dismantle *syn* STRIP, divest, denude, bare

dismay *vb* • to unnerve and check by arousing fear, apprehension, or aversion *syn* appall, horrify, daunt *rel* perplex, confound, bewilder, nonplus, dumbfound, mystify, puzzle; disconcert, rattle, faze, abash, discomfit, embarrass; alarm, frighten, terrify *ant* cheer

dismay *n*, *syn* FEAR, alarm, consternation, panic, dread, fright, terror, horror, trepidation *rel* perturbing, perturbation, agitation, disquieting, disquietude, discomposing, discomposure, upsetting, upset; apprehension, foreboding

dismiss 1 • to let go from one's employ or service *syn* discharge, cashier, drop, sack, fire, bounce 2 *syn* EJECT, oust, expel, evict *rel* discard, cast, shed, slough; spurn, repudiate, reject, refuse; scorn, scout

dismount *syn* DESCEND, alight *rel* mount

disorder *vb* • to undo the fixed or proper order of something *syn* derange, disarrange, disorganize, unsettle, disturb *rel* order

disorder *n* 1 *syn* CONFUSION, disarray, clutter, jumble, chaos, snarl, muddle *rel* derangement, disarrangement, disorganization, disturbance, unsettlement; anarchy, chaos, lawlessness *ant* order 2 *syn* DISEASE, condition, affection, ailment, malady, complaint, distemper, syndrome

disorganize *syn* DISORDER, disturb, unsettle, derange, disarrange *rel* organize

disown *syn* DISCLAIM, disavow, repudiate, disallow *rel* reject, spurn, refuse, decline *ant* own

disparage *syn* DECRY, depreciate, derogate, detract, belittle, minimize *rel* asperse, malign, traduce, defame, slander, libel; deprecate, disapprove *ant* applaud

disparaging *syn* DEROGATORY, depreciatory, depreciative, slighting, pejorative *rel* belittling, decrying, minimizing; underestimating, undervaluing, underrating

disparate *syn* DIFFERENT, diverse, divergent, various *rel* inconsonant, incompatible, incongruous, discrepant, discordant, inconsistent; distinct, separate *ant* comparable, analogous

dispassionate *syn* FAIR, unbiased, impartial, objective, uncolored, just, equitable *rel* disinterested, detached, aloof, indifferent; cool, collected, composed; candid, open, frank *ant* passionate; intemperate

dispatch *vb* 1 *syn* SEND, forward, transmit, remit, route, ship *rel* hasten, quicken, speed 2 *syn* KILL, slay, murder, assassinate, execute

dispatch *n* 1 *syn* HASTE, speed, expedition, hurry *rel* celerity, alacrity, legerity; quickness, fleetness, swiftness, rapidity; diligence *ant* delay 2 *syn* LETTER, message, note, epistle, report, memorandum, missive

dispel *syn* SCATTER, dissipate, disperse *rel* expel, eject, oust, dismiss; disintegrate, crumble, decay

dispense *syn* DISTRIBUTE, divide, deal, dole *rel* allot, assign, apportion, allocate; portion, parcel, ration, prorate 2 *syn* ADMINISTER

disperse *syn* SCATTER, dissipate, dispel *rel* separate, part, divide; dismiss, discharge *ant* assemble, congregate; collect

dispirit *syn* DISCOURAGE, dishearten, deject *rel* depress, weigh *ant* inspirit

dispirited *syn* DOWNCAST, depressed, dejected, disconsolate, woebegone *rel* sad, melancholy; gloomy, glum, morose, sullen; discouraged, disheartened *ant* high-spirited

dispiriting *syn* DISMAL, dreary, cheerless, bleak, desolate *rel* disheartening, discouraging, dejecting; depressing, oppressing, oppressive *ant* inspiriting

displace *syn* REPLACE, supplant, supersede *rel* transpose, reverse, invert; shift, remove, transfer, move; derange, disarrange, disorder; eject, oust, expel, dismiss

display *vb, syn* SHOW, exhibit, expose, parade, flaunt *rel* manifest, evidence, evince, demonstrate; reveal, disclose, discover

display *n* • a striking or spectacular

show or exhibition for the sake of effect *syn* parade, array, pomp *rel* ostentatiousness, ostentation, pretentiousness, pretension, showiness, show

disport *n, syn* PLAY, sport, frolic, rollick, romp, gambol *rel* recreation, diversion, amusement, entertainment; merriment, jollity

disport *vb, syn* PLAY, sport, frolic, rollick, romp, gambol *rel* divert, amuse, recreate, entertain

disposal · the act or the power of disposing of something *syn* disposition *rel* destroying, destruction, demolishing, demolition

dispose *syn* INCLINE, predispose, bias *rel* influence, affect, sway

disposition **1** *syn* DISPOSAL *rel* administering, administration, dispensing, dispensation; management, direction, controlling, control, conducting, conduct; arrangement, ordering **2** · the prevailing and dominant quality or qualities which distinguish or identify a person or group *syn* temperament, temper, complexion, character, personality, individuality

disprove · to show by presenting evidence that something is not true *syn* refute, confute, rebut, controvert *rel* negative, traverse, impugn, contravene *ant* prove, demonstrate

disputation *syn* ARGUMENTATION, debate, forensic, dialectic *rel* argument, dispute, controversy

dispute *vb, syn* DISCUSS, argue, debate, agitate *ant* concede

dispute *n, syn* ARGUMENT, controversy *rel* argumentation, disputation, debate, forensic, dialectic; contention, dissension, strife, discord, conflict

disquiet *syn* DISCOMPOSE, disturb, agitate, perturb, upset, fluster, flurry *rel* annoy, vex, irk, bother; worry, harass, harry; trouble, distress *ant* tranquilize, soothe

disquisition *syn* DISCOURSE, dissertation, thesis, treatise, monograph *rel* paper, essay, article; inquiry, investigation

disrate *syn* DEGRADE, demote, reduce, declass

disregard *syn* NEGLECT, ignore, overlook, slight, forget, omit

disrepute *syn* DISGRACE, dishonor, shame, infamy, ignominy, opprobrium, obloquy, odium *rel* repute

dissect *syn* ANALYZE, break down, resolve *rel* scrutinize, examine, inspect; pierce, penetrate, probe

dissection *syn* ANALYSIS, breakdown, resolution

dissemble *syn* DISGUISE, mask, cloak, camouflage *rel* simulate, feign, counterfeit, sham, pretend, assume, affect *ant* betray

disseminate *syn* SPREAD, circulate, diffuse, propagate, radiate *rel* scatter, disperse; distribute, dispense, divide; share, participate

dissension *syn* DISCORD, difference, variance, strife, conflict, contention *rel* altercation, wrangle, quarrel, bickering; argument, dispute, controversy *ant* accord; comity

dissent *syn* DIFFER, vary, disagree *rel* object, protest; demur, balk, boggle, shy, stickle *ant* concur; assent; consent

dissenter *syn* HERETIC, nonconformist, sectarian, sectary, schismatic

dissertation *syn* DISCOURSE, disquisition, thesis, treatise, monograph *rel* exposition; argumentation, disputation; article, paper, essay

dissimilarity · lack of agreement or correspondence or an instance of this *syn* unlikeness, difference, divergence, divergency, distinction *rel* diversity, disparity; discrepancy, discordance, inconsonance *ant* similarity

dissimulation *syn* DECEIT, duplicity, cunning, guile *rel* dissembling, cloaking, masking, disguising, camouflaging; hiding, concealing, secreting; pretending, pretense, feigning, shamming; hypocrisy, pharisaism, sanctimony

dissipate 1 *syn* SCATTER, dispel, disperse *rel* disintegrate, crumble; separate, part, divide; deliquesce, melt *ant* accumulate; absorb; concentrate 2 *syn* WASTE, squander, fritter, consume *rel* spend, expend, disburse; scatter, disperse; vanish, evanesce, disappear, evaporate

dissolute *syn* ABANDONED, profligate, reprobate *rel* licentious, libertine, wanton, lewd; inebriated, intoxicated, drunken, drunk; debauched, depraved, corrupt, debased, perverted

dissuade • to turn one aside from a purpose, a project, or a plan *syn* deter, discourage, divert *rel* advise, counsel; urge, exhort, prick *ant* persuade

distant • not close in space, time, or relationship *syn* far, faraway, far-off, remote, removed

distaste *syn* DISLIKE, aversion, disfavor *rel* repugnance, repulsion, abhorrence; antipathy, hostility, enmity *ant* taste

distasteful *syn* REPUGNANT, obnoxious, repellent, abhorrent, invidious *rel* hateful, odious, detestable, abominable; offensive, loathsome, repulsive, repugnant, revolting *ant* agreeable; palatable

distemper *syn* DISEASE, complaint, syndrome, malady, ailment, disorder, condition, affection

distend *syn* EXPAND, swell, dilate, inflate, amplify *rel* enlarge, increase, augment; extend, lengthen *ant* constrict

distinct 1 • capable of being distinguished as differing *syn* separate, several, discrete *rel* individual, distinctive, peculiar; single, sole, separate, particular; special, especial; different, diverse, disparate, divergent 2 *syn* EVIDENT, manifest, patent, obvious, apparent, palpable, plain, clear *rel* defined, prescribed; explicit, definite, express, specific, categorical; perspicuous, clear, lucid; clear-cut, incisive, trenchant *ant* indistinct; nebulous

distinction *syn* DISSIMILARITY, difference, divergence, divergency, unlikeness *rel* resemblance

distinctive *syn* CHARACTERISTIC, peculiar, individual *rel* special, particular, specific, especial; unique, separate, single; distinct, several, discrete *ant* typical

distinguish 1 • to recognize the differences between *syn* differentiate, discriminate, demarcate *rel* separate, part, divide; detach, disengage *ant* confound 2 *syn* CHARACTERIZE, mark, qualify *rel* individualize, peculiarize

distort *syn* DEFORM, contort, warp *rel* twist, bend, curve; disfigure, deface; injure, damage, mar, impair; misinterpret, misconstrue

distract *syn* PUZZLE, bewilder, nonplus, confound, dumbfound, mystify, perplex *rel* confuse, muddle, addle, fuddle, befuddle; baffle, balk, frustrate; agitate, upset, fluster, flurry, perturb, discompose *ant* collect (*one's thoughts, one's powers*)

distraught *syn* ABSTRACTED, absentminded, absent, preoccupied *rel* distracted, bewildered, nonplused; muddled, addled, confused; agitated, perturbed, discomposed, flustered *ant* collected

distress *n* • the state of being in great trouble or in mental or physical anguish *syn* suffering, misery, agony, dolor, passion *rel* affliction, trial, tribulation; sorrow, grief, anguish, woe, heartbreak; strait, pass, pinch, exigency; hardship, difficulty, rigor, vicissitude; pain, pang, ache

distress *vb, syn* TROUBLE, ail *rel*

afflict, try, torment, torture, rack; worry, annoy, harass, harry, plague, pester; depress, oppress, weigh

distribute • to give out, usu. in shares, to each member of a group *syn* dispense, divide, deal, dole *rel* apportion, allot, allocate, assign; ration, portion, parcel, prorate administer, *ant* collect; amass

district *syn* LOCALITY, vicinity, neighborhood *rel* area, tract, region, zone, belt; section, sector, division, parcel; field, province, territory, sphere

distrust *vb* • to lack trust or confidence in *syn* mistrust, doubt, misdoubt, suspect

distrust *n* • a lack of trust or confidence *syn* mistrust *rel* doubt, uncertainty, dubiety, dubiosity, suspicion; apprehension, foreboding, misgiving, presentiment

disturb **1** *syn* DISORDER, unsettle, derange, disarrange, disorganize *rel* displace, replace; shift, remove, move; arrest, interrupt, check; meddle, intermeddle, interfere, tamper **2** *syn* DISCOMPOSE, perturb, upset, disquiet, agitate, fluster, flurry *rel* frighten, alarm, terrify, scare; perplex, puzzle, bewilder, distract; discomfit, rattle, faze, disconcert; discommode, incommode, trouble, inconvenience

dither *syn* SHAKE, tremble, quake, quiver, shiver, quaver, wobble, teeter, shimmy, shudder, totter

diurnal *syn* DAILY, quotidian

divagation *syn* DIGRESSION, episode, excursus

dive *syn* PLUNGE, pitch *rel* leap, jump, spring, bound; move, drive, impel; push, propel

diverge *syn* SWERVE, veer, deviate, depart, digress *rel* differ, disagree, vary; divide, part, separate *ant* converge; conform

divergence **1** *syn* DEVIATION, deflection, aberration *rel* division, separation, parting; differing, disagreeing, varying *ant* convergence **2** *syn* DISSIMILARITY, divergency, difference, unlikeness, distinction *rel* diversity, variety *ant* conformity, correspondence

divergency *syn* DISSIMILARITY, divergence, difference, unlikeness, distinction *rel, ant* see DIVERGENCE 2

divergent *syn* DIFFERENT, diverse, disparate, various *rel* opposite, contradictory, contrary, antithetical *ant* convergent

divers *syn* MANY, several, sundry, various, numerous, multifarious

diverse *syn* DIFFERENT, divergent, disparate, various *rel* contrasted, contrasting; contrary, opposite, contradictory; distinct, separate *ant* identical, selfsame

diversion *syn* AMUSEMENT, recreation, entertainment *rel* play, sport, disport; levity, frivolity

diversity *syn* VARIETY *rel* divergence, divergency, difference, dissimilarity, unlikeness, distinction; multifariousness *ant* uniformity; identity

divert **1** *syn* TURN, deflect, avert, sheer *rel* bend, curve, twist; deviate, digress, diverge, swerve, veer; change, alter, modify **2** *syn* AMUSE, entertain, recreate *rel* beguile, while, wile, fleet; regale, delight, gladden, tickle, please **3** *syn* DISSUADE, deter, discourage *rel* detach, disengage, abstract

divest *syn* STRIP, denude, bare, dismantle *ant* invest, vest (*in robes of office, with power or authority*); apparel, clothe

divide **1** *syn* SEPARATE, part, sever, sunder, divorce *rel* cleave, split, rend, rive, tear; cut, carve, chop *ant* unite **2** *syn* DISTRIBUTE, dispense, deal, dole *rel* apportion, portion, prorate, ration, parcel; share, participate, partake; allot, assign, allocate

divine *adj, syn* HOLY, sacred, spiritual, religious, blessed

divine *vb, syn* FORESEE, foreknow, apprehend, anticipate *rel* discern, perceive, descry; predict, prophesy, prognosticate, presage, foretell

division *syn* PART, section, segment, sector, portion, piece, detail, member, fraction, fragment, parcel

divorce *syn* SEPARATE, sever, sunder, part, divide *rel* alienate, estrange, wean, disaffect

divulge *syn* REVEAL, tell, disclose, betray, discover *rel* impart, communicate; announce, declare, publish, advertise, proclaim; blab, tattle, gossip

dizzy *syn* GIDDY, vertiginous, swimming, dazzled *rel* reeling, whirling; confounded, bewildered, puzzled

docile *syn* OBEDIENT, biddable, tractable, amenable *rel* compliant, acquiescent; pliant, pliable, adaptable; yielding, submitting, submissive *ant* indocile; unruly, ungovernable

dock *syn* WHARF, pier, quay, slip, berth, jetty, levee

doctor *syn* ADULTERATE, sophisticate, load, weight

doctrinaire *syn* DICTATORIAL, dogmatic, magisterial, oracular, authoritarian

doctrine • a principle accepted as valid and authoritative *syn* dogma, tenet *rel* teaching, instruction; principle, fundamental

document • something preserved and serving as evidence (as of an event, a situation, or the culture of the period) *syn* monument, record, archive *rel* evidence, testimony

dodge • to avoid or evade by some maneuver or shift *syn* parry, sidestep, duck, shirk, fence, malinger *rel* evade, avoid, elude, escape; slide, slip *ant* face

dogged *syn* OBSTINATE, pertinacious, mulish, stubborn, stiff-necked, pigheaded, bullheaded *rel* determined, resolved, decided; tenacious; persevering, persistent; resolute, steadfast *ant* faltering

dogma *syn* DOCTRINE, tenet *rel* belief, conviction, persuasion, view; principle, fundamental

dogmatic *syn* DICTATORIAL, magisterial, doctrinaire, oracular, authoritarian *rel* peremptory, masterful, imperative, imperious, domineering

doldrums *syn* TEDIUM, boredom, ennui *rel* dejection, depression, gloom, blues, dumps *ant* spirits, high spirits

dole *n, syn* RATION, allowance, pittance *rel* apportioning, apportionment, parceling, parcel, portioning, portion; sharing, share

dole *vb, syn* DISTRIBUTE, dispense, deal, divide *rel* apportion, ration, portion, parcel, prorate; bestow, confer, present, give

doleful *syn* MELANCHOLY, lugubrious, dolorous, plaintive, rueful *rel* mourning, mournful, sorrowing, sorrowful, grieving; piteous, pitiful *ant* cheerful, cheery

dolor *syn* DISTRESS, agony, suffering, passion, misery *rel* anguish, woe, sorrow, grief; tribulation, trial, affliction, cross, visitation *ant* beatitude, blessedness

dolorous *syn* MELANCHOLY, doleful, plaintive, lugubrious, rueful *rel, ant* see DOLEFUL

domain *syn* FIELD, sphere, province, territory, bailiwick *rel* area, region, zone; district, locality; jurisdiction, dominion

domicile *syn* HABITATION, dwelling, abode, residence, house, home

dominant • superior to all others in power, influence, position, or rank *syn* predominant, paramount, preponderant, preponderating, sovereign *rel* prevailing, prevalent; preeminent, supreme, transcendent, surpassing; outstanding, salient, signal; governing, ruling *ant* subordinate

domineering *syn* MASTERFUL, imperious, imperative, peremptory *rel* arrogant, overbearing, lordly, insolent; magisterial, dictatorial *ant* subservient

dominion *syn* POWER, control, command, sway, authority, jurisdiction *rel* ascendancy, supremacy; sovereignty

donate *syn* GIVE, present, bestow, confer, afford *rel* grant, accord, award

donation · a gift of money or its equivalent for a charitable, philanthropic, or humanitarian object *syn* benefaction, contribution, alms *rel* grant, subvention, appropriation, subsidy

doom *n, syn* FATE, destiny, lot, portion

doom *vb, syn* SENTENCE, damn, condemn, proscribe

door · an entrance to a place *syn* gate, portal, postern, doorway, gateway *rel* entrance, entry, entrée, ingress, access

doorway *syn* DOOR, portal, postern, gate, gateway

dormant **1** *syn* LATENT, quiescent, abeyant, potential *rel* inactive, inert, passive, idle *ant* active, live **2** *syn* PRONE, couchant, recumbent, supine, prostrate

dormer *syn* WINDOW, casement, oriel

dotage *syn* AGE, senility, senescence *ant* infancy

dote *syn* LIKE, love, relish, enjoy, fancy *ant* loathe

doting *syn* LOVING, fond, devoted, affectionate *rel* infatuated, enamored; fatuous, foolish, silly, asinine, simple

double *syn* SUBSTITUTE, understudy, stand-in, supply, locum tenens, alternate, pinch hitter

double-cross *syn* DECEIVE, delude, betray, beguile, mislead

double-dealing *syn* DECEPTION, chicanery, chicane, trickery, fraud *rel* duplicity, dissimulation, deceit, guile, cunning

double entendre *syn* AMBIGUITY, equivocation, tergiversation

doubt *n, syn* UNCERTAINTY, skepticism, suspicion, mistrust, dubiety, dubiosity *rel* dubiousness, doubtfulness, questionableness; incredulity, unbelief, disbelief *ant* certitude; confidence

doubt *vb, syn* DISTRUST, mistrust, misdoubt, suspect

doubtful · not affording assurance of the worth, soundness, success, or certainty of something or someone *syn* dubious, problematic, questionable *rel* distrusting, distrustful, mistrusting, mistrustful; fearful, apprehensive, afraid *ant* cocksure, positive

doughty *syn* BRAVE, courageous, unafraid, fearless, intrepid, valiant, valorous, dauntless, undaunted, bold, audacious *rel* venturesome, adventurous, daring

dour *syn* SULLEN, saturnine, glum, gloomy, morose, surly, sulky, crabbed *rel* severe, stern, austere; rigorous, strict, rigid; grim, implacable

dowdy *syn* SLATTERNLY, frowzy, blowsy *rel* slovenly, slipshod, unkempt, disheveled, sloppy *ant* smart (*in dress, appearance*)

dower · to furnish or provide with a gift *syn* endow, endue *rel* furnish, equip, outfit, appoint, accouter

downcast · very low in spirits *syn* dispirited, dejected, depressed, disconsolate, woebegone *rel* weighed down, oppressed; distressed, troubled; despondent, forlorn *ant* elated

downright *syn* FORTHRIGHT *rel* blunt, bluff, brusque, curt; candid, plain, open, frank; straightforward, aboveboard

doze *syn* SLEEP, drowse, snooze, slumber, nap, catnap

draft *n, syn* SKETCH, outline, diagram, delineation, tracing, plot, blueprint

draft *vb, syn* SKETCH, outline, diagram, delineate, trace, plot, blueprint

drag *syn* PULL, draw, haul, hale, tug, tow

drain *syn* DEPLETE, exhaust, impoverish, bankrupt *rel* sap, undermine, debilitate, weaken

dramatic · of, relating to, or suggestive of plays, or the performance of a play *syn* theatrical, dramaturgic, melodramatic, histrionic

dramaturgic *syn* DRAMATIC, theatrical, histrionic, melodramatic

draw *vb, syn* PULL, drag, tug, tow, haul, hale *rel* bring, fetch; attract, allure; lure, entice; extract, elicit, evoke, educe

draw *n* · an indecisive ending to a contest or competition *syn* tie, stalemate, deadlock, standoff

drawback *syn* DISADVANTAGE, detriment, handicap *rel* evil, ill; inconvenience, trouble; obstruction, hindrance

dread *syn* FEAR, horror, terror, fright, alarm, trepidation, panic, consternation, dismay *rel* apprehension, foreboding, misgiving, presentiment; timidity, timorousness

dreadful *syn* FEARFUL, horrible, horrific, appalling, awful, frightful, terrible, terrific, shocking

dream *syn* FANCY, fantasy, phantasy, phantasm, vision, daydream, nightmare *rel* delusion, illusion, hallucination

dreary **1** *syn* DISMAL, cheerless, dispiriting, bleak, desolate *rel* discouraging, disheartening; barren, bare; forlorn, hopeless **2** *syn* DULL, humdrum, monotonous, pedestrian, stodgy *rel* irksome, tiresome, wearisome, tedious, boring; fatiguing, exhausting, fagging, tiring

dregs *syn* DEPOSIT, sediment, precipitate, lees, grounds

drench *syn* SOAK, saturate, sop, steep, impregnate, waterlog *rel* permeate, pervade, penetrate, impenetrate

dress *vb, syn* CLOTHE, attire, apparel, array, robe *ant* undress

dress *n, syn* CLOTHES, clothing, attire, apparel, raiment

drift *syn* TENDENCY, trend, tenor *rel* flow, stream, current; movement, motion, progression, progress; intention, purpose, end, objective, goal, intent, aim

drill *vb* **1** *syn* PERFORATE, bore, punch, puncture, prick *rel* pierce, penetrate, enter, probe **2** *syn* PRACTICE, exercise *rel* train, discipline, teach, instruct, school; habituate, accustom

drill *n, syn* PRACTICE, exercise

drive *vb, syn* MOVE, impel, actuate *rel* push, shove, propel; compel, force, coerce; incite, instigate

drive *n* **1** *syn* RIDE **2** *syn* VIGOR, vim, spirit, dash, esprit, verve, punch, élan *rel* power, force, energy, strength, might; impetus, momentum, speed, velocity

drivel *syn* NONSENSE, twaddle, bunk, balderdash, poppycock, gobbledygook, trash, rot, bull *rel* gibberish, mummery, abracadabra

droll *syn* LAUGHABLE, risible, comic, comical, funny, ludicrous, ridiculous, farcical *rel* amusing, diverting, entertaining; absurd, preposterous; humorous, witty, facetious

droop · to become literally or figuratively limp through loss of vigor or freshness *syn* wilt, flag, sag *rel* sink, slump, subside, fall, drop; languish; wither, shrivel, wizen

drop **1** *syn* FALL, sink, slump, subside *rel* descend, dismount; lapse, relapse, backslide; slip, slide; expire, elapse *ant* mount **2** *syn* DIS-

MISS, discharge, cashier, sack, fire, bounce

drowse *syn* SLEEP, doze, snooze, slumber, nap, catnap

drowsy *syn* SLEEPY, somnolent, slumberous *rel* comatose, lethargic, sluggish, torpid

drudgery *syn* WORK, toil, travail, labor, grind *rel* exertion, effort, pains, trouble

drug · a substance used by itself or in a mixture for the treatment or in the diagnosis of disease *syn* medicinal, pharmaceutical, biologic, simple *rel* medicine, medicament, medication, remedy, physic, specific, cure

druggist · one who deals in medicinal drugs *syn* pharmacist, apothecary, chemist

drunk · having the faculties impaired by alcohol *syn* drunken, intoxicated, inebriated, tipsy, tight *rel* fuddled, befuddled, confused; maudlin, soppy *ant* sober

drunkard · one who is habitually drunk *syn* inebriate, alcoholic, dipsomaniac, sot, soak, toper, tosspot, tippler *ant* teetotaler

drunken *syn* DRUNK, intoxicated, inebriated, tipsy, tight *rel, ant* see DRUNK

dry *adj* **1** · devoid of moisture *syn* arid *rel* barren, bare, bald; dehydrated, desiccated, dried, parched, baked; drained, depleted, exhausted, impoverished; sapped *ant* wet **2** *syn* SOUR, acid, acidulous, tart *ant* sweet (*wine*)

dry *vb* · to treat or to affect so as to deprive of moisture *syn* desiccate, dehydrate, bake, parch *rel* drain, deplete, exhaust; wither, shrivel, wizen *ant* moisten, wet

dubiety *syn* UNCERTAINTY, dubiosity, doubt, skepticism, suspicion, mistrust *rel* hesitation, hesitancy; wavering, vacillation, faltering *ant* decision

dubiosity *syn* UNCERTAINTY, dubiety, doubt, skepticism, suspicion, mistrust *rel* confusion, muddlement, addlement; wavering, vacillation, faltering, hesitation *ant* decidedness

dubious *syn* DOUBTFUL, questionable, problematic *rel* suspicious, skeptical, mistrustful, uncertain; hesitant, reluctant, disinclined *ant* cocksure; reliable; trustworthy

duck **1** *syn* DIP, immerse, submerge, souse, dunk **2** *syn* DODGE, parry, shirk, sidestep, fence, malinger *rel* avoid, elude, shun, evade, escape; avert, ward, prevent

duct *syn* CHANNEL, canal, conduit, aqueduct

ductile *syn* PLASTIC, pliable, pliant, malleable, adaptable *rel* tractable, amenable; responsive; yielding, submitting; fluid, liquid; flexible, elastic, resilient

dude *syn* FOP, dandy, beau, coxcomb, exquisite, buck

dudgeon *syn* OFFENSE, umbrage, huff, pique, resentment *rel* anger, indignation, wrath, rage, fury, ire; temper, humor, mood

due *adj* · being in accordance with what is just and appropriate *syn* rightful, condign *rel* appropriate, meet, suitable, fit, fitting, proper; right, good; just, fair, equitable

due *n* · what is justly owed to a person (sometimes a thing), esp. as a recompense or compensation *syn* desert, merit *rel* compensation, recompensing, recompense, repayment, satisfaction, payment; retribution, retaliation, reprisal, vengeance, revenge; reward, meed, guerdon

dulcet *syn* SWEET, engaging, winning, winsome *rel* soft, gentle, mild, balmy, lenient; serene, calm, tranquil; harmonious, consonant, accordant, concordant *ant* grating

dull **1** *syn* STUPID, slow, dumb, dense, crass *rel* lethargic, sluggish, comatose; phlegmatic, stolid, impassive, apathetic; backward; retarded *ant* clever, bright **2** • lacking sharpness of edge or point *syn* blunt, obtuse *ant* sharp; poignant (*sensation, feeling, reaction*) **3** • being so unvaried and uninteresting as to provoke boredom or tedium *syn* humdrum, dreary, monotonous, pedestrian, stodgy *rel* irksome, tiresome, wearisome, tedious, boring; prosy, prosaic, matter-of-fact *ant* lively

dumb 1 • lacking the power to speak *syn* mute, speechless, inarticulate **2** *syn* STUPID, dull, slow, dense, crass *rel ant* articulate

dumbfound *syn* PUZZLE, confound, nonplus, bewilder, distract, mystify, perplex *rel* astound, flabbergast, amaze, astonish, surprise; confuse, muddle, addle, fuddle; disconcert, rattle, faze, discomfit

dumps *syn* SADNESS, dejection, gloom, blues, depression, melancholy, melancholia *rel* despondency, forlornness, hopelessness, despair; doldrums, ennui, boredom, tedium

dumpy *syn* STOCKY, thickset, thick, chunky, stubby, squat

dunk *syn* DIP, immerse, souse, submerge, duck *rel* soak, saturate, sop

dupe • mean to delude by underhanded means or methods *syn* gull, befool, trick, hoax, hoodwink, bamboozle *rel* deceive, beguile, delude, mislead, double-cross, betray; cheat, cozen, defraud, overreach; outwit, baffle, circumvent

duplicate *syn* REPRODUCTION, facsimile, copy, carbon copy, transcript, replica *rel* counterpart, parallel, analogue

duplicity *syn* DECEIT, dissimulation, cunning, guile *rel* double-dealing, chicanery, chicane, trickery, deception, fraud; treacherousness, treachery, perfidiousness, perfidy, faithlessness

durable *syn* LASTING, perdurable, permanent, stable, perpetual *rel* enduring, abiding, persisting; strong, stout, tenacious

duress *syn* FORCE, constraint, coercion, compulsion, violence, restraint

dusky *syn* DARK, dim, obscure, murky, gloomy

duty 1 *syn* OBLIGATION *rel* responsibility, accountability, amenability, answerability, liability **2** *syn* FUNCTION, office, province *rel* concern, business, affair **3** *syn* TASK, assignment, job, stint, chore *rel* work, business, employment, occupation, calling; trade, craft, art, profession

dwarf • an individual and usu. a person of very small size *syn* pygmy, midget, manikin, homunculus, runt

dwell *syn* RESIDE, live, lodge, sojourn, stay, put up, stop

dwelling *syn* HABITATION, abode, residence, domicile, home, house

dwindle *syn* DECREASE, diminish, lessen, reduce, *rel* wane, ebb, abate, subside; attenuate, extenuate, thin; moderate; disappear

dynamic *syn* ACTIVE, live, operative *rel* potent, forceful, forcible, powerful; intense, vehement, fierce, exquisite, violent; vitalizing, energizing, activating

E

each *adj, syn* ALL, every

each *adv* • by, for, or to every one of the many *syn* apiece, severally, individually, respectively

eager • moved by a strong and urgent desire or interest *syn* avid, keen, anxious, agog, athirst *rel* desiring, coveting, craving; longing, yearning, hungering, thirsting; impatient, restless, restive *ant* listless

early • at or nearly at the beginning of a specified or implied period of time *syn* soon, beforehand, betimes *ant* late

earn *syn* DESERVE, merit, rate *rel* gain, win, get

earnest *adj, syn* SERIOUS, solemn, grave, somber, sober, sedate, staid *rel* zealous, enthusiastic, passionate; diligent, busy, industrious, assiduous, sedulous; sincere, wholehearted, whole-souled *ant* frivolous

earnest *n, syn* PLEDGE, token, pawn, hostage

earsplitting *syn* LOUD, stentorian, hoarse, raucous, strident, stertorous

earth • the entire area or extent of space in which human beings think of themselves as living and acting *syn* world, globe, planet *rel* universe, cosmos, macrocosm

earthly • of, belonging to, or characteristic of the earth or life on earth *syn* terrestrial, earthy, mundane, worldly, sublunary *rel* temporal, profane, secular; material, physical, corporeal

earthy *syn* EARTHLY, mundane, worldly, terrestrial, sublunary *rel* material, physical, corporeal; fleshly, carnal, sensual; gross, coarse

ease **1** *syn* REST, comfort, relaxation, repose, leisure *rel* inactivity, idleness, inertness, passiveness, supineness; tranquillity, serenity, placidity, calmness, peacefulness **2** *syn* READINESS, facility, dexterity *rel* effortlessness, smoothness, easiness; grace, elegance; expertness, adeptness, skillfulness, proficiency; deftness, adroitness *ant* effort

easy **1** *syn* COMFORTABLE, restful, cozy, snug *rel* soft, lenient, gentle; commodious, spacious; calm, tranquil, serene, placid; unconstrained, spontaneous *ant* disquieting, disquieted **2** • causing or involving little or no difficulty *syn* facile, simple, light, effortless, smooth *ant* hard

eat • to take food into the stomach through the mouth *syn* swallow, ingest, devour, consume *rel* bite, champ, gnaw

ebb *syn* ABATE, subside, wane *rel* dwindle, diminish, decrease, lessen; recede, retrograde, retreat *ant* flow

eccentric *syn* STRANGE, erratic, odd, queer, peculiar, singular, unique, quaint, outlandish, curious *rel* abnormal, atypical, aberrant; irregular, anomalous, unnatural; exceptional, exceptionable; fantastic, bizarre, grotesque

eccentricity • an act, a practice, or a characteristic that impresses the observer as strange or singular *syn* idiosyncrasy *rel* deviation, aberration, divergence; peculiarity, oddity, queerness, singularity; freak, conceit, vagary, crotchet, caprice, fancy, whim, whimsy

echelon *syn* LINE, row, rank, file, tier

éclat *syn* FAME, renown, glory, celebrity, notoriety, repute, reputation, honor *rel* prominence, conspicuousness, remarkableness, noticeableness; illustriousness, luster, eminence

eclipse *syn* OBSCURE, dim, bedim, darken, cloud, becloud, fog, befog, obfuscate *rel* hide, conceal, screen; cloak, mask, camouflage

economical *syn* SPARING, frugal, thrifty *rel* prudent, provident; close, cheeseparing, parsimonious, penurious, stingy *ant* extravagant

ecstasy • a feeling or a state of intense, sometimes excessive or extreme, mental and emotional exaltation *syn* rapture, transport *rel* bliss, beatitude, blessedness, felicity, happiness; joy, delectation, delight, pleasure; inspiration, fury, frenzy, afflatus

ecumenical *syn* UNIVERSAL, cosmic, catholic, cosmopolitan *ant* provincial; diocesan

eddy *n* • a swirling mass esp. of water *syn* whirlpool, maelstrom, vortex

eddy *vb, syn* TURN, rotate, gyrate, circle, spin, whirl, revolve, twirl, wheel, swirl, pirouette

edge **1** *syn* BORDER, verge, rim, brink, margin, brim *rel* limit, end, bound, confine; circumference, periphery, compass **2** *syn* ADVANTAGE, odds, handicap, allowance

edifice *syn* BUILDING, structure, pile

edit • to prepare material for publication *syn* compile, revise, redact, rewrite, adapt *rel* make, fabricate, fashion, form

edition • the total number of copies of the same work printed during a stretch of time *syn* impression, reprinting, printing, reissue

educate *syn* TEACH, train, discipline, school, instruct

educe • to bring or draw out what is hidden, latent, or reserved *syn* evoke, elicit, extract, extort *rel* draw, drag, pull; produce, bear, yield, turn out; summon, call

eerie *syn* WEIRD, uncanny *rel* fantastic, bizarre, grotesque; mysterious, inscrutable, arcane; fearful, awful, dreadful, horrific; strange, odd, queer, curious, peculiar

efface *syn* ERASE, obliterate, expunge, blot out, delete, cancel *rel* remove, move, shift; eradicate, extirpate, wipe out; eliminate, exclude, rule out

effect *n* **1** • a condition, situation, or occurrence, ascribable to a cause *syn* result, consequence, upshot, aftereffect, aftermath, sequel, issue, outcome, event *ant* cause **2** *pl* **effects** *syn* POSSESSIONS, belongings, means, resources, assets

effect *vb, syn* PERFORM, accomplish, achieve, execute, discharge, fulfill *rel* reach, attain, achieve, compass, gain; finish, complete, conclude, end, terminate, close; implement, enforce; realize, actualize

effective • producing or capable of producing a result *syn* effectual, efficient, efficacious *rel* forceful, forcible, potent, powerful; producing, productive, bearing; telling, cogent, convincing, compelling; operative, active, dynamic *ant* ineffective; futile

effectual *syn* EFFECTIVE, efficacious, efficient *rel* effecting, accomplishing, achieving, fulfilling; operative, dynamic, active; decisive, determinative, conclusive *ant* ineffectual; fruitless

effervescent *syn* ELASTIC, volatile, buoyant, expansive, resilient *rel* lively, vivacious, sprightly, gay, animated; hilarious, jolly, gleeful, mirthful *ant* subdued

efficacious *syn* EFFECTIVE, effectual, efficient *rel* potent, powerful, puissant; cogent, telling, sound, convincing, compelling *ant* inefficacious; powerless

efficient *syn* EFFECTIVE, effectual, efficacious *rel* competent, qualified, able, capable; expert, skillful, skilled, proficient, adept, masterly *ant* inefficient

effort • the active use or expenditure of physical or mental power to produce a desired result *syn* exertion, pains, trouble *rel* work, labor, toil, travail; energy, force, power, might, puissance; endeavor, essay *ant* ease

effortless *syn* EASY, smooth, facile, simple, light *rel* proficient, skilled, skillful, expert, adept, masterly *ant* painstaking

effrontery *syn* TEMERITY, audacity, hardihood, nerve, cheek, gall *rel* impudence, brazenness, brashness; impertinence, intrusiveness, officiousness

effulgent *syn* BRIGHT, radiant, luminous, brilliant, lustrous, refulgent, beaming, lambent, lucent, incandescent *rel* flaming, blazing, glowing, flaring; flashing, gleaming; resplendent, splendid, glorious

egg *syn* URGE, exhort, goad, spur, prod, prick, sic *rel* stimulate, excite, provoke, pique; incite, instigate; rally, arouse, rouse, stir

egoism *syn* CONCEIT, egotism, amour propre, self-love, self-esteem *rel* self-confidence, self-assurance, self-possession; self-satisfaction, self-complacency, complacency, smugness, priggishness *ant* altruism

egotism *syn* CONCEIT, egoism, self-love, amour propre, self-esteem *rel* vanity, vainglory, pride; boasting, boastfulness, vaunting, vauntfulness, gasconading; pluming, piquing, priding, preening *ant* modesty

eject • to force or thrust something or someone out *syn* expel, oust, evict, dismiss *rel* exclude, eliminate, shut out, rule out, debar, disbar; dismiss, discharge, cashier, fire, sack; discard, cast, shed; reject, repudiate, spurn *ant* admit

elaborate *syn* UNFOLD, evolve, develop, perfect *rel* expand, amplify, dilate; enlarge, augment, increase; heighten, enhance

élan *syn* VIGOR, vim, spirit, dash, esprit, verve, punch, drive

elapse *syn* PASS, pass away, expire *rel* slip, slide, glide; end, terminate

elastic **1** • able to endure strain without being permanently affected or injured *syn* resilient, springy, flexible, supple *rel* pliable, pliant, ductile; plastic, malleable; limber, lithe, supple *ant* rigid **2** • able to recover quickly from depression and maintain high spirits *syn* expansive, resilient, buoyant, volatile, effervescent *rel* spirited, high-spirited, mettlesome; lively, vivacious, sprightly, animated, gay *ant* depressed

elbowroom *syn* ROOM, berth, play, leeway, margin, clearance

elderly *syn* AGED, old, superannuated *ant* youthful

elect *adj, syn* SELECT, picked, exclusive *rel* choice, exquisite, rare; selected, preferred, chosen, singled out; redeemed, saved, delivered *ant* reprobate (*in theology*)

elect *vb* **1** *syn* CHOOSE, select, pick, prefer, single, opt, cull *rel* decide, determine, settle, resolve; conclude, judge; receive, accept, admit, take *ant* abjure **2** *syn* DESIGNATE, name, nominate, appoint

election *syn* CHOICE, selection, option, preference, alternative *rel* deciding, decision, determining, determination, settling, settlement

electrify *syn* THRILL, enthuse *rel* galvanize, excite, stimulate, quicken, provoke; stir, rouse, arouse, rally

eleemosynary *syn* CHARITABLE, benevolent, humane, humanitarian, philanthropic, altruistic

elegance · impressive beauty of form, appearance, or behavior *syn* grace, dignity *rel* beautifulness, beauty, handsomeness, comeliness; fastidiousness, niceness, nicety, daintiness; perfection, excellence; taste

elegant *syn* CHOICE, exquisite, recherché, rare, dainty, delicate *rel* majestic, stately, noble, august, grand; beautiful, handsome; fastidious, nice; consummate, finished; sumptuous, luxurious, opulent

element · one of the parts of a compound or complex whole *syn* component, constituent, ingredient, factor *rel* principle, fundamental; part, portion, member; item, detail, particular *ant* compound (*in science*); composite

elemental **1** · of, relating to, or being an ultimate or irreducible element *syn* basic, elementatry, essential, fundamental, primitive, underlying **2** *syn* ELEMENTARY, basal, beginning, rudimentary

elementary **1** · of, relating to, or dealing with the simplest principles *syn* basal, beginning, elemental, rudimentary **2** *syn* ELEMENTAL, basic, essential, fundamental, primitive, underlying

elephantine *syn* HUGE, vast, immense, enormous, mammoth, giant, gigantic, gigantean, colossal, gargantuan, Herculean, cyclopean, titanic, Brobdingnagian

elevate *syn* LIFT, raise, rear, hoist, heave, boost *rel* exalt, aggrandize, magnify; heighten, enhance; rise, mount, ascend, tower, soar, rocket *ant* lower

elevation **1** *syn* HEIGHT, altitude *rel* ascension, ascent **2** *syn* ADVANCEMENT, promotion, preferment *rel* exaltation, aggrandizement *ant* degradation

elicit *syn* EDUCE, evoke, extract, extort *rel* draw, drag, pull; bring, fetch

eliminate *syn* EXCLUDE, rule out, debar, blackball, disbar, suspend, shut out *rel* eject, oust, dismiss, expel, evict; eradicate, extirpate, exterminate, uproot, wipe; expunge, erase, delete, efface

elite *syn* ARISTOCRACY, society, nobility, gentry, county *ant* rabble

ell *syn* ANNEX, wing, extension

elongate *syn* EXTEND, lengthen, prolong, protract *ant* abbreviate, shorten

eloquent **1** *syn* VOCAL, articulate, voluble, fluent, glib *rel* impassioned, passionate, fervid, perfervid, ardent, fervent; expressing, voicing, venting, uttering; forceful, forcible, potent, powerful **2** *syn* EXPRESSIVE, significant, meaningful, pregnant, sententious *rel* revealing, disclosing, telling, betraying; impressive, moving, poignant, touching, affecting

elucidate *syn* EXPLAIN, interpret, construe, expound, explicate *rel* illustrate, exemplify; demonstrate, prove

elude *syn* ESCAPE, evade, avoid, shun, eschew *rel* thwart, foil, outwit, circumvent, baffle; flee, fly, escape

emanate *syn* SPRING, issue, proceed, rise, arise, originate, derive, flow, stem *rel* emerge, loom, appear; begin, commence, start, initiate

emancipate *syn* FREE, manumit, liberate, release, discharge *rel* deliver, enfranchise

emasculate **1** *syn* STERILIZE, castrate, spay, alter, mutilate, geld **2** *syn* UNNERVE, enervate, unman *rel* weaken, enfeeble, debilitate, sap, undermine

embarrass · to distress by confusing or confounding *syn* discomfit, abash, disconcert, rattle, faze *rel* discompose, disturb, perturb, fluster, flurry; bewilder, nonplus, perplex; trouble, distress; vex, annoy, bother, irk; impede, obstruct, block, hinder; hamper, fetter, shackle, hog-tie *ant* relieve; facilitate

embellish *syn* ADORN, beautify, deck, bedeck, garnish, decorate, ornament *rel* enhance, heighten, intensify; apparel, array

embers *syn* ASH, cinders, clinkers

emblem *syn* SYMBOL, attribute, type *rel* device, motif, design, figure, pattern; sign, mark, token, badge

embody **1** *syn* REALIZE, incarnate, materialize, externalize, objectify, actualize, hypostatize, reify *rel* invest, clothe; illustrate, exemplify; manifest, demonstrate, evidence, evince, show *ant* disembody **2** *syn* IDENTIFY, incorporate, assimilate *rel* add, annex, superadd, append; introduce, insert, interpolate, interject; comprehend, include, embrace, involve, imply

embolden *syn* ENCOURAGE, inspirit, hearten, cheer, nerve, steel *rel* strengthen, fortify; venture, chance, hazard *ant* abash

embrace **1** *syn* ADOPT, espouse *rel* accept, receive; seize, grasp, take *ant* spurn **2** *syn* INCLUDE, comprehend, involve, imply, subsume *rel* contain, hold, accommodate; embody, incorporate

emend *syn* CORRECT, rectify, revise, amend, remedy, redress, reform *rel* mend, repair; improve, better, ameliorate *ant* corrupt (*a text, passage*)

emerge *syn* APPEAR, loom *rel* issue, emanate, spring, flow, arise, rise, proceed, stem, derive, originate

emergency *syn* JUNCTURE, exigency, contingency, crisis, pass, pinch, strait *rel* situation, condition, posture, state; difficulty, vicissitude

emigrant • a person who leaves one country in order to settle in another *syn* immigrant, migrant *rel* foreigner, alien, emigré, exile, expatriate, fugitive, refugee

emigrate *syn* MIGRATE immigrate

émigré *syn* STRANGER, immigrant, alien, foreigner, outlander, outsider

eminent *syn* FAMOUS, illustrious, renowned, celebrated, famed *rel* signal, outstanding, prominent, remarkable, conspicuous, noticeable

emolument *syn* WAGE, stipend, salary, fee, pay, hire *rel* compensation, remuneration, recompensing, recompense; reward, meed, guerdon

emotion *syn* FEELING, affection, passion, sentiment

empathy *syn* SYMPATHY, pity, compassion, commiseration, ruth, condolence *rel* imagination, fancy, fantasy; appreciation, understanding, comprehension

emphasis • exerted force or special stress that gives impressiveness or importance to something *syn* stress, accent, accentuation

employ *syn* USE, utilize, apply, avail *rel* practice, exercise, drill; engross, absorb, monopolize; choose, select, pick

employment *syn* WORK, occupation, business, calling, pursuit *rel* trade, craft, handicraft, art, profession

empower *syn* ENABLE *rel* authorize, commission, accredit, license; train, instruct, discipline, teach; endow, endue

empty **1** • lacking the contents that could or should be present *syn* vacant, blank, void, vacuous *rel* devoid, destitute, void; bare, barren; exhausted, drained, depleted *ant* full **2** *syn* VAIN, idle, hollow, nugatory, otiose *rel* inane, insipid, vapid, flat, jejune, banal; trifling, trivial, paltry, petty; fruitless, futile, bootless

empyrean, empyreal *syn* CELESTIAL, heavenly

emulate *syn* RIVAL, compete, vie *rel* imitate, copy, ape; match, equal, approach, touch

emulous *syn* AMBITIOUS *rel* aspiring, aiming, panting; eager, avid, keen, anxious, athirst, agog

enable • to render able often by giving power, strength, or means to *syn* empower *rel* permit, allow, let

enamored • possessed by a strong or unreasoning love or admiration *syn* infatuated *rel* bewitched, captivated, fascinated; fond, devoted, doting, loving

enchant *syn* ATTRACT, charm, captivate, allure, fascinate, bewitch *rel* delight, rejoice, gladden, gratify, please *ant* disenchant

enchanting *syn* ATTRACTIVE, charming, captivating, alluring, fascinating, bewitching, *rel* delightful, delectable; pleasant, pleasing, grateful, gratifying

encircle *syn* SURROUND, environ, circle, encompass, compass, hem, gird, girdle, ring *rel* enclose, envelop; circumscribe, confine, limit

enclose • to shut in or confine by or as if by barriers *syn* envelop, fence, pen, coop, corral, cage, wall *rel* confine, circumscribe, limit, restrict; environ, surround, encircle, circle, encompass, compass, hem

encomium • a more or less formal and public expression of praise *syn* eulogy, panegyric, tribute, citation *rel* lauding, laudation, extolling, extollation, praising, praise; plaudits, applause, acclaim, acclamation; commending, commendation, complimenting, compliment

encompass *syn* SURROUND, environ, encircle, circle, compass, hem, gird, girdle, ring *rel* envelop, enclose, wall; circumscribe, confine

encounter *vb, syn* MEET, face, confront *rel* collide, conflict, clash, bump; brave, beard, defy, challenge

encounter *n* • a sudden, hostile, and usu. brief confrontation or dispute between factions or persons *syn* skirmish, brush *rel* battle, engagement; contest, combat, conflict, fight, fray; clash, collision, impact, impingement

encourage 1 • to fill with courage or strength of purpose esp. in preparation for a hard task *syn* inspirit, hearten, embolden, cheer, nerve, steel *rel* stimulate, excite, provoke, quicken, pique, galvanize; strengthen, fortify, energize, invigorate; rally, stir *ant* discourage 2 *syn* FAVOR, countenance *rel* sanction, endorse, approve; incite, instigate, abet; induce, prevail *ant* discourage

encroach *syn* TRESPASS, entrench, infringe, invade *rel* enter, penetrate, pierce, probe; intrude, butt in, obtrude, interlope; interfere, intervene, interpose

encumber *syn* BURDEN, cumber, weigh, weight, load, lade, tax, charge, saddle *rel* discommode, incommode, inconvenience; clog, fetter, hamper; impede, obstruct, block, hinder

end *n* 1 *syn* LIMIT, bound, term, confine *rel* extreme, extremity 2 • the point at which something ceases *syn* termination, ending, terminus *rel* closing, close, concluding, conclusion, finishing, finish, completion; culmination, climax; term, bound, limit *ant* beginning 3 *syn* INTENTION, objective, goal, aim, object, intent, purpose, design *rel* destiny, fate, lot, doom, portion; function, office, duty

end *vb, syn* CLOSE, conclude, terminate, finish, complete *ant* begin

endanger *syn* VENTURE, hazard, risk, chance, jeopardize, imperil *rel* encounter, confront, meet, face; dare, brave; incur, contract, catch

endeavor *vb, syn* ATTEMPT, try, essay, strive, struggle *rel* apply, devote, direct, address; determine, resolve, decide

endeavor *n, syn* ATTEMPT, essay, striving, struggle, try *rel* toil, labor, travail, work; effort, exertion, pains, trouble

endemic *syn* NATIVE, indigenous, autochthonous, aboriginal *ant* exotic; pandemic

ending *syn* END, terminus, termination

endless *syn* EVERLASTING, interminable, unceasing *rel* lasting, perdurable, perpetual, permanent; eternal, illimitable, boundless, infinite; immortal, deathless, undying

endorse *syn* APPROVE, sanction, accredit, certify *rel* vouch, attest, witness; commend, recommend; support, uphold, champion, back, advocate

endow *syn* DOWER, endue *rel* bestow, confer, give; grant, award, accord; empower, enable; furnish, equip

endue *syn* DOWER, endow *rel* clothe, invest, vest; furnish, equip, outfit, accouter; bestow, confer, give

endure **1** *syn* CONTINUE, last, abide, persist *rel* survive, outlast, outlive; stay, remain, wait, linger, tarry *ant* perish **2** *syn* BEAR, abide, tolerate, suffer, stand, brook *rel* accept, receive, take; submit, yield

enemy • an individual or a group that is hostile toward another *syn* foe *rel* opponent, adversary, antagonist; rival, competitor

energetic *syn* VIGOROUS, strenuous, lusty, nervous *rel* forceful, forcible, powerful, potent; active, dynamic, live; busy, industrious, diligent; strong, stout, sturdy, stalwart, tough, tenacious *ant* lethargic

energize **1** *syn* VITALIZE, activate *rel* stimulate, quicken, galvanize, excite, provoke; stir, arouse, rouse, rally **2** *syn* STRENGTHEN, invigorate, fortify, reinforce *rel* empower, enable; stir, rally, rouse, arouse

energy *syn* POWER, force, strength, might, puissance *rel* dynamism, activity, operativeness, operation; momentum, impetus, speed, velocity, headway *ant* inertia

enervate *syn* UNNERVE, emasculate, unman *rel* weaken, enfeeble, debilitate, undermine, sap, disable; abase, demean, debase, degrade; exhaust, jade, fatigue, tire, weary *ant* harden, inure

enervated *syn* LANGUID, languishing, languorous, lackadaisical, spiritless, listless *rel* decadent, degenerated, deteriorated; enfeebled, debilitated, weakened

enfeeble *syn* WEAKEN, debilitate, sap, undermine, cripple, disable *rel* impair, mar, harm, injure; enervate, emasculate, unnerve, unman *ant* fortify

enforce • to put something into effect or operation *syn* implement *rel* execute, fulfill, discharge, perform; compel, constrain, oblige, force *ant* relax (*discipline, rules, demands*)

engage *syn* PROMISE, pledge, plight, covenant, contract *rel* bind, tie; agree, accede, acquiesce, assent, consent, subscribe

engagement **1** • a promise to be in an agreed place at a specified time, usu. for a particular purpose *syn* appointment, rendezvous, tryst, assignation, date **2** *syn* BATTLE, action *rel* encounter, skirmish, brush; contest, conflict, combat, fight

engaging *syn* SWEET, winning, winsome, dulcet *rel* alluring, attractive, enchanting, charming, captivating; interesting, intriguing *ant* loathsome

engender *syn* GENERATE, breed, beget, get, sire, procreate, propagate, reproduce *rel* produce, bear, yield; provoke, excite, stimulate, quicken; rouse, arouse, stir

engine *syn* MACHINE, mechanism, machinery, apparatus, motor

engineer *syn* GUIDE, pilot, lead, steer *rel* manage, direct, conduct, control

engrave *syn* CARVE, incise, etch, sculpture, sculpt, sculp, chisel *rel* delineate, depict, limn, portray; imprint, impress, print

engross *syn* MONOPOLIZE, absorb, consume *rel* utilize, employ, use, apply; control, manage

engrossed *syn* INTENT, absorbed, rapt *rel* monopolized, consumed; fixed, set, settled; busy, industrious, diligent, sedulous, assiduous

engrossing *syn* INTERESTING, absorbing, intriguing *rel* monopolizing, consuming; controlling, managing, directing; transporting, ravishing, enrapturing, entrancing *ant* irksome

enhance *syn* INTENSIFY, heighten, aggravate *rel* lift, elevate, raise; exalt, magnify, aggrandize; augment, increase; adorn, embellish, beautify

enigma *syn* MYSTERY, riddle, puzzle, conundrum, problem

enigmatic *syn* OBSCURE, cryptic, dark, vague, ambiguous, equivocal *rel* puzzling, perplexing, mystifying, bewildering; abstruse, occult, esoteric, recondite; dubious, problematic, doubtful *ant* explicit

enjoin **1** *syn* COMMAND, direct, order, bid, instruct, charge *rel* advise, counsel; admonish, reprove; warn, forewarn, caution **2** *syn* FORBID, interdict, prohibit, inhibit, ban *rel* debar, shut out, rule out; bar, hinder, impede

enjoy **1** *syn* LIKE, love, relish, fancy, dote *rel* delight, rejoice, gratify, gladden, regale, tickle, please *ant* loathe, abhor, abominate **2** *syn* HAVE, possess, own, hold

enjoyment *syn* PLEASURE, delight, joy, delectation, fruition *rel* delighting, rejoicing, gratifying, regaling, gladdening, pleasing; happiness, felicity, bliss, beatitude; zest, relish, gusto, taste *ant* abhorrence

enlarge *syn* INCREASE, augment, multiply *rel* extend, lengthen, elongate, prolong, protract; amplify, expand, distend, dilate, inflate; magnify, aggrandize

enlighten *syn* ILLUMINATE, illustrate, illume, light, lighten *rel* educate, instruct, train, teach, school; inform, apprise, acquaint, advise *ant* confuse, muddle

enliven *syn* QUICKEN, animate, vivify *rel* refresh, renew, restore, rejuvenate; stimulate, excite, galvanize, provoke; entertain, recreate, divert, amuse; inspire, fire, inform *ant* deaden; subdue

enmesh *syn* ENTANGLE, involve *rel* ensnare, entrap, snare, trap, capture, catch; hamper, clog, hog-tie, fetter

enmity • deep-seated dislike or ill will or a manifestation of such a feeling *syn* hostility, antipathy, antagonism, animosity, rancor, animus *rel* hate, hatred, detestation, abhorrence, loathing; aversion, antipathy; malignity, malignancy, ill will, malevolence, malice *ant* amity

ennoble *syn* DIGNIFY, honor, glorify *rel* exalt, magnify; elevate, raise, lift; heighten, enhance, intensify

ennui *syn* TEDIUM, doldrums, boredom *rel* depression, dejection, dumps, blues, melancholy, sadness; listlessness, languidness, languorousness, languor, spiritlessness; satiation, satiety, surfeiting, surfeit, cloying

enormous *syn* HUGE, vast, immense, elephantine, mammoth, giant, gigantic, gigantean, colossal, gargantuan, Herculean, cyclopean, titanic, Brobdingnagian *rel* prodigious, stupendous, tremendous, monstrous, monumental; inordinate, exorbitant, excessive, extravagant

enough *syn* SUFFICIENT, adequate, competent

enrage *syn* ANGER, infuriate, madden, incense *rel* exasperate, provoke, aggravate, rile, irritate *ant* placate

enrapture *syn* TRANSPORT, ravish, entrance *rel* rejoice, delight, gladden, please, gratify; charm, enchant, captivate, fascinate, attract

enroll *syn* RECORD, register, list, catalog *rel* enter; insert

ensconce *syn* HIDE, screen, secrete, conceal, cache, bury *rel* shield, guard, safeguard, protect, defend; shelter, lodge, harbor

ensign *syn* FLAG, standard, banner, color, streamer, pennant, pendant, pennon, jack

ensnare *syn* CATCH, snare, entrap, trap, bag, capture *rel* lure, entice, inveigle, decoy

ensue *syn* FOLLOW, succeed, supervene *rel* issue, emanate, proceed, stem, spring, derive, originate, rise, arise; pursue, chase

ensure • to make a person or thing certain or sure *syn* insure, assure, secure

entangle • to catch or hold as if in a net from which it is difficult to escape *syn* involve, enmesh *rel* hamper, trammel, fetter, clog, hog-tie; embarrass, discomfit; ensnare, snare, entrap, trap, capture, catch *ant* disentangle

entente *syn* CONTRACT, treaty, pact, compact, concordat, convention, cartel, bargain

enter **1** • to make way into something so as to reach or pass through the interior *syn* penetrate, pierce, probe *rel* invade, entrench, trespass, encroach; intrude, butt in; begin, commence, start *ant* issue from **2** • to cause or permit to go in or get in *syn* introduce, admit *rel* insert, interpolate, intercalate, insinuate, introduce

enterprise *syn* ADVENTURE, quest *rel* exploit, feat, achievement; struggle, striving, endeavor, essay, attempt

entertain **1** *syn* HARBOR, shelter, lodge, house, board *rel* receive, admit; cultivate, cherish, foster, nurse; feed, nourish **2** *syn* AMUSE, divert, recreate *rel* please, delight, gratify, rejoice, gladden, regale; beguile, while, wile

entertainment *syn* AMUSEMENT, diversion, recreation *rel* dinner, banquet, feast; play, sport, disport

enthuse *syn* THRILL, electrify

enthusiasm *syn* PASSION, fervor, ardor, zeal *ant* apathy

enthusiast • a person who manifests excessive ardor, fervor, or devotion in an attachment to some cause, idea, party, or church *syn* fanatic, zealot, bigot *rel* devotee, votary, addict

entice *syn* LURE, inveigle, decoy, tempt, seduce *rel* snare, ensnare, trap, entrap, catch; cajole, blandish, coax, wheedle *ant* scare

entire **1** *syn* WHOLE, total, all, gross *rel* complete, full, plenary *ant* partial **2** *syn* PERFECT, whole, intact *rel* integrated, concatenated; unified, consolidated, compacted *ant* impaired

entity • one that has real and independent existence *syn* being, creature, individual, person

entrance *n* • the act or fact of going

in or coming in *syn* entry, entrée, ingress, access *ant* exit

entrance *vb, syn* TRANSPORT, ravish, enrapture *rel* delight, gladden, rejoice, please; enchant, captivate, bewitch, charm, attract

entrap *syn* CATCH, trap, snare, ensnare, bag, capture *rel* seize, take, clutch; lure, inveigle, decoy, entice

entreat *syn* BEG, beseech, implore, supplicate, importune, adjure *rel* ask, request, solicit; pray, appeal, plead, petition, sue

entrée *syn* ENTRANCE, entry, ingress, access *rel* admission, admittance

entrench *syn* TRESPASS, encroach, infringe, invade *rel* monopolize, engross, consume, absorb; interpose, interfere, intervene

entrust *syn* COMMIT, confide, consign, relegate *rel* allot, assign, allocate; rely, trust, depend, count, bank, reckon

entry *syn* ENTRANCE, entrée, ingress, access *rel* door, doorway, gate, gateway, portal, postern

entwine *syn* WIND, coil, curl, twist, twine, wreathe *rel* curve, bend; interweave, weave; entangle, enmesh

enumerate *syn* COUNT, tell, number *rel* compute, calculate, reckon; add, sum, total, figure; rehearse, recount, recite, relate

enunciate *syn* ARTICULATE, pronounce

envelop **1** *syn* COVER, overspread, wrap, shroud, veil *rel* surround, environ, encompass; cloak, mask, disguise **2** *syn* ENCLOSE, fence, pen, coop, corral, cage, wall *rel* confine, circumscribe; protect, shield, guard

envious • maliciously grudging another's advantages *syn* jealous *rel* covetous, grasping, greedy; grudging, coveting, envying; malign, malignant, spiteful, malicious, malevolent

environ *syn* SURROUND, encircle, circle, encompass, compass, hem, gird, girdle, ring *rel* enclose, envelop, fence; circumscribe, confine

environment *syn* BACKGROUND, setting, milieu, backdrop, mise-en-scène

envisage, envision *syn* THINK, conceive, imagine, realize, fancy *rel* view, behold, survey, contemplate, see; objectify, externalize, materialize, realize

envoy *syn* AMBASSADOR, legate, minister, nuncio, internuncio, chargé d'affaires

envy *syn* COVET, grudge, begrudge *rel* long, pine, hanker, yearn

ephemeral *syn* TRANSIENT, transitory, passing, fugitive, fleeting, evanescent, momentary, short-lived *rel* brief, short

epicene *syn* BISEXUAL, hermaphroditic, hermaphrodite, androgynous

epicure • one who takes great pleasure in eating and drinking *syn* gourmet, gourmand, glutton, bon vivant, gastronome *rel* connoisseur, aesthete, dilettante

epicurean *syn* SENSUOUS, sybaritic, luxurious, sensual, voluptuous *rel* fastidious, dainty, nice, particular *ant* gross

epigram *syn* SAYING, aphorism, apothegm, saw, maxim, adage, proverb, motto

episode **1** *syn* DIGRESSION, divagation, excursus *rel* deviation, divergence, deflection; departing, departure **2** *syn* OCCURRENCE, incident, event, circumstance

epistle *syn* LETTER, missive, note, message, dispatch, report, memorandum

epitome *syn* ABRIDGMENT, conspectus, synopsis, abstract, brief *rel* précis, aperçu, sketch, digest, compendium

epoch *syn* PERIOD, era, age, aeon

equable *syn* STEADY, even, constant, uniform *rel* regular, orderly, methodical, systematic; invariable, immutable, unchangeable; same, equal, equivalent *ant* variable, changeable

equal *adj, syn* SAME, equivalent, very, identical, identic, tantamount *rel* equable, even, uniform; like, alike; proportionate, commensurate, proportional *ant* unequal

equal *vb, syn* MATCH, rival, approach, touch *rel* compare; square, accord, tally, correspond, agree

equanimity • the characteristic quality of one who is self-possessed or not easily disturbed or perturbed *syn* composure, sangfroid, phlegm *rel* poise, equipose, balance, equilibrium; self-possession, self-assurance, aplomb, confidence; tranquillity, serenity, placidity, calmness

equilibrium *syn* BALANCE, equipoise, poise, tension *rel* stableness, stability; stabilization, steadying; counterbalancing, counterbalance, counterpoising, counterpoise

equip *syn* FURNISH, outfit, appoint, accouter, arm

equipment • items needed for the performance of a task or useful in effecting a given end *syn* apparatus, machinery, paraphernalia, outfit, tackle, gear, matériel

equipoise *syn* BALANCE, equilibrium, poise, tension

equitable *syn* FAIR, just, impartial, unbiased, dispassionate, uncolored, objective *rel* proportional, proportionate, commensurate, commensurable; equal, equivalent, same, identical *ant* inequitable, unfair

equity *syn* JUSTICE

equivalent *syn* SAME, equal, identical, identic, selfsame, very, tantamount *rel* like, alike, comparable, parallel, uniform, similar; proportionate, commensurate, proportional; reciprocal, corresponding, convertible *ant* different

equivocal *syn* OBSCURE, ambiguous, dark, vague, enigmatic, cryptic *rel* dubious, questionable, doubtful *ant* unequivocal

equivocate *syn* LIE, prevaricate, palter, fib *rel* deceive, mislead, delude; evade, elude, escape

equivocation *syn* AMBIGUITY, tergiversation, double entendre *rel* prevarication, lying, lie, paltering, fibbing, fib; duplicity, dissimulation, deceit

era *syn* PERIOD, age, epoch, aeon

eradicate *syn* EXTERMINATE, uproot, deracinate, extirpate, wipe *rel* abolish, annihilate, extinguish, abate; destroy, demolish, raze; obliterate, efface, erase, blot out

erase • to strike, rub, or scrape out something so that it no longer has effect or existence *syn* expunge, cancel, efface, obliterate, blot out, delete *rel* annul, nullify, negate; abolish, extinguish

erect *syn* BUILD, construct, frame, raise, rear *rel* fabricate, fashion, form, make; lift, raise, elevate *ant* raze

eremite *syn* RECLUSE, hermit, anchorite, cenobite

erotic • of, devoted to, affected by, or tending to arouse sexual love or desire *syn* amatory, amorous, amative, aphrodisiac *rel* passionate, impassioned, fervid, perfervid, ardent, fervent; carnal, fleshly, sensual

erratic *syn* STRANGE, eccentric, odd, queer, singular, peculiar, unique, quaint, outlandish, curious *rel* aberrant, abnormal, atypical; irregular, unnatural, anomalous; capricious, fickle, mercurial, inconstant

error • something (as an act, statement, or belief) that departs from what is or is generally held to be acceptable *syn* mistake, blunder, slip, lapse, faux pas, bull, howler, boner

errorless *syn* IMPECCABLE, flawless, faultless *rel* correct, accurate, exact, precise, right, nice

ersatz *syn* ARTIFICIAL, synthetic, factitious

erudite *syn* LEARNED, scholarly

erudition *syn* KNOWLEDGE, learning, scholarship, science, information, lore

escape **1** • to run away esp. from something that limits one's freedom or threatens one's well-being *syn* flee, fly, decamp, abscond **2** • to get away or keep away from what one does not wish to incur, endure, or encounter *syn* avoid, evade, elude, shun, eschew

eschew **1** *syn* ESCAPE, shun, elude, avoid, evade *ant* choose **2** *syn* FORGO, forbear, abnegate, sacrifice *rel* abstain, refrain

escort *syn* ACCOMPANY, conduct, convoy, chaperon, attend *rel* protect, shield, guard, safeguard, defend; lead, guide, pilot, steer

esoteric *syn* RECONDITE, occult, abstruse *rel* mystic, mystical, anagogic, cabalistic; arcane, mysterious

especial *syn* SPECIAL, specific, particular, individual *rel* preeminent, surpassing, supreme; paramount, dominant, predominant, preponderant, sovereign; exceptional

espousal *syn* MARRIAGE, matrimony, nuptial, wedding, wedlock

espouse *syn* ADOPT, embrace *rel* support, uphold, advocate, champion, back

esprit *syn* VIGOR, vim, spirit, dash, verve, punch, élan, drive *rel* wit, brain, intelligence, mind; courage, mettle, tenacity; ardor, fervor, passion, enthusiasm

esprit de corps *syn* MORALE, discipline

espy *syn* SEE, descry, behold, perceive, discern, notice, remark, note, observe, survey, view, contemplate

essay *vb, syn* ATTEMPT, endeavor, strive, struggle, try *rel* work, labor, toil, travail

essay *n* **1** *syn* ATTEMPT, endeavor, striving, struggle, try *rel* effort, exertion, trouble, pains; toil, labor, work, travail **2** • a relatively brief discourse written for others' reading or consideration *syn* article, paper, theme, composition

essential **1** *syn* INHERENT, intrinsic, constitutional, ingrained *rel* innate, inborn, inbred, congenital; inner, inward; elemental, elementary; characteristic, individual, peculiar, distinctive *ant* accidental **2** • so important as to be indispensable *syn* fundamental, vital, cardinal *rel* basic, basal, underlying; principal, foremost, capital, chief, main, leading; prime, primary, primal **3** *syn* NEEDFUL, indispensable, requisite, necessary *rel* required, needed, wanted *ant* nonessential **4** *syn* ELEMENTAL, basic, elementary, fundamental, primitive, underlying

establish **1** *syn* SET, settle, fix *rel* implant, inculcate, instill; secure, rivet, anchor, moor *ant* uproot; abrogate **2** *syn* FOUND, institute, organize, create *rel* start, inaugurate, begin, commence, initiate *ant* abolish

esteem *n, syn* REGARD, respect, admiration *rel* honor, homage, reverence, deference, obeisance; veneration, reverence, worship, adoration *ant* abomination; contempt

esteem *vb, syn* REGARD, respect, admire *rel* prize, value, appreciate, treasure, cherish; revere, reverence, venerate *ant* abominate

estimate *vb* **1** • to judge a thing with respect to its worth *syn* appraise, evaluate, value, rate, assess, assay *rel* judge, adjudge, adjudicate; determine, discover, ascertain; settle, decide **2** *syn* CALCULATE, reckon, compute *rel* figure, cast, sum, add; count, enumerate; conjecture, surmise, guess

estimate *n, syn* ESTIMATION *rel* valuation, evaluation, appraisal, assessment; cost, expense, price

estimation • the act of valuing or appraising *syn* estimate *rel* esteem, regard, respect; opinion, view; conjecture, guess, surmise

estrange • to cause one to break a bond or tie of affection or loyalty *syn* alienate, disaffect, wean *rel* separate, part, divide, sunder, sever, divorce *ant* reconcile

etch *syn* CARVE, incise, engrave, chisel, sculpture, sculpt, sculp

eternal *syn* INFINITE, sempiternal, boundless, illimitable, uncircumscribed *rel* everlasting, endless, unceasing, interminable; lasting, perdurable, perpetual, permanent; immortal, deathless, undying *ant* mortal

ethereal *syn* AIRY, aerial *rel* celestial, heavenly, empyrean, empyreal; tenuous, rare, thin *ant* substantial

ethical *syn* MORAL, righteous, virtuous, noble *ant* unethical

etiolate *syn* WHITEN, decolorize, blanch, bleach

etiquette *syn* DECORUM, propriety, decency, dignity *rel* deportment, demeanor, mien, bearing

eulogize *syn* PRAISE, extol, acclaim, laud *rel* exalt, magnify, aggrandize; commend, applaud, compliment *ant* calumniate, vilify

eulogy *syn* ENCOMIUM, panegyric, tribute, citation *rel* compliment, flattery, adulation; lauding, laudation, extolling, extollation, praising, praise *ant* calumny; tirade

euphuistic *syn* RHETORICAL, flowery, aureate, grandiloquent, magniloquent, bombastic

evade *syn* ESCAPE, elude, avoid, shun, eschew *rel* flee, fly; thwart, foil, circumvent, outwit

evaluate *syn* ESTIMATE, appraise, value, rate, assess, assay *rel* judge, adjudge; criticize

evanesce *syn* VANISH, evaporate, disappear, fade *rel* escape, flee, fly; scatter, dissipate, dispel, disperse; squander, dissipate, consume, waste

evanescent *syn* TRANSIENT, ephemeral, passing, fugitive, fleeting, transitory, momentary, short-lived

evaporate *syn* VANISH, evanesce, disappear, fade *rel* escape, decamp, flee, fly; dissipate, dispel

even **1** *syn* LEVEL, smooth, flat, plane, plain, flush *ant* uneven **2** *syn* STEADY, uniform, equable, constant *rel* same, equal, identical; continuous, constant, incessant, continual

event **1** *syn* OCCURRENCE, incident, episode, circumstance *rel* action, act, deed; exploit, feat, achievement; chance, accident, fortune; happening, befalling, transpiring **2** *syn* EFFECT, result, consequence, upshot, aftereffect, aftermath, sequel, issue, outcome

eventual *syn* LAST, ultimate, concluding, terminal, final, latest *rel* ensuing, succeeding; terminating, closing, ending

everlasting • continuing on and on without end *syn* endless, interminable, unceasing *rel* eternal, boundless, infinite; lasting, perdurable, perpetual; immortal, deathless, undying *ant* transitory

every *syn* ALL, each

evict *syn* EJECT, oust, expel, dismiss *rel* exclude, eliminate, shut out; reject, repudiate, spurn; fire, cashier, discharge

evidence *syn* SHOW, evince, manifest, demonstrate *rel* reveal, disclose, betray, divulge; display, exhibit, expose, prove, indicate, betoken, attest, bespeak

evident · readily perceived or apprehended *syn* manifest, patent, distinct, obvious, apparent, palpable, plain, clear *rel* perceptible, sensible, tangible, appreciable, ponderable; conspicuous, prominent, noticeable

evil *adj, syn* BAD, ill, wicked, naughty *rel* base, low, vile; iniquitous, nefarious, flagitious, vicious, villainous, infamous; pernicious, baneful; execrable, damnable *ant* exemplary; salutary

evil *n* · whatever is harmful or disastrous to morals or well-being *syn* ill *ant* good

evince *syn* SHOW, manifest, evidence, demonstrate *rel* betoken, indicate, attest, prove, argue, bespeak; display, exhibit, expose disclose, reveal, discover, betray

evoke *syn* EDUCE, elicit, extract, extort *rel* provoke, excite, stimulate; arouse, rouse, rally, awaken, waken, stir

evolution *syn* DEVELOPMENT

evolve *syn* UNFOLD, develop, elaborate, perfect *rel* progress, advance; mature, ripen

exact *vb, syn* DEMAND, require, claim *rel* ask, request, solicit; compel, force, constrain, coerce, oblige

exact *adj, syn* CORRECT, accurate, right, precise, nice *rel* careful, meticulous, scrupulous, punctilious; agreeing, squaring, tallying, jibing, conforming

exacting *syn* ONEROUS, burdensome, oppressive *rel* severe, stern; rigid, rigorous, strict, stringent; arduous, difficult, hard *ant* easy; lenient

exaggeration · an overstepping of the bounds of truth, especially in describing the goodness or badness or the greatness or the smallness of something *syn* overstatement, hyperbole *rel* misrepresentation, untruth; fallacy, sophistry

exalt · to increase in importance or in prestige *syn* magnify, aggrandize *rel* elevate, raise, lift; heighten, enhance, intensify; extol, laud, praise *ant* abase

examination *syn* SCRUTINY, inspection, scanning, audit *rel* questioning, interrogation, inquiry, catechism, quizzing, quiz

examine 1 *syn* SCRUTINIZE, inspect, scan, audit *rel* analyze, dissect, resolve; contemplate, observe, survey, view, notice, note 2 *syn* ASK, question, interrogate, quiz, catechize, query, inquire *rel* penetrate, probe; test, try

example 1 *syn* INSTANCE, sample, specimen, case, illustration 2 *syn* MODEL, exemplar, pattern, ideal, standard, beau ideal, mirror *rel* paragon, apotheosis

exasperate *syn* IRRITATE, provoke, nettle, aggravate, rile, peeve *rel* vex, annoy, irk, bother; anger, incense, enrage, madden, infuriate *ant* mollify

excavate *syn* DIG, delve, spade, grub

exceed · to go or to be beyond a stated or implied limit, measure, or degree *syn* surpass, transcend, excel, outdo, outstrip

excel *syn* EXCEED, surpass, transcend, outdo, outstrip

excellence · the quality of especial worth or value *syn* merit, virtue, perfection *rel* value, worth; property, quality, character *ant* fault

exceptionable *syn* OBJECTIONABLE, unacceptable, undesirable, unwanted, unwelcome *rel* offensive, repugnant, loathsome, repulsive, revolting; repellent, distasteful, obnoxious, invidious, repugnant *ant* unexceptionable; exemplary

exceptional · being out of the ordinary *syn* extraordinary, phenomenal, unusual, unwonted *rel* outstanding, remarkable, noticeable, conspicuous, prominent, salient, signal; rare, infrequent, uncommon, scarce; singular, unique, strange; anomalous, irregular *ant* common; average

excerpt *syn* EXTRACT

excess · whatever exceeds a limit, measure, bound, or usual degree *syn* superfluity, surplus, surplusage, overplus *rel* lavishness, prodigality, profuseness, profusion, luxuriance, exuberance; inordinateness, immoderation, extravagance *ant* deficiency; dearth, paucity

excessive · going beyond a normal or acceptable limit *syn* immoderate, inordinate, extravagant, exorbitant, extreme *rel* superfluous, surplus, supernumerary, extra, spare; intense, vehement, fierce, exquisite, violent; redundant *ant* deficient

exchange · to give and receive reciprocally *syn* interchange, bandy

excitant *syn* STIMULUS, stimulant, incitement, impetus

excite *syn* PROVOKE, stimulate, pique, quicken, galvanize *rel* stir, rouse, arouse, rally, waken, awaken; agitate, disturb, perturb, discompose, disquiet; animate, inspire, fire *ant* soothe, quiet; allay (*fears, anxiety*)

exclude · to prevent the participation, consideration, or inclusion of *syn* debar, blackball, eliminate, rule out, shut out, disbar, suspend *rel* hinder, bar, block; preclude, obviate, ward, prevent; banish, exile, ostracize, deport *ant* admit; include

exclusive *syn* SELECT, elect, picked *rel* excluding, eliminating, debarring, shutting out, ruling out; aristocratic, patrician *ant* inclusive

excogitate *syn* CONSIDER, weigh, study, contemplate *rel* ponder, meditate, ruminate, muse; cogitate, reflect, deliberate, speculate, think

excoriate *syn* ABRADE, chafe, fret, gall *rel* strip, divest, denude, bare; flay, skin; torture, torment, rack; tongue-lash, revile, berate, scold

excruciating · intensely or unbearably painful *syn* agonizing, racking *rel* torturing, tormenting; intense, vehement, fierce, exquisite, violent

exculpate · to free from alleged fault or guilt *syn* absolve, exonerate, acquit, vindicate *rel* justify, explain, rationalize; excuse, condone, pardon, forgive, remit *ant* inculpate; accuse

excursion *syn* JOURNEY, trip, jaunt, tour, cruise, voyage, expedition, pilgrimage *rel* ride, drive

excursus *syn* DIGRESSION, divagation, episode

excuse *vb* · to exact neither punishment nor redress for or from *syn* condone, pardon, forgive, remit *rel* justify, explain, account, rationalize; acquit, vindicate, exculpate, absolve, exonerate; palliate, extenuate, gloss, whitewash *ant* punish

excuse *n, syn* APOLOGY, plea, pretext, apologia, alibi *rel* explanation, justification, rationalization; palliation, extenuation, whitewashing, glossing

execrable · so odious as to be utterly detestable *syn* damnable, accursed, cursed *rel* outrageous, atrocious, heinous, monstrous; base, low, vile; loathsome, revolting, repulsive, offensive, repugnant

execrate · to denounce violently *syn* curse, damn, anathematize, objurgate *rel* denounce, condemn, reprobate, censure, reprehend; revile, berate, rate

execute **1** *syn* PERFORM, effect, fulfill, discharge, accomplish, achieve *rel* complete, finish, conclude, close; realize, actualize, externalize, objectify **2** *syn* KILL, dispatch, slay, murder, assassinate

exemplar *syn* MODEL, pattern, ideal, beau ideal, example, mirror, standard *rel* apotheosis, paragon, nonpareil, nonesuch; type, symbol

exemplify · to use examples or show instances of in order to clarify *syn* illustrate

exemption · freeing or the state of being free or freed from a charge or obligation to which others are subject *syn* immunity

exercise *n* · repeated activity or exertion *syn* practice, drill *rel* action, act, deed; using, use, employment, utilization, application; operation, functioning, behavior

exercise *vb, syn* PRACTICE, drill *rel* use, employ, utilize; display, exhibit, show; wield, ply, manipulate, handle

exertion *syn* EFFORT, pains, trouble *rel* labor, toil, travail, work, grind, drudgery; struggle, striving, endeavor

exhaust **1** *syn* DEPLETE, drain, impoverish, bankrupt *rel* sap, undermine, weaken; consume, absorb, engross, monopolize; dissipate, disperse, dispel, scatter **2** *syn* TIRE, fatigue, jade, weary, fag, tucker *rel* unnerve, enervate, emasculate; disable, cripple, debilitate, enfeeble

exhibit *vb, syn* SHOW, display, expose, parade, flaunt *rel* reveal, disclose, discover, divulge; manifest, evidence, evince, demonstrate

exhibit *n, syn* EXHIBITION, show, exposition, fair

exhibition · a public display of objects of interest *syn* show, exhibit, exposition, fair

exhort *syn* URGE, egg, goad, spur, prod, prick, sic *rel* plead, appeal; entreat, implore, beseech, beg; stimulate, excite, provoke; advise, counsel

exigency **1** *syn* JUNCTURE, pass, emergency, pinch, strait, crisis, contingency *rel* difficulty, vicissitude, rigor, hardship; predicament, plight, fix, quandary, dilemma, jam, pickle, scrape **2** *syn* NEED, necessity *rel* demanding, demand, requirement, exacting, exaction, claiming, claim; compulsion, coercion, constraint, duress

exigent *syn* PRESSING, urgent, imperative, crying, importunate, insistent, instant *rel* critical, crucial, acute; threatening, menacing; compelling, constraining

exiguous *syn* MEAGER, scant, scanty, skimpy, scrimpy, spare, sparse *rel* diminutive, tiny, small, little; tenuous, slender, slight, thin; limited, restricted, confined *ant* capacious, ample

exile *syn* BANISH, expatriate, ostracize, deport, transport, extradite *rel* proscribe, condemn; expel, eject, oust

exist *syn* BE, live, subsist

existence · the state or fact of having independent reality *syn* being, actuality *rel* state, condition, situation, status; subsisting, subsistence, living, life *ant* nonexistence

exonerate *syn* EXCULPATE, acquit, vindicate, absolve *rel* relieve, lighten, alleviate; excuse, remit *ant* charge

exorbitant *syn* EXCESSIVE, inordinate, extravagant, immoderate, extreme *rel* onerous, burdensome, oppressive, exacting; greedy, grasping, covetous; extorting, extortionate *ant* just

exordium *syn* INTRODUCTION, preamble, preface, foreword, prologue, prelude

expand · to increase or become increased in size, bulk, or volume *syn* amplify, swell, distend, inflate, dilate *rel* enlarge, increase, augment; extend, protract, prolong *ant* contract; abridge; circumscribe

expanse · a significantly large area or range *syn* amplitude, spread, stretch *rel* range, reach, scope, compass, sweep, orbit; domain, territory, sphere, field

expansive *syn* ELASTIC, resilient, buoyant, volatile, effervescent *rel* exuberant, luxuriant, lavish, prodigal; generous, liberal, bountiful, bounteous, open-handed; exalted, magnified, aggrandized *ant* tense; reserved

expatiate *syn* DISCOURSE, descant, dilate *rel* speak, talk, converse; expand, amplify; discuss, argue, dispute; expound, explain; relate, narrate, recount, recite, rehearse

expatriate *syn* BANISH, exile, ostracize, deport, transport, extradite *ant* repatriate

expect · to anticipate in the mind *syn* hope, look, await *rel* foresee, foreknow, anticipate, apprehend, divine *ant* despair of

expedient *adj* · dictated by practical wisdom or by motives of prudence *syn* politic, advisable *rel* advantageous, beneficial, profitable; useful, utilitarian; seasonable, opportune, timely, well-timed; feasible, practicable, possible *ant* inexpedient

expedient *n, syn* RESOURCE, resort, shift, makeshift, stopgap, substitute, surrogate *rel* device, contrivance, contraption; mean, agency, instrument, instrumentality, medium

expedition **1** *syn* HASTE, dispatch, speed, hurry *rel* celerity, legerity, alacrity; agility, nimbleness, briskness *ant* procrastination **2** *syn* JOURNEY, voyage, tour, trip, jaunt, excursion, cruise, pilgrimage

expeditious *syn* FAST, speedy, swift, rapid, fleet, quick, hasty *rel* efficient, effective, efficacious, effectual; brisk, agile, nimble; quick, ready, prompt *ant* sluggish

expel *syn* EJECT, oust, dismiss, evict *rel* banish, exile, ostracize; discharge, cashier, fire; discard, cast out; exclude, shut out, eliminate *ant* admit

expend *syn* SPEND, disburse *rel* pay, repay, compensate, reimburse, remunerate; distribute, dispense

expense *syn* PRICE, cost, charge

expensive *syn* COSTLY, dear, valuable, precious, invaluable, priceless *rel* exorbitant, extravagant, excessive, immoderate *ant* inexpensive

experience · to pass through the process of actually coming to know or to feel *syn* undergo, sustain, suffer *rel* see, perceive, behold, view, survey

expert *adj, syn* PROFICIENT, adept, skilled, skillful, masterly *rel* practiced, drilled; trained, schooled; dexterous, deft, adroit *ant* amateurish

expert *n* · one who shows mastery in a subject, an art, or a profession or who reveals extraordinary skill in execution, performance, or technique *syn* adept, artist, artiste, virtuoso, wizard *ant* amateur

expiate · to make amends or give satisfaction for wrong done *syn* atone *rel* redress, remedy, rectify, correct, amend; redeem, deliver, save

expiation · the making of amends or the giving of satisfaction for wrongs done *syn* atonement *rel* penitence, repentance, contrition; trial, tribulation, cross, visitation

expire *syn* PASS, pass away, elapse *rel* end, terminate, close; cease, discontinue, stop

explain **1** · to make the meaning of something understood or more comprehensible *syn* expound, explicate, elucidate, interpret, construe *rel* analyze, resolve, dissect, break down; discuss, argue, dispute; exemplify, illustrate **2** · to give the reason for or cause of *syn* account, justify, rationalize *rel* excuse, condone; exculpate, exonerate, acquit, absolve

explicate *syn* EXPLAIN, expound, elucidate, interpret, construe

explicit · characterized by full precise expression and meaning that is perfectly clear *syn* express, specific, definite, categorical *rel* precise, exact, accurate; clear, lucid, perspicuous *ant* ambiguous

exploit *syn* FEAT, achievement *rel* act, deed, action; adventure, enterprise, quest

expose *syn* SHOW, display, exhibit, parade, flaunt *rel* reveal, disclose, discover, divulge; demonstrate, evince, manifest, evidence; air, ventilate, vent, voice, utter, express; publish, advertise, proclaim, broadcast, declare

exposé *syn* EXPOSITION, exposure

exposed *syn* LIABLE, open, subject, prone, susceptible, sensitive *rel* threatened, menaced

exposition **1** *syn* EXHIBITION, fair, exhibit, show **2** · a setting forth or laying open of a thing or things hitherto not known or fully understood *syn* exposure, exposé

expostulate *syn* OBJECT, remonstrate, protest, kick *rel* oppose, resist, combat, fight; argue, debate, dispute, discuss

exposure *syn* EXPOSITION, exposé *ant* cover; covering

expound *syn* EXPLAIN, explicate, elucidate, interpret, construe *rel* dissect, break down, analyze, resolve; illustrate, exemplify

express *adj, syn* EXPLICIT, definite, specific, categorical *rel* expressed, voiced, uttered; lucid, clear, perspicuous; distinct, plain, evident; precise, exact, accurate

express *vb* · to let out what one feels or thinks *syn* vent, utter, voice, broach, air, ventilate *rel* speak, talk; pronounce, articulate, enunciate; reveal, disclose, divulge, tell; declare, proclaim, announce *ant* imply

expression *syn* PHRASE, locution, idiom

expressive · clearly conveying or manifesting a thought, idea, or feeling or a combination of these *syn* eloquent, significant, meaningful, pregnant, sententious *rel* revealing, revelatory, disclosing, divulging; graphic, vivid, picturesque, pictorial; suggesting, suggestive, adumbrating, shadowing

expunge *syn* ERASE, cancel, efface, obliterate, blot out, delete *rel* wipe, eradicate, extirpate, exterminate

exquisite *adj* **1** *syn* CHOICE, recherché, rare, dainty, delicate, elegant *rel* precious, valuable, priceless, costly; consummate, finished; flawless, impeccable, faultless; perfect, intact, whole, entire **2** *syn* INTENSE, vehement, fierce, violent *rel* consummate; perfect; supreme, superlative; heightened, aggravated, intensified, enhanced; exalted, magnified

exquisite *n, syn* FOP, coxcomb, beau, dandy, dude, buck

extemporaneous · composed, devised, or done at the moment rather than beforehand *syn* extempore, extemporary, improvised, impromptu, offhand, unpremeditated *rel* spontaneous, impulsive; ready, prompt, apt, quick

extemporary, extempore *syn* EXTEMPORANEOUS, improvised, impromptu, offhand, unpremeditated

extend · to make or become longer *syn* lengthen, elongate, prolong, protract *rel* increase, enlarge, augment; expand, amplify, distend, dilate *ant* abridge, shorten

extension *syn* ANNEX, wing, ell

extent *syn* SIZE, dimensions, area, magnitude, volume *rel* range, scope, compass, sweep, reach, radius; stretch, spread, amplitude, expanse

extenuate *syn* THIN, attenuate, dilute, rarefy *rel* diminish, lessen, reduce, decrease; weaken, enfeeble, debilitate; moderate, temper, qualify *ant* intensify **2** *syn* PALLIATE, gloze, gloss, whitewash, whiten *rel* condone, excuse; rationalize, explain, justify

exterior *syn* OUTER, external, outward, outside *rel* extrinsic, extraneous, foreign, alien *ant* interior

exterminate • to destroy utterly *syn* extirpate, eradicate, uproot, deracinate, wipe *rel* abolish, extinguish, annihilate, abate; obliterate, efface, expunge, blot out, erase; destroy, demolish, raze

external *syn* OUTER, exterior, outward, outside *rel* extrinsic, extraneous, foreign, alien *ant* internal

externalize *syn* REALIZE, materialize, actualize, embody, incarnate, objectify, hypostatize, reify

extinguish **1** *syn* CRUSH, quell, suppress, quench, quash *rel* obliterate, expunge, efface, delete; destroy; ruin, wreck *ant* inflame **2** *syn* ABOLISH, annihilate, abate *rel* extirpate, exterminate, eradicate, uproot, wipe; obliterate, efface, blot out, expunge, erase; suppress, repress

extirpate *syn* EXTERMINATE, eradicate, uproot, deracinate, wipe *rel* extinguish, abolish, annihilate; obliterate, efface, expunge, erase, blot out; destroy, demolish, raze

extol *syn* PRAISE, laud, eulogize, acclaim *rel* applaud, commend, compliment; exalt, magnify, aggrandize *ant* decry; abase (*oneself*)

extort *syn* EDUCE, extract, elicit, evoke *rel* draw, drag, pull; compel, force, constrain, oblige, coerce; exact, demand, require

extra *syn* SUPERFLUOUS, supernumerary, spare, surplus

extract *vb, syn* EDUCE, extort, elicit, evoke *rel* draw, pull, drag; demand, require, exact; obtain, procure, gain, win, acquire, get

extract *n* • a passage transcribed or quoted from a book or document *syn* excerpt

extradite *syn* BANISH, deport, transport, expatriate, exile, ostracize *rel* surrender, relinquish, yield, resign

extraneous *syn* EXTRINSIC, foreign, alien *rel* external, exterior, outside, outer, outward; adventitious, accidental, incidental *ant* relevant

extraordinary *syn* EXCEPTIONAL, phenomenal, unusual, unwonted *rel* amazing, stupendous, terrific, wonderful

extravagant *syn* EXCESSIVE, inordinate, immoderate, exorbitant, extreme *rel* preposterous, absurd, foolish, silly; profuse, prodigal, lavish, exuberant *ant* restrained

extreme *adj, syn* EXCESSIVE, exorbitant, inordinate, immoderate, extravagant

extreme *n* • the utmost limit or degree of something *syn* extremity

extremity *syn* EXTREME

extricate • to free or release from what binds or holds back *syn* disentangle, untangle, disencumber, disembarrass *rel* disengage, detach, abstract; liberate, release, free; rescue, deliver

extrinsic • external to a thing, its essential nature, or its original character *syn* extraneous, foreign, alien *rel* external, outer, outside, exterior, outward; acquired, gained *ant* intrinsic

exuberant *syn* PROFUSE, lavish, prodigal, luxuriant, lush *rel* prolific, fertile, fruitful, fecund; vigorous, lusty, energetic, nervous; rampant, rank; copious, plentiful *ant* austere; sterile

eyewitness *syn* SPECTATOR, witness, onlooker, looker-on, observer, beholder, bystander, kibitzer

F

fable 1 *syn* FICTION, fabrication, figment 2 *syn* ALLEGORY, myth, parable

fabricate *syn* MAKE, fashion, forge, form, shape, manufacture *rel* invent, create; produce, turn out; devise, contrive

fabrication *syn* FICTION, figment, fable *rel* invention, creation; art, craft, handicraft, trade; work, product, production, opus, artifact

fabulous *syn* FICTITIOUS, mythical, legendary, apocryphal *rel* astonishing, amazing, astounding, surprising; extravagant, inordinate, excessive; monstrous, prodigious, stupendous

face *n* · the front part of a human or, sometimes, animal head including the mouth, nose, eyes, forehead, and cheeks *syn* countenance, visage, physiognomy, mug, puss

face *vb* 1 *syn* MEET, encounter, confront *rel* look, watch, see; gaze, stare, glare; await, look, expect 2 · to confront with courage or boldness *syn* brave, challenge, dare, defy, beard *rel* confront, encounter, meet; oppose, withstand, resist; contend, fight *ant* avoid

facet *syn* PHASE, aspect, side, angle

facetious *syn* WITTY, humorous, jocose, jocular *rel* joking, jesting, quipping, wisecracking; jolly, jovial, jocund, merry, blithe; comical, comic, droll, funny, ludicrous, laughable *ant* lugubrious

facile *syn* EASY, smooth, light, simple, effortless *rel* adroit, deft, dexterous; fluent, voluble, glib, vocal; superficial, shallow, uncritical, cursory *ant* arduous; constrained, clumsy

facility *syn* READINESS, ease, dexterity *rel* spontaneity, unconstraint, abandon; address, poise, tact; lightness, effortlessness, smoothness

facsimile *syn* REPRODUCTION, copy, carbon copy, duplicate, replica, transcript

faction *syn* COMBINATION, bloc, party, combine, ring *rel* clique, set, coterie, circle

factious *syn* INSUBORDINATE, contumacious, seditious, mutinous, rebellious *rel* contending, fighting, warring; contentious, quarrelsome, belligerent; disaffected, estranged, alienated *ant* cooperative

factitious *syn* ARTIFICIAL, synthetic, ersatz *rel* manufactured, fabricated; forced, compelled, constrained; simulated, feigned, counterfeited, shammed, pretended, affected, assumed *ant* bona fide, veritable

factor 1 *syn* AGENT, attorney, deputy, proxy 2 *syn* ELEMENT, constituent, component, ingredient *rel* determinant, cause, antecedent; influence; agency, agent, instrument, instrumentality, mean

faculty 1 *syn* POWER, function 2 *syn* GIFT, aptitude, knack, bent, turn, genius, talent *rel* ability, capacity, capability; property, quality; penchant, flair, propensity, proclivity, leaning; predilection

fad *syn* FASHION, vogue, style, rage, craze, mode, dernier cri, cry *rel* fancy, whim, whimsy, caprice, conceit, vagary

fade *syn* VANISH, evanesce, evaporate, disappear *rel* deliquesce, melt, liquefy; thin, rarefy, attenuate; reduce, lessen, decrease

faded *syn* SHABBY, dilapidated, dingy, seedy, threadbare *rel* worn, wasted, haggard; dim, murky, gloomy, dark; colorless, achromatic; pale, pallid, ashen, wan

fag *syn* TIRE, exhaust, jade, fatigue, weary, tucker

failing *syn* FAULT, frailty, foible, vice *rel* blemish, flaw, defect; weakness, infirmity *ant* perfection

failure • an omission on the part of someone or something of what is expected or required *syn* neglect, default, miscarriage, dereliction *rel* fault, failing; shortcoming, deficiency, imperfection; lack, want, absence, privation, dearth; negligence, laxness, slackness, remissness; indifference, unconcernedness, unconcern

faineant *syn* LAZY, indolent, slothful *rel* supine, passive, inactive, inert, idle; apathetic, impassive, phlegmatic; lethargic, sluggish; languorous, lackadaisical, languid

fair *adj* **1** *syn* BEAUTIFUL, comely, lovely, pretty, bonny, handsome, beauteous, pulchritudinous, good-looking *rel* delicate, dainty, exquisite, choice; charming, attractive, enchanting; pure, chaste *ant* foul; ill-favored **2** • characterized by honesty, justice, and freedom from improper influence *syn* just, equitable, impartial, unbiased, dispassionate, uncolored, objective *rel* disinterested, detached, indifferent; reasonable, rational *ant* unfair **3** *syn* MEDIUM, average, middling, mediocre, second-rate, moderate, indifferent *rel* ordinary, common

fair *n, syn* EXHIBITION, exposition, show, exhibit

faith **1** *syn* BELIEF, credence, credit *rel* assurance, conviction, certainty, certitude; assenting, assent, acquiescence, agreement *ant* doubt **2** *syn* TRUST, dependence, reliance, confidence *rel* assurance, certitude, certainty **3** *syn* RELIGION, creed, persuasion, church, denomination, sect, cult, communion *rel* tenets, dogmas, doctrines

faithful • firm in adherence to whatever one is bound to by duty or promise *syn* loyal, true, constant, staunch, steadfast, resolute *rel* devoted, loving, affectionate; tried, trustworthy, reliable, dependable *ant* faithless

faithless • not true to allegiance or duty *syn* false, disloyal, traitorous, treacherous, perfidious *rel* inconstant, unstable, fickle, capricious; wavering, fluctuating; changeable, changeful *ant* faithful

fake *n, syn* IMPOSTURE, sham, humbug, counterfeit, cheat, fraud, deceit, deception

fake *adj, syn* COUNTERFEIT, spurious, bogus, sham, pseudo, pinchbeck, phony *rel* fabricated, forged; framed, invented, concocted, contrived

faker *syn* IMPOSTOR, mountebank, charlatan, quack *rel* defrauder, cheater, cheat, swindler, cozener

fall • to go or to let go downward freely *syn* drop, sink, slump, subside *rel* descend, dismount, alight; droop, sag, flag, wilt; ebb, abate, wane; recede *ant* rise

fallacious • contrary to or devoid of logic *syn* sophistical, casuistical *rel* irrational, unreasonable; misleading, deceptive, delusive, delusory; equivocal, ambiguous, obscure *ant* sound, valid

fallacy · unsound and misleading reasoning or line of argument *syn* sophism, sophistry, casuistry

false 1 · not in conformity with what is true or right *syn* wrong *rel* misleading, deceptive, delusive, delusory; fallacious, sophistical; mendacious, deceitful, dishonest, untruthful; factitious, artificial *ant* true 2 *syn* FAITHLESS, perfidious, disloyal, traitorous, treacherous *rel* recreant, apostate, renegade, backsliding; inconstant, unstable; crooked, devious *ant* true

falsehood *syn* LIE, untruth, fib, misrepresentation, story *ant* truth

falsify *syn* MISREPRESENT, belie, garble *rel* change, alter, modify, vary; distort, contort, warp, deform; pervert, corrupt, debase; contradict, contravene, traverse, deny

falter *syn* HESITATE, waver, vacillate *rel* flinch, blench, recoil, quail, shrink; fluctuate, oscillate, swing; shake, tremble, quake, shudder

fame · the state of being widely known for one's deeds *syn* renown, honor, glory, celebrity, reputation, repute, notoriety, éclat *rel* acclaim, acclamation, applause; recognizing, recognition, acknowledgment; eminence, illustriousness *ant* infamy; obscurity

famed *syn* FAMOUS, renowned, celebrated, eminent, illustrious *ant* obscure

familiar 1 · near to one another because of frequent association or shared interests *syn* intimate, close, confidential, chummy, thick *rel* friendly, neighborly, amicable; sociable, cordial, genial, affable, gracious; easy, comfortable, cozy, snug; intrusive, obtrusive, officious, impertinent *ant* aloof 2 *syn* COMMON, ordinary, popular, vulgar *rel* usual, wonted, accustomed, customary, habitual *ant* unfamiliar; strange

famous · widely known and honored for achievement *syn* famed, renowned, celebrated, eminent, illustrious *ant* obscure

fanatic *syn* ENTHUSIAST, bigot, zealot

fanciful *syn* IMAGINARY, visionary, fantastic, chimerical, quixotic *rel* fictitious, fabulous, mythical, apocryphal, legendary; bizarre, grotesque, fantastic; preposterous, absurd, foolish; false, wrong *ant* realistic

fancy *n* 1 *syn* CAPRICE, freak, whim, whimsy, conceit, vagary, crotchet 2 *syn* IMAGINATION, fantasy *ant* experience 3 · a vivid idea or image present in the mind but having no concrete or objective reality *syn* fantasy, phantasy, phantasm, vision, dream, daydream, nightmare *rel* figment, fabrication, fable, fiction; notion, conception, idea, concept *ant* reality

fancy *vb* 1 *syn* LIKE, dote, love, enjoy, relish *rel* approve, endorse, sanction 2 *syn* THINK, imagine, conceive, envisage, envision, realize *rel* conjecture, surmise, guess

fantastic 1 *syn* IMAGINARY, chimerical, visionary, fanciful, quixotic *rel* extravagant, extreme, excessive; incredible, unbelievable, implausible; preposterous, absurd, foolish; irrational, unreasonable; delusory, delusive, deceptive, misleading 2 · conceived or made without reference to reality *syn* bizarre, grotesque, antic *rel* imagined, fancied, conceived; externalized, objectified, realized; ingenious, adroit, clever; eccentric, erratic, singular, strange, odd, queer

fantasy 1 *syn* IMAGINATION, fancy

rel imagining, fancying, conceiving, envisioning; externalizing, objectifying, realizing **2** *syn* FANCY, phantasy, phantasm, vision, dream, daydream, nightmare *rel* delusion, illusion, hallucination; vagary, caprice, whimsy, whim, freak, fancy; grotesquerie, bizarrerie

far, faraway, far-off *syn* DISTANT, remote, removed *ant* near, nigh, nearly

farcical *syn* LAUGHABLE, comical, comic, ludicrous, ridiculous, risible, droll, funny

farfetched *syn* FORCED, labored, strained *rel* fantastic, grotesque, bizarre; eccentric, erratic, strange, queer

farming *syn* AGRICULTURE, husbandry

farther • at or to a greater distance or more avanced point *syn* further, beyond

fascinate *syn* ATTRACT, charm, bewitch, enchant, captivate, allure *rel* influence, impress, affect, sway, strike, touch; delight, rejoice, gladden, please

fascinating *syn* ATTRACTIVE, charming, bewitching, enchanting, captivating, alluring *rel* delightful, delectable; luring, enticing, seducing, seductive, tempting

fashion *n* **1** *syn* METHOD, manner, way, mode, system *rel* practice, habit, custom, usage, wont **2** • the prevailing or accepted custom *syn* style, mode, vogue, fad, rage, craze, dernier cri, cry *rel* trend, drift, tendency; convention, form, usage

fashion *vb, syn* MAKE, form, shape, fabricate, manufacture, forge *rel* devise, contrive; design, plan, plot; produce, turn out

fashionable *syn* STYLISH, modish, smart, chic, dashing *ant* unfashionable; old-fashioned

fast • moving, proceeding, or acting with great celerity *syn* rapid, swift, fleet, quick, speedy, hasty, expeditious *ant* slow

fasten • to cause one thing to hold to another *syn* fix, attach, affix *rel* secure, rivet, moor, anchor; join, connect, link, unite; adhere, cleave, cling, stick, cohere; bind, tie *ant* unfasten; loosen, loose

fastidious *syn* NICE, finicky, finicking, finical, particular, fussy, dainty, squeamish, persnickety, pernickety *rel* exacting, demanding; critical, hypercritical, captious; careful, meticulous, punctilious, scrupulous

fastness *syn* FORT, stronghold, fortress, citadel

fat *syn* FLESHY, stout, portly, plump, corpulent, obese, rotund, chubby *ant* lean

fatal *syn* DEADLY, mortal, lethal *rel* killing, slaying; destroying, destructive; baneful, pernicious

fate • whatever is destined or inevitably decreed for one *syn* destiny, lot, portion, doom *rel* issue, outcome, upshot, consequence, result, effect; end, ending, termination

fateful *syn* OMINOUS, portentous, inauspicious, unpropitious *rel* momentous, significant, important; decisive, determinative, conclusive; crucial, critical, acute

fathom • to measure depth typically with a weighted line *syn* sound, plumb

fatigue *syn* TIRE, exhaust, jade, weary, fag, tucker *rel* deplete, drain; debilitate, disable, weaken *ant* rest

fatuous *syn* SIMPLE, asinine, silly, foolish *rel* idiotic, imbecile, moronic; fond, infatuated, besotted, insensate *ant* sensible

fault **1** *syn* IMPERFECTION, deficiency, shortcoming *rel* flaw, defect, blemish; weakness, infirmity *ant* excellence **2** • an imperfection in character or an ingrained moral weakness *syn* failing, frailty, foible, vice *rel* weakness, infirmity; flaw, defect, blemish *ant* merit **3** *syn* BLAME, culpability, guilt *rel* responsibility, answerability, accountability; sin, offense, crime

faultfinding *syn* CRITICAL, captious, caviling, carping, censorious, hypercritical *rel* exacting, demanding, requiring; fussy, particular, finicky, pernickety, nice

faultless *syn* IMPECCABLE, flawless, errorless *rel* correct, right, nice, accurate, exact, precise; perfect, intact, entire, whole *ant* faulty

faux pas *syn* ERROR, blunder, slip, mistake, lapse, bull, howler, boner

favor *n*, *syn* GIFT, boon, largess, present, gratuity *rel* token, pledge, earnest; concession, allowance; honor, homage, deference; benefaction, donation, contribution

favor *vb* **1** · to give the support of one's approval to *syn* countenance, encourage *rel* approve, endorse; support, uphold, back *ant* disapprove **2** *syn* OBLIGE, accommodate *rel* help, aid, assist; indulge, pamper, humor; benefit, profit

favorable · being of good omen or presaging a happy or successful outcome *syn* benign, auspicious, propitious *rel* advantageous, beneficial, profitable; salutary, wholesome, healthful; benignant, kindly, kind *ant* unfavorable; antagonistic

favorite *syn* PARASITE, sycophant, toady, lickspittle, bootlicker, hanger-on, leech, sponge, sponger

fawn · to behave abjectly before a superior *syn* toady, truckle, cringe, cower *rel* blandish, cajole, wheedle, coax; defer, bow, cave, yield, submit; court, woo, invite *ant* domineer

faze *syn* EMBARRASS, disconcert, discomfit, rattle, abash *rel* nonplus, confound, dumbfound, perplex, mystify, puzzle; confuse, muddle; fluster, flurry, perturb, discompose

fealty *syn* FIDELITY, loyalty, devotion, allegiance, piety *rel* faithfulness, faith, trueness, truth, constancy, staunchness, steadfastness; obligation, duty *ant* perfidy

fear **1** · agitation or dismay which overcomes one in the anticipation or in the presence of danger *syn* dread, fright, alarm, dismay, consternation, panic, terror, horror, trepidation *rel* apprehension, foreboding, misgiving, presentiment; anxiety, worry, concern, care *ant* fearlessness **2** *syn* REVERENCE, awe *rel* veneration, worship, adoration; admiration, wonder, amazement; respect, esteem, regard *ant* contempt

fearful **1** · inspired or moved by fear *syn* apprehensive, afraid *rel* timid, timorous; anxious, worried, concerned, care; hesitant, reluctant, disinclined *ant* fearless; intrepid **2** · causing fear *syn* awful, dreadful, frightful, terrible, terrific, horrible, horrific, shocking, appalling *rel* frightening, terrifying, alarming; ghastly, gruesome, grisly, grim, macabre, lurid; sinister, baleful, malign; sublime, splendid

fearless *syn* BRAVE, unafraid, dauntless, undaunted, bold, intrepid, audacious, courageous, valiant, valorous, doughty *rel* daring, venturesome, adventurous; heroic, gallant; plucky, gritty *ant* fearful

feasible *syn* POSSIBLE, practicable *rel* practical, practicable; advisable, expedient, politic; advantageous, beneficial, profitable; suitable, appropriate, fitting, fit *ant* unfeasible, infeasible; chimerical

feast *syn* DINNER, banquet

feat · a remarkable deed or performance *syn* exploit, achievement *rel* deed, act, action; triumph, conquest, victory; enterprise, adventure, quest

feature *syn* CHARACTERISTIC, trait *rel* detail, particular, item; speciality, particularity; quality, character, property

fecund *syn* FERTILE, fruitful, prolific *rel* bearing, producing, yielding; breeding, propagating, reproducing, generating *ant* barren

fecundity *syn* FERTILITY, fruitfulness, prolificacy *rel* producing, productiveness; profuseness, profusion, luxuriance, lavishness, prodigality, lushness, exuberance *ant* barrenness

federation *syn* ALLIANCE, confederacy, confederation, coalition, fusion

fee *syn* WAGE, stipend, emolument, salary, wages, pay, hire *rel* remuneration, compensation; charge, price, cost, expense

feeble *syn* WEAK, infirm, decrepit, frail, fragile *rel* unnerved, enervated, emasculated, unmanned; debilitated, weakened, enfeebled, disabled, crippled; powerless, impotent *ant* robust

feed *vb* · to provide the food that one needs or desires *syn* nourish, pasture, graze *rel* nurse, nurture, foster, cherish; support, sustain, maintain *ant* starve

feed *n, syn* FOOD, fodder, forage, provender, victuals, viands, provisions, comestibles

feel *vb, syn* TOUCH, palpate, handle, paw *rel* apprehend, comprehend; perceive, observe, notice, see

feel *n, syn* ATMOSPHERE, feeling, aura *rel* see FEELING 3

feeling **1** *syn* SENSATION, sensibility, sense *rel* reacting, reaction, behaving, behavior; responsiveness; sensitiveness, susceptibility **2** · subjective response or reaction *syn* affection, emotion, sentiment, passion *rel* impressing, impression, touching, affecting, affection; mood, humor, temper, vein **3** *syn* ATMOSPHERE, feel, aura *rel* impression, impress, imprint; peculiarity, individuality, characteristic; quality, property, character, attribute

feign *syn* ASSUME, simulate, counterfeit, sham, pretend, affect *rel* fabricate, manufacture, forge, make; dissemble, disguise, cloak, mask, camouflage

feint *syn* TRICK, artifice, wile, ruse, gambit, ploy, stratagem, maneuver *rel* pretense, pretension, make-believe; hoaxing, hoax, hoodwinking, befooling, dupe; resort, expedient, shift

felicitate · to express one's pleasure in the joy, success, elevation, or prospects of another *syn* congratulate

felicitous *syn* FIT, happy, apt, fitting, appropriate, suitable, meet, proper *rel* telling, convincing, valid; pat, timely, opportune, seasonable, well-timed; apposite, pertinent, relevant *ant* infelicitous; inept, maladroit

felicity *syn* HAPPINESS, bliss, beatitude, blessedness *rel* rapture, transport, ecstasy; joy, delight, delectation, pleasure, fruition *ant* misery

fell *syn* FIERCE, cruel, inhuman, savage, barbarous, ferocious, truculent *rel* baleful, malign, malefic, maleficent, sinister; pitiless, ruthless; relentless, unrelenting, merciless, grim, implacable

felon *syn* CRIMINAL, convict, malefactor, culprit, delinquent

female *n* · a person and esp. an adult who belongs to the sex that is the counterpart of the male sex *syn* woman, lady

female *adj* · of, characteristic of, or like a female esp. of the human species *syn* feminine, womanly, womanlike, womanish, ladylike *ant* male

feminine *syn* FEMALE, womanly, womanish, ladylike, womanlike *ant* masculine

fence **1** *syn* ENCLOSE, envelop, pen, coop, corral, cage, wall *rel* confine, circumscribe, limit; surround, gird, environ **2** *syn* DODGE, parry, sidestep, duck, shirk, malinger *rel* evade, avoid, shun, elude, escape; maneuver, feint; baffle, foil, outwit, frustrate

feral *syn* BRUTAL, brute, brutish, bestial, beastly *rel* fierce, ferocious

ferocious *syn* FIERCE, truculent, barbarous, savage, inhuman, cruel, fell *rel* infuriated, maddened, enraged; rapacious, voracious, ravening, ravenous; relentless, implacable, merciless, grim

ferret out *syn* SEEK, search, scour, hunt, comb, ransack, rummage *rel* extract, elicit, educe; penetrate, pierce, probe, enter

fertile · marked by abundant productivity *syn* fecund, fruitful, prolific *rel* producing, bearing, yielding; inventing, inventive, creating, creative; quickening, stimulating, provoking, exciting, galvanizing *ant* infertile, sterile

fertility · the quality or state of being fertile *syn* fruitfulness, fecundity, prolificacy *ant* infertility, sterility

fervent *syn* IMPASSIONED, ardent, fervid, perfervid, passionate *rel* devout, pious, religious; warm, warmhearted, tender, responsive; sincere, wholehearted, heartfelt, hearty, whole-souled, unfeigned; intense, vehement, fierce, exquisite, violent

fervid *syn* IMPASSIONED, fervent, ardent, perfervid, passionate *rel* intense, vehement, fierce, exquisite, violent; earnest, serious, solemn; sincere, heartfelt, hearty, wholehearted, whole-souled

fervor *syn* PASSION, ardor, enthusiasm, zeal *rel* devoutness, piousness, piety; earnestness, seriousness, solemnity; sincerity, heartiness, wholeheartedness

fetch *syn* BRING, take *rel* get, obtain, procure; transfer, shift, move, remove; convey, transport, transmit, carry, bear

fetid *syn* MALODOROUS, noisome, stinking, putrid, rank, rancid, fusty, musty *rel* foul, nasty, dirty; offensive, loathsome, repulsive, repugnant, revolting *ant* fragrant

fetish · an object believed to be endowed with the virtue of averting evil or of bringing good fortune *syn* talisman, charm, amulet

fetter *syn* HAMPER, shackle, trammel, clog, manacle, hog-tie *rel* hinder, impede, obstruct, block, bar, dam; restrain, curb, check; baffle, balk, thwart, foil, frustrate; bind, tie

fib *n, syn* LIE, untruth, falsehood, misrepresentation, story

fib *vb, syn* LIE, equivocate, palter, prevaricate

fickle *syn* INCONSTANT, unstable, capricious, mercurial *rel* changeable, changeful, variable, protean; fitful, spasmodic; light, light-minded, frivolous, flighty, volatile *ant* constant, true

fiction · a story, account, explanation, or conception which is an invention of the human mind *syn* figment, fabrication, fable *rel* narrative, story, tale, anecdote, yarn

fictitious · having the character of something invented or imagined as opposed to something true or genuine *syn* fabulous, legendary, mythical, apocryphal *rel* invented, created; imaginary, fanciful, fantastic; fabricated, fashioned *ant* historical

fidelity · faithfulness to something to which one is bound by a pledge or duty *syn* allegiance, fealty, loyalty, devotion, piety *rel* faithfulness, constancy, staunchness, steadfastness *ant* faithlessness; perfidy

fidgety *syn* IMPATIENT, restless, restive, uneasy, jumpy, jittery, nervous, unquiet

field • a limited area of knowledge or endeavor to which pursuits, activities, and interests are confined *syn* domain, province, sphere, territory, bailiwick *rel* limits, bounds, confines; extent, area, size, magnitude

fiendish • having or manifesting qualities associated with devils, demons, and fiends *syn* devilish, diabolical, diabolic, demoniac, demonic *rel* hellish, infernal; malign, malefic, maleficent, baleful, sinister; malignant, malevolent, malicious

fierce 1 • displaying fury or malignity in looks or actions *syn* truculent, ferocious, barbarous, savage, inhuman, cruel, fell *rel* menacing, threatening; infuriated, maddened, enraged; ravening, ravenous, rapacious, voracious; fearful, terrible, horrible, horrific *ant* tame; mild 2 *syn* INTENSE, vehement, exquisite, violent *rel* extreme, excessive, inordinate; penetrating, piercing; supreme, superlative, transcendent

fiery *syn* SPIRITED, high-spirited, peppery, gingery, mettlesome, spunky *rel* impetuous, precipitate, headlong; passionate, perfervid, ardent, impassioned, fervid; vehement, intense, fierce, violent

fight *vb* 1 *syn* CONTEND, battle, war *rel* struggle, strive, attempt; dispute, debate, discuss; wrangle, squabble, quarrel, altercate 2 *syn* RESIST, withstand, contest, oppose, combat, conflict, antagonize

fight *n, syn* CONTEST, combat, fray, affray, conflict *rel* struggle, striving; strife, contention, conflict, dissension, discord, difference, variance

figment *syn* FICTION, fabrication, fable *rel* fancy, fantasy, dream, daydream, nightmare; invention, creation

figure *n* 1 *syn* NUMBER, numeral, digit, integer *rel* symbol, character 2 *syn* FORM, shape, configuration, conformation *rel* outline, contour, profile, silhouette; character, symbol, sign, mark 3 • a unit in a decorative composition (as in fabric) *syn* pattern, design, motif, device

figure *vb, syn* ADD, cast, sum, total, tot, foot *rel* compute, calculate, reckon, estimate; count, enumerate, number

filch *syn* STEAL, purloin, lift, pilfer, pinch, snitch, swipe, cop *rel* snatch, grab, take, seize, grasp; rob, plunder, loot, rifle

file *syn* LINE, row, rank, echelon, tier

fillet *syn* STRIP, band, ribbon, stripe

filthy *syn* DIRTY, foul, squalid, nasty *rel* slovenly, unkempt, disheveled, sloppy, slipshod; offensive, loathsome, repulsive, revolting *ant* neat, spick-and-span

final *syn* LAST, terminal, concluding, latest, ultimate, eventual *rel* closing, ending, terminating; decisive, determinative, conclusive, definitive

financial • of or relating to the possession, making, borrowing, lending, or expenditure of money *syn* monetary, pecuniary, fiscal

fine *n* • a pecuniary penalty exacted by an authority *syn* amercement

fine *vb, syn* PENALIZE, amerce, mulct

finicky, finicking, finical *syn* NICE, particular, fussy, fastidious, dainty, squeamish, persnickety, pernickety *rel* exacting, demanding; captious, carping, hypercritical, critical; meticulous, punctilious, careful; conscientious, scrupulous, upright

finish *syn* CLOSE, complete, conclude, end, terminate *rel* achieve, accomplish, effect, fulfill, perform

finished *syn* CONSUMMATE, accomplished *rel* perfect, entire, intact, whole; refined, cultivated, cultured; suave, urbane, smooth; elegant, exquisite, choice *ant* crude

fire *n* · a destructive burning *syn* conflagration, holocaust *rel* blaze, glare, flame, flare; burning, charring, scorching

fire *vb* **1** *syn* LIGHT, kindle, ignite *rel* burn, scorch, char; blaze, flame, flare, glare, glow; illuminate, lighten **2** *syn* INFORM, animate, inspire *rel* excite, provoke, stimulate, galvanize; thrill, electrify; stir, rouse, arouse; enliven, quicken, vivify *ant* daunt **3** *syn* DISMISS, discharge, cashier, drop, sack, bounce *rel* eject, oust, expel; discard

firm · having a texture or consistency that resists deformation by external force *syn* hard, solid *rel* compact, close, dense, thick; tough, tenacious, strong; stiff, rigid, inflexible *ant* loose, flabby

fiscal *syn* FINANCIAL, monetary, pecuniary

fish · to attempt to catch fish *syn* angle

fissure *syn* CRACK, cleft, crevasse, crevice, cranny, chink *rel* break, gap; breach, split, rent, rupture, rift

fit *n* · an episode of bodily or mental disorder or excess *syn* attack, access, accession, paroxysm, spasm, convulsion

fit *adj* · right with respect to some end, need, use, or circumstances *syn* suitable, meet, proper, appropriate, fitting, apt, happy, felicitous *rel* adapted, adaptable, adjusted, adjustable, conformed, conformable; qualified, capable, able, competent *ant* unfit

fit *vb*, *syn* PREPARE, qualify, condition, ready *rel* endow, endue; furnish, provide, supply

fitful · lacking steadiness or regularity in course, movement, or succession *syn* spasmodic, convulsive *rel* intermittent, periodic, recurrent; desultory, hit-or-miss, random, haphazard *ant* constant

fitting *syn* FIT, appropriate, proper, meet, suitable, apt, happy, felicitous *rel* relevant, pertinent, germane, apposite, apropos; seemly, decorous, decent, proper; congruous, consonant; harmonious, concordant, accordant *ant* unfitting

fix *vb* **1** *syn* SET, settle, establish *rel* stabilize, steady; determine, decide, rule, settle; prescribe, define *ant* alter; abrogate (*a custom, rule, law*) **2** *syn* FASTEN, attach, affix *rel* implant, instill, inculcate; secure, rivet, anchor, moor **3** *syn* ADJUST, regulate *rel* repair, mend, patch, rebuild; correct, rectify, revise, amend, emend

fix *n*, *syn* PREDICAMENT, plight, dilemma, quandary, scrape, jam, pickle

flabbergast *syn* SURPRISE, amaze, astound, astonish *rel* dumbfound, confound, bewilder, nonplus, perplex, puzzle; disconcert, rattle, faze, discomfit, embarrass

flabby *syn* LIMP, flaccid, floppy, flimsy, sleazy *rel* loose, relaxed, slack, lax; soft; yielding, caving in; powerless, impotent; spiritless, listless, enervated, languid *ant* firm

flaccid *syn* LIMP, flabby, floppy, flimsy, sleazy *rel* slack, relaxed, lax, loose; unnerved, enervated, emasculated, unnerved; weakened, debilitated, enfeebled, sapped *ant* resilient

flag *n* · a piece of fabric that is used as a symbol (as of a nation) or as a signaling device *syn* ensign, standard, banner, color, streamer, pennant, pendant, pennon, jack

flag *vb, syn* DROOP, wilt, sag *rel* fall, subside, slump, sink, drop; ebb, wane, abate

flagitious *syn* VICIOUS, nefarious, infamous, iniquitous, villainous, corrupt, degenerate *rel* scandalous, criminal, sinful; shameful, disgraceful; flagrant, gross, glaring

flagrant • bad or objectionable *syn* glaring, gross, rank *rel* heinous, outrageous, atrocious, monstrous; nefarious, flagitious, infamous, vicious

flair *syn* LEANING, proclivity, propensity, penchant

flamboyant *syn* ORNATE, florid, rococo, baroque *rel* luxuriant, exuberant, profuse; resplendent, gorgeous, glorious, splendid; dashing, stylish; ostentatious, showy, pretentious; flashy, gaudy

flame *n, syn* BLAZE, flare, glare, glow *rel* effulgence, radiance, brilliance, brilliancy, refulgence, luminosity, brightness; ardor, fervor, passion; flashing, coruscation, gleaming, scintillation

flame *vb, syn* BLAZE, flare, glare, glow *rel* flash, gleam, glance, glint, coruscate; burn; fire, ignite, kindle, light

flammable *syn* COMBUSTIBLE, inflammable, incendiary, inflammatory

flare *vb, syn* BLAZE, glare, flame, glow *rel* dart, shoot, fly; flutter, flicker, flit; rise, arise, spring; flash, glance, glint, coruscate, scintillate; kindle, light, fire *ant* gutter out

flare *n, syn* BLAZE, glare, flame, glow *rel* rising, rise, surging, surge, towering; darting, dart, shooting; flashing, flash, coruscation, scintillation

flash *vb* • to shoot forth light (as in rays or sparks) *syn* gleam, glance, glint, sparkle, glitter, glisten, scintillate, coruscate, twinkle *rel* shoot, dart, fly; rise, surge, tower, rocket; blaze, flame, flare, glare, glow

flash *n, syn* INSTANT, second, moment, minute, jiffy, twinkling, split second

flashy *syn* GAUDY, garish, tawdry, meretricious *rel* showy, pretentious, ostentatious; flamboyant, ornate, florid; glittering, flashing, sparkling

flat **1** *syn* LEVEL, plane, plain, even, smooth, flush **2** *syn* INSIPID, vapid, jejune, banal, wishy-washy, inane

flattery *syn* COMPLIMENT, adulation *rel* blandishment, cajolery; fawning, toadying, truckling; eulogy, panegyric, encomium; homage, obeisance, deference, honor

flatulent *syn* INFLATED, tumid, turgid *rel* empty, hollow, vain; superficial, shallow; bombastic, grandiloquent, magniloquent, rhetorical

flaunt *syn* SHOW, parade, expose, display, exhibit *rel* boast, brag, vaunt, gasconade; reveal, disclose, discover, divulge; advertise, publish, broadcast, proclaim, declare

flavor *syn* TASTE, savor, tang, relish, smack

flavorsome *syn* PALATABLE, toothsome, tasty, savory, sapid, relishing, appetizing

flaw *syn* BLEMISH, defect *rel* cleaving, cleavage, riving, splitting, split, rending, rent, ripping, rip, tearing, tear

flawless *syn* IMPECCABLE, faultless, errorless *rel* intact, entire, whole, perfect; correct, accurate, precise, right, nice, exact

flay *syn* SKIN, decorticate, peel, pare *rel* abrade, excoriate, chafe; rack, torture, torment, afflict; chastise, castigate, punish

fleck *syn* SPOT, spatter, sprinkle,

mottle, stipple, marble, speckle, spangle, bespangle

flecked *syn* SPOTTED, spattered, sprinkled, mottled, stippled, marbled, speckled, spangled, bespangled *rel* dappled, freaked, variegated

flee *syn* ESCAPE, fly, decamp, abscond *rel* evade, elude, avoid, escape

fleer *syn* SCOFF, jeer, gibe, gird, sneer, flout *rel* deride, mock, ridicule; grin, smile, smirk

fleet *vb, syn* WHILE, wile, beguile *rel* speed, hasten, hurry, quicken, accelerate

fleet *adj, syn* FAST, swift, rapid, quick, speedy, hasty, expeditious *rel* agile, brisk, nimble, spry; darting, skimming, scudding, flying

fleeting *syn* TRANSIENT, evanescent, fugitive, passing, transitory, ephemeral, momentary, short-lived *ant* lasting

fleshly *syn* CARNAL, sensual, animal *rel* physical, bodily, corporeal, corporal, somatic; sensuous, sensual, voluptuous, luxurious, sybaritic, epicurean

fleshy · thick and heavy in body because of superfluous fat *syn* fat, stout, portly, plump, rotund, chubby, corpulent, obese *rel* muscular, brawny, burly, husky *ant* skinny, scrawny

flex · to bend *syn* crook, bow, buckle *rel* bend, curve, twist *ant* extend

flexible *syn* ELASTIC, supple, resilient, springy *rel* pliable, pliant, malleable, ductile, plastic; tractable, obedient; limber, lithe, supple *ant* inflexible

flexuous *syn* WINDING, sinuous, serpentine, tortuous

flicker *syn* FLIT, flutter, flitter, hover *rel* waver, vibrate, oscillate, fluctuate, swing; flare, flame, glare, blaze; flash, gleam, glance, glint, coruscate; quiver, quaver, tremble, shake

flightiness *syn* LIGHTNESS, light-mindedness, volatility, levity, frivolity, flippancy *rel* capriciousness, unstableness, instability, fickleness, mercurialness, mercuriality, inconstancy; effervescence, buoyancy, elasticity; liveliness, gaiety, sprightliness *ant* steadiness; steadfastness

flimsy *syn* LIMP, sleazy, floppy, flaccid, flabby *rel* thin, slight, tenuous; loose, slack; weak, feeble

flinch *syn* RECOIL, shrink, wince, blench, quail *rel* falter, hesitate, vacillate; evade, elude, shun, eschew, avoid, escape; withdraw, retire, go; retreat, recede

fling *syn* THROW, hurl, sling, toss, cast, pitch *rel* thrust, shove, propel, push; impel, drive, move

flippancy *syn* LIGHTNESS, levity, light-mindedness, frivolity, volatility, flightiness *rel* sauciness, pertness, archness; impishness, waggishness, roguishness, mischievousness, playfulness *ant* seriousness

flirt *syn* TRIFLE, coquet, dally, toy *rel* play, sport, disport; caress, fondle, pet

flit · to move or fly briskly, irregularly, and usu. intermittently *syn* flutter, flitter, flicker, hover *rel* fly, dart, skim, float, scud

flitter *syn* FLIT, flutter, flicker, hover *rel* fly, dart, skim; quiver, quaver, teeter, shake

float *syn* FLY, skim, sail, dart, scud, shoot *rel* glide, slide, slip; flit, hover, flitter

flood **1** *syn* FLOW, stream, current, tide, flux *rel* excess, superfluity, surplus; incursion, invasion **2** · a great or overwhelming flow of or as if of water *syn* deluge, inundation, torrent, spate, cataract *rel* flow, stream, tide, current

floppy *syn* LIMP, flabby, flaccid, flimsy, sleazy *rel* loose, relaxed, lax, slack

florid *syn* ORNATE, flamboyant,

rococo, baroque *rel* aureate, flowery, euphuistic, grandiloquent, magniloquent, rhetorical, bombastic; sumptuous, luxurious, opulent; showy, ostentatious, pretentious *ant* chaste (*in style, decoration*)

flounder *syn* STUMBLE, trip, blunder, lurch, lumber, galumph, lollop, bumble *rel* struggle, strive, attempt; toil, travail, labor; wallow, welter

flourish **1** *syn* SUCCEED, prosper, thrive *rel* bloom, flower, blossom, blow; increase, augment, multiply; expand, amplify *ant* languish **2** *syn* SWING, brandish, shake, wave, thrash *rel* wield, manipulate, ply, handle; flaunt, display, exhibit, show

flout *syn* SCOFF, jeer, gibe, fleer, gird, sneer *rel* scout, scorn, despise, contemn, disdain; spurn, repudiate, decline; deride, ridicule, mock *ant* revere

flow *vb, syn* SPRING, issue, emanate, proceed, stem, derive, arise, rise, originate *rel* emerge, appear, loom; start, begin, commence

flow *n* · something suggestive of running water *syn* stream, current, flood, tide, flux *rel* succession, progression, series, sequence; continuity, continuation, continuance

flower *n, syn* BLOSSOM, bloom, blow

flower *vb, syn* BLOSSOM, bloom, blow *rel* flourish, prosper, succeed

flowery *syn* RHETORICAL, aureate, grandiloquent, magniloquent, euphuistic, bombastic *rel* florid, ornate, flamboyant; inflated, tumid, turgid; wordy, verbose, redundant, prolix, diffuse

fluctuate *syn* SWING, oscillate, sway, vibrate, pendulate, waver, undulate *rel* alternate, rotate; waver, vacillate, hesitate

fluent *syn* VOCAL, eloquent, voluble, glib, articulate *rel* facile, effortless, smooth, easy; quick, prompt, ready, apt

fluid *syn* LIQUID *rel* liquefied, melted, fused, deliquesced, deliquescent

flurry *n, syn* STIR, bustle, fuss, ado, pother *rel* perturbation, agitation, disturbance, discomposure; haste, hurry

flurry *vb, syn* DISCOMPOSE, fluster, agitate, perturb, disturb, disquiet *rel* bewilder, distract, perplex, puzzle; quicken, excite, galvanize, stimulate, provoke

flush *n, syn* BLUSH *rel* color, tinge, tint

flush *vb, syn* BLUSH *rel* color, tinge, tint; surge, rise; betray, divulge, disclose, reveal

flush *adj, syn* LEVEL, even, flat, plane, plain, smooth

fluster *syn* DISCOMPOSE, upset, agitate, perturb, flurry, disturb, disquiet *rel* bewilder, distract, confound, nonplus, mystify, perplex, puzzle; rattle, faze, disconcert, discomfit, embarrass; confuse, muddle, addle, fuddle

flutter *syn* FLIT, flitter, flicker, hover *rel* shake, tremble, quiver, quaver, wobble; beat, throb, pulsate, palpitate; fluctuate, vibrate, oscillate, swing

flux *syn* FLOW, current, tide, stream, flood *rel* swinging, swing, fluctuation, oscillation, wavering, swaying, sway; shifting, moving; motion, movement, stir

fly **1** · to pass lightly or quickly over or above a surface *syn* dart, float, skim, scud, shoot, sail *rel* flit, flutter, flitter, flicker, hover; soar, mount, rise, arise, ascend; glide, slide, slip **2** *syn* ESCAPE, flee, decamp, abscond

flying field *syn* AIRPORT, airdrome, airfield, airstrip, landing strip, landing field

foam · a mass of bubbles gathering in or on the surface of a liquid or something as insubstantial as such a mass *syn* froth, spume, scum, lather, suds, yeast

focal *syn* CENTRAL, pivotal *rel* significant, important, momentous; salient, signal, striking, arresting, outstanding, noticeable

focus *n, syn* CENTER, heart, nucleus, core, middle, midst, hub

focus *vb, syn* CENTER, centralize, concentrate *rel* fix, set, settle, establish

fodder *syn* FOOD, forage, feed, provender, provisions, comestibles, victuals, viands

foe *syn* ENEMY *rel* antagonist, opponent, adversary; assailant, attacker; rival, competitor *ant* friend

fog *n, syn* HAZE, smog, mist

fog *vb, syn* OBSCURE, dim, bedim, darken, eclipse, cloud, becloud, befog, obfuscate *rel* puzzle, perplex, mystify, bewilder, distract; confuse, muddle, addle

foible *syn* FAULT, failing, frailty, vice *rel* weakness, infirmity; defect, flaw, blemish; aberration, deviation

foil *syn* FRUSTRATE, thwart, circumvent, balk, baffle, outwit *rel* discomfit, embarrass, disconcert, faze, rattle; curb, check, restrain, inhibit

follow **1** · to come after in time *syn* succeed, ensue, supervene **2** · to go after or on the trail of *syn* pursue, chase, trail, tag, tail *rel* attend, accompany, convoy; copy, imitate, ape; practice, exercise *ant* precede; forsake (*a teacher or teachings*)

follower · one who attaches himself to another *syn* adherent, disciple, sectary, partisan, henchman, satellite *rel* devotee, votary, addict, habitué; parasite, sycophant, toady *ant* leader

following · the body of persons who attach themselves to another esp. as disciples, patrons, or admirers *syn* clientele, public, audience

foment *syn* INCITE, abet, instigate *rel* goad, spur; stimulate, quicken, excite, galvanize, provoke; nurture, nurse, foster, cultivate *ant* quell

fond **1** · made blindly or stupidly foolish *syn* infatuated, besotted, insensate *rel* foolish, silly, fatuous, asinine, simple; stupid, dumb **2** *syn* LOVING, devoted, affectionate, doting *rel* enamored, infatuated; tender, sympathetic, warm, responsive; ardent, passionate, impassioned

fondle *syn* CARESS, pet, cosset, cuddle, dandle

food **1** · things that are edible for human beings or animals *syn* feed, victuals, viands, provisions, comestibles, provender, fodder, forage **2** · material which feeds and supports the mind or the spirit *syn* aliment, pabulum, nutriment, nourishment, sustenance, pap

fool · one regarded as lacking sense or good judgment *syn* idiot, imbecile, moron, simpleton, natural

foolhardy *syn* ADVENTUROUS, daring, daredevil, rash, reckless, venturesome *rel* bold, audacious, brave; headlong, precipitate, impetuous *ant* wary

foolish **1** *syn* SIMPLE, silly, fatuous, asinine *rel* idiotic, imbecilic, moronic **2** · felt to be ridiculous because not exhibiting good sense *syn* silly, absurd, preposterous *rel* ridiculous, ludicrous, laughable *ant* sensible

foot *syn* ADD, figure, cast, sum, total, tot

fop · a man who is conspicuously fashionable or elegant in dress or manners *syn* dandy, beau, coxcomb, exquisite, dude, buck

for *syn* BECAUSE, since, as, inasmuch as

forage *syn* FOOD, fodder, provender, feed, provisions, comestibles, victuals, viands

forbear 1 *syn* FORGO, abnegate, eschew, sacrifice *rel* restrain, curb, bridle, inhibit; avoid, escape, evade, shun; desist, cease, stop 2 *syn* REFRAIN, abstain *rel* suffer, tolerate, endure, bear

forbearance 1 *syn* PATIENCE, long-suffering, longanimity, resignation *rel, ant* see FORBEARANCE 2 2 · a disinclination to be severe or rigorous *syn* tolerance, clemency, mercifulness, leniency, indulgence *rel* patience, long-suffering, longanimity; mercy, lenity, grace, charity *ant* vindictiveness; anger

forbearing · disinclined by nature, disposition, or circumstances to be severe or rigorous *syn* tolerant, clement, merciful, lenient, indulgent *rel* gentle, mild, soft; patient, long-suffering, longanimous *ant* unrelenting

forbearingly · in a forbearing manner *syn* tolerantly, clemently, mercifully, leniently, indulgently

forbid · to debar one from using, doing, or entering or something from being used, done, or entered *syn* prohibit, enjoin, interdict, inhibit, ban *rel* debar, rule out, exclude; preclude, obviate, prevent; prevent, forestall *ant* permit; bid

force *n* 1 *syn* POWER, energy, strength, might, puissance *rel* stress, strain, pressure, tension; speed, velocity, momentum, impetus, headway 2 · the exercise of power in order to impose one's will on a person or to have one's will with a thing *syn* violence, compulsion, coercion, duress, constraint, restraint *rel* intensity, vehemence, fierceness; effort, exertion, pains, trouble

force *vb* · to cause a person or thing to yield to pressure *syn* compel, coerce, constrain, oblige *rel* impel, drive, move; command, order, enjoin; exact, demand, require

forced · produced or kept up through effort *syn* labored, strained, farfetched *rel* compelled, coerced, constrained; factitious, artificial; fatiguing, exhausting, tiring

forceful *syn* POWERFUL, potent, forcible, puissant *rel* compelling, constraining; virile, manful; cogent, telling, convincing, compelling, valid; effective, efficient *ant* feeble

forcible *syn* POWERFUL, forceful, potent, puissant *rel* vehement, intense, violent; energetic, strenuous, vigorous; aggressive, militant, assertive, self-assertive; coercing, coercive

forebear *syn* ANCESTOR, forefather, progenitor

forebode *syn* FORETELL, portend, presage, augur, prognosticate, predict, forecast, prophesy *rel* betoken, bespeak, indicate; import, signify, mean; fear, dread

foreboding *syn* APPREHENSION, misgiving, presentiment *rel* foretoken, presage, omen, portent, augury, prognostic; forewarning, warning

forecast *syn* FORETELL, predict, prophesy, prognosticate, augur, presage, portend, forebode *rel* foresee, foreknow, anticipate, apprehend, divine; surmise, conjecture, guess; infer, gather, conclude

forefather *syn* ANCESTOR, forebear, progenitor

foregoing *syn* PRECEDING, antecedent, precedent, previous, prior, former, anterior *ant* following

foreign *syn* EXTRINSIC, alien, extraneous *rel* external, outside, outer; inconsonant, inconsistent, incongruous, incompatible; repugnant, repellent, obnoxious, distasteful;

adventitious, accidental *ant* germane

foreigner *syn* STRANGER, alien, outlander, outsider, immigrant, émigré

foreknow *syn* FORESEE, divine, anticipate, apprehend *rel* foretell, predict, forecast, prophesy, prognosticate; infer, gather, conclude

foremost *syn* CHIEF, leading, principal, main, capital

forensic *syn* ARGUMENTATION, debate, disputation, dialectic

forerunner · one that goes before or in some way announces the coming of another *syn* precursor, harbinger, herald *rel* anticipator; announcer, announcement, advertiser, advertisement; portent, prognostic, omen, foretoken, presage, augury; forewarning, warning

foresee · to know or expect in advance that something will happen or come into existence or be made manifest *syn* foreknow, divine, apprehend, anticipate *rel* forecast, predict, foretell, prophesy, prognosticate; perceive, discern, descry, espy, see

foreshore *syn* SHORE, beach, strand, coast, littoral

foresight *syn* PRUDENCE, forethought, providence, discretion *rel* sagacity, perspicacity, shrewdness, astuteness; acumen, clairvoyance, discernment, perception *ant* hindsight

foresighted *syn* PRUDENT, forethoughtful, provident, discreet *rel* sagacious, perspicacious, shrewd, astute; intelligent, alert, quick-witted, brilliant, knowing; wise, judicious, sage, sapient *ant* hindsighted

forestall *syn* PREVENT, anticipate *rel* ward, avert, prevent, preclude, obviate; frustrate, thwart, foil, circumvent

foretaste *syn* PROSPECT, anticipation, outlook *rel* realization, actualization; token, earnest, pledge; presentiment, foreboding, apprehension

foretell · to tell something before it happens through special knowledge or occult power *syn* predict, forecast, prophesy, prognosticate, augur, presage, portend, forebode *rel* divine, foreknow, foresee, anticipate, apprehend; announce, declare, proclaim; reveal, divulge, disclose, discover; forewarn, warn

forethought *syn* PRUDENCE, foresight, providence, discretion *rel* premeditatedness, premeditation, deliberateness, deliberation; wisdom, judgment, sense, gumption

forethoughtful *syn* PRUDENT, foresighted, provident, discreet *rel* cautious, circumspect, wary, calculating; deliberate, premeditated, considered, advised, studied

foretoken · something that serves as a sign of future happenings *syn* presage, prognostic, omen, augury, portent *rel* sign, symptom, token, mark, badge, note; forerunner, harbinger, precursor, herald

forewarn *syn* WARN, caution *rel* notify, advise, apprise, inform; admonish, reprove; advise, counsel

foreword *syn* INTRODUCTION, preface, exordium, prologue, prelude, preamble

forge *syn* MAKE, fabricate, fashion, manufacture, form, shape *rel* beat, pound; produce, turn out, bear; counterfeit, simulate; copy, imitate

forget *syn* NEGLECT, overlook, ignore, disregard, omit, slight *ant* remember

forgetful · losing or letting go from one's mind something once known or learned *syn* oblivious, unmindful *rel* remiss, negligent, neglectful, lax, slack; heedless, thoughtless, careless

forgive *syn* EXCUSE, pardon, remit,

condone *rel* absolve, exculpate, acquit, exonerate, vindicate

forgo · to deny oneself something for the sake of an end *syn* forbear, abnegate, eschew, sacrifice *rel* waive, relinquish, surrender, abandon; renounce, resign, abdicate

forlorn **1** *syn* ALONE, lorn, lone, desolate, lonesome, lonely, solitary *rel* separated, parted, divorced, severed, sundered; forsaken, deserted, abandoned; wretched, miserable; depressed, weighed down, oppressed **2** *syn* DESPONDENT, hopeless, despairing, desperate *rel* pessimistic, cynical; futile, vain, fruitless

forlornness *syn* DESPONDENCY, hopelessness, despair, desperation *rel* dejection, depression, gloom, melancholy, blues, dumps, sadness

form *n* **1** · outward appearance of something as distinguished from the substance of which it is made *syn* figure, shape, conformation, configuration *rel* contour, outline, profile, silhouette; structure, anatomy, framework, skeleton; organism, system, economy, scheme **2** · conduct regulated by an external control (as custom or a formal protocol of procedure) *syn* formality, ceremony, ceremonial, rite, ritual, liturgy *rel* proceeding, procedure, process; practice, usage, custom, habit; rule, regulation, precept, law, canon; method, mode; decorum, propriety, etiquette **3** · a fixed or accepted way of doing or sometimes of expressing something *syn* usage, convention, convenance

form *vb*, *syn* MAKE, shape, fashion, fabricate, manufacture, forge *rel* devise, contrive; invent, create; produce, turn out, bear; design, project, scheme, plan, plot; organize, found, establish

formal *syn* CEREMONIAL, conventional, ceremonious, solemn *rel* systematic, methodical, orderly, regular; decorous, proper, seemly *ant* informal

formality *syn* FORM, ceremony, ceremonial, rite, liturgy, ritual *rel* convention, convenance, usage, form; practice, custom, habit, use, wont

former *syn* PRECEDING, prior, previous, antecedent, precedent, foregoing, anterior *ant* latter

formless · having no definite or recognizable form *syn* unformed, shapeless *rel* fluid, liquid; rough, raw, crude, rude

forsake *syn* ABANDON, desert *rel* repudiate, spurn, reject, decline; abdicate, renounce, resign; quit, leave, go *ant* return to; revert to

forswear **1** *syn* ABJURE, renounce, recant, retract *rel* abandon, desert, forsake; repudiate, spurn, reject, decline; deny, contravene, traverse, gainsay **2** *syn* PERJURE

fort · a structure or place offering resistance to a hostile force *syn* fortress, citadel, stronghold, fastness

forth *syn* ONWARD, forward

forthright *syn* STRAIGHTFORWARD, aboveboard *rel* honest, upright, conscientious, just, honorable *ant* furtive

fortify *syn* STRENGTHEN, invigorate, energize, reinforce *rel* rally, stir, arouse, rouse; stimulate, quicken, provoke; renew, restore, refresh *ant* enfeeble

fortitude · a quality of character combining courage and staying power *syn* grit, backbone, pluck, guts, sand *rel* courage, mettle, spirit, resolution, tenacity; bravery, courageousness, intrepidity, dauntlessness, valorousness *ant* pusillanimity

fortress *syn* FORT, citadel, stronghold, fastness

fortuitous *syn* ACCIDENTAL, contingent, casual, incidental *rel* random, haphazard, chance, chancy, hit-or-miss

fortunate *syn* LUCKY, providential, happy *rel* auspicious, propitious, favorable, benign; advantageous, beneficial, profitable; felicitous, happy, fit *ant* unfortunate; disastrous

fortune *syn* CHANCE, accident, luck, hap, hazard *rel* fate, destiny, lot, portion, doom; opportunity, occasion, break, time

forward *adj, syn* PREMATURE, advanced, untimely, precocious *ant* backward

forward *adv* **1** *syn* BEFORE, ahead *ant* backward **2** *syn* ONWARD, forth *ant* backward

forward *vb* **1** *syn* ADVANCE, promote, further *rel* speed, accelerate, quicken, hasten; help, aid, assist; support, uphold, back, champion *ant* hinder; balk **2** *syn* SEND, dispatch, transmit, remit, route, ship

foster *syn* NURSE, nurture, cherish, cultivate *rel* support, uphold, back, champion; harbor, shelter, entertain, lodge, house; promote, further, forward, advance; favor, accommodate, oblige

foul *adj, syn* DIRTY, filthy, nasty, squalid *rel* putrid, stinking, fetid, noisome, malodorous; offensive, revolting, repulsive, loathsome; obscene, gross, vulgar, coarse *ant* fair; undefiled

foul *vb, syn* SOIL, dirty, sully, tarnish, befoul, smirch, besmirch, grime, begrime *rel* pollute, defile, contaminate; profane, desecrate

found **1** *syn* BASE, ground, bottom, stay, rest *rel* set, fix, settle, establish; sustain, support; build, erect, raise, rear **2** · to set going or to bring into existence *syn* establish, institute, organize, create *rel* begin, commence, start, initiate, inaugurate; form, fashion, make

foundation *syn* BASE, basis, ground, groundwork *ant* superstructure

foxy *syn* SLY, insidious, wily, guileful, tricky, crafty, cunning, artful *rel* devious, crooked, oblique; deceitful, dishonest

fracas *syn* BRAWL, broil, melee, row, rumpus, scrap *rel* fray, affray, fight, conflict, combat, contest; altercation, wrangle, quarrel, squabble; contention, dissension, strife, discord

fraction *syn* PART, fragment, piece, portion, section, segment, sector, detail, member, division, parcel

fractious *syn* IRRITABLE, peevish, snappish, waspish, petulant, pettish, huffy, fretful, querulous *rel* unruly, refractory, recalcitrant, ungovernable, intractable, willful; perverse, contrary, froward, restive, wayward

fragile **1** · easily broken *syn* frangible, brittle, crisp, short, friable *ant* tough **2** *syn* WEAK, frail, feeble, decrepit, infirm *rel* impotent, powerless; delicate, dainty, choice; evanescent, ephemeral, transient, transitory *ant* durable

fragment *syn* PART, fraction, piece, portion, section, segment, sector, division, detail, member, parcel *rel* remnant, remainder

fragrance · a sweet or pleasant odor *syn* perfume, incense, redolence, bouquet *rel* smell, scent, odor, aroma *ant* stench, stink

fragrant *syn* ODOROUS, aromatic, redolent, balmy *rel* delicious, delectable, delightful *ant* fetid

frail *syn* WEAK, fragile, feeble, infirm, decrepit *rel* slight, slender, tenuous, thin, slim; puny, petty; flimsy, sleazy, limp; powerless, impotent *ant* robust

frailty *syn* FAULT, failing, foible, vice *rel* defect, flaw, blemish; infirmity, fragility, feebleness, weakness

frame **1** *syn* BUILD, construct, erect, raise, rear *rel* fabricate, manufacture, fashion, make **2** *syn* CONTRIVE, devise, invent, concoct *rel* plan, scheme, project; conceive, envisage, think

framework *syn* STRUCTURE, skeleton, anatomy

franchise *syn* SUFFRAGE, vote, ballot

frangible *syn* FRAGILE, brittle, crisp, short, friable

frank • marked by free, forthright, and sincere expression *syn* candid, open, plain *rel* ingenuous, naïve, unsophisticated, simple, natural; forthright, downright; straightforward, aboveboard *ant* reticent

frantic *syn* FURIOUS, frenzied, wild, frenetic, delirious, rabid *rel* crazy, crazed, mad, insane; hysterical; irrational, unreasonable

fraud 1 *syn* DECEPTION, trickery, chicanery, chicane, double-dealing *rel* duplicity, deceit, guile, dissimulation; defrauding, swindling, cheating, cozening, overreaching 2 *syn* IMPOSTURE, cheat, sham, fake, humbug, deceit, deception, counterfeit *rel* hoaxing, hoax, bamboozling, bamboozlement, hoodwinking, duping, dupery; trick, ruse, stratagem, maneuver, gambit, ploy, wile, artifice

fray *syn* CONTEST, affray, fight, conflict, combat *rel* fracas, broil, brawl, melee; altercation, wrangle, quarrel; contention, strife, dissension, discord

freak *syn* CAPRICE, fancy, whim, whimsy, conceit, vagary, crotchet *rel* notion, idea; fancy, fantasy, dream, daydream

freaked *syn* VARIEGATED, parti-colored, motley, checkered, checked, pied, piebald, skewbald, dappled *rel* spotted, flecked, speckled, spattered, sprinkled

free *adj* • not subject to the rule or control of another *syn* independent, sovereign, autonomous, autarchic, autarkic *rel* liberated, emancipated, delivered, freed, released, enfranchised *ant* bond

free *vb* • to relieve from constraint or restraint *syn* release, liberate, emancipate, manumit, discharge *rel* deliver, enfranchise

freebooter *syn* PIRATE, buccaneer, privateer, corsair

freedom 1 • the state or condition of not being subject to external rule or control *syn* independence, autonomy, sovereignty, autarchy, autarky *rel* liberation, emancipation, release, delivery, enfranchisement, manumission; liberty, license *ant* bondage 2 • the power or condition of acting without compulsion *syn* liberty, license *rel* exemption, immunity; scope, range, compass, sweep *ant* necessity

freethinker *syn* ATHEIST, unbeliever, agnostic, deist, infidel

freezing *syn* COLD, frigid, frosty, gelid, icy, glacial, arctic, chilly, cool

freight *syn* LOAD, cargo, burden, lading

frenetic *syn* FURIOUS, frantic, frenzied, wild, delirious, rabid *rel* demented, insane, mad; irrational, unreasonable; provoked, excited, stimulated

frenzied *syn* FURIOUS, frantic, wild, frenetic, delirious, rabid *rel* demented, deranged, insane, crazed, mad; distracted, bewildered

frenzy 1 *syn* MANIA, delirium, hysteria 2 *syn* INSPIRATION, fury, afflatus *rel* ecstasy, rapture, transport

frequently *syn* OFTEN, oft, oftentimes *ant* rarely, seldom

fresh *syn* NEW, novel, new-fashioned, newfangled, modern, modernistic, original *rel* gleaming, glistening, sparkling; virginal, youthful; raw, green, crude, uncouth, rude; naïve, unsophisticated, artless, natural *ant* stale

fret *syn* ABRADE, excoriate, chafe,

gall *rel* eat, devour, consume; worry, harass

fretful *syn* IRRITABLE, peevish, petulant, querulous, fractious, snappish, waspish, pettish, huffy *rel* cross, cranky, touchy, choleric, irascible; captious, carping, caviling, faultfinding, critical; contrary, perverse

friable *syn* FRAGILE, short, frangible, crisp, brittle *rel* crumbling, crumbly, disintegrating

friar *syn* RELIGIOUS, monk, nun

friend · a person, esp. not related by blood, with whom one is on good and usu. familiar terms *syn* acquaintance, intimate, confidant *rel* comrade, companion, crony, associate; ally, colleague, partner *ant* foe

friendly *syn* AMICABLE, neighborly *rel* familiar, intimate, close; loving, affectionate, devoted; loyal, true, steadfast, faithful *ant* unfriendly; belligerent

friendship · the relation existing between persons, communities, states, or peoples that are in accord and in sympathy with each other *syn* amity, comity, goodwill *rel* sympathy, affinity, attraction; empathy; accord, concord, consonance, harmony; alliance, league, coalition, fusion, federation *ant* animosity

fright *n, syn* FEAR, alarm, consternation, panic, dread, dismay, terror, horror, trepidation *rel* scaring, scare, startling, affrighting, frightening

fright *vb, syn* FRIGHTEN, scare, alarm, terrify, terrorize, startle, affray, affright *rel* see FRIGHTEN

frighten · to strike or to fill with fear or dread *syn* fright, scare, alarm, terrify, terrorize, startle, affray, affright *rel* appall, horrify, dismay, daunt; intimidate, cow, browbeat, bulldoze; agitate, perturb, upset, disquiet, discompose

frightful *syn* FEARFUL, dreadful, awful, terrible, terrific, horrible, horrific, shocking, appalling *rel* ghastly, grisly, gruesome, macabre, grim, lurid; sinister, baleful, malign

frigid *syn* COLD, freezing, gelid, icy, glacial, arctic, cool, chilly, frosty *ant* torrid (*temperature*); amorous (*persons*)

fritter *syn* WASTE, squander, dissipate, consume *rel* disperse, scatter; dispense, distribute; disburse, spend, expend

frivolity *syn* LIGHTNESS, levity, flippancy, light-mindedness, volatility, flightiness *rel* trifling, flirting, dallying, coquetting, toying; play, sport, fun, jest, game; gaiety, liveliness, vivaciousness, sprightliness *ant* seriousness, staidness

frolic *vb, syn* PLAY, sport, disport, rollick, romp, gambol

frolic *n, syn* PLAY, sport, disport, rollick, romp, gambol *rel* fun, jest, game, play, sport; caper, prank, antic, monkeyshine, dido; levity, lightness, frivolity

frolicsome *syn* PLAYFUL, sportive, roguish, waggish, impish, mischievous *rel* merry, blithe, jocund, jovial, jolly; mirthful, gleeful, hilarious; lively, vivacious, sprightly, gay

frosty *syn* COLD, chilly, cool, frigid, freezing, gelid, icy, glacial, arctic

froth *syn* FOAM, spume, scum, lather, suds, yeast *rel* lightness, levity, frivolity, flippancy

froward *syn* CONTRARY, perverse, balky, restive, wayward *rel* obstinate, stubborn, mulish, pigheaded, stiff-necked; willful, headstrong, refractory, unruly, ungovernable, intractable, recalcitrant; contumacious, insubordinate, rebellious *ant* compliant

frown · to put on a dark or malignant countenance or aspect *syn* scowl, glower, lower, gloom *ant* smile

frowzy *syn* SLATTERNLY, blowsy,

dowdy *rel* slovenly, unkempt, disheveled, sloppy, slipshod; squalid, dirty, filthy; negligent, neglectful, lax, slack, remiss *ant* trim; smart

frugal *syn* SPARING, thrifty, economical *rel* careful, meticulous; provident, prudent, discreet; saving, preserving, conserving; parsimonious, cheeseparing, penny-pinching, stingy *ant* wasteful

fruitful *syn* FERTILE, fecund, prolific *rel* reproducing, reproductive, propagating, breeding; bearing, producing, productive, yielding; teeming, abounding; luxuriant, lush, exuberant, profuse *ant* unfruitful; fruitless

fruitfulness *syn* FERTILITY, prolificacy, fecundity

fruition *syn* PLEASURE, enjoyment, delectation, delight, joy *rel* realization, actualization, materialization; fulfillment, accomplishment; attainment, achievement; possession, enjoyment

fruitless *syn* FUTILE, vain, bootless, abortive *rel* unfruitful, barren, infertile, sterile; vain, idle, otiose, nugatory, empty, hollow; frustrated, thwarted, foiled *ant* fruitful

frustrate • to come between a person and his or her aim or desire or to defeat another's plan *syn* thwart, foil, baffle, balk, circumvent, outwit *rel* negative, counteract, neutralize; defeat, beat, overcome, conquer; forbid, prohibit, inhibit; prevent, preclude, obviate; hinder, impede, obstruct, block, bar *ant* fulfill

fuddle *syn* CONFUSE, muddle, addle *rel, ant* see BEFUDDLE

fugitive *syn* TRANSIENT, evanescent, transitory, fleeting, passing, ephemeral, momentary, short-lived

fulfill **1** *syn* PERFORM, effect, achieve, accomplish, execute, discharge *rel* enforce, implement; compass, attain, reach, gain; realize, actualize; finish, complete, close *ant* frustrate; fail (in) **2** *syn* SATISFY, meet, answer *rel* equal, approach, match, touch, rival *ant* fall short (of)

full • containing all that is wanted or needed or possible *syn* complete, plenary, replete *rel* including, inclusive, comprehending, comprehensive; teeming, abounding; glutted, cloyed, gorged, surfeited, sated *ant* empty

fulsome • too obviously extravagant or ingratiating to be accepted as genuine or sincere *syn* oily, unctuous, oleaginous, slick, soapy *rel* lavish, profuse, exuberant; excessive, extravagant; cloying, satiating, sating; bombastic, grandiloquent, magniloquent, rhetorical

fumble *syn* BOTCH, bungle, muff, cobble *rel* blunder, flounder, stumble

fumigate *syn* STERILIZE, disinfect, sanitize

fun • action or speech that is intended to amuse or arouse laughter *syn* jest, sport, game, play *rel* amusement, diversion, recreation, entertainment; merriment, jocundity, blitheness, joviality; mirth, glee, hilarity, jollity

function *n* **1** • acts or operations expected of a person or thing *syn* office, duty, province *rel* end, goal, object, objective, purpose, intention; business, concern, affair; task, job **2** *syn* POWER, faculty *rel* ability, capacity, capability; action, behavior, operation

function *vb, syn* ACT, operate, work, behave, react

fundamental *adj* **1** • forming or affecting the groundwork, roots, or lowest part of something *syn* basic, basal, underlying, radical *rel* primary, primal, primordial, prime; elementary, elemental **2** *syn* ESSENTIAL, vital, cardinal *rel* requisite, needful, necessary, indispensable; paramount, dominant; principal, capital, foremost, chief **3** *syn* ELEMENTAL, basic, elementary, essential, primitive, underlying

fundamental *n, syn* PRINCIPLE, axiom, law, theorem *rel* element, constituent, component, factor; ground, basis, foundation, base, groundwork

funny *syn* LAUGHABLE, risible, ludicrous, ridiculous, comic, comical, farcical, droll *rel* humorous, witty, jocose, jocular, facetious; amusing, diverting, entertaining; grotesque, bizarre, fantastic, antic

furious · marked by uncontrollable excitement esp. under the stress of a powerful emotion *syn* frantic, frenzied, wild, frenetic, delirious, rabid *rel* excited, stimulated, provoked; infuriated, enraged, maddened; violent, fierce, vehement, intense

furnish **1** *syn* PROVIDE, supply *rel* get, obtain, procure, acquire, secure; prepare, fit, ready, qualify, condition *ant* strip **2** · to supply one with what is needed (as for daily living or a particular activity) *syn* equip, outfit, appoint, accouter, arm *rel* endue, endow, dower; array, apparel, clothe

further *adv, syn* FARTHER, beyond

further *vb, syn* ADVANCE, forward, promote *rel* help, aid, assist; back, champion, support, uphold; propagate, generate, engender; accelerate, speed, hasten, quicken *ant* hinder; retard

furthermore *syn* ALSO, moreover, besides, likewise, too

furtive *syn* SECRET, stealthy, clandestine, surreptitious, underhand, underhanded, covert *rel* sly, cunning, crafty, wily, guileful, artful; cautious, calculating, wary, circumspect; disguised, cloaked, masked *ant* forthright; brazen

furuncle *syn* ABSCESS, boil, carbuncle, pimple, pustule

fury **1** *syn* ANGER, rage, ire, wrath, indignation *rel* passion; exasperation, irritation, aggravation; acrimony, asperity, acerbity **2** *syn* INSPIRATION, frenzy, afflatus

fuse **1** *syn* LIQUEFY, melt, deliquesce, thaw **2** *syn* MIX, amalgamate, merge, coalesce, blend, mingle, commingle *rel* consolidate, unify, compact; unite, combine, conjoin

fusion *syn* ALLIANCE, coalition, league, federation, confederation, confederacy

fuss *syn* STIR, pother, ado, flurry, bustle *rel* agitation, perturbation, disturbance, flustering, fluster; haste, hurry, speed

fussy *syn* NICE, finicky, finicking, finical, particular, persnickety, pernickety, dainty, fastidious, squeamish *rel* exacting, demanding, requiring; querulous, fretful, irritable

fustian *syn* BOMBAST, rant, rodomontade, rhapsody

fusty *syn* MALODOROUS, musty, rancid, putrid, fetid, stinking, noisome, rank *rel* dirty, squalid, nasty, filthy, foul; slovenly, unkempt, disheveled, sloppy, slipshod

futile · barren of result *syn* vain, fruitless, bootless, abortive *rel* vain, idle, otiose, nugatory; ineffective, ineffectual, inefficacious

G

gab *syn* CHAT, chatter, patter, prate, prattle, babble, gabble, jabber, gibber

gabble *syn* CHAT, babble, gab, chatter, patter, prate, prattle, jabber, gibber

gad *syn* WANDER, stray, roam, ramble, rove, range, prowl, gallivant, traipse, meander

gadget *syn* DEVICE, contraption, contrivance

gag *syn* JOKE, jest, jape, quip, witticism, wisecrack, crack

gain **1** *syn* GET, win, obtain, procure, secure, acquire *rel* achieve, accomplish, effect, perform; endeavor, strive, struggle, attempt, try *ant* forfeit; lose **2** *syn* REACH, compass, achieve, attain *rel, ant* see GAIN 1 **3** *syn* IMPROVE, recover, recuperate, convalesce *rel* progress, advance; cure, heal, remedy; strengthen, invigorate

gainful *syn* PAYING, remunerative, lucrative, profitable *rel* productive, yielding, bearing

gainsay *syn* DENY, contradict, impugn, contravene, negative, traverse *rel* controvert, refute, confute, disprove; oppose, combat, resist, withstand, fight *ant* admit

gall *n, syn* TEMERITY, effrontery, nerve, cheek, hardihood, audacity

gall *vb, syn* ABRADE, chafe, excoriate, fret *rel* injure, hurt, harm, damage; worry, harass

gallant *syn* CIVIL, courtly, chivalrous, courteous, polite *rel* attentive, considerate, thoughtful; spirited, mettlesome, high-spirited; urbane, suave

gallantry **1** *syn* HEROISM, valor, prowess *rel* bravery, intrepidity, valorousness, dauntlessness; courage, mettle, spirit, resolution *ant* dastardliness **2** *syn* COURTESY, attention, amenity *rel* chivalrousness, chivalry, courtliness; deference, homage, honor; suavity, urbanity; address, poise, tact, savoir faire

gallery *syn* PASSAGE, passageway, corridor, arcade, cloister, ambulatory, aisle, hall, hallway

gallivant *syn* WANDER, stray, roam, ramble, rove, range, prowl, gad, traipse, meander

galumph *syn* STUMBLE, trip, blunder, lurch, flounder, lumber, lollop, bumble

galvanize *syn* PROVOKE, excite, stimulate, quicken, pique *rel* rouse, arouse, rally, stir, awaken, waken; electrify, thrill, enthuse; kindle, fire, light

gambit *syn* TRICK, ruse, stratagem, maneuver, ploy, artifice, wile, feint

gambol *n, syn* PLAY, frolic, disport, sport, rollick, romp

gambol *vb, syn* PLAY, frolic, disport, sport, rollick, romp

game **1** *syn* FUN, sport, play, jest *rel* diversion, amusement, recreation, entertainment **2** *pl* **games** *syn* ATHLETICS, sports *rel* contest, conflict

gamut *syn* RANGE, reach, radius, compass, sweep, scope, orbit, horizon, ken, purview

gap *syn* BREAK, interruption, interval, interim, hiatus, lacuna *rel* breach, split, rent, rift; hole, hollow, cavity; division, separation; pass, passage, way

gape *syn* GAZE, stare, glare, gloat, peer *rel* regard, admire; look, watch, see

garbage *syn* REFUSE, waste, offal, rubbish, trash, debris

garble *syn* MISREPRESENT, falsify, belie *rel* distort, contort, warp, deform; misinterpret, misconstrue

gargantuan *syn* HUGE, vast, immense, enormous, elephantine, mammoth, giant, gigantic, gigantean, colossal, Herculean, cyclopean, titanic, Brobdingnagian

garish *syn* GAUDY, tawdry, flashy, meretricious *rel* resplendent, gorgeous, splendid; showy, ostentatious, pretentious *ant* somber

garner *syn* REAP, glean, gather, harvest *rel* amass, accumulate

garnish *syn* ADORN, embellish, beautify, deck, bedeck, decorate, ornament *rel* enhance, heighten, intensify

garrulity, garrulousness *syn* TALKATIVENESS, loquacity, volubility, glibness *rel* verbiage; prolixity, verboseness, diffuseness, wordiness; chattering, prating, babbling, jabbering

garrulous *syn* TALKATIVE, loquacious, voluble, glib *rel* fluent, vocal, articulate, eloquent *ant* taciturn

gasconade *syn* BOAST, vaunt, brag, crow

gastronome *syn* EPICURE, gourmet, gourmand, bon vivant, glutton

gate *syn* DOOR, portal, gateway, postern, doorway

gateway *syn* DOOR, gate, portal, postern, doorway

gather **1** • to come or bring together *syn* collect, assemble, congregate *rel* accumulate, amass, hoard; heap, pile, stack, mass **2** *syn* REAP, glean, garner, harvest *rel* see GATHER 1 **3** *syn* INFER, deduce, conclude, judge

gathering • a number of individuals come or brought together *syn* collection, assemblage, assembly, congregation *rel* crowd, throng, press, horde, mob, rout, crush; accumulation

gauche *syn* AWKWARD, maladroit, clumsy, inept

gaudy • vulgar or cheap in its showiness *syn* tawdry, garish, flashy, meretricious *rel* showy, pretentious, ostentatious; vulgar, coarse, gross; resplendent, gorgeous, splendid *ant* quiet (*in taste or style*)

gauge *syn* STANDARD, criterion, yardstick, touchstone

gaunt *syn* LEAN, rawboned, angular, lank, lanky, spare, scrawny, skinny *rel* cadaverous, wasted, haggard, worn; thin, slim, slender, slight

gay *syn* LIVELY, vivacious, sprightly, animated *rel* merry, blithe, jocund, jovial, jolly; playful, frolicsome, sportive *ant* grave, sober

gaze • to look at long and attentively *syn* gape, stare, glare, peer, gloat *rel* watch, look, see; observe, survey, contemplate; regard, admire

gear *syn* EQUIPMENT, tackle, paraphernalia, outfit, apparatus, machinery *rel* appurtenances, accessories, adjuncts, appendages; possessions, belongings, effects, means

geld *syn* STERILIZE, castrate, spay, emasculate, alter, mutilate

gelid *syn* COLD, icy, frigid, freezing, frosty, glacial, arctic, cool, chilly

general *syn* UNIVERSAL, generic, common *rel* regular, typical, normal, natural

generally *syn* LARGELY, mostly, chiefly, mainly, principally, greatly

generate • to give life or origin to or to bring into existence by or as if by natural processes *syn* engender, breed, beget, get, sire, procreate, propagate, reproduce *rel* bear, produce, yield; teem, abound

generic *syn* UNIVERSAL, general, common *rel* typical, regular, normal; specific, special

generous *syn* LIBERAL, bountiful, bounteous, openhanded, munificent, handsome *rel* lavish, prodigal, profuse, exuberant; benevolent, philanthropic, eleemosynary, charitable, altruistic *ant* stingy

genesis *syn* BEGINNING, rise, initiation *rel* origin, source, root, inception, provenance, provenience; derivation, origination; commencement, start

genial *syn* GRACIOUS, sociable, affable, cordial *rel* kind, kindly, benign, benignant; friendly, neighborly, amicable; jocund, jovial, jolly, blithe, merry; cheerful, happy, glad *ant* saturnine; caustic

genius *syn* GIFT, talent, faculty, aptitude, knack, bent, turn *rel* ability, capacity, capability; originality; inspiration, afflatus

gentle *syn* SOFT, mild, smooth, lenient, bland, balmy *rel* moderate, temperate; pleasant, agreeable, grateful, pleasing, welcome; calm, tranquil, serene, placid, peaceful, halcyon *ant* rough, harsh

gentleman • a person of good or noble birth *syn* patrician, aristocrat *ant* boor

gentry *syn* ARISTOCRACY, county, nobility, elite, society

genuine *syn* AUTHENTIC, bona fide, veritable *rel* true, real, actual; unadulterated, unsophisticated; pure, sheer, absolute; sincere, unfeigned *ant* counterfeit; fraudulent

germane *syn* RELEVANT, pertinent, material, apposite, applicable, apropos *rel* appropriate, fitting, apt, happy, felicitous, fit; akin, analogous, comparable, parallel, like; related, allied, cognate, kindred *ant* foreign

gesticulation *syn* GESTURE

gesture • an expressive movement of the body or the use of such a movement *syn* gesticulation

get **1** • to come into possession of *syn* obtain, procure, secure, acquire, gain, win *rel* fetch, bring; extract, elicit, extort, educe, evoke; receive, accept; seize, take, grasp, grab, clutch; effect, accomplish, achieve; incur, contract, catch **2** *syn* GENERATE, beget, procreate, sire, engender, breed, propagate, reproduce *rel* see BEGET **3** *syn* INDUCE, persuade, prevail *rel* move, actuate, drive, impel; incite, instigate, abet

ghastly • horrifying and repellent in appearance or aspect *syn* grisly, gruesome, macabre, grim, lurid *rel* deathly, deadly; frightful, horrible, horrific, dreadful, fearful, appalling; repellent, repugnant; repulsive, revolting, loathsome, offensive

ghost *syn* APPARITION, spirit, specter, shade, phantasm, phantom, wraith, revenant

giant *syn* HUGE, vast, immense, enormous, elephantine, mammoth, gigantic, gigantean, colossal, gargantuan, Herculean, cyclopean, titanic, Brobdingnagian

gibber *syn* CHAT, prate, chatter, gab, patter, prattle, babble, gabble, jabber

gibberish • speech or actions that are esoteric in nature and suggest the magical, strange, or unknown *syn* mummery, hocus-pocus, abracadabra

gibe *syn* SCOFF, jeer, sneer, flout, gird, fleer *rel* ridicule, deride, mock, taunt, twit, rally

giddy • affected by a sensation of being whirled about or around *syn* dizzy, vertiginous, swimming, dazzled *rel* whirling, reeling; confusing, addling, fuddling, muddling; bewildering, distracting, mystifying; frivolous, flighty

gift **1** • something, often of value but not necessarily material, given freely to another for his benefit or pleasure *syn* present, gratuity, favor, boon, largess *rel* donation, benefaction, contribution, alms **2** • a special ability or a capacity for a definite kind of activity or achievement *syn* faculty, aptitude, genius, talent, knack, bent, turn *rel* endowment, dowry; power, faculty, function; acquirement, attainment, accomplishment, acquisition

gigantic, gigantean *syn* HUGE, vast, immense, enormous, elephantine, mammoth, giant, colossal, gargantuan, Herculean, cyclopean, titanic, Brobdingnagian *rel* prodigious, stupendous, tremendous, monstrous, monumental

gingery *syn* SPIRITED, fiery, peppery, high-spirited, mettlesome, spunky

gird *vb, syn* SURROUND, environ, encircle, circle, encompass, compass, hem, girdle, ring *rel* enclose, envelop, wall; confine, circumscribe, limit

gird *vb, syn* SCOFF, sneer, flout, jeer, gibe, fleer *rel* deride, mock, taunt, twit, rally, ridicule

girdle *syn* SURROUND, environ, encircle, circle, encompass, compass, hem, gird, ring *rel* see GIRD (to surround)

gist *syn* SUBSTANCE, purport, burden, core, pith *rel* center, heart, nucleus; import, significance; theme, topic, subject

give • to convey something or make something over or available to another *syn* present, donate, bestow, confer, afford *rel* award, accord, vouchsafe, grant, concede; assign, allot, apportion, allocate; distribute, dispense, deal, dole

glacial *syn* COLD, arctic, icy, gelid, frigid, freezing, frosty, cool, chilly

glad • characterized by or expressing the mood of one who is pleased or delighted *syn* happy, cheerful, lighthearted, joyful, joyous *rel* pleased, delighted, gratified, tickled, rejoiced; blithe, jocund, merry, jolly, jovial; gleeful, mirthful, hilarious *ant* sad

gladden *syn* PLEASE, delight, rejoice, gratify, tickle, regale *rel* comfort, console, solace; enliven, animate, quicken, vivify *ant* sadden

glance *vb* **1** *syn* BRUSH, graze, shave, skim *rel* slide, slip, glide; touch, contact; dart, fly **2** *syn* FLASH, glint, gleam, sparkle, glitter, glisten, scintillate, coruscate, twinkle

glance *n, syn* LOOK, glimpse, peep, peek, sight, view

glare *vb* **1** *syn* BLAZE, glow, flare, flame *rel* flash, gleam, glitter, glisten, scintillate, coruscate, sparkle **2** *syn* GAZE, stare, peer, gloat, gape *rel* glower, lower, scowl, frown

glare *n, syn* BLAZE, flare, glow, flame *rel* effulgence, refulgence, radiance, brilliance; glittering, glitter, sparkling, sparkle, flashing, flash

glaring *syn* FLAGRANT, gross, rank *rel* noticeable, conspicuous, outstanding; obtrusive, impertinent; extreme, excessive, inordinate

glaze *syn* LUSTER, gloss, sheen

gleam *syn* FLASH, glance, glint, sparkle, glitter, glisten, scintillate, coruscate, twinkle

glean *syn* REAP, gather, garner, harvest *rel* pick, choose; strip, divest

glee *syn* MIRTH, jollity, hilarity *rel* delight, joy, pleasure, enjoyment, delectation; merriment, jocundity, blitheness, joviality; gladness, happiness, cheerfulness, joyfulness, joyousness *ant* gloom

glib **1** *syn* VOCAL, fluent, voluble, articulate, eloquent *rel* garrulous, loquacious, voluble, talkative; facile, smooth, effortless, easy **2** *syn* TALKATIVE, loquacious, garrulous, voluble

glibness *syn* TALKATIVENESS, loquacity, garrulity, volubility

glide *syn* SLIDE, slip, skid, glissade, slither, coast, toboggan *rel* float, fly, skim, scud, sail, shoot

glimpse *syn* LOOK, glance, peep, peek, sight, view

glint *syn* FLASH, glance, gleam, sparkle, glitter, glisten, scintillate, coruscate, twinkle

glissade *syn* SLIDE, glide, slip, skid, slither, coast, toboggan

glisten *syn* FLASH, sparkle, glitter, gleam, glance, glint, scintillate, coruscate, twinkle

glitter *syn* FLASH, glisten, sparkle, gleam, glance, glint, scintillate, coruscate, twinkle

gloat *syn* GAZE, gape, stare, glare, peer

globe *syn* EARTH, world, planet

gloom *vb, syn* FROWN, lower, glower, scowl

gloom *n, syn* SADNESS, dejection, depression, melancholy, melancholia, blues, dumps *rel* despondency, forlornness, hopelessness, despair, desperation *ant* glee

gloomy **1** *syn* DARK, murky, obscure, dim, dusky *ant* brilliant **2** *syn* SULLEN, glum, morose, saturnine, dour, surly, sulky, crabbed *rel* depressed, weighed down, oppressed *ant* cheerful

glorify *syn* DIGNIFY, ennoble, honor *rel* extol, laud, acclaim, praise; exalt, magnify

glorious *syn* SPLENDID, resplendent, sublime, superb, gorgeous *rel* radiant, brilliant, effulgent, lustrous, bright; transcendent, superlative, surpassing, peerless, supreme; illustrious, renowned, eminent, famous *ant* inglorious

glory *syn* FAME, renown, honor, celebrity, éclat, reputation, repute, notoriety *ant* ignominy, shame

gloss *n, syn* LUSTER, sheen, glaze *rel* sleekness, slickness, glossiness

gloss *vb, syn* PALLIATE, gloze, extenuate, whitewash, whiten *rel* disguise, cloak, mask, dissemble, camouflage; rationalize, account, justify, explain

gloss *n, syn* ANNOTATION *rel* commentary, comment, note, remark, observation

gloss *vb, syn* ANNOTATE *rel* interpret, construe, explain, elucidate, expound, explicate

glossy *syn* SLEEK, slick, velvety, silken, silky, satiny *rel* lustrous, bright, brilliant, lucent, lambent

glow *vb, syn* BLAZE, flame, flare, glare *rel* burn; kindle, ignite, light; illuminate, lighten, illumine

glow *n, syn* BLAZE, flame, flare, glare *rel* brightness, brilliance, radiance, effulgence, luminosity, incandescence; fervor, ardor, passion

glower *syn* FROWN, lower, scowl, gloom *rel* glare, stare, gaze; watch, look, see

gloze *syn* PALLIATE, gloss, whitewash, extenuate, whiten *rel* condone, excuse; justify, rationalize, explain, account; dissemble, cloak, mask, disguise, camouflage

glum *syn* SULLEN, gloomy, morose, saturnine, dour, surly, sulky, crabbed *rel* silent, taciturn, close-lipped, tight-lipped; depressed, weighed down, oppressed; scowling, frowning, lowering, glowering, glooming *ant* cheerful

glut *syn* SATIATE, gorge, surfeit, sate, cloy, pall

glutton *syn* EPICURE, gourmand, gastronome, bon vivant, gourmet

gluttonous *syn* VORACIOUS, ravenous, ravening, rapacious *rel* greedy, covetous, grasping *ant* abstemious

gnash *syn* BITE, gnaw, champ *rel* grind, grate, rasp, scrape; strike, smite

gnaw *syn* BITE, champ, gnash *rel* fret, abrade; worry, annoy

go *vb* **1** · to move out of or away from where one is *syn* leave, depart, quit, withdraw, retire *rel* escape, decamp, abscond, flee, fly *ant* come **2** *syn* RESORT, refer, apply, turn

go *n, syn* SPELL, shift, tour, trick, turn, stint, bout

goad *n, syn* MOTIVE, spur, incentive, inducement, spring, impulse *rel* impelling, impulsion, driving, drive; urge, lust, passion, desire *ant* curb

goad *vb, syn* URGE, egg, exhort, spur, prod, prick, sic *rel* drive, impel, move; coerce, compel, constrain, force; incite, instigate; worry, harass

goal *syn* INTENTION, objective, object, end, aim, intent, purpose, design *rel* limit, bound, confine, end, term; aspiration, ambition

gob *syn* MARINER, sailor, seaman, tar, bluejacket

gobbledygook *syn* NONSENSE, twaddle, drivel, bunk, balderdash, poppycock, trash, rot, bull

godless *syn* IRRELIGIOUS, ungodly, unreligious, nonreligious *rel* atheistic, agnostic, infidel

good · in accordance with one's standard of what is satisfactory *syn* right *ant* bad; poor

good-looking *syn* BEAUTIFUL, comely, pretty, bonny, fair, beauteous, pulchritudinous, handsome, lovely *rel* attractive, alluring, charming; pleasing, pleasant, agreeable

good-natured *syn* AMIABLE, obliging, complaisant *rel* compliant, acquiescent; kindly, kind; altruistic, benevolent, charitable *ant* contrary

goodness · moral excellence *syn* virtue, rectitude, morality *rel* righteousness, nobility, virtuousness; honesty, integrity, probity, honor *ant* badness, evil

good sense *syn* SENSE

goodwill *syn* FRIENDSHIP, amity, comity *ant* animosity

gorge *syn* SATIATE, surfeit, sate, glut, cloy, pall

gorgeous *syn* SPLENDID, resplendent, glorious, sublime, superb *rel* luxurious, sumptuous, opulent; showy, ostentatious, pretentious

gory *syn* BLOODY, sanguinary, sanguine, sanguineous

gossip *n, syn* REPORT, rumor, hearsay *rel* talk, conversation; tattling, blabbing

gossip *vb* · to disclose something, often of questionable veracity, that is better kept to oneself *syn* blab, tattle

gourmand *syn* EPICURE, glutton, gastronome, bon vivant, gourmet

gourmet *syn* EPICURE, bon vivant, gastronome, gourmand, glutton

govern · to exercise sovereign authority *syn* rule *rel* conduct, direct, control, manage; restrain, curb, inhibit

grab *syn* TAKE, grasp, clutch, seize, snatch *rel* catch, capture

grace *n* **1** *syn* MERCY, clemency, lenity, charity *rel* kindliness, kindness, benignity, benignancy; tenderness, compassionateness, responsiveness; indulgence, forbearance, leniency **2** *syn* ELEGANCE, dignity *rel* loveliness, beautifulness, beauty, fairness, comeliness; suppleness, litheness, lithesomeness, lissomeness; attractiveness, alluringness, allurement, charmingness, charm

gracious · marked by kindly courtesy *syn* cordial, affable, genial, sociable *rel* obliging, complaisant, amiable; benignant, benign, kindly, kind; courteous, courtly, chivalrous, civil *ant* ungracious

gradate *syn* CLASS, grade, rank, rate, graduate *rel* order, arrange; divide, separate; classify, assort, sort; differentiate, discriminate, demarcate, distinguish

gradation · difference or variation between two things that are nearly alike *syn* shade, nuance *rel* difference, divergence, distinction, dissimilarity; variation, modification, change

grade *syn* CLASS, rank, rate, graduate, gradate *rel* order, arrange; divide, separate; assort, sort, classify

graduate *syn* CLASS, grade, rank, rate, gradate *rel* order, arrange; divide, separate; distinguish, differentiate, demarcate, discriminate

grand • large, handsome, dignified, and impressive *syn* magnificent, imposing, stately, majestic, august, noble, grandiose *rel* sumptuous, luxurious, opulent; sublime, superb, splendid, gorgeous; monumental, tremendous, stupendous, prodigious, monstrous

grandiloquent *syn* RHETORICAL, magniloquent, aureate, flowery, euphuistic, bombastic *rel* grandiose, imposing, grand; inflated, turgid, tumid

grandiose *syn* GRAND, imposing, stately, august, magnificent, majestic, noble *rel* ostentatious, pretentious, showy; grandiloquent, magniloquent, rhetorical

grant *vb* **1** • to give as a favor or as a right *syn* concede, vouchsafe, accord, award *rel* bestow, confer, give, present, donate; allot, assign, apportion, allocate; cede, yield, surrender, relinquish **2** • to admit something in question, esp. a contention of one's opponent in an argument *syn* concede, allow *rel* admit, acknowledge; agree, concur, coincide

grant *n, syn* APPROPRIATION, subvention, subsidy *rel* donation, benefaction, contribution

graph *n, syn* CHART, map *rel* plot, scheme, design, plan; diagram, outline, sketch

graph *vb, syn* CHART, map *rel* see GRAPH *n*

graphic • giving a clear visual impression esp. in words *syn* vivid, picturesque, pictorial *rel* lucid, perspicuous, clear; clear-cut, incisive; telling, convincing, compelling, cogent, valid

grapple *syn* WRESTLE, tussle, scuffle *rel* battle, fight, contend; vie, compete, rival; oppose, combat, resist

grasp *vb, syn* TAKE, clutch, grab, seize, snatch *rel* catch, capture; apprehend, arrest; comprehend

grasp *n, syn* HOLD, grip, clutch *rel* control, power, sway; comprehension, understanding, appreciation

grasping *syn* COVETOUS, greedy, avaricious, acquisitive *rel* rapacious, ravening, ravenous, voracious; extorting, extortionate

grate *syn* SCRAPE, scratch, rasp, grind *rel* abrade, chafe, gall; harass, annoy, harry, worry; offend, outrage; exasperate, irritate

grateful **1** • feeling or expressing gratitude *syn* thankful *rel* appreciating, appreciative, valuing, prizing, cherishing; gratified, pleased, delighted; satisfied, contented *ant* ungrateful **2** *syn* PLEASANT, agreeable, gratifying, pleasing, welcome *rel* comforting, consoling, solacing; refreshing, restoring, restorative, renewing, rejuvenating; delicious, delightful, delectable *ant* obnoxious

gratify *syn* PLEASE, delight, rejoice, gladden, tickle, regale *rel* content, satisfy; indulge, humor, pamper *ant* anger; offend, affront; disappoint

gratifying *syn* PLEASANT, grateful, agreeable, pleasing, welcome *rel* satisfying, contenting; delighting, rejoicing, gladdening, regaling

gratuitous *syn* SUPEREROGATORY, uncalled-for, wanton *rel* voluntary, willing; unrecompensed, unremunerated; unprovoked, unexcited; unjustified, unwarranted

gratuity *syn* GIFT, largess, boon, favor, present

grave *syn* SERIOUS, solemn, somber, sedate, sober, earnest, staid *rel* austere, stern, ascetic, severe; saturnine, dour, sullen *ant* gay

graze *vb, syn* FEED, pasture, nourish

graze *vb, syn* BRUSH, glance, shave, skim *rel* touch, contact; injure, hurt, harm; deface, disfigure; wound, bruise, contuse

grease *syn* OIL, lubricate, anoint, cream

great *syn* LARGE, big *rel* enormous, immense, huge, mammoth; tremendous, prodigious, stupendous, monumental, monstrous; eminent, illustrious, renowned, famous; supreme, superlative, surpassing, transcendent *ant* little

greatly *syn* LARGELY, mostly, chiefly, mainly, principally, generally

greed *syn* CUPIDITY, rapacity, avarice *rel* greediness, covetousness, avariciousness, acquisitiveness; voraciousness, ravenousness, rapaciousness, gluttonousness, gluttony

greedy *syn* COVETOUS, acquisitive, grasping, avaricious *rel* rapacious, ravening, ravenous, voracious, gluttonous; stingy, parsimonious, miserly, close, closefisted

green *syn* RUDE, callow, raw, crude, rough, uncouth *ant* experienced; seasoned

greet *syn* ADDRESS, salute, hail, accost

greeting • the ceremonial words or acts of one who meets, welcomes, or formally addresses another *syn* salutation, salute

gregarious *syn* SOCIAL, cooperative, convivial, companionable, hospitable

grief *syn* SORROW, anguish, woe, heartache, heartbreak, regret *rel* mourning, grieving, sorrowing; lamenting, lamentation, bewailing, bemoaning, deploring

grievance *syn* INJUSTICE, wrong, injury *rel* hardship, rigor, difficulty; trial, tribulation, affliction, cross

grieve • to feel or express sorrow or grief *syn* mourn, sorrow *rel* suffer, bear, endure; lament, bemoan, bewail, deplore; cry, weep, wail, keen *ant* rejoice

grim **1** • being extremely obdurate or firm in action or purpose *syn* implacable, relentless, unrelenting, merciless *rel* inexorable, obdurate, adamant, inflexible; inevitable, certain; fierce, ferocious, cruel, fell; malignant, malevolent, malicious *ant* lenient **2** *syn* GHASTLY, grisly, gruesome, macabre, lurid *rel* fierce, truculent, savage; repellent, repugnant; repulsive, revolting, loathsome, offensive

grime *syn* SOIL, dirty, sully, tarnish, foul, befoul, smirch, besmirch, begrime *rel* pollute, defile, contaminate

grin *vb, syn* SMILE, smirk, simper

grin *n, syn* SMILE, smirk, simper

grind *vb, syn* SCRAPE, scratch, grate, rasp *rel* abrade; sharpen; press, bear, squeeze; gnash, gnaw, bite

grind *n, syn* WORK, drudgery, toil, travail, labor *rel* pains, trouble, exertion, effort

grip *syn* HOLD, grasp, clutch *rel* tenaciousness, toughness, stoutness; power, force; duress, coercion, restraint, constraint, force

grisly *syn* GHASTLY, gruesome, macabre, grim, lurid *rel* horrific, horrible, horrendous, horrid; uncanny, eerie, weird

grit *syn* FORTITUDE, pluck, backbone, guts, sand *rel* courage, resolution, tenacity, mettle, spirit *ant* faintheartedness

groan *vb, syn* SIGH, moan, sob *rel* wail, weep, cry; lament, bemoan, bewail, deplore

groan *n, syn* SIGH, moan, sob

gross **1** *syn* WHOLE, total, entire, all *ant* net **2** *syn* COARSE, vulgar, obscene, ribald *rel* fleshly, carnal, sensual, animal; material, physical, corporeal; loathsome, offensive, revolting, repulsive *ant* delicate, dainty; ethereal **3** *syn* FLAGRANT, glaring, rank *rel* extreme, excessive, inordinate, immoderate, exorbitant; outrageous, atrocious, monstrous, heinous *ant* petty

grotesque *syn* FANTASTIC, bizarre, antic *rel* baroque, rococo, flamboyant, ornate; weird, eerie, uncanny; extravagant, extreme, excessive; preposterous, absurd, foolish; ludicrous, ridiculous, comical, comic, droll, laughable

ground *n* **1** *syn* BASE, basis, foundation, groundwork *rel* background, backdrop **2** *syn* REASON, argument, proof *rel* evidence, testimony; determinant, cause, antecedent; demonstration, proof, trial, test **3** *pl* **grounds** *syn* DEPOSIT, precipitate, sediment, dregs, lees

ground *vb, syn* BASE, found, bottom, stay, rest *rel* establish, fix, settle, set; implant; sustain, support, buttress

groundless *syn* BASELESS, unfounded, unwarranted *rel* unsupported, unsustained

groundwork *syn* BASE, foundation, basis, ground *ant* superstructure

group • a collection or assemblage of persons or things *syn* cluster, bunch, parcel, lot *rel* company, party, band, troop, troupe; set, circle, coterie, clique; crowd, mob, horde

grovel *syn* WALLOW, welter *rel* fawn, cringe, cower, toady, truckle; crawl, creep; abase, demean, humble

growl *syn* BARK, bay, howl, snarl, yelp, yap *rel* threaten, menace; irritate

grown-up *syn* MATURE, adult, matured, ripe, mellow *ant* childish; callow

grub *syn* DIG, delve, spade, excavate

grudge *vb, syn* COVET, begrudge, envy *rel* deny; refuse, decline

grudge *n, syn* MALICE, ill will, malevolence, spite, despite, malignity, malignancy, spleen *rel* animus, antipathy, animosity, rancor, enmity; hate, hatred; grievance, injustice, injury

gruesome *syn* GHASTLY, macabre, grisly, grim, lurid *rel* daunting, appalling, horrifying, horrendous, horrific, horrible; baleful, sinister

gruff *syn* BLUFF, crusty, brusque, blunt, curt *rel* surly, morose, sullen, saturnine, crabbed, dour; churlish, boorish; truculent, fierce

guarantee • an assurance for the fulfillment of a condition or a person who provides such assurance *syn* guaranty, surety, security, bond, bail *rel* pledge, earnest, token; guarantor, surety, sponsor

guarantor *syn* SPONSOR, surety, patron, backer, angel *rel* guarantee

guaranty *syn* GUARANTEE, surety, security, bond, bail *rel* pledge, earnest, token; contract, bargain

guard *syn* DEFEND, shield, protect, safeguard *rel* watch, attend, tend, mind; convoy, escort, chaperon, conduct, accompany

guerdon *syn* PREMIUM, reward, meed, bounty, award, prize, bonus

guess *vb, syn* CONJECTURE, surmise *rel* speculate, think, reason; imagine, fancy; gather, infer, deduce; estimate, reckon, calculate

guess *n, syn* CONJECTURE, surmise *rel* hypothesis, theory; belief, opinion, view *ant* certainty

guest *syn* VISITOR, caller, visitant

guide • to put or lead on a course or into the way to be followed *syn* lead, steer, pilot, engineer *rel* conduct, convoy, escort, chaperon, accompany; direct, manage, control, conduct *ant* misguide

guile *syn* DECEIT, duplicity, dissimulation, cunning *rel* trickery, double-dealing, chicanery, chicane, deception; craft, artifice, art *ant* ingenuousness; candor

guileful *syn* SLY, cunning, crafty, tricky, foxy, insidious, wily, artful

guilt *syn* BLAME, culpability, fault *rel* sin, crime, offense; responsibility, answerability, liability *ant* innocence; guiltlessness

guilty *syn* BLAMEWORTHY, culpable *rel* responsible, answerable, accountable; indicted, impeached, incriminated, accused *ant* innocent

gulf · a hollow place of vast width and depth *syn* chasm, abysm, abyss

gull *syn* DUPE, befool, trick, hoax, hoodwink, bamboozle *rel* delude, beguile, deceive, mislead, double-cross, betray

gullibility *syn* CREDULITY *ant* astuteness

gullible *syn* CREDULOUS *rel* duped, befooled, hoaxed, hoodwinked; deluded, beguiled, deceived, misled; impressionable, susceptible, sentient *ant* astute

gumption *syn* SENSE, common sense, good sense, judgment, wisdom *rel* sagaciousness, sagacity, shrewdness, perspicaciousness, perspicacity, astuteness

gunman *syn* ASSASSIN, cutthroat, bravo

gush *syn* POUR, stream, sluice *rel* flow, stream, flood; spring, issue, emanate

gusto *syn* TASTE, relish, zest, palate *rel* enjoyment, delight, delectation, pleasure; enthusiasm, fervor, ardor, passion, zeal

gut **1** *syn* ABDOMEN, belly, stomach, paunch **2** *pl* **guts** *syn* FORTITUDE, grit, pluck, backbone, sand *rel* tenacity, resolution, mettle, spirit, courage

gyrate *syn* TURN, rotate, revolve, spin, whirl, wheel, circle, twirl, eddy, swirl, pirouette

H

habit **1** · a mode of behaving or doing that has become fixed by constant repetition *syn* habitude, practice, usage, custom, use, wont *rel* instinct; convention, convenance, usage, form **2** *syn* PHYSIQUE, build, constitution *rel* body, carcass; structure, anatomy, framework; figure, form, shape; outline, contour

habitat · the place in which a particular kind of organism lives or grows *syn* biotope, range, station

habitation · the place where one lives *syn* dwelling, abode, residence, domicile, home, house

habitual *syn* USUAL, customary, wonted, accustomed *rel* habituated, addicted; practiced, drilled; confirmed, inveterate, chronic, deep-seated, deep-rooted *ant* occasional

habituate · to make used to something *syn* accustom, addict, inure *rel* train, discipline, school, teach; harden, season, acclimatize, acclimate; practice, exercise, drill

habitude *syn* HABIT, practice, usage, custom, use, wont *rel* attitude, stand, position; state, condition, situation

habitué *syn* ADDICT, votary, devotee

hack *syn* MERCENARY, hireling,

venal *rel* toiling, drudging, grinding, laboring; hired, employed; mean, abject, sordid

hackneyed *syn* TRITE, stereotyped, threadbare, shopworn *rel* antiquated, archaic, obsolete, antediluvian, old; worn, wasted, haggard; attenuated, diluted, thin

Hadean *syn* INFERNAL, chthonian, Tartarean, stygian, hellish, chthonic

haggard · thin and drawn by or as if by worry, fatigue, hunger, or illness *syn* worn, careworn, pinched, wasted, cadaverous *rel* gaunt, scrawny, skinny, lean; fatigued, exhausted, wearied, fagged, jaded, tired; wan, pallid, ashen, pale

hail *syn* ADDRESS, salute, greet, accost

halcyon *syn* CALM, serene, placid, tranquil, peaceful

hale *adj, syn* HEALTHY, robust, sound, wholesome, well *rel* lusty, vigorous; sturdy, stalwart, strong, stout; spry, agile *ant* infirm

hale *vb, syn* PULL, haul, draw, drag, tug, tow

hall, hallway *syn* PASSAGE, passageway, corridor, gallery, arcade, cloister, aisle, ambulatory

hallow *syn* DEVOTE, consecrate, dedicate

hallucination *syn* DELUSION, mirage, illusion *rel* apparition, phantasm, phantom, wraith; fantasy, fancy, vision, dream, nightmare

hamper · to hinder or impede in moving, progressing, or acting freely *syn* trammel, clog, fetter, shackle, manacle, hog-tie *rel* hinder, impede, obstruct, block, bar; embarrass, discomfit; baffle, balk, thwart, foil, frustrate *ant* assist (*persons*); expedite (*work, projects*)

hand *syn* WORKER, operative, workman, workingman, laborer, craftsman, handicraftsman, mechanic, artisan, roustabout

handicap **1** *syn* ADVANTAGE, allowance, odds, edge **2** *syn* DISADVANTAGE, detriment, drawback *rel* burden, encumbrance, load; disability, inability; impediment, obstacle *ant* asset, advantage

handicraft *syn* TRADE, craft, art, profession

handicraftsman *syn* WORKER, craftsman, workman, artisan, mechanic, workingman, laborer, operative, hand, roustabout

handle **1** · to deal with or manage usu. with dexterity or efficiency *syn* manipulate, wield, swing, ply *rel* swing, flourish, brandish, shake, wave; direct, aim, point, level, train, lay **2** *syn* TREAT, deal *rel* manage, control, conduct, direct **3** *syn* TOUCH, feel, palpate, paw *rel* inspect, examine, scrutinize; try, test, prove

handsome **1** *syn* LIBERAL, generous, bountiful, bounteous, openhanded, munificent *rel* lavish, prodigal, profuse **2** *syn* BEAUTIFUL, pulchritudinous, beauteous, comely, good-looking, lovely, pretty, bonny, fair *rel* majestic, stately, august, noble, grand; elegant, exquisite, choice; smart, modish, fashionable, stylish

handy *syn* DEXTEROUS, deft, adroit *rel* adept, skillful, skilled, proficient; able, capable, competent

hang **1** · to place or be placed so as to be supported at one point or side usu. at the top *syn* suspend, sling, dangle *rel* stick, adhere, cling; hover, flit **2** *syn* DEPEND, hinge, turn

hanger-on *syn* PARASITE, sycophant, leech, sponge, sponger, favorite, toady, lickspittle, bootlicker

hanker *syn* LONG, yearn, pine, hunger, thirst *rel* crave, desire, covet, wish, want; aspire, pant, aim

hap *syn* CHANCE, fortune, luck, accident, hazard *rel* fate, destiny, lot, portion

haphazard *syn* RANDOM, chance, chancy, casual, desultory, hit-or-miss, happy-go-lucky *rel* accidental, fortuitous, casual

hapless *syn* UNLUCKY, disastrous, ill-starred, ill-fated, unfortunate, calamitous, luckless *rel* unhappy, infelicitous, unfit; miserable, wretched

happen • to come to pass or to come about *syn* chance, occur, befall, betide, transpire

happiness • a state of well-being or pleasurable satisfaction *syn* felicity, beatitude, blessedness, bliss *rel* contentedness, content, satisfiedness, satisfaction; pleasure, enjoyment, delight, delectation, joy, fruition *ant* unhappiness

happy **1** *syn* LUCKY, fortunate, providential *rel* accidental, incidental, fortuitous, casual; favorable, auspicious, propitious, benign; opportune, timely, seasonable *ant* unhappy **2** *syn* FIT, felicitous, apt, appropriate, fitting, suitable, meet, proper *rel* effective, efficacious, efficient, effectual; telling, cogent, convincing, valid; pat, seasonable, well-timed; right, correct, nice *ant* unhappy **3** *syn* GLAD, cheerful, lighthearted, joyful, joyous *rel* contented, satisfied; gratified, delighted, pleased, gladdened, rejoiced *ant* unhappy; disconsolate

happy-go-lucky *syn* RANDOM, haphazard, hit-or-miss, chance, chancy, casual, desultory

harangue *syn* SPEECH, oration, address, lecture, talk, sermon, homily *rel* rant, rodomontade, bombast

harass *syn* WORRY, harry, annoy, plague, pester, tease, tantalize *rel* bait, badger, hound, ride, hector, chivy, heckle; vex, irk, bother, annoy

harbinger *syn* FORERUNNER, precursor, herald

harbor *n* • a place where seacraft may ride secure *syn* haven, port

harbor *vb* • to provide with shelter or refuge *syn* shelter, entertain, lodge, house, board *rel* foster, cherish, nurture, nurse; hide, conceal, secrete; protect, shield, defend

hard **1** *syn* FIRM, solid *rel* compact, dense, close; consolidated, compacted, concentrated; hardened, indurated, callous *ant* soft **2** • demanding great toil or effort *syn* difficult, arduous *rel* onerous, burdensome, oppressive, exacting; intricate, knotty, complicated, involved, complex; exhausting, fatiguing, wearying, tiring *ant* easy

harden **1** • to make or to become physically hard or solid *syn* solidify, indurate, petrify, cake *rel* compact, consolidate, concentrate; compress, condense, contract *ant* soften **2** • to make proof against hardship, strain, or exposure *syn* season, acclimatize, acclimate *rel* habituate, accustom, inure; adapt, adjust, accommodate *ant* soften

hardened • grown or become hard *syn* indurated, callous *rel* consolidated, compacted, concentrated *ant* softened.

hardihood *syn* TEMERITY, audacity, effrontery, nerve, cheek, gall *rel* boldness, intrepidity; brazenness, impudence, brashness; guts, sand, grit, pluck, fortitude

hardship *syn* DIFFICULTY, rigor, vicissitude *rel* adversity, misfortune, mischance; peril, danger, jeopardy, hazard; trial, tribulation, affliction; toil, travail, drudgery, work

harm *n, syn* INJURY, damage, hurt, mischief *rel* detrimentalness, detriment, deleteriousness, perniciousness, noxiousness; misfortune, mischance, mishap; impairing, impairment, marring *ant* benefit

harm *vb, syn* INJURE, impair, hurt, damage, mar, spoil *rel* abuse, maltreat, mistreat, misuse; ruin, dilapidate; discommode, incommode, inconvenience; sap, undermine, weaken *ant* benefit

harmless · not having hurtful or injurious qualities *syn* innocuous, innocent, inoffensive, unoffending *ant* harmful

harmonize 1 *syn* AGREE, accord, correspond, square, conform, tally, jibe *rel* reconcile, adjust, adapt, accommodate; match, equal, approach, touch, rival *ant* clash; conflict 2 · to bring into consonance or accord *syn* tune, attune *rel* adjust, reconcile, adapt

harmony 1 · the effect produced when different things come together without clashing or disagreement *syn* consonance, accord, concord *rel* integration, articulation, concatenation; congruousness, congruity, consonance, compatibility; concurrence, agreement *ant* conflict 2 *syn* SYMMETRY, proportion, balance *rel* grace, elegance, dignity; unity, integrity

harry *syn* WORRY, harass, annoy, plague, pester, tease, tantalize *rel* torment, torture, rack, afflict, try; trouble, distress; bait, badger, hound, ride, hector; fret, gall, chafe, abrade

harsh *syn* ROUGH, rugged, scabrous, uneven *rel* repellent, repugnant, distasteful, abhorrent, obnoxious; coarse, gross; strident, vociferous, blatant; rigorous, strict, stringent, rigid *ant* pleasant; mild

harvest *syn* REAP, glean, gather, garner *rel* collect, assemble; accumulate, amass, hoard

haste · rapidity of motion or action *syn* hurry, speed, expedition, dispatch *rel* celerity, alacrity, legerity; rapidity, swiftness, quickness, expeditiousness; readiness, promptness; agility, briskness *ant* deliberation

hasten *syn* SPEED, accelerate, quicken, hurry, precipitate *ant* delay

hasty 1 *syn* FAST, speedy, quick, expeditious, rapid, swift, fleet *rel* agile, brisk, nimble; hurried, quickened 2 *syn* PRECIPITATE, headlong, abrupt, impetuous, sudden

hate *n, syn* ABHORRENCE, hatred, detestation, abomination, loathing *rel* antipathy, aversion; animosity, rancor, hostility, enmity; despite, contempt, scorn, disdain *ant* love

hate *vb* · to feel extreme enmity or dislike *syn* detest, abhor, abominate, loathe *rel* despise, contemn, scorn, disdain; disapprove, deprecate *ant* love

hateful · deserving of or arousing hate *syn* odious, abhorrent, detestable, abominable *rel* antipathetic, unsympathetic, averse; repellent, repugnant, obnoxious, distasteful *ant* lovable; sympathetic

hatred *syn* ABHORRENCE, hate, detestation, abomination, loathing *rel* animosity, enmity, hostility, rancor; aversion, antipathy; malevolence, malignity, malignancy, ill will, despite, malice; envy, jealousy

haughty *syn* PROUD, arrogant, insolent, lordly, overbearing, supercilious, disdainful *rel* aloof, detached, indifferent; vain, vainglorious, proud; contemptuous, scornful *ant* lowly

haul *syn* PULL, hale, draw, drag, tug, tow *rel* move, remove, shift; lift, raise, hoist, heave, boost, elevate; convey, transport, carry

have · to keep, control, or experience as one's own *syn* hold, own, possess, enjoy

haven *syn* HARBOR, port *rel* asylum, refuge, retreat, shelter, cover

havoc *syn* RUIN, devastation, destruction *rel* calamity, cataclysm, catastrophe, disaster; ravaging, pillaging, despoiling

hazard *n* 1 *syn* CHANCE, accident, fortune, luck, hap 2 *syn* DAN-

GER, jeopardy, peril, risk *rel* possibility, probability, likelihood; contingency, exigency, emergency, juncture

hazard *vb, syn* VENTURE, risk, chance, jeopardize, endanger, imperil *rel* dare, beard, face; confront, encounter, meet; expose, open, subject

hazardous *syn* DANGEROUS, precarious, risky, perilous *rel* venturesome, adventurous; chancy, chance, haphazard, happy-go-lucky, random

haze · an atmospheric condition that is characterized by the presence of fine particulate material in the air and that deprives the air of its transparency *syn* mist, fog, smog

head, headman *syn* CHIEF, leader, chieftain, master

headlong *syn* PRECIPITATE, impetuous, abrupt, hasty, sudden *rel* rash, reckless, daring, daredevil, foolhardy, adventurous

headstrong *syn* UNRULY, ungovernable, intractable, refractory, recalcitrant, willful *rel* perverse, contrary, froward, wayward; stubborn, obstinate, pigheaded, stiff-necked

headway *syn* SPEED, pace, velocity, momentum, impetus *rel* advance, progress; motion, movement

heal *syn* CURE, remedy

healthful · conducive or beneficial to the health or soundness of body or mind *syn* healthy, wholesome, salubrious, salutary, hygienic, sanitary *rel* beneficial, advantageous, profitable; remedying, remedial, correcting, corrective; helping, helpful, aiding

healthy 1 *syn* HEALTHFUL, wholesome, salubrious, salutary, hygienic, sanitary *rel* see HEALTHFUL 2 · having or manifesting health of mind or body or indicative of such health *syn* sound, wholesome, robust, hale, well *rel* vigorous, lusty, energetic; strong, sturdy, stalwart, tough, tenacious *ant* unhealthy

heap *n* · a quantity of things brought together into a more or less compact group *syn* pile, stack, shock, cock, mass, bank *rel* aggregate, aggregation, conglomerate, conglomeration; collection, assemblage

heap *vb* · to bring a number of things together into a more or less compact group or collection *syn* pile, stack, shock, cock, mass, bank *rel* accumulate, amass, hoard; collect, assemble, gather

hearing · an opportunity to be heard *syn* audience, audition

hearsay *syn* REPORT, rumor, gossip

heart *syn* CENTER, middle, core, hub, nucleus, midst, focus

heartache, heartbreak *syn* SORROW, grief, anguish, woe, regret

hearten *syn* ENCOURAGE, inspirit, embolden, cheer, nerve, steel *rel* strengthen, fortify, invigorate, energize; rally, arouse, rouse, stir *ant* dishearten

heartfelt *syn* SINCERE, hearty, unfeigned, wholehearted, whole-souled *rel* genuine, veritable, authentic, bona fide; profound, deep

hearty *syn* SINCERE, heartfelt, unfeigned, wholehearted, whole-souled *rel* warm, warmhearted, responsive, tender, deep, profound; exuberant, profuse *ant* hollow

heave *syn* LIFT, raise, hoist, elevate, boost, rear

heavenly *syn* CELESTIAL, empyrean, empyreal

heavy · having great weight *syn* weighty, ponderous, cumbrous, cumbersome, hefty *rel* solid, hard, firm; oppressing, oppressive, weighing down, depressing *ant* light

heckle *syn* BAIT, badger, hector, chivy, hound, ride *rel* plague, pester, harass, harry, worry, annoy; disconcert, rattle, faze, discomfit, embarrass; rack, torment, afflict

hector *syn* BAIT, badger, chivy, heckle, hound, ride *rel* tease, tantalize, plague, pester, worry; bother, vex, irk, annoy; fret, chafe, gall, abrade

heedless *syn* CARELESS, thoughtless, inadvertent *rel* forgetful, oblivious, unmindful; abstracted, absent, absentminded, distraught; frivolous, light-minded, flippant, volatile; remiss, lax, slack, negligent, neglectful *ant* heedful

hefty *syn* HEAVY, weighty, ponderous, cumbrous, cumbersome *rel, ant* see HEAVY

height · the distance a thing rises above the level on which it stands *syn* altitude, elevation

heighten *syn* INTENSIFY, enhance, aggravate *rel* exalt, magnify, aggrandize; elevate, lift, raise; improve, better

heinous *syn* OUTRAGEOUS, atrocious, monstrous *rel* flagrant, glaring, gross, rank; nefarious, flagitious, infamous, vicious *ant* venial

hellish *syn* INFERNAL, chthonian, chthonic, Hadean, Tartarean, stygian *rel* devilish, diabolical, fiendish, demoniac

help *vb* **1** · to give assistance or support *syn* aid, assist *rel* support, uphold, back, champion; benefit, profit, avail; forward, further, promote, advance *ant* hinder **2** *syn* IMPROVE, better, ameliorate *rel* palliate, gloss, extenuate, whitewash, whiten; alleviate, relieve, mitigate

help *n* · an act or instance of giving what will benefit or assist *syn* aid, assistance *rel* cooperation, uniting, union; supporting, support, backing

helper *syn* ASSISTANT, coadjutor, aid, aide, aide-de-camp

hem *syn* SURROUND, environ, encircle, circle, encompass, compass, gird, girdle, ring *rel* enclose, envelop, wall, cage, fence; confine, circumscribe, restrict, limit

hence *syn* THEREFORE, consequently, then, accordingly, so

henchman *syn* FOLLOWER, adherent, disciple, partisan, satellite, sectary

herald *syn* FORERUNNER, harbinger, precursor

Herculean *syn* HUGE, vast, immense, enormous, elephantine, mammoth, giant, gigantic, gigantean, colossal, gargantuan, cyclopean, titanic, Brobdingnagian

hereditary *syn* INNATE, congenital, inborn, inherited, inbred *rel* transmitted, conveyed; inherent, constitutional, intrinsic, ingrained

heretic · one who is not orthodox in his beliefs *syn* schismatic, sectarian, sectary, dissenter, nonconformist *rel* freethinker, deist, unbeliever, atheist; renegade, apostate

heretical *syn* HETERODOX

heritage · something which one receives or is entitled to receive by succession *syn* inheritance, patrimony, birthright

hermaphroditic, hermaphrodite *syn* BISEXUAL, androgynous, epicene

hermit *syn* RECLUSE, eremite, anchorite, cenobite

heroism · conspicuous courage or bravery *syn* valor, prowess, gallantry *rel* bravery, intrepidity, dauntlessness, doughtiness; courage, tenacity, resolution, mettle, spirit; fortitude, pluck, grit, guts, sand

hesitancy *syn* HESITATION *rel* reluctance, averseness, indisposedness, indisposition; faltering, wavering, vacillation

hesitant *syn* DISINCLINED, reluctant, loath, averse, indisposed *rel* fearful, afraid, apprehensive; diffident, shy, bashful; recoiling, flinching, blenching, shrinking

hesitate · to show irresolution or uncertainty *syn* waver, vacillate, falter *rel* balk, boggle, stick, stickle, scruple, demur, shy; fluctuate, oscillate, swing

hesitation · an act or action of hesitating *syn* hesitancy *rel* uncertainty, doubt, dubiety, dubiosity, mistrust; procrastination, delaying, delay, dawdling

heterodox · not in conformity with orthodox beliefs or teachings *syn* heretical *ant* orthodox

heterogeneous *syn* MISCELLANEOUS, motley, promiscuous, assorted *rel* diverse, disparate, various, divergent, different; mixed, mingled, commingled; multifarious, divers, many *ant* homogeneous

hew *syn* CUT, chop, carve, slit, slash *rel* cleave, rive, split, tear

hiatus *syn* BREAK, gap, interruption, interval, interim, lacuna

hick *syn* BOOR, bumpkin, yokel, rube, clodhopper, clown, lout, churl

hide *vb* · to withdraw or to withhold from sight or observation *syn* conceal, screen, secrete, cache, bury, ensconce *rel* cloak, mask, disguise, dissemble, camouflage; suppress, repress

hide *n, syn* SKIN, pelt, rind, bark, peel

hidebound *syn* ILLIBERAL, narrow-minded, narrow, intolerant, bigoted *rel* restricted, circumscribed, limited

hideous *syn* UGLY, ill-favored, unsightly *rel* revolting, repulsive, offensive, loathsome; repellent, obnoxious, abhorrent, distasteful, repugnant; homely, plain *ant* fair

high · having a relatively great upward extension *syn* tall, lofty *rel* elevated, lifted, raised, reared; deep, profound, abysmal; heightened, enhanced, intensified; increased, augmented *ant* low

high-spirited *syn* SPIRITED, mettlesome, spunky, fiery, peppery, gingery *rel* gallant, chivalrous, courtly, courteous, civil; audacious, bold, brave, intrepid

hilarity *syn* MIRTH, jollity, glee *rel* merriment, blitheness, jocundity; cheerfulness, gladness, joyfulness, joyousness, lightheartedness; fun, play, sport, jest, game

hind *syn* POSTERIOR, hinder, rear, after, back *ant* fore, front

hinder *vb* · to put obstacles in the way *syn* impede, obstruct, block, bar, dam *rel* arrest, check, interrupt; hamper, fetter, clog, trammel, shackle, manacle, hog-tie; restrain, inhibit, curb, check; baffle, balk, frustrate *ant* further

hinder *adj, syn* POSTERIOR, hind, rear, after, back *ant* front, fore

hinge *syn* DEPEND, hang, turn *rel* swing, fluctuate, undulate

hint *syn* SUGGEST, intimate, insinuate, imply *rel* allude, advert, refer

hire *n, syn* WAGE, wages, pay, salary, stipend, fee, emolument

hire *vb* · to take or engage something or grant the use of something for a stipulated price or rate *syn* let, lease, rent, charter *rel* secure, obtain, get, procure; engage, contract, promise

hireling *syn* MERCENARY, venal, hack *rel* servile, menial, subservient; mean, abject, sordid

history · a chronological record of events *syn* chronicle, annals

histrionic *syn* DRAMATIC, theatrical, dramaturgic, melodramatic *rel* acting, playing, impersonating

hit *syn* STRIKE, smite, punch, slug, slog, swat, clout, slap, cuff, box *rel* beat, buffet, pound, pummel, thrash

hit-or-miss *syn* RANDOM, haphazard, happy-go-lucky, desultory, casual, chance, chancy

hoard *syn* ACCUMULATE, amass *rel* collect, assemble, gather; pile, heap, stack, mass

hoarse *syn* LOUD, raucous, strident, stentorian, earsplitting, stertorous *rel* harsh, rough; gruff, crusty, bluff

hoax *syn* DUPE, hoodwink, bamboozle, gull, befool, trick *rel* delude, mislead, deceive; cheat, cozen, overreach, defraud

hobo *syn* VAGABOND, tramp, vagrant, truant, bum

hocus-pocus *syn* GIBBERISH, mummery, abracadabra

hog-tie *syn* HAMPER, trammel, clog, fetter, shackle, manacle *rel* impede, hinder, obstruct, block, bar, dam; curb, check, restrain; tie, bind

hoist *syn* LIFT, raise, elevate, boost, heave, rear *rel* rise, arise, ascend, mount, levitate

hold *vb* **1** *syn* KEEP, hold back, withhold, reserve, detain, retain, keep back, keep out *rel* restrain, inhibit, curb, check; preserve, conserve, save **2** *syn* CONTAIN, accommodate *rel* carry, bear, convey; receive, admit, take; house, lodge, harbor, shelter; include, comprehend **3** *syn* HAVE, own, possess, enjoy *rel* control, direct, manage, conduct

hold *n* • the act or manner of grasping or holding *syn* grip, grasp, clutch *rel* possession, ownership; control, command, power, authority

hold back *syn* KEEP, hold, withhold, reserve, detain, retain, keep back, keep out

hole • a space within the substance of a body or mass *syn* hollow, cavity, pocket, void, vacuum *rel* aperture, orifice, interstice; perforation, puncture, bore, prick; slit, slash, cut

holiness • a state of spiritual soundness and unimpaired virtue *syn* sanctity *rel* sacredness, divineness, divinity, spirituality, blessedness, religiousness; devoutness, devotion, piousness, piety; goodness, virtue, rectitude

holler *vb, syn* SHOUT, yell, shriek, scream, screech, squeal, whoop *rel* vociferate, clamor, bellow, roar

holler *n, syn* SHOUT, yell, shriek, scream, screech, squeal, whoop *rel* bellow, roar, vociferation, bawl

hollow *adj, syn* VAIN, empty, nugatory, otiose, idle *rel* see EMPTY *adj* 2

hollow *n, syn* HOLE, cavity, pocket, void, vacuum *rel* excavation, digging; gulf, chasm, abyss; orifice, aperture

holocaust *syn* FIRE, conflagration

holy • dedicated to the service of or set apart by religion *syn* sacred, divine, spiritual, religious, blessed *rel* hallowed, consecrated, dedicated; adored, worshiped, venerated, reverenced, revered; devout, pious, religious *ant* unholy

homage *syn* HONOR, reverence, deference, obeisance *rel* worship, adoration, veneration, reverence; fealty, fidelity, devotion, loyalty, allegiance; tribute, panegyric, eulogy, encomium

home *syn* HABITATION, house, dwelling, abode, residence, domicile

homely *syn* PLAIN, simple, unpretentious *rel* familiar, intimate, close; usual, wonted, customary, habitual; ill-favored, ugly *ant* comely, bonny

homily *syn* SPEECH, sermon, talk, address, oration, harangue, lecture

homunculus *syn* DWARF, manikin, midget, pygmy, runt

honest *syn* UPRIGHT, just, conscientious, scrupulous, honorable *rel* truthful, veracious; candid, open, plain, frank; straightforward, aboveboard, forthright; fair, equitable, dispassionate, objective *ant* dishonest

honesty • uprightness as evidenced in character and actions *syn* honor, integrity, probity *rel* veracity, truth, verity; uprightness, justness, conscientiousness, scrupulousness; candidness, candor, openness, plainness, frankness; reliability, trustworthiness, dependability; rectitude, virtue, goodness *ant* dishonesty

honor *n* **1** *syn* FAME, glory, renown, celebrity, éclat, reputation, repute, notoriety *rel* esteem, respect, regard, admiration; reverence, veneration, worship, adoration; prestige, credit, authority, influence, weight *ant* dishonor **2** · respect or esteem shown one as his or her due or claimed by one as a right *syn* homage, reverence, deference, obeisance *rel* recognition, acknowledgment; adulation, compliment; tribute, panegyric, eulogy, encomium **3** *syn* HONESTY, integrity, probity *rel* uprightness, justness, honorableness, scrupulousness, conscientiousness; truth, veracity; straightforwardness, forthrightness; rectitude, virtue, goodness

honor *vb, syn* DIGNIFY, ennoble, glorify *rel* exalt, magnify, aggrandize; extol, laud, acclaim, praise; reverence, revere, venerate

honorable *syn* UPRIGHT, just, scrupulous, conscientious, honest *rel* trustworthy, reliable, dependable; noble, virtuous, righteous, moral, ethical *ant* dishonorable

hoodwink *syn* DUPE, hoax, trick, gull, befool, bamboozle *rel* delude, deceive, mislead; cozen, cheat, overreach; confuse, muddle, fuddle, befuddle; baffle, outwit, circumvent, frustrate

hop *syn* SKIP, bound, curvet, lope, lollop, ricochet

hope *syn* EXPECT, look, await *rel* aspire, aim, pant; yearn, long, hunger, thirst, pine; rely, trust, depend, count, bank, reckon; anticipate, foresee, foreknow, divine *ant* despair (*of*); despond

hopeful · having or showing confidence that the end or outcome will be favorable *syn* optimistic, roseate, rose-colored *rel* expecting, hoping, awaiting; anticipating, foreseeing, divining; sanguine, sure, confident, assured *ant* hopeless, despairing

hopeless *syn* DESPONDENT, despairing, desperate, forlorn *rel* dejected, depressed, melancholy, sad; gloomy, glum, morose, sullen; acquiescent, compliant *ant* hopeful

hopelessness *syn* DESPONDENCY, despair, desperation, forlornness *rel* dejection, depression, melancholy, gloom, sadness *ant* hopefulness

horde *syn* CROWD, mob, throng, crush, press, rout

horizon *syn* RANGE, gamut, reach, radius, compass, sweep, scope, orbit, ken, purview *rel* limit, bound, confine, term, end; spread, stretch, amplitude, expanse

horrendous *syn* HORRIBLE, horrific, horrid

horrible **1** · inspiring horror or abhorrence *syn* horrid, horrific, horrendous *rel* abhorrent, abominable, detestable, hateful; repugnant, repellent, obnoxious; offensive, repulsive, revolting, loathsome *ant* fascinating **2** *syn* FEARFUL, horrific, shocking, appalling, awful, dreadful, frightful, terrible, terrific *rel, ant* see HORRIBLE 1

horrid *syn* HORRIBLE, horrific, horrendous *rel* distasteful, repellent, repugnant, obnoxious; loathsome, offensive, revolting, repulsive *ant* delightful

horrific **1** *syn* HORRIBLE, horrid, horrendous *rel* horrifying, appalling, dismaying, daunting; terrorizing, terrifying, frightening, alarming **2** *syn* FEARFUL, horrible, terrible, terrific, shocking, appalling, awful, dreadful, frightful *rel* see HORRIFIC 1

horrify *syn* DISMAY, daunt, appall *rel* agitate, upset, perturb, discompose; offend, outrage

horror *syn* FEAR, terror, dread, fright, alarm, dismay, consternation, panic, trepidation *rel* aversion, antipathy; repugnance, abhorrence, repellency, repulsion, distastefulness, distaste; recoiling, recoil, flinching, shrinking, blenching *ant* fascination

hors d'oeuvre *syn* APPETIZER, aperitif

horse sense *syn* SENSE, common sense, good sense, gumption, judgment, wisdom

hospitable *syn* SOCIAL, gregarious,

convivial, cooperative, companionable *rel* sociable, gracious, cordial, genial, affable; generous, liberal, bountiful, bounteous, openhanded; friendly, neighborly, amicable *ant* inhospitable

host *syn* MULTITUDE, army, legion

hostage *syn* PLEDGE, pawn, earnest, token *rel* surety, security, guarantee, guaranty

hostility *syn* ENMITY, animosity, antagonism, antipathy, rancor, animus *rel* hatred, hate; ill will, malevolence, malignity, malignancy, malice; aggression, attack; opposing, opposition, combating, resisting, resistance

hound *syn* BAIT, ride, hector, badger, heckle, chivy *rel* harry, harass, worry, annoy; torment, torture, try, afflict; persecute, oppress, wrong

house *n, syn* HABITATION, home, dwelling, abode, residence, domicile

house *vb, syn* HARBOR, lodge, board, shelter, entertain *rel* accommodate, hold, contain

hover *syn* FLIT, flutter, flitter, flicker *rel* hang, suspend; poise, balance, stabilize; float, fly, skim, sail

howl 1 *syn* BARK, bay, growl, snarl, yelp, yap 2 *syn* ROAR, bellow, bluster, bawl, vociferate, clamor, ululate *rel* wail, blubber, cry; lament, bewail, deplore

howler *syn* ERROR, boner, mistake, blunder, slip, lapse, faux pas, bull

hub *syn* CENTER, core, middle, nucleus, heart, focus, midst

hubbub *syn* DIN, uproar, pandemonium, hullabaloo, babel, clamor, racket

hue *syn* COLOR, shade, tint, tinge, tone

huff *syn* OFFENSE, dudgeon, pique, resentment, umbrage *rel* petulance, huffiness, irritability, fractiousness; anger, indignation, rage, wrath

huffy *syn* IRRITABLE, petulant, pettish, fractious, peevish, snappish, waspish, fretful, querulous *rel* angry, mad, indignant, irate

huge • exceedingly or excessively large *syn* vast, immense, enormous, elephantine, mammoth, giant, gigantic, gigantean, colossal, gargantuan, Herculean, cyclopean, titanic, Brobdingnagian *rel* stupendous, tremendous, prodigious, monumental, monstrous; big, great, large

hullabaloo *syn* DIN, uproar, pandemonium, babel, hubbub, clamor, racket

humane *syn* CHARITABLE, humanitarian, benevolent, philanthropic, eleemosynary, altruistic *rel* compassionate, tender, warmhearted; gentle, lenient, mild, soft; clement, merciful, tolerant, forbearing; kindly, kind, benign, benignant *ant* barbarous, inhuman; atrocious

humanitarian *syn* CHARITABLE, humane, benevolent, philanthropic, eleemosynary, altruistic

humble *adj* • lacking all signs of pride, aggressiveness, or self-assertiveness *syn* meek, modest, lowly *rel* submissive, subdued, tame; resigned, acquiescent, compliant

humble *vb, syn* ABASE, humiliate, demean, debase, degrade *rel* abash, discomfit, embarrass; chagrin, mortify

humbug *syn* IMPOSTURE, fake, sham, cheat, fraud, deceit, deception, counterfeit *rel* pretense, pretension, make-believe; impostor, faker, charlatan, mountebank; hocus-pocus, mummery, gibberish, abracadabra

humdrum *syn* DULL, dreary, monotonous, pedestrian, stodgy *rel* irksome, tiresome, wearisome, tedious, boring

humid *syn* WET, moist, damp, dank

humiliate *syn* ABASE, humble, degrade, debase, demean *rel* mortify, chagrin; confound, bewilder, nonplus, puzzle; embarrass, discomfit, abash, disconcert, faze, rattle

humor *n* **1** *syn* MOOD, temper, vein *rel* caprice, freak, fancy, whim, whimsy, conceit, vagary, crotchet; attitude, position, stand **2** *syn* WIT, irony, satire, sarcasm, repartee

humor *vb, syn* INDULGE, pamper, spoil, baby, mollycoddle *rel* gratify, delight, please, rejoice, gladden, tickle; content, satisfy

humorous *syn* WITTY, facetious, jocular, jocose *rel* droll, comic, comical, farcical, funny, laughable; amusing, diverting, entertaining

hunger *syn* LONG, yearn, hanker, pine, thirst *rel* crave, desire, covet, wish, want

hunt *syn* SEEK, search, ransack, rummage, scour, comb, ferret out *rel* pursue, chase, follow, trail

hurl *syn* THROW, fling, cast, pitch, toss, sling

hurricane • a violent rotating storm originating in the tropics and often moving into temperate latitudes *syn* tropical storm, typhoon *rel* whirlwind, whirly; cyclone, tornado, twister

hurry *vb, syn* SPEED, quicken, precipitate, hasten *rel* impel, drive, move *ant* delay

hurry *n, syn* HASTE, speed, dispatch, expedition *rel* swiftness, rapidity, expeditiousness, quickness, speediness; celerity, alacrity, legerity; flurry, stir, bustle, pother, ado

hurt *vb, syn* INJURE, harm, damage, impair, mar, spoil *rel* afflict, torture, torment; trouble, distress; wrong, oppress, persecute, aggrieve

hurt *n, syn* INJURY, harm, damage, mischief *rel* pain, ache, pang, throe, twinge, stitch; injustice, wrong, grievance

husbandry *syn* AGRICULTURE, farming

husky *syn* MUSCULAR, brawny, sinewy, athletic, burly *rel* stalwart, stout, strong, sturdy, tough; powerful, puissant, potent, forceful

hygienic *syn* HEALTHFUL, sanitary, healthy, wholesome, salubrious, salutary

hymeneal *syn* MATRIMONIAL, nuptial, marital, connubial, conjugal

hymn *syn* SING, troll, carol, descant, warble, trill, chant, intone *rel* extol, laud, acclaim, praise

hyperbole *syn* EXAGGERATION, overstatement

hypercritical *syn* CRITICAL, captious, caviling, carping, censorious, faultfinding *rel* finicky, fastidious, fussy, pernickety, squeamish, particular, nice

hypochondriac *syn* MELANCHOLIC, melancholy, atrabilious

hypocrisy • the pretense or affectation of having virtues, principles, or beliefs that one does not actually have *syn* sanctimony, pharisaism, cant *rel* dissimulation, duplicity, guile, deceit; pretense, pretension, make-believe

hypocritical • characterized by hypocrisy *syn* sanctimonious, pharisaical, canting *rel* unctuous, oily, slick, fulsome; feigned, affected, assumed, simulated, shammed, counterfeited, pretended

hypostatize *syn* REALIZE, reify, externalize, materialize, incarnate, actualize, embody, objectify

hypothetical *syn* SUPPOSED, conjectural, supposititious, reputed, putative, purported *rel* theoretical, speculative, academic; doubtful, dubious, problematic, questionable

hysteria *syn* MANIA, delirium, frenzy

I

icon *syn* IMAGE, portrait, effigy, statue, photograph, mask

iconoclast *syn* REBEL, insurgent

icy *syn* COLD, glacial, arctic, gelid, frigid, freezing, frosty, cool, chilly *ant* fiery

idea · what exists in the mind as a representation as of something comprehended or as a formulation as of a plan *syn* concept, conception, thought, notion, impression *rel* opinion, view, belief, conviction, sentiment; hypothesis, theory, law

ideal *adj, syn* ABSTRACT, transcendent, transcendental *rel* utopian; surpassing, peerless, supreme *ant* actual

ideal *n, syn* MODEL, pattern, exemplar, example, standard, beau ideal, mirror *rel* truth, verity; perfection, excellence

identical 1 *also* identic *syn* SAME, selfsame, very, equivalent, equal, tantamount *rel* corresponding, correlative, convertible, reciprocal *ant* diverse 2 *syn* LIKE, alike, similar, analogous, comparable, akin, parallel, uniform *rel* matching, equaling; agreeing, squaring, tallying, jibing, corresponding *ant* different

identification *syn* RECOGNITION, apperception, assimilation *rel* perception, discernment, discrimination; image, percept, sense-datum, sensum, sensation

identify · to bring (one or more things) into union with another thing *syn* incorporate, embody, assimilate *rel* fuse, blend, merge, mix; mistake, confuse, confound

idiom 1 *syn* LANGUAGE, dialect, speech, tongue *rel* jargon, patois, cant, argot 2 *syn* PHRASE, expression, locution

idiosyncrasy *syn* ECCENTRICITY *rel* peculiarity, individuality, distinctiveness, distinction, characteristicness, characteristic; manner, way, method, mode; mannerism, affectation, pose

idiot *syn* FOOL, imbecile, moron, simpleton, natural

idle *adj* 1 *syn* VAIN, nugatory, otiose, empty, hollow *rel* fruitless, bootless, futile; ineffective, ineffectual, inefficacious; trivial, paltry, petty, trifling 2 *syn* INACTIVE, inert, passive, supine *rel* indolent, faineant, lazy, slothful; dawdling, lagging, procrastinating *ant* busy

idle *vb* · to spend time not in work but in idleness *syn* loaf, lounge, loll, laze *rel* rest, relax, repose; saunter, stroll, amble

idolize *syn* ADORE, worship *rel* dote, love, like; venerate, revere, reverence

ignite *syn* LIGHT, kindle, fire *ant* stifle; extinguish

ignoble *syn* MEAN, sordid, abject *rel* base, low, vile; churlish, boorish, loutish; petty, puny, paltry, measly, trivial; abased, debased, degraded *ant* noble; magnanimous

ignominy *syn* DISGRACE, infamy, shame, opprobrium, dishonor, disrepute, obloquy, odium *rel* humiliation, degradation, abasement; contempt, scorn, disdain, despite; mortification, chagrin

ignorant · lacking knowledge or education *syn* illiterate, unlettered, uneducated, untaught, untutored, unlearned *rel* rude, crude, raw, callow, green, uncouth; simple, ingenuous, unsophisticated, naïve *ant* cognizant (*of something*); conversant; informed

ignore *syn* NEGLECT, disregard, overlook, slight, omit, forget *rel* blink, wink; evade, elude, escape, avoid, shun, eschew *ant* heed (*a warning, a sign, a symptom*); acknowledge

ilk *syn* TYPE, kind, sort, nature, description, character, stripe, kidney

ill *adj, syn* BAD, evil, wicked, naughty *rel* see EVIL *ant* good

ill *n, syn* EVIL *ant* good

illegal *syn* UNLAWFUL, illegitimate, illicit *ant* legal

illegitimate *syn* UNLAWFUL, illegal, illicit *ant* legitimate

ill-fated *syn* UNLUCKY, ill-starred, disastrous, unfortunate, calamitous, luckless, hapless *rel* ominous, portentous, fateful; malefic, malign, baleful, sinister

ill-favored *syn* UGLY, hideous, unsightly *rel* plain, homely *ant* well-favored; fair

illiberal · unwilling or unable to understand the point of view of others *syn* narrow-minded, narrow, intolerant, bigoted, hidebound *ant* liberal

illicit *syn* UNLAWFUL, illegal, illegitimate *ant* licit

illimitable *syn* INFINITE, boundless, uncircumscribed, eternal, sempiternal *rel* endless, everlasting, interminable

illiterate *syn* IGNORANT, unlettered, uneducated, untaught, untutored, unlearned *ant* literate

ill-mannered *syn* RUDE, uncivil, ungracious, impolite, discourteous *rel* boorish, loutish, churlish *ant* well-bred

ill-starred *syn* UNLUCKY, ill-fated, disastrous, unfortunate, calamitous, luckless, hapless *rel* malefic, malign, baleful, sinister; ominous, portentous, fateful

ill-treat *syn* ABUSE, maltreat, mistreat, misuse, outrage *rel* wrong, oppress, persecute, aggrieve; injure, harm, hurt

illuminate, illumine · to fill with or to throw light upon *syn* light, lighten, enlighten, illustrate *rel* fire, kindle; elucidate, explain; exemplify *ant* darken, obscure

illusion *syn* DELUSION, mirage, hallucination *rel* imagination, fancy, fantasy; sensation, percept, sense-datum, sensum, image

illusory *syn* APPARENT, seeming, ostensible *rel* chimerical, fanciful, visionary, imaginary, fantastic; delusory, delusive, misleading, deceptive *ant* factual; matter-of-fact

illustrate 1 *syn* ILLUMINATE, enlighten, illumine, light, lighten *rel* adorn, embellish; expose, exhibit, display, show; reveal, disclose, discover *ant* dim 2 *syn* EXEMPLIFY *rel* elucidate, interpret, explain, expound; vivify, enliven; demonstrate, manifest, show

illustration *syn* INSTANCE, example, case, sample, specimen

illustrious *syn* FAMOUS, eminent, renowned, celebrated, famed *rel* glorious, splendid, resplendent, sublime; outstanding, signal, striking, conspicuous *ant* infamous

ill will *syn* MALICE, malevolence, malignity, malignancy, spite, despite, spleen, grudge *rel* animosity, antipathy, rancor, animus, hostility, enmity; hate, hatred *ant* goodwill; charity

image 1 · a lifelike representation esp. of a living being *syn* effigy, statue, icon, portrait, photograph, mask *rel* reproduction, copy, duplicate, facsimile, replica; form, figure, shape 2 *syn* SENSATION, percept, sense-datum, sensum *rel* idea, concept, impression, conception, notion; fabrication, figment; phantasy, fancy, fantasy

imaginary · unreal or unbelievable or conceiving such unreal or unbelievable things *syn* fanciful, visionary, fantastic, chimerical, quixotic *rel* fictitious, fabulous, mythical, legendary, apocryphal; ideal, transcendent, transcendental, abstract; utopian; delusory, delusive, misleading; illusory, seeming, apparent *ant* real, actual

imagination · the power or function of the mind by which mental images of things are formed or the exercise of that power *syn* fancy, fantasy *rel* invention, creation; conceiving, conception, realizing, realization

imagine *syn* THINK, conceive, fancy, realize, envisage, envision *rel* invent, create; fabricate, form, fashion, shape, make; conjecture, surmise, guess

imbecile *syn* FOOL, idiot, moron, simpleton, natural

imbibe *syn* ABSORB, assimilate *rel* receive, take, admit, accept; soak, saturate, steep, impregnate; permeate, pervade, penetrate, impenetrate; acquire, obtain, get *ant* ooze, exude

imbue *syn* INFUSE, inoculate, leaven, ingrain, suffuse *rel* inform, inspire, fire, animate; impregnate, saturate, permeate, pervade

imitate *syn* COPY, mimic, ape, mock *rel* impersonate; simulate, feign, counterfeit; caricature, burlesque, parody, travesty

immaterial · not composed of matter *syn* spiritual, incorporeal *ant* material

immature · not fully developed *syn* unmatured, unripe, unmellow *rel* crude, callow, green, rude; premature, precocious, untimely; childish, childlike *ant* mature

immediate *syn* DIRECT *rel* nearest, next; intuitive, instinctive *ant* mediate (*knowledge, relation, operation*); distant (*relatives*)

immense *syn* HUGE, vast, enormous, elephantine, mammoth, giant, gigantic, gigantean, colossal, gargantuan, Herculean, cyclopean, titanic, Brobdingnagian *rel* tremendous, prodigious, stupendous, monstrous; large, big, great

immerse *syn* DIP, submerge, duck, souse, dunk *rel* drench, soak, saturate, sop, impregnate; infuse, imbue, ingrain; engross, absorb

immigrant **1** *syn* STRANGER, alien, foreigner, outlander, outsider, émigré **2** *syn* EMIGRANT, migrant

immigrate *syn* MIGRATE, emigrate

imminent *syn* IMPENDING *rel* threatening, menacing; likely, probable, possible; inevitable, ineluctable, inescapable, unescapable, unavoidable; expected, awaited

immobile *syn* IMMOVABLE, immotive *ant* mobile

immoderate *syn* EXCESSIVE, inordinate, exorbitant, extreme, extravagant *rel* profuse, lavish, prodigal, exuberant; teeming, overflowing *ant* moderate

immortal · not subject to death or decay *syn* deathless, undying, unfading *rel* everlasting, endless *ant* mortal

immotive *syn* IMMOVABLE, immobile

immovable · incapable of moving or being moved *syn* immobile, immotive *ant* movable

immunity *syn* EXEMPTION *ant* susceptibility

immure *syn* IMPRISON, incarcerate, jail, intern *rel* confine, circumscribe, limit, restrict

impact · a forcible or enforced contact between two or more things *syn* impingement, collision, clash, shock, concussion, percussion, jar, jolt *rel* hitting, hit, striking, stroke, smiting, slapping, slap; beating, pounding, buffeting

impair *syn* INJURE, damage, mar, harm, hurt, spoil *rel* weaken, enfeeble, debilitate, sap, undermine, disable, cripple; deface, disfigure; deform, distort, contort, warp *ant* improve, amend; repair

impalpable *syn* IMPERCEPTIBLE, insensible, intangible, inappreciable, imponderable *rel* tenuous, rare, slight, thin; attenuated, extenuated, rarefied *ant* palpable

impart *syn* COMMUNICATE *rel* share, participate, partake; distribute, dispense, divide; convey, transfer; instill, inculcate, implant; imbue, inoculate, leaven, infuse

impartial *syn* FAIR, equitable, unbiased, objective, just, dispassionate, uncolored *rel* disinterested, detached, aloof, indifferent *ant* partial

impassable · not allowing passage *syn* impenetrable, impervious, impermeable *ant* passable

impassible *syn* INSENSIBLE, insensitive, anesthetic

impassioned · actuated by or showing intense feeling *syn* passionate, ardent, fervent, fervid, perfervid *rel* vehement, intense, fierce, violent; deep, profound; sentimental, romantic, maudlin *ant* unimpassioned

impassive · unresponsive to what might normally excite interest or emotion *syn* stoic, phlegmatic, apathetic, stolid *rel* cool, composed, collected, imperturbable; reserved, taciturn, silent, reticent; callous, hardened, indurated; insensible, insensitive *ant* responsive

impassivity, impassiveness · unresponsiveness to something that might normally excite interest or emotion *syn* apathy, stolidity, phlegm, stoicism

impatient · manifesting signs of unrest or an inability to keep still or quiet *syn* nervous, unquiet, restless, restive, uneasy, fidgety, jumpy, jittery *rel* fretful, querulous, irritable, snappish, waspish; eager, anxious, avid, keen; impetuous, precipitate, headlong, hasty, sudden, abrupt *ant* patient

impeach *syn* ACCUSE, indict, incriminate, charge, arraign *rel* condemn, denounce, blame, censure; try, test, prove

impeccable · absolutely correct and beyond criticism *syn* faultless, flawless, errorless *rel* inerrant, unerring, infallible; correct, accurate, precise, right, nice; perfect, entire, whole, intact

impecunious *syn* POOR, indigent, needy, destitute, penniless, poverty-stricken, necessitous *ant* flush

impede *syn* HINDER, obstruct, block, bar, dam *rel* clog, hamper, fetter, trammel, shackle, manacle, hog-tie; embarrass, discomfit, disconcert, rattle, faze; thwart, baffle, balk, frustrate *ant* assist; promote

impediment *syn* OBSTACLE, obstruction, bar, snag *rel* difficulty, hardship, rigor, vicissitude; barrier, bar; handicap *ant* aid, assistance; advantage

impel *syn* MOVE, drive, actuate *rel* compel, constrain, force; provoke, excite, stimulate; incite, instigate, foment; goad, spur *ant* restrain

impending · likely to occur soon or without further warning *syn* imminent *rel* close, near, nigh; approaching, nearing; likely, probable; threatening, menacing

impenetrable *syn* IMPASSABLE, impervious, impermeable *rel* close, dense, compact, thick; solid, hard, firm; compacted, concentrated, consolidated; callous, hardened, indurated; obdurate, adamant, inflexible *ant* penetrable

impenetrate *syn* PERMEATE, interpenetrate, penetrate, pervade, impregnate, saturate *rel* enter, pierce, probe; invade, entrench trespass; drench, soak

imperative 1 *syn* MASTERFUL, peremptory, imperious, domineering *rel* commanding, ordering, bidding; magisterial, dictatorial, dogmatic, oracular; arbitrary, autocratic, despotic, absolute 2 *syn* PRESSING, urgent, crying, importunate, insistent, exigent, instant *rel* compelling, constraining; critical, crucial, acute

imperceptible · incapable of being apprehended by the senses or intellect *syn* insensible, impalpable, intangible, inappreciable, imponderable *ant* perceptible

imperfection · an instance of failure to reach a standard of excellence or perfection *syn* deficiency, shortcoming, fault *rel* failure, neglect, dereliction; failing, frailty, foible; blemish, flaw, defect; weakness, infirmity *ant* perfection

imperial *syn* KINGLY, regal, royal, queenly, princely *rel* majestic, august, stately, noble, grand; sovereign, dominant

imperil *syn* VENTURE, hazard, risk, chance, jeopardize, endanger *rel* dare, brave; encounter, confront, meet, face; threaten, menace

imperious *syn* MASTERFUL, domineering, peremptory, imperative *rel* dictatorial, authoritarian, magisterial; despotic, tyrannical, arbitrary, autocratic, absolute; lordly, overbearing *ant* abject

impermeable *syn* IMPASSABLE, impervious, impenetrable *rel* solid, hard, firm; tight

impersonate *syn* ACT, play *rel* imitate, mimic, ape, copy; simulate, counterfeit, feign; caricature, burlesque

impersonator *syn* ACTOR, player, mummer, mime, mimic, performer, thespian, trouper

impertinent · given to thrusting oneself into the affairs of others *syn* officious, meddlesome, intrusive, obtrusive *rel* interfering, meddling; arrogant, insolent; brazen, impudent, brash, barefaced, shameless; offensive, repugnant

imperturbable *syn* COOL, composed, collected, unruffled, unflappable, nonchalant *rel* immobile, immovable; serene, calm, tranquil, placid; complacent, self-satisfied, smug *ant* choleric, touchy

impervious *syn* IMPASSABLE, impenetrable, impermeable *rel* resisting, resistant, withstanding, opposing, combating, fighting; hardened, indurated, callous; obdurate, adamant, adamantine, inflexible

impetuous *syn* PRECIPITATE, headlong, abrupt, hasty, sudden *rel* impulsive, spontaneous; vehement, intense, violent; forceful, forcible, powerful; violent; impatient, restive; impassioned, passionate, fervid, ardent

impetus 1 *syn* SPEED, momentum, velocity, pace *rel* energy, force, power; impelling, impulsion, driving, moving 2 *syn* STIMULUS, excitant, incitement, stimulant *rel* incentive, impulse, spur, goad, motive, spring

impingement *syn* IMPACT, collision, clash, shock, concussion, percussion, jar, jolt *rel* hitting, hit, striking, stroke, smiting; encroachment, entrenchment; impression, impress, imprint, stamp, print

impious · lacking in reverence for what is sacred or divine *syn* profane, blasphemous, sacrilegious *rel* nefarious, iniquitous, flagitious; irreligious, ungodly, godless *ant* pious; reverent

impish *syn* PLAYFUL, roguish, waggish, mischievous, frolicsome, sportive *rel* saucy, pert, arch; naughty, bad; sly, cunning, tricky

implacable *syn* GRIM, relentless, unrelenting, merciless *rel* inflexible, inexorable, obdurate, adamant; pitiless, ruthless, compassionless

implant · to introduce into the mind *syn* inculcate, instill *rel* infuse, imbue, inoculate, ingrain, leaven; impregnate, saturate, impenetrate, penetrate, permeate, pervade

implement *n* · a relatively simple device for performing work *syn* tool, instrument, appliance, utensil *rel* machine, mechanism, apparatus; contrivance, device, contraption, gadget

implement *vb, syn* ENFORCE *rel* effect, fulfill, execute, achieve, accomplish, perform; realize, actualize, materialize

implicate *syn* INVOLVE *rel* concern, affect; incriminate, accuse

implication · something hinted at but not explicitly stated *syn* inference *rel* hinting, hint, suggestion, intimation; insinuation, innuendo

implicit · understood though not directly stated *syn* virtual, constructive *rel* implied, suggested, intimated, hinted; inferred, deduced, gathered *ant* explicit

implore *syn* BEG, entreat, beseech, supplicate, importune, adjure *rel* pray, plead, sue, appeal, petition; ask, request, solicit

imply **1** *syn* INCLUDE, involve, comprehend, embrace, subsume *rel* import, mean, signify, denote; contain, hold; convey, carry, bear **2** *syn* SUGGEST, hint, intimate, insinuate *rel* connote, denote; presuppose, presume, assume, postulate; betoken, bespeak, indicate, attest, argue, prove *ant* express

impolite *syn* RUDE, uncivil, discourteous, ill-mannered, ungracious *rel* churlish, boorish, loutish; curt, gruff, brusque, blunt, bluff *ant* polite

imponderable *syn* IMPERCEPTIBLE, impalpable, inappreciable, insensible, intangible *ant* ponderable, appreciable

import *vb, syn* MEAN, denote, signify *rel* connote; involve, imply, include, comprehend; suggest, intimate, hint; intend

import *n* **1** *syn* MEANING, significance, sense, acceptation, signification *rel* denotation, connotation; interpreting, interpretation, construing, construction; drift, tenor; implication **2** *syn* IMPORTANCE, significance, consequence, moment, weight *rel* worth, value; purpose, intent, design, object, objective, intention; emphasis, stress

importance · the quality or state of being of notable worth or influence *syn* consequence, moment, weight, significance, import *rel* prominence, conspicuousness, saliency; eminence, illustriousness; seriousness, gravity; magnitude, size, extent *ant* unimportance

importunate *syn* PRESSING, urgent, imperative, crying, insistent, exigent, instant *rel* demanding, claiming, requiring; persistent, persevering; pertinacious, dogged, obstinate

importune *syn* BEG, entreat, beseech, implore, supplicate, adjure *rel* tease, pester, plague, harry, worry; hound, hector, badger; plead, appeal, sue

impose *syn* DICTATE, prescribe, ordain, decree *rel* order, enjoin, command, charge; exact, demand, require; constrain, oblige, compel, force

imposing *syn* GRAND, stately, majestic, august, noble, magnificent, grandiose *rel* showy, pretentious, ostentatious; impressive, moving; regal, imperial; monumental, stupendous, prodigious *ant* unimposing

impostor · a person who fraudulently pretends to be someone or something else *syn* faker, quack, mountebank, charlatan *rel* cheat, fraud, fake, humbug, imposture; deceiver, beguiler, misleader

imposture · a thing made to seem other than it is *syn* cheat, fraud, sham, fake, humbug, deceit, deception, counterfeit *rel* trick, ruse, feint, artifice, wile, stratagem, maneuver, gambit, ploy

impotent **1** *syn* POWERLESS *rel* ineffective, ineffectual, inefficacious, inefficient; incapable, incompetent; disabled, crippled, debilitated, enfeebled *ant* potent **2** *syn* STERILE, barren, unfruitful, infertile *ant* virile

impoverish *syn* DEPLETE, bankrupt, exhaust, drain *ant* enrich

imprecation *syn* CURSE, malediction, anathema *rel* execration, damning, objurgation; blasphemy, profanity, swearing *ant* prayer

impregnable *syn* INVINCIBLE, inexpugnable, unassailable, invulnerable, unconquerable, indomitable *rel* secure, safe; protected, shielded, guarded, safeguarded, defended

impregnate **1** *syn* PERMEATE, saturate, pervade, penetrate, impenetrate, interpenetrate *rel* imbue, inoculate, ingrain, infuse, suffuse, leaven; enter, pierce, probe **2** *syn* SOAK, saturate, drench, steep, sop, waterlog *rel* immerse, submerge, dip, souse

impress *vb, syn* AFFECT, touch, strike, influence, sway *rel* move, actuate; thrill, electrify, enthuse; provoke, excite, stimulate, galvanize, pique

impress *n, syn* IMPRESSION, imprint, print, stamp *rel* see IMPRESSION 1

impressible *syn* SENTIENT, sensitive, impressionable, responsive, susceptible *rel* subject, exposed, open, liable, prone; predisposed, disposed, inclined

impression **1** · the perceptible trace or traces left by pressure *syn* impress, imprint, print, stamp *rel* trace, vestige, track; mark, token, sign; stigma, brand, blot, stain **2** *syn* IDEA, notion, thought, concept, conception *rel* image, percept, sense-datum, sensum, sensation; sentiment, opinion, view **3** *syn* EDITION, reprinting, printing, reissue

impressionable *syn* SENTIENT, sensitive, impressible, responsive, susceptible *rel* affectable, influenceable; open, liable, subject, exposed, prone; predisposed, disposed, inclined

impressive *syn* MOVING, affecting, poignant, touching, pathetic *rel* imposing, majestic, august, noble, magnificent, grandiose, grand; sublime, superb, glorious, splendid; striking, arresting, remarkable, noticeable *ant* unimpressive

imprint *syn* IMPRESSION, print, impress, stamp

imprison · to confine closely so that escape is impossible or unlikely *syn* incarcerate, jail, immure, intern *rel* confine, circumscribe, restrict, limit; restrain, curb, check

impromptu *syn* EXTEMPORANEOUS, unpremeditated, offhand, improvised, extempore, extemporary *rel* spontaneous, impulsive; ready, prompt, quick, apt

improper **1** *syn* UNFIT, inappropriate, unfitting, unsuitable, inapt, unhappy, infelicitous *rel* wrong, bad, poor; amiss, astray; incongruous, inconsonant *ant* proper **2** *syn* INDECOROUS, indecent, unseemly, unbecoming, indelicate *rel* unconventional, unceremonious, informal; shameless, brazen, impudent, brash, barefaced; obscene, ribald, coarse, vulgar, gross *ant* proper

impropriety *syn* BARBARISM, corruption, solecism, vulgarism, vernacular

improve 1 · to make more acceptable or bring nearer to some standard *syn* better, help, ameliorate *rel* benefit, profit; amend, correct, rectify, reform, revise; enhance, heighten *ant* impair; worsen 2 · to grow or become better (as in health or well-being) *syn* recover, recuperate, convalesce, gain

improvised *syn* EXTEMPORANEOUS, unpremeditated, impromptu, offhand, extempore, extemporary *rel* see IMPROMPTU

impudent *syn* SHAMELESS, brazen, barefaced, brash *rel* impertinent, intrusive, obtrusive, officious, meddlesome; rude, impolite, discourteous, uncivil, ungracious *ant* respectful

impugn *syn* DENY, gainsay, contradict, negative, traverse, contravene *rel* attack, assail; refute, rebut, confute, controvert, disprove *ant* authenticate; advocate

impulse *syn* MOTIVE, spring, incentive, inducement, spur, goad *rel* impetus, stimulus, incitement, stimulant, excitant; urge, passion, lust, desire, appetite; moving, movement, driving, drive, impelling, impulsion, actuation

impulsive *syn* SPONTANEOUS, instinctive, automatic, mechanical *rel* impetuous, precipitate, headlong, abrupt, sudden, hasty *ant* deliberate

impute *syn* ASCRIBE, attribute, assign, refer, credit, accredit, charge *rel* attach, fasten, affix; accuse, indict; allege, advance, adduce; intimate, insinuate, hint, suggest

inactive · not engaged in work or activity *syn* idle, inert, passive, supine *rel* latent, quiescent, dormant, abeyant, potential; torpid, comatose, sluggish, lethargic *ant* active, live

inadvertent *syn* CARELESS, heedless, thoughtless

inane *syn* INSIPID, banal, wishy-washy, jejune, vapid, flat *rel* foolish, silly, fatuous, asinine, simple; vain, idle, empty, hollow, nugatory; vacuous, blank, empty

inanimate *syn* DEAD, lifeless, defunct, deceased, departed, late *rel* inert, inactive *ant* animate

inappreciable *syn* IMPERCEPTIBLE, imponderable, impalpable, insensible, intangible *ant* appreciable, ponderable

inappropriate *syn* UNFIT, unfitting, inapt, improper, unsuitable, unhappy, infelicitous *rel* unbecoming, unseemly, indecorous; incongruous, discordant, inconsonant *ant* appropriate

inapt *syn* UNFIT, unhappy, infelicitous, inappropriate, unfitting, unsuitable, improper *rel* inept, maladroit, gauche, awkward, clumsy; banal, flat, jejune, insipid *ant* apt

inarticulate *syn* DUMB, speechless, mute *rel* silent, taciturn, reserved *ant* articulate

inasmuch as *syn* BECAUSE, since, for, as

inaugurate 1 *syn* INITIATE, install, induct, invest *rel* introduce, admit, enter 2 *syn* BEGIN, start, commence *rel* found, establish, institute, organize

inauspicious *syn* OMINOUS, unpropitious, portentous, fateful *rel* threatening, menacing; sinister, malign, malefic, maleficent, baleful *ant* auspicious

inborn *syn* INNATE, congenital, hereditary, inherited, inbred *rel* inherent, intrinsic, constitutional, essential; natural, normal, regular, typical; native, indigenous *ant* acquired

inbred *syn* INNATE, inborn, congenital, hereditary, inherited *rel* ingrained, inherent, constitutional, intrinsic; deep-rooted, deep-seated, inveterate, confirmed, chronic

incapable • mentally or physically unfit, or untrained to do a given kind of work *syn* incompetent, unqualified *rel* inefficient, ineffective; disabled, crippled, debilitated *ant* capable

incarcerate *syn* IMPRISON, jail, immure, intern *rel* confine, circumscribe, restrict, limit

incarnate *syn* REALIZE, embody, hypostatize, materialize, externalize, objectify, actualize, reify

incendiary *syn* COMBUSTIBLE, inflammable, flammable, inflammatory

incense *n, syn* FRAGRANCE, redolence, perfume, bouquet *rel* odor, aroma, smell

incense *vb, syn* ANGER, enrage, infuriate, madden *rel* exasperate, irritate, rile, provoke, nettle, aggravate; offend, outrage, affront, insult *ant* placate

incentive *syn* MOTIVE, inducement, spring, spur, goad, impulse *rel* stimulus, incitement, stimulant, excitant, impetus; provoking, provocation, excitement, stimulation; reason, cause, determinant

inception *syn* ORIGIN, source, root, provenance, provenience *rel* beginning, commencement, starting, start, initiation, inauguration; rising, rise, origination, derivation *ant* termination

incessant *syn* CONTINUAL, continuous, constant, unremitting, perpetual, perennial *rel* unceasing, interminable, endless, everlasting; steady, constant; vexing, irking, annoying, bothering *ant* intermittent

incident *syn* OCCURRENCE, episode, event, circumstance

incidental *syn* ACCIDENTAL, casual, fortuitous, contingent *rel* subordinate, secondary, collateral; associated, related, linked, connected *ant* essential

incise *syn* CARVE, engrave, etch, chisel, sculpture, sculpt, sculp *rel* imprint, print, stamp, impress; depict, delineate, limn, represent

incisive • having, manifesting, or suggesting a keen alertness of mind *syn* trenchant, clear-cut, cutting, biting, crisp *rel* terse, succinct, laconic, concise; poignant, pungent, piquant

incite • to spur to action *syn* instigate, abet, foment *rel* stimulate, excite, provoke, pique, galvanize; arouse, rouse, stir *ant* restrain

incitement *syn* STIMULUS, stimulant, excitant, impetus *rel* spur, goad, incentive, inducement, impulse, motive, spring; provoking, provocation, excitement, stimulation, piquing; motivation, activation, actuation *ant* restraint; inhibition

incline **1** *syn* SLANT, lean, slope *rel* bend, curve; swerve, veer, deviate; deflect, turn **2** • to influence one to have or to take an attitude toward something *syn* bias, dispose, predispose *rel* influence, affect, sway; move, drive, impel *ant* disincline, indispose

include • to contain within as part of the whole *syn* comprehend, embrace, involve, imply, subsume *rel* contain, hold, accommodate *ant* exclude

incognito *syn* PSEUDONYM, alias, nom de guerre, pen name, nom de plume

incommode *syn* INCONVENIENCE, discommode, trouble *rel* hinder, impede, obstruct, block; disturb, discompose; bother, irk, vex, annoy *ant* accommodate

incomparable *syn* SUPREME, peerless, superlative, transcendent, surpassing, preeminent *rel* unrivaled, unmatched, unapproached, unequaled

incompatible *syn* INCONSONANT, incongruous, inconsistent, discordant, discrepant, uncongenial, unsympathetic *rel* antagonistic, counter, adverse; antipathetic, averse; contrary, contradictory, antithetical, antipodal, antipodean, opposite; irreconcilable, unconformable, unadaptable *ant* compatible

incompetent *syn* INCAPABLE, unqualified *rel* inefficient, ineffective *ant* competent

incongruous *syn* INCONSONANT, uncongenial, incompatible, inconsistent, discordant, discrepant, unsympathetic *rel* alien, foreign, extraneous; grotesque, bizarre, fantastic *ant* congruous

inconsistent *syn* INCONSONANT, incompatible, incongruous, uncongenial, unsympathetic, discordant, discrepant *rel* divergent, disparate, diverse, different; irreconcilable *ant* consistent

inconsonant · not in agreement with or not agreeable to *syn* inconsistent, incompatible, incongruous, uncongenial, unsympathetic, discordant, discrepant *ant* consonant

inconstant · lacking firmness or steadiness (as in purpose or devotion) *syn* fickle, capricious, mercurial, unstable *rel* changeable, changeful, variable, protean, mutable; faithless, disloyal, false, treacherous, traitorous, perfidious; volatile, frivolous, light, light-minded *ant* constant

inconvenience · to subject to disturbance or discomfort *syn* incommode, discommode, trouble *rel* disturb, discompose; interfere, intermeddle, meddle

incorporate *syn* IDENTIFY, embody, assimilate *rel* merge, blend, fuse, coalesce, mix; unite, combine, conjoin; consolidate, unify, compact

incorporeal *syn* IMMATERIAL, spiritual *ant* corporeal

increase · to make or become greater *syn* enlarge, augment, multiply *rel* intensify, aggravate, heighten, enhance; expand, swell, amplify, dilate, distend, inflate; extend, lengthen, elongate, prolong, protract *ant* decrease

incredulity *syn* UNBELIEF, disbelief *rel* doubt, dubiety, dubiosity, skepticism, uncertainty *ant* credulity

increment *syn* ADDITION, accretion, accession

incriminate *syn* ACCUSE, impeach, indict, charge, arraign *rel* involve, implicate

inculcate *syn* IMPLANT, instill *rel* infuse, inoculate, imbue, leaven; teach, instruct, educate; impart, communicate

incur · to bring upon oneself something usu. unpleasant or injurious *syn* contract, catch *rel* get, obtain, acquire

incurious *syn* INDIFFERENT, unconcerned, aloof, detached, uninterested, disinterested *rel* abstracted, preoccupied, absent, absentminded, distraught *ant* curious, inquisitive

incursion *syn* INVASION, raid, inroad

indebtedness *syn* DEBT, debit, obligation, liability, arrear

indecent *syn* INDECOROUS, unseemly, indelicate, improper, unbecoming *rel* obscene, ribald, coarse, gross, vulgar; lewd, lascivious, licentious; immoral; offensive, revolting, repulsive, repugnant, loathsome *ant* decent

indecorous · not conforming to what is accepted as right, fitting, or in good taste *syn* improper, unseemly, indecent, unbecoming, indelicate *rel* unfitting, inappropriate, unsuitable, unfit; incongruous, inconsonant; rude, ill-mannered, uncivil, discourteous, impolite; coarse, vulgar, gross *ant* decorous

indefatigable · capable of prolonged and arduous effort *syn* tireless, weariless, untiring, unwearying, unwearied, unflagging *rel* diligent, assiduous, sedulous, industrious, busy; dogged, pertinacious, obstinate; energetic, strenuous, vigorous

indefinable *syn* UNUTTERABLE, inexpressible, unspeakable, ineffable, indescribable

indelicate *syn* INDECOROUS, indecent, unseemly, improper, unbecoming *rel* coarse, gross, vulgar, obscene; rude, rough, crude, callow, uncouth; lewd, wanton, licentious *ant* delicate, refined

indemnify *syn* PAY, reimburse, recompense, compensate, remunerate, repay, satisfy

indemnity *syn* REPARATION, redress, amends, restitution

indentured *syn* BOUND, articled, bond

independence *syn* FREEDOM, autonomy, sovereignty, autarchy, autarky *rel* liberty, license *ant* dependence

independent *syn* FREE, autonomous, sovereign, autarchic, autarkic *rel* alone, solitary; self-governed, self-ruled *ant* dependent

indescribable *syn* UNUTTERABLE, inexpressible, ineffable, unspeakable, indefinable

indicate · to give evidence of or to serve as ground for a valid or reasonable inference *syn* betoken, attest, bespeak, argue, prove *rel* intimate, hint, suggest; evince, evidence, demonstrate, manifest, show; import, signify, denote, mean

indict *syn* ACCUSE, incriminate, impeach, charge, arraign *rel* blame, denounce, condemn

indifferent **1** · not showing or feeling interest *syn* unconcerned, incurious, aloof, detached, uninterested, disinterested *rel* impartial, unbiased, dispassionate, fair; apathetic, impassive, phlegmatic; cool, nonchalant *ant* avid **2** *syn* MEDIUM, average, moderate, middling, fair, mediocre, second-rate *rel* ordinary, common *ant* choice **3** *syn* NEUTRAL

indigence *syn* POVERTY, penury, want, destitution, privation *rel* strait, exigency, emergency, pass *ant* affluence, opulence

indigenous *syn* NATIVE, autochthonous, endemic, aboriginal *ant* naturalized; exotic

indigent *syn* POOR, needy, destitute, penniless, impecunious, poverty-stricken, necessitous *ant* opulent

indignant *syn* ANGRY, irate, wrathful, wroth, acrimonious, mad *rel* incensed, infuriated, enraged, angered, maddened; exasperated, riled, provoked, nettled; roused, aroused, stirred

indignation *syn* ANGER, wrath, ire, rage, fury *rel* resentment, dudgeon, offense; passion

indignity *syn* AFFRONT, insult *rel* injury, wrong, injustice, grievance; offending, offense, outraging, outrage

indirect · deviating from a direct line or straightforward course *syn* circuitous, roundabout *rel* devious, oblique, crooked; winding, sinuous, tortuous *ant* direct; forthright, straightforward

indiscriminate · including all or nearly all within the range of choice, operation, or effectiveness *syn* wholesale, sweeping *rel* promiscuous, motley, heterogeneous, assorted, miscellaneous; uncritical, superficial, shallow *ant* selective; discriminating

indispensable *syn* NEEDFUL, essential, necessary, requisite *rel* vital, cardinal, fundamental, *ant* dispensable

indisposed *syn* DISINCLINED, loath, averse, hesitant, reluctant *rel* inimical, hostile, antagonistic, antipathetic *ant* disposed

individual *adj* **1** *syn* SPECIAL, particular, specific, especial *rel* single, sole, separate *ant* general **2** *syn* CHARACTERISTIC, peculiar, distinctive *rel* unique, singular, strange; distinct, separate, several *ant* common

individual *n*, *syn* ENTITY, being, creature, person *rel* aggregate

individuality *syn* DISPOSITION, personality, temperament, temper, complexion, character

individually *syn* EACH, apiece, severally, respectively

indolent *syn* LAZY, faineant, slothful *rel* lethargic, sluggish, comatose; inactive, inert, idle, passive, supine; languid, languorous, lackadaisical, listless *ant* industrious

indomitable *syn* INVINCIBLE, unconquerable, impregnable, inexpugnable, unassailable, invulnerable *rel* stubborn, dogged, pertinacious, obstinate; resolute, staunch, steadfast, faithful; undaunted, dauntless, intrepid, doughty, brave

induce • to move another to do or agree to something *syn* persuade, prevail, get *rel* incite, instigate, abet; move, actuate, drive, impel; motivate, activate

inducement *syn* MOTIVE, incentive, spur, goad, spring, impulse *rel* temptation, enticement, seduction, luring, lure; stimulus, incitement, impetus, stimulant, excitant

induct *syn* INITIATE, inaugurate, install, invest

indulge • to show undue favor to a person's desires and feelings *syn* pamper, humor, spoil, baby, mollycoddle *rel* favor, accommodate, oblige; gratify, please, regale, delight *ant* discipline (*others*); abstain (*with reference to oneself, one's appetite*)

indulgence *syn* FORBEARANCE, tolerance, clemency, mercifulness, leniency *rel* mercy, charity, lenity, grace; kindness, benignancy, benignity, benignness, kindliness; mildness, gentleness *ant* strictness

indulgent *syn* FORBEARING, lenient, tolerant, clement, merciful *rel* humoring, pampering; forgiving, pardoning, condoning, excusing; benignant, benign, kind, kindly; mild, gentle, soft *ant* strict

indulgently *syn* FORBEARINGLY, tolerantly, clemently, mercifully, leniently

indurate *syn* HARDEN, solidify, petrify, cake *rel* season; fix, establish, set

indurated *syn* HARDENED, callous *rel* rigid, stiff, inflexible; obdurate, adamant, adamantine, inexorable, inflexible *ant* pliable

industrious *syn* BUSY, diligent, assiduous, sedulous *rel* active, operative, live, dynamic; persevering, persisting, persistent; indefatigable, tireless, untiring, unflagging, unwearied *ant* slothful, indolent

industry *syn* BUSINESS, trade, commerce, traffic

inebriate *syn* DRUNKARD, alcoholic, dipsomaniac, sot, soak, toper, tosspot, tippler *ant* teetotaler

inebriated *syn* DRUNK, drunken, intoxicated, tipsy, tight

ineffable *syn* UNUTTERABLE, inexpressible, unspeakable, indescribable, indefinable *rel* celestial, heavenly, empyrean, empyreal; ethereal; spiritual, divine, holy, sacred; transcendent, transcendental, ideal, abstract

ineffective • not producing or incapable of producing an intended result *syn* ineffectual, inefficient, inefficacious *rel* futile, vain, fruitless, bootless, abortive; nugatory, otiose, idle, empty, hollow; sterile, barren, unfruitful, infertile *ant* effective

ineffectual *syn* INEFFECTIVE, inefficacious, inefficient *rel* see INEFFECTIVE *ant* effectual

inefficacious *syn* INEFFECTIVE, ineffectual, inefficient *rel* inactive, inert, idle; futile, vain, fruitless, bootless, abortive; powerless, impotent *ant* efficacious

inefficient *syn* INEFFECTIVE, ineffectual, inefficacious *rel* incompetent, unqualified, incapable; infirm, decrepit, feeble, weak; indolent, slothful, faineant, lazy; remiss, lax, slack, negligent, neglectful *ant* efficient

ineluctable *syn* INEVITABLE, inescapable, unescapable, unavoidable *rel* certain, necessary

inept *syn* AWKWARD, clumsy, maladroit, gauche *rel* inapt, unfit, unsuitable, inappropriate; impertinent, intrusive, obtrusive; vain, nugatory, idle, empty, hollow, otiose; fatuous, asinine, foolish, silly *ant* apt; adept; able

inerrable *syn* INFALLIBLE, inerrant, unerring

inerrant *syn* INFALLIBLE, unerring *rel* impeccable, flawless, faultless; accurate, exact, correct, precise; reliable, dependable, trustworthy; inevitable, certain

inert *syn* INACTIVE, passive, idle, supine *rel* lifeless, inanimate, dead; impotent, powerless; apathetic, impassive, phlegmatic, stolid *ant* dynamic; animated

inescapable *syn* INEVITABLE, ineluctable, unescapable, unavoidable *rel* certain, necessary; inexorable, inflexible *ant* escapable

inevitable **1** • incapable of being avoided or escaped *syn* ineluctable, inescapable, unescapable, unavoidable *rel* certain, necessary; determined, settled, decided; inexorable, inflexible *ant* evitable **2** *syn* CERTAIN, necessary *rel* infallible, inerrant, unerring; perfect, entire, whole; definitive, determinative, decisive, conclusive

inexorable *syn* INFLEXIBLE, obdurate, adamant, adamantine *rel* rigid, rigorous, strict; resolute, steadfast, faithful; immovable, immobile; implacable, unrelenting, relentless, merciless, grim *ant* exorable

inexpressible *syn* UNUTTERABLE, ineffable, unspeakable, indescribable, indefinable *rel* tenuous, rare; infinite, boundless, illimitable *ant* expressible

inexpugnable *syn* INVINCIBLE, unassailable, impregnable, unconquerable, invulnerable, indomitable *rel* uncombatable, irresistible, unopposable *ant* expugnable

infallible • incapable of making mistakes or errors *syn* inerrable, inerrant, unerring *rel* certain, inevitable, necessary; impeccable, flawless, faultless *ant* fallible

infamous *syn* VICIOUS, nefarious, flagitious, iniquitous, villainous, corrupt, degenerate *rel* ignominious, disgraceful, disreputable, shameful *ant* illustrious

infamy *syn* DISGRACE, ignominy, shame, dishonor, disrepute, opprobrium, obloquy, odium *rel* notoriety; degradation, humiliation, debasement, abasement

infancy • the state or period of being under the age established by law for the attainment of full civil rights *syn* minority, nonage

infatuated **1** *syn* FOND, besotted, insensate *rel* deluded, deceived, beguiled, misled; duped, gulled, befooled; foolish, silly, fatuous, asinine **2** *syn* ENAMORED

infectious **1** • transmissible by infection *syn* contagious, communicable, catching *rel* toxic, mephitic, pestilent, pestilential, virulent, poisonous **2** • capable of infecting or tending to infect *syn* infective

infective *syn* INFECTIOUS *rel* contaminating, tainting, polluting, defiling; corrupting, vitiating; poisonous, virulent, toxic, mephitic

infelicitous *syn* UNFIT, unhappy,

inapt, inappropriate, unfitting, unsuitable, improper *rel* unbecoming, unseemly, indecorous, improper, indelicate, indecent; inept, maladroit, gauche, awkward *ant* felicitous

infer · to arrive at by reasoning from evidence or from premises *syn* deduce, conclude, judge, gather *rel* reason, speculate, think; surmise, conjecture, guess

inference 1 · the deriving of a conclusion by reasoning *syn* deduction, conclusion, judgment 2 · the process of arriving at conclusions from data or premises *syn* ratiocination *rel* deduction, conclusion, judgment; reasoning, thinking, speculation, cogitation; surmise, conjecture 3 *syn* IMPLICATION

inferential · deduced or deducible by reasoning *syn* ratiocinative *rel* hypothetical, putative, purported, conjectural, supposititious, supposed; theoretical, speculative, academic; implicit, constructive, virtual

inferior · one who is lower than another esp. in station or rank *syn* underling, subordinate *rel* dependent, subject *ant* superior

infernal · of or relating to a nether world of the dead *syn* chthonian, chthonic, hellish, Hadean, Tartarean, stygian *rel* fiendish, devilish, diabolical, demoniac; damnable, accursed, cursed, execrable; nefarious, flagitious, iniquitous, villainous, vicious *ant* supernal

infertile *syn* STERILE, barren, impotent, unfruitful *rel* dry, arid; impoverished, exhausted, drained, depleted *ant* fertile

infest · to spread or swarm over in a troublesome manner *syn* overrun, beset *rel* teem, swarm, abound; harass, harry, pester, plague, worry, annoy *ant* disinfest

infidel *syn* ATHEIST, unbeliever, freethinker, agnostic, deist

infinite · being without known limits *syn* eternal, sempiternal, boundless, illimitable, uncircumscribed *ant* finite

infirm *syn* WEAK, feeble, decrepit, frail, fragile *rel* debilitated, disabled, crippled *ant* hale

inflammable *syn* COMBUSTIBLE, flammable, incendiary, inflammatory *rel* igniting, kindling, firing, lighting; flaring, blazing; infuriating, enraging, incensing *ant* extinguishable

inflammatory *syn* COMBUSTIBLE, inflammable, flammable, incendiary *rel* inciting, instigating; stimulating, exciting; sensitive, susceptible

inflate *syn* EXPAND, distend, swell, amplify, dilate *rel* enlarge, increase, augment; magnify, aggrandize, exalt *ant* deflate

inflated · swollen with or as if with something insubstantial *syn* flatulent, tumid, turgid *rel* bombastic, grandiloquent, magniloquent, aureate, flowery, rhetorical; pretentious, ostentatious, showy; rhapsodical, ranting, fustian; wordy, verbose, prolix, diffuse *ant* pithy

inflection · a particular manner of employing the sounds of the voice in speech *syn* intonation, accent *rel* enunciation, pronunciation, articulation

inflexible 1 *syn* STIFF, rigid, tense, stark, wooden *rel* hard, solid, firm; rigorous, strict, stringent; tough, tenacious, stout, strong; immobile, immovable *ant* flexible 2 · unwilling to alter a predetermined course or purpose *syn* inexorable, obdurate, adamant, adamantine *rel* rigid, strict, rigorous, stringent; intractable, refractory, headstrong, unruly, ungovernable; implacable, relentless, unrelenting, grim; stubborn, obstinate, dogged, stiff-necked, mulish *ant* flexible

influence *n* • power exerted over the minds or behavior of others *syn* authority, prestige, weight, credit *rel* driving, drive, impelling, impulsion, actuation; power, control, dominion, sway, authority; ascendancy, supremacy; dominance

influence *vb, syn* AFFECT, sway, impress, touch, strike *rel* move, actuate, drive, impel; stimulate, provoke, excite; stir, arouse, rouse; incline, dispose, predispose, bias

inform **1** • to stimulate (as mental powers) to higher or more intense activity *syn* animate, inspire, fire *rel* infuse, inoculate, imbue, leaven; instill, implant, inculcate; enlighten, illuminate; fire, kindle; endue, endow, dower **2** • to make one aware of something *syn* acquaint, apprise, advise, notify *rel* communicate, impart; teach, instruct, school, discipline, educate, train; warn, forewarn, caution

information *syn* KNOWLEDGE, lore, learning, science, erudition, scholarship *rel* news, tidings, intelligence, advice

infraction *syn* BREACH, violation, transgression, infringement, trespass, contravention *rel* offense, sin, crime, vice, scandal; slip, lapse, faux pas, error *ant* observance

infrequent • not common or abundant *syn* uncommon, scarce, rare, occasional, sporadic *rel* exceptional; singular, unique, strange; irregular, anomalous, unnatural *ant* frequent

infringe *syn* TRESPASS, encroach, entrench, invade *rel* intrude, obtrude, butt in, interlope; violate, break, transgress

infringement *syn* BREACH, infraction, violation, trespass, transgression, contravention *rel* encroachment, invading, invasion, entrenchment; intruding, intrusion, obtruding, obtrusion

infuriate *syn* ANGER, enrage, incense, madden *rel* provoke, rile, exasperate, aggravate, irritate; outrage, insult, affront, offend

infuse • to introduce one thing into another so as to affect it throughout *syn* suffuse, imbue, ingrain, inoculate, leaven *rel* impregnate, saturate, impenetrate, permeate, pervade; inform, inspire, animate, fire; instill, inculcate, implant

ingeminate *syn* REPEAT, iterate, reiterate

ingenious *syn* CLEVER, cunning, adroit *rel* inventing, inventive, creating, creative, discovering; dexterous, handy, deft; skillful, adept, skilled, expert, proficient, masterly

ingenuous *syn* NATURAL, simple, naïve, unsophisticated, artless *rel* open, frank, candid, plain; transparent, clear; childlike, childish; straightforward, aboveboard; sincere, unfeigned *ant* disingenuous; cunning

ingest *syn* EAT, swallow, devour, consume *rel* introduce, insert; receive, take, accept

ingrain *syn* INFUSE, suffuse, imbue, inoculate, leaven *rel* impregnate, saturate, permeate, pervade, impenetrate, interpenetrate; instill, inculcate, implant; incorporate, embody

ingrained *syn* INHERENT, constitutional, essential, intrinsic *rel* confirmed, inveterate, deep-seated, deep-rooted, chronic; implanted; imbued, inoculated

ingredient *syn* ELEMENT, constituent, component, factor *rel* item, detail, particular

ingress *syn* ENTRANCE, entry, entrée, access *ant* egress

inhabitant • one that occupies a particular place regularly *syn* denizen, resident, citizen

inherent · being a part, element, or quality of a thing's inmost being *syn* ingrained, intrinsic, essential, constitutional *rel* innate, inborn, inbred, congenital; inner, inward, internal; natural, typical, normal, regular; integrated, integral *ant* adventitious

inheritance *syn* HERITAGE, patrimony, birthright

inherited *syn* INNATE, hereditary, inborn, inbred, congenital *rel* transmitted, conveyed; generated, engendered, bred

inhibit **1** *syn* FORBID, prohibit, interdict, ban, enjoin *rel* prevent, preclude, obviate, avert, ward; debar, rule out, exclude; hinder, impede, obstruct, block, bar *ant* allow **2** *syn* RESTRAIN, curb, check, bridle *rel* suppress, repress; prevent, forestall; arrest *ant* animate; activate

inhuman *syn* FIERCE, savage, barbarous, truculent, ferocious, cruel, fell *rel* pitiless, ruthless; malign, malignant, malicious; merciless, relentless, unrelenting, implacable, grim; fiendish, diabolical, devilish *ant* humane

iniquitous *syn* VICIOUS, nefarious, flagitious, villainous, infamous, corrupt, degenerate *rel* wicked, evil, ill, bad; atrocious, heinous, outrageous, monstrous; ungodly, godless, irreligious *ant* righteous

initial · marking a beginning or constituting a start *syn* original, primordial *rel* starting, beginning, commencing; primary, primal, primeval, pristine; elementary *ant* final

initiate **1** *syn* BEGIN, commence, start, inaugurate *rel* found, establish, organize, institute *ant* consummate **2** · to put through the formalities for becoming a member or an official *syn* induct, inaugurate, install, invest *rel* introduce, admit, enter

initiation *syn* BEGINNING, genesis, rise *rel* starting, start, commencing, commencement; introducing, introduction, entering, entrance

initiative *syn* MANDATE, referendum, plebiscite

injunction *syn* COMMAND, order, bidding, behest, mandate, dictate *rel* instruction, direction, charging, charge; warning; precept, rule, regulation, law, statute, ordinance, canon

injure · to deplete the soundness, strength, effectiveness, or perfection of something *syn* harm, hurt, damage, impair, mar, spoil *rel* deface, disfigure; deform, distort, contort; afflict, torture, torment; maim, cripple, mutilate, mangle, batter; abuse, ill-treat, maltreat, outrage, mistreat, misuse *ant* aid

injury **1** · the act or the result of inflicting something that causes loss or pain *syn* hurt, damage, harm, mischief *rel* distress, suffering, agony, misery; pain, pang; violation, transgression, trespass, infringement, breach; detriment; evil, ill **2** *syn* INJUSTICE, wrong, grievance *rel* see INJURY 1

injustice · an act that inflicts undeserved hurt *syn* injury, wrong, grievance *rel* damage, hurt, harm, mischief; infringement, trespass, transgression, violation, infraction, breach; unfairness, inequitableness

innate · not acquired after birth *syn* inborn, inbred, congenital, hereditary, inherited *rel* constitutional, inherent, intrinsic, essential, ingrained; instinctive, intuitive; natural, typical, regular, normal; native, indigenous *ant* acquired

inner · situated further in *syn* inward, inside, interior, internal, intestine *rel* central, middle, focal, nuclear; intimate, close, familiar; intrinsic, constitutional, essential, inherent; instinctive, intuitive;

deep-seated, deep-rooted *ant* outer

innocent *syn* HARMLESS, innocuous, inoffensive, unoffending

innocuous *syn* HARMLESS, innocent, inoffensive, unoffending *ant* pernicious

innuendo *syn* INSINUATION *rel* hinting, hint, intimation, suggestion; implication, inference; allusion

inoculate *syn* INFUSE, imbue, ingrain, leaven, suffuse *rel* impregnate, saturate, impenetrate, interpenetrate, permeate, pervade; introduce, admit, enter; instill, inculcate, implant

inoffensive *syn* HARMLESS, innocuous, innocent, unoffending *ant* offensive

inordinate *syn* EXCESSIVE, immoderate, exorbitant, extreme, extravagant *rel* irrational, unreasonable; supererogatory, wanton, uncalled-for, gratuitous; superfluous, surplus, extra *ant* temperate

inquest *syn* INQUIRY, investigation, probe, inquisition, research *rel* examination, inspection, scrutiny, audit; questioning, interrogation, catechizing, examining

inquire *syn* ASK, query, question, interrogate, catechize, quiz, examine

inquiry · a search for truth, knowledge, or information *syn* inquisition, investigation, inquest, probe, research *rel* questioning, interrogation, catechizing; examination, inspection, scrutiny, audit

inquisition *syn* INQUIRY, inquest, probe, investigation, research *rel*

inquisitive *syn* CURIOUS, prying, snoopy, nosy *rel* impertinent, intrusive, meddlesome; interfering, meddling, intermeddling *ant* incurious

inroad *syn* INVASION, incursion, raid *rel* intrusion, butting in; encroachment, entrenchment, infringement, trespassing, trespass; entrance, entry, ingress

insane · afflicted by or manifesting unsoundness of mind or an inability to control one's rational processes *syn* mad, crazy, crazed, demented, deranged, lunatic, maniac, non compos mentis *rel* irrational, unreasonable; distracted, bewildered *ant* sane

insanity · a deranged state of mind or serious mental disorder *syn* lunacy, psychosis, mania, dementia *rel* alienation, derangement, aberration; frenzy, delirium, hysteria *ant* sanity

inscription · something written, printed, or engraved (as on a coin or a medal or under or over a picture) to indicate or describe the purpose or the nature of the thing *syn* legend, caption

inscrutable *syn* MYSTERIOUS, arcane *rel* profound, abysmal, deep; baffling, balking, thwarting, frustrating, foiling; hidden, concealed, secreted; enigmatic, cryptic, dark, obscure, vague; mystifying, perplexing, puzzling

insensate *syn* FOND, besotted, infatuated *rel* fatuous, asinine, foolish, silly; stupid, slow, dense, crass, dull, dumb; irrational, unreasonable

insensible **1** · unresponsive to stimuli or to external influences *syn* insensitive, impassible, anesthetic *rel* obtuse, dull, blunt; impassive, apathetic, phlegmatic, stolid, stoic; hardened, indurated, callous; engrossed, absorbed, intent, rapt *ant* sensible (*to or of something*) **2** *syn* IMPERCEPTIBLE, impalpable, intangible, inappreciable, imponderable *rel* tenuous, rare, slight, slender, thin; attenuated, extenuated, diluted, rarefied *ant* sensible, palpable

insensitive *syn* INSENSIBLE, impassible, anesthetic *rel* hardened, indurated, callous; indifferent, unconcerned, aloof, incurious; impassive, stoic, apathetic, phlegmatic, stolid *ant* sensitive

insert *syn* INTRODUCE, interpolate, intercalate, insinuate, interpose, interject *rel* intrude, obtrude, interlope; instill, inculcate, implant; enter, admit *ant* abstract; extract

inside *syn* INNER, interior, internal, intestine, inward *ant* outside

insidious *syn* SLY, cunning, crafty, tricky, foxy, wily, guileful, artful *rel* treacherous, perfidious; dangerous, perilous; furtive, stealthy, covert, underhand, underhanded

insight *syn* DISCERNMENT, penetration, acumen, discrimination, perception *rel* intuition, understanding, reason; comprehension, apprehension; appreciation, understanding; perspicaciousness, sagacity, shrewdness *ant* obtuseness

insinuate **1** *syn* INTRODUCE, insert, interject, interpolate, intercalate, interpose *rel* infuse, inoculate, imbue, leaven; instill, inculcate, implant **2** *syn* SUGGEST, intimate, hint, imply *rel* allude, advert, refer; impute, ascribe

insinuation · a subtle or covert hinting or suggestion *syn* innuendo *rel* hinting, hint, implying, implication, suggestion, intimation; animadversion, aspersion, reflection; imputation, ascription; allusion

insipid · devoid of qualities that make for spirit and character *syn* vapid, flat, jejune, banal, wishy-washy, inane *rel* thin, slight, tenuous, rare; weak, feeble; tame, subdued; bland, mild, soft *ant* sapid; zestful

insistent *syn* PRESSING, urgent, imperative, crying, importunate, exigent, instant *rel* persistent, persevering; pertinacious, dogged, obstinate; obtrusive, impertinent

insolent *syn* PROUD, arrogant, overbearing, supercilious, disdainful, haughty, lordly *rel* domineering, masterful, imperious, peremptory, imperative; pretentious, ostentatious, showy; dictatorial, magisterial; scornful, contemptuous *ant* deferential

inspect *syn* SCRUTINIZE, examine, scan, audit *rel* survey, view, observe, notice; probe, penetrate; inquire, interrogate, question, catechize, ask

inspection *syn* SCRUTINY, examination, scanning, audit *rel* investigation, probe, inquest, inquiry, inquisition, research; surveillance, oversight, supervision

inspiration · a divine or seemingly divine imparting of knowledge or power *syn* afflatus, fury, frenzy *rel* enlightenment, illumination; ecstasy, rapture, transport; revelation, vision, apocalypse, prophecy

inspire *syn* INFORM, animate, fire *rel* enlighten, illuminate; quicken, stimulate, excite, galvanize, provoke; activate, energize, vitalize; endue, endow

inspirit *syn* ENCOURAGE, hearten, embolden, cheer, nerve, steel *rel* enliven, animate, quicken, vivify; stimulate, excite, galvanize *ant* dispirit

in spite of *syn* NOTWITHSTANDING, despite

install *syn* INITIATE, induct, inaugurate, invest

instance *n* · something that exhibits distinguishing characteristics in its category *syn* case, illustration, example, sample, specimen *rel* proof, reason, ground; evidence; particular, item, detail

instance *vb, syn* MENTION, name, specify *rel* exemplify, illustrate; cite, quote

instant *n* · an almost imperceptible point or stretch of time *syn* moment, minute, second, flash, jiffy, twinkling, split second

instant *adj, syn* PRESSING, urgent,

imperative, crying, importunate, insistent, exigent *rel* immediate, direct; compelling, constraining, obliging

instigate *syn* INCITE, abet, foment *rel* activate, actuate, motivate; suggest, hint, insinuate; plan, plot, scheme

instill *syn* IMPLANT, inculcate *rel* infuse, inoculate, imbue, ingrain, leaven; impregnate, permeate, saturate, pervade, impenetrate, interpenetrate

instinctive 1 • prompted by natural instinct or propensity *syn* intuitive *rel* innate, inborn, congenital; constitutional, inherent, ingrained *ant* reasoned 2 *syn* SPONTANEOUS, impulsive, automatic, mechanical *rel* natural, normal, typical, regular; habitual, customary, wonted, accustomed, usual *ant* intentional

institute *syn* FOUND, establish, organize, create *rel* begin, commence, start, initiate, inaugurate; introduce *ant* abrogate

instruct 1 *syn* TEACH, train, educate, discipline, school *rel* impart, communicate; inform, acquaint, apprise; lead, guide, steer, pilot, engineer; practice, drill, exercise 2 *syn* COMMAND, direct, enjoin, bid, order, charge *rel* prescribe, assign, define

instrument 1 *syn* MEAN, instrumentality, agency, medium, agent, organ, vehicle, channel *rel* method, system, mode, way, manner, fashion; machinery, apparatus, tackle, gear, equipment, paraphernalia; device, contrivance, contraption 2 *syn* IMPLEMENT, tool, appliance, utensil 3 *syn* PAPER, document

instrumentality *syn* MEAN, agent, agency, instrument, medium, organ, vehicle, channel *rel* work, labor, toil; effort, exertion, trouble, pains; power, energy, force, might; action, deed, act

insubordinate • unwilling to submit to authority *syn* rebellious, mutinous, seditious, factious, contumacious *rel* recalcitrant, refractory, unruly, ungovernable, intractable

insular • having the narrow and limited outlook characteristic of geographic isolation *syn* provincial, parochial, local, small-town *rel* isolated, insulated, secluded; circumscribed, limited, restricted, confined; narrow, narrow-minded, illiberal; aloof, unconcerned, indifferent

insulate *syn* ISOLATE, segregate, seclude, sequester *rel* separate, part, sever, sunder; detach, disengage

insult *vb, syn* OFFEND, affront, outrage *rel* humiliate, humble, debase, degrade, abase; flout, scoff, jeer, gird, gibe, fleer, sneer; mock, taunt, deride, ridicule *ant* honor

insult *n, syn* AFFRONT, indignity *rel* abuse, vituperation, invective, obloquy; dishonor, shame, ignominy, opprobrium, disgrace; insolence, superciliousness, disdainfulness; contempt, despite, scorn, disdain

insure *syn* ENSURE, assure, secure *rel* protect, shield, guard, safeguard, defend; indemnify, compensate

insurgent *syn* REBEL, iconoclast

insurrection *syn* REBELLION, uprising, revolt, mutiny, revolution, putsch, coup

intact *syn* PERFECT, whole, entire *rel* flawless, faultless, impeccable; complete, replete, full; consummate, finished *ant* defective

intangible *syn* IMPERCEPTIBLE, impalpable, insensible, inappreciable, imponderable *rel* tenuous, rare, slight, slender, thin; ethereal, airy, aerial; eluding, elusive, evading, evasive *ant* tangible

integer *syn* NUMBER, numeral, figure, digit

integrate • to join together systematically *syn* articulate, concatenate *rel* unite, combine, conjoin; unify, consolidate, concentrate, compact; fuse, blend, merge, coalesce, mix; organize, systematize *ant* disintegrate

integration · the act or process of operating as a unit or whole *syn* articulation, concatenation *rel* unification, consolidation, concentration; integrity, union, unity, solidarity

integrity 1 *syn* UNITY, solidarity, union *rel* wholeness, entirety, perfection, intactness; consummateness; purity, simplicity, absoluteness 2 *syn* HONESTY, probity, honor *rel* uprightness, justness, conscientiousness, scrupulousness, scrupulosity; rectitude, virtue, goodness, morality; truth, veracity, verity *ant* duplicity

intellect *syn* MIND, soul, psyche, brain, intelligence, wit *rel* reason, understanding, intuition

intellectual *syn* MENTAL, psychic, cerebral, intelligent *ant* carnal

intelligence 1 *syn* MIND, brain, intellect, soul, psyche, wit *rel* sense, judgment, wisdom, gumption; discernment, penetration, insight, acumen; sagaciousness, sagacity, perspicaciousness, perspicacity, astuteness, shrewdness 2 *syn* NEWS, tidings, advice

intelligent 1 *syn* MENTAL, intellectual, cerebral, psychic 2 · mentally quick or keen *syn* clever, alert, quick-witted, bright, smart, knowing, brilliant *rel* sharp, keen, acute; shrewd, sagacious, perspicacious, astute; cunning, ingenious, adroit *ant* unintelligent

intend · to have in mind as a purpose or goal *syn* mean, design, propose, purpose *rel* aim, aspire; attempt, try, endeavor, strive, essay; plan, design, scheme, plot

intense · extreme in degree, power, or effect *syn* vehement, fierce, exquisite, violent *rel* intensified, enhanced, heightened, aggravated; accentuated, emphasized, stressed *ant* subdued

intensify · to increase markedly in degree or measure *syn* aggravate, heighten, enhance *rel* accentuate, emphasize, stress, accent; magnify, aggrandize, exalt *ant* temper; mitigate, allay; abate

intent *n*, *syn* INTENTION, purpose, design, aim, end, object, objective, goal *rel* will, volition, conation *ant* accident

intent *adj* · having one's mind or attention deeply fixed *syn* engrossed, absorbed, rapt *rel* attending, attentive, minding, watching; abstracted, preoccupied; concentrated; riveted *ant* distracted

intention · what one intends to accomplish or attain *syn* intent, purpose, design, aim, end, object, objective, goal *rel* plan, scheme, project; desiring, desire, wishing, wish

intentional *syn* VOLUNTARY, deliberate, willful, willing *rel* intended, meant, purposed, proposed; considered, premeditated, advised, studied, designed, deliberate *ant* instinctive

intercalate *syn* INTRODUCE, interpolate, insert, interpose, interject, insinuate

intercede *syn* INTERPOSE, mediate, intervene, interfere *rel* plead, petition, sue, pray

interchange *syn* EXCHANGE, bandy *rel* transpose, reverse

intercourse · connection or dealing between persons or groups *syn* commerce, traffic, dealings, communication, communion, conversation, converse, correspondence

interdict *syn* FORBID, ban, inhibit, enjoin, prohibit *rel* proscribe, sentence; debar, rule out, exclude; restrain, curb, check *ant* sanction

interesting · holding the attention for some time *syn* engrossing, absorbing, intriguing *rel* stimulating, exciting, provoking, quickening; stirring, rousing, awakening; thrilling, electrifying; amusing, diverting, entertaining; inspiring, animating *ant* boring

interfere 1 *syn* INTERPOSE, intervene, mediate, intercede *rel* impede, obstruct, block, hinder, bar 2 *syn* MEDDLE, intermeddle, tamper *rel* intrude, interlope, butt in, obtrude; incommode, discommode, inconvenience, trouble; thwart, foil, balk, baffle, frustrate

interim *syn* BREAK, gap, interruption, interval, hiatus, lacuna

interior *syn* INNER, inside, internal, inward, intestine *rel* intimate, familiar; spiritual; intrinsic, constitutional, inherent *ant* exterior

interject *syn* INTRODUCE, interpolate, interpose, insert, intercalate, insinuate *rel* throw, cast, toss; obtrude, intrude, interlope, butt in; comment, remark, animadvert

interlope *syn* INTRUDE, butt in, obtrude *rel* trespass, encroach, invade, entrench, infringe; interfere, interpose, intervene

intermeddle *syn* MEDDLE, interfere, tamper *rel* intrude, obtrude, butt in, interlope; entrench, encroach, trespass, invade

interminable *syn* EVERLASTING, unceasing, endless *rel* perpetual, lasting, perdurable, permanent; incessant, continual, continuous, constant; eternal, infinite

intermission *syn* PAUSE, recess, respite, lull *rel* interruption, interval, gap, break; ceasing, cessation, stopping, stop

intermit *syn* DEFER, suspend, stay, postpone *rel* interrupt, arrest, check; stop, discontinue; abate, reduce, lessen, decrease

intermittent • occurring or appearing in interrupted sequence *syn* recurrent, periodic, alternate *rel* interrupted, checked, arrested; fitful, spasmodic; sporadic, occasional, infrequent; discontinuing, discontinuous, stopping, quitting *ant* incessant, continual

intern *syn* IMPRISON, immure, incarcerate, jail *rel* confine, circumscribe, restrict, limit; restrain, curb, check; fetter, manacle, shackle, hamper

internal *syn* INNER, interior, intestine, inward, inside *rel* intrinsic, constitutional, inherent, essential *ant* external

internuncio *syn* AMBASSADOR, nuncio, legate, minister, envoy, chargé d'affaires

interpenetrate *syn* PERMEATE, impenetrate, penetrate, pervade, impregnate, saturate *rel* see IMPENETRATE

interpolate *syn* INTRODUCE, insert, intercalate, insinuate, interpose, interject *rel* enter, introduce, admit; intrude, interlope; add, superadd, annex, append

interpose 1 *syn* INTRODUCE, interject, insert, insinuate, interpolate, intercalate *rel* throw, toss, cast; intrude, obtrude; push, shove, thrust 2 • to come or go between *syn* interfere, intervene, mediate, intercede *rel* intrude, butt in, interlope; meddle, intermeddle; interrupt

interpret *syn* EXPLAIN, elucidate, construe, expound, explicate *rel* illustrate, exemplify; gloss, annotate; comment, commentate

interrogate *syn* ASK, question, catechize, quiz, examine, query, inquire

interrupt *syn* ARREST, check *rel* suspend, stay, intermit, defer, postpone; intrude, obtrude, interlope, butt in; interfere, interpose, intervene

interruption *syn* BREAK, gap, interval, interim, hiatus, lacuna *rel* pause, recess, respite, lull, intermission; breach, rupture, rent, split, rift

interstice *syn* APERTURE, orifice

interval *syn* BREAK, gap, interruption, interim, hiatus, lacuna *rel* period, epoch, age, era; pause, respite, lull, intermission, recess; distance, remoteness, removedness; aperture, interstice, orifice

intervene *syn* INTERPOSE, mediate, intercede, interfere *rel* separate, part, divide, sever; intrude, interlope, butt in, obtrude

intestine *syn* INNER, internal, interior, inside *ant* foreign

intimate *vb, syn* SUGGEST, imply, hint, insinuate *rel* indicate, betoken, attest, bespeak; allude, advert, refer

intimate *adj, syn* FAMILIAR, close, confidential, chummy, thick *rel* nearest, next; devoted, fond, affectionate, loving; secret, privy; friendly, neighborly, amicable; companionable, convivial, social, hospitable, cooperative

intimate *n, syn* FRIEND, confidant, acquaintance *rel* comrade, companion, crony, associate *ant* stranger, outsider

intimidate • to frighten into submission *syn* cow, bulldoze, bully, browbeat *rel* terrorize, terrify, frighten; hector, hound, ride, chivy, bait, badger; coerce, force, compel, constrain, oblige

intolerant *syn* ILLIBERAL, narrow-minded, narrow, bigoted, hidebound *rel* obdurate, inflexible; antipathetic, unsympathetic, averse *ant* tolerant

intonation *syn* INFLECTION, accent

intone *syn* SING, troll, carol, descant, warble, trill, hymn, chant

intoxicated *syn* DRUNK, drunken, inebriated, tipsy, tight *rel* fuddled, befuddled, confused, muddled; maudlin, sentimental

intractable *syn* UNRULY, ungovernable, refractory, recalcitrant, willful, headstrong *rel* obstreperous, boisterous, vociferous; contumacious, rebellious, factious, insubordinate; froward, perverse, contrary, wayward, balky *ant* tractable

intrepid *syn* BRAVE, courageous, unafraid, fearless, valiant, valorous, dauntless, undaunted, doughty, bold, audacious *rel* daring, venturesome, adventurous, daredevil; mettlesome, high-spirited, spirited, fiery; plucky, gritty

intricate *syn* COMPLEX, complicated, involved, knotty *rel* perplexing, puzzling, mystifying, bewildering; tortuous, winding; difficult, hard, arduous

intrigue **1** *syn* PLOT, conspiracy, machination, cabal *rel* scheme, design, plan; stratagem, maneuver, ruse, artifice, trick, feint, gambit, ploy **2** *syn* AMOUR, liaison, affair

intriguing *syn* INTERESTING, engrossing, absorbing *rel* provoking, provocative, piquing, exciting; mystifying, puzzling; luring, tempting, enticing, inveigling

intrinsic *syn* INHERENT, ingrained, constitutional, essential *rel* inner, inward, internal, interior, inside, intestine; innate, inborn, inbred, congenital; natural, normal, typical, regular *ant* extrinsic

introduce **1** *syn* ENTER, admit *rel* induct, install, inaugurate, initiate; instill, inculcate, implant; infuse, inoculate, imbue **2** • to put among or between others *syn* insert, insinuate, interpolate, intercalate, interpose, interject *ant* withdraw; abstract

introduction • something that serves as a preliminary or antecedent *syn* prologue, prelude, preface, foreword, exordium, preamble

introductory *syn* PRELIMINARY, preparatory, prefatory *ant* closing, concluding

intrude • to thrust or force in or upon without permission, welcome, or fitness *syn* obtrude, interlope, butt in *rel* trespass, invade, encroach, entrench, infringe; interject, interpose, insinuate, interpolate, intercalate, introduce; interfere, intervene; meddle, intermeddle, tamper *ant* stand off

intrusive *syn* IMPERTINENT, officious, meddlesome, obtrusive *rel* intruding, butting in, interloping, obtruding; inquisitive, prying, snoopy, nosy, curious; interfering, meddling, intermeddling *ant* retiring; unintrusive

intuition *syn* REASON, understanding *rel* intellect, soul, mind; insight, acumen, discernment *ant* ratiocination

intuitive *syn* INSTINCTIVE *rel* immediate, direct *ant* ratiocinative

inundation *syn* FLOOD, deluge, torrent, spate, cataract

inure *syn* HABITUATE, accustom, addict *rel* adapt, adjust, accommodate

invade *syn* TRESPASS, encroach, entrench, infringe *rel* intrude, obtrude, butt in, interlope; enter, penetrate, pierce, probe; permeate, pervade, impenetrate, interpenetrate

invalidate *syn* NULLIFY, negate, annul, abrogate *rel* negative, counteract, neutralize; void, vacate, quash, annul *ant* validate

invaluable *syn* COSTLY, priceless, precious, valuable, dear, expensive *ant* worthless

invasion • a hostile entrance into the territory of another *syn* incursion, raid, inroad *rel* aggression, attack, offense, offensive; trespass, violation, transgression, infringement, infraction, breach; intruding, intrusion, interloping, butting in, obtruding, obtrusion; encroachment, entrenchment

invective *syn* ABUSE, vituperation, obloquy, scurrility, billingsgate *rel* vilifying, vilification, maligning, calumniation, traducing; animadversion, stricture, aspersion, reflection

inveigle *syn* LURE, decoy, entice, tempt, seduce *rel* snare, ensnare, trap, entrap; beguile, mislead, delude, deceive, betray; cajole, wheedle, blandish, coax

invent *syn* CONTRIVE, devise, frame, concoct *rel* initiate, inaugurate, begin; institute, found, establish

inventory *syn* LIST, register, schedule, catalog, table, roll, roster

invert *syn* REVERSE, transpose *rel* upset, overturn, capsize; interchange, exchange; derange, disarrange

invest **1** *syn* INITIATE, induct, install, inaugurate *rel* endue, endow; consecrate, devote *ant* divest, strip unfrock **2** *syn* BESIEGE, beleaguer, blockade

investigation *syn* INQUIRY, probe, inquest, inquisition, research *rel* inspection, examination, scrutiny, audit; surveying, survey, observing, observation

inveterate • so firmly established that change is almost impossible *syn* confirmed, chronic, deep-seated, deep-rooted *rel* habituated, accustomed, addicted; habitual, customary, usual; hardened, indurated; settled, set, fixed, established; inbred, innate; persisting, persistent, enduring, abiding

invidious *syn* REPUGNANT, distasteful, obnoxious, repellent, abhorrent *rel* hateful, odious, abominable, detestable; offensive, loathsome, revolting, repulsive

invigorate *syn* STRENGTHEN, fortify, energize, reinforce *rel* renew, restore, refresh, rejuvenate; stir, rally, rouse; vitalize, activate *ant* debilitate

invincible • incapable of being conquered *syn* unconquerable, indomitable, impregnable, inexpugnable, unassailable, invulnerable *rel* dauntless, undaunted, intrepid

inviolable *syn* SACRED, inviolate, sacrosanct *rel* hallowed, consecrated, dedicated; holy, blessed, divine, religious; pure, chaste

inviolate *syn* SACRED, sacrosanct, inviolable *ant* violated

invite · to request the presence or participation of *syn* bid, solicit, court, woo *rel* ask, request; lure, tempt, entice, inveigle; excite, provoke, stimulate

involve **1** *syn* ENTANGLE, enmesh *rel* complicate; confuse, confound, mistake; perplex, mystify, nonplus, puzzle **2** *syn* INCLUDE, comprehend, embrace, imply, subsume *rel* import, mean, signify, denote; bespeak, attest, betoken, indicate, argue, prove **3** · to bring a person or thing into circumstances or a situation from which extrication is difficult *syn* implicate *rel* ensnare, entrap, snare, trap, catch; connect, link, associate, relate, join; embarrass; fetter, shackle, hamper

involved *syn* COMPLEX, intricate, complicated, knotty *rel* confused, muddled; perplexing, puzzling, bewildering, mystifying; difficult, hard, arduous

invunerable *syn* INVINCIBLE, impregnable, inexpugnable, unassailable, unconquerable, indomitable *ant* vulnerable

inward *syn* INNER, interior, internal, inside, intestine *rel* inbred, innate, inborn; ingrained, inherent, intrinsic, constitutional; intimate, familiar; objective, sensible, material; heartfelt, unfeigned, sincere; impalpable, imperceptible *ant* outward

iota *syn* PARTICLE, jot, tittle, whit, bit, mite, smidgen, atom

irascible · easily aroused to anger *syn* choleric, splenetic, testy, touchy, cranky, cross *rel* irritable, fractious, snappish, waspish, huffy, querulous, petulant, peevish; impatient, restive, jumpy, jittery, nervous; crabbed, surly

irate *syn* ANGRY, wrathful, wroth, mad, indignant, acrimonious *rel* provoked, exasperated, nettled, irritated; incensed, infuriated, enraged

ire *syn* ANGER, rage, fury, indignation, wrath *rel* passion; temper, humor, mood

irenic *syn* PACIFIC, peaceable, peaceful, pacifist, pacifistic *rel* conciliating, conciliatory, placating, placatory, propitiating, propitiatory *ant* acrimonious

iridescent *syn* PRISMATIC, opalescent, opaline

irk *syn* ANNOY, vex, bother *rel* perturb, disturb, upset, discompose; discommode, incommode, trouble, inconvenience; fret, chafe, abrade

irksome · tending to cause boredom or tedium *syn* tiresome, wearisome, tedious, boring *rel* dull, stupid, slow; fatiguing, exhausting, fagging, tiring *ant* absorbing, engrossing

ironic *syn* SARCASTIC, satiric, sardonic *rel* biting, cutting, incisive, trenchant; caustic, mordant, scathing

irony *syn* WIT, satire, sarcasm, humor, repartee

irrational · not governed or guided by reason *syn* unreasonable *rel* absurd, preposterous, foolish, silly; fatuous, asinine, simple; crazy, demented, mad, insane *ant* rational

irregular · not conforming to rule, law, or custom *syn* anomalous, unnatural *rel* aberrant, abnormal, atypical; exceptional; singular, unique, strange, peculiar, odd, queer *ant* regular

irreligious · lacking religious emotions, doctrines, or practices *syn* unreligious, nonreligious, ungodly, godless *rel* impious, profane, blasphemous, sacrilegious;

immoral, amoral, unmoral *ant* religious

irritable · easily exasperated *syn* fractious, peevish, snappish, waspish, petulant, pettish, huffy, fretful, querulous *rel* cranky, cross, testy, touchy, choleric, splenetic, irascible *ant* easygoing

irritate · to excite a feeling of anger or annoyance *syn* exasperate, nettle, provoke, aggravate, rile, peeve *rel* annoy, vex, irk, bother; incense, anger, madden, enrage, infuriate; offend, affront; fret, chafe, abrade

isolate · to set apart from others *syn* segregate, seclude, insulate, sequester *rel* detach, disengage, abstract; separate, part, sever, sunder

isolation *syn* SOLITUDE, alienation, seclusion *rel* loneliness, solitariness, loneness, desolateness, desolation

issue *n* **1** *syn* EFFECT, outcome, result, consequence, upshot, aftereffect, aftermath, sequel, event *rel* ending, end, termination, concluding, conclusion, closing **2** *syn* OFFSPRING, young, progeny, descendant, posterity

issue *vb, syn* SPRING, emanate, proceed, flow, derive, originate, arise, rise, stem *rel* emerge, appear, loom

item · one of the distinct parts of a whole *syn* detail, particular *rel* thing, object, article; constituent, component, element, factor

itemized *syn* CIRCUMSTANTIAL, detailed, particularized, minute, particular *ant* summarized

iterate *syn* REPEAT, reiterate, ingeminate

itinerant · traveling from place to place *syn* peripatetic, ambulatory, ambulant, nomadic, vagrant *rel* wandering, roving, rambling, straying, roaming, ranging; moving, shifting

J

jabber *syn* CHAT, chatter, gab, patter, prate, prattle, babble, gabble, gibber

jack *syn* FLAG, ensign, standard, banner, color, streamer, pennant, pendant, pennon

jade *syn* TIRE, exhaust, fatigue, weary, fag, tucker *rel* oppress, depress, weigh; enervate, unnerve, unman, emasculate; sate, satiate, surfeit, pall, cloy *ant* refresh

jail *syn* IMPRISON, incarcerate, immure, intern *rel* confine, circumscribe, restrict, limit; shackle, manacle, fetter

jam *vb, syn* PRESS, crowd, squeeze, bear, bear down *rel* crush, squash; pack, cram, stuff, ram, tamp

jam *n, syn* PREDICAMENT, plight, fix, dilemma, quandary, scrape, pickle *rel* difficulty, vicissitude; pinch, strait, exigency

jape *syn* JOKE, jest, quip, witticism, wisecrack, crack, gag

jar *syn* IMPACT, jolt, impingement, collision, clash, shock, concussion, percussion *rel* shaking, shake, quaking, quake; vibration, fluctuation, swaying, sway; agitation, disturbance, upsetting, upset

jargon *syn* DIALECT, vernacular, patois, lingo, cant, argot, slang *rel* idiom, speech, language; abracadabra, gibberish

jaunt *syn* JOURNEY, excursion,

trip, tour, voyage, cruise, expedition, pilgrimage

jaw *syn* SCOLD, upbraid, rate, berate, tongue-lash, bawl, chew out, wig, rail, revile, vituperate *rel* censure, denounce, reprobate, reprehend, criticize, blame, condemn; reprove, reproach, chide, reprimand, rebuke

jealous *syn* ENVIOUS *rel* suspicious, mistrustful; doubtful, dubious; vigilant, watchful, alert; distrusting, mistrusting

jeer *syn* SCOFF, gibe, fleer, gird, sneer, flout *rel* deride, ridicule, mock, taunt, twit, rally

jejune *syn* INSIPID, vapid, flat, wishy-washy, inane, banal *rel* thin, slight, slim, tenuous; arid, dry; attenuated, extenuated, diluted, thinned; meager, skimpy, exiguous

jell, jelly *syn* COAGULATE, congeal, set, curdle, clot *rel* solidify, harden; cohere, stick; compact, consolidate

jeopardize *syn* VENTURE, hazard, risk, chance, endanger, imperil *rel* brave, dare; meet, encounter, confront, face

jeopardy *syn* DANGER, peril, hazard, risk *rel* threatening, threat, menacing, menace; exposure; liability, susceptibility, sensitiveness, openness; chance, accident, hap

jeremiad *syn* TIRADE, diatribe, philippic

jerk · to make a sudden sharp quick movement *syn* snap, twitch, yank *rel* pull, drag; toss, sling, fling, throw; wrench, wrest, wring

jest 1 *syn* JOKE, jape, quip, witticism, wisecrack, crack, gag *rel* badinage, persiflage, raillery; bantering, banter, chaffing, chaff, jollying, jolly; twitting, twit, ridiculing, ridicule, deriding, derision 2 *syn* FUN, sport, game, play *rel* diversion, entertainment, amusement; joviality, merriment

jetty *syn* WHARF, dock, pier, quay, slip, berth, levee

jib *syn* DEMUR, balk, shy, boggle, stickle, stick, strain, scruple

jibe *syn* AGREE, harmonize, accord, conform, square, tally, correspond

jiffy *syn* INSTANT, moment, minute, second, flash, twinkling, split second

jittery *syn* IMPATIENT, jumpy, nervous, unquiet, restless, restive, uneasy, fidgety *rel* unnerved, unmanned; perturbed, agitated, disquieted, upset, discomposed

job *syn* TASK, duty, assignment, stint, chore *rel* office, function, province; business, concern, affair, matter, thing

jocose *syn* WITTY, jocular, facetious, humorous *rel* waggish, sportive, playful, roguish; comic, comical, laughable, ludicrous, droll, funny; merry, jolly, jovial, jocund, blithe

jocular *syn* WITTY, jocose, humorous, facetious *rel* jovial, jolly, merry; playful, sportive; funny, droll, comic, comical, laughable, ludicrous, ridiculous

jocund *syn* MERRY, blithe, jolly, jovial *rel* joyful, joyous, cheerful, lighthearted, happy, glad; mirthful, hilarious, gleeful; sportive, playful, mischievous

jog *vb, syn* POKE, prod, nudge *rel* shake, agitate; push, shove

jog *n, syn* POKE, prod, nudge

join · to bring or come together into some manner of union *syn* conjoin, combine, unite, connect, link, associate, relate *rel* cooperate, concur, articulate, concatenate, integrate; attach, affix, fasten; knit, weave; tie, bind *ant* disjoin; part

joint · a place where two or more things are united *syn* articulation, suture

joke · something said or done to provoke laughter *syn* jest, jape, quip, witticism, wisecrack, crack, gag *rel* prank, caper, antic, monkeyshine, dido; trick, ruse, wile; travesty, parody, burlesque, caricature; raillery, badinage, persiflage; jocoseness, jocularity, facetiousness, wittiness, humorousness; wit, humor, repartee, sarcasm

jollity *syn* MIRTH, hilarity, glee *rel* merriment, joviality, jocundity, blitheness; sport, disport, play, frolic, rollick, gambol, romp; diversion, amusement, recreation, entertainment; fun, jest, game

jolly *adj, syn* MERRY, jovial, jocund, blithe *rel* bantering, chaffing, jollying, joshing; jocular, jocose, witty, humorous, facetious; sportive, playful, mischievous, roguish, waggish, frolicsome; gay, lively, vivacious, animated, sprightly

jolly *vb, syn* BANTER, chaff, kid, rag, rib, josh *rel* blandish, cajole; deride, ridicule, twit, rally, mock, taunt

jolt *syn* IMPACT, jar, shock, impingement, collision, clash, concussion, percussion *rel* shaking, shake, rocking, rock, convulsing, convulsion

josh *syn* BANTER, chaff, kid, rag, rib, jolly

jot *syn* PARTICLE, tittle, iota, bit, mite, smidgen, whit, atom

journal • a publication that appears at regular intervals *syn* periodical, newspaper, magazine, review, organ

journey • travel or a passage from one place to another *syn* voyage, tour, trip, jaunt, excursion, cruise, expedition, pilgrimage

jovial *syn* MERRY, jolly, jocund, blithe *rel* jocular, jocose, facetious, humorous, witty; genial, sociable, affable; good-natured, amiable; bantering, chaffing, jollying, joshing

joy *syn* PLEASURE, delight, enjoyment, delectation, fruition *rel* bliss, beatitude, happiness, felicity; ecstasy, rapture, transport *ant* sorrow; misery; abomination

joyful *syn* GLAD, joyous, cheerful, happy, lighthearted *rel* blithe, jocund, merry, jolly; buoyant, effervescent, expansive *ant* joyless

joyous *syn* GLAD, joyful, happy, cheerful, lighthearted *rel* blithe, jocund, merry; rapturous, ecstatic, transported *ant* lugubrious

judge *vb* **1** • to decide something in dispute or controversy upon its merits and upon evidence *syn* adjudge, adjudicate, arbitrate *rel* determine, decide, settle, rule **2** *syn* INFER, conclude, deduce, gather *rel* prove, demonstrate, try, test

judge *n* • a person who impartially decides unsettled questions or controversial issues *syn* arbiter, arbitrator, referee, umpire

judgment **1** *syn* INFERENCE, conclusion, deduction *rel* decision, determination, ruling; opinion, conviction, persuasion, view, belief **2** *syn* SENSE, wisdom, gumption *rel* intelligence, wit, brain, mind; sagaciousness, sagacity, perspicaciousness, perspicacity, shrewdness, astuteness; acumen, discernment, insight, penetration; prudence, discretion

judicious *syn* WISE, sage, sapient, prudent, sensible, sane *rel* rational, reasonable; just, fair, equitable, dispassionate, objective; sagacious, perspicacious, astute, shrewd; discreet, prudent *ant* injudicious; asinine

jumble *syn* CONFUSION, disorder, chaos, disarray, clutter, snarl, muddle

jump *vb* • to move suddenly through space by or as if by muscular action *syn* leap, spring, bound, vault

jump *n* • a sudden move through space *syn* leap, spring, bound, vault

jumpy *syn* IMPATIENT, jittery, nervous, restless, uneasy, fidgety, unquiet, restive *ant* steady

junction · the act, state, or place of meeting or uniting *syn* confluence, concourse

juncture · a critical or crucial time or state of affairs *syn* pass, exigency, emergency, contingency, pinch, strait, crisis *rel* state, posture, situation, condition, status; predicament, plight, quandary

junk *syn* DISCARD, scrap, cast, shed, molt, slough

jurisdiction *syn* POWER, authority, control, command, sway, dominion *rel* limits, bounds, confines; range, scope, compass, reach; circuit, periphery; province, office, function, duty; domain, territory, field, sphere, bailiwick

just 1 *syn* UPRIGHT, honorable, conscientious, scrupulous, honest *rel* strict, rigid; virtuous, righteous, moral, ethical, noble; reliable, dependable, tried, trustworthy 2 *syn* FAIR, equitable, impartial, unbiased, dispassionate, uncolored, objective *rel* detached, disinterested, aloof, indifferent; due, rightful, condign; rational, reasonable *ant* unjust

justice · awarding each what is rightly due *syn* equity

justify 1 *syn* MAINTAIN, vindicate, defend, assert *rel* prove, demonstrate; support, uphold, back 2 *syn* EXPLAIN, account, rationalize *rel* excuse, condone; exculpate, exonerate, absolve, acquit, vindicate; extenuate, gloze, gloss, whitewash, palliate 3 · to constitute sufficient grounds *syn* warrant *rel* allow, permit, let; sanction, approve; authorize

jut *syn* BULGE, stick out, protrude, project, over-hang, beetle *rel* extend, lengthen, elongate; swell, distend, dilate, expand

juvenile *syn* YOUTHFUL, puerile, boyish, virgin, virginal, maiden *rel* immature, unmatured; callow, green, crude *ant* adult; senile

juxtaposed *syn* ADJACENT, adjoining, contiguous, abutting, tangent, conterminous *rel* close, near, nigh

K

keen *adj* 1 *syn* SHARP, acute *rel* piercing, penetrating, probing; pungent, poignant, piquant; cutting, biting, incisive, trenchant *ant* blunt 2 *syn* EAGER, avid, agog, athirst, anxious *rel* ardent, fervent, fervid, perfervid, impassioned; intense, vehement, fierce; fired

keen *vb*, *syn* CRY, wait, weep, whimper, blubber *rel* lament, bewail, bemoan; mourn, sorrow, grieve

keep *vb* 1 · to notice or honor a day, occasion, or deed *syn* observe, celebrate, solemnize, commemorate *rel* regard, respect *ant* break 2 · to hold in one's possession or under one's control *syn* keep back, keep out, retain, detain, withhold, reserve, hold back *rel* save, preserve, conserve; hold, have, enjoy, possess, own; control, direct, manage, conduct *ant* relinquish

keep *n*, *syn* LIVING, livelihood, subsistence, sustenance, maintenance, support, bread

keep back, keep out *syn* KEEP, retain, detain, withhold, reserve, hold, hold back

keepsake *syn* REMEMBRANCE, remembrancer, reminder, memorial, memento, token, souvenir

ken *syn* RANGE, gamut, reach, radius, compass, sweep, scope, orbit, horizon, purview *rel* field, sphere, province, domain; view, sight

kibitzer *syn* SPECTATOR, onlooker, looker-on, bystander, observer, beholder, witness, eyewitness

kick *syn* OBJECT, protest, remonstrate, expostulate *rel* oppose, combat, resist, withstand, fight; criticize, denounce, condemn; objurgate, execrate, curse, damn, anathematize

kid *syn* BANTER, chaff, rag, rib, josh, jolly *rel* tease, plague, pester, harry, worry

kidnap *syn* ABDUCT

kidney *syn* TYPE, kind, sort, nature, description, character, stripe, ilk

kill • to deprive of life *syn* slay, murder, assassinate, dispatch, execute

kind *n, syn* TYPE, sort, stripe, kidney, ilk, description, nature, character

kind *adj* • showing or having a gentle considerate nature *syn* kindly, benign, benignant *rel* benevolent, charitable, humane, altruistic, philanthropic, eleemosynary, humanitarian; sympathetic, warm, warmhearted, responsive, tender, compassionate; clement, lenient, indulgent, merciful, forbearing, tolerant; amiable, good-natured, complaisant, obliging *ant* unkind

kindle *syn* LIGHT, ignite, fire *rel* blaze, flame, flare, glow; provoke, excite, stimulate; arouse, rouse, stir; incite, foment, instigate *ant* smother, stifle

kindly *syn* KIND, benign, benignant *rel* gracious, cordial, genial, affable, sociable; amiable, good-natured, complaisant, obliging; friendly, neighborly, amicable; considerate, thoughtful, attentive *ant* unkindly; acrid (*of temper, attitudes, comments*)

kindred *syn* RELATED, cognate, allied, affiliated *ant* alien

kingly • of, relating to, or befitting one who occupies a throne *syn* regal, royal, queenly, imperial, princely

knack *syn* GIFT, bent, turn, faculty, aptitude, genius, talent *rel* ability, capacity, capability; aptness, readiness, quickness; facility, dexterity, ease *ant* ineptitude

knave *syn* VILLAIN, scoundrel, blackguard, rascal, rogue, scamp, rapscallion, miscreant

knit *syn* WEAVE, crochet, braid, plait, tat *rel* join, connect, link, unite

knock *vb, syn* TAP, rap, thump, thud *rel* strike, hit, smite; beat, pound, pummel

knock *n, syn* TAP, rap, thump, thud *rel* pounding, beating

knotty *syn* COMPLEX, intricate, involved, complicated

knowing *syn* INTELLIGENT, alert, bright, smart, clever, quick-witted, brilliant *rel* shrewd, astute, perspicacious, sagacious; watchful, vigilant; discerning, observing, observant, perceiving, perceptive

knowledge • what is or can be known by an individual or by mankind *syn* science, learning, erudition, scholarship, information, lore *ant* ignorance

L

label *n, syn* MARK, brand, stamp, tag, ticket
label *vb, syn* MARK, brand, stamp, tag, ticket
labor *syn* WORK, toil, travail, drudgery, grind *rel* effort, exertion, pains, trouble; endeavor, striving, struggle
labored *syn* FORCED, strained, farfetched *rel* heavy, ponderous, weighty; awkward, clumsy, maladroit, inept; stiff, wooden, rigid
laborer *syn* WORKER, working man, workman, craftsman, handicraftsman, mechanic, artisan, operative, hand, roustabout
lack *vb* · to be without something, esp. something essential or greatly needed *syn* want, need, require
lack *n* · the fact or state of being wanting or deficient *syn* want, dearth, absence, defect, privation *rel* need, necessity, exigency; deficiency; exhaustion, impoverishment, draining, depletion
lackadaisical *syn* LANGUID, listless, spiritless, enervated, languishing, languorous *rel* indifferent, unconcerned, incurious; indolent, slothful, faineant, lazy; inert, inactive, passive, supine, idle; sentimental, romantic; emasculated
laconic *syn* CONCISE, succinct, terse, summary, pithy, compendious *rel* curt, brusque, bluff; brief, short *ant* verbose
lacuna *syn* BREAK, gap, hiatus, interruption, interval, interim
lade *syn* BURDEN, load, encumber, cumber, weigh, weight, tax, charge, saddle *ant* unlade
lading *syn* LOAD, freight, cargo, burden
ladle *syn* DIP, scoop, spoon, dish, bail
lady *syn* FEMALE, woman
ladylike *syn* FEMALE, feminine, womanly, womanlike, womanish *rel* dainty, fastidious, finicky, particular, nice; fashionable, modish, smart, chic, stylish; decorous, proper, seemly
lag *syn* DELAY, loiter, dawdle, procrastinate *rel* slow, slacken, retard; tarry, linger, wait, stay
laggard *syn* SLOW, dilatory, leisurely, deliberate *rel* dawdling, loitering, delaying, procrastinating; lethargic, sluggish, comatose; phlegmatic, apathetic, impassive *ant* prompt, quick
lambent *syn* BRIGHT, beaming, luminous, brilliant, radiant, lustrous, effulgent, refulgent, lucent, incandescent *rel* gleaming, glistening
lament *syn* DEPLORE, bewail, bemoan *rel* weep, keen, wail, cry; grieve, mourn, sorrow *ant* exult; rejoice
lampoon *syn* LIBEL, skit, squib, pasquinade
land *syn* ALIGHT, light, perch, roost *rel* arrive, come; reach, gain, achieve, attain; appear, emerge
landing field, landing strip *syn* AIRPORT, airdrome, airfield, airstrip, flying field
language 1 · a body or system of words and phrases used by a large community or by a people, a nation, or a group of nations *syn* dialect, tongue, speech, idiom *rel* vernacular, patois, lingo, jargon, cant, argot, slang 2 · oral or written expression or a quality of such expression that is dependent on the variety, or arrangement, or expressiveness of words *syn*

vocabulary, phraseology, phrasing, diction, style

languid · lacking in vim or energy *syn* languishing, languorous, lackadaisical, listless, spiritless, enervated *rel* lethargic, sluggish, comatose, torpid; phlegmatic, apathetic, impassive; inert, inactive, supine *ant* vivacious; chipper

languishing *syn* LANGUID, languorous, lackadaisical, listless, spiritless, enervated *rel* weakened, enfeebled, debilitated; indolent, faineant, lazy; inert, inactive, supine; sentimental, romantic; pining, longing, yearning *ant* thriving, flourishing; unaffected

languor *syn* LETHARGY, lassitude, stupor, torpor, torpidity *rel* exhaustion, fatigue, weariness; ennui, doldrums, tedium; depression, blues, dumps *ant* alacrity

languorous *syn* LANGUID, languishing, lackadaisical, listless, spiritless, enervated *rel* leisurely, laggard, slow, dilatory; indolent, slothful, faineant, lazy; passive, inert, inactive, supine; relaxed, slack, lax, loose; pampered, indulged *ant* vigorous; strenuous (*of times, seasons*)

lank, lanky *syn* LEAN, gaunt, rawboned, spare, angular, scrawny, skinny *rel* thin, slim, slender, slight; attenuated, extenuated *ant* burly

lapse *n* **1** *syn* ERROR, slip, mistake, blunder, faux pas, bull, howler, boner *rel* offense, sin, vice, crime; fault, failing, frailty, foible; transgression, breach, violation, trespass **2** · a fall back into a state or condition from which one has been raised *syn* relapse, backsliding *rel* deterioration, decline, declension, decadence, degeneration, devolution; retrograding, retrogradation, receding, recession; retrogressiveness, retrogression, regressiveness, regression

lapse *vb* · to fall from a better or higher state into a lower or poorer one *syn* relapse, backslide *rel* revert, return; slip, slide; deteriorate, degenerate, decline; descend; recede, retrograde

larcener, larcenist *syn* THIEF, robber, burglar

larceny *syn* THEFT, robbery, burglary

large · above the average of its kind in magnitude *syn* big, great *rel* vast, immense, enormous, huge, mammoth, colossal, gigantic; tremendous, prodigious, monumental, stupendous, monstrous; inordinate, excessive, exorbitant, extreme, immoderate, extravagant *ant* small

largely · in a reasonably inclusive manner *syn* greatly, mostly, chiefly, mainly, principally, generally

largess *syn* GIFT, boon, present, gratuity, favor *rel* benefaction, donation, contribution; grant, subvention

lascivious *syn* LICENTIOUS, lewd, libertine, lustful, libidinous, lecherous, wanton *rel* immoral, unmoral, amoral; sensual, carnal, fleshly, animal; obscene, gross, coarse

lassitude *syn* LETHARGY, languor, stupor, torpor, torpidity *rel* exhaustion, weariness, fatigue; ennui, doldrums, tedium; dumps, blues, depression; impotence, powerlessness *ant* vigor

last *vb*, *syn* CONTINUE, endure, abide, persist *rel* survive, outlast, outlive; remain, stay *ant* fleet

last *adj* · following all others as in time, order, or importance *syn* latest, final, terminal, concluding, eventual, ultimate *ant* first

lasting · enduring so long as to seem fixed or established *syn* permanent, perdurable, durable, stable, perpetual *rel* enduring, abiding, persisting, persistent, continuing; everlasting, endless, unceasing; continual, continuous, incessant, unremitting, perennial; eternal, sempiternal *ant* fleeting

late 1 *syn* TARDY, behindhand, overdue *rel* delayed, retarded, detained *ant* early; punctual, prompt 2 *syn* DEAD, departed, deceased, defunct, lifeless, inanimate 3 *syn* MODERN, recent

latent · not now showing signs of activity or existence *syn* dormant, quiescent, potential, abeyant *rel* hidden, concealed; inactive, inert, idle; unripe, unmatured, immature *ant* patent

latest *syn* LAST, final, terminal, concluding, eventual, ultimate *ant* earliest

lather *syn* FOAM, suds, froth, spume, scum, yeast

laud *syn* PRAISE, extol, eulogize, acclaim *rel* magnify, aggrandize, exalt; worship, adore, venerate, revere, reverence; commend, applaud, compliment *ant* revile

laughable · provoking laughter or mirth *syn* risible, ludicrous, ridiculous, comic, comical, farcical, droll, funny *rel* amusing, diverting, entertaining; humorous, witty, facetious, jocular, jocose

lavish *syn* PROFUSE, prodigal, luxuriant, lush, exuberant *rel* liberal, bountiful, bounteous, openhanded, generous, munificent, handsome; sumptuous, opulent, luxurious; excessive, inordinate, extravagant *ant* sparing

law 1 · a principle governing action or procedure *syn* rule, regulation, precept, statute, ordinance, canon *rel* mandate, dictate, command 2 *syn* PRINCIPLE, axiom, fundamental, theorem *rel* necessity, exigency *ant* chance

lawful · being in accordance with law *syn* legal, legitimate, licit *rel* rightful, due, condign; allowed, allowable, permitted, permissible; justified, justifiable, warranted, warrantable *ant* unlawful

lawlessness *syn* ANARCHY, chaos *rel* discord, strife, dissension, contention, conflict, difference, variance; confusion, disorder *ant* discipline; order

lawsuit *syn* SUIT, action, cause, case

lawyer · a person authorized to practice law in the courts or to serve clients in the capacity of legal agent or adviser *syn* counselor, barrister, counsel, advocate, attorney, solicitor

lax 1 *syn* LOOSE, relaxed, slack *rel* limp, floppy, flabby, flaccid *ant* rigid 2 *syn* NEGLIGENT, remiss, neglectful *rel* careless, heedless, thoughtless; indifferent, unconcerned; forgetful, unmindful, oblivious *ant* strict, stringent

lay *vb, syn* DIRECT, aim, point, level, train

lay *adj, syn* PROFANE, secular, temporal

laze *syn* IDLE, loaf, lounge, loll *rel* relax, rest, repose

lazy · not easily aroused to activity *syn* indolent, slothful, faineant *rel* inert, idle, inactive, supine, passive; torpid, comatose, sluggish, lethargic; languid, languorous, lackadaisical, listless; slack, remiss, lax, negligent, neglectful

lead *syn* GUIDE, pilot, engineer, steer *rel* conduct, direct, manage, control; set, fix, establish; command, order; induce, persuade, prevail, get *ant* follow

leader *syn* CHIEF, head, chieftain, master *ant* follower

leading *syn* CHIEF, principal, main, foremost, capital *rel* governing, ruling; conducting, directing, managing, controlling; prominent, outstanding; eminent, famous; preeminent, supreme, superlative *ant* subordinate

league *syn* ALLIANCE, coalition, fusion, confederacy, confederation, federation

lean *vb, syn* SLANT, slope, incline *rel* bend, curve; turn, deflect, divert, sheer

lean *adj* • thin because of an absence of excess flesh *syn* spare, lank, lanky, gaunt, rawboned, angular, scrawny, skinny *rel* slender, slim, thin, slight; cadaverous, wasted, pinched, haggard *ant* fleshy

leaning • a strong instinct or liking for something *syn* propensity, proclivity, penchant, flair *rel* bias, predilection, partiality, prepossession, prejudice; inclining, inclination, predisposition; bent, turn, aptitude, faculty, gift *ant* distaste

leap *vb, syn* JUMP, spring, bound, vault *rel* rise, arise, mount, soar, ascend

leap *n, syn* JUMP, spring, bound, vault

learn *syn* DISCOVER, ascertain, determine, unearth

learned • possessing or manifesting unusually wide and deep knowledge *syn* scholarly, erudite *rel* cultivated, cultured; pedantic, academic, scholastic, bookish; recondite, abstruse, esoteric

learning *syn* KNOWLEDGE, erudition, scholarship, science, information, lore *rel* culture, cultivation, breeding, refinement; enlightenment

lease *syn* HIRE, let, charter, rent

leave *vb* **1** *syn* WILL, bequeath, devise, legate *rel* commit, entrust, confide, consign; assign, allot, apportion **2** *syn* RELINQUISH, resign, surrender, abandon, yield, cede, waive *rel* forsake, desert; forgo, forbear, sacrifice, abnegate, eschew; neglect, ignore, forget, omit; grant, concede, vouchsafe; relegate, commit, confide, entrust **3** *syn* GO, depart, quit, withdraw, retire *rel* escape, flee, fly, abscond, decamp **4** *syn* LET, allow, permit, suffer

leave *n, syn* PERMISSION, sufferance *rel* consenting, consent, assenting, assent; sanctioning, sanction, endorsement, approval; authorization

leaven *syn* INFUSE, imbue, inoculate, ingrain, suffuse *rel* temper, qualify, moderate; inform, animate, inspire; pervade, permeate, impregnate, saturate; vivify, enliven, quicken

leavings *syn* REMAINDER, remains, residue, residuum, rest, balance, remnant *rel* fragments, pieces, portions; discardings, discards, scrappings, scraps, junkings; junk

lecherous *syn* LICENTIOUS, libidinous, lascivious, lustful, lewd, wanton, libertine *rel* dissolute, abandoned, reprobate, profligate; degenerate, corrupt

lecture *syn* SPEECH, address, oration, harangue, talk, sermon, homily

leech *syn* PARASITE, sponge, sponger, sycophant, toady, lickspittle, bootlicker, hanger-on, favorite

lees *syn* DEPOSIT, precipitate, sediment, dregs, grounds *rel* refuse, waste

leeway *syn* ROOM, berth, play, elbowroom, margin, clearance

legal *syn* LAWFUL, legitimate, licit *ant* illegal

legal tender *syn* MONEY, cash, currency, specie, coin, coinage

legate *n, syn* AMBASSADOR, nuncio, internuncio, chargé d'affaires, minister, envoy

legate *vb, syn* WILL, bequeath, devise, leave

legend **1** *syn* MYTH, saga **2** *syn* INSCRIPTION, caption

legendary *syn* FICTITIOUS, mythical, apocryphal, fabulous

legerity *syn* CELERITY, alacrity *rel* nimbleness, agility, briskness, spryness; swiftness, fleetness, rapidity; dexterity, ease, readiness, facility; dispatch, expedition, speed *ant* deliberateness; sluggishness

legion *syn* MULTITUDE, host, army

legitimate *syn* LAWFUL, legal, licit *rel* justified, justifiable, warranted, warrantable; valid, sound, cogent; recognized, acknowledged; customary, usual; regular, normal, typical, natural *ant* illegitimate; arbitrary

leisure *syn* REST, relaxation, repose, ease, comfort *ant* toil

leisurely *syn* SLOW, deliberate, dilatory, laggard *rel* relaxed, slack, lax, loose; slackened, retarded, delayed; easy, comfortable, restful *ant* hurried; abrupt

leitmotiv *syn* SUBJECT, motive, motif, theme, matter, subject matter, argument, topic, text

lengthen *syn* EXTEND, elongate, prolong, protract *rel* increase, augment; expand, amplify, distend *ant* shorten

leniency *syn* FORBEARANCE, clemency, mercifulness, tolerance, indulgence *rel* lenity, mercy, charity, grace; kindliness, benignity, benignancy, kindness; compassionateness, tenderness

lenient **1** *syn* SOFT, gentle, smooth, mild, bland, balmy *rel* assuaging, alleviating, relieving; grateful, agreeable, welcome, gratifying, pleasing, pleasant *ant* caustic **2** *syn* FORBEARING, indulgent, merciful, clement, tolerant *rel* forgiving, excusing, condoning, pardoning; kindly, benign, benignant; compassionate, tender; indulging, pampering, humoring, spoiling, mollycoddling; lax *ant* stern; exacting

leniently *syn* FORBEARINGLY, tolerantly, clemently, mercifully, indulgently

lenity *syn* MERCY, clemency, charity, grace *rel* leniency, indulgence, clemency, mercifulness, forbearance, tolerance; benignity, benignancy, kindliness, kindness; compassionateness, compassion, tenderness; benevolence, humaneness, charitableness; laxity *ant* severity

lesion *syn* WOUND, trauma, traumatism, bruise, contusion *rel* injury, hurt, damage

lessen *syn* DECREASE, diminish, reduce, abate, dwindle *rel* shorten, curtail, retrench, abridge, abbreviate; shrink, contract; lighten, mitigate, alleviate, relieve; thin, dilute, attenuate

let **1** *syn* HIRE, lease, rent, charter **2** · to neither forbid nor prevent *syn* allow, permit, suffer, leave *rel* sanction, endorse, approve, accredit, certify; authorize, license, commission

lethal *syn* DEADLY, fatal, mortal *rel* destroying, destructive; killing, slaying; pernicious, baneful, noxious; poisonous, virulent, venomous, toxic

lethargic · deficient in alertness or activity *syn* sluggish, torpid, comatose *rel* inert, idle, inactive, supine, passive; phlegmatic, stolid, impassive, apathetic; languid, languorous, lackadaisical, listless; slow, dilatory, laggard *ant* energetic, vigorous

lethargy · physical or mental inertness *syn* languor, lassitude, stupor, torpor, torpidity *rel* sluggishness, comatoseness; indolence, slothfulness, sloth, laziness; inertness, inertia, inactivity, idleness, passiveness, supineness; apathy, phlegm, impassivity *ant* vigor

letter · a direct or personal written or printed message addressed to a person or organization *syn* epistle, missive, note, message, dispatch, report, memorandum

levee *syn* WHARF, dock, pier, quay, slip, berth, jetty

level *vb, syn* DIRECT, point, train, aim, lay

level *adj* · having a surface without bends, curves, or irregularities *syn* flat, plane, plain, even, smooth, flush *rel* parallel, uniform, like, alike, akin, identical, similar; same, equivalent, equal

levitate *syn* RISE, arise, ascend, mount, soar, tower, rocket, surge *ant* gravitate, sink

levity *syn* LIGHTNESS, light-mindedness, frivolity, flippancy, volatility, flightiness *rel* foolishness, folly, silliness, absurdity; gaiety, liveliness, sprightliness, vivaciousness, vivacity *ant* gravity

lewd *syn* LICENTIOUS, lustful, lascivious, libidinous, lecherous, wanton, libertine *rel* immoral, unmoral, amoral; gross, coarse, obscene; indecent, indelicate, indecorous *ant* chaste

liability *syn* DEBT, indebtedness, obligation, debit, arrear *ant* asset (*or plural* assets)

liable **1** *syn* RESPONSIBLE, amenable, answerable, accountable *rel* obliged, constrained, compelled; bound, tied **2** · being by nature or through circumstances likely to experience something adverse *syn* open, exposed, subject, prone, susceptible, sensitive *ant* exempt, immune **3** *syn* APT, likely

liaison *syn* AMOUR, intrigue, affair

libel *n* · a public and often satirical presentation of the faults or weaknesses, esp. of an individual *syn* skit, squib, lampoon, pasquinade *rel* scurrility, invective, vituperation, abuse; burlesque, travesty, caricature

libel *vb, syn* MALIGN, defame, slander, traduce, asperse, vilify, calumniate *rel* revile, vituperate; decry, disparage, derogate, detract; caricature, travesty, burlesque

liberal **1** · giving or given freely and unstintingly *syn* generous, bountiful, bounteous, openhanded, munificent, handsome *rel* lavish, prodigal, profuse, exuberant; benevolent, philanthropic, eleemosynary, charitable *ant* close **2** · not bound by what is orthodox, established, or traditional *syn* progressive, advanced, radical *rel* tolerant, forbearing, indulgent, lenient *ant* authoritarian

liberate *syn* FREE, release, emancipate, manumit, discharge *rel* deliver, enfranchise; disengage, detach; extricate, disentangle, untangle, disencumber, disembarrass; rescue, redeem, ransom

libertine *syn* LICENTIOUS, lewd, wanton, lustful, lascivious, libidinous, lecherous *rel* debauched, corrupted, corrupt; abandoned, dissolute, profligate, reprobate; immoral, unmoral, amoral *ant* straitlaced

liberty *syn* FREEDOM, license *rel* independence, autonomy; exemption, immunity; liberation, emancipation, enfranchisement, delivery; scope, range, compass, sweep *ant* restraint

libidinous *syn* LICENTIOUS, lecherous, lustful, lascivious, lewd, wanton, libertine *rel* sensual, animal, carnal; immoral; gross, obscene, coarse; dissolute, abandoned, profligate, reprobate

license *n, syn* FREEDOM, liberty *rel* exemption, immunity; looseness, laxity, slackness, relaxedness, relaxation; privilege, prerogative, right *ant* decorum

license *vb, syn* AUTHORIZE, commission, accredit *rel* permit, let, allow, suffer; approve, endorse, sanction, certify; empower, enable *ant* ban

licentious · lacking moral restraint esp. in a disregarding of sexual restraints *syn* libertine, lewd, wanton, lustful, lascivious, libidinous, lecherous *rel* profligate, reprobate, dissolute, abandoned; debauched, depraved, corrupted, corrupt; lax, loose, relaxed; immoral, unmoral, amoral *ant* continent

licit *syn* LAWFUL, legitimate, legal *rel* permitted, allowed; sanctioned, approved; authorized, licensed; regulated *ant* illicit

lick *syn* CONQUER, beat, defeat, vanquish, subdue, subjugate, reduce, overcome, surmount, overthrow, rout

lickspittle *syn* PARASITE, sycophant, toady, bootlicker, hanger-on, leech, sponge, sponger, favorite

lie *vb* · to tell an untruth *syn* prevaricate, equivocate, palter, fib *rel* deceive, delude, mislead, beguile

lie *n* · a statement or declaration that is not true *syn* falsehood, untruth, fib, misrepresentation, story *rel* prevarication, equivocation, fibbing, fib; mendaciousness, mendacity, untruthfulness, dishonesty, deceitfulness *ant* truth

life *syn* BIOGRAPHY, memoir, autobiography, confessions

lifeless *syn* DEAD, inanimate, defunct, deceased, departed, late *rel* inert, inactive, passive; stiff, rigid, stark, wooden, inflexible; torpid *ant* living

lift **1** · to move from a lower to a higher place or position *syn* raise, rear, elevate, hoist, heave, boost *rel* rise, arise, ascend, levitate, mount, soar, tower, rocket, surge; exalt, magnify, aggrandize; heighten, enhance, intensify *ant* lower **2** *syn* STEAL, purloin, filch, pilfer, pinch, snitch, swipe, cop

light *vb* **1** · to cause something to start burning *syn* kindle, ignite, fire **2** *syn* ILLUMINATE, lighten, illumine, enlighten, illustrate

light *adj, syn* EASY, simple, facile, effortless, smooth *rel* slight; trivial, trifling, petty, puny *ant* heavy; arduous; burdensome

light *vb, syn* ALIGHT, land, perch, roost

lighten *vb, syn* ILLUMINATE, illumine, light, enlighten, illustrate *ant* darken

lighten *vb, syn* RELIEVE, alleviate, mitigate, assuage, allay *rel* lessen, reduce, diminish, decrease, abate; moderate, temper, qualify; attenuate, extenuate, thin, dilute

lighthearted *syn* GLAD, cheerful, happy, joyful, joyous *rel* buoyant, resilient, volatile, effervescent, expansive; blithe, jocund, merry, jolly; high-spirited, spirited; gay, sprightly, vivacious, lively *ant* despondent

light-mindedness *syn* LIGHTNESS, levity, frivolity, flippancy, volatility, flightiness

lightness · gaiety or indifference where seriousness and attention are called for *syn* light-mindedness, levity, frivolity, flippancy, volatility, flightiness *rel* buoyancy, resiliency, elasticity, effervescence, expansiveness; gaiety, liveliness, vivaciousness, vivacity; lightheartedness, cheerfulness *ant* seriousness

like *vb* · to feel attraction toward or take pleasure in *syn* love, enjoy, relish, fancy, dote *rel* prefer, choose, select, elect; admire, esteem, respect, regard; approve, endorse; appreciate, comprehend, understand *ant* dislike

like *adj* · the same or nearly the same (as in appearance, character, or quantity) *syn* alike, similar, analogous, comparable, akin, parallel, uniform, identical *rel* equivalent, equal, same, selfsame; cognate, allied, related *ant* unlike

likely **1** *syn* PROBABLE, possible *rel* credible, believable, colorable, plausible; reasonable, rational *ant* unlikely **2** *syn* APT, liable

likeness · agreement or correspondence in details *syn* similarity, resemblance, similitude, analogy, affinity *rel* equivalence, equality, sameness, identicalness, identity; agreement, conformity, correspondence; analogousness, comparableness, uniformity, parallelism *ant* unlikeness

likewise *syn* ALSO, too, besides, moreover, furthermore

limb *syn* SHOOT, bough, branch

limber *syn* SUPPLE, lithe, lithesome, lissome *rel* pliant, pliable, plastic; flexible, elastic, resilient, springy

limit *n* • a material or immaterial point beyond which something does not or cannot extend *syn* bound, confine, end, term *rel* limitation, restriction, circumscription, confinement; border, margin, verge, edge, rim, brim, brink

limit *vb* • to set bounds for *syn* restrict, circumscribe, confine *rel* define, prescribe, assign; restrain, curb, check *ant* widen

limn *syn* REPRESENT, depict, portray, delineate, picture

limp • deficient in firmness of texture, substance, or structure *syn* floppy, flaccid, flabby, flimsy, sleazy *rel* loose, slack, relaxed, lax; limber, supple

limpid *syn* CLEAR, transparent, translucent, lucid, pellucid, diaphanous *rel* pure, sheer; perspicuous *ant* turbid

line *n* • a series of things arranged in continuous or uniform order *syn* row, rank, file, echelon, tier *rel* succession, progression, series, sequence, chain

line *vb* • to arrange in a line or in lines *syn* line up, align, range, array *rel* marshal, arrange, order

lineage *syn* ANCESTRY, pedigree

line up *syn* LINE, align, range, array

linger *syn* STAY, tarry, wait, remain, abide *rel* delay, procrastinate, loiter, dawdle, lag

lingo *syn* DIALECT, vernacular, patois, jargon, cant, argot, slang

link *syn* JOIN, connect, relate, associate, conjoin, combine, unite *rel* concatenate, articulate, integrate; tie, bind *ant* sunder

liquefy • to convert or to become converted to a liquid state *syn* melt, deliquesce, fuse, thaw

lissome *syn* SUPPLE, lithesome, lithe, limber

list *n* • a series of items (as names) written down or printed as a memorandum or record *syn* table, catalog, schedule, register, roll, roster, inventory

list *vb, syn* RECORD, register, enroll, catalog

listless *syn* LANGUID, spiritless, languishing, languorous, lackadaisical, enervated *rel* apathetic, impassive, phlegmatic; heedless, thoughtless, careless; inert, inactive, passive, supine, idle *ant* eager

lithe, lithesome *syn* SUPPLE, lissome, limber *rel* slender, slim, slight, thin; lean, spare; pliant, pliable, plastic; nimble, agile, brisk, spry; graceful, elegant

little *syn* SMALL, diminutive, wee, tiny, minute, miniature *rel* petty, paltry, puny, trivial, trifling; slight, slim, slender, thin; meager, scanty, scrimpy, skimpy *ant* big

littoral *syn* SHORE, coast, beach, strand, bank, foreshore

liturgy *syn* FORM, ritual, rite, ceremony, ceremonial, formality

live *vb* **1** *syn* BE, exist, subsist *rel* endure, abide, persist, continue **2** *syn* RESIDE, dwell, sojourn, lodge, stay, put up, stop

live *adj, syn* ACTIVE, operative, dynamic *rel* vigorous, energetic, lusty, strenuous; powerful, potent, forcible, forceful; effective, efficacious, effectual, efficient *ant* inactive, inert; dormant; defunct

livelihood *syn* LIVING, subsistence, sustenance, maintenance, support, keep, bread *rel* trade, craft, handicraft, art, profession; wage, wages, salary, pay, stipend, fee, emolument

lively • keenly alive and spirited

syn animated, vivacious, sprightly, gay *rel* agile, nimble, brisk, spry; buoyant, effervescent, volatile, expansive, resilient, elastic; merry, blithe, jocund, jolly; mirthful, gleeful, hilarious *ant* dull

livid *syn* PALE, ashen, ashy, pallid, wan *rel* ghastly, grisly, lurid; murky, gloomy, dusky, dark

living *adj* · having or showing life *syn* alive, animate, animated, vital *rel* existing, being, subsisting; active, live, operative, dynamic *ant* lifeless

living *n* · supplies or resources needed to live *syn* livelihood, subsistence, sustenance, maintenance, support, keep, bread, bread and butter

load *n* · something which is carried, conveyed, or transported from one place to another *syn* burden, freight, cargo, lading

load *vb* **1** *syn* BURDEN, encumber, cumber, weigh, weight, lade, tax, charge, saddle *rel* bear, convey, carry, transport *ant* unload **2** *syn* ADULTERATE, weight, sophisticate, doctor

loaf *syn* IDLE, lounge, loll, laze *rel* rest, repose, relax; saunter, stroll, amble

loath *syn* DISINCLINED, indisposed, averse, hesitant, reluctant *rel* adverse, averse; antipathetic, unsympathetic *ant* anxious

loathe *syn* HATE, abominate, detest, abhor *rel* despise, contemn, scorn, disdain; refuse, reject, spurn, repudiate, decline; recoil, shrink, flinch, blench, quail *ant* dote on

loathing *syn* ABHORRENCE, detestation, abomination, hate, hatred *rel* aversion, antipathy; repugnance, repellency, distaste *ant* tolerance

loathsome *syn* OFFENSIVE, repulsive, repugnant, revolting *rel* abominable, abhorrent, detestable, odious, hateful; repellent, repugnant, distasteful, obnoxious, invidious *ant* engaging, inviting

local *syn* INSULAR, provincial, parochial, small-town *rel* narrow, narrow-minded; circumscribed, limited, restricted, confined *ant* cosmopolitan

locality · a more or less definitely circumscribed place or region *syn* district, vicinity, neighborhood *rel* region, area, zone, belt, tract; section, sector; territory, field, bailiwick, province, sphere, domain

location *syn* PLACE, position, situation, site, spot, station

locomotion *syn* MOTION, movement, move, stir

locum tenens *syn* SUBSTITUTE, supply, alternate, understudy, pinch hitter, double, stand-in

locution *syn* PHRASE, idiom, expression

lodge **1** *syn* HARBOR, house, board, shelter, entertain *rel* receive, take, accept, admit; accommodate, contain, hold **2** *syn* RESIDE, live, dwell, sojourn, stay, put up, stop

lofty *syn* HIGH, tall *rel* elevated, raised, lifted; exalted, magnified, aggrandized; imposing, stately, august, majestic, grand; sublime, glorious, superb, splendid

logical · having or showing skill in thinking or reasoning *syn* analytical, subtle *rel* cogent, valid, sound, telling, convincing, compelling; clear, lucid, perspicuous; rational, reasonable; inferential, ratiocinative *ant* illogical

logistic, logistical *syn* STRATEGIC, tactical

logistics *syn* STRATEGY, tactics

loiter *syn* DELAY, dawdle, lag, procrastinate *rel* tarry, linger, wait

loll *syn* IDLE, loaf, lounge, laze *rel* relax, rest, repose; lean, incline

lollop **1** *syn* SKIP, bound, hop, curvet, lope, ricochet **2** *syn* STUM-

BLE, trip, blunder, lurch, flounder, lumber, galumph, bumble

lone 1 *syn* ALONE, lonely, lonesome, forlorn, lorn, solitary, desolate 2 *syn* SINGLE, sole, unique, solitary, separate, particular

lonely *syn* ALONE, lonesome, lone, solitary, forlorn, lorn, desolate *rel* abandoned, deserted, forsaken; secluded, isolated

lonesome *syn* ALONE, lonely, lone, solitary, forlorn, lorn, desolate *rel* see LONELY

long · to have a strong desire for something *syn* yearn, hanker, pine, hunger, thirst *rel* crave, desire, wish, want, covet; pant, aspire, aim

longanimity *syn* PATIENCE, long-suffering, forbearance, resignation *rel* fortitude, sand, grit, pluck, backbone; endurance, toleration, tolerance; submissiveness

long-suffering *syn* PATIENCE, resignation, forbearance *rel* submissiveness, subduedness; meekness, humbleness, humility, lowliness; fortitude, grit; endurance, toleration

look *vb* 1 *syn* SEE, watch *rel* gaze, gape, stare, glare, peer; scrutinize, scan, inspect, examine 2 *syn* SEEM, appear *rel* indicate, betoken, bespeak; show, manifest, evidence, evince, demonstrate 3 *syn* EXPECT, hope, await *rel* foresee, foreknow, anticipate, divine

look *n* 1 · the directing of one's eyes in order to see *syn* sight, view, glance, glimpse, peep, peek *rel* gazing, gaze, staring, stare; scrutiny, inspection, examination 2 *syn* APPEARANCE, aspect, semblance *rel* bearing, demeanor, mien; posture, attitude, pose; face, countenance, visage, physiognomy

looker-on *syn* SPECTATOR, onlooker, beholder, observer, witness, eyewitness, bystander, kibitzer

loom *syn* APPEAR, emerge *ant* vanish

loose · not tightly bound, held, restrained, or stretched *syn* relaxed, slack, lax *rel* limp, flabby, flaccid, flimsy; free, independent; disengaged, detached; casual, desultory, hit-or-miss, happy-go-lucky, random, haphazard; negligent, remiss, careless, heedless, thoughtless *ant* tight; strict

loot *n, syn* SPOIL, booty, plunder, swag, prize

loot *vb, syn* ROB, plunder, rifle, burglarize *rel* sack, pillage, despoil, ravage, spoliate, devastate, waste; steal, pilfer, filch, purloin

lop *syn* SHEAR, poll, clip, trim, prune, snip, crop *rel* cut, slash, chop, hew; shorten, curtail

lope *syn* SKIP, bound, hop, curvet, lollop, ricochet

loquacious *syn* TALKATIVE, garrulous, voluble, glib *rel* fluent, vocal, articulate, glib, eloquent, voluble; chatting, chatty, gabbing, gabby, chattering, prating, jabbering

loquacity, loquaciousness *syn* TALKATIVENESS, garrulity, volubility, glibness *rel* chattering, chatter, chatting, chat, gabbing, gab, prating, prate, jabbering, jabber; fluency, articulateness, volubleness; readiness, ease, facility

lordly *syn* PROUD, haughty, arrogant, overbearing, insolent, supercilious, disdainful *rel* pretentious, showy; dictatorial, magisterial, authoritarian; imperious, domineering, masterful

lore *syn* KNOWLEDGE, science, learning, erudition, scholarship, information

lorn *syn* ALONE, forlorn, lonely, lonesome, lone, solitary, desolate *rel* see FORLORN

lot 1 *syn* FATE, destiny, portion,

doom *rel* fortune, luck, hap, chance, hazard **2** *syn* GROUP, cluster, bunch, parcel *rel* collection, assemblage; aggregate, aggregation, conglomeration, conglomerate

loud · marked by intensity or volume of sound *syn* stentorian, earsplitting, hoarse, raucous, strident, stertorous *ant* low-pitched, low

lounge *syn* IDLE, loaf, loll, laze *rel* incline, lean; relax, repose, rest

lout *syn* BOOR, churl, clown, clodhopper, bumpkin, hick, yokel, rube

loutish *syn* BOORISH, churlish, clownish *rel* clumsy, gauche, maladroit, inept, awkward; burly, brawny, husky, muscular; rude, rough, crude, raw, callow, green, uncouth

love *n, syn* ATTACHMENT, affection *rel* devotion, piety, fidelity, allegiance, loyalty; adoration, worship, idolatry; passion, fervor, ardor, enthusiasm, zeal *ant* hate

love *vb, syn* LIKE, enjoy, dote, relish, fancy *rel* adore, worship, idolize; cherish, treasure, value, prize, appreciate *ant* hate

lovely *syn* BEAUTIFUL, fair, comely, pretty, bonny, handsome, beauteous, pulchritudinous, good-looking *rel* alluring, enchanting, charming, attractive; delightful, delectable; exquisite, delicate, dainty, rare *ant* unlovely; plain

loving · feeling or expressing love *syn* affectionate, devoted, fond, doting *rel* amorous, amatory, erotic; enamored, infatuated; attentive, considerate, thoughtful; impassioned, passionate, ardent, fervent; true, constant, faithful *ant* unloving

low *syn* BASE, vile *rel* abject, ignoble, mean, sordid; coarse, vulgar, gross, obscene, ribald; crooked, devious, oblique

lower *syn* FROWN, glower, scowl, gloom *rel* glare, stare, peer

lowly *syn* HUMBLE, meek, modest *rel* submissive, subdued, tame; retiring, withdrawing; reverential, deferential, obeisant *ant* pompous

loyal *syn* FAITHFUL, true, constant, staunch, steadfast, resolute *ant* disloyal

loyalty *syn* FIDELITY, allegiance, fealty, devotion, piety *rel* trueness, truth, faithfulness, constancy, staunchness, steadfastness; attachment, affection, love *ant* disloyalty

lubricate *syn* OIL, grease, anoint, cream

lucent *syn* BRIGHT, brilliant, radiant, luminous, lustrous, effulgent, refulgent, beaming, lambent, incandescent *rel* glowing, blazing, flaming; splendid, resplendent, glorious

lucid **1** *syn* CLEAR, pellucid, transparent, translucent, diaphanous, limpid *rel* luminous, bright, brilliant, lucent **2** *syn* CLEAR, perspicuous *rel* distinct, plain, manifest, evident *ant* obscure, vague, dark

luck *syn* CHANCE, fortune, hap, accident, hazard *rel* break, chance, occasion, opportunity; lot, portion, destiny, fate

luckless *syn* UNLUCKY, disastrous, ill-starred, ill-fated, unfortunate, calamitous, hapless *rel* unhappy, infelicitous; miserable, wretched

lucky · meeting with unforeseen success *syn* fortunate, happy, providential *rel* favorable, benign, auspicious, propitious; advantageous, beneficial, profitable; felicitous, meet *ant* unlucky

lucrative *syn* PAYING, gainful, remunerative, profitable

ludicrous *syn* LAUGHABLE, risible, ridiculous, comic, comical, farcical, droll, funny *rel* absurd, preposterous, foolish, silly; grotesque, bizarre, antic, fantastic; amusing, diverting, entertaining

lugubrious *syn* MELANCHOLY, doleful, dolorous, rueful, plaintive *rel* depressing, oppressing, oppressive; sorrowful, woeful; gloomy, saturnine, dour, morose, glum, sullen *ant* joyous; facetious

lull *vb, syn* CALM, compose, quiet, quieten, still, soothe, settle, tranquilize *rel* pacify, placate, appease, mollify; moderate, qualify, temper; allay, assuage, alleviate, relieve *ant* agitate

lull *n, syn* PAUSE, recess, respite, intermission *rel* quiescence, abeyance; period, epoch, era; interval, interruption, break

lumber *syn* STUMBLE, trip, blunder, lurch, flounder, galumph, lollop, bumble

luminous *syn* BRIGHT, brilliant, radiant, lustrous, effulgent, lucent, refulgent, beaming, lambent, incandescent *rel* glowing, blazing, flaming; gleaming, glittering, flashing, scintillating; resplendent, glorious, splendid

lunacy *syn* INSANITY, psychosis, mania, dementia *rel* alienation, derangement, aberration; delirium, frenzy, hysteria

lunatic *syn* INSANE, mad, crazy, crazed, demented, deranged, maniac, non compos mentis

lurch *syn* STUMBLE, trip, blunder, flounder, lumber, galumph, lollop, bumble *rel* reel, stagger, totter; plunge, pitch, dive

lure *n* · something that leads an animal or a person into a place or situation from which escape is difficult *syn* bait, decoy, snare, trap

lure *vb* · to lead astray from one's true course *syn* entice, inveigle, decoy, tempt, seduce *rel* ensnare, snare, entrap, trap, capture, catch, bag; bewitch, fascinate, allure, captivate, attract; blandish, wheedle, cajole, coax *ant* revolt, repel

lurid *syn* GHASTLY, grisly, gruesome, macabre, grim *rel* livid, pale, pallid, wan, ashy, ashen; sinister, malign, baleful, malefic, maleficent

lurk · to behave so as to escape attention *syn* skulk, slink, sneak *rel* hide, conceal, secrete; ambush, waylay, surprise

luscious *syn* DELIGHTFUL, delicious, delectable *rel* sapid, flavorsome, toothsome, palatable, appetizing; grateful, gratifying, pleasing, pleasant *ant* austere; tasteless

lush *syn* PROFUSE, luxuriant, lavish, prodigal, exuberant *rel* abounding, abundant, teeming, swarming; sumptuous, opulent, luxurious

lust *syn* DESIRE, appetite, passion, urge *rel* cupidity, greed, avarice, rapacity; yearning, longing, hankering, thirsting, thirst, hungering, hunger; craving, coveting; gusto, zest, taste

luster · the quality or condition of shining by reflected light *syn* sheen, gloss, glaze *rel* iridescence, opalescence; brilliancy, radiance, luminosity, effulgence, refulgence

lustful *syn* LICENTIOUS, lascivious, libidinous, lecherous, wanton, lewd, libertine *rel* carnal, fleshly, sensual, animal; immoral, unmoral, amoral

lustrous *syn* BRIGHT, luminous, radiant, brilliant, effulgent, refulgent, beaming, lambent, lucent, incandescent *rel* glorious, resplendent, splendid; glowing, blazing, flaming

lusty *syn* VIGOROUS, energetic, strenuous, nervous *rel* robust, sound, healthy, hale; stout, sturdy, strong, stalwart; husky, brawny, muscular, sinewy, athletic *ant* effete

luxuriant *syn* PROFUSE, lush, exuberant, lavish, prodigal *rel* fruitful, fecund, fertile, prolific; rank, rampant; abounding, abundant, teeming

luxurious 1 *syn* SENSUOUS, voluptuous, sybaritic, epicurean, sensual *rel* self-indulging, self-indulgent, self-pampering; languorous, languishing *ant* ascetic 2 • ostentatiously rich or magnificent *syn* sumptuous, opulent *rel* ostentatious, pretentious, showy; magnificent, stately, imposing, majestic, grand; costly, expensive, valuable, precious

luxury *syn* AMENITY *rel* pleasure, joy, delight; agreeableness, gratification, gratefulness *ant* hardship

lying *syn* DISHONEST, mendacious, untruthful, deceitful *rel* false, wrong; deceptive, misleading, delusive, delusory *ant* truthtelling

M

macabre *syn* GHASTLY, gruesome, grisly, grim, lurid *rel* horrifying, daunting, appalling, dismaying; horrific, horrendous, horrible, horrid

macerate *syn* CRUSH, mash, smash, bruise, squash *rel* separate, part, divide; stew, seethe, simmer; soften

machination *syn* PLOT, intrigue, conspiracy, cabal *rel* trick, ruse, stratagem, maneuver, gambit, ploy, artifice, feint, wile

machine • a device or system by which energy can be converted into useful work *syn* mechanism, machinery, apparatus, engine, motor *rel* contrivance, device, contraption, gadget; implement, tool, instrument, utensil, appliance

machinery 1 *syn* EQUIPMENT, apparatus, paraphernalia, outfit, tackle, gear, matériel *rel* mean, instrument, instrumentality, agency, medium, vehicle, organ, channel, agent; machine, mechanism, engine, motor; device, contrivance, contraption, gadget; implement, tool, instrument, utensil, appliance 2 *syn* MACHINE, mechanism, apparatus, engine, motor

mad 1 *syn* INSANE, crazy, crazed, demented, deranged, lunatic, maniac, non compos mentis *rel* frenzied, hysterical, delirious; irrational, unreasonable 2 *syn* ANGRY, irate, wrathful, wroth, indignant, acrimonious *rel* maddened, incensed, infuriated, enraged; offended, outraged, affronted

madden *syn* ANGER, incense, enrage, infuriate *rel* vex, annoy, irk; exasperate, provoke, rile, aggravate, irritate

maelstrom *syn* EDDY, whirlpool, vortex

magazine *syn* JOURNAL, periodical, review, organ, newspaper

magic • the use of means (as charms or spells) believed to have supernatural power over natural forces *syn* sorcery, witchcraft, witchery, wizardry, alchemy, thaumaturgy

magisterial *syn* DICTATORIAL, authoritarian, dogmatic, doctrinaire, oracular *rel* masterful, domineering, imperious, imperative, peremptory; directing, controlling, conducting, managing

magnificent *syn* GRAND, imposing, stately, majestic, august, noble, grandiose *rel* splendid, resplendent, glorious, sublime, superb; opulent, sumptuous, luxurious; ostentatious, pretentious, showy *ant* modest

magnify *syn* EXALT, aggrandize *rel* extol, praise, laud, acclaim, eulogize; enlarge, increase, augment; expand, amplify, distend, swell, inflate, dilate *ant* minimize, belittle

magniloquent *syn* RHETORICAL, grandiloquent, aureate, flowery, euphuistic, bombastic *rel* turgid, tumid, inflated, flatulent; theatrical, histrionic, melodramatic, dramatic

magnitude *syn* SIZE, volume, extent, dimensions, area *rel* amplitude, expanse, stretch, spread; bulk, mass, volume

maiden **1** *syn* UNMARRIED, single, celibate, virgin **2** *syn* YOUTHFUL, juvenile, virgin, virginal, puerile, boyish *ant* experienced

maim • to injure so severely as to cause lasting damage *syn* cripple, mutilate, batter, mangle *rel* mar, spoil, damage, injure; deface, disfigure

main *syn* CHIEF, principal, leading, foremost, capital *rel* cardinal, vital, essential, fundamental; prime, primary, primal

mainly *syn* LARGELY, greatly, mostly, chiefly, principally, generally

maintain • to uphold as true, right, just, or reasonable *syn* assert, defend, vindicate, justify *rel* affirm, aver, protest, avow, declare, profess, avouch; contend, fight, battle, war; persist, persevere

maintenance *syn* LIVING, sustenance, support, livelihood, subsistence, keep, bread

majestic *syn* GRAND, stately, august, noble, magnificent, imposing, grandiose *rel* lofty, high; sublime, superb, glorious, splendid, resplendent; monumental, tremendous; exceptional

make • to bring something into being by forming, shaping, combining, or altering materials *syn* form, shape, fashion, fabricate, manufacture, forge *rel* produce, turn out, yield, bear; accomplish, achieve, effect, fulfill

make-believe *syn* PRETENSE, pretension

maker • one who brings something into being or existence *syn* creator, author

makeshift *syn* RESOURCE, shift, expedient, resort, stopgap, substitute, surrogate *rel* device, contrivance, contraption, gadget; mean, instrument, agency, instrumentality

maladroit *syn* AWKWARD, clumsy, gauche, inept *ant* adroit

malady *syn* DISEASE, ailment, disorder, condition, affection, complaint, distemper, syndrome

male • of, characteristic of, or like a male, esp. of the human species *syn* masculine, manly, manlike, mannish, manful, virile *ant* female

malediction *syn* CURSE, imprecation, anathema *ant* benediction

malefactor *syn* CRIMINAL, felon, convict, culprit, delinquent *rel* miscreant, scoundrel, villain, blackguard *ant* benefactor; well-doer

malefic, maleficent *syn* SINISTER, malign, baleful

malevolence *syn* MALICE, ill will, malignity, malignancy, spite, despite, spleen, grudge *rel* animosity, rancor, animus, antipathy, antagonism, enmity, hostility; hate, hatred, detestation, abhorrence, abomination *ant* benevolence

malevolent *syn* MALICIOUS, malignant, malign, spiteful *rel* sinister, baleful, malefic, maleficent *ant* benevolent

malice • the desire to see another experience pain, injury, or distress *syn* ill will, malevolence, spite, despite, malignity, malignancy, spleen, grudge *rel* maliciousness, spitefulness; venom, bane, poison; animosity, animus, rancor, antipathy, enmity *ant* charity

malicious • having, showing, or indicative of intense often vicious ill will *syn* malevolent, malignant, malign, spiteful *rel* poisonous, venomous, virulent, toxic; pernicious, noxious, baneful, deleterious, detrimental; envious, jealous; wanton, gratuitous, uncalled-for, supererogatory

malign *adj* **1** *syn* MALICIOUS, malignant, malevolent, spiteful *rel* inimical, hostile, rancorous, antipathetic, antagonistic; venomous, virulent, poisonous, toxic *ant* benign **2** *syn* SINISTER, baleful, malefic, maleficent *rel* threatening, menacing; baneful, noxious, pernicious, deleterious; disastrous, catastrophic, cataclysmic, calamitous *ant* benign

malign *vb* • to injure by speaking ill of *syn* traduce, asperse, vilify, calumniate, defame, slander, libel *rel* detract, decry, disparage, depreciate, derogate; vituperate, revile; defile, pollute, contaminate *ant* defend

malignancy *syn* MALICE, malignity, ill will, malevolence, spite, despite, spleen, grudge *rel, ant* see MALIGNITY

malignant *syn* MALICIOUS, malign, malevolent, spiteful *rel* virulent, venomous, poisonous; envious, jealous; baneful, noxious, pernicious; diabolical, devilish, fiendish *ant* benignant

malignity *syn* MALICE, malignancy, ill will, malevolence, spite, despite, spleen, grudge *rel* rancor, animus, animosity, enmity, hostility; maliciousness, spitefulness; hatred, hate; vindictiveness, revengefulness, vengefulness *ant* benignity

malinger *syn* DODGE, parry, sidestep, duck, shirk, fence *rel* evade, avoid, elude, escape, shun

malleable *syn* PLASTIC, pliable, pliant, ductile, adaptable *rel* tractable, amenable *ant* refractory

malodorous • having an unpleasant smell *syn* stinking, fetid, noisome, putrid, rank, rancid, fusty, musty *ant* odorous

maltreat *syn* ABUSE, mistreat, ill-treat, misuse, outrage

mammoth *syn* HUGE, vast, immense, enormous, elephantine, giant, gigantic, gigantean, colossal, gargantuan, Herculean, cyclopean, titanic, Brobdingnagian *rel* monstrous, monumental, stupendous, tremendous, prodigious; ponderous, weighty, cumbrous, cumbersome, heavy

manacle *syn* HAMPER, trammel, clog, fetter, shackle, hog-tie *rel* hinder, impede, obstruct, bar, block; tie, bind; restrain, inhibit, curb, check

manage *syn* CONDUCT, control, direct *rel* govern, rule; guide, lead, steer, pilot, engineer; handle, manipulate, wield, swing, ply

mandate **1** *syn* COMMAND, dictate, order, injunction, bidding, behest *rel* charging, charge, direction, instruction; sanctioning, sanction, endorsement, approval **2** • an authorization to take a political action given to a representative *syn* initiative, referendum, plebiscite

maneuver *syn* TRICK, stratagem, ruse, gambit, ploy, artifice, wile, feint *rel* device, contrivance; expedient, resort, resource, shift, makeshift; intrigue, machination, plot

manful *syn* MALE, virile, mannish, manlike, manly, masculine *rel* sturdy, stout, tenacious, stalwart, tough, strong; resolute, steadfast, staunch; intrepid, bold, brave

mangle *syn* MAIM, batter, mutilate, cripple *rel* injure, damage, mar, impair; deface, disfigure; deform, contort, distort

mania 1 *syn* INSANITY, lunacy, psychosis, dementia *rel* alienation, derangement, aberration *ant* lucidity 2 • a state of mind in which there is loss of control over emotional, nervous, or mental processes *syn* delirium, frenzy, hysteria *rel* depression, dejection, melancholia, melancholy, sadness; ecstasy, transport; excitement, provocation

maniac *syn* INSANE, mad, crazy, crazed, demented, deranged, lunatic, non compos mentis *rel* irrational, unreasonable

manifest *adj, syn* EVIDENT, patent, distinct, obvious, apparent, palpable, plain, clear *rel* revealed, disclosed, divulged, told; shown, evidenced, evinced; conspicuous, noticeable, prominent *ant* latent; constructive

manifest *vb, syn* SHOW, evidence, evince, demonstrate *rel* exhibit, display, expose; express, vent, utter, voice; reveal, discover, disclose, divulge *ant* suggest

manikin *syn* DWARF, midget, pygmy, homunculus, runt *ant* giant

manipulate *syn* HANDLE, wield, swing, ply *rel* flourish, brandish, shake, wave, thrash

manlike *syn* MALE, mannish, manful, virile, manly, masculine

manly *syn* MALE, manlike, manful, virile, masculine, mannish *rel* mature, matured, grown-up, adult; sturdy, strong, stout, stalwart *ant* unmanly, womanly

manner *syn* METHOD, mode, way, fashion, system *rel* custom, usage, use, wont, practice, habit, habitude

mannerism *syn* POSE, air, affectation *rel* eccentricity, idiosyncrasy; peculiarity, singularity, oddness, queerness

mannish *syn* MALE, manlike, virile, masculine, manful, manly *ant* womanish

manufacture *syn* MAKE, fabricate, forge, form, shape, fashion *rel* produce, turn out, yield

manumit *syn* FREE, emancipate, enfranchise, deliver, discharge, release, liberate *ant* enslave

many • amounting to or being one of a large indefinite number *syn* several, sundry, various, divers, numerous, multifarious *ant* few

many-sided *syn* VERSATILE, all-around

map *syn* CHART, graph *rel* plan, plot, scheme, design; sketch, outline, diagram

mar *syn* INJURE, damage, hurt, harm, impair, spoil *rel* deface, disfigure; deform, contort, distort, warp; ruin, wreck

marble *syn* SPOT, spatter, sprinkle, mottle, fleck, stipple, speckle, spangle, bespangle

marbled *syn* SPOTTED, spattered, sprinkled, mottled, flecked, stippled, speckled, spangled, bespangled

margin 1 *syn* BORDER, verge, edge, rim, brim, brink *rel* bound, end, term, confine, limit; penumbra 2 *syn* ROOM, berth, play, elbowroom, leeway, clearance

marine • of or relating to the navigation of the sea *syn* maritime, nautical, naval

mariner • a person engaged in sailing or handling a ship *syn* sailor, seaman, tar, gob, bluejacket

marital *syn* MATRIMONIAL, conjugal, connubial, nuptial, hymeneal

maritime *syn* MARINE, nautical, naval

mark *n* 1 *syn* SIGN, symptom, note, token, badge *rel* stigma, brand, blot, stain; criterion, touchstone, gauge, yardstick, standard; trace, vestige, track;

stamp, print, imprint, impress, impression 2 *syn* CHARACTER, symbol, sign *rel* device, contrivance 3 · a symbol or device used for identification or indication of ownership *syn* brand, stamp, label, tag, ticket

mark *vb* 1 · to affix, attach, or impress something which serves for identification *syn* brand, stamp, label, tag, ticket *rel* imprint, impress, print; recognize, identify 2 *syn* CHARACTERIZE, distinguish, qualify *rel* indicate, betoken, attest, bespeak, prove, argue; intimate, hint, suggest

marriage · acts by which a man and woman become husband and wife or the state of being husband and wife *syn* matrimony, wedlock, wedding, nuptial, espousal

marshal *syn* ORDER, arrange, organize, systematize, methodize *rel* array, range, align, line, line up

martial · of, relating to, or suited for war or a warrior *syn* warlike, military *rel* belligerent, bellicose, pugnacious, combative; aggressive, militant; spirited, high-spirited, mettlesome

marvel *syn* WONDER, prodigy, miracle, phenomenon *rel* astonishment, amazement, surprise; perplexity, mystification, puzzle

masculine *syn* MALE, virile, manful, manly, manlike, mannish *rel* vigorous, energetic, lusty, strenuous; robust, healthy, sound *ant* feminine

mash *syn* CRUSH, smash, bruise, squash, macerate *rel* pound, beat

mask *syn* DISGUISE, cloak, dissemble, camouflage *rel* conceal, hide, secrete, screen; protect, shield, defend, guard, safeguard

mass *n* 1 *syn* BULK, volume *rel* aggregate, aggregation, conglomerate, conglomeration; sum, amount, total, whole 2 *syn* HEAP, pile, stack, shock, cock, bank *rel* accumulation, hoarding, hoard, amassment

mass *vb, syn* HEAP, pile, stack, shock, cock, bank *rel* gather, collect, assemble, congregate; accumulate, amass, hoard; merge, blend, fuse, coalesce, mix; consolidate, compact, unify, concentrate

massacre · the act or an instance of killing a number of usu. helpless or unresisting human beings under circumstances of atrocity or cruelty *syn* slaughter, butchery, carnage, pogrom *rel* assassination, murdering, murder, slaying, killing

massive · impressively large or heavy *syn* massy, bulky, monumental, substantial *rel* heavy, weighty, ponderous; solid, hard, firm; immense, enormous, huge, gigantic, colossal

massy *syn* MASSIVE, bulky, monumental, substantial *rel* ponderous, hefty, cumbrous, cumbersome, weighty, heavy; large, big, great; solid, firm, hard

master *syn* CHIEF, chieftain, head, leader

masterful · tending to impose one's will on others *syn* domineering, imperious, peremptory, imperative *rel* magisterial, dictatorial, authoritarian, oracular, dogmatic, doctrinaire; arbitrary, absolute, despotic, tyrannical

masterly *syn* PROFICIENT, adept, skilled, skillful, expert *rel* dexterous, deft, adroit; preeminent, superlative, transcendent, supreme

match · to come up to or nearly up to the level or standard of *syn* rival, equal, approach, touch *rel* correspond, harmonize, agree, conform, square, accord

material *adj* 1 · of or belonging to actuality *syn* physical, corporeal, phenomenal, sensible, objective *rel* carnal, fleshly, sensual, animal; actual, true, real; tangible, perceptible, appreciable, palpable *ant* immaterial **2** *syn* RELEVANT, germane, pertinent, apposite, applicable, apropos *rel* important, significant, consequential, momentous; vital, cardinal, essential, fundamental *ant* immaterial

material *n, syn* MATTER, substance, stuff *rel* element, constituent, ingredient, component

materialize *syn* REALIZE, externalize, objectify, incarnate, embody, actualize, hypostatize, reify

matériel *syn* EQUIPMENT, apparatus, machinery, paraphernalia, outfit, tackle, gear

matrimonial • of, relating to, or characteristic of marriage *syn* marital, conjugal, connubial, nuptial, hymeneal

matrimony *syn* MARRIAGE, wedlock, wedding, nuptial, espousal

matter **1** • what goes into the makeup or forms the being of a thing whether physical or not *syn* substance, material, stuff **2** *syn* AFFAIR, business, concern, thing **3** *syn* SUBJECT, subject matter, argument, topic, text, theme, motive, motif, leitmotiv

matter-of-fact *syn* PROSAIC, prosy *rel* stolid, phlegmatic, impassive; arid, dry; downright, forthright

mature *adj* • having attained the normal peak of natural growth and development *syn* matured, ripe, mellow, adult, grown-up *ant* immature; childish

mature *vb* • to become fully developed or ripe *syn* develop, ripen, age *rel* harden, season, acclimatize, acclimate; habituate, accustom, inure, addict

matured *syn* MATURE, ripe, mellow, adult, grown-up *rel* completed, finished; deliberate, considered, advised, designed, studied, premeditated *ant* unmatured; premature

maudlin *syn* SENTIMENTAL, mawkish, romantic, soppy, mushy, slushy *rel* confused, muddled, fuddled, addled, befuddled; embarrassed, rattled, fazed, discomfited, disconcerted

mawkish *syn* SENTIMENTAL, maudlin, romantic, soppy, mushy, slushy *rel* flat, vapid, jejune, insipid, banal, inane

maxim *syn* SAYING, saw, adage, proverb, motto, epigram, aphorism, apothegm

meager falling short of what is normal, necessary, or desirable *syn* scanty, scant, skimpy, scrimpy, exiguous, spare, sparse *rel* thin, slender, slim, slight, tenuous, rare; thinned, attenuated, extenuated, diluted; jejune, flat, insipid, inane; penurious, stingy, parsimonious *ant* ample; copious

mean *adj* • being below the normal standards of human decency and dignity *syn* ignoble, abject, sordid *rel* base, low, vile; contemptible, despicable, sorry, scurvy, cheap, beggarly, shabby, pitiable

mean *vb* **1** *syn* INTEND, design, propose, purpose *rel* wish, want, desire; aim, aspire, plan **2** • to convey (as an idea) to the mind *syn* denote, signify, import *rel* carry, convey, bear, transmit; connote; define, assign, prescribe; suggest, imply, intimate, hint

mean *n* **1** *syn* AVERAGE, median, norm, par **2** • one by which work is accomplished or an end effected *syn* instrument, instrumentality, agent, agency, medium, organ, vehicle, channel *rel* method, mode, manner, way, fashion, system; machinery, apparatus, equipment, paraphernalia **3** *in plural form* **means** *syn* POSSESSIONS, resources, assets, effects, belongings *rel* money, cash, currency; riches, wealthiness, affluence, opulence

mean *adj, syn* AVERAGE, median, par *ant* extreme

meander *syn* WANDER, stray, roam,

ramble, rove, range, prowl, gad, gallivant, traipse

meaning · the idea that something conveys to the mind *syn* sense, acceptation, signification, significance, import *rel* suggestion, implication, intimation, hinting, hint; denotation, connotation

meaningful *syn* EXPRESSIVE, significant, pregnant, sententious, eloquent *rel* important, consequential, momentous, weighty *ant* meaningless

measly *syn* PETTY, paltry, trifling, trivial, puny, picayunish, picayune *rel* contemptible, despicable, sorry, scurvy, cheap, beggarly, shabby; stingy, parsimonious, penurious, miserly

mechanic *syn* WORKER, workman, workingman, artisan, operative, hand, laborer, craftsman, handicraftsman, roustabout

mechanical *syn* SPONTANEOUS, automatic, instinctive, impulsive *rel* stereotyped, hackneyed, trite; dull, slow, stupid, dense, crass, dumb

mechanism *syn* MACHINE, machinery, apparatus, engine, motor

meddle · to interest oneself in what is not one's concern *syn* interfere, intermeddle, tamper *rel* intrude, obtrude, interlope, butt in; interpose, intervene; discommode, incommode, trouble, inconvenience

meddlesome *syn* IMPERTINENT, intrusive, obtrusive, officious *rel* interfering, meddling, intermeddling, tampering; prying, snoopy, nosy, inquisitive, curious

median *n, syn* AVERAGE, mean, norm, par

median *adj, syn* AVERAGE, mean, par

mediate *syn* INTERPOSE, intercede, intervene, interfere *rel* arbitrate, judge, adjudge, adjudicate; conciliate, propitiate, pacify; reconcile, accommodate, adapt

medicament, medication *syn* REMEDY, medicine, cure, specific, physic

medicinal *syn* DRUG, pharmaceutical, biologic, simple

medicine *syn* REMEDY, cure, medicament, medication, specific, physic

mediocre *syn* MEDIUM, middling, second-rate, moderate, average, fair, indifferent *rel* poor, wrong, bad; common, ordinary, vulgar

meditate *syn* PONDER, muse, ruminate *rel* contemplate, consider, study, weigh; reflect, reason, speculate, deliberate, think, cogitate; examine, inspect, scrutinize

meditative *syn* THOUGHTFUL, contemplative, speculative, reflective, pensive *rel* pondering, musing, ruminating

medium *n, syn* MEAN, instrument, instrumentality, agent, agency, organ, vehicle, channel

medium *adj* · about midway between the extremes of a scale, measurement, or evaluation *syn* middling, mediocre, second-rate, moderate, average, fair, indifferent *rel* mean, median, average, par; common, ordinary, vulgar, popular

meed *syn* PREMIUM, guerdon, prize, award, reward, bounty, bonus *rel* recompensing, recompense, remuneration, satisfaction

meek *syn* HUMBLE, modest, lowly *rel* gentle, mild, soft; subdued, submissive, tame; compliant, acquiescent, resigned; forbearing, tolerant, lenient; patient, long-suffering *ant* arrogant

meet *vb* **1** · to come together face-to-face or as if face-to-face *syn* face, encounter, confront *rel* accost, greet, salute, address; collide, bump, clash; experience, undergo, sustain, suffer; wrestle, grapple, tussle; forestall, anticipate *ant* avoid **2** *syn* SATISFY, fulfill, answer *rel* equal, approach, match, touch; gratify, please; content *ant* disappoint

meet *adj, syn* FIT, suitable, proper, appropriate, fitting, apt, happy, felicitous *rel* adapted, adjusted, accommodated, conformed, reconciled; right, good; just, equitable, fair *ant* unmeet

melancholia *syn* SADNESS, melancholy, depression, dejection, gloom, blues, dumps

melancholic · gloomy or depressed, esp. as a manifestation of one's temperament or state of health *syn* melancholy, atrabilious, hypochondriac *rel* despondent, despairing, hopeless, forlorn, desperate; pessimistic, misanthropic, cynical, misogynic

melancholy *n, syn* SADNESS, melancholia, dejection, gloom, depression, blues, dumps *rel* miserableness, misery, wretchedness; despondency, despair, hopelessness, forlornness, desperation; tedium, boredom, ennui, doldrums *ant* exhilaration

melancholy *adj* **1** *syn* MELANCHOLIC, atrabilious, hypochondriac *rel* morose, gloomy, glum, sullen, dour, saturnine; depressed, oppressed, weighed down; despondent, despairing, hopeless, forlorn, desperate **2** · expressing or suggesting sorrow or mourning *syn* dolorous, doleful, lugubrious, rueful, plaintive *rel* pathetic, poignant, moving, touching; hopeless, forlorn, despairing, despondent; pensive, reflective, thoughtful; discomposing, disquieting, perturbing, disturbing

melee *syn* BRAWL, fracas, row, broil, rumpus, scrap *rel* altercation, quarrel, wrangle, squabble; confusion, disorder

mellow *syn* MATURE, ripe, matured, adult, grown-up *rel* tender, warm, sympathetic, responsive, warmhearted *ant* unmellow; green

melodramatic *syn* DRAMATIC, histrionic, theatrical, dramaturgic *rel* showy, pretentious, ostentatious; sentimental, romantic, maudlin, mawkish

melody · a rhythmic succession of single tones organized as an aesthetic whole *syn* air, tune

melt *syn* LIQUEFY, deliquesce, fuse, thaw

member *syn* PART, portion, piece, detail, division, section, segment, sector, fraction, fragment, parcel *rel* element, component, constituent; branch, limb, shoot, bough

memento *syn* REMEMBRANCE, remembrancer, reminder, memorial, token, keepsake, souvenir *rel* earnest, pledge; gift, present, favor

memoir *syn* BIOGRAPHY, life, autobiography, confessions

memorable *syn* NOTEWORTHY, notable *rel* remembered, recollected, recalled; salient, remarkable, noticeable, outstanding, striking, arresting; exceptional

memorandum *syn* LETTER, epistle, missive, note, message, dispatch, report

memorial *syn* REMEMBRANCE, remembrancer, reminder, memento, token, keepsake, souvenir *rel* monument, record; sign, mark

memory · the capacity for or the act of remembering, or the thing remembered *syn* remembrance, recollection, reminiscence, mind, souvenir *rel* intellect, soul, intelligence, brain, wit; remembering, minding, recalling, reminding; awareness, consciousness, cognizance *ant* oblivion

menace *syn* THREATEN *rel* alarm, terrify, scare, frighten; intimidate, cow; presage, portend, forebode, forecast, foretell

mend · to put into good order something that is injured, damaged, or defective *syn* repair, patch, rebuild *rel* improve, better, ameliorate, help; emend, remedy, redress, correct, rectify, reform; renew, restore, renovate, rejuvenate, refurbish; fix, adjust, regulate

mendacious *syn* DISHONEST, lying, untruthful, deceitful *rel* false, wrong; prevaricating, equivocating, paltering, fibbing *ant* veracious

menial *syn* SUBSERVIENT, servile, slavish, obsequious *rel* abject, mean, sordid, ignoble; base, low, vile; groveling, wallowing

mental · of or relating to the mind *syn* intellectual, psychic, intelligent, cerebral

mention · to refer to someone or something in a clear unmistakable manner *syn* name, instance, specify *rel* refer, allude, advert; cite, quote

mephitic *syn* POISONOUS, toxic, venomous, virulent, pestilent, pestilential, miasmic, miasmatic, miasmal *rel* offensive, loathsome, revolting, repulsive, repugnant; fetid, noisome, putrid, malodorous; noxious, pernicious, baneful

mercantile *syn* COMMERCIAL

mercenary · serving merely for pay or sordid advantage *syn* hireling, venal, hack *rel* abject, mean, sordid, ignoble; covetous, greedy, acquisitive, grasping, avaricious; debased, corrupt, corrupted, depraved

merciful *syn* FORBEARING, clement, tolerant, lenient, indulgent *rel* compassionate, tender; benignant, benign, kind, kindly; forgiving, pardoning, condoning *ant* merciless

mercifully *syn* FORBEARINGLY, tolerantly, clemently, leniently, indulgently

mercifulness *syn* FORBEARANCE, clemency, tolerance, leniency, indulgence *rel* mercy, lenity, charity, grace; compassion, commiseration, pity, ruth, sympathy

merciless *syn* GRIM, implacable, relentless, unrelenting *rel* pitiless, ruthless, compassionless; wanton, uncalled-for, gratuitous, supererogatory; cruel, fell, fierce; inexorable, obdurate, inflexible, adamant, adamantine *ant* merciful

mercurial *syn* INCONSTANT, fickle, capricious, unstable *rel* volatile, effervescent, buoyant, expansive, elastic, resilient; changeable, changeful, variable, protean, mutable; mobile, movable; clever, adroit, cunning, ingenious *ant* saturnine

mercy · a disposition to show compassion or kindness *syn* charity, grace, clemency, lenity *rel* compassion, ruth, pity, commiseration, sympathy; mercifulness, forbearance, tolerance, leniency, indulgence

mere · being as stated with nothing more added or extra *syn* bare, very

meretricious *syn* GAUDY, tawdry, garish, flashy *rel* showy, pretentious, ostentatious; vulgar, coarse, gross; deceptive, delusive, delusory, misleading

merge *syn* MIX, blend, fuse, coalesce, amalgamate, commingle, mingle *rel* consolidate, concentrate, compact, unify; unite, combine, conjoin; integrate, concatenate, articulate

merger *syn* CONSOLIDATION, amalgamation

meridian *syn* SUMMIT, culmination, zenith, apogee, peak, pinnacle, climax, apex, acme

merit *n* **1** *syn* DUE, desert *rel* meed, reward, guerdon; worth, value; gaining, gainings, winning, winnings **2** *syn* EXCELLENCE, virtue, perfection *ant* fault; defect

merit *vb, syn* DESERVE, earn, rate *rel* reward, award; requite, recompense, repay, pay

merry · showing high spirits or

lightheartedness *syn* blithe, jocund, jovial, jolly *rel* gay, vivacious, lively, sprightly, animated; joyful, joyous, cheerful, glad, happy, lighthearted; mirthful, gleeful, hilarious

mesa *syn* MOUNTAIN, mount, peak, alp, volcano

message *syn* LETTER, missive, note, epistle, dispatch, report, memorandum

metamorphose *syn* TRANSFORM, transmute, convert, transmogrify, transfigure *rel* change, vary, alter, modify; develop, mature, age, ripen

metamorphosis *syn* TRANSFORMATION, transmutation, conversion, transmogrification, transfiguration *rel* change, mutation, alternation, permutation, vicissitude; variation, alteration, modification

metaphor *syn* ANALOGY, simile

metaphrase *syn* TRANSLATION, version, paraphrase

meter *syn* RHYTHM, cadence

method • the means taken or procedure followed in achieving an end *syn* mode, manner, way, fashion, system *rel* process, procedure, proceeding; classification; disposition, disposal

methodical *syn* ORDERLY, systematic, regular *rel* methodized, systematized, organized; careful, meticulous, scrupulous; logical, analytical *ant* unmethodical; desultory

methodize *syn* ORDER, systematize, organize, arrange, marshal *rel* regulate, adjust; set, settle, fix, establish

meticulous *syn* CAREFUL, scrupulous, punctilious, punctual *rel* fastidious, finicky, particular, fussy, pernickety, nice; accurate, exact, precise, correct

mettle *syn* COURAGE, spirit, resolution, tenacity *rel* fortitude, backbone, sand, grit, pluck, guts; nerve, hardihood, temerity, audacity; gallantry, valor, heroism

mettlesome *syn* SPIRITED, high-spirited, spunky, fiery, peppery, gingery *rel* courageous, bold, audacious, intrepid, brave; impassioned, passionate, ardent, fervent; restive, impatient, restless

miasmic, miasmatic, miasmal *syn* POISONOUS, toxic, venomous, virulent, pestilent, pestilential, mephitic *rel* contagious, infectious, catching; noxious, pernicious, baneful, deleterious

microscopic *syn* SMALL, minute, little, diminutive, miniature, petite, wee, tiny, teeny, weeny

middle *syn* CENTER, midst, core, hub, focus, nucleus, heart

middling *syn* MEDIUM, mediocre, second-rate, moderate, average, fair, indifferent

midget *syn* DWARF, manikin, pygmy, homunculus, runt

midst *syn* CENTER, middle, core, hub, focus, nucleus, heart

mien *syn* BEARING, demeanor, deportment, port, presence *rel* air, pose, affectation, mannerism; aspect, appearance, semblance, look

might *syn* POWER, strength, energy, force, puissance *rel* vigorousness, vigor, strenuousness, energeticness, lustiness; potency, powerfulness, forcibleness, forcefulness

migrant *syn* EMIGRANT, immigrant

migrate • to move from one country, place, or locality to another *syn* emigrate, immigrate

mild *syn* SOFT, gentle, smooth, lenient, bland, balmy *rel* forbearing, tolerant, clement, merciful, lenient, indulgent; delicate, dainty, exquisite, choice; temperate, moderate; calm, serene, tranquil, placid *ant* harsh; fierce

milieu *syn* BACKGROUND, environment, setting, mise-en-scène, backdrop

militant *syn* AGGRESSIVE, assertive,

self-assertive, pushing, pushy *rel* bellicose, pugnacious, combative, contentious, belligerent; combating, opposing, antagonizing, antagonistic; fighting, warring, contending, battling

military *syn* MARTIAL, warlike

mime *syn* ACTOR, player, performer, mummer, mimic, thespian, impersonator, trouper

mimic *n, syn* ACTOR, player, performer, mummer, mime, thespian, impersonator, trouper

mimic *vb, syn* COPY, imitate, ape, mock *rel* play, impersonate, act; counterfeit, feign, simulate, sham, pretend, assume

mind *n* **1** *syn* MEMORY, remembrance, recollection, reminiscence, souvenir **2** • the element or complex of elements in an individual that feels, perceives, thinks, wills, and esp. reasons *syn* intellect, soul, psyche, brain, intelligence, wit *rel* power, function, faculty; reason, understanding, intuition; wisdom, judgment, sense, gumption

mind *vb* **1** *syn* REMEMBER, recollect, recall, remind, reminisce, bethink **2** *syn* OBEY, comply *rel* defer, yield, submit, bow; accede, assent, consent, agree, acquiesce **3** *syn* TEND, attend, watch

mingle *syn* MIX, commingle, blend, merge, coalesce, amalgamate, fuse *rel* join, combine, unite, conjoin, connect; consolidate, compact, unify, concentrate

miniature *syn* SMALL, minute, diminutive, little, wee, tiny, teeny, weeny

minimize *syn* DECRY, depreciate, belittle, disparage, derogate, detract *ant* magnify

minister *syn* AMBASSADOR, envoy, legate, nuncio, internuncio, chargé d'affaires

minority *syn* INFANCY, nonage *ant* majority

minstrel *syn* POET, bard, troubadour, versifier, rhymer, rhymester, poetaster

minute *n, syn* INSTANT, moment, second, flash, jiffy, twinkling, split second

minute *adj* **1** *syn* SMALL, little, diminutive, miniature, wee, tiny, teeny, weeny **2** *syn* CIRCUMSTANTIAL, particular, particularized, detailed, itemized *rel* meticulous, scrupulous, careful, punctilious; precise, accurate, exact, right, nice, correct

miracle *syn* WONDER, marvel, prodigy, phenomenon

miraculous *syn* SUPERNATURAL, supranatural, preternatural, superhuman

mirage *syn* DELUSION, hallucination, illusion

mirror *syn* MODEL, example, pattern, exemplar, ideal, standard, beau ideal

mirth • a mood or temper characterized by joy and high spirits and usu. manifested in laughter and merrymaking *syn* glee, jollity, hilarity *rel* cheerfulness, cheer, lightheartedness, joyfulness, gladness, happiness; joy, pleasure, delight; merriment, blitheness, jocundity, joviality

misanthropic *syn* CYNICAL, pessimistic *ant* philanthropic

miscarriage *syn* FAILURE, neglect, default, dereliction *rel* abuse, maltreatment, misuse

miscellaneous • consisting of diverse things or members *syn* assorted, heterogeneous, motley, promiscuous *rel* various, diverse, divergent, disparate, different; multifarious, divers, sundry, many

mischance *syn* MISFORTUNE, adversity, mishap *rel* accident, casualty; disaster, calamity, catastrophe, cataclysm

mischief *syn* INJURY, hurt, damage, harm *rel* perniciousness, detrimentalness, detriment, deleteriousness, noxiousness, banefulness, bane; evil, ill; impairment, marring, spoiling

mischievous *syn* PLAYFUL, roguish, waggish, impish, frolicsome, sportive *rel* annoying, bothering, bothersome, vexing, vexatious, irking, irksome; naughty, bad, evil, ill, wicked; tricky, foxy, insidious, artful, sly

miscreant *syn* VILLAIN, scoundrel, blackguard, knave, rascal, rogue, scamp, rapscallion *rel* criminal, malefactor, culprit, delinquent

misdoubt *syn* DISTRUST, mistrust, doubt, suspect

mise-en-scène *syn* BACKGROUND, setting, environment, milieu, backdrop

miserable • being in a pitiable state of distress or unhappiness (as from want or shame) *syn* wretched *rel* forlorn, hopeless, despairing, despondent; pitiable, piteous, pitiful; doleful, dolorous, melancholy *ant* comfortable

miserly *syn* STINGY, penurious, parsimonious, niggardly, tight, tightfisted, close, closefisted, cheeseparing, penny-pinching *rel* avaricious, greedy, covetous, grasping; mean, sordid, abject, ignoble

misery *syn* DISTRESS, suffering, agony, dolor, passion *rel* adversity, misfortune; affliction, visitation, trial, tribulation; melancholy, dejection, sadness, depression *ant* felicity, blessedness

misfortune • adverse fortune or an instance of this *syn* mischance, adversity, mishap *rel* disaster, calamity, catastrophe, cataclysm; accident, casualty; trial, tribulation, cross, affliction, visitation *ant* happiness; prosperity

misgiving *syn* APPREHENSION, foreboding, presentiment *rel* mistrust, distrust; suspicion, doubt, skepticism, uncertainty; fear, alarm, dread, fright

mishap **1** *syn* MISFORTUNE, mischance, adversity **2** *syn* ACCIDENT, casualty *rel* misfortune, mischance; disaster, calamity; chance, fortune, hap, hazard

mislay *syn* MISPLACE

mislead *syn* DECEIVE, delude, beguile, betray, double-cross *rel* entice, inveigle, lure, tempt, seduce; dupe, gull, hoodwink, hoax, bamboozle

misleading having an appearance or character that leads one astray or into error *syn* deceptive, delusive, delusory *rel* fallacious, casuistical, sophistical; false, wrong; confounding, bewildering, distracting, perplexing, puzzling

misplace • to put in the wrong place *syn* mislay *rel* displace; derange, disarrange, disorder

misrepresent • to give a false or misleading representation of usu. with an intent to deceive *syn* falsify, belie, garble *rel* disguise, dissemble, cloak, mask, camouflage; simulate, counterfeit, feign; lie, prevaricate, equivocate, palter

misrepresentation *syn* LIE, falsehood, untruth, fib, story *rel* dishonesty, deceitfulness, mendaciousness, mendacity; sophistication, doctoring, loading, weighting, adulteration; sophistry, casuistry

missive *syn* LETTER, epistle, note, message, dispatch, report, memorandum

mist *syn* HAZE, fog, smog

mistake *vb* • to take one thing to be another *syn* confuse, confound *rel* addle, muddle *ant* recognize

mistake *n, syn* ERROR, slip, lapse, blunder, faux pas, bull, howler, boner *rel* confusion, confounding, mistaking; inadvertence; neglecting, neglect, omitting, omission, disregarding, slighting, slight

mistreat *syn* ABUSE, maltreat, ill-treat, misuse, outrage *rel* see ILL-TREAT

mistrust *n* **1** *syn* UNCERTAINTY, suspicion, skepticism, doubt, dubiety, dubiosity *rel* misgiving, presentiment, foreboding, apprehension *ant* trust; assurance **2** *syn* DISTRUST

mistrust *vb, syn* DISTRUST, doubt, suspect, misdoubt *rel* apprehend, anticipate, foresee; alarm, frighten, scare; appall, dismay

misuse *syn* ABUSE, mistreat, maltreat, ill-treat, outrage *rel* hurt, injure, harm, damage, impair, mar, spoil; pervert, debase, corrupt *ant* respect

mite *syn* PARTICLE, bit, smidgen, whit, atom, iota, jot, tittle

mitigate *syn* RELIEVE, allay, alleviate, lighten, assuage *rel* temper, moderate; abate, reduce, lessen, diminish, decrease; palliate, extenuate *ant* intensify

mix • to combine or be combined into a more or less uniform whole *syn* mingle, commingle, blend, merge, coalesce, amalgamate, fuse *rel* join, combine, unite, conjoin

mixture • a product formed by the combination of two or more things *syn* admixture, blend, compound, composite, amalgam *rel* joining, combining, uniting

moan *n, syn* SIGH, groan, sob *rel* crying, cry, wailing, wail; lamenting, lament, bemoaning, bewailing

moan *vb, syn* SIGH, groan, sob *rel* mourn, grieve, sorrow; bemoan, bewail, lament, deplore

mob *syn* CROWD, throng, press, crush, rout, horde *rel* multitude, army, host, legion

mobile *syn* MOVABLE, motive *rel* fluid, liquid; changeable, changeful, protean, variable; inconstant, unstable, mercurial, fickle, capricious *ant* immobile

mock **1** *syn* RIDICULE, taunt, deride, twit, rally *rel* flout, scoff, jeer, gird, gibe; caricature, parody, travesty, burlesque **2** *syn* COPY, imitate, mimic, ape *rel* counterfeit, feign, affect, simulate, assume

mode *n* **1** *syn* STATE, condition, situation, posture, status **2** *syn* METHOD, manner, way, fashion, system *rel* trend, drift, tendency, tenor; procedure, process

mode *n, syn* FASHION, style, vogue, fad, rage, craze, dernier cri, cry

model • someone or something set before one for guidance or imitation *syn* example, pattern, exemplar, ideal, standard, beau ideal, mirror *rel* criterion, touchstone, gauge, standard

moderate *adj* **1** • not excessive in degree, amount, or intensity *syn* temperate *rel* ordinary, common, familiar; gentle, mild, bland, soft; sparing, economical *ant* immoderate **2** *syn* MEDIUM, middling, mediocre, second-rate, average, fair, indifferent *rel* decent, decorous, proper; steady, even, equable, constant

moderate *vb* • to modify something so as to avoid an extreme or to keep within bounds *syn* qualify, temper *rel* abate, reduce, lessen, diminish, decrease; mitigate, alleviate, lighten, relieve; slow, slacken, delay

modern **1** • having taken place, existed, or developed in times close to the present *syn* recent, late **2** *syn* NEW, modernistic, novel, new-fashioned, newfangled, original, fresh *rel* contemporary, contemporaneous, coincident, concomitant, concurrent; prevailing, current, prevalent *ant* antique; ancient

modernistic *syn* NEW, new-fashioned, newfangled, novel, modern, original, fresh *ant* antiquated

modest **1** *syn* HUMBLE, meek, lowly *rel* retiring, withdrawing; moderate, temperate *ant* ambitious **2** *syn* SHY, bashful, diffident, coy *rel* reserved, reticent, silent; shrinking, recoiling; nice, seemly, proper, decorous **3** *syn* CHASTE, decent, pure *rel* moral, virtuous; decorous, proper, seemly *ant* immodest

modification *syn* CHANGE, alteration, variation *rel* transformation, metamorphosis, conversion, transmogrification; qualification, tempering

modify *syn* CHANGE, alter, vary *rel* temper, moderate, qualify; transform, convert, metamorphose, transmogrify

modish *syn* STYLISH, fashionable, smart, chic, dashing *ant* antiquated

moist *syn* WET, damp, humid, dank

mollify *syn* PACIFY, appease, placate, propitiate, conciliate *rel* relieve, allay, mitigate, lighten; moderate, temper, qualify; abate, lessen, reduce, decrease *ant* exasperate

mollycoddle *syn* INDULGE, humor, pamper, spoil, baby

molt *syn* DISCARD, cast, shed, slough, scrap, junk

moment **1** *syn* INSTANT, minute, second, flash, jiffy, twinkling, split second **2** *syn* IMPORTANCE, consequence, significance, import, weight *rel* value, worth; advantage, profit, avail, use

momentary *syn* TRANSIENT, transitory, passing, ephemeral, fugitive, fleeting, evanescent, short-lived *ant* agelong

momentum *syn* SPEED, impetus, velocity, pace, headway

monastery *syn* CLOISTER, convent, nunnery, abbey, priory

monetary *syn* FINANCIAL, pecuniary, fiscal

money • something (as pieces of stamped metal or paper certificates) customarily and legally used as a medium of exchange *syn* cash, currency, legal tender, specie, coin, coinage

monk *syn* RELIGIOUS, friar, nun *rel* recluse, hermit, eremite, anchorite, cenobite

monkeyshine *syn* PRANK, caper, antic, dido

monograph *syn* DISCOURSE, treatise, disquisition, dissertation, thesis *rel* article, paper, essay

monopolize • to take up completely *syn* engross, absorb, consume *rel* possess, own, have, hold; utilize, use, employ; control, manage, conduct

monopoly • exclusive possession or control *syn* corner, pool, syndicate, trust, cartel

monotonous *syn* DULL, dreary, pedestrian, humdrum, stodgy *rel* wearisome, boring, irksome, tedious, tiresome

monstrous **1** • extremely impressive *syn* prodigious, tremendous, stupendous, monumental *rel* enormous, immense, huge, vast, colossal, mammoth, gigantic **2** *syn* OUTRAGEOUS, heinous, atrocious *rel* flagrant, glaring, gross, rank; ominous, portentous, fateful; flagitious, nefarious, infamous

monument *syn* DOCUMENT, record, archive

monumental **1** *syn* MONSTROUS, prodigious, tremendous, stupendous *rel* colossal, gigantic, enormous, mammoth, huge; impressive, moving **2** *syn* MASSIVE, massy, bulky, substantial *rel* imposing, stately, majestic, august, magnificent, grand

mood • a state of mind in which an emotion or set of emotions gains ascendancy *syn* humor, temper, vein *rel* disposition, temperament, character, personality, individuality; soul, spirit; emotion, feeling, affection

moor *syn* SECURE, anchor, rivet *rel* tie, bind; attach, fasten, affix, fix; balance, steady, stabilize, trim

moral • conforming to a standard

of what is right and good *syn* ethical, virtuous, righteous, noble *rel* right, good; upright, honest, just, honorable, scrupulous, conscientious; chaste, pure, modest, decent; ideal, abstract

morale • a sense of common purpose or dedication with respect to a group *syn* discipline, esprit de corps *rel* vigor, spirit, drive; self-confidence, self-possession, assurance, confidence; nerving, steeling

morality *syn* GOODNESS, virtue, rectitude *rel* integrity, probity, honor, honesty; excellence, perfection, merit

morally *syn* VIRTUALLY, practically

morbid *syn* UNWHOLESOME, sickly, diseased, pathological *rel* hypochondriac, atrabilious, melancholic; gloomy, morose, saturnine, sullen *ant* sound

mordant *syn* CAUSTIC, acrid, scathing *rel* incisive, trenchant, cutting, biting, clear-cut, crisp; pungent, poignant, piquant, racy, spicy, snappy; sharp, keen, acute

moreover *syn* ALSO, besides, furthermore, likewise, too

moron *syn* FOOL, imbecile, idiot, simpleton, natural

morose *syn* SULLEN, glum, gloomy, saturnine, dour, surly, sulky, crabbed *rel* splenetic, choleric, irascible, testy, cranky, cross; peevish, snappish, waspish, petulant, irritable; brusque, gruff

mortal *syn* DEADLY, fatal, lethal *rel* destructive; virulent, venomous, poisonous; implacable, unrelenting, relentless, grim *ant* venial (*especially of a sin*)

mortified *syn* ASHAMED, chagrined *rel* harassed, harried, worried, annoyed; humiliated, humbled, abased; abashed, embarrassed, discomfited

mostly *syn* LARGELY, greatly, chiefly, mainly, princially, generally

motif 1 *syn* FIGURE, device, design, pattern 2 *syn* SUBJECT, matter, subject matter, argument, topic, text, theme, motive, leitmotiv

motion • the act or an instance of moving *syn* movement, move, locomotion, stir *rel* impetus, momentum, speed, velocity, pace, headway

motivate *syn* ACTIVATE, actuate *rel* stimulate, quicken, provoke, excite; arouse, rouse, stir; inspire, animate, fire, inform

motive *n* 1 • a stimulus to action *syn* spring, impulse, incentive, inducement, spur, goad *rel* cause, determinant, antecedent, reason; desire, appetite, urge, passion, lust; feeling, emotion; purpose, intent, intention, aim, end 2 *syn* SUBJECT, matter, subject matter, argument, topic, text, theme, motif, leitmotiv

motive *adj, syn* MOVABLE, mobile *rel* active, operative, dynamic; moving, driving, impelling, impulsive

motley 1 *syn* VARIEGATED, parti-colored, checkered, checked, pied, piebald, skewbald, dappled, freaked 2 *syn* MISCELLANEOUS, heterogeneous, assorted, promiscuous *rel* different, diverse, divergent, disparate, various; discrepant, incompatible, uncongenial, incongruous, inconsonant

motor *syn* MACHINE, mechanism, machinery, apparatus, engine

motorcade *syn* PROCESSION, parade, cortege, cavalcade

mottle *syn* SPOT, spatter, sprinkle, fleck, stipple, marble, speckle, spangle, bespangle

mottled *syn* SPOTTED, spattered, sprinkled, flecked, stippled, marbled, speckled, spangled, bespangled

motto *syn* SAYING, proverb, adage, saw, maxim, epigram, aphorism, apothegm

mount *n, syn* MOUNTAIN, peak, alp, volcano, mesa

mount *vb* **1** *syn* RISE, ascend, soar, arise, tower, rocket, levitate, surge *ant* drop **2** *syn* ASCEND, climb, scale *ant* dismount

mountain • a relatively steep and high elevation of land *syn* mount, peak, alp, volcano, mesa *rel* height, altitude, elevation

mountebank *syn* IMPOSTOR, faker, charlatan, quack

mourn *syn* GRIEVE, sorrow *rel* lament, bewail, bemoan; weep, keen, wail, cry

movable • capable of moving or of being moved *syn* mobile, motive *rel* changeable, changeful, variable, mutable *ant* immovable; stationary

move *vb* **1** • to set or keep in motion *syn* actuate, drive, impel *rel* activate, motivate; provoke, excite, quicken, stimulate; induce, persuade, prevail, get **2** • to change or to cause to change from one place to another *syn* remove, shift, transfer *rel* displace, replace, supplant, supersede; convey, carry, bear, transport, transmit

move *n, syn* MOTION, movement, locomotion, stir *rel* change, alteration, variation, modification; transformation, metamorphosis, conversion, transmogrification

movement *syn* MOTION, move, locomotion, stir *rel* action, act, deed; change, alteration, variation, modification; activity, operativeness, operation, dynamism, liveness

moving • having the power to produce deep emotion *syn* impressive, poignant, affecting, touching, pathetic *rel* exciting, stimulating, quickening, provoking; thrilling, electrifying; stirring, arousing, rousing, awakening, rallying

muddle *vb, syn* CONFUSE, addle, fuddle, befuddle *rel* puzzle, perplex, mystify, bewilder, distract, nonplus, confound, dumbfound; faze, rattle, discomfit, embarrass; fluster, flurry, upset, agitate, discompose *ant* enlighten

muddle *n, syn* CONFUSION, disorder, chaos, disarray, jumble, clutter, snarl

muddy *syn* TURBID, roily *rel* murky, gloomy, obscure, dark; confused, muddled, addled, dirty, filthy, foul, nasty, squalid

muff *syn* BOTCH, bungle, fumble, cobble

mug *syn* FACE, countenance, visage, physiognomy, puss

mulct *syn* PENALIZE, fine, amerce *rel* exact, require, demand, claim

mulish *syn* OBSTINATE, dogged, stubborn, pertinacious, stiff-necked, pigheaded, bullheaded *rel* headstrong, intractable, recalcitrant, refractory, ungovernable, unruly; fixed, set

multifarious *syn* MANY, divers, numerous, various, several, sundry *rel* disparate, diverse, divergent, different; incongruous, incompatible, uncongenial, discrepant, discordant, inconsonant, inconsistent

multiply *syn* INCREASE, augment, enlarge *rel* propagate, reproduce, breed, generate; expand, spread, stretch

multitude • a very large number of individuals or things *syn* army, host, legion *rel* horde, throng, press, mob, crush, crowd

mummer *syn* ACTOR, performer, mime, mimic, player, thespian, impersonator, trouper

mummery *syn* GIBBERISH, hocus-pocus, abracadabra

mundane *syn* EARTHLY, worldly, earthy, terrestrial, sublunary *rel* fleshly, sensual, carnal, animal; secular, temporal, profane *ant* eternal

munificent *syn* LIBERAL, bountiful,

bounteous, openhanded, generous, handsome *rel* benevolent, charitable, philanthropic, eleemosynary, altruistic; profuse, lavish, prodigal

murder *syn* KILL, slay, assassinate, dispatch, execute

murky *syn* DARK, obscure, gloomy, dim, dusky *rel* turbid, muddy, roily; lowering, glowering, glooming, gloomy; lurid, grim, ghastly

muscular · strong and powerful in build or action *syn* brawny, sinewy, athletic, burly, husky *rel* robust, healthy, hale, sound; strong, sturdy, stalwart, stout; vigorous, lusty

muse *syn* PONDER, meditate, ruminate *rel* consider, study, contemplate, weigh, excogitate; reflect, reason, think

mushy *syn* SENTIMENTAL, romantic, mawkish, maudlin, soppy, slushy

muster *syn* SUMMON, summons, call, cite, convoke, convene *rel* collect, congregate, assemble, gather; marshal, organize, arrange, order; align, line, line up, range, array

musty *syn* MALODOROUS, fusty, stinking, fetid, noisome, putrid, rank, rancid *rel* dirty, filthy, foul, nasty, squalid; sloppy, slipshod, unkempt, slovenly

mutable *syn* CHANGEABLE, changeful, variable, protean *rel* unstable, inconstant, fickle; fluctuating, wavering, swinging, swaying *ant* immutable

mutation *syn* CHANGE, permutation, vicissitude, alternation *rel* shifting, shift, moving, move, removing, remove; variation, modification, alteration

mute *syn* DUMB, speechless, inarticulate

mutilate **1** *syn* MAIM, cripple, batter, mangle *rel* injure, damage, hurt, spoil, mar; disfigure, deface **2** *syn* STERILIZE, castrate, spay, emasculate, alter, geld

mutinous *syn* INSUBORDINATE, rebellious, seditious, factious, contumacious *rel* recalcitrant, refractory, intractable, unruly, ungovernable; disaffected, alienated

mutiny *syn* REBELLION, revolution, uprising, revolt, insurrection, putsch, coup *rel* sedition, treason; traitorousness, treacherousness, perfidiousness, perfidy, faithlessness

mutual *syn* RECIPROCAL, common *rel* shared, participated, partaken; joined, joint, united, connected, related, associated

mysterious · being beyond one's power to discover, understand, or explain *syn* inscrutable, arcane *rel* occult, esoteric, recondite, abstruse; cryptic, enigmatic, ambiguous, equivocal, obscure; mystical, mystic, anagogical, cabalistic

mystery · something which baffles or perplexes *syn* problem, enigma, riddle, puzzle, conundrum

mystic *syn* MYSTICAL, anagogic, cabalistic *rel* occult, esoteric, recondite, abstruse; mysterious, inscrutable; visionary, quixotic, imaginary

mystical · having a spiritual meaning or reality that is neither apparent to the senses nor obvious to the intelligence *syn* mystic, anagogic, cabalistic *rel* profound, deep, abysmal; ultimate, absolute, categorical; spiritual, divine, sacred, holy; supernatural, supranatural, miraculous

mystify *syn* PUZZLE, bewilder, perplex, distract, nonplus, confound, dumbfound *rel* discomfit, faze, rattle, embarrass; discompose, disquiet, perturb, disturb, agitate, upset *ant* enlighten

myth **1** · a traditional story of ostensibly historical content whose origin has been lost *syn* legend, saga *rel* fiction, fable, fabrication, figment; invention, creation **2** *syn* ALLEGORY, parable, fable

mythical *syn* FICTITIOUS, fabulous, legendary, apocryphal *rel* imaginary, visionary, fanciful, fantastic; invented, created

N

naïve *syn* NATURAL, unsophisticated, artless, ingenuous, simple *rel* sincere, unfeigned; spontaneous, impulsive, instinctive; fresh, original, new

naked *syn* BARE, nude, bald, barren *rel* revealed, disclosed, discovered; evident, manifest, palpable, obvious; uncolored, colorless; pure, simple, sheer

name *n* • the word or combination of words by which something is called and by means of which it can be distinguished or identified *syn* designation, denomination, appellation, title, style

name *vb* **1** *syn* DESIGNATE, nominate, elect, appoint *rel* choose, select, prefer, opt; declare, announce, publish, advertise **2** *syn* MENTION, instance, specify *rel* refer, allude, advert; designate; identify, recognize; cite, quote

nap *syn* SLEEP, catnap, doze, drowse, snooze, slumber

narcotic *syn* ANODYNE, opiate, nepenthe

narrate *syn* RELATE, rehearse, recite, recount, describe, state, report *rel* tell, reveal, disclose, discover; discourse, expatiate, dilate, descant

narrative *syn* STORY, tale, anecdote, yarn *rel* chronicle, account, report, story, version; fiction, fabrication, figment, fable

narrow, narrow-minded *syn* ILLIBERAL, intolerant, bigoted, hidebound *rel* rigorous, rigid, strict, stringent; obdurate, inflexible, inexorable; provincial, parochial, local, small-town, insular *ant* broad, broad-minded

narrows *syn* STRAIT, sound, channel, passage

nasty *syn* DIRTY, filthy, squalid, foul *rel* coarse, gross, vulgar, obscene, ribald; tainted, contaminated, polluted, defiled; indelicate, indecent, unseemly, improper, indecorous

national *syn* CITIZEN, subject

native • belonging to a particular place by birth or origin *syn* indigenous, endemic, aboriginal, autochthonous *ant* alien, foreign

natural *adj* **1** *syn* REGULAR, normal, typical *rel* ordinary, common, familiar; usual, customary, habitual, accustomed, wonted *ant* unnatural; artificial; adventitious **2** • free from pretension or calculation *syn* simple, ingenuous, naïve, unsophisticated, artless, unaffected *rel* spontaneous, impulsive, instinctive; ingrained, constitutional, inherent

natural *n, syn* FOOL, idiot, imbecile, moron, simpleton

nature *syn* TYPE, kind, sort, stripe, kidney, ilk, description, character *rel* structure, anatomy, framework; disposition, temperament, personality; form, figure, shape, conformation

naughty *syn* BAD, evil, ill, wicked *rel* mischievous, roguish, impish, waggish; froward, balky, restive, wayward, contrary, perverse

nauseate *syn* DISGUST, sicken *rel* vomit, disgorge, belch; offend, outrage

nautical *syn* MARINE, maritime, naval

naval *syn* MARINE, nautical, maritime

near *adj & adv, syn* CLOSE, nigh, nearby *ant* far

near *vb, syn* APPROACH, approximate *rel* rival, match, touch, equal

nearby *syn* CLOSE, near, nigh *ant* far off

nearly · very close to *syn* almost, approximately, well-nigh

neat · manifesting care and orderliness *syn* tidy, trim, trig, snug, shipshape, spick-and-span *rel* clean, cleanly; fastidious, nice, dainty, finicky; exact, precise, correct, accurate *ant* filthy

neb *syn* BILL, beak, nib

necessary **1** *syn* NEEDFUL, requisite, indispensable, essential *rel* compelling, compulsory, obliging, obligatory, constraining; important, significant, momentous; cardinal, vital, fundamental **2** *syn* CERTAIN, inevitable *rel* unavoidable, unescapable, inescapable, ineluctable; infallible, inerrable, inerrant, unerring

necessitous *syn* POOR, indigent, needy, destitute, penniless, impecunious, poverty-stricken *rel* impoverished, drained, depleted, exhausted, bankrupt

necessity *syn* NEED, exigency *rel* compelling, compulsion, constraining, constraint, obliging, obligation, coercing, coercion; indispensableness, requisiteness, requisition, needfulness

need *n* · a pressing lack of something essential *syn* necessity, exigency *rel* stress, strain, pressure; lack, want, dearth, absence, defect, privation; poverty, indigence, penury, destitution

need *vb, syn* LACK, want, require *rel* demand, claim, exact; long, hanker, pine, yearn, hunger, thirst; crave, covet, desire, wish

needful · required for supply or relief *syn* necessary, requisite, indispensable, essential *rel* wanted, needed, required, lacked; vital, cardinal, fundamental

needy *syn* POOR, indigent, destitute, penniless, impecunious, poverty-stricken, necessitous *rel, ant* see NECESSITOUS

nefarious *syn* VICIOUS, iniquitous, flagitious, infamous, corrupt, degenerate, villainous *rel* heinous, outrageous, atrocious, monstrous; flagrant, glaring, gross, rank

negate *syn* NULLIFY, annul, abrogate, invalidate *rel* negative, neutralize, counteract

negative **1** *syn* DENY, gainsay, traverse, contradict, impugn, contravene **2** *syn* NEUTRALIZE, counteract *rel* nullify, negate, annul, abrogate, invalidate

neglect *vb* · to pass over without giving due attention *syn* omit, disregard, ignore, overlook, slight, forget *ant* cherish

neglect *n* **1** *syn* FAILURE, default, miscarriage, dereliction *rel* omitting, omission, disregarding, disregard, ignoring, slighting, forgetting, overlooking; forgetfulness, obliviousness **2** *syn* NEGLIGENCE *rel* neglecting, omitting, omission, disregarding, disregard, ignoring, slighting, forgetting, overlooking

neglectful *syn* NEGLIGENT, lax, slack, remiss *rel* careless, heedless, thoughtless *ant* attentive

negligence · a failure to exercise proper or due care *syn* neglect *rel* laxness, slackness, remissness; indifference, unconcernedness, unconcern, incuriousness *ant* attention; solicitude

negligent · culpably careless or indicative of such carelessness *syn* neglectful, lax, slack, remiss *rel* careless, heedless, thoughtless, inadvertent; indifferent, unconcerned, incurious; slipshod, slovenly

negotiate 1 *syn* CONFER, parley, treat, commune, consult, advise 2 · to bring about by mutual agreement *syn* arrange, concert

neighborhood *syn* LOCALITY, district, vicinity

neighborly *syn* AMICABLE, friendly *rel* peaceful, peaceable, pacific; social, hospitable, gregarious, cooperative; cordial, sociable, gracious *ant* unneighborly; ill-disposed

neophyte *syn* NOVICE, novitiate, probationer, postulant, apprentice

nepenthe *syn* ANODYNE, opiate, narcotic

nerve *n, syn* TEMERITY, effrontery, audacity, hardihood, cheek, gall *rel* boldness, intrepidity; fortitude, grit, pluck, sand, guts; foolhardiness, recklessness

nerve *vb, syn* ENCOURAGE, inspirit, hearten, embolden, cheer, steel *rel* strengthen, invigorate, fortify, energize; rally, stir, rouse, arouse; renew, restore, refresh *ant* unnerve

nervous 1 *syn* VIGOROUS, lusty, energetic, strenuous *rel* forceful, forcible, potent, powerful; spirited, mettlesome; virile, manly 2 *syn* IMPATIENT, restless, restive, unquiet, uneasy, fidgety, jumpy, jittery *rel* excited, excitable, stimulated, provoked, provocative; inconstant, unstable, mercurial *ant* steady

nettle *syn* IRRITATE, provoke, exasperate, aggravate, rile, peeve *rel* annoy, irk, bother, vex; disturb, perturb, agitate, upset, discompose; fret, chafe, gall, abrade

network *syn* SYSTEM, scheme, complex, organism

neutral · lacking decisiveness or distinctiveness in character, quality, action, or effect *syn* indifferent

neutralize · to make inoperative or ineffective usu. by means of an opposite force, influence, or effect *syn* counteract, negative *rel* offset, countervail, counterbalance, counterpoise, compensate; defeat, overcome, subdue, conquer

new · having recently come into existence or use *syn* novel, new-fashioned, newfangled, modern, modernistic, original, fresh *ant* old

newfangled *syn* NEW, novel, new-fashioned, modernistic, modern, original, fresh

new-fashioned *syn* NEW, novel, newfangled, modernistic, modern, original, fresh

news · a report of events or conditions not previously known *syn* tidings, intelligence, advice

newspaper *syn* JOURNAL, periodical, magazine, review, organ

nib *syn* BILL, beak, neb

nice 1 · having or displaying exacting standards *syn* dainty, fastidious, finicky, finicking, finical, particular, fussy, squeamish, persnickety, pernickety *rel* wise, judicious, sage, sapient; punctilious, meticulous, scrupulous, careful; discriminating, discerning, penetrating 2 *syn* CORRECT, precise, exact, accurate, right *rel* strict, rigid, rigorous, stringent; exquisite, delicate, rare, choice 3 *syn* DECOROUS, proper, seemly, decent *rel* fitting, fit, appropriate, suitable, meet

niggardly *syn* STINGY, parsimonious, penurious, miserly, close, closefisted, tight, tightfisted, cheeseparing, penny-pinching *rel* covetous, avaricious, grasping, greedy; sparing, economical, frugal, thrifty; mean, ignoble *ant* bountiful

nigh *syn* CLOSE, near, nearby *ant* far

night *syn* NIGHTLY, nocturnal

nightly • of, relating to, or associated with the night *syn* nocturnal, night *ant* daily

nightmare *syn* FANCY, dream, vision, fantasy, phantasy, phantasm, daydream *rel* delusion, hallucination, illusion; threatening, threat, menacing, menace

nimble *syn* AGILE, brisk, spry *rel* sprightly, lively, animated; alert, wide-awake, vigilant, watchful; supple, limber, lithe

nip *vb, syn* BLAST, blight *rel* check, arrest; squeeze, press; frustrate, thwart, balk

nip *n, syn* BLAST, blight *rel* arresting, checking; frigidity, freezing

nobility *syn* ARISTOCRACY, gentry, county, elite, society

noble **1** *syn* GRAND, stately, majestic, imposing, august, magnificent, grandiose *rel* glorious, splendid, resplendent, superb, sublime; illustrious, eminent, famous *ant* ignoble; cheap **2** *syn* MORAL, virtuous, righteous, ethical *rel* honorable, upright, just, honest *ant* base (*of actions*); atrocious (*of acts, deeds*)

nocturnal *syn* NIGHTLY *ant* diurnal

noise *syn* SOUND *rel* din, uproar, babel, hubbub, clamor, racket, pandemonium

noiseless *syn* STILL, silent, quiet, stilly *rel* calm, tranquil, serene, placid

noisome *syn* MALODOROUS, fetid, stinking, putrid, rank, rancid, fusty, musty *rel* foul, nasty, squalid, filthy, dirty; noxious, baneful, pernicious, deleterious; loathsome, offensive, revolting *ant* balmy

nomadic *syn* ITINERANT, peripatetic, ambulatory, ambulant, vagrant

nom de guerre, nom de plume *syn* PSEUDONYM, alias, pen name, incognito

nominate *syn* DESIGNATE, name, elect, appoint *rel* propose, intend, mean, purpose; present, tender, offer, proffer

nominee *syn* CANDIDATE, aspirant, applicant

nonage *syn* INFANCY, minority *ant* age

nonchalant *syn* COOL, unruffled, imperturbable, unflappable, composed, collected *rel* unconcerned, indifferent, aloof, detached; lighthearted, cheerful, glad; easy, effortless, light, smooth

non compos mentis *syn* INSANE, mad, crazy, crazed, demented, deranged, lunatic, maniac

nonconformist *syn* HERETIC, dissenter, sectary, sectarian, schismatic

nonesuch *syn* PARAGON, apotheosis, nonpareil

nonpareil *syn* PARAGON, apotheosis, nonesuch

nonplus *syn* PUZZLE, bewilder, distract, confound, dumbfound, mystify, perplex *rel* faze, rattle, embarrass, discomfit, disconcert; confuse, muddle; baffle, balk, frustrate

nonreligious *syn* IRRELIGIOUS, unreligious, ungodly, godless *rel* secular, profane, lay, temporal

nonsense • something said or proposed that seems senseless or absurd *syn* twaddle, drivel, bunk, balderdash, poppycock, gobbledygook, trash, rot, bull *rel* absurdity, preposterousness, silliness, foolishness; asininity, fatuousness

nonsocial *syn* UNSOCIAL, asocial, antisocial

norm *syn* AVERAGE, mean, median, par

normal *syn* REGULAR, typical, natural *rel* ordinary, common, familiar; usual, customary, habitual, wonted, accustomed *ant* abnormal

nosy *syn* CURIOUS, inquisitive, prying, snoopy *rel* meddlesome, impertinent, intrusive, obtrusive

notable *syn* NOTEWORTHY, memorable *rel* noticeable, remarkable, prominent, outstanding, extraordinary; eminent, celebrated, famous

note *vb, syn* SEE, remark, notice, perceive, discern, observe, contemplate, survey, view, behold, descry, espy

note *n* **1** *syn* SIGN, mark, token, badge, symptom *rel* indication, betokening, bespeaking, attesting; character, quality, property, attribute, accident **2** *syn* REMARK, observation, comment, commentary, obiter dictum *rel* annotation, gloss; remembering, reminding, reminder, recalling **3** *syn* LETTER, epistle, missive, message, dispatch, report, memorandum

noteworthy • having some quality that attracts one's attention *syn* notable, memorable *rel* noticeable, remarkable, prominent, conspicuous; patent, manifest, evident

notice *syn* SEE, remark, observe, note, perceive, discern, behold, descry, espy, view, survey, contemplate *rel* recognize, acknowledge; refer, advert, allude

noticeable • attracting notice or attention *syn* remarkable, prominent, outstanding, conspicuous, salient, signal, striking, arresting *rel* evident, manifest, obvious, palpable, patent

notify *syn* INFORM, apprise, advise, acquaint *rel* announce, declare, proclaim, publish, promulgate, broadcast; reveal, disclose, discover, divulge, tell

notion *syn* IDEA, concept, conception, thought, impression *rel* opinion, view, belief, conviction, persuasion, sentiment

notoriety *syn* FAME, reputation, repute, éclat, celebrity, renown, honor, glory *rel* publicity, ballyhoo, promotion, propaganda

notwithstanding • without being prevented or obstructed by *syn* in spite of, despite

nourish *syn* FEED, pasture, graze *rel* nurse, nurture, foster, cultivate

nourishment *syn* FOOD, nutriment, sustenance, aliment, pabulum, pap *rel* support, keep, maintenance, living

novel *syn* NEW, new-fashioned, newfangled, modern, modernistic, original, fresh *rel* strange, singular, unique, peculiar

novice • one who is just entering a field in which he or she has no previous experience *syn* novitiate, apprentice, probationer, postulant, neophyte *rel* beginner, starter, commencer; amateur, dilettante, dabbler, tyro

novitiate *syn* NOVICE, apprentice, probationer, postulant, neophyte

noxious *syn* PERNICIOUS, baneful, deleterious, detrimental *rel* injurious, hurtful, harmful; poisonous, virulent, venomous, toxic, pestilent, miasmatic; noisome, stinking, fetid, putrid, malodorous *ant* wholesome, sanitary

nuance *syn* GRADATION, shade *rel* distinction, difference, dissimilarity; touch, suggestion, suspicion, soupçon, dash, tinge; trace, vestige

nucleus *syn* CENTER, middle, midst, core, hub, focus, heart

nude *syn* BARE, naked, bald, barren *ant* clothed

nudge *vb, syn* POKE, prod, jog *rel* push, thrust, shove

nudge *n, syn* POKE, prod, jog

nugatory *syn* VAIN, otiose, idle, empty, hollow *rel* worthless, valueless; trifling, trivial, petty, paltry; ineffectual, ineffective, inefficacious; fruitless, bootless, futile, vain, abortive

nullify • to deprive of effective or continued existence *syn* negate, annul, abrogate, invalidate *rel* neutralize, negative, counteract; offset, countervail, counterbalance, compensate; limit, restrict, confine

number *n* **1** *syn* SUM, quantity, whole, total, aggregate, amount **2** • a character by which an arithmetical value is designated *syn* numeral, figure, digit, integer

number *vb, syn* COUNT, tell, enumerate *rel* calculate, compute, estimate, reckon

numeral *syn* NUMBER, figure, digit, integer

numerous *syn* MANY, several, sundry, various, divers, multifarious *rel* large, great, big; abundant, plentiful, plenteous

nun *syn* RELIGIOUS, monk, friar

nuncio *syn* AMBASSADOR, legate, internuncio, chargé d'affaires, minister, envoy

nunnery *syn* CLOISTER, monastery, convent, abbey, priory

nuptial *adj, syn* MATRIMONIAL, conjugal, connubial, hymeneal, marital

nuptial *n, syn* MARRIAGE, matrimony, wedlock, wedding, espousal

nurse • to promote the growth, development, or progress of *syn* nurture, foster, cherish, cultivate *rel* feed, nourish; promote, advance, further, forward; indulge, pamper, humor

nurture *syn* NURSE, foster, cherish, cultivate *rel* raise, rear; train, educate, school, discipline, teach; support, uphold, back

nutriment *syn* FOOD, nourishment, sustenance, aliment, pabulum, pap *rel* maintenance, support, keep, bread and butter, living

O

obdurate *syn* INFLEXIBLE, inexorable, adamant, adamantine *rel* hardened, indurated, callous; obstinate, stubborn, mulish, stiff-necked; immovable, immobile

obedient • submissive to the will of another *syn* docile, tractable, amenable, biddable *rel* compliant, acquiescent, resigned; submissive, subdued, tame; deferential, obeisant *ant* disobedient; contumacious

obeisance *syn* HONOR, deference, homage, reverence *rel* allegiance, fealty, loyalty, fidelity; respect, esteem, regard; veneration, reverence

obese *syn* FLESHY, corpulent, rotund, chubby, fat, stout, portly, plump *ant* scrawny

obey • to follow the wish, direction, or command of another *syn* comply, mind *rel* submit, yield, defer, bow, succumb; accede, acquiesce, subscribe, agree, assent *ant* command, order

obfuscate *syn* OBSCURE, dim, bedim, darken, eclipse, cloud, becloud, fog, befog *rel* confuse, muddle, befuddle, fuddle, addle; stupefy, bemuse, daze; perplex, mystify, bewilder, puzzle

obiter dictum *syn* REMARK, observation, comment, commentary, note

object *n* **1** *syn* THING, article *rel* affair, concern, matter; form, figure, shape, configuration **2** *syn* INTENTION, objective, goal, end, aim, design, purpose, intent *rel* motive, incentive, inducement

object *vb* • to oppose by arguing against *syn* protest, remonstrate, expostulate, kick *rel* demur, balk, scruple, jib, boggle, shy, stick, stickle; criticize, denounce, reprobate *ant* acquiesce

objectify *syn* REALIZE, externalize, materialize, incarnate, embody, actualize, hypostatize, reify

objectionable · arousing or likely to arouse objection *syn* exceptionable, unacceptable, undesirable, unwanted, unwelcome

objective *adj* **1** *syn* MATERIAL, physical, corporeal, phenomenal, sensible *rel* external, outside, outer, outward; tangible, palpable, perceptible *ant* subjective **2** *syn* FAIR, impartial, unbiased, dispassionate, uncolored, just, equitable *rel, ant* see OBJECTIVE 1

objective *n, syn* INTENTION, object, end, goal, aim, design, purpose, intent

objurgate *syn* EXECRATE, curse, damn, anathematize *rel* revile, vituperate, scold; condemn, denounce, reprobate, criticize

obligation **1** · something one is bound to do or forbear *syn* duty *rel* compulsion, constraint, restraint; responsibility, accountability, answerability **2** *syn* DEBT, indebtedness, liability, debit, arrear *rel* burden, load; promising, promise, engagement, pledging, pledge

oblige **1** *syn* FORCE, constrain, coerce, compel *rel* tie, bind **2** · to do a service or courtesy *syn* accommodate, favor *rel* gratify, please; benefit, profit, avail; help, aid, assist; support, uphold, back *ant* disoblige

obliging *syn* AMIABLE, good-natured, complaisant *rel* helping, helpful, aiding, assisting; accommodating, favoring; compliant, acquiescent; thoughtful, considerate *ant* disobliging; inconsiderate

oblique *syn* CROOKED, devious *rel* awry, askance, askew; indirect, circuitous, roundabout

obliterate *syn* ERASE, efface, cancel, expunge, blot out, delete *rel* abolish, annihilate, extinguish; destroy, raze; annul, abrogate, negate, invalidate, nullify

oblivious *syn* FORGETFUL, unmindful *rel* disregarding, ignoring, forgetting, neglecting, overlooking

obloquy **1** *syn* ABUSE, vituperation, invective, scurrility, billingsgate *rel* censuring, censure, condemning, condemnation, denouncing, denunciation, criticizing, criticism; calumny, detraction, backbiting, slander, scandal **2** *syn* DISGRACE, dishonor, disrepute, shame, infamy, ignominy, opprobrium, odium *rel* stigma, brand, blot, stain; humiliation, humbling, degradation

obnoxious *syn* REPUGNANT, distasteful, invidious, abhorrent, repellent *rel* hateful, odious, detestable, abominable; offensive, loathsome, repulsive, revolting *ant* grateful

obscene *syn* COARSE, gross, vulgar, ribald *rel* indecent, indelicate, indecorous; lewd, lascivious, wanton, licentious; foul, nasty, dirty *ant* decent

obscure *adj* **1** *syn* DARK, murky, gloomy, dim, dusky *rel* shady, shadowy, umbrageous **2** · not clearly understandable *syn* dark, vague, enigmatic, cryptic, ambiguous, equivocal *rel* abstruse, recondite, occult, esoteric; difficult, hard; complicated, intricate, involved, complex; mysterious, inscrutable *ant* distinct, obvious

obscure *vb* · to make dark, dim, or indistinct *syn* dim, bedim, darken, eclipse, cloud, becloud, fog, befog, obfuscate *rel* hide, conceal, screen; disguise, cloak, mask, camouflage; misrepresent, belie, falsify *ant* illuminate, illumine

obsequious *syn* SUBSERVIENT, servile, slavish, menial *rel* deferential, obeisant; compliant, acquiescent; sycophantic, parasitic, toadyish; cringing, fawning, truckling, cowering *ant* contumelious

observation *syn* REMARK, comment, commentary, note, obiter dictum *rel* opinion, view, belief; annotation, gloss; criticism, critique

observe **1** *syn* KEEP, celebrate, solemnize, commemorate *rel* respect, esteem, regard; revere, reverence, venerate *ant* violate **2** *syn* SEE, survey, view, contemplate, notice, remark, note, perceive, discern, behold, descry, espy *rel* scrutinize, examine, scan, inspect

observer *syn* SPECTATOR, beholder, looker-on, onlooker, witness, eyewitness, bystander, kibitzer

obsolete *syn* OLD, antiquated, archaic, antique, ancient, venerable, antediluvian *ant* current

obstacle • something that seriously hampers action or progress *syn* obstruction, impediment, bar, snag *rel* barrier, hindering, hindrance, blocking, block

obstinate • fixed and unyielding in course or purpose *syn* dogged, stubborn, pertinacious, mulish, stiff-necked, pigheaded, bullheaded *rel* headstrong, willful, recalcitrant, unruly; obdurate, inexorable, inflexible; resolute, steadfast, staunch *ant* pliant, pliable

obstreperous *syn* VOCIFEROUS, clamorous, blatant, strident, boisterous *rel* unruly, ungovernable, intractable, headstrong, refractory; uproarious, rackety

obstruct *syn* HINDER, impede, block, bar, dam *rel* prevent, preclude, obviate, avert; restrain, check, curb, inhibit

obstruction *syn* OBSTACLE, impediment, bar, snag *rel* hindering, hindrance, blocking, block; arresting, arrest, checking, check, interruption *ant* assistance

obtain *syn* GET, procure, secure, acquire, gain, win *rel* reach, achieve, attain; effect, fulfill, accomplish, perform

obtrude *syn* INTRUDE, interlope, butt in *rel* interpose, interfere, intervene, mediate

obtrusive *syn* IMPERTINENT, intrusive, meddlesome, officious *rel* inquisitive, curious, prying, snoopy, nosy; blatant, strident *ant* unobtrusive; shy

obtuse *syn* DULL, blunt *rel* insensitive, insensible, anesthetic, impassible; stolid, phlegmatic, impassive *ant* acute

obviate *syn* PREVENT, preclude, avert, ward *rel* evade, elude, avoid, escape; forestall, anticipate; interpose, interfere, intervene

obvious *syn* EVIDENT, manifest, patent, distinct, apparent, palpable, plain, clear *rel* prominent, conspicuous, salient, signal, striking, noticeable *ant* obscure; abstruse

occasion **1** *syn* OPPORTUNITY, chance, break, time *rel* juncture, pass; situation, posture, condition, state; moment, instant **2** *syn* CAUSE, determinant, antecedent, reason *rel* incident, occurrence, event; origin, source, inception

occasional *syn* INFREQUENT, uncommon, scarce, rare, sporadic *rel* casual, desultory, random; incidental, accidental *ant* customary

occult *syn* RECONDITE, esoteric, abstruse *rel* mysterious, inscrutable, arcane; mystic, cabalistic, mystical, anagogic

occupation *syn* WORK, employment, calling, pursuit, business

occur *syn* HAPPEN, chance, befall, betide, transpire *rel* rise, arise, spring, emanate, issue, proceed; follow, succeed, ensue, supervene

occurrence • something that happens or takes place *syn* event, incident, episode, circumstance *rel* appearance, emergence; juncture, pass, exigency, emergency, contingency; posture, situation, condition, state

odd *syn* STRANGE, queer, quaint, singular, unique, peculiar, eccentric, erratic, outlandish, curious *rel* bizarre, grotesque, fantastic; anomalous, irregular, unnatural

odds *syn* ADVANTAGE, handicap, allowance, edge

odious *syn* HATEFUL, abhorrent, abominable, detestable *rel* repugnant, repellent, distasteful, obnoxious; offensive, loathsome, repulsive, revolting

odium *syn* DISGRACE, obloquy, opprobrium, ignominy, infamy, dishonor, disrepute, shame *rel* hate, hatred; antipathy, aversion; abhorrence, abomination, detestation, loathing

odor *syn* SMELL, scent, aroma *rel* fragrance, perfume, redolence, incense, bouquet

odorous • emitting and diffusing scent *syn* fragrant, redolent, aromatic, balmy *ant* malodorous; odorless

offal *syn* REFUSE, waste, rubbish, trash, debris, garbage

offend • to cause hurt feelings or deep resentment *syn* outrage, affront, insult *rel* annoy, vex, irk, bother; exasperate, nettle, irritate; pique, provoke, excite; chafe, fret, gall

offense 1 *syn* ATTACK, offensive, aggression *rel* assault, onslaught, onset 2 • an emotional response to a slight or indignity *syn* resentment, umbrage, pique, dudgeon, huff *rel* affront, insult, indignity; indignation, wrath, anger 3 • a transgression of law *syn* sin, vice, crime, scandal *rel* injustice, injury, wrong, grievance; breach, infraction, violation, transgression, trespass, infringement, contravention

offensive *adj* 1 *syn* ATTACKING, aggressive *rel* invasive, incursive; assaulting, assailing, attacking, bombarding, storming 2 • utterly distasteful or unpleasant to the senses or sensibilities *syn* loathsome, repulsive, repugnant, revolting *rel* repellent, abhorrent, distasteful, obnoxious, invidious; hateful, odious, abominable, detestable

offensive *n* *syn* ATTACK, aggression, offense *rel* assault, onslaught, onset

offer • to put something before another for acceptance or consideration *syn* proffer, tender, present, prefer *rel* give, bestow, confer; adduce, advance; propose, design, purpose, intend

offhand *syn* EXTEMPORANEOUS, extempore, extemporary, improvised, impromptu, unpremeditated *rel* casual, desultory, random; abrupt, hasty, sudden, precipitate, impetuous; brusque, curt, blunt, bluff

office *syn* FUNCTION, duty, province *rel* work, business, calling; task, job, chore, stint

officious *syn* IMPERTINENT, meddlesome, intrusive, obtrusive *rel* meddling, interfering, intermeddling, tampering; annoying, vexing, irking, bothering; pushing, assertive, aggressive

offset *syn* COMPENSATE, countervail, balance, counterbalance, counterpoise *rel* neutralize, negative, counteract; nullify, negate; redeem, reclaim, save, rescue

offspring • those who follow in direct parental line *syn* young, progeny, issue, descendants, posterity

oft *syn* OFTEN, frequently, oftentimes

often • many times *syn* frequently, oft, oftentimes

oftentimes *syn* OFTEN, frequently, oft

oil · to smear, rub over, or lubricate with oil or an oily substance *syn* grease, lubricate, anoint, cream

oily *syn* FULSOME, unctuous, oleaginous, slick, soapy *rel* hypocritical, pharisaical, sanctimonious; bland, politic, diplomatic, smooth, suave

old **1** *syn* AGED, elderly, superannuated *rel* weak, feeble, infirm, decrepit *ant* young **2** · having come into existence or use in the more or less distant past *syn* ancient, venerable, antique, antiquated, antediluvian, archaic, obsolete *rel* primitive, primeval, pristine, primal *ant* new

oleaginous *syn* FULSOME, oily, unctuous, slick, soapy *rel*

oligarchy · government by, or a state governed by, the few *syn* aristocracy, plutocracy

omen *syn* FORETOKEN, augury, portent, presage, prognostic *rel* sign, mark, token, badge, note, symptom; foreboding, apprehension, presentiment, misgiving

ominous · having a menacing or threatening aspect *syn* portentous, fateful, inauspicious, unpropitious *rel* sinister, baleful, malign, malefic, maleficent; threatening, menacing

omit *syn* NEGLECT, disregard, ignore, overlook, slight, forget *rel* cancel, delete, efface, erase; exclude, eliminate

omnipresent · present at all places at all times *syn* ubiquitous

onerous · imposing great hardship or strain *syn* burdensome, oppressive, exacting *rel* heavy, weighty, ponderous, cumbrous, cumbersome, hefty; arduous, hard, difficult

onlooker *syn* SPECTATOR, looker-on, observer, beholder, witness, eyewitness, bystander, kibitzer

only · being one or more of which there are no others *syn* alone *rel* solitary; single, sole, lone, unique

onset *syn* ATTACK, assault, onslaught *rel* aggression, offensive, offense; storming, bombarding, assailing; invasion, raid, incursion

onslaught *syn* ATTACK, assault, onset *rel* see ONSET

onward · toward or at a point lying ahead in space or time *syn* forward, forth

opalescent, opaline *syn* PRISMATIC, iridescent

open **1** *syn* LIABLE, exposed, subject, prone, susceptible, sensitive *ant* closed **2** *syn* FRANK, plain, candid *rel* straightforward, aboveboard, forthright; natural, simple, ingenuous, naïve, unsophisticated; fair, equitable, impartial *ant* close, closemouthed, close-lipped; clandestine

openhanded *syn* LIBERAL, bountiful, bounteous, generous, munificent, handsome *ant* closefisted, tightfisted

operate *syn* ACT, behave, work, function, react

operative *adj, syn* ACTIVE, dynamic, live *rel* effective, effectual, efficacious, efficient; fertile, fecund, fruitful *ant* abeyant

operative *n, syn* WORKER, mechanic, artisan, hand, workman, workingman, laborer, craftsman, handicraftsman, roustabout

opiate *syn* ANODYNE, narcotic, nepenthe

opinion · a judgment one holds as true *syn* view, belief, conviction, persuasion, sentiment *rel* thought, notion, impression, idea, concept, conception; inference, deduction, conclusion, judgment; deciding, decision, determining, determination, settling, settlement

opponent · one who expresses or manifests opposition *syn* antagonist, adversary *rel* enemy, foe; rival, competitor, emulator

opportune *syn* SEASONABLE, timely, well-timed, pat *rel* happy, felicitous, appropriate, fitting, fit; propitious, auspicious, favorable; ready, prompt, quick, apt *ant* inopportune

opportunity · a state of affairs or a combination of circumstances favorable to some end *syn* occasion, chance, break, time *rel* juncture, pass, contingency, emergency; posture, situation, condition, state

oppose *syn* RESIST, contest, fight, combat, conflict, antagonize, withstand *rel* contend, fight, battle, war; attack, assail, assault, storm, bombard; defend, protect, shield, guard, safeguard

opposite *n* · something that is exactly opposed or contrary *syn* contradictory, contrary, antithesis, antipode, antonym, converse, counter, reverse

opposite *adj* · so far apart as to be or to seem irreconcilable *syn* contradictory, contrary, antithetical, antipodal, antipodean, antonymous *rel* reverse, converse; antagonistic, adverse, counter, counteractive

oppress **1** *syn* DEPRESS, weigh *rel* abuse, mistreat, maltreat, ill-treat, outrage; worry, annoy, harass, harry **2** *syn* WRONG, persecute, aggrieve *rel* afflict, torment, torture; overcome, subdue, subjugate, reduce, overthrow, conquer

oppressive *syn* ONEROUS, burdensome, exacting *rel* extorting, extortionate, extracting; compelling, compulsory, coercing, coercion, constraining, obliging, obligatory; despotic, tyrannical, absolute, arbitrary

opprobrious *syn* ABUSIVE, vituperative, contumelious, scurrilous *rel* reviling, vituperating, railing, berating; malicious, malevolent, malign, malignant; execrable, damnable, accursed

opprobrium *syn* DISGRACE, obloquy, odium, ignominy, infamy, shame, dishonor, disrepute *rel* abuse, invective, vituperation, obloquy, scurrility; censure, denunciation, condemnation, reprehension

opt *syn* CHOOSE, select, elect, pick, cull, prefer, single *rel* take, accept, receive; adopt, embrace, espouse

optimistic *syn* HOPEFUL, roseate, rose-colored *rel* confident, sanguine, assured; cheerful, lighthearted, joyous, glad *ant* pessimistic

option *syn* CHOICE, alternative, preference, selection, election *rel* right, prerogative, privilege

opulent **1** *syn* RICH, affluent, wealthy *rel* lavish, profuse, prodigal; showy, pretentious, ostentatious *ant* destitute; indigent **2** *syn* LUXURIOUS, sumptuous *rel* luxuriant, lush, exuberant, profuse; splendid, resplendent, gorgeous, superb

opus *syn* WORK, product, production, artifact

oracular *syn* DICTATORIAL, doctrinaire, dogmatic, authoritarian, magisterial *rel* positive, certain, sure, cocksure

oral *syn* VOCAL, articulate *ant* written

oration *syn* SPEECH, address, harangue, lecture, talk, sermon, homily

orbit *syn* RANGE, gamut, reach, radius, compass, sweep, scope, horizon, ken, purview

ordain *syn* DICTATE, prescribe, decree, impose *rel* order, command, enjoin, direct

order *n* **1** *syn* ASSOCIATION, society, club **2** *syn* COMMAND, injunction, bidding, behest, mandate, dictate *rel* instruction, direction, charging, charge

order *vb* **1** · to put persons or things into their proper places in relation to each other *syn* arrange, marshal, organize, systematize, methodize *rel* adjust, regulate; line, line up, align, range, array **2** *syn* COMMAND, bid, enjoin, direct, instruct, charge *rel* prohibit, forbid, interdict, inhibit, ban

orderly · following a set arrangement, design, or pattern *syn* methodical, systematic, regular *rel* tidy, neat, trim, spick-and-span; formal, conventional, ceremonious, ceremonial; peaceable, pacific, peaceful *ant* disorderly; chaotic

ordinance *syn* LAW, canon, precept, rule, regulation, statute

ordinary *syn* COMMON, familiar, popular, vulgar *rel* usual, customary, habitual, wonted, accustomed *ant* extraordinary

organ **1** *syn* MEAN, medium, vehicle, channel, instrument, instrumentality, agent, agency **2** *syn* JOURNAL, periodical, newspaper, magazine, review

organism *syn* SYSTEM, scheme, network, complex

organize **1** *syn* ORDER, systematize, methodize, arrange, marshal *rel* design, project, plan, scheme; form, fashion, shape, make *ant* disorganize **2** *syn* FOUND, institute, establish, create *rel* begin, commence, start, initiate, inaugurate; adjust, regulate

oriel *syn* WINDOW, casement, dormer

orifice *syn* APERTURE, interstice

origin · the point at which something begins its course or its existence *syn* source, inception, root, provenance, provenience, prime mover *rel* beginning, commencement, initiation, starting; derivation, origination, rising, rise; ancestry, lineage

original **1** *syn* INITIAL, primordial *rel* beginning, commencing, starting; primary, primal, pristine, primeval; basic, fundamental **2** *syn* NEW, fresh, novel, new-fashioned, newfangled, modern, modernistic *ant* dependent; banal; trite

originate *syn* SPRING, rise, derive, arise, flow, issue, emanate, proceed, stem *rel* begin, commence, start

ornament *syn* ADORN, decorate, embellish, beautify, deck, bedeck, garnish *rel* enhance, heighten, intensify

ornate · elaborately and often pretentiously decorated or designed *syn* rococo, baroque, flamboyant, florid *rel* adorned, decorated, ornamented, embellished; flowery, aureate; luxurious, sumptuous, opulent; showy, ostentatious *ant* chaste; austere

orotund *syn* RESONANT, sonorous, ringing, resounding, vibrant *rel* loud, stentorian, strident

oscillate *syn* SWING, sway, vibrate, fluctuate, pendulate, waver, undulate *rel* vacillate, hesitate, falter; shake, tremble, quiver, quaver

ostensible *syn* APPARENT, seeming, illusory *rel* specious, plausible, colorable; pretended, assumed, affected, simulated, feigned

ostentatious *syn* SHOWY, pretentious *rel* vainglorious, vain, proud; flaunting, parading, displaying; boasting, bragging, gasconading

ostracize *syn* BANISH, exile, expatriate, deport, transport, extradite

otiose *syn* VAIN, nugatory, idle, empty, hollow *rel* superfluous, supernumerary, surplus; futile, vain, fruitless, bootless

oust *syn* EJECT, expel, evict, dismiss *rel* exclude, eliminate, shut out, rule out, debar, disbar; discharge, fire, cashier, sack

out-and-out *syn* OUTRIGHT, unmitigated, arrant

outcast · one that is cast out or refused acceptance by society *syn* castaway, derelict, reprobate, pariah, untouchable *rel* vagabond, vagrant, tramp, hobo

outcome *syn* EFFECT, result, consequence, upshot, aftereffect, aftermath, sequel, issue, event *rel* fate, lot, portion, destiny; termination, end

outdo *syn* EXCEED, excel, outstrip, transcend, surpass

outer · being or located outside something *syn* outward, outside, external, exterior *rel* extrinsic, extraneous, foreign, alien *ant* inner

outfit *n, syn* EQUIPMENT, apparatus, paraphernalia, tackle, machinery, gear, matériel

outfit *vb, syn* FURNISH, equip, appoint, accouter, arm

outlander *syn* STRANGER, foreigner, alien, outsider, immigrant, émigré

outlandish *syn* STRANGE, singular, unique, peculiar, eccentric, erratic, odd, queer, quaint, curious *rel* bizarre, grotesque, fantastic, antic; alien, foreign, extraneous, extrinsic

outlast *syn* OUTLIVE, survive *rel* endure, persist, abide, continue; withstand, resist

outline *n* **1** · the line that bounds and gives form to something *syn* contour, profile, skyline, silhouette *rel* figure, form, shape, conformation, configuration **2** *syn* SKETCH, diagram, delineation, draft, tracing, plot, blueprint

outline *vb, syn* SKETCH, diagram, delineate, draft, trace, plot, blueprint

outlive · to remain in existence longer than *syn* outlast, survive *rel* endure, persist, abide, continue; surpass, exceed

outlook *syn* PROSPECT, anticipation, foretaste *rel* forecasting, forecast, predicting, prediction, prophesying, prophecy, presaging, presage; possibility, probability, likelihood

outrage **1** *syn* ABUSE, misuse, mistreat, maltreat, ill-treat *rel* wrong, persecute, oppress, aggrieve; corrupt, pervert, vitiate, deprave, debase **2** *syn* OFFEND, affront, insult *rel* vex, annoy, irk, bother; mortify, chagrin

outrageous · enormously or flagrantly bad or horrible *syn* monstrous, heinous, atrocious *rel* flagrant, glaring, gross, rank; excessive, inordinate, immoderate, extreme; flagitious, nefarious, iniquitous, vicious

outright · being exactly what is stated *syn* out-and-out, unmitigated, arrant

outside *syn* OUTER, outward, external, exterior *rel* extrinsic, extraneous, alien, foreign *ant* inside

outsider *syn* STRANGER, foreigner, alien, outlander, immigrant, émigré

outstanding *syn* NOTICEABLE, prominent, conspicuous, salient, signal, striking, arresting, remarkable *rel* exceptional *ant* commonplace

outstrip *syn* EXCEED, outdo, surpass, transcend, excel

outward *syn* OUTER, outside, external, exterior *rel* extraneous, extrinsic, alien, foreign *ant* inward

outwit *syn* FRUSTRATE, thwart, foil, baffle, balk, circumvent *rel* defeat, overcome, surmount, conquer; prevent, preclude, obviate, avert; overreach, cheat, defraud

over *syn* ABOVE *ant* beneath

overbearing *syn* PROUD, supercilious, disdainful, lordly, arrogant, haughty, insolent *rel* domineering, masterful, imperious; scorning, scornful, despising, despiteful, contemning; autocratic, despotic, tyrannical, absolute *ant* subservient

overcome *syn* CONQUER, surmount, overthrow, subjugate, rout, vanquish, defeat, beat, lick, subdue *rel* capture, catch; outstrip, outdo, exceed; suppress, repress

overdue *syn* TARDY, behindhand, late *rel* delayed, retarded, detained, slowed, slackened; deferred, postponed

overflow *syn* TEEM, swarm, abound

overhang *syn* BULGE, jut, stick out, protrude, project, beetle *rel* threaten, menace; suspend, hang, dangle

overlay · to lay or spread over or across *syn* superpose, superimpose, appliqué

overlook *syn* NEGLECT, slight, forget, ignore, disregard, omit

overplus *syn* EXCESS, superfluity, surplus, surplusage

overreach *syn* CHEAT, cozen, defraud, swindle

overrun *syn* INFEST, beset

oversight · the function or duty of watching or guarding for the sake of proper control or direction *syn* supervision, surveillance *rel* management, direction, controlling, control; inspection, scrutiny, examination

overspread *syn* COVER, envelop, wrap, shroud, veil *rel* hide, conceal, screen; cloak, mask, disguise, camouflage

overstatement *syn* EXAGGERATION, hyperbole *ant* understatement

overthrow **1** *syn* OVERTURN, subvert, upset, capsize *rel* throw, cast, fling, hurl, toss **2** *syn* CONQUER, rout, surmount, overcome, vanquish, defeat, beat, lick, subdue, subjugate, reduce

overture · an action taken to win the favor or approval of another person or party *syn* approach, advance, tender, bid *rel* proposal, proposition; offering, offer, proffering

overturn · to turn from an upright or proper position *syn* upset, capsize, overthrow, subvert *rel* invert, reverse, transpose

own **1** *syn* HAVE, possess, hold, enjoy *rel* control, manage, direct, conduct; keep, retain **2** *syn* ACKNOWLEDGE, avow, admit, confess *rel* concede, grant, allow; reveal, disclose, divulge *ant* disown; repudiate

P

pabulum *syn* FOOD, aliment, nutriment, nourishment, sustenance, pap

pace *syn* SPEED, velocity, momentum, impetus, headway

pacific · affording or promoting peace *syn* peaceable, peaceful, irenic, pacifist, pacifistic *rel* calm, placid, serene, tranquil; conciliating, conciliatory, propitiating, propitiatory, appeasing, pacifying, pacificatory *ant* bellicose

pacifist, pacifistic *syn* PACIFIC, peaceable, peaceful, irenic

pacify · to ease the anger or disturbance of *syn* appease, placate, mollify, propitiate, conciliate *rel* assuage, alleviate, allay, mitigate, relieve; moderate, qualify, temper *ant* anger

pack *n*, *syn* BUNDLE, bunch, package, packet, bale, parcel

pack *vb* · to fill a limited space with more than is practicable or fitting *syn* crowd, cram, stuff, ram, tamp *rel* compact, consolidate; press, squeeze, jam; compress, constrict, contract

package *syn* BUNDLE, packet, bunch, bale, parcel, pack

packet *syn* BUNDLE, package, pack, bunch, bale, parcel

pact *syn* CONTRACT, compact, bargain, treaty, entente, convention, cartel, concordat

pain **1** · a bodily sensation that causes acute discomfort or suffering *syn* ache, pang, throe, twinge, stitch *rel* agony, distress, suffering, passion; anguish, sorrow, grief, heartbreak **2** *pl* **pains** *syn* EFFORT, exertion, trouble *rel* labor, toil, travail, work; industriousness, industry, diligence, sedulousness, assiduousness

pair *syn* COUPLE, brace, yoke

palatable · agreeable or pleasant to the taste *syn* appetizing, savory, sapid, tasty, toothsome, flavorsome, relishing *rel* delightful, delicious, delectable, luscious; piquant, pungent, spicy *ant* unpalatable; distasteful

palate *syn* TASTE, relish, gusto, zest

pale **1** · deficient in color or in intensity of color *syn* pallid, ashen, ashy, wan, livid *rel* ghastly, macabre; cadaverous, haggard, worn **2** · being weak and thin in substance or in vital qualities *syn* anemic, bloodless *rel* insipid, wishy-washy, inane, jejune; ineffective, ineffectual

pall *syn* SATIATE, cloy, surfeit, sate, glut, gorge

palliate · to give a speciously fine appearance to what is base, evil, or erroneous *syn* extenuate, gloze, gloss, whitewash, whiten *rel* mitigate, alleviate, lighten, relieve; condone, excuse; moderate, qualify, temper; cloak, mask, disguise, dissemble, camouflage

pallid *syn* PALE, ashen, ashy, wan, livid

palpable **1** *syn* PERCEPTIBLE, sensible, tangible, appreciable, ponderable *rel* apparent, ostensible, seeming; believable, credible, colorable, plausible *ant* insensible **2** *syn* EVIDENT, plain, clear, apparent, manifest, patent, obvious, distinct *rel* sure, certain, positive; noticeable, remarkable, striking, arresting *ant* impalpable

palpate *syn* TOUCH, feel, handle, paw

palpitate *syn* PULSATE, beat, throb, pulse *rel* vibrate, oscillate, fluctuate, swing, sway

palpitation *syn* PULSATION, beat, throb, pulse *rel* vibration, oscillation, fluctuation, swinging, swaying

palter *syn* LIE, prevaricate, equivocate, fib *rel* evade, elude, escape; trifle, dally

paltry *syn* PETTY, trifling, trivial, puny, measly, picayunish, picayune *rel* contemptible, despicable, sorry, scurvy, cheap, beggarly, shabby; abject, ignoble, mean; base, low, vile

pamper *syn* INDULGE, humor, spoil, baby, mollycoddle *rel* gratify, tickle, regale, please; fondle, pet, cosset, caress, dandle *ant* chasten

pandect *syn* COMPENDIUM, syllabus, digest, survey, sketch, précis, aperçu

pandemonium *syn* DIN, uproar, hullabaloo, babel, hubbub, clamor, racket

pander *syn* CATER, purvey *rel* truckle, toady, fawn, cringe; gratify, tickle, regale, please

panegyric *syn* ENCOMIUM, tribute, eulogy, citation *rel* commendation, applauding, applause, complimenting, compliment; acclaiming, acclaim, laudation, praising, praise, extolling, extollation

pang *syn* PAIN, ache, throe, twinge, stitch *rel* agony, distress, suffering; anguish, sorrow, grief, heartache, heartbreak; torturing, torture, tormenting, torment

panic *syn* FEAR, terror, horror, trepidation, consternation, dismay, alarm, fright, dread *rel* agitation, upsetting, upset, perturbation, disquieting, disquiet, discomposing, discomposure

pant *syn* AIM, aspire *rel* thirst, hunger, long, yearn, pine; crave, covet, desire, wish, want

pap *syn* FOOD, aliment, pabulum, nutriment, nourishment, sustenance

paper **1** · a written or printed statement that is of value as a source of information or proof of a right, contention, or claim *syn* instrument, document **2** *syn* ESSAY, article, theme, composition

par *n, syn* AVERAGE, norm, mean, median

par *adj, syn* AVERAGE, mean, median

parable *syn* ALLEGORY, myth, fable

parade *n* **1** *syn* DISPLAY, array, pomp *rel* showiness, ostentatiousness, ostentation, pretentiousness **2** *syn* PROCESSION, cavalcade, cortege, motorcade

parade *vb, syn* SHOW, flaunt, expose, display, exhibit *rel* reveal, disclose, divulge; declare, proclaim, publish, advertise; vaunt, boast, brag, gasconade

paradox · an expression or revelation of an inner or inherent contradiction *syn* antinomy, anomaly

paragon · a model of excellence or perfection *syn* apotheosis, nonpareil, nonesuch

paragraph · one of the several and individually distinct statements of a discourse or instrument, each of which deals with a particular point or item *syn* verse, article, clause, plank, count

parallel *adj, syn* LIKE, alike, similar, analogous, comparable, akin, uniform, identical *rel* same, equal, equivalent;

parallel *n* **1** *syn* COMPARISON, contrast, antithesis, collation *rel* likeness, similarity, resemblance, similitude **2** · one that corresponds to or closely resembles another *syn* counterpart, analogue, correlate

paralyze *syn* DAZE, stun, bemuse, stupefy, benumb, petrify *rel* dismay, daunt, appall, horrify; disable, cripple, weaken, enfeeble; astound, flabbergast, surprise; dumbfound, confound, nonplus, puzzle

paramount *syn* DOMINANT, preponderant, preponderating, predominant, sovereign *rel* supreme, surpassing, preeminent, superlative; capital, foremost, principal, main, leading, chief

parapet *syn* BULWARK, rampart, breastwork, bastion

paraphernalia *syn* EQUIPMENT, apparatus, machinery, outfit, tackle, gear, matériel

paraphrase *syn* TRANSLATION, metaphrase, version

parasite · a usu. obsequious flatterer or self-seeker *syn* sycophant, favorite, toady, lickspittle, bootlicker, hanger-on, leech, sponge, sponger *rel* fawner, cringer, truckler

parboil *syn* BOIL, seethe, simmer, stew

parcel *n* **1** *syn* PART, portion, piece, detail, member, division, section, segment, sector, fraction, fragment **2** *syn* BUNDLE, bunch, pack, package, packet, bale **3** *syn* GROUP, cluster, bunch, lot *rel* collection, assemblage; aggregate, aggregation, conglomerate, conglomeration

parcel *vb, syn* APPORTION, portion, ration, prorate *rel* allot, assign, allocate; grant, accord, award

parch *syn* DRY, desiccate, dehydrate, bake *rel* sear, scorch, char, burn; shrivel, wizen, wither

pardon *n* · a remission of penalty or punishment *syn* amnesty, absolution

pardon *vb, syn* EXCUSE, forgive, remit, condone *rel* free, release, liberate; acquit, absolve, exculpate *ant* punish

pardonable *syn* VENIAL

pare *syn* SKIN, peel, decorticate, flay

pariah *syn* OUTCAST, castaway, derelict, reprobate, untouchable

parley *syn* CONFER, treat, negotiate, commune, consult, advise *rel* discuss, debate, dispute, argue, agitate; converse, talk, speak

parochial *syn* INSULAR, provincial, local, small-town *rel* circumscribed, restricted, limited, confined; narrow, narrow-minded, illiberal, intolerant, hidebound, bigoted *ant* catholic

parody *n, syn* CARICATURE, travesty, burlesque *rel* skit, squib, lampoon, libel

parody *vb, syn* CARICATURE, travesty, burlesque

paroxysm *syn* FIT, spasm, convulsion, attack, access, accession

parry *syn* DODGE, shirk, sidestep, duck, fence, malinger *rel* ward, avert, prevent, preclude; forestall, anticipate; elude, evade, avoid, shun, escape

parsimonious *syn* STINGY, niggardly, penurious, close, closefisted, tight, tightfisted, miserly, cheeseparing, penny-pinching *rel* avaricious, covetous, grasping, greedy; sparing, frugal; mean, ignoble, sordid, abject *ant* prodigal

part *n* • something less than the whole *syn* portion, piece, detail, member, division, section, segment, sector, fraction, fragment, parcel *ant* whole

part *vb, syn* SEPARATE, divide, sever, sunder, divorce *rel* detach, disengage; apportion, allot, allocate, assign; tear, rend, cleave

partake *syn* SHARE, participate *rel* separate, part, divide; take, receive, accept; have, hold, own, possess, enjoy; get, obtain, procure, acquire

partiality *syn* PREDILECTION, prepossession, prejudice, bias *rel* approving, approval, endorsing, endorsement *ant* impartiality

participate *syn* SHARE, partake *rel* separate, divide, part; take, receive, accept; have, hold, own, possess, enjoy

particle • a tiny or insignificant amount, part, or piece *syn* bit, mite, smidgen, whit, atom, iota, jot, tittle

parti-colored *syn* VARIEGATED, motley, checkered, checked, pied, piebald, skewbald, dappled, freaked

particular *adj* **1** *syn* SINGLE, sole, separate, unique, lone, solitary *ant* general **2** *syn* SPECIAL, individual, specific, especial *ant* general, universal **3** *syn* CIRCUMSTANTIAL, particularized, detailed, itemized, minute *rel* scrupulous, meticulous, careful, punctilious **4** *syn* NICE, fussy, squeamish, dainty, fastidious, finicky, finicking, finical, persnickety, pernickety *rel* exacting, demanding, requiring; strict, rigid, rigorous

particular *n, syn* ITEM, detail *ant* universal; whole; aggregate

particularized *syn* CIRCUMSTANTIAL, particular, detailed, itemized, minute *rel* accurate, precise, exact, correct *ant* generalized

partisan *syn* FOLLOWER, adherent, disciple, sectary, henchman, satellite *rel* supporter, upholder, backer, champion; helper, aider, aid, assistant

partner • one associated in action with another *syn* copartner, colleague, ally, confederate *ant* rival

party **1** *syn* COMPANY, band, troop, troupe *rel* clique, set, coterie, circle; gathering, collection, assembly, assemblage, congregation **2** *syn* COMBINATION, combine, bloc, faction, ring

pasquinade *syn* LIBEL, lampoon, squib, skit

pass *vb* · move or come to a termination or end *syn* pass away, elapse, expire *rel* depart, leave, quit, go, withdraw; end, terminate, close

pass *n, syn* WAY, passage, route, course, artery

pass *n, syn* JUNCTURE, exigency, emergency, contingency, pinch, strait, crisis *rel* situation, condition, state, posture; plight, predicament, quandary

passage **1** *syn* WAY, pass, route, course, artery **2** · a typically long narrow way connecting parts of a building *syn* passageway, corridor, hall, hallway, gallery, arcade, cloister, aisle, ambulatory **3** *syn* STRAIT, sound, channel, narrows

passageway *syn* PASSAGE, corridor, hall, hallway, gallery, arcade, cloister, aisle, ambulatory

pass away *syn* PASS, elapse, expire

passing *n, syn* DEATH, decease, demise

passing *adj, syn* TRANSIENT, transitory, ephemeral, momentary, fugitive, fleeting, evanescent, short-lived

passion **1** *syn* DISTRESS, suffering, agony, dolor, misery *rel* trial, tribulation, cross, visitation, affliction **2** *syn* FEELING, emotion, affection, sentiment *rel* inspiration, frenzy; ecstasy, rapture, transport **3** *syn* DESIRE, lust, appetite, urge *rel* craving, coveting; longing, yearning, hungering, hunger, thirsting, thirst; panting, aspiring, aiming **4** · intense emotion compelling action *syn* fervor, ardor, enthusiasm, zeal *rel* ecstasy, rapture, transport; anger, rage, fury, wrath; eroticism, amorousness

passionate *syn* IMPASSIONED, ardent, fervent, fervid, perfervid *rel* intense, vehement, fierce, violent; impetuous, headlong, precipitate, abrupt; excited, quickened, stimulated

passive *syn* INACTIVE, inert, idle, supine *rel* impassive, phlegmatic, stolid, apathetic *ant* active

pastoral *syn* RURAL, rustic, bucolic

pasture *syn* FEED, graze, nourish

pat *syn* SEASONABLE, timely, well-timed, opportune *rel* apt, happy, felicitous, appropriate, fitting, fit; pertinent, apposite, apropos, applicable, relevant

patch *syn* MEND, repair, rebuild *rel* emend, remedy, redress, amend, correct; fix, adjust, regulate

patent *syn* EVIDENT, manifest, distinct, obvious, apparent, palpable, plain, clear *rel* noticeable, conspicuous, salient, prominent; flagrant, glaring, gross, rank *ant* latent

pathetic *syn* MOVING, poignant, affecting, touching, impressive *rel* pitiful, piteous, pitiable; plaintive, melancholy, doleful *ant* comical

pathological *syn* UNWHOLESOME, morbid, sickly, diseased

pathos · a quality that moves one to pity and sorrow *syn* poignancy, bathos

patience · the power or capacity to endure without complaint something difficult or disagreeable *syn* long-suffering, longanimity, forbearance, resignation *rel* perseverance, persistence; fortitude, backbone, pluck, grit, sand, guts; equanimity, composure *ant* impatience

patois *syn* DIALECT, vernacular, lingo, jargon, cant, argot, slang

patrician *syn* GENTLEMAN, aristocrat

patrimony *syn* HERITAGE, inheritance, birthright

patron *syn* SPONSOR, surety, guarantor, backer, angel *rel* supporter, upholder, champion; benefactor, contributor; protector, defender *ant* client; protégé

patter *syn* CHAT, chatter, prate, gab, prattle, babble, gabble, jabber, gibber

pattern **1** *syn* MODEL, exemplar,

example, ideal, standard, beau ideal, mirror *rel* paragon, apotheosis **2** *syn* FIGURE, design, motif, device *rel* form, shape, conformation, configuration

paunch *syn* ABDOMEN, belly, stomach, gut

pause • a temporary cessation of activity or of an activity *syn* recess, respite, lull, intermission *rel* interruption, gap, interval, break, interim; stopping, stop, ceasing, cessation

paw *syn* TOUCH, feel, palpate, handle

pawn *syn* PLEDGE, hostage, earnest, token

pay *vb* • to give money or its equivalent in return for something *syn* compensate, remunerate, satisfy, reimburse, indemnify, repay, recompense

pay *n, syn* WAGE, wages, salary, stipend, fee, hire, emolument *rel* reparation, restitution, indemnity, redress, amends

paying • yielding a profit *syn* gainful, remunerative, lucrative, profitable

peace *syn* TRUCE, cease-fire, armistice

peaceable *syn* PACIFIC, peaceful, pacifist, pacifistic, irenic *rel* amicable, friendly, neighborly; amiable, complaisant; calm, placid, serene, tranquil *ant* contentious; acrimonious

peaceful **1** *syn* CALM, tranquil, serene, placid, halcyon *rel* soft, gentle, mild; still, stilly, quiet, silent, noiseless *ant* turbulent **2** *syn* PACIFIC, peaceable, pacifist, pacifistic, irenic *rel* composed, collected, unruffled, cool; equable, constant, steady

peak **1** *syn* MOUNTAIN, mount, alp, volcano, mesa **2** *syn* SUMMIT, pinnacle, climax, apex, acme, culmination, meridian, zenith, apogee

peculiar **1** *syn* CHARACTERISTIC, individual, distinctive *rel* special, especial, particular, specific; idiosyncratic, eccentric **2** *syn* STRANGE, eccentric, odd, queer, singular, unique, quaint, outlandish, curious *rel* bizarre, grotesque, fantastic; abnormal, atypical, aberrant; unusual, uncustomary

pecuniary *syn* FINANCIAL, monetary, fiscal

pedantic • too narrowly concerned with scholarly matters *syn* academic, scholastic, bookish *rel* learned, erudite; recondite, abstruse

pedestrian *syn* DULL, humdrum, dreary, monotonous, stodgy *rel* commonplace, platitudinous, truistic; banal, jejune, inane, wishy-washy, insipid; irksome, wearisome, tiresome, boring

pedigree *syn* ANCESTRY, lineage

peek *syn* LOOK, peep, glimpse, glance, sight, view

peel *vb, syn* SKIN, decorticate, pare, flay

peel *n, syn* SKIN, bark, rind, hide, pelt

peep *vb, syn* CHIRP, chirrup, cheep, tweet, twitter, chitter

peep *n, syn* CHIRP, chirrup, cheep, tweet, twitter, chitter

peep *n, syn* LOOK, glance, glimpse, peek, sight, view *rel* peering, peer, gazing, gaze, staring, stare

peer *syn* GAZE, gape, stare, glare, gloat *rel* peep, glance, glimpse, look

peerless *syn* SUPREME, surpassing, preeminent, superlative, transcendent, incomparable *rel* paramount, sovereign, dominant, predominant; unmatched, unrivaled, unequaled

peeve *syn* IRRITATE, exasperate, nettle, provoke, aggravate, rile *rel* vex, annoy, irk, bother; chafe, fret, gall, abrade

peevish *syn* IRRITABLE, fractious, snappish, waspish, petulant, pettish, huffy, fretful, querulous *rel* captious, carping, caviling, faultfinding, critical

pejorative *syn* DEROGATORY, depreciatory, depreciative, disparaging, slighting *rel* contemptuous, despiteful, scornful, disdainful; decrying, belittling, minimizing

pellucid *syn* CLEAR, transparent, translucent, lucid, diaphanous, limpid *rel* pure, sheer; bright, brilliant, luminous, radiant

pelt *syn* SKIN, hide, rind, bark, peel

pen *syn* ENCLOSE, envelop, fence, coop, corral, cage, wall *rel* confine, circumscribe, restrict, limit

penalize • to inflict a penalty on *syn* fine, amerce, mulct *rel* punish, discipline, correct, chasten

penchant *syn* LEANING, propensity, proclivity, flair *rel* bent, turn, talent, knack, gift; bias, prepossession, predilection, prejudice

pendant *syn* FLAG, ensign, standard, banner, color, streamer, pennant, pennon, jack

pendent *syn* SUSPENDED, pendulous

pendulate *syn* SWING, sway, oscillate, vibrate, fluctuate, waver, undulate

pendulous *syn* SUSPENDED, pendent

penetrate **1** *syn* ENTER, pierce, probe *rel* invade, entrench, encroach, trespass; perforate, puncture, bore, prick **2** *syn* PERMEATE, pervade, impenetrate, interpenetrate, impregnate, saturate *rel* insert, insinuate, interpolate, introduce; soak, saturate, drench, steep

penetration *syn* DISCERNMENT, insight, acumen, discrimination, perception *rel* sharpness, keenness, acuteness; shrewdness, astuteness, perspicaciousness, perspicacity, sagaciousness, sagacity

penitence • regret for sin or wrongdoing *syn* repentance, contrition, attrition, compunction, remorse *rel* regret, sorrow, anguish; humiliation, humbling, degradation, debasement; qualm, scruple

pen name *syn* PSEUDONYM, nom de plume, alias, nom de guerre, incognito

pennant *syn* FLAG, ensign, standard, banner, color, streamer, pendant, pennon, jack

penniless *syn* POOR, indigent, needy, destitute, impecunious, poverty-stricken, necessitous *rel* impoverished, bankrupt, drained; penurious

pennon *syn* FLAG, ensign, standard, banner, color, streamer, pennant, pendant, jack

penny-pinching *syn* STINGY, close, closefisted, tight, tightfisted, niggardly, parsimonious, penurious, miserly, cheeseparing

pensive *syn* THOUGHTFUL, reflective, speculative, contemplative, meditative *rel* solemn, somber, serious, earnest, sober, grave; musing, pondering, ruminating

penumbra *syn* SHADE, umbra, adumbration, umbrage, shadow

penurious *syn* STINGY, parsimonious, niggardly, close, closefisted, tight, tightfisted, miserly, cheeseparing, penny-pinching *rel* avaricious, grasping, greedy, covetous; mercenary, venal; mean, abject, sordid, ignoble

penury *syn* POVERTY, indigence, want, destitution, privation *rel* need, necessity, exigency; pinch, strait, pass, juncture *ant* luxury

peppery *syn* SPIRITED, fiery, gingery, high-spirited, mettlesome, spunky *rel* impetuous, headlong, precipitate, abrupt; pungent, piquant, spicy, snappy

perceive *syn* SEE, discern, note, remark, notice, observe, contemplate, behold, descry, espy, view, survey *rel* grasp, seize, take; apprehend, comprehend; enter, penetrate, pierce, probe

percept *syn* SENSATION, sense-datum, sensum, image *rel* idea, concept, notion; recognition, acknowledgment

perceptible · apprehensible as real or existent *syn* sensible, palpable, tangible, appreciable, ponderable *rel* clear, lucid, perspicuous; noticeable, conspicuous, signal; discerned, discernible, noted, notable, observed, observable *ant* imperceptible

perception *syn* DISCERNMENT, penetration, insight, acumen, discrimination *rel* appreciation, comprehension, understanding; sharpness, keenness, acuteness

perch *syn* ALIGHT, light, land, roost

percussion *syn* IMPACT, concussion, clash, shock, impingement, collision, jar, jolt *rel* striking, hitting, smiting; vibration, oscillation, fluctuation

perdurable *syn* LASTING, durable, permanent, stable, perpetual *rel* enduring, abiding, persisting, continuing; everlasting, endless, interminable *ant* fleeting

peremptory *syn* MASTERFUL, imperative, imperious, domineering *rel* decisive, decided; positive, certain, sure; dictatorial, dogmatic, oracular

perennial *syn* CONTINUAL, perpetual, incessant, unremitting, constant, continuous *rel* lasting, perdurable, stable; everlasting, unceasing

perfect *adj* · not lacking or faulty in any particular *syn* whole, entire, intact *rel* pure, absolute, simple, sheer; consummate, finished, accomplished; impeccable, flawless, faultless, errorless *ant* imperfect

perfect *vb, syn* UNFOLD, evolve, develop, elaborate *rel* complete, finish

perfection *syn* EXCELLENCE, virtue, merit *ant* failing

perfervid *syn* IMPASSIONED, fervid, passionate, ardent, fervent *rel* intense, vehement, fierce, violent; heightened, enhanced, intensified

perfidious *syn* FAITHLESS, false, disloyal, traitorous, treacherous *rel* mercenary, venal; disaffected, alienated, estranged; deceitful, dishonest; perjured, forsworn

perforate · to pierce through so as to leave a hole *syn* puncture, punch, prick, bore, drill *rel* enter, penetrate, pierce, probe

perform · to carry out or into effect *syn* execute, discharge, accomplish, achieve, effect, fulfill *rel* reach, gain, compass, attain; finish, complete, conclude

performer *syn* ACTOR, player, mummer, mime, mimic, thespian, impersonator, trouper

perfume *syn* FRAGRANCE, bouquet, redolence, incense *rel* odor, scent, aroma, smell

peril *syn* DANGER, jeopardy, hazard, risk *rel* menacing, menace, threatening, threat; exposure, subjection, openness, liability

perilous *syn* DANGEROUS, hazardous, risky, precarious *rel* desperate, forlorn, hopeless; chancy, chance, haphazard, random

perimeter *syn* CIRCUMFERENCE, periphery, circuit, compass

period · a division of time *syn* epoch, era, age, aeon

periodic *syn* INTERMITTENT, recurrent, alternate *rel* fitful, spasmodic, convulsive; sporadic, occasional, infrequent

periodical *syn* JOURNAL, magazine, newspaper, review, organ

peripatetic *syn* ITINERANT, ambulatory, ambulant, nomadic, vagrant

periphery *syn* CIRCUMFERENCE, perimeter, circuit, compass *rel* limit, confine, bound, end

periphrasis *syn* VERBIAGE, redundancy, tautology, pleonasm, circumlocution

perjure · to make a false swearer of oneself by violating one's oath to tell the truth *syn* forswear *rel* deceive, delude, mislead, beguile; lie, prevaricate

permanent *syn* LASTING, perdurable, durable, stable, perpetual *rel* perennial, constant, continuous, continual *ant* temporary; ad interim (*of persons*)

permeate • to pass or cause to pass through every part of a thing *syn* pervade, penetrate, impenetrate, interpenetrate, impregnate, saturate *rel* infuse, imbue, ingrain; drench, steep, soak, saturate; inform, animate, inspire, fire

permission • a sanctioning to act or do something that is granted by one in authority *syn* leave, sufferance *rel* authorization, commissioning, commission, licensing, license; letting, allowing; sanctioning, approval, endorsement *ant* prohibition

permit *syn* LET, allow, suffer, leave *rel* authorize, license, commission; sanction, endorse, approve *ant* prohibit, forbid

permutation *syn* CHANGE, mutation, vicissitude, alternation *rel* moving, move, shifting, shift, removing, remove; transformation, conversion, metamorphosis

pernicious • exceedingly harmful or destructive *syn* baneful, noxious, deleterious, detrimental *rel* baleful, malign, sinister, malefic, maleficent; poisonous, venomous, toxic, pestilent, miasmatic; injurious, hurtful, harmful, mischievous *ant* innocuous

pernickety *syn* NICE, persnickety, fastidious, finicky, finicking, finical, dainty, particular, fussy, squeamish *rel* exacting, demanding, requiring; annoyed, vexed, irked

perpendicular *syn* VERTICAL, plumb *rel* steep, abrupt, precipitous, sheer *ant* horizontal

perpetrate *syn* COMMIT *rel* accomplish, achieve, effect

perpetual **1** *syn* LASTING, permanent, perdurable, durable, stable *rel* everlasting, endless, unceasing, interminable; eternal, sempiternal, infinite **2** *syn* CONTINUAL, continuous, constant, incessant, unremitting, perennial *rel* enduring, persisting, abiding, continuing; set, settled, fixed, established *ant* transitory, transient

perplex *syn* PUZZLE, mystify, bewilder, distract, nonplus, confound, dumbfound *rel* disturb, perturb, upset, discompose; baffle, balk, thwart, frustrate; astound, amaze, astonish, surprise

perquisite *syn* RIGHT, prerogative, privilege, appanage, birthright

persecute *syn* WRONG, oppress, aggrieve *rel* worry, annoy, harass, harry; torture, torment, rack; bait, badger, hound, ride

persevere • to continue in a given course in the face of difficulty or opposition *syn* persist *rel* continue, abide, endure, last

persiflage *syn* BADINAGE, raillery *rel* bantering, banter, chaffing, chaff; ridiculing, ridicule, twitting, deriding, derision

persist **1** *syn* PERSEVERE *ant* desist **2** *syn* CONTINUE, last, endure, abide *ant* desist

persnickety *syn* NICE, pernickety, fastidious, finicky, finicking, finical, dainty, particular, fussy, squeamish *rel* exacting, demanding, requiring; annoyed, vexed, irked

person *syn* ENTITY, being, creature, individual

personality *syn* DISPOSITION, character, individuality, temperament, temper, complexion

perspicacious *syn* SHREWD, sagacious, astute *rel* sharp, keen, acute; penetrating, piercing, probing *ant* dull

perspicuous *syn* CLEAR, lucid *rel* manifest, evident, plain, distinct; explicit, express, specific, definite

persuade *syn* INDUCE, prevail, get

rel influence, affect, touch, sway, impress; move, drive, impel, actuate *ant* dissuade

persuasion 1 *syn* OPINION, conviction, belief, view, sentiment *rel* predilection, prepossession, bias, partiality, prejudice; tenet, dogma, doctrine 2 *syn* RELIGION, denomination, sect, cult, communion, faith, creed, church

port *syn* SAUCY, arch *rel* flippant, frivolous, volatile, light-minded; impertinent, intrusive; brash, impudent, shameless *ant* coy

pertain *syn* BEAR, relate, appertain, belong, apply *rel* connect, join, combine, associate

pertinacious *syn* OBSTINATE, stubborn, dogged, mulish, stiff-necked, pigheaded, bullheaded *rel* tenacious, tough, stout, sturdy, strong; persistent, persevering; resolute, steadfast, staunch; headstrong, willful, unruly

pertinent *syn* RELEVANT, germane, material, apposite, applicable, apropos *rel* fitting, apt, happy, felicitous, fit; pat, seasonable, opportune, timely, well-timed *ant* impertinent; foreign

perturb *syn* DISCOMPOSE, disturb, agitate, upset, disquiet, fluster, flurry *rel* annoy, vex, irk, bother; confuse, muddle, addle; confound, nonplus, distract, bewilder, dumbfound, puzzle

pervade *syn* PERMEATE, penetrate, impenetrate, interpenetrate, impregnate, saturate *rel* infuse, imbue, ingrain, leaven; inform, animate, inspire, fire

perverse *syn* CONTRARY, restive, balky, froward, wayward *rel* unruly, ungovernable, recalcitrant, refractory; obstinate, stubborn, mulish, pigheaded, stiff-necked; fractious, irritable, peevish

pervert *syn* DEBASE, deprave, corrupt, vitiate, debauch *rel* abuse, misuse, ill-treat, maltreat, mistreat, outrage; contort, distort, warp, deform

perverted *syn* DEBASED, corrupted, depraved, vitiated, debauched *rel* distorted, contorted, warped; abused, misused, outraged

pessimistic *syn* CYNICAL, misanthropic *rel* gloomy, morose, sullen; depressed, oppressed, weighed down *ant* optimistic

pester *syn* WORRY, plague, tease, tantalize, annoy, harass, harry *rel* bait, badger, hector, heckle, chivy; fret, gall, chafe; perturb, disturb, agitate, upset, discompose

pestilent, pestilential *syn* POISONOUS, venomous, virulent, toxic, mephitic, miasmic, miasmatic, miasmal *rel* infectious, contagious, catching; noxious, pernicious, baneful, deleterious

pet *syn* CARESS, fondle, cosset, cuddle, dandle *rel* indulge, humor, pamper, mollycoddle, baby

petite *syn* SMALL, little, diminutive, wee, tiny, teeny, weeny, minute, microscopic, miniature

petition *n, syn* PRAYER, suit, plea, appeal

petition *vb, syn* PRAY, sue, plead, appeal

petrify 1 *syn* HARDEN, solidify, indurate, cake *rel* deposit, precipitate; compact, consolidate 2 *syn* DAZE, stun, bemuse, stupefy, benumb, paralyze *rel* terrify, alarm, frighten, startle; appall, horrify, dismay

pettish *syn* IRRITABLE, fractious, peevish, petulant, snappish, waspish, huffy, fretful, querulous

petty · being often contemptibly insignificant or unimportant *syn* puny, trivial, trifling, paltry, measly, picayunish, picayune *rel* small, little, diminutive, minute *ant* important, momentous; gross

petulant *syn* IRRITABLE, fractious, peevish, pettish, snappish, waspish, huffy, fretful, querulous *rel* cross, cranky, touchy, testy, irascible; impatient, restive, fidgety

phantasm 1 *syn* APPARITION, phantom, wraith, ghost, spirit, specter, shade, revenant *rel* delusion, illusion, hallucination 2 *syn* FANCY, fantasy, phantasy, vision, dream, daydream, nightmare

phantasy *syn* FANCY, fantasy, phantasm, vision, dream, daydream, nightmare

phantom *syn* APPARITION, phantasm, wraith, ghost, spirit, specter, shade, revenant *rel* counterfeit, deception, imposture; delusion, illusion, hallucination

pharisaical *syn* HYPOCRITICAL, sanctimonious, canting

pharisaism *syn* HYPOCRISY, sanctimony, cant

pharmaceutical *syn* DRUG, medicinal, biologic, simple

pharmacist *syn* DRUGGIST, apothecary, chemist

phase · one of the possible ways of viewing or being presented to view *syn* aspect, side, facet, angle *rel* state, condition, situation, posture; appearance, look, semblance

phenomenal 1 *syn* MATERIAL, physical, corporeal, sensible, objective *rel* actual, real *ant* noumenal 2 *syn* EXCEPTIONAL, extraordinary, unusual, unwonted

phenomenon *syn* WONDER, marvel, prodigy, miracle *rel* abnormality; anomaly, paradox; singularity, peculiarity, uniqueness

philanthropic *syn* CHARITABLE, benevolent, humane, humanitarian, eleemosynary, altruistic *rel* liberal, munificent, bountiful, bounteous, openhanded, generous; lavish, profuse, prodigal *ant* misanthropic

philanthropy *syn* CHARITY *ant* misanthropy

philippic *syn* TIRADE, diatribe, jeremiad *rel* harangue, speech, address, oration; condemnation, denunciation

phlegm 1 *syn* IMPASSIVITY, impassiveness, stolidity, apathy, stoicism *rel* insensibility, insensitiveness, impassibility, anesthesia 2 *syn* EQUANIMITY, composure, sangfroid *rel* imperturbability, nonchalance, coolness, collectedness; calmness, calm, tranquillity, serenity

phlegmatic *syn* IMPASSIVE, stolid, apathetic, stoic *rel* indifferent, unconcerned, incurious, aloof; cool, chilly, cold, frigid; sluggish, lethargic

phony *syn* COUNTERFEIT, spurious, bogus, fake, sham, pseudo, pinchbeck

phrase · a group of words which, taken together, express a notion and may be used as a part of a sentence *syn* idiom, expression, locution

phraseology, **phrasing** *syn* LANGUAGE, vocabulary, diction, style

physic *syn* REMEDY, cure, medicine, medicament, medication, specific

physical 1 *syn* BODILY, corporeal, corporal, somatic *rel* fleshly, carnal, sensual, animal 2 *syn* MATERIAL, corporeal, phenomenal, sensible, objective *rel* actual, real, true; elemental, elementary

physiognomy *syn* FACE, countenance, visage, mug, puss

physique · bodily makeup or type *syn* build, habit, constitution *rel* body; structure, framework, anatomy; system, organism

picayunish, picayune *syn* PETTY, trivial, trifling, puny, paltry, measly

pick *syn* CHOOSE, select, elect, opt, cull, prefer, single *rel* take, seize, grasp; determine, decide, settle

picked *syn* SELECT, elect, exclusive

pickle *syn* PREDICAMENT, plight, dilemma, quandary, scrape, fix, jam

pictorial *syn* GRAPHIC, vivid, picturesque

picture *syn* REPRESENT, depict, portray, delineate, limn *rel* describe, relate, narrate, recount; sketch, outline

picturesque *syn* GRAPHIC, vivid, pictorial *rel* charming, attractive, alluring; conspicuous, salient, striking, arresting

piece *syn* PART, portion, detail, member, division, section, segment, sector, fraction, fragment, parcel

pied, piebald *syn* VARIEGATED, parti-colored, motley, checkered, checked, skewbald, dappled, freaked

pier 1 *syn* BUTTRESS, abutment 2 *syn* WHARF, dock, quay, slip, berth, jetty, levee

pierce *syn* ENTER, penetrate, probe *rel* perforate, bore, drill, puncture; rend, tear, cleave, split, rive

pietistic *syn* DEVOUT, sanctimonious, pious, religious *rel* reverencing, reverential, venerating, adoring, worshiping; fervid, perfervid, ardent, fervent, impassioned; sentimental, maudlin, romantic

piety *syn* FIDELITY, devotion, allegiance, fealty, loyalty *rel* obedience, docility; fervor, ardor, zeal, enthusiasm, passion; holiness, sanctity *ant* impiety

pigeonhole *syn* ASSORT, sort, classify *rel* systematize, methodize, organize, arrange, order

pigheaded *syn* OBSTINATE, stubborn, mulish, stiff-necked, bullheaded, dogged, pertinacious *rel* headstrong, willful, recalcitrant, refractory; contrary, perverse, froward

pilaster *syn* PILLAR, column

pile *n* 1 *syn* HEAP, stack, mass, bank, shock, cock 2 *syn* BUILDING, edifice, structure

pile *vb, syn* HEAP, stack, mass, bank, shock, cock *rel* gather, collect, assemble, congregate; accumulate, amass, hoard

pilfer *syn* STEAL, filch, purloin, lift, pinch, snitch, swipe, cop *rel* seize, take, grasp, grab, snatch; catch, capture; rob, rifle, loot, plunder

pilgrimage *syn* JOURNEY, voyage, tour, trip, jaunt, excursion, cruise, expedition

pillage *syn* RAVAGE, devastate, waste, sack, despoil, spoliate *rel* plunder, loot, rob, rifle; invade, encroach, trespass; confiscate, arrogate, appropriate, usurp

pillar • a firm upright support for a superstructure *syn* column, pilaster

pilot *syn* GUIDE, steer, lead, engineer *rel* direct, manage, conduct, control; handle, manipulate

pimple *syn* ABSCESS, boil, furuncle, carbuncle, pustule

pinch *vb, syn* STEAL, pilfer, filch, purloin, lift, snitch, swipe, cop

pinch *n, syn* JUNCTURE, pass, exigency, emergency, contingency, strait, crisis *rel* difficulty, hardship, rigor, vicissitude

pinchbeck *syn* COUNTERFEIT, spurious, bogus, fake, sham, pseudo, phony

pinched *syn* HAGGARD, cadaverous, worn, careworn, wasted *rel* gaunt, scrawny, skinny, angular, rawboned, lean

pinch hitter *syn* SUBSTITUTE, supply, locum tenens, alternate, understudy, double, stand-in

pine *syn* LONG, yearn, hanker, hunger, thirst *rel* crave, covet, desire; languish, enervate

pinnacle *syn* SUMMIT, peak, apex, acme, climax, culmination, meridian, zenith, apogee

pious *syn* DEVOUT, religious, pietistic, sanctimonious *rel* holy, sacred, divine; worshiping, adoring, reverencing, venerating, revering; fervent, ardent, fervid, impassioned *ant* impious

piquant *syn* PUNGENT, poignant,

racy, spicy, snappy *rel* incisive, trenchant, cutting, biting, clear-cut *ant* bland

pique *n, syn* OFFENSE, resentment, umbrage, dudgeon, huff *rel* annoyance, vexation, irking, irk; irritation, exasperation, provocation

pique *vb* **1** *syn* PROVOKE, excite, stimulate, quicken, galvanize *rel* stir, rouse, arouse; prick, punch; kindle, ignite **2** *syn* PRIDE, plume, preen

pirate · a robber on the high seas *syn* freebooter, buccaneer, privateer, corsair

pirouette *syn* TURN, revolve, rotate, gyrate, circle, spin, twirl, whirl, wheel, eddy, swirl

pitch **1** *syn* THROW, hurl, fling, cast, toss, sling *rel* heave, lift, raise, hoist; move, drive, impel **2** *syn* PLUNGE, dive *rel* fall, drop, sink; descend; jump, leap, spring

piteous *syn* PITIFUL, pitiable *rel* imploring, supplicating, entreating, beseeching; melancholy, doleful, dolorous, plaintive

pith *syn* SUBSTANCE, purport, gist, burden, core *rel* center, nucleus, heart, focus; spirit, soul

pithy *syn* CONCISE, summary, compendious, terse, succinct, laconic *rel* sententious, pregnant, meaningful, expressive; brief, short

pitiable **1** *syn* PITIFUL, piteous *rel* sad, depressed, dejected, melancholy; forlorn, hopeless, despairing, desperate, despondent **2** *syn* CONTEMPTIBLE, despicable, sorry, scurvy, cheap, beggarly, shabby *rel* miserable, wretched; deplorable, lamentable

pitiful · arousing or deserving pity *syn* piteous, pitiable *rel* touching, moving, pathetic, affecting; tender, compassionate, responsive, sympathetic *ant* cruel

pittance *syn* RATION, allowance, dole

pity *syn* SYMPATHY, compassion, commiseration, condolence, ruth, empathy *rel* sadness, melancholy, dejection, depression; pathos, poignancy; charity, mercy, clemency, lenity

pivotal *syn* CENTRAL, focal *rel* essential, cardinal, vital; important, significant, momentous; capital, principal, chief

placate *syn* PACIFY, appease, mollify, propitiate, conciliate *ant* enrage

place · the portion of space occupied by or chosen for something *syn* position, location, situation, site, spot, station *rel* locality, vicinity, district; region, tract, area, zone; field, territory, province

placid *syn* CALM, tranquil, serene, peaceful, halcyon *rel* imperturbable, nonchalant, cool, collected, composed; gentle, mild, lenient, smooth; steady, equable, even, constant *ant* choleric (*of persons*); ruffled (*of things*)

plague *syn* WORRY, pester, tease, tantalize, harry, harass, annoy *rel* gall, fret, chafe; bait, badger, hector, hound, ride; torment, afflict, try

plain **1** *syn* LEVEL, plane, flat, even, smooth, flush *ant* solid **2** *syn* EVIDENT, clear, distinct, obvious, manifest, patent, apparent, palpable *rel* clear, lucid, perspicuous; explicit, express, definite, specific, categorical *ant* abstruse **3** · free from all ostentation or superficial embellishment *syn* homely, simple, unpretentious *rel* ugly, ill-favored, unsightly, hideous; barren, bare, bald; unembellished, unadorned, undecorated, unornamented, ungarnished *ant* lovely **4** *syn* FRANK, candid, open *rel* forthright, straightforward, aboveboard; blunt, bluff; sincere, unfeigned

plaintive *syn* MELANCHOLY, dolorous, doleful, lugubrious, rueful *rel* pensive, reflective, meditative, thoughtful; lamenting, deploring; pitiful, piteous

plait *syn* WEAVE, knit, crochet, braid, tat

plan *n* · a method devised for making or doing something or achieving an end *syn* design, plot, scheme, project *rel* intention, intent, purpose; idea, conception, notion; chart, map, graph; diagram, outline, sketch

plan *vb* · to formulate a plan for arranging, realizing, or achieving something *syn* design, plot, scheme, project *rel* propose, purpose, intend; sketch, outline, diagram, delineate

plane *syn* LEVEL, plain, flat, even, smooth, flush *ant* solid

planet *syn* EARTH, world, globe

plank *syn* PARAGRAPH, verse, article, clause, count

plastic · susceptible of being modified in form or nature *syn* pliable, pliant, ductile, malleable, adaptable *rel* flexible, supple, elastic, resilient; tractable, amenable

platitude *syn* COMMONPLACE, truism, bromide, cliché *rel* banality, inanity, vapidity, insipidity; mawkishness, sentimentality

plaudits *syn* APPLAUSE, acclamation, acclaim *rel* cheering

plausible · appearing worthy of belief *syn* credible, believable, colorable, specious *rel* smooth, bland, politic, diplomatic, suave; likely, probable, possible; unctuous, fulsome, slick, oily

play *n* **1** · activity engaged in for amusement *syn* sport, disport, frolic, rollick, romp, gambol *rel* enjoyment, delectation, pleasure, delight; amusement, diversion, recreation, entertainment; athletics, sports, games *ant* work **2** *syn* FUN, jest, sport, game *ant* earnest **3** *syn* ROOM, berth, elbowroom, leeway, margin, clearance

play *vb* **1** · to engage in an activity for amusement or recreation *syn* sport, disport, frolic, rollick, romp, gambol *rel* divert, entertain, recreate, amuse; trifle, toy, dally **2** *syn* ACT, impersonate *rel* feign, simulate, counterfeit, assume

player *syn* ACTOR, performer, mummer, mime, mimic, thespian, impersonator, trouper

playful · given to or characterized by play, jests, or tricks *syn* frolicsome, sportive, roguish, waggish, impish, mischievous *rel* gay, sprightly, lively; merry, blithe, jocund, jolly, jovial; mirthful, gleeful, hilarious

plea **1** *syn* APOLOGY, apologia, excuse, pretext, alibi *rel* explanation, justification, rationalization; defense, vindication **2** *syn* PRAYER, suit, petition, appeal *rel* entreaty, supplication, imploring, beseeching, begging

plead *syn* PRAY, sue, petition, appeal *rel* entreat, implore, supplicate, beseech, beg; intercede, mediate, intervene, interpose

pleasant · highly acceptable to the mind or the senses *syn* pleasing, agreeable, grateful, gratifying, welcome *rel* charming, attractive, alluring; soft, gentle, mild, balmy, smooth *ant* unpleasant; distasteful; harsh

please · to give or be a source of pleasure to *syn* gratify, delight, rejoice, gladden, tickle, regale *rel* satisfy, content; beguile, while, wile *ant* displease; anger; vex

pleasing *syn* PLEASANT, agreeable, grateful, gratifying, welcome *rel* winning; charming, attractive, alluring, enchanting *ant* displeasing; repellent

pleasure · the agreeable emotion accompanying the expectation, acquisition, or possession of something good or greatly desired *syn* delight, joy, delectation, enjoyment, fruition *rel* happiness, felicity, bliss; amusement, diversion, recreation, entertainment *ant* displeasure; anger; vexation

plebiscite *syn* MANDATE, initiative, referendum

pledge *n* · something given or held as a sign of another's good faith or intentions *syn* earnest, token, pawn, hostage *rel* guarantee, guaranty, security, surety, bond, bail

pledge *vb, syn* PROMISE, engage, plight, covenant, contract *rel* bind, tie; commit, consign, confide, entrust *ant* abjure

plenary *syn* FULL, complete, replete *ant* limited

plenteous *syn* PLENTIFUL, ample, abundant, copious *rel, ant* see PLENTIFUL

plentiful · more than sufficient without being excessive *syn* plenteous, ample, abundant, copious *rel* fruitful, prolific; sumptuous, opulent, luxurious; profuse, lavish, prodigal *ant* scanty, scant

pleonasm *syn* VERBIAGE, redundancy, tautology, circumlocution, periphrasis

pliable *syn* PLASTIC, pliant, ductile, malleable, adaptable *rel* lithe, limber, supple; elastic, resilient, springy, flexible; compliant, acquiescent *ant* obstinate

pliant *syn* PLASTIC, pliable, ductile, malleable, adaptable *rel* see PLIABLE

plight *vb, syn* PROMISE, engage, pledge, covenant, contract

plight *n, syn* PREDICAMENT, dilemma, quandary, scrape, fix, jam, pickle *rel* situation, condition, state, posture; difficulty, rigor, hardship, vicissitude

plot *n* **1** *syn* PLAN, design, scheme, project *rel* chart, map, graph **2** · a plan secretly devised to accomplish an evil or treacherous end *syn* intrigue, machination, conspiracy, cabal *rel* contrivance, device, contraption; maneuver, stratagem, trick, ruse, artifice **3** *syn* SKETCH, outline, diagram, delineation, draft, tracing, blueprint

plot *vb* **1** *syn* PLAN, design, scheme, project *rel* fashion, fabricate, forge, form, shape, make **2** *syn* SKETCH, outline, diagram, delineate, draft, trace, blueprint *rel* create, invent; chart, map, graph

ploy *syn* TRICK, ruse, stratagem, maneuver, gambit, artifice, wile, feint

pluck *syn* FORTITUDE, grit, backbone, guts, sand *rel* courage, spirit, mettle, resolution, tenacity; hardihood, audacity, temerity

plumb *vb, syn* FATHOM, sound

plumb *adj, syn* VERTICAL, perpendicular

plume *syn* PRIDE, pique, preen *rel* appreciate, value, prize

plump *syn* FLESHY, stout, portly, rotund, chubby, fat, corpulent, obese *ant* cadaverous

plunder *vb, syn* ROB, rifle, loot, burglarize *rel* despoil, spoliate, sack, pillage, ravage; strip, denude, bare

plunder *n, syn* SPOIL, booty, prize, loot, swag *rel* robbery, larceny, theft

plunge · to thrust or cast oneself or something into or as if into deep water *syn* dive, pitch *rel* submerge, immerse, dip; throw, cast, fling, hurl; push, thrust, shove, propel

plutocracy *syn* OLIGARCHY, aristocracy

ply *syn* HANDLE, manipulate, wield, swing *rel* exercise, practice, drill; operate, work, function; manage, direct, control, conduct

pocket *syn* HOLE, hollow, cavity, void, vacuum

poet · a writer of verse *syn* versifier, rhymer, rhymester, poetaster, bard, minstrel, troubadour *rel* maker, creator, author; writer, composer

poetaster *syn* POET, versifier, rhymer, rhymester, bard, minstrel, troubadour

pogrom *syn* MASSACRE, slaughter, butchery, carnage

poignancy *syn* PATHOS, bathos

poignant **1** *syn* PUNGENT, piquant, racy, spicy, snappy *rel* penetrating, piercing, probing; sharp, keen, acute; incisive, trenchant, cutting, biting, crisp *ant* dull **2** *syn* MOVING, touching, pathetic, impressive, affecting *rel* exciting, stimulating, provoking; disturbing, agitating, perturbing

point *syn* DIRECT, aim, level, train, lay *rel* bend; direct, address, devote; steer, pilot, engineer, guide

point of view • a position from which something is considered or evaluated *syn* viewpoint, standpoint, angle, slant *rel* position, stand, attitude

poise *vb, syn* STABILIZE, steady, balance, ballast, trim *rel* support, uphold, back

poise *n* **1** *syn* BALANCE, equilibrium, equipoise, tension *rel* suspending, suspension, hanging; equanimity, composure **2** *syn* TACT, address, savoir faire *rel* self-possession, aplomb, assurance, confidence; calmness, tranquillity, serenity; grace, dignity, elegance

poison • something that harms, interferes with, or destroys the activity, progress, or welfare of something else *syn* venom, virus, toxin, bane

poisonous • having the properties or effects of poison *syn* venomous, virulent, toxic, mephitic, pestilent, pestilential, miasmic, miasmatic, miasmal *rel* mortal, fatal, lethal, deadly; pernicious, baneful, noxious, deleterious, detrimental

poke *vb* • to thrust something into so as to stir up, urge on, or attract attention *syn* prod, nudge, jog *rel* push, shove, thrust; stir, arouse, rouse, awaken; provoke, excite, stimulate, galvanize, quicken

poke *n* • a quick thrust with or as if with the hand *syn* prod, nudge, jog

polite *syn* CIVIL, courteous, courtly, gallant, chivalrous *rel* suave, urbane, diplomatic, politic; thoughtful, considerate, attentive *ant* impolite

politic **1** *syn* EXPEDIENT, advisable *rel* practical, practicable; possible, feasible; shrewd, astute, perspicacious, sagacious **2** *syn* SUAVE, diplomatic, bland, smooth, urbane *rel* unctuous, slick, oily, fulsome; wise, prudent, judicious

politician • a person engaged in the art or science of government *syn* statesman, politico

politico *syn* POLITICIAN, statesman

poll *syn* SHEAR, clip, trim, prune, lop, snip, crop *rel* cut, slash; sever, separate

pollute *syn* CONTAMINATE, defile, taint, attaint *rel* debase, vitiate, corrupt, deprave, pervert; abuse, outrage, mistreat; profane, desecrate, blaspheme

pomp *syn* DISPLAY, parade, array *rel* ceremony, ceremonial, liturgy, ritual, formality, form; ostentatiousness, ostentation, showiness, show

ponder • to consider or examine attentively or deliberately *syn* meditate, muse, ruminate *rel* weigh, consider, contemplate; reflect, deliberate, speculate, think, cogitate

ponderable *syn* PERCEPTIBLE, appreciable, sensible, palpable, tangible *rel* important, significant, momentous, weighty, consequential

ponderous *syn* HEAVY, cumbrous, cumbersome, weighty, hefty *rel* massive, massy, bulky, substantial; clumsy, awkward, maladroit; onerous, burdensome, oppressive, exacting

pool *syn* MONOPOLY, corner, syndicate, trust, cartel

poor **1** · lacking money or material possessions *syn* indigent, needy, destitute, penniless, impecunious, poverty-stricken, necessitous *ant* rich **2** *syn* BAD, wrong *rel* deficient, defective; petty, puny, trivial, trifling, paltry; base, low, vile

poppycock *syn* NONSENSE, twaddle, drivel, bunk, balderdash, gobbledygook, trash, rot, bull

popular *syn* COMMON, ordinary, familiar, vulgar *rel* general, universal, generic, common; accepted, received, admitted; prevalent, prevailing, current *ant* unpopular; esoteric

port *n, syn* HARBOR, haven

port *n, syn* BEARING, presence, deportment, demeanor, mien

portal *syn* DOOR, gate, doorway, gateway, postern

portend *syn* FORETELL, presage, augur, prognosticate, predict, forecast, prophesy, forebode *rel* betoken, indicate, bespeak, attest; signify, import, mean, denote

portent *syn* FORETOKEN, presage, prognostic, omen, augury *rel* presentiment, foreboding, misgiving, apprehension; forewarning, warning, cautioning, caution

portentous *syn* OMINOUS, unpropitious, inauspicious, fateful *rel* threatening, menacing; prodigious, monstrous; prophesying, prophetic, presaging, foreboding, predicting, foretelling

portion *n* **1** *syn* PART, piece, detail, member, division, section, segment, sector, fraction, fragment, parcel *rel* quantity, amount, sum; apportionment, rationing, ration; allotment, assignment, allocation **2** *syn* FATE, destiny, lot, doom *rel* distribution, dispensation, division, dealing; fortune, hap, chance, luck

portion *vb, syn* APPORTION, parcel, ration, prorate *rel* allot, assign, allocate; distribute, dispense, divide, deal

portly *syn* FLESHY, stout, plump, rotund, chubby, fat, corpulent, obese *rel* burly, husky, brawny, muscular

portray *syn* REPRESENT, depict, delineate, picture, limn *rel* image, photograph; describe, relate, narrate; reproduce, copy, duplicate

pose *vb, syn* PROPOSE, propound *rel* ask, question, query; puzzle, confound; baffle, frustrate

pose *n* **1** · an adopted way of speaking or behaving *syn* air, affectation, mannerism **2** *syn* POSTURE, attitude

posit *vb, syn* PRESUPPOSE, presume, assume, postulate, premise

posit *n, syn* ASSUMPTION, presupposition, presumption, postulate, premise

position **1** · a firmly held point of view or way of regarding something *syn* stand, attitude *rel* point of view, viewpoint, standpoint, angle, slant **2** *syn* PLACE, location, situation, site, spot, station

positive *syn* SURE, certain, cocksure *rel* confident, assured, sanguine; dogmatic, doctrinaire, oracular, dictatorial *ant* doubtful

possess *syn* HAVE, own, enjoy, hold *rel* control, manage, direct, conduct; retain, keep, reserve, withhold

possessions · all the items that taken together constitute a person's or group's property or wealth *syn* belongings, effects, means, resources, assets

possible **1** · capable of being realized *syn* practicable, feasible *rel* practical; expedient, advisable **2** *syn* PROBABLE, likely *rel* credible, believable, colorable, plausible; potential, dormant, latent

posterior · situated at or toward the back *syn* rear, hind, hinder, after, back *ant* anterior

posterity *syn* OFFSPRING, young, progeny, issue, descendant *ant* ancestry

postern *syn* DOOR, gate, gateway, doorway, portal

postpone *syn* DEFER, suspend, stay, intermit *rel* delay, retard, slow, slacken

postulant *syn* NOVICE, novitiate, probationer, neophyte, apprentice

postulate *vb, syn* PRESUPPOSE, presume, assume, premise, posit *rel* affirm, aver, predicate, assert

postulate *n, syn* ASSUMPTION, presupposition, presumption, premise, posit *rel* principle, axiom, theorem, fundamental, law; theory, hypothesis

posture **1** · the position or bearing of the body *syn* attitude, pose *rel* bearing, deportment, mien **2** *syn* STATE, situation, condition, mode, status *rel* position, stand, attitude; readiness, quickness, promptness

pot *syn* BET, wager, stake, ante

potent *syn* POWERFUL, puissant, forceful, forcible *rel* vigorous, energetic, strenuous, lusty; effective, efficacious, effectual; strong, sturdy, tenacious *ant* impotent

potential *syn* LATENT, dormant, quiescent, abeyant *ant* active, actual

pother *syn* STIR, flurry, fuss, ado, bustle *rel* haste, hurry, speed, dispatch; agitation, upset, perturbation, disturbance

pouch *syn* BAG, sack

pound *syn* BEAT, pummel, buffet, baste, belabor, thrash *rel* strike, hit, smite, slug; batter, mutilate, maim

pour · to send forth or come forth abundantly *syn* stream, gush, sluice *rel* emerge, appear; flow, issue, proceed, spring

poverty · the state of one with insufficient resources *syn* indigence, penury, want, destitution, privation *rel* necessity, need, exigency; strait, pass, pinch, juncture *ant* riches

poverty-stricken *syn* POOR, indigent, needy, destitute, penniless, impecunious, necessitous

power **1** · the ability to exert effort *syn* force, energy, strength, might, puissance *rel* ability, capacity, capability; gift, genius, talent, faculty; qualification, competence *ant* impotence **2** · the ability of a living being to perform in a given way or a capacity for a particular kind of performance *syn* faculty, function **3** · the right to govern or rule or determine *syn* authority, jurisdiction, control, command, sway, dominion *rel* right, privilege, prerogative, birthright; management, direction; ascendancy, supremacy

powerful · having or manifesting power to effect great or striking results *syn* potent, puissant, forceful, forcible *rel* able, capable, competent; efficacious, effectual, effective, efficient; vigorous, energetic, strenuous *ant* powerless; inefficacious

powerless · unable to effect one's purpose, intention, or end *syn* impotent *rel* inert, inactive, passive, supine; feeble, weak, infirm, decrepit *ant* powerful; efficacious

practicable *syn* POSSIBLE, feasible *rel* operating, operable, working, workable, functioning *ant* impracticable

practically *syn* VIRTUALLY, morally

practice *vb* · to perform or cause one to perform an act or series of acts repeatedly in order to master or strengthen a skill or ability *syn* exercise, drill *rel* perform, execute, fulfill; follow, pursue; repeat, iterate

practice *n* **1** *syn* HABIT, habitude, usage, custom, use, wont *rel* procedure, process, proceeding; method, system, way, fashion, mode, manner **2** • repeated activity or exertion in order to develop or improve a strength or skill *syn* exercise, drill *rel* use, utility, usefulness; usage, form, convention, convenance; pursuit, calling, work *ant* theory; precept

praise • to express approval of or esteem for *syn* laud, acclaim, extol, eulogize *rel* commend, applaud, compliment; exalt, magnify, aggrandize *ant* blame

prank • a playful, often a mischievous, act or trick *syn* caper, antic, monkeyshine, dido *rel* frolic, gambol, rollick, sport, play; levity, lightness, frivolity; vagary, caprice, freak, fancy, whim, whimsy, conceit

prate *syn* CHAT, chatter, gab, patter, prattle, babble, gabble, jabber, gibber

prattle *syn* CHAT, chatter, patter, prate, gab, babble, gabble, jabber, gibber

pray • to request or make a request for in a humble, beseeching manner *syn* plead, petition, appeal, sue *rel* supplicate, entreat, beseech, implore, beg

prayer • an earnest and usu. a formal request for something *syn* suit, plea, petition, appeal *rel* supplication, entreaty, beseeching, imploring, begging; worship, adoration

preamble *syn* INTRODUCTION, prologue, prelude, preface, foreword, exordium

precarious *syn* DANGEROUS, hazardous, perilous, risky *rel* doubtful, dubious, questionable; distrustful, mistrustful; chance, chancy, haphazard, random

precedence *syn* PRIORITY *rel* leading, lead, guiding; guide; antecedence, foregoing

precedent *syn* PRECEDING, antecedent, foregoing, previous, prior, former, anterior

preceding • being before, esp. in time or in arrangement *syn* antecedent, precedent, foregoing, previous, prior, former, anterior *ant* following

precept *syn* LAW, rule, canon, regulation, statute, ordinance *rel* principle, fundamental, axiom; doctrine, tenet, dogma; injunction, behest, bidding, command *ant* practice; counsel

precious *syn* COSTLY, expensive, dear, valuable, invaluable, priceless *rel* choice, exquisite, recherché, rare; valued, prized, appreciated, cherished

precipitate *vb, syn* SPEED, accelerate, quicken, hasten, hurry *rel* drive, impel, move; force, compel, coerce, constrain

precipitate *n, syn* DEPOSIT, sediment, dregs, lees, grounds

precipitate *adj* • showing undue haste or unexpectedness *syn* headlong, abrupt, impetuous, hasty, sudden *rel* headstrong, willful, refractory *ant* deliberate

precipitous *syn* STEEP, abrupt, sheer *rel* soaring, towering, rocketing, ascending, rising

précis *syn* COMPENDIUM, sketch, aperçu, survey, syllabus, digest, pandect

precise *syn* CORRECT, exact, accurate, nice, right *rel* definite, express, explicit; strict, rigid, rigorous, stringent *ant* loose

preciseness *syn* PRECISION

precision • the quality or character of what is precise *syn* preciseness

preclude *syn* PREVENT, obviate, avert, ward *rel* hinder, obstruct, impede, block, bar; stop, discontinue, quit, cease; exclude, eliminate, shut out, debar

precocious *syn* PREMATURE, untimely, forward, advanced *rel* immature, unmatured, unripe *ant* backward

precursor *syn* FORERUNNER, harbinger, herald *rel* sign, mark, token, symptom; antecedent, determinant, cause, reason

predicament · a difficult, perplexing, or trying situation *syn* dilemma, quandary, plight, scrape, fix, jam, pickle *rel* state, situation, condition, posture; pass, pinch, strait, emergency, exigency, juncture

predicate *syn* ASSERT, affirm, declare, profess, aver, protest, avouch, avow, warrant

predict *syn* FORETELL, forecast, prophesy, prognosticate, augur, presage, portend, forebode *rel* foresee, foreknow, divine; warn, forewarn, caution; surmise, conjecture, guess

predilection · an attitude of mind that predisposes one to favor something *syn* partiality, prepossession, prejudice, bias *rel* leaning, propensity, proclivity, flair; bent, turn, knack, aptitude, gift *ant* aversion

predispose *syn* INCLINE, dispose, bias *rel* influence, sway, affect, touch, impress, strike

predominant *syn* DOMINANT, paramount, preponderant, preponderating, sovereign *rel* controlling, directing, conducting, managing; prevailing, prevalent; chief, principal, leading, main, foremost

preeminent *syn* SUPREME, surpassing, transcendent, superlative, peerless, incomparable *rel* dominant, predominant, paramount; excelling, excellent, outdoing, outstripping; consummate, finished

preempt *syn* ARROGATE, usurp, appropriate, confiscate *rel* take, seize, grasp, grab; exclude, eliminate, shut out, debar

preen *syn* PRIDE, plume, pique *rel* congratulate, felicitate

preface *syn* INTRODUCTION, prologue, prelude, foreword, exordium, preamble

prefatory *syn* PRELIMINARY, introductory, preparatory *rel* preparing, fitting, readying

prefer **1** *syn* CHOOSE, select, elect, opt, pick, cull, single *rel* accept, receive, admit, take; approve, endorse, sanction; favor, oblige, accommodate **2** *syn* OFFER, proffer, tender, present

preferable *syn* BETTER, superior

preference *syn* CHOICE, selection, election, option, alternative *rel* predilection, prepossession, partiality

preferment *syn* ADVANCEMENT, promotion, elevation *rel* advance, progress; rising, rise, ascending, ascent

pregnant *syn* EXPRESSIVE, meaningful, significant, eloquent, sententious *rel* weighty, momentous, consequential, significant, important

prejudice *syn* PREDILECTION, bias, partiality, prepossession *rel* predisposition, disposition, inclination; leaning, penchant

preliminary · serving to make ready the way for something that follows *syn* introductory, preparatory, prefatory *rel* primary, primal; elementary, elemental; basic, fundamental

prelude *syn* INTRODUCTION, prologue, preface, foreword, exordium, preamble

premature · unduly early in coming, happening, or developing *syn* untimely, forward, advanced, precocious *rel* immature, unmatured, unripe, unmellow; abortive, fruitless; precipitate, hasty, sudden, abrupt *ant* matured

premeditated *syn* DELIBERATE, considered, advised, designed, studied *rel* intended, purposed, meant; voluntary, intentional, willful *ant* unpremeditated; casual, accidental

premise *n*, *syn* ASSUMPTION, postulate, posit, presupposition, presumption *rel* ground, reason; proposition, proposal

premise *vb, syn* PRESUPPOSE, postulate, posit, presume, assume

premium · something that is offered or given for some service or attainment *syn* prize, award, reward, meed, guerdon, bounty, bonus *rel* gift, present, gratuity, favor; enhancement, intensification, heightening

preoccupied *syn* ABSTRACTED, absent, absentminded, distraught *rel* intent, engrossed, absorbed; forgetful, oblivious, unmindful

preparatory *syn* PRELIMINARY, introductory, prefatory *rel* fitting, preparing, qualifying, readying, conditioning

prepare · to make ready beforehand usu. for some purpose, use, or activity *syn* fit, qualify, condition, ready *rel* provide, supply, furnish; endow, endue, dower; equip, outfit; predispose, dispose, incline

preponderant, preponderating *syn* DOMINANT, predominant, paramount, sovereign *rel* supreme, preeminent, transcendent, surpassing; outstanding, salient, signal

prepossession *syn* PREDILECTION, partiality, prejudice, bias *rel* bent, turn, knack, aptitude, gift; leaning, penchant; predisposition, inclination

preposterous *syn* FOOLISH, absurd, silly *rel* irrational, unreasonable; bizarre, grotesque, fantastic

prerequisite *syn* REQUIREMENT, requisite *rel* necessity, need, exigency

prerogative *syn* RIGHT, privilege, perquisite, appanage, birthright *rel* immunity, exemption; claim, title; freedom, license, liberty

presage *n, syn* FORETOKEN, prognostic, omen, augury, portent *rel* sign, symptom, mark, token; forewarning, warning

presage *vb, syn* FORETELL, augur, portend, forebode, prognosticate, predict, forecast, prophesy *rel* indicate, betoken, bespeak; signify, import, denote, mean

prescribe **1** *syn* DICTATE, ordain, decree, impose *rel* order, command, enjoin, bid; exact, demand, require **2** · to fix arbitrarily or authoritatively for the sake of order or of a clear understanding *syn* assign, define *rel* set, settle, fix, establish; direct, enjoin, instruct, order, command

prescription *syn* RECEIPT, recipe

presence *syn* BEARING, deportment, demeanor, mien, port *rel* personality, individuality, disposition; aspect, appearance, look

present *n, syn* GIFT, gratuity, favor, boon, largess *rel* contribution, donation, benefaction; grant, subvention, appropriation

present *vb* **1** *syn* GIVE, bestow, confer, donate, afford *rel* grant, award, accord **2** *syn* OFFER, tender, proffer, prefer *rel* exhibit, display, parade, show; advance, adduce, allege, cite

presentiment *syn* APPREHENSION, misgiving, foreboding *rel* fear, dread, alarm, terror; foretaste, anticipation, prospect; disquieting, disquietude, discomposing, discomposure, disturbance, perturbation

presently · without undue time lapse *syn* shortly, soon, directly

preserve *syn* SAVE, conserve *rel* rescue, deliver, redeem, ransom; protect, guard, safeguard, defend

press *n, syn* CROWD, throng, crush, mob, rout, horde *rel* multitude, army, host, legion

press *vb* · to act upon through steady pushing or thrusting force exerted in contact *syn* bear, bear down, squeeze, crowd, jam *rel* push, thrust, propel, shove; drive, impel, move; pack, cram, stuff, ram

pressing · demanding or claiming esp. immediate attention *syn* urgent, imperative, crying, importunate, insistent, exigent, instant *rel* immediate, direct; demanding, claiming, requiring, exacting; compelling, constraining, forcing, obliging

pressure *syn* STRESS, strain, tension

prestige *syn* INFLUENCE, authority, weight, credit *rel* ascendancy, supremacy, power, sway, dominion; reputation, repute, honor, glory, fame

presume *syn* PRESUPPOSE, postulate, premise, posit, assume *rel* surmise, conjecture; deduce, infer, judge, gather, conclude

presumption *syn* ASSUMPTION, presupposition, postulate, premise, posit *rel* view, opinion, conviction, belief; conjecture, surmise

presumptuous *syn* CONFIDENT, assured, sanguine, sure *rel* self-confident, self-assured, self-possessed; presuming, assuming; positive, cocksure, certain, sure; arrogant, insolent, overbearing, proud

presuppose · to take something for granted or as true or existent esp. as a basis for action or reasoning *syn* presume, assume, postulate, premise, posit *rel* surmise, conjecture, guess; infer, deduce, gather, judge

presupposition *syn* ASSUMPTION, presumption, postulate, premise, posit *rel* surmise, conjecture, guess; inference, deduction, judgment; belief, conviction, opinion, view

pretend *syn* ASSUME, affect, simulate, feign, counterfeit, sham *rel* disguise, dissemble, cloak, mask, camouflage; deceive, delude, mislead, beguile

pretense **1** *syn* CLAIM, pretension, title *rel* plea, pretext, excuse, apology, apologia; right, birthright, privilege **2** · the offering of something false as real or true *syn* pretension, make-believe *rel* humbug, fake, sham, fraud, deceit, deception, imposture; affectation, pose, air, mannerism

pretension **1** *syn* CLAIM, title, pretense *rel* right, privilege, prerogative; assertion, affirmation, declaration, protestation **2** *syn* PRETENSE, make-believe *rel* hypocrisy, sanctimony, cant; dissimulation, duplicity, guile, deceit **3** *syn* AMBITION, aspiration *rel* hoping, hope, expectation; dream, vision, fancy

pretentious **1** *syn* SHOWY, ostentatious *rel* gaudy, garish, flashy; ornate, flamboyant, florid, baroque, rococo *ant* unpretentious **2** *syn* AMBITIOUS, utopian *rel* aiming, aspiring, panting; conspicuous, striking, arresting, noticeable

preternatural *syn* SUPERNATURAL, supranatural, miraculous, superhuman *rel* unnatural, anomalous, irregular; abnormal, atypical; outstanding, remarkable, salient, noticeable; exceptional

pretext *syn* APOLOGY, excuse, plea, alibi, apologia *rel* ruse, trick, maneuver, stratagem; deception; justification, vindication, defending, defense

pretty *syn* BEAUTIFUL, bonny, comely, fair, lovely, handsome, good-looking, beauteous, pulchritudinous *rel* charming, attractive, alluring; dainty, delicate, exquisite, choice

prevail *syn* INDUCE, persuade, get *rel* move, actuate, drive, impel; influence, affect, impress, sway

prevailing · general (as in circulation, acceptance, or use) in a given place or at a given time *syn* prevalent, rife, current *rel* dominant, predominant, preponderant; common, ordinary, familiar; general, universal

prevalent *syn* PREVAILING, rife, current *rel* common, ordinary, familiar; pervading, impregnating, saturating; usual, wonted, accustomed, customary

prevaricate *syn* LIE, equivocate, palter, fib *rel* evade, elude, escape; misrepresent, falsify, belie, garble

prevent **1** · to deal with beforehand *syn* anticipate, forestall *rel* frustrate, thwart, foil, baffle, balk; arrest, check, interrupt; avoid, shun, eschew, evade, escape **2** · to stop from advancing or occurring *syn* preclude, obviate, avert, ward *rel* hinder, impede, obstruct, block, bar, dam; debar, shut out, exclude; prohibit, forbid, interdict, inhibit *ant* permit

previous *syn* PRECEDING, foregoing, prior, antecedent, precedent, former, anterior *ant* subsequent; consequent

prey *syn* VICTIM, quarry *rel* spoil, booty, prize

price · the quantity of one thing that is exchanged or demanded in barter or sale for another *syn* charge, cost, expense

priceless *syn* COSTLY, invaluable, precious, expensive, dear, valuable *rel* cherished, treasured, prized, valued

prick **1** *syn* PERFORATE, punch, puncture, bore, drill *rel* enter, pierce, probe, penetrate; cut, slit, slash **2** *syn* URGE, egg, exhort, goad, spur, prod, sic *rel* stimulate, excite, pique, provoke; activate, actuate, motivate; compel, constrain, force

pride *n* · an attitude of inordinate self-esteem or superiority *syn* vanity, vainglory *rel* arrogance, haughtiness, superciliousness, disdainfulness, disdain, insolence; complacency, smugness, priggishness; self-esteem, self-love, egotism, egoism, conceit *ant* humility; shame

pride *vb* · to congratulate oneself because of something one is, has, or has done or achieved *syn* plume, pique, preen *rel* boast, brag, vaunt, crow, gasconade; congratulate, felicitate

priggish **1** *syn* COMPLACENT, smug, self-complacent, self-satisfied *rel* righteous, ethical, moral; conceited, egotistic, self-esteeming, self-loving **2** *syn* PRIM, prissy, prudish, puritanical, straitlaced, stuffy *rel* see PRIGGISH 1

prim · excessively concerned with what one regards as proper or right *syn* priggish, prissy, prudish, puritanical, straitlaced, stuffy *rel* precise, correct, nice; decorous, proper; stiff, rigid, wooden

primal *syn* PRIMARY, primordial, primitive, pristine, primeval, prime *rel* ultimate, absolute, categorical; original, fresh, new

primary · first in some respect (as order, character, or importance) *syn* primal, primordial, primitive, pristine, primeval, prime *rel* initiating, initial, beginning, commencing, starting; elemental, elementary; basic, fundamental, radical; chief, leading, principal

prime *syn* PRIMARY, primal, primordial, primitive, pristine, primeval *rel* chief, leading, principal, main; choice, exquisite, recherché

prime mover *syn* ORIGIN, source, provenance, provenience, inception, root

primeval *syn* PRIMARY, pristine, primitive, primordial, primal, prime *rel* aboriginal, native, indigenous, autochthonous; original, new

primitive **1** *syn* PRIMARY, primal, primordial, pristine, primeval, prime *rel* fundamental, basic, radical; elemental, elementary; aboriginal, native **2** *syn* ELEMENTAL, basic, elementary, essential, fundamental, underlying

primordial 1 *syn* PRIMARY, primeval, pristine, primitive, primal, prime 2 *syn* INITIAL, original

princely *syn* KINGLY, regal, royal, queenly, imperial *rel* luxurious, sumptuous, opulent; munificent, bountiful, bounteous, openhanded, liberal

principal *syn* CHIEF, main, leading, foremost, capital *rel* dominant, predominant, paramount; vital, cardinal, fundamental, essential; preeminent, supreme, superlative

principally *syn* LARGELY, mainly, chiefly, mostly, greatly, generally

principle • a comprehensive and fundamental rule, doctrine, or assumption *syn* axiom, fundamental, law, theorem *rel* basis, foundation, ground; law, rule, canon, precept; form, usage, convention

print *syn* IMPRESSION, impress, imprint, stamp *rel* mark, token, sign; trace, vestige

printing *syn* EDITION, impression, reprinting, reissue

prior *syn* PRECEDING, previous, foregoing, precedent, anterior, former, antecedent *rel* ahead, before, forward

priority • the act, the fact, or the right of preceding another *syn* precedence *rel* ordering, order, arrangement; ascendancy, supremacy; preeminence, transcendence

priory *syn* CLOISTER, monastery, nunnery, convent, abbey

prismatic • marked by or displaying a variety of colors *syn* iridescent, opalescent, opaline

prisoner • one who is deprived of liberty and kept under involuntary restraint *syn* captive

prissy *syn* PRIM, priggish, prudish, puritanical, straitlaced, stuffy *rel* womanish, effeminate, ladylike, female; finicky, fastidious, nice, squeamish; scrupulous, punctilious, meticulous, careful

pristine *syn* PRIMARY, primeval, primordial, primitive, primal, prime *rel* original, fresh, new

privateer *syn* PIRATE, freebooter, buccaneer, corsair

privation 1 *syn* LACK, want, dearth, absence, defect *rel* negation, nullification, annulling, abrogation 2 *syn* POVERTY, want, destitution, indigence, penury *rel* depletion, draining, exhaustion, impoverishment; need, necessity, exigency, pinch, strait

privilege *syn* RIGHT, prerogative, birthright, perquisite, appanage *rel* concession, allowance; favor, boon, gift; claim, title

prize *n*, *syn* PREMIUM, award, reward, meed, guerdon, bounty, bonus *rel* recompensing, recompense, compensation; winning, winnings *ant* forfeit

prize *vb*, *syn* APPRECIATE, value, treasure, cherish *rel* esteem, respect, admire, regard; estimate, evaluate, assess, assay, rate

prize *n*, *syn* SPOIL, booty, plunder, loot, swag

probable • almost sure to be or to become true or real *syn* possible, likely *rel* credible, believable, colorable, plausible; reasonable, rational *ant* certain; improbable

probationer *syn* NOVICE, novitiate, apprentice, postulant, neophyte

probe *n*, *syn* INQUIRY, investigation, inquisition, inquest, research

probe *vb*, *syn* ENTER, pierce, penetrate *rel* examine, inspect, scrutinize; prove, try, test

probity *syn* HONESTY, honor, integrity *rel* uprightness, justness, conscientiousness, scrupulousness; truth, veracity; rectitude, goodness, virtue

problem *syn* MYSTERY, enigma, fiddle, puzzle, conundrum *rel* perplexity, mystification, bewilderment, distraction; predicament, dilemma, plight, quandary *ant* solution

problematic *syn* DOUBTFUL, dubious, questionable *rel* ambiguous, equivocal, obscure, vague, cryptic, enigmatic; uncertain, suspicious, mistrustful

procedure *syn* PROCESS, proceeding *rel* ordering, order, arrangement; method, system, manner, way; conducting, conduct, management

proceed *syn* SPRING, issue, emanate, stem, flow, derive, arise, rise, originate *rel* follow, succeed, ensue; come, arrive

proceeding *syn* PROCESS, procedure *rel* action, act, deed; affair, business, concern; operation, functioning, working

process · the series of actions, operations, or motions involved in the accomplishment of an end *syn* procedure, proceeding *rel* progress, advance; conducting, conduct, management, controlling, control, direction; performance, execution, accomplishment, fulfillment

procession · a body (as of persons and vehicles) moving along in a usu. ceremonial order *syn* parade, cortege, cavalcade, motorcade *rel* succession, sequence, train; pomp, array, display

proclaim *syn* DECLARE, announce, publish, advertise, promulgate, broadcast *rel* reveal, disclose, discover, divulge, tell; voice, utter, vent, ventilate, express; inform, apprise

proclamation *syn* DECLARATION, announcement, publication, advertisement, promulgation, broadcasting

proclivity *syn* LEANING, propensity, penchant, flair *rel* knack, aptitude, gift, bent, turn; inclination, disposition, predisposition; predilection, prepossession, prejudice, bias

procrastinate *syn* DELAY, lag, dawdle, loiter *rel* defer, suspend, stay, postpone; protract, prolong, extend *ant* hasten, hurry

procreate *syn* GENERATE, engender, beget, get, sire, breed, propagate, reproduce

procure *syn* GET, obtain, secure, acquire, gain, win *rel* negotiate, arrange, concert; reach, compass, achieve, attain

prod *vb* **1** *syn* POKE, nudge, jog *rel* prick, punch, bore, perforate; goad, spur; pierce, penetrate **2** *syn* URGE, egg, exhort, goad, spur, prick, sic *rel* incite, instigate; stimulate, excite, pique, provoke

prod *n, syn* POKE, nudge, jog *rel* stimulus, stimulant, incitement, impetus

prodigal *adj, syn* PROFUSE, lavish, exuberant, luxuriant, lush *rel* extravagant, exorbitant, immoderate, excessive; abundant, plentiful, plenteous, ample, copious; supererogatory, uncalled-for, gratuitous *ant* parsimonious; frugal

prodigal *n, syn* SPENDTHRIFT, profligate, waster, wastrel *rel* spender, expender, disburser

prodigious *syn* MONSTROUS, tremendous, stupendous, monumental *rel* enormous, immense, huge, vast, gigantic, mammoth, colossal; amazing, astounding, flabbergasting

prodigy *syn* WONDER, marvel, miracle, phenomenon *rel* abnormality; monstrosity; anomaly, paradox

produce *vb, syn* BEAR, yield, turn out *rel* generate, breed, propagate; make, form, shape, fabricate, manufacture; create, invent

produce *n, syn* PRODUCT, production

product **1** *syn* WORK, production, opus, artifact *rel* forming, form, fabrication, manufacturing, manufacture; article, object, thing **2** · something produced by physical labor or intellectual effort *syn* production, produce

production 1 *syn* WORK, product, opus, artifact *rel* execution, fulfillment, performance; effort, exertion 2 *syn* PRODUCT, produce

profanation · a violation or a misuse of something normally held sacred *syn* desecration, sacrilege, blasphemy *rel* defilement, pollution, contamination; debasement, vitiation, corruption, perversion; violation, transgression, trespass, breach

profane 1 · not concerned with religion or religious purposes *syn* secular, lay, temporal *rel* worldly, mundane, earthly, terrestrial *ant* sacred 2 *syn* IMPIOUS, blasphemous, sacrilegious *rel* foul, filthy, dirty, nasty; ungodly, godless, irreligious; iniquitous, nefarious, villainous, vicious

profanity *syn* BLASPHEMY, cursing, swearing *rel* imprecation, curse, malediction; execration, objurgation, damning

profess *syn* ASSERT, declare, affirm, aver, protest, avouch, avow, predicate, warrant *rel* allege, adduce, advance

profession *syn* TRADE, art, handicraft, craft

proffer *syn* OFFER, tender, present, prefer *rel* propose, design, intend; confer, bestow, give

proficient · having great knowledge and experience in a trade or profession *syn* adept, skilled, skillful, expert, masterly *rel* efficient, effectual, effective; capable, able, competent, qualified; finished, accomplished, consummate; practiced, drilled, exercised

profile *syn* OUTLINE, contour, silhouette, skyline

profit *n, syn* USE, service, advantage, account, avail *rel* reward, award, meed, guerdon, premium; gaining, gain, winning

profit *vb, syn* BENEFIT, avail *rel* get, gain, win; advance, progress

profitable 1 *syn* BENEFICIAL, advantageous *rel* favorable, auspicious, propitious; expedient, advisable, politic *ant* unprofitable 2 *syn* PAYING, gainful, remunerative, lucrative *rel* fruitful; compensating, recompensing, repaying; valuable, precious, costly

profligate *adj, syn* ABANDONED, dissolute, reprobate *rel* debauched, corrupted, depraved, debased, perverted; degenerate, corrupt, vicious; loose, relaxed, slack, lax

profligate *n, syn* SPENDTHRIFT, prodigal, wastrel, waster *rel* debauchee, pervert, corrupter; libertine, lecher

profound *syn* DEEP, abysmal *rel* penetrating, probing, piercing; scrutinizing, inspecting, examining *ant* shallow

profuse · giving or given out in great abundance *syn* lavish, prodigal, luxuriant, lush, exuberant *rel* copious, abundant, plentiful; excessive, immoderate, extravagant; liberal, bountiful, bounteous, openhanded, munificent, generous *ant* spare, scanty, scant

progenitor *syn* ANCESTOR, forefather, forebear *ant* progeny

progeny *syn* OFFSPRING, young, issue, descendant, posterity *ant* progenitor

prognostic *syn* FORETOKEN, presage, omen, augury, portent *rel* indication, betokening, bespeaking; symptom, sign, mark, token

prognosticate *syn* FORETELL, predict, forecast, prophesy, augur, presage, portend, forebode *rel* indicate, betoken, bespeak; foresee, foreknow, apprehend, divine, anticipate

program · a formulated plan listing things to be done or to take place esp. in chronological order *syn* schedule, timetable, agenda

progress *n* 1 *syn* ADVANCE *rel*

improvement, betterment; headway, impetus **2** • a movement forward (as in time or space) *syn* progression

progress *vb, syn* ADVANCE *rel* move, drive, impel; further, forward, promote, advance; develop, mature *ant* retrogress

progression **1** *syn* SUCCESSION, series, sequence, chain, train, string **2** *syn* PROGRESS

progressive *syn* LIBERAL, advanced, radical *ant* reactionary

prohibit *syn* FORBID, inhibit, enjoin, interdict, ban *rel* prevent, preclude, obviate; debar, shut out, exclude; hinder, impede, obstruct; restrain, curb, check *ant* permit

project *n, syn* PLAN, scheme, design, plot *rel* sketch, delineation, draft, outline, diagram; device, contrivance

project *vb* **1** *syn* PLAN, scheme, design, plot *rel* propose, purpose, intend; sketch, outline, diagram, delineate **2** *syn* BULGE, jut, stick out, protrude, overhang, beetle *rel* extend, prolong, lengthen; swell, distend, expand

projection • an extension beyond the normal line or surface *syn* protrusion, protuberance, bulge

prolific *syn* FERTILE, fruitful, fecund *rel* teeming, swarming, abounding; generating, breeding, propagating, reproducing, reproductive *ant* barren, unfruitful

prolificacy *syn* FERTILITY, fruitfulness, fecundity *ant* barrenness, unfruitfulness

prolix *syn* WORDY, verbose, diffuse, redundant *rel* tedious, irksome, tiresome, wearisome; prolonged, protracted; pleonastic, circumlocutory, redundant, tautological

prologue *syn* INTRODUCTION, prelude, preface, foreword, exordium, preamble

prolong *syn* EXTEND, protract, lengthen, elongate *rel* continue, last, persist, endure; increase, augment, enlarge; expand, amplify *ant* curtail

prominent *syn* NOTICEABLE, remarkable, conspicuous, salient, outstanding, signal, striking, arresting *rel* chief, leading, main, principal; important, significant

promiscuous *syn* MISCELLANEOUS, heterogeneous, motley *rel* mixed, mingled, blended, merged; random, haphazard, desultory, casual; indiscriminate, wholesale, sweeping; licentious, lewd, wanton, lascivious

promise • to give one's word to do, bring about, or provide *syn* engage, pledge, plight, covenant, contract *rel* agree, consent, assent, accede; assure, ensure, insure

promote *syn* ADVANCE, forward, further *rel* help, aid, assist; speed, quicken, hasten, hurry *ant* impede

promotion **1** *syn* ADVANCEMENT, preferment, elevation *rel* progress, progression; exaltation, magnifying, aggrandizement *ant* demotion **2** *syn* PUBLICITY, ballyhoo, propaganda *rel* advertisement, promulgation, broadcasting

prompt *syn* QUICK, ready, apt *rel* alert, wide-awake, vigilant, watchful; expeditious, speedy, swift, fast; trained, disciplined; eager, keen, avid

promulgate *syn* DECLARE, proclaim, announce, publish, advertise, broadcast *rel* reveal, disclose, divulge, discover; profess, affirm, aver, avow, avouch, assert; communicate, impart

promulgation *syn* DECLARATION, proclamation, announcement, publication, advertisement, broadcasting

prone **1** *syn* LIABLE, subject, exposed, open, susceptible, sensitive *rel* inclined, predisposed, disposed; addicted, habituated, accustomed **2** • lying down *syn* supine, prostrate, recumbent, couchant, dormant *rel* flat, level; groveling, wallowing, weltering; *ant* erect

pronounce *syn* ARTICULATE, enunciate

proof **1** *syn* REASON, ground, argument *rel* demonstration, trial, test; corroboration, confirmation, substantiation, verification **2** • something that serves as evidence compelling the acceptance of a truth or fact *syn* demonstration, test, trial *ant* disproof

prop *syn* SUPPORT, sustain, bolster, buttress, brace *rel* uphold, back; hoist, heave, boost, lift

propaganda *syn* PUBLICITY, ballyhoo, promotion *rel* propagation, engendering, generating; spread, stretch, expanse; inculcation, instillment, implanting

propagate **1** *syn* GENERATE, engender, breed, beget, procreate, sire, reproduce *rel* increase, multiply, augment; continue, persist; extend, lengthen, prolong **2** *syn* SPREAD, circulate, disseminate, diffuse, radiate *rel* scatter, disperse, dissipate; distribute, dispense; teach, instruct, educate; communicate, impart; inculcate, instill, implant

propel *syn* PUSH, shove, thrust *rel* move, drive, impel; force, compel, constrain, oblige

propensity *syn* LEANING, proclivity, penchant, flair *rel* predilection, prejudice, bias, prepossession; gift, aptitude, bent, turn, knack; predisposition, disposition, inclination *ant* antipathy

proper **1** *syn* FIT, meet, appropriate, fitting, apt, happy, felicitous, suitable *rel* congruous, congenial, compatible, consonant; correct, nice, right; due, rightful, condign *ant* improper **2** *syn* DECOROUS, seemly, decent, nice *rel* formal, conventional, ceremonious, ceremonial

property *syn* QUALITY, character, attribute, accident *rel* peculiarity, individuality, characteristic

prophecy *syn* REVELATION, vision, apocalypse *rel* communication, impartation; inspiration

prophesy *syn* FORETELL, predict, forecast, prognosticate, augur, presage, portend, forebode *rel* foresee, foreknow, divine, apprehend, anticipate

propinquity *syn* PROXIMITY *rel* closeness, nearness; relatedness, relationship, kindredness, kindred

propitiate *syn* PACIFY, appease, placate, mollify, conciliate *rel* reconcile, conform, adjust, adapt; satisfy, content; intercede, mediate, interpose

propitious *syn* FAVORABLE, auspicious, benign *rel* benignant, kind, kindly; fortunate, lucky, providential, happy *ant* unpropitious; adverse

proportion *syn* SYMMETRY, balance, harmony

proportional • corresponding in size, degree, or intensity *syn* proportionate, commensurate, commensurable *rel* corresponding, correlative, reciprocal; relative, contingent, dependent

proportionate *syn* PROPORTIONAL, commensurate, commensurable *rel* corresponding, correlative, reciprocal *ant* disproportionate

proposal • something put forward, offered, or otherwise stated for consideration *syn* proposition

propose **1** *syn* INTEND, purpose, mean, design *rel* aim, aspire; plan, plot, scheme, project **2** • to set before the mind for consideration *syn* propound, pose *rel* state; offer, tender, present

proposition *syn* PROPOSAL

propound *syn* PROPOSE, pose *rel* ask, question, query; state

propriety *syn* DECORUM, decency, etiquette, dignity *rel* grace, elegance; form, usage, convention, convenance

prorate *syn* APPORTION, portion, parcel, ration

prosaic · having a plain, practical, everyday character or quality *syn* prosy, matter-of-fact *rel* practical, practicable; boring, tedious, irksome

proscribe *syn* SENTENCE, condemn, damn, doom

proselyte *syn* CONVERT

prospect · an advance realization of something to come *syn* outlook, anticipation, foretaste *rel* hope, expectation; foreseeing, foresight, foreknowing, foreknowledge, divining, divination

prosper *syn* SUCCEED, thrive, flourish *rel* increase, augment, multiply; bear, yield, produce, turn out

prostrate *syn* PRONE, supine, recumbent, couchant, dormant *rel* flat, level; abject, mean

prosy *syn* PROSAIC, matter-of-fact *rel* insipid, jejune, banal, inane; irksome, boring, tedious

protean *syn* CHANGEABLE, changeful, variable, mutable

protect *syn* DEFEND, shield, guard, safeguard *rel* save, preserve, conserve; ensure, insure, assure; shelter, harbor

protest **1** *syn* ASSERT, avouch, avow, profess, affirm, aver, declare, predicate, warrant **2** *syn* OBJECT, remonstrate, expostulate, kick *rel* oppose, resist, combat, fight; demur, scruple, balk *ant* agree

protract *syn* EXTEND, prolong, lengthen, elongate *rel* delay, retard, slow, slacken; defer, suspend, stay, postpone *ant* curtail

protrude *syn* BULGE, jut, stick out, project, overhang, beetle *rel* obtrude, intrude; extend, prolong; swell, distend, expand

protrusion *syn* PROJECTION, protuberance, bulge

protuberance *syn* PROJECTION, protrusion, bulge

protuberate *syn* BULGE, jut, stick out, protrude, project, overhang, beetle *rel* swell, distend, expand

proud **1** · showing scorn for inferiors *syn* arrogant, haughty, lordly, insolent, overbearing, supercilious, disdainful *rel* contemptuous, scornful; pretentious, ostentatious, showy; imperious, domineering, masterful *ant* humble; ashamed **2** · having or exhibiting undue or excessive pride esp. in one's appearance or achievements *syn* vain, vainglorious *rel* exalted, magnified, aggrandized; self-satisfied, complacent, smug; contented, satisfied *ant* ashamed; humble

prove **1** · to establish a point by appropriate objective means *syn* try, test, demonstrate *rel* corroborate, verify, substantiate, confirm; justify, warrant *ant* disprove **2** *syn* INDICATE, betoken, attest, bespeak, argue *rel* evidence, manifest, evince, show, demonstrate

provenance, provenience *syn* ORIGIN, source, inception, root, prime mover *rel* beginning, commencement, starting

provender *syn* FOOD, fodder, forage, feed, victuals, viands, provisions, comestibles

proverb *syn* SAYING, maxim, adage, motto, saw, epigram, aphorism, apothegm

provide · to give or acquire and make available something wanted or needed *syn* supply, furnish *rel* prepare, fit, ready; equip, outfit, arm, furnish; purvey, cater

providence *syn* PRUDENCE, foresight, forethought, discretion *rel* care, solicitude, concern; thoughtfulness, consideration; frugality, thriftiness, economy *ant* improvidence

provident *syn* PRUDENT, foresighted, forethoughtful, discreet *rel* careful, solicitous, concerned; thoughtful, considerate; sparing, economical, frugal, thrifty *ant* improvident

providential *syn* LUCKY, fortunate, happy *rel* benign, auspicious, propitious, favorable; benignant, kindly, kind

providing *syn* IF

province 1 *syn* FIELD, domain, sphere, territory, bailiwick *rel* limit, confine, bound, end 2 *syn* FUNCTION, office, duty *rel* work, calling, pursuit, business; task, job

provincial *syn* INSULAR, parochial, local, small-town *rel* circumscribed, confined, limited, restricted; narrow, narrow-minded, illiberal, intolerant, hidebound, bigoted *ant* catholic

provision 1 *syn* CONDITION, stipulation, terms, proviso, reservation, strings *rel* clause, article, paragraph; prerequisite, requisite, requirement 2 *pl* **provisions** *syn* FOOD, feed, victuals, viands, comestibles, provender, fodder, forage

provisional 1 • not final or definitive *syn* tentative *rel* temporary; conditional, dependent, contingent *ant* definitive 2 *syn* TEMPORARY, ad interim, acting

proviso *syn* CONDITION, stipulation, terms, provision, reservation, strings *rel* clause, article, paragraph; limitation, restriction; contingency, exigency

provoke 1 • to arouse as if pricking *syn* excite, stimulate, pique, quicken, galvanize *rel* arouse, rouse, stir; thrill, electrify, enthuse; incite, instigate, foment 2 *syn* IRRITATE, exasperate, nettle, aggravate, rile, peeve *rel* affront, offend, insult, outrage; anger, incense, madden; agitate, upset, perturb, discompose *ant* gratify

prowess *syn* HEROISM, valor, gallantry *rel* bravery, boldness, audacity, intrepidity; courage, mettle, spirit; strength, might, puissance, power

prowl *syn* WANDER, stray, roam, ramble, rove, range, gad, gallivant, traipse, meander

proximity • the quality or state of being near *syn* propinquity *rel* nearness, closeness; adjacency, contiguousness, juxtaposition *ant* distance

proxy *syn* AGENT, deputy, attorney, factor

prudence • good sense or shrewdness in the management of affairs *syn* providence, foresight, forethought, discretion *rel* caution, circumspection, calculation; expediency, advisableness; frugality, thriftiness, thrift

prudent 1 *syn* WISE, judicious, sensible, sane, sage, sapient *rel* intelligent, brilliant, bright, smart, alert; shrewd, perspicacious, sagacious, astute; disciplined, schooled 2 • making provision for the future *syn* provident, foresighted, forethoughtful, discreet *rel* cautious, circumspect, calculating, wary; politic, expedient, advisable; economical, frugal, thrifty, sparing

prudish *syn* PRIM, priggish, prissy, puritanical, straitlaced, stuffy *rel* rigid, strict; stern, severe, austere; formal, conventional, solemn, ceremonial

prune *syn* SHEAR, trim, lop, poll, clip, snip, crop *rel* enhance, heighten, intensify; eliminate, exclude

prying *syn* CURIOUS, inquisitive, snoopy, nosy *rel* meddlesome, officious, impertinent, intrusive, obtrusive

pseudo *syn* COUNTERFEIT, spurious, bogus, fake, sham, pinchbeck, phony *rel* false, wrong;

misleading, deceptive, delusive, delusory

pseudonym · a fictitious or assumed name *syn* alias, nom de guerre, pen name, nom de plume, incognito

psyche *syn* MIND, intellect, soul, brain, intelligence, wit

psychic *syn* MENTAL, intellectual, intelligent, cerebral

psychosis *syn* INSANITY, lunacy, mania, dementia

puberty, pubescence *syn* YOUTH, adolescence

public *syn* FOLLOWING, clientele, audience

publication *syn* DECLARATION, announcement, advertisement, proclamation, promulgation, broadcasting

publicity · an act or device designed to attract public interest and to mold public opinion *syn* ballyhoo, promotion, propaganda *rel* advertisement, publication, announcement, promulgation, broadcasting

publish *syn* DECLARE, announce, advertise, proclaim, promulgate, broadcast *rel* divulge, disclose, reveal, discover; communicate, impart; vent, ventilate, utter, broach, express

puerile *syn* YOUTHFUL, juvenile, boyish, virgin, virginal, maiden *rel* immature, unmatured, unripe; raw, callow, green, rude *ant* adult

puff *syn* CRITICISM, critique, review, blurb

pugnacious *syn* BELLIGERENT, combative, bellicose, quarrelsome, contentious *rel* aggressive, militant, assertive, self-assertive, pushing, pushy *ant* pacific

puissance *syn* POWER, might, strength, force, energy

puissant *syn* POWERFUL, potent, forceful, forcible *ant* impuissant

pulchritudinous *syn* BEAUTIFUL, beauteous, good-looking, comely, bonny, pretty, handsome, fair, lovely

pull · to cause to move toward or after an applied force *syn* draw, drag, haul, hale, tug, tow

pulsate · to course or move with or as if with rhythmic strokes *syn* pulse, beat, throb, palpitate *rel* vibrate, fluctuate, waver, oscillate, swing; quiver, shudder, quaver, tremble, shake

pulsation · a rhythmical movement or one single step in recurring rhythmic steps *syn* pulse, beat, throb, palpitation

pulse *n, syn* PULSATION, beat, throb, palpitation *rel* rhythm, cadence, meter; vibration, fluctuation

pulse *vb, syn* PULSATE, beat, throb, palpitate *rel* move, drive, impel; vibrate, fluctuate, oscillate, swing

pummel *syn* BEAT, pound, buffet, baste, belabor, thrash *rel* strike, hit, smite, slug, punch

punch *vb* **1** *syn* STRIKE, hit, smite, slug, slog, swat, clout, slap, box, cuff *rel* beat, pound, pummel, baste, belabor **2** *syn* PERFORATE, puncture, prick, bore, drill *rel* pierce, penetrate, probe, enter

punch *n, syn* VIGOR, vim, spirit, dash, esprit, verve, élan, drive

punctilious *syn* CAREFUL, punctual, meticulous, scrupulous *rel* particular, fussy, squeamish, fastidious, nice; formal, conventional, ceremonious, ceremonial

punctual *syn* CAREFUL, punctilious, meticulous, scrupulous *rel* quick, prompt, ready; precise, correct, nice, right

puncture *syn* PERFORATE, punch, prick, bore, drill *rel* pierce, penetrate, enter; deflate, shrink, contract

pungent · sharp and stimulating to the mind or the senses *syn* piquant, poignant, racy, spicy, snappy *rel* incisive, trenchant, biting, cutting; penetrating, piercing, probing; exciting, stimulating, provoking, provocative *ant* bland

punish · to inflict a penalty on in requital for wrongdoing *syn* chastise, castigate, chasten, discipline, correct *rel* penalize, fine, amerce, mulct; imprison, incarcerate, immure; avenge, revenge *ant* excuse; pardon

puny *syn* PETTY, trivial, trifling, paltry, measly, picayunish, picayune *rel* feeble, weak, frail, infirm; small, little, diminutive; slight, tenuous, thin

purblind *syn* BLIND, sightless

purchase *syn* BUY *rel* gain, win, get, obtain, procure, secure

pure **1** · containing nothing that does not properly belong *syn* absolute, simple, sheer *rel* elemental, elementary; clear, transparent, lucid, limpid; genuine, authentic *ant* contaminated, polluted; adulterated applied (*of science*) **2** *syn* CHASTE, modest, decent *rel* clean, cleanly; virtuous, moral, ethical *ant* impure; immoral

purge *syn* RID, clear, unburden, disabuse *rel* cleanse, clean; eliminate, exclude, debar, shut out, rule out; eject, oust, dismiss, expel; expunge, erase, efface, delete

puritanical *syn* PRIM, priggish, prissy, prudish, straitlaced, stuffy *rel* rigid, rigorous, strict; plain, simple, homely, unpretentious; illiberal, narrow, narrow-minded, hidebound, intolerant, bigoted

purloin *syn* STEAL, pilfer, filch, lift, pinch, snitch, swipe, cop *rel* abstract, detach; rob, plunder, rifle, loot, burglarize

purport *syn* SUBSTANCE, gist, burden, core, pith *rel* significance, import, meaning, signification; tenor, tendency, drift, trend

purported *syn* SUPPOSED, supposititious, suppositious, reputed, putative, conjectural, hypothetical

purpose *n, syn* INTENTION, intent, design, aim, end, object, objective, goal *rel* ambition, aspiration; proposition, proposal; plan, project, scheme

purpose *vb, syn* INTEND, propose, design, mean *rel* meditate, ponder; weigh, consider, contemplate; plan, plot, scheme, project; determine, decide

pursue *syn* FOLLOW, chase, trail, tag, tail *rel* persevere, persist, practice, exercise; persecute, oppress; hound, ride, bait, badger

pursuit *syn* WORK, calling, occupation, employment, business

purvey *syn* CATER, pander *rel* furnish, equip, outfit

purview *syn* RANGE, gamut, reach, radius, compass, sweep, scope, orbit, horizon, ken

push · to press against with force so as to cause to move ahead or aside *syn* shove, thrust, propel *rel* move, drive, impel; force, compel, constrain, oblige

pushing, pushy *syn* AGGRESSIVE, militant, assertive, self-assertive *rel* vigorous, energetic, strenuous; officious, intrusive, obtrusive, impertinent; self-confident, confident, self-assured, assured

puss *syn* FACE, countenance, visage, physiognomy, mug

pustule *syn* ABSCESS, boil, furuncle, carbuncle, pimple

putative *syn* SUPPOSED, supposititious, suppositious, reputed, purported, conjectural, hypothetical *rel* alleged, advanced; assumed, pretended, simulated

putrefy *syn* DECAY, rot, decompose, spoil, disintegrate, crumble *rel* corrupt, vitiate, deprave, debase; deliquesce

putrid *syn* MALODOROUS, fetid, noisome, stinking, rank, rancid, fusty, musty *rel* decomposed, decayed, rotten, putrefied; corrupted, vitiated

putsch *syn* REBELLION, revolution,

uprising, revolt, insurrection, mutiny, coup

put up *syn* RESIDE, live, dwell, sojourn, lodge, stay, stop

puzzle *vb* · to baffle and disturb mentally *syn* perplex, mystify, bewilder, distract, nonplus, confound, dumbfound *rel* amaze, astound, flabbergast, surprise; confuse, muddle, addle; embarrass, disconcert, discomfit

puzzle *n, syn* MYSTERY, problem, enigma, riddle, conundrum

pygmy *syn* DWARF, midget, manikin, homunculus, runt

Q

quack *syn* IMPOSTOR, faker, mountebank, charlatan *rel* pretender, simulator, counterfeiter, shammer; deceit, duplicity, dissimulation, cunning, guile

quail *syn* RECOIL, shrink, flinch, wince, blench *rel* cower, cringe, fawn; falter, waver, vacillate, hesitate; quake, quaver, tremble, shudder, shake

quaint *syn* STRANGE, odd, queer, outlandish, curious, peculiar, eccentric, erratic, singular, unique *rel* fantastic, bizarre, grotesque; droll, funny, laughable; archaic, antiquated, antique, old

quake *syn* SHAKE, tremble, totter, quiver, shiver, shudder, quaver, wobble, teeter, shimmy, dither *rel* quail, shrink, recoil; vibrate, fluctuate, waver, swing; falter, vacillate, hesitate

qualified *syn* ABLE, competent, capable *rel* trained, instructed, disciplined; examined, quizzed, catechized; tested, tried, proved *ant* unqualified

qualify **1** *syn* MODERATE, temper *rel* modify, vary, alter, change; adapt, adjust, conform, accommodate, reconcile **2** *syn* CHARACTERIZE, distinguish, mark *rel* ascribe, impute, attribute, assign; predicate, assert **3** *syn* PREPARE, fit, condition, ready *rel* empower, enable; endow, endue, dower; train, instruct, teach

quality **1** · an intelligible feature by which a thing may be identified *syn* property, character, attribute, accident *rel* predication, affirmation; peculiarity, individuality, characteristic **2** · a usu. high level of merit or superiority *syn* stature, caliber *rel* excellence, virtue; value, worth

qualm · a misgiving about what one is doing or is going to do *syn* scruple, compunction, demur *rel* misgiving, apprehension, foreboding, presentiment; doubt, mistrust, suspicion, uncertainty

quandary *syn* PREDICAMENT, dilemma, plight, scrape, fix, jam, pickle *rel* juncture, pass, exigency, emergency, contingency, crisis; difficulty, hardship, vicissitude; puzzling, puzzle, mystification, perplexity, bewilderment

quantity *syn* SUM, amount, aggregate, total, whole, number

quarrel *n* · a usu. verbal dispute marked by anger or discord *syn* wrangle, altercation, squabble, bickering, spat, tiff *rel* brawl, broil, fracas, melee, row, rumpus, scrap; contention, dissension, conflict, difference, variance, strife, discord

quarrel *vb, syn* wrangle, altercate,

squabble, bicker, spat, tiff *rel* contend, fight, battle, war; dispute, agitate, argue, discuss

quarrelsome *syn* BELLIGERENT, pugnacious, combative, bellicose, contentious *rel* antagonistic, adverse, counter; hostile, inimical, antipathetic, rancorous

quarry *syn* VICTIM, prey

quash **1** *syn* ANNUL, abrogate, void, vacate **2** *syn* CRUSH, quell, extinguish, suppress, quench *rel* destroy; ruin, wreck; repress

quaver *syn* SHAKE, tremble, shudder, quake, totter, quiver, shiver, wobble, teeter, shimmy, dither *rel* falter, waver, vacillate, hesitate; vibrate, fluctuate, sway, swing

quay *syn* WHARF, dock, pier, slip, berth, jetty, levee

queenly *syn* KINGLY, regal, royal, imperial, princely

queer *syn* STRANGE, odd, erratic, eccentric, peculiar, quaint, outlandish, curious *rel* dubious, doubtful, questionable; droll, funny, laughable; bizarre, grotesque, fantastic

quell *syn* CRUSH, extinguish, suppress, quench, quash *rel* destroy; wreck, ruin; subdue, subjugate, overcome, vanquish, conquer *ant* foment

quench *syn* CRUSH, quell, extinguish, suppress, quash *rel* repress, suppress; end, terminate

querulous *syn* IRRITABLE, fretful, petulant, pettish, huffy, peevish, fractious, snappish, waspish *rel* crying, weeping, wailing, whimpering, blubbering; touchy, cranky, cross, irascible; lamenting, deploring, bemoaning

query *syn* ASK, question, interrogate, inquire, examine, quiz, catechize

quest *syn* ADVENTURE, enterprise *rel* exploit, feat, achievement

question *syn* ASK, interrogate, query, inquire, examine, quiz, catechize *ant* answer

questionable *syn* DOUBTFUL, dubious, problematic *rel* uncertain, suspicious; obscure, vague, equivocal *ant* authoritative; unquestioned

quick **1** *syn* FAST, fleet, swift, rapid, speedy, expeditious, hasty *rel* brisk, nimble, agile; abrupt, impetuous, precipitate, headlong **2** • able to respond without delay or hesitation or indicative of such ability *syn* prompt, ready, apt *rel* intelligent, clever, smart, quick-witted; deft, adroit, dexterous; sharp, acute, keen *ant* sluggish

quicken **1** • to make alive or lively *syn* animate, enliven, vivify *rel* activate, vitalize, energize; rouse, arouse, stir *ant* deaden **2** *syn* PROVOKE, excite, stimulate, pique, galvanize *rel* activate, actuate, motivate; spur, goad, induce; incite, foment *ant* arrest **3** *syn* SPEED, hasten, hurry, accelerate, precipitate *ant* slacken

quick-witted *syn* INTELLIGENT, clever, bright, smart, alert, knowing, brilliant *rel* ready, prompt, quick, apt; sharp, keen, acute; witty, humorous, facetious

quiescent *syn* LATENT, dormant, potential, abeyant *rel* quiet, still, silent; inert, inactive, passive, supine

quiet *adj, syn* STILL, silent, noiseless, stilly *rel* calm, serene, placid, tranquil, peaceful *ant* unquiet

quiet, quieten *vb, syn* CALM, compose, still, lull, soothe, settle, tranquilize *rel* allay, alleviate, assuage, relieve; abate, lessen, decrease *ant* disquiet; arouse, rouse

quip *syn* JOKE, jest, jape, witticism, wisecrack, crack, gag

quit **1** *syn* BEHAVE, acquit, comport, deport, demean, conduct *rel, ant* see ACQUIT **2** *syn* GO, leave, depart, withdraw, retire *rel* forsake, desert, abandon; relinquish, surrender, resign; escape, flee, fly, abscond **3** *syn* STOP, cease, discontinue, desist

quiver *syn* SHAKE, shiver, shudder, quaver, totter, tremble, quake, wobble, teeter, shimmy, dither *rel* pulsate, pulse, beat, throb, palpitate; flutter, flicker, flitter, flit

quixotic *syn* IMAGINARY, chimerical, fantastic, visionary, fanciful *rel* sentimental, romantic; utopian, ambitious; ideal, transcendental, abstract

quiz *syn* ASK, question, interrogate, examine, catechize, query, inquire

quote • to speak or write again something already said or written by another *syn* cite, repeat *rel* adduce, allege, advance

quotidian *syn* DAILY, diurnal, circadian

R

rabid *syn* FURIOUS, frantic, frenzied, wild, frenetic, delirious *rel* maddened, enraged, infuriated, incensed, angered; violent, compulsive; insane, crazed, crazy, demented, deranged

race *syn* VARIETY, subspecies, breed, cultivar, strain, clone, stock

rack *syn* AFFLICT, torment, torture, try *rel* persecute, oppress, wrong; harry, harass, worry, annoy

racket *syn* DIN, uproar, pandemonium, hullabaloo, babel, hubbub, clamor

racking *syn* EXCRUCIATING, agonizing *rel* torturing, tormenting; intense, vehement, fierce, exquisite, violent; fierce, ferocious, barbarous, savage, cruel, inhuman

racy *syn* PUNGENT, piquant, poignant, spicy, snappy *rel* exciting, stimulating, quickening, provoking, provocative; spirited, mettlesome, fiery, gingery, peppery

radiant *syn* BRIGHT, brilliant, luminous, lustrous, effulgent, refulgent, beaming, lambent, lucent, incandescent *rel* splendid, resplendent, glorious, sublime; sparkling, glittering, gleaming, flashing, scintillating

radiate *syn* SPREAD, circulate, disseminate, diffuse, propagate *rel* distribute, dispense; disperse, scatter, dissipate; diverge

radical **1** *syn* FUNDAMENTAL, basic, basal, underlying *rel* cardinal, essential, vital; inherent, intrinsic, constitutional *ant* superficial **2** *syn* LIBERAL, advanced, progressive

radius *syn* RANGE, gamut, reach, compass, sweep, scope, orbit, horizon, ken, purview

rag *syn* BANTER, chaff, kid, rib, josh, jolly

rage **1** *syn* ANGER, ire, fury, indignation, wrath *rel* acrimony, asperity, acerbity; frenzy, mania, hysteria; agitation, upset, perturbation **2** *syn* FASHION, style, mode, vogue, craze, cry, dernier cri, fad *rel* caprice, freak, conceit, vagary, crotchet, whim, fancy

raid *syn* INVASION, incursion, inroad *rel* attack, assault, onslaught, onset

rail *syn* SCOLD, revile, vituperate, rate, berate, upbraid, tongue-lash, jaw, bawl, chew out, wig *rel* censure, denounce, condemn, reprobate, reprehend, criticize; reprimand, rebuke, reprove, reproach

raillery *syn* BADINAGE, persiflage *rel* bantering, banter, chaffing, chaff; sport, fun, game, jest, play; satire, sarcasm, irony, wit

raiment *syn* CLOTHES, apparel, attire, clothing, dress

raise **1** *syn* LIFT, elevate, hoist, heave, rear, boost *rel* rise, ascend, mount, soar; exalt, magnify, aggrandize; advance, promote, forward, further **2** *syn* BUILD, construct, erect, frame, rear *ant* raze

rally *vb, syn* STIR, rouse, arouse, awaken, waken *rel* excite, stimulate, quicken, provoke; fire, light; renew, restore, refresh

rally *vb, syn* RIDICULE, deride, mock, taunt, twit *rel* scoff, jeer, gibe, flout; tease, tantalize, worry, harass, harry

ram *syn* PACK, crowd, cram, stuff, tamp *rel* press, squeeze, jam; compact, concentrate, consolidate; compress

ramble *syn* WANDER, stray, roam, rove, range, prowl, gad, gallivant, traipse, meander

rampant *syn* RANK *rel* luxuriant, lush, exuberant, profuse, lavish; immoderate, excessive, inordinate

rampart *syn* BULWARK, breastwork, parapet, bastion

rancid *syn* MALODOROUS, stinking, fetid, rank, noisome, putrid, fusty, musty *rel* decomposed, decayed, spoiled; offensive, loathsome, repulsive

rancor *syn* ENMITY, antagonism, animosity, animus, antipathy, hostility *rel* hate, hatred, detestation, abhorrence, abomination; spite, malice, malevolence, malignity, malignancy, spleen, grudge

random · determined by accident rather than by design *syn* haphazard, chance, chancy, casual, desultory, hit-or-miss, happy-go-lucky *rel* fortuitous, accidental, casual; vagrant, vagabond, truant

range *n* **1** *syn* HABITAT, biotope, station **2** · the extent that lies within the powers of something to cover or control *syn* gamut, reach, radius, compass, sweep, scope, orbit, horizon, ken, purview *rel* extent, area; field, domain, province, sphere, territory; spread, stretch, expanse, amplitude

range *vb* **1** *syn* LINE, line up, align, array *rel* arrange, order, marshal; assort, sort, classify; incline, dispose, predispose, bias **2** *syn* WANDER, rove, ramble, roam, stray, prowl, gad, gallivant, traipse, meander

rank *adj* **1** · growing or increasing at an immoderate rate *syn* rampant *rel* coarse, gross, vulgar; exuberant, profuse, lavish, luxuriant **2** *syn* MALODOROUS, fusty, musty, rancid, stinking, fetid, noisome, putrid *rel* dank, humid, wet; offensive, loathsome, repulsive; decomposed, decayed, spoiled *ant* balmy **3** *syn* FLAGRANT, glaring, gross *rel* conspicuous, outstanding, noticeable; foul, filthy, squalid, nasty, dirty; outrageous, heinous, atrocious, monstrous

rank *n, syn* LINE, row, file, echelon, tier

rank *vb, syn* CLASS, grade, rate, graduate, gradate *rel* order, arrange; classify, assort, sort; divide, separate

ransack *syn* SEEK, search, hunt, rummage, scour, comb, ferret out *rel* investigate; penetrate, pierce, probe; examine, inspect, scrutinize

ransom *syn* RESCUE, deliver, redeem, reclaim, save *rel* free, release, liberate, emancipate, manumit; expiate, atone

rant *syn* BOMBAST, fustian, rodomontade, rhapsody *rel* inflatedness, inflation, turgidity, tumidity, flatulence

rap *n, syn* TAP, knock, thump, thud *rel* beating, pummeling, pounding

rap *vb, syn* TAP, knock, thump,

thud *rel* smite, strike; pummel, beat

rapacious *syn* VORACIOUS, ravening, ravenous, gluttonous *rel* ferocious, fierce; greedy, grasping, covetous

rapacity *syn* CUPIDITY, greed, avarice *rel* covetousness, avariciousness, greediness, graspingness; exaction, demanding, demand, claiming, claim

rapid *syn* FAST, swift, fleet, quick, speedy, hasty, expeditious *rel* brisk, nimble, agile; hurried, quickened *ant* deliberate; leisurely

rapscallion *syn* VILLAIN, scoundrel, blackguard, knave, rascal, rogue, scamp, miscreant *rel* vagabond, vagrant, tramp, hobo, bum

rapt *syn* INTENT, absorbed, engrossed *rel* ecstatic, transported, rapturous; enchanted, captivated, fascinated

rapture *syn* ECSTASY, transport *rel* bliss, beatitude, blessedness, felicity, happiness

rare **1** *syn* THIN, tenuous, slight, slender, slim **2** *syn* CHOICE, delicate, dainty, exquisite, elegant, recherché *rel* excelling, excellent, transcending, transcendent, surpassing; superlative, supreme, incomparable **3** *syn* INFREQUENT, scarce, uncommon, occasional, sporadic *rel* exceptional; singular, unique, curious, strange

rarefy *syn* THIN, attenuate, extenuate, dilute *rel* diminish, reduce, lessen, decrease; expand, distend, inflate

rascal *syn* VILLAIN, scoundrel, blackguard, knave, rogue, scamp, rapscallion, miscreant

rash *syn* ADVENTUROUS, daring, daredevil, reckless, foolhardy, venturesome *rel* precipitate, abrupt, impetuous, sudden, hasty; desperate, forlorn, despondent *ant* calculating

rasp *syn* SCRAPE, scratch, grate, grind *rel* abrade, excoriate, chafe, fret; irritate, exasperate, aggravate; annoy, vex, irk, bother

rate *vb, syn* SCOLD, berate, upbraid, tongue-lash, jaw, bawl, chew out, wig, rail, revile, vituperate *rel* reprove, reproach, rebuke, reprimand, admonish, chide; censure, condemn, denounce, reprehend, reprobate, criticize

rate *vb* **1** *syn* ESTIMATE, value, evaluate, appraise, assess, assay *rel* calculate, compute, reckon; decide, determine, settle **2** *syn* CLASS, grade, rank, graduate, gradate *rel* order, arrange, systematize, methodize; assort, sort, classify

ratify • to make something legally valid or operative usu. by formal approval or sanctioning *syn* confirm *rel* authorize, accredit, license, commission; sanction, approve, endorse; validate, authenticate, confirm

ratiocination *syn* INFERENCE *ant* intuition

ratiocinative *syn* INFERENTIAL *ant* intuitive

ration *n* • an amount allotted or made available esp. from a limited supply *syn* allowance, dole, pittance *rel* apportionment, portioning, portion; sharing, share, participation, partaking

ration *vb, syn* APPORTION, portion, prorate, parcel *rel* divide, distribute, dispense, deal, dole; share, partake, participate

rational • relating to, based on, or agreeable to reason *syn* reasonable *ant* irrational; animal (*of nature*); demented (*of state of mind*); absurd (*of actions, behavior*)

rationalize *syn* EXPLAIN, account, justify

rattle *syn* EMBARRASS, faze, discomfit, disconcert, abash *rel* confuse, muddle, addle; agitate, upset, perturb, disturb, fluster, flurry, discompose; bewilder, distract, perplex, puzzle

raucous *syn* LOUD, stentorian, earsplitting, hoarse, strident, stertorous *rel* rough, harsh; gruff, brusque, bluff

ravage · to lay waste by plundering or destroying *syn* devastate, waste, sack, pillage, despoil, spoliate *rel* destroy, demolish, raze; plunder, loot, rob; ruin, wreck; invade, trespass, encroach

ravening *syn* VORACIOUS, rapacious, ravenous, gluttonous *rel* greedy, acquisitive, grasping, covetous

ravenous *syn* VORACIOUS, ravening, rapacious, gluttonous *rel* grasping, greedy, acquisitive, covetous; fierce, ferocious

ravish *syn* TRANSPORT, enrapture, entrance *rel* rejoice, delight, regale, please

raw *syn* RUDE, crude, callow, green, rough, uncouth *rel* elementary, elemental; ignorant, untaught, untutored; immature, unmatured, unripe

rawboned *syn* LEAN, gaunt, angular, lank, lanky, spare, scrawny, skinny

ray · a shaft of light *syn* beam

raze *syn* DESTROY, demolish *rel* efface, obliterate, erase; eradicate, extirpate, exterminate; ruin, wreck; abolish, extinguish, annihilate

reach *vb* · to arrive at a point by effort or work *syn* gain, compass, achieve, attain *rel* effect, fulfill, execute, accomplish, perform; get, obtain, procure, secure

reach *n, syn* RANGE, gamut, radius, compass, sweep, scope, orbit, horizon, ken, purview *rel* extent, area, magnitude, size; spread, stretch, expanse; capacity, capability, ability

react *syn* ACT, operate, work, function, behave

readiness · the power of doing something without evidence of effort *syn* ease, facility, dexterity *rel* quickness, promptness, aptness; alacrity, celerity, legerity; fluency, eloquence, volubility

ready *adj, syn* QUICK, prompt, apt *rel* expert, adept, skilled, skillful, proficient, masterly; active, live, dynamic

ready *vb, syn* PREPARE, fit, qualify, condition

real · corresponding to known facts *syn* actual, true *rel* being, existing, existent, subsisting, subsistent; certain, necessary, inevitable *ant* unreal; apparent; imaginary

realize **1** · to bring into concrete existence something that has existed as an abstraction or a conception or a possibility *syn* actualize, embody, incarnate, materialize, externalize, objectify, hypostatize, reify *rel* effect, fulfill, execute, accomplish, achieve, perform **2** *syn* THINK, conceive, imagine, fancy, envisage, envision *rel* understand, comprehend, appreciate

reap · to do the work of collecting ripened crops *syn* glean, gather, garner, harvest *rel* collect, assemble

rear *vb* **1** *syn* BUILD, construct, erect, frame, raise **2** *syn* LIFT, raise, elevate, hoist, heave, boost *rel* rise, ascend, mount, soar; nurse, nurture, foster; breed, propagate

rear *adj, syn* POSTERIOR, after, back, hind, hinder *ant* front

reason *n* **1** · a point or points that support something open to question *syn* ground, argument, proof *rel* explanation, justification, rationalization **2** *syn* CAUSE, determinant, antecedent, occasion *rel* motive, incentive, inducement, impulse; basis, foundation, ground **3** · the power of the mind by which man attains truth or knowledge *syn* understanding, intuition *rel* mind, intellect, intelligence, brain; ratiocination, inference

reason *vb, syn* THINK, reflect, deliberate, speculate, cogitate *rel* infer, deduce, conclude, judge, gather

reasonable *syn* RATIONAL *rel* sensible, sane, prudent, judicious, wise; fair, equitable, just *ant* unreasonable

rebate *syn* DEDUCTION, abatement, discount

rebel · one who rises up against constituted authority or the established order *syn* insurgent, iconoclast *rel* opponent, antagonist, adversary; assailant, attacker

rebellion · an outbreak against authority *syn* revolution, uprising, revolt, insurrection, mutiny, putsch, coup *rel* sedition, treason; resistance, opposition, combating, withstanding

rebellious *syn* INSUBORDINATE, mutinous, seditious, factious, contumacious *rel* recalcitrant, refractory, intractable, unruly, ungovernable; estranged, alienated, disaffected *ant* acquiescent, resigned; submissive

rebound · to spring back to an original position or shape *syn* reverberate, recoil, resile, repercuss *rel* bound, skip, ricochet

rebuild *syn* MEND, repair, patch *rel* renew, restore, renovate, refresh

rebuke *syn* REPROVE, reprimand, admonish, reproach, chide *rel* rate, upbraid, scold, berate; criticize, reprehend, reprobate

rebut *syn* DISPROVE, refute, confute, controvert

recalcitrant *syn* UNRULY, refractory, intractable, headstrong, willful, ungovernable *rel* rebellious, insubordinate, factious, contumacious; obstinate, stubborn; resisting, opposing, withstanding *ant* amenable

recall **1** *syn* REMEMBER, recollect, remind, reminisce, bethink, mind *rel* evoke, elicit, extract, educe; stir, rouse, arouse, waken, awaken **2** *syn* REVOKE, reverse, repeal, rescind *rel* annul, abrogate, void; retract, abjure, recant

recant *syn* ABJURE, retract, renounce, forswear *rel* withdraw, remove

recede · to move backward *syn* retreat, retrograde, retract, back *rel* withdraw, retire, depart; rebound, recoil *ant* proceed; advance

receipt · a formula or set of directions for the compounding of ingredients esp. in cookery and medicine *syn* recipe, prescription

receive · to bring and accept into one's possession, one's presence, a group, or the mind *syn* accept, admit, take *rel* enter, penetrate; seize, grasp

recent *syn* MODERN, late *rel* fresh, new, new-fashioned

recess *syn* PAUSE, respite, lull, intermission *rel* withdrawal, retirement; break, interruption, interval, gap; relaxation, leisure, rest

recherché *syn* CHOICE, elegant, exquisite, delicate, dainty, rare *rel* fresh, original, new, novel; select, exclusive, picked *ant* banal

recipe *syn* RECEIPT, prescription

reciprocal **1** · shared, felt, or shown by both sides concerned *syn* mutual, common *rel* shared, participated, partaken; interchanged, exchanged; balancing, compensating, counterpoising **2** · like, equivalent, or similarly related to each other (as in kind, quality, or value) *syn* corresponding, correlative, complementary, complemental, convertible *rel* equivalent, identical, same; related, associated, linked, united

reciprocate · to give back usu. in kind or in quantity *syn* retaliate, requite, return *rel* interchange, exchange; repay, compensate, recompense

recite *syn* RELATE, rehearse, recount, narrate, describe, state, report *rel* enumerate, tell, count, number; detail, itemize, particularize

reckless *syn* ADVENTUROUS, daring, daredevil, rash, foolhardy, venturesome *rel* precipitate, sudden, hasty, headlong, impetuous, abrupt; desperate, hopeless, despondent *ant* calculating

reckon **1** *syn* CALCULATE, compute, estimate *rel* enumerate, count, number; figure, total, add, sum, cast, foot **2** *syn* CONSIDER, regard, account, deem *rel* think, conceive, imagine, envision; conjecture, surmise, guess **3** *syn* RELY, count, bank, trust, depend

reclaim *syn* RESCUE, save, ransom, redeem, deliver *rel* renew, restore, renovate; reform, rectify, remedy, correct, amend *ant* abandon

recluse · a person who leads a secluded or solitary life *syn* hermit, eremite, anchorite, cenobite

recognition · a learning process that relates a perception of something new to knowledge already possessed *syn* identification, assimilation, apperception

recognize *syn* ACKNOWLEDGE *rel* accept, admit, receive; notice, note, observe, remark, see

recoil **1** · to draw back in fear or distaste *syn* shrink, flinch, wince, blench, quail *rel* waver, falter, hesitate; shy, balk, stick, stickle, demur *ant* confront; defy **2** *syn* REBOUND, reverberate, resile, repercuss *rel* retreat, recede, back, retract; return, revert

recollect *syn* REMEMBER, recall, remind, reminisce, bethink, mind *rel* stir, rouse, arouse, rally, waken, awaken

recollection *syn* MEMORY, remembrance, reminiscence, mind, souvenir

recommend *syn* COMMEND, compliment, applaud *rel* approve, endorse, sanction; praise, extol, acclaim

recommendation *syn* CREDENTIAL, testimonial, character, reference *rel* approval, endorsement; commendation

recompense *syn* PAY, reimburse, indemnify, repay, satisfy, remunerate, compensate *rel* award, accord, vouchsafe, grant; balance, offset

reconcile *syn* ADAPT, conform, accommodate, adjust *rel* harmonize, accord, square, agree; correct, rectify, amend, revise

recondite · beyond the reach of the average intelligence *syn* abstruse, occult, esoteric *rel* scholarly, erudite, learned; pedantic, scholastic, academic

record *vb* · to set down in writing usu. for the purpose of written evidence or official record of *syn* register, list, enroll, catalog *rel* enter, admit, introduce

record *n, syn* DOCUMENT, monument, archive

recount *syn* RELATE, recite, rehearse, narrate, describe, state, report *rel* enumerate, count, number, tell; detail, itemize, particularize

recoup *syn* RECOVER, recruit, retrieve, regain *rel* compensate, balance, offset, counterpoise

recover **1** · to get back again *syn* regain, retrieve, recoup, recruit *rel* redeem, reclaim, rescue; compensate, offset, balance **2** *syn* IMPROVE, recuperate, convalesce, gain *rel* restore, refresh, rejuvenate, renew; revive, resuscitate, revivify

recreant *syn* RENEGADE, apostate, turncoat, backslider *rel* treacherousness, treachery, perfidiousness, perfidy, traitorousness

recreate *syn* AMUSE, divert, entertain *rel* renew, restore, refresh, rejuvenate; enliven, quicken, animate

recreation *syn* AMUSEMENT, diversion, entertainment *rel* relaxation, repose, ease, rest; play, sport, frolic, rollick; mirth, jollity, hilarity

recrudesce *syn* RETURN, revert, recur *rel* renew, renovate, refurbish

recrudescence *syn* RETURN, reversion, recurrence *rel* renewal, restoration, refreshment, renovation

recruit *syn* RECOVER, regain, retrieve, recoup *rel* renew, restore, renovate, refresh; repair, mend, rebuild

rectify *syn* CORRECT, emend, amend, reform, revise, remedy, redress *rel* improve, better, help, ameliorate; mend, repair, rebuild; adjust, regulate, fix

rectitude *syn* GOODNESS, virtue, morality *rel* integrity, probity, honesty, honor; righteousness, nobility; uprightness, justness, conscientiousness, scrupulousness

recumbent *syn* PRONE, supine, prostrate, couchant, dormant *ant* upright, erect

recuperate *syn* IMPROVE, recover, convalesce, gain *rel* invigorate, strengthen, fortify, energize

recur *syn* RETURN, revert, recrudesce *rel* repeat, iterate, reiterate

recurrence *syn* RETURN, reversion, recrudescence *rel* relapse; repeating, repetition, iteration

recurrent *syn* INTERMITTENT, periodic, alternate *rel* rhythmic, metrical; returning, reverting, recrudescing; fitful, spasmodic

redact *syn* EDIT, compile, revise, rewrite, adapt

redeem *syn* RESCUE, deliver, ransom, save, reclaim *rel* free, liberate, release, emancipate, manumit; restore, renew, renovate; recover, regain

redolence *syn* FRAGRANCE, perfume, incense, bouquet *rel* odor, aroma, smell; balminess, aromaticness, aromaticity

redolent *syn* ODOROUS, aromatic, balmy, fragrant *rel* pungent, poignant, piquant, racy, spicy; penetrating, piercing

redress *vb, syn* CORRECT, emend, remedy, amend, rectify, reform, revise *rel* relieve, lighten, alleviate, assuage, mitigate, allay; repair, mend

redress *n, syn* REPARATION, amends, restitution, indemnity *rel* compensation, offsetting, balancing; retaliation, reprisal, vengeance, retribution

reduce **1** *syn* DECREASE, lessen, diminish, abate, dwindle *rel* shorten, abridge, abbreviate, curtail, retrench; contract, shrink, condense **2** *syn* CONQUER, vanquish, defeat, subjugate, beat, overcome, lick, subdue, surmount, overthrow, rout *rel* weaken, cripple, disable, undermine, enfeeble; humble, humiliate, degrade, debase, abase **3** *syn* DEGRADE, demote, declass, disrate *rel* humble, humiliate, debase, abase

redundancy *syn* VERBIAGE, tautology, pleonasm, circumlocution, periphrasis *rel* wordiness, verbosity, prolixity, diffuseness; inflatedness, inflation, turgidity, tumidity, flatulence; bombast, rant, fustian

redundant *syn* WORDY, verbose, prolix, diffuse *rel* superfluous, surplus, supernumerary, extra, spare; repeating, repetitious, iterating, reiterating *ant* concise

reef *syn* SHOAL, bank, bar

reel · to move uncertainly or uncontrollably or unsteadily (as from weakness or intoxication) *syn* whirl, stagger, totter *rel* turn, spin, revolve, rotate; sway, waver, swing; wobble, teeter, quiver, shake

refer **1** *syn* ASCRIBE, assign, credit, accredit, attribute, impute, charge *rel* associate, relate, connect, join; direct, aim, point, lay **2** *syn* RESORT, apply, go, turn *rel* consult, confer, commune, advise; address, direct **3** • to call or direct attention to something *syn* allude, advert *rel* introduce, insert, interpolate; quote, cite

referee *syn* JUDGE, umpire, arbiter, arbitrator

reference *syn* CREDENTIAL, testimonial, recommendation, character

referendum *syn* MANDATE, initiative, plebiscite

refinement *syn* CULTURE, cultivation, breeding *rel* suavity, urbanity; courtesy, politeness, civility; elegance, grace, dignity *ant* vulgarity

reflect *syn* THINK, cogitate, reason, speculate, deliberate *rel* consider, contemplate, study, weigh; ponder, muse, meditate, ruminate

reflection *syn* ANIMADVERSION, stricture, aspersion *rel* imputing, imputation, ascribing, ascription; criticizing, criticism, reprehending, reprehension, blaming, blame; attack, assault, onslaught, onset; disparagement, derogation, depreciation

reflective *syn* THOUGHTFUL, contemplative, meditative, pensive, speculative *rel* thinking, reasoning, deliberating, cogitating; analytical, logical, subtle

reform *syn* CORRECT, rectify, emend, amend, remedy, redress, revise *rel* mend, repair, rebuild; better, improve, help, ameliorate

refractory *syn* UNRULY, recalcitrant, intractable, ungovernable, headstrong, willful *rel* contrary, perverse, froward, wayward; insubordinate, rebellious, contumacious *ant* malleable; amenable

refrain • to hold oneself back from doing or indulging in *syn* abstain, forbear *rel* check, arrest, interrupt; restrain, curb, inhibit

refresh *syn* RENEW, restore, rejuvenate, renovate, refurbish *rel* enliven, quicken, animate, vivify; recruit, recover, regain; recreate, amuse, divert *ant* jade, addle

refuge *syn* SHELTER, asylum, sanctuary, cover, retreat *rel* safety, security; stronghold, citadel, fort, fortress; harbor, haven, port

refulgent *syn* BRIGHT, effulgent, luminous, radiant, lustrous, brilliant, beaming, lambent, lucent, incandescent

refurbish *syn* RENEW, renovate, refresh, restore, rejuvenate

refuse *vb, syn* DECLINE, reject, repudiate, spurn *rel* deny, gainsay; balk, baffle, frustrate, thwart, foil; debar, exclude, shut out

refuse *n* • matter that is regarded as worthless and fit only for throwing away *syn* waste, rubbish, trash, debris, garbage, offal

refute *syn* DISPROVE, confute, rebut, controvert *rel* contradict, impugn, traverse, negative, contravene, deny

regain *syn* RECOVER, recruit, recoup, retrieve *rel* gain, reach, compass, attain, achieve; redeem, reclaim, save, rescue; restore, renew

regal *syn* KINGLY, royal, queenly, imperial, princely *rel* majestic, imposing, stately, magnificent, august, grand; splendid, resplendent, glorious, sublime

regale *syn* PLEASE, tickle, gratify, delight, rejoice, gladden *ant* vex

regard *n* • a feeling of deferential approval and liking *syn* respect, esteem, admiration *rel* deference, honor, homage, reverence; appreciation, cherishing, prizing, valuing *ant* despite

regard *vb* **1** • to recognize the worth of a person or thing *syn* respect, esteem, admire *rel* appreciate, cherish, value, prize, treasure *ant* despise **2** *syn* CONSIDER, account, reckon, deem *rel* rate, estimate, value, assess, assay

regarding *syn* ABOUT, concerning, respecting

region *syn* AREA, tract, zone, belt *rel* locality, vicinity, district, neighborhood; section, sector, division, part; field, territory, province

register *n, syn* LIST, table, catalog, schedule, roll, roster, inventory

register *vb, syn* RECORD, list, enroll, catalog *rel* enter, admit; insert, introduce; fix, establish, set; preserve, conserve, save

regressive *syn* BACKWARD, retrogressive, retrograde *ant* progressive

regret *syn* SORROW, grief, heartache, heartbreak, anguish, woe *rel* compunction, remorse, penitence, repentance, contrition; qualm, scruple, demur

regular **1** · being of the sort or kind that is expected as usual, ordinary, or average *syn* normal, typical, natural *rel* usual, habitual, customary; common, ordinary, familiar *ant* irregular **2** *syn* ORDERLY, methodical, systematic, regular *rel* fixed, set, settled; constant, even, equable, steady, uniform *ant* irregular

regulate *syn* ADJUST, fix *rel* order, arrange, organize, systematize, methodize; temper, moderate; correct, rectify

regulation *syn* LAW, rule, precept, statute, ordinance, canon *rel* instruction, direction, bidding; deciding, decision, determination, ruling

regurgitate *syn* BELCH, burp, vomit, disgorge, spew, throw up

rehearse *syn* RELATE, narrate, describe, recite, recount, state, report *rel* repeat, iterate, reiterate; detail, itemize, particularize

reify *syn* REALIZE, actualize, embody, incarnate, materialize, externalize, objectify, hypostatize

reimburse *syn* PAY, indemnify, repay, recompense, compensate, remunerate, satisfy *rel* recoup, recover; balance, offset

reinforce *syn* STRENGTHEN, invigorate, fortify, energize *rel* increase, augment, multiply, enlarge; support, sustain, prop, bolster, buttress

reissue *syn* EDITION, impression, reprinting, printing

reiterate *syn* REPEAT, iterate, ingeminate

reject *syn* DECLINE, repudiate, spurn, refuse *rel* discard, cast, shed; oust, expel, dismiss, eject; exclude, debar, shut out, eliminate *ant* accept; choose, select

rejoice *syn* PLEASE, delight, gladden, gratify, tickle, regale *ant* grieve; aggrieve; bewail

rejoin *syn* ANSWER, respond, reply, retort

rejoinder *syn* ANSWER, response, reply, retort *rel* returning, return, reverting, reversion; retaliation, reprisal

rejuvenate *syn* RENEW, restore, refresh, renovate, refurbish

relapse *n, syn* LAPSE, backsliding *rel* reversion, atavism, throwback; degeneration, decline, declension, decadence, deterioration

relapse *vb, syn* LAPSE, backslide *rel* revert, return; degenerate, decline, deteriorate

relate **1** · to tell orally or in writing the details or circumstances of a situation *syn* rehearse, recite, recount, narrate, describe, state, report *rel* tell, reveal, disclose, divuige; detail, itemize, particularize **2** *syn* JOIN, associate, link, connect, conjoin, combine, unite *rel* attach, fasten, fix; refer, assign, credit, impute, ascribe **3** *syn* BEAR, pertain, appertain, belong, apply

related · connected by or as if by family ties *syn* cognate, kindred, allied, affiliated *rel* associated, connected; reciprocal, corresponding, correlative, convertible, complementary; akin, identical, alike, analogous, like; relevant, germane, pertinent

relative *syn* DEPENDENT, contingent, conditional *ant* absolute

relaxation *syn* REST, repose, leisure, ease, comfort *rel* amusement, diversion, recreation; relieving, relief, assuagement, alleviation, mitigation

relaxed *syn* LOOSE, slack, lax *rel* mitigated, lightened, alleviated, assuaged, relieved; flexuous, sinuous; soft, mild, gentle, lenient *ant* stiff

release *syn* FREE, liberate, emancipate, manumit, discharge, *rel* detach, disengage; exculpate, exonerate, acquit; surrender, resign, yield, relinquish; deliver, enfranchise *ant* detain; check; oblige

relegate *syn* COMMIT, entrust, confide, consign *rel* refer, assign, credit, accredit, charge, ascribe

relent *syn* YIELD, submit, capitulate, succumb, defer, bow, cave *rel* comply, acquiesce; forbear, refrain, abstain; abate, subside, wane, ebb

relentless *syn* GRIM, unrelenting, merciless, implacable *rel* inexorable, obdurate, adamant, inflexible; strict, stringent, rigid, rigorous; fierce, ferocious, cruel, inhuman

relevant · relating to or bearing upon the matter in hand *syn* germane, material, pertinent, apposite, applicable, apropos *rel* related, cognate, allied; fitting, appropriate, proper; important, significant, weighty *ant* extraneous

reliable · having qualities that merit confidence or trust *syn* dependable, trustworthy, trusty, tried *rel* safe, secure; infallible, inerrable, inerrant, unerring; cogent, valid, sound, convincing, compelling, telling *ant* dubious

reliance *syn* TRUST, confidence, dependence, faith *rel* credence, credit, belief, faith; assurance, conviction, certitude, certainty

relieve · to make something more tolerable or less grievous *syn* alleviate, lighten, assuage, mitigate, allay *rel* comfort, console, solace; moderate, qualify, temper; diminish, reduce, lessen, decrease *ant* intensify; embarrass; alarm

religion · a system of religious belief or the body of persons who accept such a system *syn* denomination, sect, cult, communion, faith, creed, persuasion, church

religious *adj* **1** *syn* DEVOUT, pious, pietistic, sanctimonious *rel* faithful, staunch, steadfast, true; virtuous, righteous, noble, moral, ethical; upright, just, honorable, honest *ant* irreligious **2** *syn* HOLY, spiritual, sacred, divine, blessed *ant* secular; profane

religious *n* · a member of a religious order usu. bound by monastic vows of poverty, chastity, and obedience *syn* monk, friar, nun

relinquish · to give up completely *syn* yield, leave, resign, surrender, cede, abandon, waive *rel* abdicate, renounce; desert, forsake; forgo, forbear, abnegate, sacrifice; discard, shed, cast *ant* keep

relish *n* **1** *syn* TASTE, savor, tang, flavor, smack **2** *syn* TASTE, palate, gusto, zest *rel* liking, loving, enjoying, relishing; predilection, partiality, prepossession, prejudice, bias; propensity, leaning, flair, penchant

relish *vb*, *syn* LIKE, fancy, dote, enjoy, love *rel* appreciate, understand, comprehend; approve, endorse, sanction

relishing *syn* PALATABLE, appetizing, savory, sapid, tasty, toothsome, flavorsome *rel* pleasing, gratifying, delighting, rejoicing, tickling, regaling

reluctant *syn* DISINCLINED, indisposed, hesitant, loath, averse *rel* cautious, circumspect, chary, wary, calculating; antipathetic, unsympathetic

rely (on *or* upon) • to have or place full confidence *syn* trust, depend, count, reckon, bank *rel* confide, entrust, commit; hope, expect, look, await

remain *syn* STAY, wait, abide, tarry, linger *ant* depart

remainder • a remaining or left-over group, part, or trace *syn* residue, residuum, remains, leavings, rest, balance, remnant

remains *syn* REMAINDER, leavings, residue, residuum, rest, balance, remnant

remark *vb* **1** *syn* SEE, notice, note, observe, perceive, discern, behold, descry, espy, view, survey, contemplate **2** • to make observations and pass judgment thereon *syn* comment, commentate, animadvert

remark *n* • an expression of opinion or judgment *syn* observation, comment, commentary, note, obiter dictum

remarkable *syn* NOTICEABLE, prominent, outstanding, conspicuous, salient, signal, striking, arresting *rel* exceptional; important, significant, weighty, momentous; singular, unique, peculiar, strange

remedial *syn* CURATIVE, restorative, sanative, corrective *rel* healing, curing

remedy *n* • something prescribed or used for the treatment of disease *syn* cure, medicine, medicament, medication, specific, physic

remedy *vb* **1** *syn* CURE, heal **2** *syn* CORRECT, rectify, emend, amend, redress, reform, revise *rel* relieve, assuage, alleviate, lighten, mitigate; restore, renew, refresh

remember • to bring an image or idea from the past into the mind *syn* recollect, recall, remind, reminisce, bethink, mind *ant* forget

remembrance **1** *syn* MEMORY, recollection, reminiscence, mind, souvenir *ant* forgetfulness **2** • something that serves to keep a person or thing in mind *syn* remembrancer, reminder, memorial, memento, token, keepsake, souvenir *rel* gift, present, favor

remembrancer *syn* REMEMBRANCE, reminder, memorial, memento, token, keepsake, souvenir

remind *syn* REMEMBER, recollect, recall, reminisce, bethink, mind *rel* suggest, intimate, hint, imply

reminder *syn* REMEMBRANCE, remembrancer, memorial, memento, token, keepsake, souvenir *rel* memorandum; intimation, hint, suggestion

reminisce *syn* REMEMBER, recollect, recall, remind, bethink, mind

reminiscence *syn* MEMORY, remembrance, recollection, mind, souvenir

remiss *syn* NEGLIGENT, lax, slack, neglectful *rel* careless, heedless, thoughtless; forgetful, oblivious, unmindful; indolent, slothful, faineant, lazy *ant* scrupulous

remit **1** *syn* EXCUSE, pardon, forgive, condone *rel* exculpate, exonerate, acquit, vindicate, absolve **2** *syn* SEND, forward, transmit, route, ship, dispatch

remnant *syn* REMAINDER, residue, residuum, remains, leavings, rest, balance *rel* part, piece, fragment, segment, section; vestige, trace

remonstrate *syn* OBJECT, expostulate, protest, kick *rel* oppose, combat, resist, withstand, fight; criticize, denounce, reprobate

remorse *syn* PENITENCE, repentance, contrition, attrition, compunction *rel* regret, sorrow, grief; qualm, scruple, demur

remote *syn* DISTANT, far, faraway, far-off, removed *ant* close

remove *syn* MOVE, shift, transfer *rel* convey, carry, bear, transport, transmit; eradicate, extirpate, uproot, exterminate

removed *syn* DISTANT, remote, far-off, faraway, far

remunerate *syn* PAY, compensate, satisfy, reimburse, indemnify, repay, recompense *rel* award, accord, vouchsafe, grant

remunerative *syn* PAYING, gainful, lucrative, profitable *rel* handsome, bountiful, munificent, liberal; lavish, prodigal, profuse

rend *syn* TEAR, split, cleave, rive, rip *rel* separate, divide, sever, sunder

rendezvous *syn* ENGAGEMENT, tryst, appointment, assignation, date

renegade · a person who forsakes his or her faith, party, cause, or allegiance and aligns with another *syn* apostate, turncoat, recreant, backslider *rel* rebel, insurgent, iconoclast; deserter, forsaker, abandoner; heretic, schismatic *ant* adherent

renew · to make like new *syn* restore, refresh, renovate, refurbish, rejuvenate *rel* mend, repair, rebuild; reform, revise, rectify, correct

renounce 1 *syn* ABDICATE, resign *rel* sacrifice, abnegate, forgo, forbear, eschew *ant* arrogate; covet 2 *syn* ABJURE, forswear, recant, retract *rel* reject, repudiate, spurn; forgo, forbear, eschew *ant* confess; claim

renovate *syn* RENEW, refurbish, rejuvenate, restore, refresh *rel* mend, repair, patch; clean, cleanse

renown *syn* FAME, honor, glory, celebrity, reputation, repute, notoriety, éclat *rel* prestige, authority, influence, weight, credit

renowned *syn* FAMOUS, famed, celebrated, eminent, illustrious *rel* praised, acclaimed, lauded, extolled; outstanding, signal, prominent

rent *vb, syn* HIRE, let, lease, charter

rent *n, syn* BREACH, break, split, schism, rupture, rift *rel* separation, severance, division; tearing, tear, cleaving, cleavage; interruption, gap, hiatus

renunciation · voluntary surrender or putting aside of something desired or desirable *syn* abnegation, self-abnegation, self-denial *rel* sacrificing, sacrifice, forgoing, forbearing, eschewing

repair *syn* MEND, patch, rebuild *rel* remedy, redress, amend, emend, rectify, correct; renew, renovate, refurbish, restore

reparation · a return for something lost or suffered, usu. through the fault of another *syn* redress, amends, restitution, indemnity *rel* expiation, atonement; compensation, remuneration, recompensing, recompense

repartee *syn* WIT, humor, irony, sarcasm, satire *rel* retort, rejoinder, response; badinage, persiflage, raillery

repay *syn* PAY, compensate, remunerate, recompense, satisfy, reimburse, indemnify *rel* balance, offset; accord, award

repeal *syn* REVOKE, reverse, rescind, recall *rel* abrogate, annul, void; cancel, expunge, erase

repeat 1 · to say or do again *syn* iterate, reiterate, ingeminate *rel* return, recur, revert, recrudesce; rehearse, recite, recount, relate 2 *syn* QUOTE, cite

repellent *syn* REPUGNANT, abhorrent, distasteful, obnoxious, invidious *rel* offensive, loathsome, repulsive, revolting *ant* attractive; pleasing

repentance *syn* PENITENCE, contrition, attrition, remorse, compunction *rel* regret, sorrow, grief

repercuss *syn* REBOUND, reverberate, recoil, resile

replace • to put out of a usual or proper place or into the place of another *syn* displace, supplant, supersede *rel* restore, renew; change, alter; recover, regain, recoup, retrieve

replete *syn* FULL, complete, plenary *rel* abundant, plentiful; sated, satiated, surfeited

replica *syn* REPRODUCTION, facsimile, duplicate, copy, carbon copy, transcript

reply *vb, syn* ANSWER, respond, rejoin, retort

reply *n, syn* ANSWER, response, rejoinder, retort *rel* acknowledgment, recognition

report *n* **1** • common talk or an instance of it that spreads rapidly *syn* rumor, gossip, hearsay *rel* talking, talk, conversing, conversation, speaking, speech; chatting, chattering, chatter, prating; news, tidings, intelligence, advice **2** *syn* ACCOUNT, story, chronicle, version **3** *syn* LETTER, dispatch, message, note, epistle, missive, memorandum

report *vb, syn* RELATE, narrate, describe, state, recite, recount, rehearse *rel* communicate, impart; reveal, disclose, discover, tell, divulge

repose *syn* REST, relaxation, leisure, ease, comfort *rel* calmness, tranquillity, serenity, placidity, peacefulness; refreshment, restoration, renewal

reprehend *syn* CRITICIZE, censure, reprobate, condemn, denounce, blame *rel* reprove, rebuke, reprimand, admonish, reproach, chide; scold, upbraid, berate, rate

represent • to present an image or lifelike imitation of (as in art) *syn* depict, portray, delineate, picture, limn *rel* exhibit, display, show; suggest, hint; sketch, outline, draft; describe, narrate, relate

representative *syn* DELEGATE, deputy

repress *syn* SUPPRESS *rel* restrain, curb, check, inhibit; subdue, overcome, conquer

reprimand *syn* REPROVE, rebuke, reproach, admonish, chide *rel* upbraid, rate, berate, scold; censure, denounce, blame, reprehend, reprobate, criticize

reprinting *syn* EDITION, impression, printing, reissue

reprisal *syn* RETALIATION, retribution, revenge, vengeance

reproach *syn* REPROVE, chide, admonish, rebuke, reprimand *rel* criticize, reprehend, censure, reprobate; warn, forewarn, caution; counsel, advise

reprobate *vb, syn* CRITICIZE, censure, reprehend, blame, condemn, denounce *rel* decry, derogate, detract, depreciate, disparage; reject, repudiate, spurn; reprimand, rebuke, reprove

reprobate *adj, syn* ABANDONED, profligate, dissolute *rel* vicious, iniquitous, corrupt, degenerate; blameworthy, guilty, culpable *ant* elect (*in theology*)

reprobate *n, syn* OUTCAST, castaway, derelict, pariah, untouchable *rel* sinner, offender; transgressor, trespasser; villain, scoundrel, blackguard

reproduce *syn* GENERATE, propagate, engender, breed, beget, get, sire, procreate *rel* produce, bear, yield; multiply, increase

reproduction • a thing made to closely resemble another *syn* duplicate, copy, carbon copy, facsimile, replica, transcript

reprove • to criticize adversely *syn* rebuke, reprimand, admonish, reproach, chide *rel* criticize, reprehend, censure, reprobate; chasten, correct, discipline, punish

repudiate 1 *syn* DECLINE, spurn, reject, refuse *rel* renounce, abjure; forgo, forbear, eschew, sacrifice *ant* adopt 2 *syn* DISCLAIM, disavow, disown, disallow *rel* abandon, desert, forsake; discard, cast *ant* own

repugnant 1 • so alien or unlikable as to arouse antagonism and aversion *syn* repellent, abhorrent, distasteful, obnoxious, invidious *rel* foreign, alien, extraneous, extrinsic; uncongenial, incompatible, incongruous, inconsonant; antipathetic, averse, unsympathetic *ant* congenial 2 *syn* OFFENSIVE, repulsive, revolting, loathsome *rel* odious, hateful, abominable, detestable; foul, nasty, dirty; vile, base, low

repulsive *syn* OFFENSIVE, repugnant, revolting, loathsome *rel* repellent, repugnant, abhorrent, obnoxious *ant* alluring, captivating

reputation *syn* FAME, repute, renown, honor, glory, celebrity, éclat, notoriety *rel* credit, weight, influence, authority, prestige

repute *syn* FAME, reputation, renown, celebrity, notoriety, éclat, honor, glory *ant* disrepute

reputed *syn* SUPPOSED, supposititious, suppositious, putative, purported, conjectural, hypothetical *rel* assumed, presumed

request *syn* ASK, solicit *rel* beg, entreat, beseech, implore, supplicate, importune; appeal, petition, sue, pray

require 1 *syn* DEMAND, exact, claim *rel* prescribe, assign, define; warrant, justify 2 *syn* LACK, want, need

requirement • something essential to the existence or occurrence of something else *syn* requisite, prerequisite

requisite *adj, syn* NEEDFUL, necessary, indispensable, essential *rel* compelled, compulsory, constrained, obliged, obligatory; fundamental, cardinal, vital

requisite *n, syn* REQUIREMENT, prerequisite

requite *syn* RECIPROCATE, retaliate, return *rel* repay, recompense, compensate, pay; satisfy, content; revenge, avenge

rescind *syn* REVOKE, reverse, repeal, recall *rel* cancel, expunge, erase; abrogate, annul, void

rescue • to set free from confinement or danger *syn* deliver, redeem, ransom, reclaim, save *rel* free, release, liberate, emancipate, manumit; preserve, conserve, save; extricate, disentangle, disembarrass

research *syn* INQUIRY, investigation, inquisition, inquest, probe

resemblance *syn* LIKENESS, similarity, similitude, analogy, affinity *rel* correspondence, agreement, harmonizing, harmony, conformity; comparison, parallel *ant* difference; distinction

resentment *syn* OFFENSE, umbrage, pique, dudgeon, huff *rel* rancor, animus, animosity, antipathy, antagonism, enmity; ill will, spite, malice, malignity, malignancy

reservation *syn* CONDITION, stipulation, terms, provision, proviso, strings *rel* limitation, restriction, circumscription; exception

reserve *syn* KEEP, keep back, keep out, hold, hold back, retain, withhold, detain *rel* save, preserve, conserve; appropriate, preempt, confiscate, arrogate

reserved *syn* SILENT, reticent, uncommunicative, taciturn, secretive, close, close-lipped, closemouthed, tight-lipped *rel* aloof, detached, uninterested, disinterested, indifferent; shy, diffident, modest, bashful; formal, ceremonious, conventional, ceremonial *ant* affable; expansive; blatant

reside • to have as one's habitation

or domicile *syn* live, dwell, sojourn, lodge, stay, put up, stop *rel* remain, abide; continue, endure

residence *syn* HABITATION, dwelling, abode, domicile, home, house

resident *syn* INHABITANT, denizen, citizen

residue, residuum *syn* REMAINDER, remains, leavings, rest, balance, remnant

resign **1** *syn* RELINQUISH, yield, surrender, leave, abandon, cede, waive *rel* forgo, eschew, sacrifice, forbear, abnegate; abjure, renounce, forswear **2** *syn* ABDICATE, renounce

resignation **1** *syn* COMPLIANCE, acquiescence *rel* submitting, submission, yielding, deferring, deference; meekness, modesty, humbleness, humility, lowliness **2** *syn* PATIENCE, long-suffering, longanimity, forbearance *rel* endurance, toleration, suffering, sufferance; fortitude, backbone, pluck

resigned *syn* COMPLIANT, acquiescent *rel* submissive, subdued, tame; reconciled, adjusted, adapted, accommodated, conformed *ant* rebellious

resile *syn* REBOUND, recoil, reverberate, repercuss

resilient **1** *syn* ELASTIC, springy, flexible, supple *rel* recoiling, resiling, rebounding; recovering, regaining, retrieving **2** *syn* ELASTIC, expansive, buoyant, volatile, effervescent *rel* responsive, sympathetic; spirited, high-spirited, mettlesome *ant* flaccid

resist · to stand firm against a person or influence *syn* withstand, contest, oppose, fight, combat, conflict, antagonize *rel* assail, attack, assault; impugn, gainsay, contravene; thwart, baffle, balk, foil, frustrate *ant* submit; abide

resolute *syn* FAITHFUL, steadfast, staunch, true, loyal *rel* determined, decided, resolved; intrepid, valiant, brave, courageous; stubborn, obstinate, pertinacious

resolution **1** *syn* ANALYSIS, dissection, breakdown *rel* separation, division; elucidation, interpretation, expounding, exposition, explaining, explanation **2** *syn* COURAGE, mettle, spirit, tenacity *rel* pluck, grit, fortitude, backbone, guts

resolve **1** *syn* ANALYZE, dissect, break down *rel* separate, part, divide; reduce, diminish, decrease; melt, fuse *ant* blend **2** *syn* DECIDE, determine, settle, rule *rel* purpose, propose, design, intend, mean; plan, scheme, project **3** *syn* SOLVE, unfold, unravel, decipher *rel* dispel, dissipate, disperse; clear, rid, purge, disabuse

resolved *syn* decided, decisive, determined

resonant · marked by conspicuously full and rich sounds or tones (as of speech or music) *syn* sonorous, ringing, resounding, vibrant, orotund *rel* full, replete; rich, opulent; intensified, enhanced, heightened

resort *n*, *syn* RESOURCE, expedient, shift, makeshift, stopgap, substitute, surrogate *rel* see RESOURCE 2

resort *vb* · to betake oneself or to have recourse when in need of help or relief *syn* refer, apply, go, turn *rel* direct, address, devote; use, employ, utilize

resounding *syn* RESONANT, sonorous, ringing, vibrant, orotund *rel* loud, stentorian, earsplitting; intensified, heightened

resource **1** *pl* **resources** *syn* POSSESSIONS, assets, belongings, effects, means **2** · something one turns to in the absence of the usual means or source of supply *syn* resort, expedient, shift, makeshift, stopgap, substitute, surrogate *rel* device, contrivance, contraption; invention, creation; method, manner, way, fashion, mode, system

respect *n, syn* REGARD, esteem, admiration *rel* reverence, awe, fear; honor, homage, deference; veneration, worship, adoration *ant* contempt

respect *vb, syn* REGARD, esteem, admire *rel* reverence, revere, venerate; value, prize, cherish, appreciate *ant* abuse; misuse

respecting *syn* ABOUT, concerning, regarding

respectively *syn* EACH, apiece, severally, individually

respite *syn* PAUSE, recess, lull, intermission *rel* leisure, ease, rest; interruption, interval, break

resplendent *syn* SPLENDID, gorgeous, glorious, sublime, superb *rel* effulgent, refulgent, radiant, brilliant, bright; blazing, glowing, flaming

respond *syn* ANSWER, reply, rejoin, retort *rel* react, behave, act

response *syn* ANSWER, reply, rejoinder, retort

responsible • subject to being held to account *syn* answerable, accountable, amenable, liable *rel* subject, open, exposed; reliable, dependable, trustworthy

responsive **1** *syn* SENTIENT, sensitive, impressible, impressionable, susceptible *rel* answering, responding, replying; reacting, acting, behaving *ant* impassive **2** *syn* TENDER, sympathetic, warm, warmhearted, compassionate *rel* gentle, mild, lenient, soft; sensible, conscious, alive, awake, aware; sensitive, susceptible, prone, liable

rest *n* • freedom from toil or strain *syn* repose, relaxation, leisure, ease, comfort *rel* intermitting, intermission, suspending, suspension, deferring; stillness, quietness, quiet, silentness, silence; calmness, calm, tranquillity, serenity

rest *vb, syn* BASE, found, ground, bottom, stay *rel* depend, hang, hinge; rely, count

rest *n, syn* REMAINDER, residue, residuum, remains, leavings, balance, remnant *rel* excess, superfluity, surplus, surplusage, overplus

restful *syn* COMFORTABLE, COZY snug, easy *rel* soft, gentle, mild, lenient; still, quiet, silent; placid, peaceful, calm, serene, tranquil

restitution *syn* REPARATION, amends, redress, indemnity *rel* repayment, recompense, reimbursement

restive **1** *syn* CONTRARY, perverse, balky, froward, wayward *rel* intractable, unruly, ungovernable, refractory; obstinate, stubborn, mulish, stiff-necked, pigheaded **2** *syn* IMPATIENT, restless, nervous, unquiet, uneasy, fidgety, jumpy, jittery *rel* see RESTLESS

restless *syn* IMPATIENT, restive, nervous, unquiet, uneasy, fidgety, jumpy, jittery *rel* fitful, spasmodic; inconstant, capricious, unstable, fickle; agitated, disquieted, perturbed, discomposed

restorative *syn* CURATIVE, remedial, corrective, sanative *rel* stimulating, quickening

restore **1** *syn* RENEW, refresh, rejuvenate, renovate, refurbish *rel* save, reclaim, redeem, rescue; reform, revise, amend, correct; recover, regain, retrieve, recoup, recruit **2** • to help or cause to regain signs of life and vigor *syn* revive, revivify, resuscitate *rel* cure, heal, remedy; arouse, rouse, rally, stir

restrain • to hold back from or control in doing something *syn* curb, check, bridle, inhibit *rel* arrest, interrupt; abstain, refrain, forbear; hinder, impede, obstruct, block *ant* impel; incite; activate; abandon (*oneself*)

restraint *syn* FORCE, constraint, compulsion, coercion, duress, violence *rel* curbing, checking, inhibiting; hindering, impeding, obstructing, blocking *ant* incitement; liberty

restrict *syn* LIMIT, circumscribe, confine *rel* bind, tie; contract, shrink; restrain, curb, check

result *syn* EFFECT, consequence, upshot, aftereffect, aftermath, sequel, issue, outcome, event *rel* concluding, conclusion, ending, end, closing, close, termination; product, production

resuscitate *syn* RESTORE, revive, revivify *rel* reanimate; rekindle

retain *syn* KEEP, keep back, keep out, detain, withhold, reserve, hold, hold back *rel* have, own, possess, enjoy; save, preserve, conserve

retaliate *syn* RECIPROCATE, requite, return *rel* revenge, avenge; repay, recompense, compensate, pay

retaliation • the act of inflicting or the intent to inflict injury in return for injury *syn* reprisal, revenge, vengeance, retribution *rel* punishment, disciplining, discipline, correcting, correction; recompensing, recompense, indemnification, repayment

retard *syn* DELAY, slow, slacken, detain *rel* reduce, lessen, decrease; arrest, check, interrupt; clog, fetter, hamper; balk, baffle, frustrate *ant* accelerate; advance, further

reticent *syn* SILENT, reserved, uncommunicative, taciturn, secretive, close, close-lipped, closemouthed, tight-lipped *rel* restrained, inhibited, curbed, checked; discreet, prudent *ant* frank

retire *syn* GO, withdraw, leave, depart, quit *rel* recede, retreat; recoil, rebound, resile; relinquish, yield, surrender, abandon

retort *vb, syn* ANSWER, rejoin, reply, respond

retort *n, syn* ANSWER, rejoinder, reply, response *rel* retaliation, reprisal, revenge; repartee

retract **1** *syn* RECEDE, retrograde, back, retreat *ant* protract **2** *syn* ABJURE, recant, renounce, forswear *rel* eliminate, exclude, suspend, rule out

retreat *n, syn* SHELTER, cover, refuge, asylum, sanctuary *rel* harbor, haven, port; safety, security; seclusion, solitude

retreat *vb, syn* RECEDE, retrograde, back, retract *rel* withdraw, retire, depart, go; recoil, shrink, quail

retrench *syn* SHORTEN, curtail, abridge, abbreviate *rel* decrease, lessen, reduce, diminish

retribution *syn* RETALIATION, reprisal, vengeance, revenge *rel* reparation, redress, amends, restitution; visitation, tribulation, trial, affliction

retrieve *syn* RECOVER, regain, recoup, recruit *rel* amend, remedy, redress, reform, correct; repair, mend, rebuild *ant* lose

retrograde *adj, syn* BACKWARD, retrogressive, regressive *rel* reversed, inverted; relapsing, lapsing, backsliding

retrograde *vb, syn* RECEDE, retreat, back, retract *rel* return, revert; reverse, invert; relapse, lapse, backslide

retrogressive *syn* BACKWARD, regressive, retrograde *rel* reversing, inverting; receding, retreating, retrograding *ant* progressive

return *vb* **1** • to go or come back (as to a person, place, or condition) *syn* revert, recur, recrudesce *rel* advert; turn, rotate, revolve; restore, renew; recover, regain; reverberate, repercuss, rebound **2** *syn* RECIPROCATE, retaliate, requite *rel* repay, recompense, compensate; give, bestow

return *n* · the act of coming back to or from a place or condition *syn* reversion, recurrence, recrudescence

reveal · to make known what has been or should be concealed *syn* discover, disclose, divulge, tell, betray *rel* impart, communicate; suggest, adumbrate, shadow, declare, announce, publish *ant* conceal

revelation · disclosure or something disclosed by or as if by divine or preternatural means *syn* vision, apocalypse, prophecy *ant* adumbration

revenant *syn* APPARITION, phantasm, phantom, wraith, ghost, spirit, specter, shade

revenge *vb, syn* AVENGE *rel* recompense, repay, pay; vindicate, defend, justify

revenge *n, syn* RETALIATION, vengeance, retribution, reprisal *rel* reparation, redress, amends; recompensing, recompense, repayment

revengeful *syn* VINDICTIVE, vengeful *rel* implacable, relentless, unrelenting, merciless, grim; inexorable, obdurate, adamant, inflexible

reverberate *syn* REBOUND, repercuss, recoil, resile *rel* return, revert, recur

revere · to honor and admire profoundly and respectfully *syn* reverence, venerate, worship, adore *rel* esteem, respect, regard, admire; cherish, prize, value, treasure, appreciate *ant* flout

reverence *n* **1** *syn* HONOR, homage, deference, obeisance *rel* piety, devotion, fealty, loyalty, fidelity; esteem, respect, regard, admiration **2** · a feeling of worshipful respect *syn* veneration, worship, adoration *rel* fervor, ardor, zeal, passion; devoutness, piousness, religiousness **3** · the emotion inspired by what arouses one's deep respect or veneration *syn* awe, fear

reverence *vb, syn* REVERE, venerate, worship, adore *rel* love, enjoy, like; esteem, respect, regard, admire

reverse *vb* **1** · to change to the opposite position *syn* transpose, invert *rel* overturn, upset, capsize **2** *syn* REVOKE, repeal, rescind, recall *rel* upset, overturn; retract, recant, abjure, forswear; abrogate, annul

reverse *n, syn* OPPOSITE, contradictory, contrary, antithesis, antipode, antonym, converse, counter

reversion **1** *syn* RETURN, recurrence, recrudescence **2** · a return to an ancestral type or condition or an instance of such return *syn* atavism, throwback *rel* relapse, lapse, backsliding

reversionary · relating to a return to an ancestral type *syn* atavistic

revert *syn* RETURN, recur, recrudesce *rel* recede, retreat, retrograde, back; lapse, relapse, backslide

review **1** *syn* CRITICISM, critique, blurb, puff **2** *syn* JOURNAL, periodical, magazine, organ, newspaper

revile *syn* SCOLD, vituperate, rail, berate, rate, upbraid, tongue-lash, jaw, bawl, chew out, wig *rel* vilify, calumniate, malign, traduce, defame, asperse, slander, libel; execrate, objurgate, curse *ant* laud

revise **1** *syn* CORRECT, rectify, emend, remedy, redress, amend, reform *rel* improve, better, ameliorate; change, alter, modify **2** *syn* EDIT, compile, redact, rewrite, adapt *rel* amend, emend, correct, rectify; improve, better

revive *syn* RESTORE, revivify, resuscitate *rel* recover, recruit, regain; recuperate, improve, gain; refresh, rejuvenate, renew

revivify *syn* RESTORE, revive, resuscitate *rel* reanimate; vitalize, activate, energize; galvanize, quicken, stimulate, provoke

revoke · to annul by recalling or taking back *syn* reverse, repeal, rescind, recall *rel* annul, abrogate, void; cancel, expunge, erase; invalidate, nullify

revolt *syn* REBELLION, revolution, uprising, insurrection, mutiny, putsch, coup *rel* insubordination, seditiousness, sedition, factiousness, contumaciousness, contumacy

revolting *syn* OFFENSIVE, loathsome, repulsive, repugnant *rel* horrible, horrid, horrific; repellent, distasteful, obnoxious, abhorrent; odious, hateful, abominable

revolution *syn* REBELLION, uprising, revolt, insurrection, mutiny, putsch, coup *rel* overthrowing, overthrow, subverting, subversion, upsetting, upset, overturning, overturn; change, modification, alteration

revolve *syn* TURN, rotate, gyrate, circle, spin, twirl, whirl, wheel, eddy, swirl, pirouette *rel* swing, sway, oscillate, vibrate

reward *syn* PREMIUM, prize, award, meed, guerdon, bounty, bonus

rewrite *syn* EDIT, compile, revise, redact, adapt

rhapsody *syn* BOMBAST, rant, fustian, rodomontade

rhetorical · emphasizing style often at the expense of thought *syn* grandiloquent, magniloquent, aureate, flowery, euphuistic, bombastic *rel* eloquent, articulate, vocal, fluent, voluble, glib; florid, ornate, flamboyant; inflated, turgid, tumid, flatulent

rhymer, rhymester *syn* POET, versifier, poetaster, bard, minstrel, troubadour

rhythm · the regular rise and fall in intensity of sounds that is associated chiefly with poetry and music *syn* meter, cadence

rib *syn* BANTER, chaff, kid, rag, josh, jolly

ribald *syn* COARSE, obscene, gross, vulgar *rel* offensive, loathsome; indecent, indelicate, indecorous; lewd, lascivious, wanton, licentious; scurrilous, opprobrious

ribbon *syn* STRIP, fillet, band, stripe

rich · having goods, property, and money in abundance *syn* wealthy, affluent, opulent *ant* poor

ricochet *syn* SKIP, bound, hop, curvet, lope, lollop

rid · to set a person or thing free of something that encumbers *syn* clear, unburden, disabuse, purge *rel* free, release, liberate; exterminate, extirpate, eradicate, uproot; abolish, extinguish

riddle *syn* MYSTERY, puzzle, conundrum, enigma, problem

ride *vb* **1** · to travel by automobile or other conveyance *syn* drive **2** *syn* BAIT, badger, heckle, hector, chivy, hound *rel* worry, annoy, harass, harry; persecute, oppress; torment, torture, afflict

ride *n* · a usu. short trip in a vehicle or by other conveyance *syn* drive *rel* journey, tour, trip, excursion, expedition

ridicule · to make an object of laughter of *syn* deride, mock, taunt, twit, rally *rel* scoff, flout, jeer, gibe; caricature, burlesque, travesty

ridiculous *syn* LAUGHABLE, risible, ludicrous, droll, funny, comic, comical, farcical *rel* absurd, preposterous, foolish, silly; amusing, diverting, entertaining; fantastic, grotesque, bizarre, antic

rife *syn* PREVAILING, prevalent, current *rel* abundant, plentiful, copious, ample; common, ordinary, familiar

rifle *syn* ROB, plunder, loot, burglarize *rel* despoil, spoilate, ravage, pillage, sack, devastate; steal, pilfer, purloin, filch

rift *syn* BREACH, break, split, schism, rent, rupture *rel* crack, cleft, fissure; gap, interval, hiatus, interruption; separation, division

right *adj* **1** *syn* GOOD *ant* wrong **2** *syn* CORRECT, accurate, exact, precise, nice *rel* fitting, proper, meet, fit; decorous, decent, seemly *ant* wrong

right *n* · something to which one has a just claim *syn* prerogative, privilege, perquisite, appanage, birthright *rel* claim, title; freedom, license, liberty

righteous *syn* MORAL, virtuous, noble, ethical *rel* upright, honest, just, honorable *ant* iniquitous

rightful *syn* DUE, condign *rel* fair, equitable, just, impartial; lawful, legal, legitimate

rigid **1** *syn* STIFF, inflexible, tense, stark, wooden *rel* firm, hard, solid; compact, close; tough, tenacious, strong *ant* elastic **2** · extremely severe or stern *syn* rigorous, strict, stringent *rel* inflexible, inexorable, obdurate, adamant, adamantine; stern, severe, austere *ant* lax

rigor *syn* DIFFICULTY, hardship, vicissitude *rel* austerity, severity, sternness; harshness, roughness; trial, tribulation, visitation, affliction *ant* amenity

rigorous *syn* RIGID, strict, stringent *rel* stiff, inflexible; stern, austere, ascetic, severe; exacting, onerous, burdensome, oppressive

rile *syn* IRRITATE, exasperate, nettle, provoke, aggravate, peeve

rim *syn* BORDER, brim, brink, margin, verge, edge

rind *syn* SKIN, bark, peel, hide, pelt

ring *n, syn* COMBINATION, combine, party, bloc, faction

ring *vb, syn* SURROUND, environ, encircle, circle, encompass, compass, hem, gird, girdle *rel* confine, circumscribe, limit, restrict; enclose, corral, wall

ringing *syn* RESONANT, sonorous, resounding, vibrant, orotund

rip *syn* TEAR, rend, split, cleave, rive

ripe *syn* MATURE, matured, mellow, adult, grown-up *rel* seasonable, timely, well-timed; consummate, finished, accomplished *ant* green; unripe

ripen *syn* MATURE, develop, age *rel* improve, better; enhance, heighten, intensify; season

rise *vb* **1** *syn* SPRING, arise, originate, derive, flow, issue, emanate, proceed, stem *rel* appear, emerge, loom *ant* abate **2** · to move or come up from a lower to a higher level *syn* arise, ascend, mount, soar, tower, rocket, levitate, surge *rel* climb, ascend, scale; increase, enlarge, augment; lift, raise, elevate *ant* decline; set (*as the sun*)

rise *n, syn* BEGINNING, genesis, initiation *rel* origin, source, inception, root, provenance, provenience; derivation, origination *ant* fall

risible *syn* LAUGHABLE, droll, funny, ludicrous, ridiculous, comic, comical, farcical *rel* amusing, diverting, entertaining

risk *n, syn* DANGER, hazard, peril, jeopardy *rel* chance, fortune, luck, accident; exposedness, exposure, liableness, liability, openness

risk *vb, syn* VENTURE, hazard, chance, jeopardize, endanger, imperil *rel* dare, brave, beard, face, defy; confront, encounter, meet

risky *syn* DANGEROUS, precarious, hazardous, perilous *rel* adventurous, venturesome; chancy, random, haphazard, hit-or-miss, happy-go-lucky

rite, ritual *syn* FORM, liturgy, ceremonial, ceremony, formality

rival **1** · to strive to equal or

surpass *syn* compete, vie, emulate *rel* strive, struggle, try, attempt; contend, fight **2** *syn* MATCH, equal, approach, touch

rive *syn* TEAR, cleave, split, rend, rip *rel* sever, sunder, divide, separate; cut, hew, chop

rivet *syn* SECURE, anchor, moor *rel* fasten, attach, affix, fix; join, unite, connect, link

roam *syn* WANDER, stray, ramble, rove, range, prowl, gad, gallivant, traipse, meander

roar *vb* • to make a very loud and often a continuous or protracted noise *syn* bellow, bluster, bawl, vociferate, clamor, howl, ululate *rel* reverberate, repercuss, rebound; yell, shout; bay, bark, growl, yelp

roar *n* • a very loud and often a continuous noise *syn* bellow, bluster, bawl, vociferation, ululation

rob • to take possessions unlawfully *syn* plunder, rifle, loot, burglarize *rel* steal, pilfer, purloin, filch, lift; defraud, swindle, cheat; despoil, pillage, sack, ravage

robber *syn* THIEF, burglar, larcener, larcenist

robbery *syn* THEFT, larceny, burglary

robe *syn* CLOTHE, attire, dress, apparel, array

robust *syn* HEALTHY, sound, wholesome, hale, well *rel* strong, sturdy, stout, stalwart; athletic, husky, muscular, sinewy; vigorous, energetic, lusty *ant* frail, feeble

rock *syn* SHAKE, agitate, convulse *rel* swing, sway, undulate, oscillate; totter, quake, tremble

rocket *syn* RISE, arise, ascend, mount, soar, tower, levitate, surge

rococo *syn* ORNATE, baroque, flamboyant, florid

rodomontade *syn* BOMBAST, rhapsody, rant, fustian *rel* boasting, bragging, vaunting; vainglory, vanity, pride; magniloquence, grandiloquence

rogue *syn* VILLAIN, scoundrel, blackguard, knave, rascal, scamp, rapscallion, miscreant *rel* vagabond, vagrant, tramp, hobo, bum; malefactor, culprit, delinquent, criminal

roguish *syn* PLAYFUL, frolicsome, sportive, waggish, impish, mischievous

roily *syn* TURBID, muddy

roll *syn* LIST, table, catalog, schedule, register, roster, inventory

rollick *vb, syn* PLAY, frolic, disport, sport, romp, gambol

rollick *n, syn* PLAY, frolic, disport, sport, romp, gambol

romantic *syn* SENTIMENTAL, mawkish, maudlin, soppy, mushy, slushy *rel* fanciful, imaginary, quixotic, fantastic, visionary; invented, created; picturesque, pictorial, vivid, graphic

romp *n, syn* PLAY, frolic, rollick, gambol, disport, sport

romp *vb, syn* PLAY, frolic, rollick, gambol, disport, sport

room **1** • space in a building enclosed or set apart by a partition *syn* chamber, apartment **2** • enough space or range for free movement *syn* berth, play, elbowroom, leeway, margin, clearance

roost *syn* ALIGHT, perch, light, land

root *n, syn* ORIGIN, source, inception, provenance, provenience, prime mover *rel* beginning, commencing, commencement, starting, start; foundation, basis, ground, base

root *vb, syn* APPLAUD, cheer

roseate *syn* HOPEFUL, optimistic, rose-colored

rose-colored *syn* HOPEFUL, optimistic, roseate

roster *syn* LIST, table, catalog, schedule, register, roll, inventory

rot *vb, syn* DECAY, decompose, putrefy, spoil, disintegrate, crumble *rel* corrupt, vitiate, debase; taint, contaminate, pollute, defile

rot *n, syn* NONSENSE, twaddle, drivel, bunk, balderdash, poppycock, gobbledygook, trash, bull

rotate **1** *syn* TURN, revolve, gyrate, circle, spin, twirl, whirl, wheel, eddy, swirl, pirouette **2** · to succeed or cause to succeed each other in turn *syn* alternate *rel* interchange, exchange, bandy; succeed, follow, ensue

rotter *syn* CAD, bounder

rotund *syn* FLESHY, plump, chubby, portly, stout, fat, corpulent, obese *ant* angular

rough **1** · not smooth or even *syn* harsh, uneven, rugged, scabrous *rel* hard, solid, firm; coarse, gross; rank, rampant *ant* smooth **2** *syn* RUDE, crude, uncouth, raw, callow, green *rel* brusque, crusty, gruff, curt, blunt, bluff; ungracious, uncivil, discourteous, impolite, rude; indecorous, unseemly, indecent, indelicate *ant* gentle

roundabout *syn* INDIRECT, circuitous *rel* sinuous, winding, tortuous, flexuous

rouse *syn* STIR, arouse, awaken, rally, waken *rel* enliven, quicken, animate, vivify; stimulate, excite, provoke; incite, foment, instigate

roustabout *syn* WORKER, workman, workingman, laborer, mechanic, artisan, operative, hand, craftsman, handicraftsman

rout *n, syn* CROWD, throng, press, crush, mob, horde

rout *vb, syn* CONQUER, vanquish, defeat, subdue, subjugate, reduce, overcome, surmount, overthrow, beat, lick

route *n, syn* WAY, course, passage, pass, artery

route *vb, syn* SEND, forward, transmit, remit, ship, dispatch

rove *syn* WANDER, stray, roam, ramble, range, prowl, gad, gallivant, traipse, meander

row *n, syn* LINE, rank, file, echelon, tier *rel* series, sequence, succession, train

row *n, syn* BRAWL, broil, fracas, melee, rumpus, scrap *rel* fight, affray, fray, combat, conflict, contest; altercation, wrangle, quarrel, squabble

royal *syn* KINGLY, regal, queenly, imperial, princely *rel* splendid, resplendent, glorious, superb; august, majestic, stately, imposing, grand

rubbish *syn* REFUSE, waste, trash, debris, garbage, offal

rube *syn* BOOR, bumpkin, hick, yokel, clodhopper, clown, lout, churl

rude **1** · lacking in social refinement *syn* rough, crude, raw, callow, green, uncouth *rel* boorish, churlish, clownish, loutish; rustic, rural, bucolic; barbarous, savage, barbarian; primitive, primary, primeval **2** · offensive in manner or action *syn* ill-mannered, impolite, discourteous, uncivil, ungracious *rel* brusque, curt, gruff, crusty, bluff; impertinent, intrusive, meddlesome; surly, crabbed, sullen *ant* civil; urbane

rudimentary *syn* ELEMENTARY, basal, beginning, elemental

rueful *syn* MELANCHOLY, dolorous, doleful, lugubrious, plaintive *rel* depressed, weighed down, oppressed; piteous, pitiful; despairing, despondent, hopeless

rugged *syn* ROUGH, scabrous, harsh, uneven *rel* robust, healthy; burly, brawny, husky, muscular; rank, rampant; arduous, hard, difficult *ant* fragile

ruin *n* · the bringing about of or the results of disaster *syn* havoc, devastation, destruction *rel* disintegration, crumbling

ruin *vb* · to subject to forces that are destructive of soundness, worth, or usefulness *syn* wreck, dilapidate *rel* destroy, demolish, raze; deface, disfigure; maim, mutilate, mangle

rule *n, syn* LAW, regulation, precept, statute, ordinance, canon *rel* order, mandate, dictate, command; principle, axiom, fundamental; etiquette, decorum, propriety

rule *vb* **1** *syn* GOVERN *rel* guide, lead; manage, direct, control, conduct **2** *syn* DECIDE, determine, settle, resolve *rel* conclude, judge, gather, deduce, infer

rule out *syn* EXCLUDE, eliminate, debar, shut out, suspend, disbar, blackball *rel* bar, block, hinder; prevent, preclude, obviate

ruminate *syn* PONDER, muse, meditate *rel* consider, weigh, excogitate; reflect, deliberate, speculate, cogitate, think

rummage *syn* SEEK, comb, ransack, search, hunt, scour, ferret out *rel* examine, inspect, scrutinize

rumor *syn* REPORT, gossip, hearsay

rumpus *syn* BRAWL, broil, fracas, melee, row, scrap

runt *syn* DWARF, pygmy, midget, manikin, homunculus

rupture *syn* BREACH, break, split, schism, rent, rift *rel* separation, division, parting, severance, divorce; estrangement, alienation

rural • relating to or characteristic of the country *syn* rustic, pastoral, bucolic

ruse *syn* TRICK, stratagem, maneuver, gambit, ploy, artifice, wile, feint *rel* chicane, trickery, deception; expedient, shift, makeshift, resource, resort

rush • to move or cause to move quickly, impetuously, and often heedlessly *syn* dash, tear, shoot, charge *rel* speed, hurry, hasten; dart, fly, scud

rustic *syn* RURAL, pastoral, bucolic

ruth *syn* SYMPATHY, commiseration, compassion, pity, condolence, empathy *rel* mercy, grace, charity, clemency, lenity; forbearance, tolerance, indulgence

S

sack *n, syn* BAG, pouch

sack *vb, syn* DISMISS, discharge, cashier, drop, fire, bounce

sack *vb, syn* RAVAGE, pillage, despoil, spoliate, devastate, waste *rel* plunder, rob, loot, rifle; destroy, demolish, raze; strip, bare, denude

sacred **1** *syn* HOLY, divine, blessed, spiritual, religious *rel* dedicated, consecrated, hallowed; cherished, treasured, valued *ant* profane **2** • protected (as by law, custom, or human respect) against abuse *syn* sacrosanct, inviolate, inviolable *rel* protected, shielded, defended, guarded; revered, reverenced, venerated

sacrifice *syn* FORGO, abnegate, forbear, eschew *rel* renounce, abdicate; surrender, yield, resign, relinquish

sacrilege *syn* PROFANATION, desecration, blasphemy *rel* defilement, pollution; violation, transgression, trespass, breach; sin, crime, scandal, offense

sacrilegious *syn* IMPIOUS, blasphemous, profane *rel* polluting, defiling; profaning, desecrating

sacrosanct *syn* SACRED, inviolate, inviolable *rel* respected, regarded, esteemed; revered, venerated, reverenced

saddle *syn* BURDEN, encumber, cumber, weigh, weight, load, lade, tax, charge

sadness • the quality, state, or instance of being unhappy or low in spirits *syn* depression, melancholy, melancholia, dejection, gloom, blues, dumps *rel* sorrow, grief, anguish, woe; despondency, despair, hopelessness, forlornness *ant* gladness

safe • affording security from threat of danger, harm, or loss *syn* secure *rel* protected, guarded, shielded; reliable, dependable, tried *ant* dangerous

safeguard *syn* DEFEND, guard, shield, protect *rel* conserve, preserve, save; secure, insure, ensure, assure

sag *syn* DROOP, wilt, flag *rel* sink, slump, subside, fall, drop; hang, dangle, suspend

saga *syn* MYTH, legend

sagacious *syn* SHREWD, perspicacious, astute *rel* sharp, keen, acute; penetrating, piercing, probing; wise, judicious, sage, sapient

sage *syn* WISE, sapient, judicious, prudent, sensible, sane *rel* intelligent, knowing, brilliant; learned, erudite; sagacious, perspicacious, shrewd

sail *syn* FLY, float, skim, scud, shoot, dart

sailor *syn* MARINER, seaman, tar, gob, bluejacket

salary *syn* WAGE, wages, stipend, pay, hire, emolument, fee

salient *syn* NOTICEABLE, conspicuous, outstanding, signal, striking, arresting, prominent, remarkable *rel* significant, important, weighty; impressive, moving; obtrusive, intrusive

salubrious *syn* HEALTHFUL, healthy, wholesome, salutary, hygienic, sanitary *rel* beneficial, advantageous; benign, favorable

salutary *syn* HEALTHFUL, wholesome, healthy, salubrious, hygienic, sanitary *rel* beneficial, advantageous, profitable *ant* deleterious; evil

salutation *syn* GREETING, salute

salute *vb, syn* ADDRESS, greet, hail, accost

salute *n, syn* GREETING, salutation

same • not different or not differing from one another *syn* selfsame, very, identical, identic, equivalent, equal, tantamount *rel* alike, like, akin, parallel, uniform *ant* different

sample *syn* INSTANCE, specimen, example, case, illustration *rel* piece, part, portion, segment, fragment

sanative *syn* CURATIVE, remedial, restorative, corrective *rel* salutary, hygienic, sanitary, healthful; healing, curing, remedying

sanctimonious 1 *syn* DEVOUT, pietistic, religious, pious *rel* see SANCTIMONIOUS 2 2 *syn* HYPOCRITICAL, pharisaical, canting *rel* affected, feigned, simulated, counterfeited, assumed, pretended; perfervid, fervid, ardent, fervent, impassioned

sanctimony *syn* HYPOCRISY, pharisaism, cant *rel* pretending, pretense, simulation, feigning, counterfeiting, affecting, affectation; enthusiasm, zealotry, fanaticism

sanction *syn* APPROVE, endorse, accredit, certify *rel* authorize, license, commission; confirm, ratify; enforce, implement *ant* interdict

sanctity *syn* HOLINESS

sanctuary *syn* SHELTER, refuge, asylum, cover, retreat *rel* safety, security; protection, shielding, shield, guarding, guard

sand *syn* FORTITUDE, grit, backbone, pluck, guts *rel* courage, mettle, spirit, resolution, tenacity

sane *syn* WISE, judicious, prudent, sensible, sage, sapient *rel* rational, reasonable; right, good; sound, cogent, convincing, compelling *ant* insane

sangfroid *syn* EQUANIMITY, phlegm, composure *rel* indifference, unconcernedness, unconcern, aloofness, detachment; self-possession, aplomb, self-assurance, assurance, self-confidence, confidence

sanguinary *syn* BLOODY, sanguine, sanguineous, gory

sanguine **1** *also* **sanguineous** *syn* BLOODY, sanguinary, gory *ant* bloodless **2** *syn* CONFIDENT, assured, sure, presumptuous *rel* hopeful, optimistic; positive, certain *ant* afraid

sanitary *syn* HEALTHFUL, hygienic, salutary, salubrious, healthy, wholesome *rel* curing, curative, healing, remedying; effective, efficacious, effectual *ant* noxious

sanitize *syn* STERILIZE, disinfect, fumigate

sap *syn* WEAKEN, undermine, enfeeble, debilitate, cripple, disable *rel* drain, deplete, exhaust, impoverish; ruin, wreck; destroy

sapid *syn* PALATABLE, appetizing, savory, tasty, toothsome, flavorsome, relishing *ant* insipid

sapient *syn* WISE, sage, judicious, prudent, sensible, sane *rel* learned, erudite, scholarly; sagacious, perspicacious, shrewd

sarcasm *syn* WIT, satire, irony, humor, repartee *rel* incisiveness, trenchancy, bitingness, cuttingness; mockery, taunting, derision

sarcastic • marked by bitterness and a power or will to cut or sting *syn* satiric, ironic, sardonic *rel* biting, cutting, trenchant, incisive; caustic, scathing, mordant

sardonic *syn* SARCASTIC, ironic, satiric *rel* bitter, acrid; deriding, derisive, mocking, taunting, ridiculing; sinister, malign

sate *syn* SATIATE, surfeit, cloy, pall, glut, gorge *rel* satisfy, content; indulge, pamper, humor; gratify, regale, please

satellite *syn* FOLLOWER, adherent, henchman, partisan, disciple, sectary *rel* sycophant, parasite, favorite, toady, lickspittle, bootlicker, hanger-on; devotee, votary, addict

satiate • to fill to repletion *syn* sate, surfeit, cloy, pall, glut, gorge *rel* satisfy, content; pamper, humor, indulge; gratify, regale, please

satiny *syn* SLEEK, silky, silken, velvety, glossy, slick

satire *syn* WIT, irony, humor, sarcasm, repartee *rel* raillery, persiflage, badinage; lampoon, pasquinade, libel, skit; ridiculing, ridicule, deriding, derision, taunting

satiric *syn* SARCASTIC, ironic, sardonic *rel* pungent, piquant, poignant; ridiculing, deriding, derisive, taunting, mocking; mordant, caustic, scathing

satisfied • showing or expressing satisfaction from the fulfillment of one's desires *syn* content, contented *rel* gratified, gladdened, pleased; appeased, pacified

satisfy **1** • to appease desires or longings *syn* content *rel* gratify, gladden, please; appease, pacify; satiate, sate *ant* tantalize **2** *syn* PAY, recompense, compensate, remunerate, repay, reimburse, indemnify *rel* balance, offset **3** • to measure up to a set of criteria or requirements *syn* fulfill, meet, answer *rel* prove, test, try, demonstrate; verify, substantiate, corroborate, confirm; match, equal, rival, approach, touch

saturate **1** *syn* SOAK, steep, impregnate, drench, sop, waterlog *rel* dip, immerse, submerge; absorb, imbibe, assimilate **2** *syn* PERMEATE, impregnate, impenetrate, interpenetrate, penetrate, pervade *rel* infuse, imbue, ingrain, inoculate; pierce, probe, enter

saturnine *syn* SULLEN, dour, gloomy, glum, morose, surly, sulky, crabbed *rel* grave, serious, solemn, somber, staid; taciturn, reserved, uncommunicative, silent *ant* genial; mercurial

saucy • flippant and bold in manner or attitude *syn* pert, arch *rel* flippant, frivolous, volatile, light-minded; intrusive, obtrusive, meddlesome, impertinent; brash, impudent, shameless; piquant, snappy

saunter • to walk slowly in an idle or aimless manner *syn* stroll, amble

savage **1** *syn* FIERCE, ferocious, barbarous, inhuman, cruel, fell, truculent *rel* implacable, relentless, unrelenting, merciless, grim; rapacious, voracious, ravenous **2** *syn* BARBARIAN, barbaric, barbarous *rel* primitive, primeval; rough, harsh; untaught, untutored, ignorant

save **1** *syn* RESCUE, deliver, redeem, ransom, reclaim *rel* free, release, liberate, emancipate; defend, protect, shield, guard, safeguard; recover, retrieve, recoup, recruit *ant* lose; waste; damn (*in theology*) **2** • to keep secure or maintain intact from injury, decay, or loss *syn* preserve, conserve *rel* have, hold, own, possess, enjoy; keep, retain, reserve *ant* spend; consume

savoir faire *syn* TACT, poise, address *rel* grace, dignity, elegance; ease, readiness, dexterity, facility; self-possession, self-assurance, aplomb, confidence

savor *syn* TASTE, flavor, tang, relish, smack *rel* quality, property, character, attribute; peculiarity, individuality, characteristic, distinctiveness; impression, impress, print, stamp

savory *syn* PALATABLE, appetizing, sapid, tasty, toothsome, flavorsome, relishing *ant* bland; acrid

saw *syn* SAYING, adage, proverb, maxim, motto, epigram, aphorism, apothegm

say • to express in words *syn* utter, tell, state *rel* pronounce, articulate, enunciate; express, voice, broach; speak, talk; declare, announce, proclaim; note, observe; comment, animadvert, remark; explain, expound; cite, quote, repeat; assert, affirm, aver, avow, protest

saying • an often repeated statement that usu. is brief and expresses a common observation or general truth *syn* saw, adage, proverb, maxim, motto, epigram, aphorism, apothegm

scabrous *syn* ROUGH, harsh, uneven, rugged *ant* glabrous; smooth

scale *syn* ASCEND, climb, mount

scamp *syn* VILLAIN, scoundrel, blackguard, knave, rascal, rogue, rapscallion, miscreant *rel* malefactor, culprit, delinquent, criminal

scamper *syn* SCUTTLE, scurry, skedaddle, sprint *rel* speed, hurry, hasten; rush, dash, shoot

scan *syn* SCRUTINIZE, examine, inspect, audit *rel* consider, study, contemplate; observe, survey, remark, notice, see

scandal **1** *syn* OFFENSE, sin, vice, crime *rel* indignity, insult, affront; offending, outraging, outrage; wrong, grievance, injury, injustice **2** *syn* DETRACTION, calumny, slander, backbiting *rel* gossiping, gossip, tattling; maligning, defaming, defamation, traducing

scanning *syn* SCRUTINY, examination, inspection, audit *rel* study, application, attention, concentration; oversight, supervision, surveillance; analysis, dissection

scant, scanty *syn* MEAGER, skimpy, scrimpy, exiguous, spare, sparse *rel* deficient, defective; scarce, rare, infrequent *ant* plentiful; profuse

scarce *syn* INFREQUENT, rare, uncommon, occasional, sporadic *rel* deficient; curtailed, abridged, shortened *ant* abundant

scare *syn* FRIGHTEN, alarm, fright, terrify, terrorize, startle, affray, affright *rel* daunt, appall, dismay; intimidate, cow, browbeat; astound, amaze, flabbergast, astonish, surprise *ant* entice

scathing *syn* CAUSTIC, mordant, acrid *ant* scorching, searing, burning; fierce, ferocious, truculent, savage; incisive, biting, cutting, trenchant

scatter **1** · to cause to separate or break up *syn* disperse, dissipate, dispel *rel* throw, cast, fling, toss; distribute, dispense, divide; discard, shed **2** *syn* STREW, straw, broadcast, sow *rel* spread, disseminate; sprinkle, besprinkle

scent *syn* SMELL, odor, aroma *rel* emanation, issuing, issue

schedule **1** *syn* LIST, table, catalog, register, roll, roster, inventory **2** *syn* PROGRAM, timetable, agenda

scheme *n* **1** *syn* PLAN, design, plot, project *rel* proposal, proposition; arrangement, ordering; device, contrivance; expedient, shift, makeshift **2** *syn* SYSTEM, network, complex, organism *rel* organization, arrangement, ordering; whole, total, sum

scheme *vb, syn* PLAN, design, plot, project *rel* propose, purpose, intend; aim, aspire; manipulate, handle, swing, wield

schism *syn* BREACH, split, rupture, break, rent, rift *rel* division, separation, severance; estrangement, alienation; discord, dissension

schismatic *syn* HERETIC, sectarian, dissenter, nonconformist

scholarly *syn* LEARNED, erudite *rel* academic, scholastic, pedantic; abstruse, recondite; accurate, exact, precise, correct

scholarship *syn* KNOWLEDGE, learning, erudition, science, information, lore

scholastic *syn* PEDANTIC, academic, bookish *rel* conversant, versed; dry, arid; formal, conventional, ceremonial

school *syn* TEACH, discipline, train, instruct, educate *rel* practice, exercise, drill; guide, lead; conduct, control, direct, manage

science *syn* KNOWLEDGE, learning, erudition, scholarship, information, lore

scintillate *syn* FLASH, gleam, glance, glint, sparkle, glitter, glisten, coruscate, twinkle

scoff · to show one's contempt in derision or mockery *syn* jeer, gibe, fleer, gird, sneer, flout *rel* ridicule, deride, mock, taunt; scorn, disdain, scout, contemn, despise

scold *n, syn* VIRAGO, shrew, vixen, termagant, amazon

scold *vb* · to reproach angrily and abusively *syn* upbraid, rate, berate, tongue-lash, jaw, bawl, chew out, wig, rail, revile, vituperate *rel* reprehend, reprobate, censure, blame, criticize; reproach, reprimand, reprove, rebuke, admonish, chide; execrate, objurgate

scoop *syn* DIP, bail, ladle, spoon, dish

scope *syn* RANGE, gamut, reach, radius, compass, sweep, orbit, horizon, ken, purview *rel* expanse, amplitude, spread, stretch; field, domain, sphere, territory, province; extent, area, size

scorch *syn* BURN, char, sear, singe *rel* wither, shrivel

scorn *n, syn* DISDAIN, contempt, despite *rel* superciliousness, insolence, disdainfulness; scoffing, flouting, jeering, gibing; deriding, derision, ridiculing, ridicule, taunting, mocking, mockery

scorn *vb, syn* DESPISE, disdain, scout, contemn *rel* repudiate, spurn, reject, decline; flout, scoff, jeer, gibe; deride, mock, taunt, ridicule

scoundrel *syn* VILLAIN, blackguard, knave, rascal, rogue, scamp, rapscallion, miscreant *rel* criminal, felon, malefactor, culprit

scour *syn* SEEK, search, hunt, ransack, rummage, comb, ferret out *rel* investigate; scrutinize, inspect, examine; range, roam, rove, wander

scout *syn* DESPISE, scorn, contemn, disdain *rel* flout, scoff, sneer, jeer; deride, taunt, mock, ridicule

scowl *syn* FROWN, glower, lower, gloom *rel* glare, stare, gaze

scrap *vb, syn* DISCARD, junk, cast, shed, molt, slough

scrap *n, syn* BRAWL, broil, fracas, melee, row, rumpus *rel* quarrel, altercation, squabble, wrangle; fight, affray, fray, combat, contest

scrape *vb* • to rub or slide against something that is harsh, rough, or sharp *syn* scratch, grate, rasp, grind *rel* erase, efface, delete; remove; rid, clear; abrade, chafe, excoriate

scrape *n, syn* PREDICAMENT, dilemma, quandary, plight, fix, jam, pickle *rel* difficulty, vicissitude; perplexity, bewilderment, distraction; embarrassment, discomfiture

scratch *syn* SCRAPE, grate, rasp, grind *rel* tear, rend; injure, damage, mar, impair, hurt; deface, disfigure

scrawny *syn* LEAN, skinny, lank, lanky, spare, gaunt, rawboned, angular *rel* thin, slim, slender; meager, exiguous *ant* brawny; fleshy; obese

scream *vb, syn* SHOUT, shriek, screech, yell, squeal, holler, whoop *rel* pierce, penetrate; vent, utter, voice, express, air

scream *n, syn* SHOUT, shriek, screech, yell, squeal, holler, whoop

screech *vb, syn* SHOUT, scream, shriek, yell, squeal, holler, whoop

screech *n, syn* SHOUT, scream, shriek, yell, squeal, holler, whoop

screen *syn* HIDE, conceal, secrete, cache, bury, ensconce *rel* defend, protect, shield, guard, safeguard; disguise, dissemble, cloak, mask, camouflage

scrimpy *syn* MEAGER, scanty, scant, skimpy, exiguous, spare, sparse *rel* thin, slight, slender, slim; niggardly, stingy, penurious, parsimonious

scruple *n, syn* QUALM, demur, compunction *rel* hesitation, hesitancy; doubt, uncertainty, suspicion, mistrust; misgiving, apprehension

scruple *vb, syn* DEMUR, balk, jib, shy, boggle, stickle, stick, strain *rel* hesitate, waver, falter, vacillate; object, protest

scrupulous **1** *syn* CAREFUL, meticulous, punctilious, punctual *rel* fastidious, particular, finicky, fussy; exact, accurate, precise, correct *ant* remiss **2** *syn* UPRIGHT, conscientious, honest, just, honorable *rel* moral, ethical, righteous, virtuous, noble; rigid, rigorous, strict *ant* unscrupulous

scrutinize • to look at or over *syn* scan, inspect, examine, audit *rel* consider, study, contemplate, weigh; analyze, resolve, dissect; penetrate, pierce, probe

scrutiny • a close study, inquiry, or visual inspection *syn* examination, scanning, inspection, audit *rel* investigation, research, probe, inquiry, inquisition; surveying, survey, observing, observation, viewing, view

scud *syn* FLY, skim, shoot, sail, dart, float

scuffle *syn* WRESTLE, tussle, grapple *rel* fight, contend; clash, conflict, collide, bump

sculpture, sculpt, sculp *syn* CARVE, chisel, engrave, incise, etch *rel* shape, fashion, form, make; depict, portray, represent

scum *syn* FOAM, froth, spume, lather, suds, yeast

scurrility *syn* ABUSE, billingsgate, invective, vituperation, obloquy *rel* vilifying, vilification, maligning, traducing, calumniation; reviling, berating, upbraiding, rating, scolding

scurrilous *syn* ABUSIVE, opprobrious, vituperative, contumelious *rel* ribald, obscene, gross, coarse, vulgar; insulting, outraging, offending, offensive; foul, filthy, dirty

scurry *syn* SCUTTLE, scamper, skedaddle, sprint *rel* rush, dash, shoot, tear, charge; dart, fly, scud; hurry, speed, hasten

scurvy *syn* CONTEMPTIBLE, despicable, pitiable, sorry, cheap, beggarly, shabby *rel* base, low, vile; mean, abject

scuttle • to move with or as if with short brisk steps *syn* scurry, scamper, skedaddle, sprint *rel* shoot, tear, dash, rush, charge; fly, scud; hurry, speed, hasten

seaman *syn* MARINER, sailor, tar, gob, bluejacket

sear *syn* BURN, scorch, char, singe

search *syn* SEEK, scour, hunt, comb, ransack, rummage, ferret out *rel* investigate; inspect, examine, scrutinize; penetrate, pierce, probe

season *syn* HARDEN, acclimatize, acclimate *rel* habituate, accustom, inure; train, school, discipline, teach; practice, exercise, drill

seasonable • done or occurring at a good, suitable, or proper time *syn* timely, well-timed, opportune, pat *rel* apropos, apposite, pertinent, relevant; appropriate, happy, felicitous, apt, fit; welcome, grateful, gratifying, pleasant *ant* unseasonable

seclude *syn* ISOLATE, segregate, insulate, sequester *rel* enclose, envelop, fence, pen, cage, wall; confine, circumscribe, limit, restrict

seclusion *syn* SOLITUDE, isolation, alienation *rel* retirement, withdrawal; separation, parting, severing, severance

second *syn* INSTANT, moment, minute, flash, jiffy, twinkling, split second

secondary *syn* SUBORDINATE, dependent, subject, tributary, collateral *rel* auxiliary, accessory, subservient, subsidiary, contributory; incidental, accidental, adventitious *ant* primary

second-rate *syn* MEDIUM, mediocre, middling, moderate, average, fair, indifferent

secret • done without attracting observation *syn* covert, stealthy, furtive, clandestine, surreptitious, underhand, underhanded *rel* mysterious, inscrutable, arcane; puzzling, perplexing, mystifying; hidden, concealed, secreted, screened

secrete *syn* HIDE, conceal, screen, cache, bury, ensconce *rel* dissemble, cloak, mask, disguise, camouflage

secretive *syn* SILENT, close, close-lipped, closemouthed, tight-lipped, uncommunicative, taciturn, reticent, reserved *rel* cautious, circumspect, wary; restrained, inhibited

sect *syn* RELIGION, denomination, cult, communion, faith, creed, persuasion, church

sectary **1** *syn* FOLLOWER, adherent, disciple, partisan, henchman, satellite *rel* devotee, votary, addict **2** *also* sectarian *syn* HERETIC, schismatic, dissenter, nonconformist *rel* enthusiast, zealot, fanatic, bigot

section *syn* PART, sector, segment, division, portion, piece, detail, member, fraction, fragment, parcel *rel* district, locality, vicinity;

region, tract, area, zone, belt; field, sphere, territory

sector *syn* PART, segment, section, division, portion, piece, detail, member, fraction, fragment, parcel

secular *syn* PROFANE, temporal, lay *rel* worldly, mundane, earthly, earthy, terrestrial *ant* religious; sacred; regular

secure *adj, syn* SAFE *rel* firm, solid; protected, shielded, guarded, safeguarded, defended, certain, positive, sure; impregnable, unassailable, invulnerable, invincible *ant* precarious, dangerous

secure *vb* **1** · to fasten or fix firmly *syn* anchor, moor, rivet *rel* establish, set, settle, fix; fasten, attach, affix **2** *syn* ENSURE, insure, assure *rel* protect, defend, safeguard, guard, shield; preserve, conserve, save; guarantee, guaranty; warrant, justify **3** *syn* GET, procure, obtain, acquire, gain, win *rel* seize, take, grasp; reach, attain, achieve; have, hold, own, possess

security *syn* GUARANTEE, surety, guaranty, bond, bail *rel* pledge, earnest, token

sedate *syn* SERIOUS, grave, staid, earnest, sober, solemn, somber *rel* placid, calm, serene, tranquil; collected, composed, imperturbable, cool; decorous, seemly, proper *ant* flighty

sediment *syn* DEPOSIT, precipitate, dregs, lees, grounds

sedition · an offense against a ruling authority to which one owes allegiance *syn* treason *rel* rebellion, revolt, revolution, uprising, insurrection, mutiny, putsch, coup; disaffection, alienation, estrangement

seditious *syn* INSUBORDINATE, mutinous, rebellious, factious, contumacious *rel* traitorous, treacherous, perfidious, disloyal, faithless; disaffected, alienated

seduce *syn* LURE, tempt, entice, inveigle, decoy *rel* mislead, beguile, delude, deceive; corrupt, debauch, deprave, pervert, debase; bewitch, captivate, allure, attract

sedulous *syn* BUSY, assiduous, diligent, industrious *rel* persevering, persistent; untiring, unwearied, indefatigable, tireless

see **1** · to take cognizance of by physical or mental vision *syn* behold, descry, espy, view, survey, contemplate, observe, notice, remark, note, perceive, discern *rel* scrutinize, scan, examine, inspect; pierce, penetrate, probe; consider, study, contemplate **2** · to perceive something by means of the eyes *syn* look, watch *rel* gaze, gape, stare, glare

seedy *syn* SHABBY, dilapidated, dingy, faded, threadbare *rel* drooping, flagging, sagging, wilting; sickly, unwholesome, morbid; worn, haggard

seek · to look for *syn* search, scour, hunt, comb, ferret out, ransack, rummage *rel* inquire, question, ask, interrogate; pursue, chase, follow, trail

seem · to give the impression of being without necessarily being so in fact *syn* look, appear *rel* infer, gather, judge, deduce, conclude

seeming *syn* APPARENT, illusory, ostensible *rel* plausible, specious, credible; dissembling, disguising, masking, cloaking, camouflaging

seemly *syn* DECOROUS, proper, nice, decent *rel* fitting, suitable, appropriate, meet, fit; congruous, compatible, congenial, consistent, consonant *ant* unseemly

seethe *syn* BOIL, simmer, parboil, stew

segment *syn* PART, section, sector, division, portion, piece, detail, member, fraction, fragment, parcel

segregate *syn* ISOLATE, seclude, insulate, sequester *rel* separate, divide, part, sever; detach, disengage; choose, select, single

seize *syn* TAKE, grasp, clutch, snatch, grab *rel* catch, capture, snare, ensnare, trap, entrap; appropriate, confiscate, usurp, arrogate

select *adj* • chosen from a number or group by fitness, superiority, or preference *syn* elect, picked, exclusive *rel* choice, exquisite, rare, delicate, dainty, recherché; superlative, surpassing, peerless, supreme *ant* indiscriminate

select *vb, syn* CHOOSE, elect, prefer, opt, pick, cull, single *rel* assort, sort, classify; discriminate, discern *ant* reject

selection *syn* CHOICE, preference, election, option, alternative *rel* choosing, culling, picking; discrimination, discernment, insight, acumen *ant* rejection

self-abnegation *syn* RENUNCIATION, abnegation, self-denial *rel* sacrificing, sacrifice, forbearance, forgoing, eschewal; surrendering, surrender, resignation, abandonment, relinquishment

self-assertive *syn* AGGRESSIVE, assertive, pushing, pushy, militant *rel* obtrusive, intrusive, officious, meddlesome, impertinent; bold, audacious, brave; positive, certain, sure, cocksure

self-assurance *syn* CONFIDENCE, assurance, self-confidence, aplomb, self-possession *rel* coolness, collectedness, imperturbability; composure, sangfroid, equanimity

self-complacent *syn* COMPLACENT, self-satisfied, smug, priggish *rel* see COMPLACENT

self-confidence *syn* CONFIDENCE, assurance, self-assurance, self-possession, aplomb *rel* composure, equanimity; sureness, sanguineness

self-denial *syn* RENUNCIATION, self-abnegation, abnegation *rel* sacrificing, sacrifice, forbearance; abstaining, refraining; restraining, restraint, curbing, curb, checking, check

self-esteem *syn* CONCEIT, self-love, egotism, egoism, amour propre *rel* pride, vanity; self-respect, self-regard, self-admiration *ant* self-distrust

self-love *syn* CONCEIT, self-esteem, egotism, egoism, amour propre *rel* pride, vanity, vainglory; complacency, self-complacency, smugness, priggishness *ant* self-forgetfulness

self-possession *syn* CONFIDENCE, self-confidence, assurance, self-assurance, aplomb *rel* equanimity, composure; coolness, collectedness, imperturbability, nonchalance; poise, savoir faire, tact

selfsame *syn* SAME, very, identical, identic, equivalent, equal, tantamount *rel* alike, like, uniform *ant* diverse

self-satisfied *syn* COMPLACENT, self-complacent, smug, priggish *rel* satisfied, content; conceited, egoistic, egotistic

semblance *syn* APPEARANCE, look, aspect *rel* likeness, similitude, resemblance, analogy, affinity; pose, affectation, air; form, figure, shape

sempiternal *syn* INFINITE, eternal, boundless, illimitable, uncircumscribed *rel* everlasting, endless, interminable, unceasing; immortal, deathless, undying; lasting, perdurable

send • to cause to go or be taken from one place, person or condition to another *syn* dispatch, forward, transmit, remit, route, ship *rel* speed, quicken; direct, order, command; go, leave, depart

senescence *syn* AGE, senility, dotage *ant* adolescence

senility *syn* AGE, dotage, senescence *rel* infirmity, feebleness, weakness, decrepitude; childishness, childlikeness; decay, disintegration

sensation 1 • awareness (as of heat or pain) due to stimulation of a sense organ *syn* percept, sense-datum, sensum, image *rel* impression, impress, print, stamp; feeling, feel; consciousness, awareness 2 • the power to respond or an act of responding to stimuli *syn* sense, feeling, sensibility *rel* perceptibleness, perceptibility, tangibleness, tangibility, palpableness, palpability, ponderableness, ponderability; reaction, action, behavior; response, answer

sense 1 *syn* SENSATION, feeling, sensibility *rel* awareness, consciousness, cognizance; perception, discernment, discrimination, penetration 2 • the ability to reach intelligent conclusions *syn* common sense, good sense, horse sense, gumption, judgment, wisdom *rel* prudence, foresight, discretion; understanding, comprehension, appreciation; intelligence, brain, wit, mind 3 *syn* MEANING, acceptation, signification, significance, import *rel* denotation, connotation

sense-datum *syn* SENSATION, sensum, percept, image

sensibility *syn* SENSATION, feeling, sense *rel* perception, discernment, penetration, discrimination, insight; sensitiveness, susceptibility; emotion, affection

sensible 1 *syn* MATERIAL, physical, corporeal, phenomenal, objective *ant* intelligible 2 *syn* PERCEPTIBLE, palpable, tangible, appreciable, ponderable *rel* sensational, perceptual, imaginal; obvious, patent, manifest, evident; carnal, fleshly, sensual *ant* insensible 3 *syn* AWARE, conscious, cognizant, alive, awake *rel* perceiving, noting, remarking, observing, seeing; knowing, intelligent; understanding, comprehending, appreciating; sensitive, susceptible, liable *ant* insensible (of *or* to) 4 *syn* WISE, prudent, sane, judicious, sage, sapient *rel* sagacious, perspicacious, astute, shrewd; foresighted, discreet, provident; reasonable, rational *ant* absurd, foolish; fatuous, asinine

sensitive 1 *syn* LIABLE, susceptible, subject, exposed, open, prone *rel* impressed, influenced, affected; predisposed, disposed, inclined *ant* insensitive 2 *syn* SENTIENT, impressible, impressionable, responsive, susceptible *rel* alert, watchful, vigilant, wide-awake; sharp, keen, acute; aware, conscious, cognizant, sensible, alive

sensual 1 *syn* CARNAL, fleshly, animal *rel* bodily, physical, corporeal, somatic; coarse, gross, vulgar; lewd, lascivious, lustful, wanton, licentious 2 *syn* SENSUOUS, luxurious, voluptuous, sybaritic, epicurean *rel* see SENSUAL 1

sensum *syn* SENSATION, sense-datum, percept, image

sensuous • relating to or providing pleasure through gratification of the senses *syn* sensual, luxurious, voluptuous, sybaritic, epicurean *rel* sensational, imaginal; delicious, delectable, luscious, delightful; aesthetic, artistic

sentence • to decree the fate or punishment of one adjudged guilty, unworthy, or unfit *syn* condemn, damn, doom, proscribe *rel* judge, adjudge, adjudicate; denounce, blame, criticize; determine, settle, rule, decide

sententious *syn* EXPRESSIVE, pregnant, meaningful, significant, eloquent *rel* formal, conventional, ceremonious, ceremonial; showy, ostentatious; terse, pithy, compendious, concise

sentient • readily affected by external stimuli *syn* sensitive, impressible, impressionable, responsive, susceptible

sentiment 1 *syn* FEELING, emotion, affection, passion *rel* thought, impression, notion, idea; ideal, standard, exemplar 2 *syn* OPINION, view, belief, conviction, persuasion *rel* truth, verity; conclusion, judgment

sentimental · unduly or affectedly emotional *syn* romantic, mawkish, maudlin, soppy, mushy, slushy *rel* emotional, affectionate, feeling, passionate; affecting, moving, pathetic, touching; affected, pretended, counterfeited, feigned, simulated

separate *vb* · to become or cause to become disunited or disjoined *syn* part, divide, sever, sunder, divorce *rel* cleave, rend, split, rive, tear; estrange, alienate; disperse, dispel, scatter; detach, disengage *ant* combine

separate *adj* 1 *syn* DISTINCT, several, discrete *rel* diverse, disparate, different, divergent, various; free, independent 2 *syn* SINGLE, solitary, particular, unique, sole, lone *rel* special, especial, specific, individual; peculiar, distinctive, characteristic; detached, disengaged

sequel *syn* EFFECT, outcome, issue, result, consequence, upshot, aftereffect, aftermath, event *rel* termination, end, ending; conclusion, closing, finishing, finish

sequence *syn* SUCCESSION, series, progression, chain, train, string *rel* ordering, order, arrangement

sequent, sequential *syn* CONSECUTIVE, successive, serial

sequester *syn* ISOLATE, segregate, seclude, insulate *rel* separate, sever, sunder

serene *syn* CALM, tranquil, peaceful, placid, halcyon *rel* still, stilly, silent, noiseless, quiet; cool, collected, composed; smooth, effortless, easy

serial *syn* CONSECUTIVE, successive, sequent, sequential *rel* following, ensuing, succeeding; continuous, continual

series *syn* SUCCESSION, progression, sequence, chain, train, string

serious · not light or frivolous (as in disposition, appearance, or manner) *syn* grave, solemn, somber, sedate, staid, sober, earnest *rel* austere, stern, severe, ascetic; thoughtful, reflective, contemplative, meditative; deep, profound *ant* light, flippant

sermon *syn* SPEECH, homily, address, oration, harangue, talk, lecture

serpentine *syn* WINDING, sinuous, tortuous, flexuous *rel* circuitous, roundabout, indirect; crooked, devious

service *syn* USE, advantage, profit, account, avail *rel* usefulness, utility; worth, value; helping, help, aiding, aid, assistance

servile *syn* SUBSERVIENT, menial, slavish, obsequious *rel* mean, abject, ignoble; fawning, cringing, truckling, cowering *ant* authoritative

servitude · the state of subjection to a master *syn* slavery, bondage

set *vb* 1 · to position (something) in a specified place *syn* settle, fix, establish *rel* implant; fasten, attach, affix; prescribe, assign, define 2 *syn* COAGULATE, congeal, curdle, clot, jelly, jell *rel* harden, solidify; compact, consolidate, concentrate

set *n* · a group of persons associated by common interest *syn* circle, coterie, clique

setting *syn* BACKGROUND, environment, milieu, mise-en-scène, backdrop

settle 1 *syn* SET, fix, establish *rel* secure, anchor, moor, rivet;

order, arrange *ant* unsettle **2** *syn* CALM, compose, quiet, quieten, still, lull, soothe, tranquilize *rel* placate, appease, pacify, mollify, conciliate *ant* unsettle **3** *syn* DECIDE, determine, rule, resolve *rel* judge, adjudge, adjudicate; close, end, conclude, terminate

sever *syn* SEPARATE, sunder, part, divide, divorce *rel* rive, cleave, rend, split, tear; cut, hew, chop; detach, disengage

several **1** *syn* DISTINCT, separate, discrete *rel* individual, particular, special, especial **2** *syn* MANY, sundry, various, divers, numerous, multifarious *rel* single, separate, particular; detached, disengaged

severally *syn* EACH, individually, respectively, apiece

severe • given to or marked by strict discipline and firm restraint *syn* stern, austere, ascetic *rel* exacting, oppressive, onerous, burdensome; rigid, rigorous, strict, stringent; hard, difficult, arduous; harsh, rugged, uneven, rough *ant* tolerant; tender

shabby **1** • being ill-kept and showing signs of wear and tear *syn* dilapidated, dingy, faded, seedy, threadbare *rel* worn, haggard; dowdy, frowzy, slatternly; shopworn, trite; decrepit **2** *syn* CONTEMPTIBLE, despicable, pitiable, sorry, scurvy, cheap, beggarly *rel* mean, sordid, ignoble; base, low, vile

shackle *syn* HAMPER, fetter, clog, trammel, manacle, hog-tie *rel* restrain, curb, check, inhibit; hinder, impede, obstruct, block, bar; restrict, circumscribe, confine, limit

shade **1** • comparative darkness or obscurity due to interception of light rays *syn* shadow, umbrage, umbra, penumbra, adumbration *rel* darkness, dimness, obscurity; shelter, cover, retreat **2** *syn* APPARITION, ghost, spirit, specter, phantasm, phantom, wraith, revenant **3** *syn* BLIND, shutter **4** *syn* COLOR, tint, hue, tinge, tone **5** *syn* GRADATION, nuance *rel* distinction, difference, dissimilarity; touch, suggestion, suspicion, soupçon, dash, tinge **6** *syn* TOUCH, suggestion, suspicion, soupçon, tinge, smack, spice, dash, vein, strain, tincture, streak *rel* trace, vestige; tint

shadow *n, syn* SHADE, umbrage, umbra, penumbra, adumbration *rel* form, figure, shape, conformation, configuration; darkness, obscurity, dimness; silhouette, contour, outline

shadow *vb, syn* SUGGEST, adumbrate *rel* foretell, forecast, predict, prognosticate; foresee, foreknow, divine

shake **1** • to exhibit vibratory, wavering, or oscillating movement often as an evidence of instability *syn* tremble, quake, totter, quiver, shiver, shudder, quaver, wobble, teeter, shimmy, dither *rel* oscillate, fluctuate, vibrate, waver, swing, sway **2** • to move up and down or to and fro with some violence *syn* agitate, rock, convulse *rel* move, drive, impel; flourish, brandish, swing, wave; disturb, derange, unsettle, disorder **3** *syn* SWING, wave, flourish, brandish, thrash

shallow *syn* SUPERFICIAL, cursory, uncritical *rel* slim, slight, slender, thin; trivial, trifling, petty, paltry; empty, hollow, idle, vain

sham *n, syn* IMPOSTURE, cheat, fake, humbug, fraud, deceit, deception, counterfeit *rel* pretense, pretension, make-believe; trick, ruse, feint, wile, gambit, ploy

sham *vb, syn* ASSUME, feign, simulate, counterfeit, pretend, affect *rel* invent, create; ape, mock, mimic, imitate, copy

sham *n, syn* COUNTERFEIT, spurious, bogus, fake, pseudo, pinchbeck, phony *rel* feigned, assumed, affected; hoaxing, bamboozling, hoodwinking, duping; deceptive, delusive, delusory, misleading

shame *syn* DISGRACE, dishonor, disrepute, infamy, ignominy, opprobrium, obloquy, odium *rel* humiliation, degradation, abasement; mortification, chagrin *ant* glory; pride

shameless • characterized by or exhibiting boldness and a lack of shame *syn* brazen, barefaced, brash, impudent *rel* abandoned, profligate, dissolute; hardened, indurated, callous; vicious, villainous, iniquitous

shape *vb, syn* MAKE, form, fashion, fabricate, manufacture, forge

shape *n, syn* FORM, figure, conformation, configuration *rel* outline, contour, profile, silhouette; appearance, look, aspect, semblance

shapeless *syn* FORMLESS, unformed *rel* rude, rough, crude *ant* shapely

share • to have, get, or use in common with another or others *syn* participate, partake *rel* communicate, impart; divide, dispense, distribute

sharp • having or showing alert competence and clear understanding *syn* keen, acute *rel* incisive, trenchant, cutting, biting; mordant, caustic, scathing; piercing, penetrating, probing; tricky, cunning, artful, wily, guileful, sly *ant* dull; blunt

shatter *syn* BREAK, shiver, crack, burst, bust, snap *rel* demolish, destroy; ruin, wreck; rend, split, rive, tear

shave *syn* BRUSH, graze, glance, skim *rel* touch, contact; escape, avoid

shear • to cut or cut off with or as if with shears *syn* poll, clip, trim, prune, lop, snip, crop *rel* cut, slit, slash, hew; split, rive, cleave, tear

shed *syn* DISCARD, cast, molt, slough, scrap, junk *rel* remove, shift, transfer, move; reject, repudiate, spurn

sheen *syn* LUSTER, gloss, glaze *rel* gleaming, gleam, glittering, glitter, flashing, flash

sheer *adj* **1** *syn* PURE, simple, absolute *rel* outright, out-and-out, arrant, unmitigated **2** *syn* STEEP, precipitous, abrupt *rel* perpendicular, vertical

sheer *vb, syn* TURN, divert, deflect, avert

shelter *n* • something that covers or affords protection *syn* cover, retreat, refuge, asylum, sanctuary *rel* protection, safeguarding, safeguard; harbor, haven, port

shelter *vb, syn* HARBOR, lodge, house, entertain, board *rel* defend, protect, shield, guard, safeguard; receive, accept, admit

shibboleth *syn* CATCHWORD, byword, slogan

shield *syn* DEFEND, protect, guard, safeguard *rel* preserve, conserve, save; harbor, shelter, lodge, house

shift *vb, syn* MOVE, remove, transfer *rel* displace, replace; change, alter, vary; veer, swerve, deviate

shift *n* **1** *syn* RESOURCE, makeshift, expedient, resort, stopgap, substitute, surrogate *rel* device, contrivance, contraption; ruse, trick, stratagem, maneuver, gambit, ploy, wile, feint, artifice **2** *syn* SPELL, tour, trick, turn, stint, bout, go *rel* change, alternation; allotment, assignment

shimmy *syn* SHAKE, tremble, quake, totter, quiver, shiver, shudder, quaver, wobble, teeter, dither

ship *n, syn* BOAT, vessel, craft

ship *vb, syn* SEND, forward, transmit, remit, route, dispatch

shipshape *syn* NEAT, tidy, trim, trig, snug, spick-and-span

shirk *syn* DODGE, parry, sidestep, duck, fence, malinger *rel* evade, elude, avoid, escape; recoil, shrink, quail, flinch

shiver *vb, syn* BREAK, shatter, crack, burst, bust, snap

shiver *vb, syn* SHAKE, quiver, shudder, quaver, tremble, quake, totter, wobble, teeter, shimmy, dither

shoal · a shallow place in a body of water *syn* bank, reef, bar

shock *n, syn* HEAP, cock, stack, pile, mass, bank

shock *vb, syn* HEAP, cock, stack, pile, mass, bank

shock *n, syn* IMPACT, collision, clash, concussion, impingement, percussion, jar, jolt *rel* encounter, skirmish; attack, assault, onslaught, onset; shaking, rocking, agitation, convulsion

shocking *syn* FEARFUL, appalling, awful, dreadful, frightful, terrible, terrific, horrible, horrific *rel* ghastly, gruesome, lurid, macabre, grisly, grim; odious, abhorrent, abominable, hateful; repugnant, repellent, distasteful, obnoxious

shoot *vb* **1** *syn* FLY, dart, float, skim, scud, sail *rel* hasten, quicken **2** *syn* RUSH, dash, tear, charge *rel* speed, hasten, hurry

shoot *n* · a branch or a part of a plant that is an outgrowth from a main stem *syn* branch, bough, limb

shopworn *syn* TRITE, hackneyed, stereotyped, threadbare *rel* wasted, haggard; attenuated, diluted, thinned; antiquated, obsolete, archaic, old

shore · land bordering a usu. large body of water *syn* coast, beach, strand, bank, littoral, foreshore

short **1** *syn* BRIEF *rel* decreased, lessened, reduced, diminished; shortened, abridged, abbreviated, curtailed; concise, terse, laconic *ant* long **2** *syn* FRAGILE, crisp, brittle, friable, frangible

shortcoming *syn* IMPERFECTION, deficiency, fault *rel* defect, flaw, blemish; failing, frailty, foible

shorten · to reduce in extent *syn* curtail, abbreviate, abridge, retrench *rel* reduce, decrease, lessen, diminish; contract, shrink, condense *ant* lengthen, elongate; extend

short-lived *syn* TRANSIENT, transitory, passing, ephemeral, momentary, fugitive, fleeting, evanescent *ant* agelong

shortly *syn* PRESENTLY, soon, directly

shout *vb* · to utter a sudden loud cry (as to attract attention) *syn* yell, shriek, scream, screech, squeal, holler, whoop *rel* roar, bellow, bawl, howl

shout *n* · a sudden loud cry *syn* yell, shriek, scream, screech, squeal, holler, whoop *rel* bellow, vociferation, clamor, bawl, roar

shove *syn* PUSH, thrust, propel *rel* force, constrain, oblige, compel, coerce; impel, drive, move

show *vb* **1** · to reveal outwardly or make apparent *syn* manifest, evidence, evince, demonstrate *rel* reveal, disclose, discover; present, offer, proffer, tender **2** · to present so as to invite notice or attention *syn* exhibit, display, expose, parade, flaunt *rel* indicate, betoken, attest, bespeak, argue, prove; intimate, hint, suggest *ant* disguise

show *n, syn* EXHIBITION, exhibit, exposition, fair

showy · given to excess outward display *syn* pretentious, ostentatious *rel* gaudy, tawdry, garish, flashy, meretricious; resplendent, gorgeous, splendid; opulent, sumptuous, luxurious

shrew *syn* VIRAGO, scold, vixen, termagant, amazon

shrewd · acute in perception and sound in judgment *syn* sagacious, perspicacious, astute *rel* knowing, intelligent, smart, clever, quick-witted; politic, diplomatic, smooth, suave; wise, prudent, sensible, judicious; penetrating, piercing, probing; sharp, keen, acute

shriek *vb, syn* SHOUT, yell, scream, screech, squeal, holler, whoop *rel* vociferate, clamor, bellow, roar; vent, ventilate, air, voice, express

shriek *n, syn* SHOUT, yell, scream, screech, squeal, holler, whoop *rel* vociferation, clamor, bellow, roar

shrink **1** *syn* CONTRACT, constrict, compress, condense, deflate *rel* decrease, reduce, diminish, lessen; shorten, abridge, retrench, curtail *ant* swell **2** *syn* RECOIL, flinch, quail, blench, wince *rel* cringe, cower; retreat, recede; balk, shy, boggle, scruple, demur

shrivel *syn* WITHER, wizen *rel* parch, desiccate, dry; sear, scorch, burn

shroud *syn* COVER, overspread, envelop, wrap, veil *rel* hide, conceal, screen, bury; cloak, mask, camouflage, disguise

shudder *syn* SHAKE, shiver, quiver, quaver, tremble, quake, totter, wobble, teeter, shimmy, dither

shun *syn* ESCAPE, avoid, evade, elude, eschew *rel* decline, refuse, reject; balk, shy, scruple, demur, stick, stickle; scorn, disdain, despise *ant* habituate

shut *syn* CLOSE

shut out *syn* EXCLUDE, eliminate, debar, rule out, blackball, disbar *rel* prevent, preclude, obviate; hinder, obstruct, block, bar

shutter *syn* BLIND, shade

shy *adj* · not inclined to be forward *syn* bashful, diffident, modest, coy *rel* timid, timorous; wary, chary, cautious, circumspect *ant* obtrusive

shy *vb, syn* DEMUR, balk, boggle, scruple, jib, stickle, stick, strain *rel* recoil, shrink, quail, blench; hesitate, waver, falter, vacillate

sic *syn* URGE, egg, exhort, goad, spur, prod, prick *rel* incite, instigate, abet; encourage, countenance, favor

sicken *syn* DISGUST, nauseate *rel* revolt, offend, repulse

sickly *syn* UNWHOLESOME, morbid, diseased, pathological *rel* ailing; weak, feeble, frail, infirm; mawkish, mushy, maudlin *ant* robust

side *syn* PHASE, aspect, facet, angle

sidereal *syn* STARRY, stellar, astral

sidestep *syn* DODGE, parry, shirk, duck, fence, malinger *rel* avoid, evade, elude, shun, escape

siege *syn* BLOCKADE

sigh *vb* · to let out a deep audible breath (as in weariness or sorrow) *syn* sob, moan, groan *rel* lament, deplore, bemoan, bewail; long, yearn, pine, hunger, thirst

sigh *n* · a usu. inarticulate sound indicating mental or physical pain or distress *syn* groan, moan, sob *rel* regret, sorrow, grief

sight *syn* LOOK, view, glance, glimpse, peep, peek *rel* prospect, outlook; vision, revelation

sightless *syn* BLIND, purblind

sign **1** · a discernible indication of what is not itself directly perceptible *syn* mark, token, badge, note, symptom *rel* indication, betokening, attesting, attestation; manifestation, evidencing, evidence, demonstration, showing, show; intimation, suggestion **2** · a motion, action, gesture, or word by which a command, thought, or wish is expressed *syn* signal *rel* gesture, gesticulation; symbol, emblem **3** *syn* CHARACTER, symbol, mark *rel* device, contrivance

signal *n, syn* SIGN *rel* alarm, tocsin, alert; gesture, gesticulation; motion, movement; device, contrivance, contraption

signal *adj, syn* NOTICEABLE, salient, striking, arresting, outstanding, prominent, remarkable, conspicuous *rel* distinctive, individual, peculiar, characteristic; eminent, illustrious, famous, renowned

significance 1 *syn* MEANING, signification, import, sense, acceptation *rel* denotation, connotation; suggestion, implication, intimation 2 *syn* IMPORTANCE, import, consequence, moment, weight *rel* worth, value; influence, authority, credit, prestige, merit, excellence, virtue, perfection

significant *syn* EXPRESSIVE, meaningful, pregnant, eloquent, sententious *rel* cogent, telling, convincing, compelling, valid, sound; forcible, forceful, powerful; important, momentous, weighty

signification *syn* MEANING, significance, import, sense, acceptation *rel* signifying, meaning, denoting; denotation, connotation

signify *syn* MEAN, import, denote *rel* convey, carry, bear; connote; imply, suggest

silent 1 • showing restraint in speaking *syn* uncommunicative, taciturn, reticent, reserved, secretive, close, close-lipped, close-mouthed, tight-lipped *rel* restrained, curbed, checked, inhibited; discreet, prudent *ant* talkative 2 *syn* STILL, stilly, quiet, noiseless *rel* calm, serene, tranquil, placid, peaceful

silhouette *syn* OUTLINE, contour, profile, skyline *rel* shadow, shade, adumbration

silken, silky *syn* SLEEK, slick, glossy, velvety, satiny *rel* lustrous, luminous, lambent, bright

silly 1 *syn* SIMPLE, foolish, fatuous, asinine *rel* irrational, unreasonable; stupid, slow, dull, dense, crass, dumb; vacuous, empty 2 *syn* FOOLISH, absurd, preposterous *rel* inane, wishy-washy, insipid; puerile, juvenile, youthful; ridiculous, ludicrous, laughable

similar *syn* LIKE, alike, analogous, comparable, akin, parallel, uniform, identical *rel* same, equivalent, equal; corresponding, correlative, complementary, reciprocal *ant* dissimilar

similarity *syn* LIKENESS, resemblance, similitude, analogy, affinity *rel* comparison, contrast, collation, parallel; agreement, accordance, harmonizing, harmony, correspondence *ant* dissimilarity

simile *syn* ANALOGY, metaphor

similitude *syn* LIKENESS, similarity, resemblance, analogy, affinity *ant* dissimilitude, dissimilarity

simmer *syn* BOIL, seethe, parboil, stew

simper *vb, syn* SMILE, smirk, grin

simper *n, syn* SMILE, smirk, grin

simple *adj* 1 *syn* PURE, absolute, sheer *rel* elemental, elementary; single, sole *ant* compound; complex 2 *syn* EASY, facile, light, effortless, smooth *rel* clear, plain, distinct, obvious, evident, manifest; lucid, perspicuous *ant* complicated; difficult 3 *syn* PLAIN, homely, unpretentious *rel* ordinary, common, familiar; lowly, humble; insignificant, unimportant 4 *syn* NATURAL, ingenuous, naïve, unsophisticated, artless *rel* sincere, unfeigned; childlike, childish; open, plain, frank, candid 5 • actually or apparently deficient in intelligence *syn* foolish, silly, fatuous, asinine *rel* childish, childlike; dull, dense, dumb, slow, stupid, crass; ignorant, illiterate, untaught *ant* wise

simple *n, syn* DRUG, medicinal, pharmaceutical, biologic

simpleton *syn* FOOL, moron, imbecile, idiot, natural

simulate *syn* ASSUME, feign, counterfeit, sham, pretend, affect *rel* dissemble, disguise, cloak, mask, camouflage; ape, mock, mimic, imitate, copy

simultaneous *syn* CONTEMPORARY,

synchronous, coincident, contemporaneous, coeval, coetaneous, concomitant, concurrent *rel* concurring, coinciding, agreeing

sin *syn* OFFENSE, vice, crime, scandal *rel* transgression, trespass, breach, violation; error, lapse, slip; fault, failing, frailty

since *syn* BECAUSE, for, as, inasmuch as

sincere · genuine in feeling *syn* wholehearted, whole-souled, heartfelt, hearty, unfeigned *rel* candid, open, frank, plain; honest, honorable, conscientious, scrupulous, upright; straightforward, aboveboard, forthright *ant* insincere

sinewy *syn* MUSCULAR, athletic, husky, brawny, burly *rel* robust, healthy, sound; strong, tough, tenacious, sturdy; nervous, vigorous, energetic

sing · to produce musical tones by or as if by means of the voice *syn* troll, carol, descant, warble, trill, hymn, chant, intone

singe *syn* BURN, sear, scorch, char

single *adj* **1** *syn* UNMARRIED, celibate, virgin, maiden **2** · one as distinguished from two or more or all others *syn* sole, unique, lone, solitary, separate, particular *rel* individual, special, especial, specific *ant* accompanied; supported; conjugal

single *vb, syn* CHOOSE, prefer, select, elect, opt, pick, cull *rel* take, seize, grasp, grab; accept, receive, admit; decide, determine, settle

singular *syn* STRANGE, unique, peculiar, eccentric, erratic, odd, queer, quaint, outlandish, curious *rel* different, diverse, divergent, disparate; exceptional; abnormal, atypical, aberrant

sinister · seriously threatening evil or disaster *syn* baleful, malign, malefic, maleficent *rel* ominous, portentous, fateful, unpropitious, inauspicious; secret, covert, furtive, underhand, underhanded; malicious, malignant, malevolent, spiteful

sink *syn* FALL, drop, slump, subside *rel* droop, sag, flag, wilt; submerge, immerse, dip; ebb, abate, wane; disappear, vanish

sinuous *syn* WINDING, flexuous, serpentine, tortuous *rel* circuitous, roundabout, indirect; crooked, devious

sire *syn* GENERATE, beget, get, procreate, engender, breed, propagate, reproduce

site *syn* PLACE, position, location, situation, spot, station *rel* area, tract, region, zone; field, territory, province; section, sector, part; locality, district

situation **1** *syn* PLACE, position, location, site, spot, station *rel* area, region, tract, zone; section, sector, part; locality, district, vicinity, neighborhood **2** *syn* STATE, condition, mode, posture, status *rel* juncture, pass, crisis, exigency, emergency; predicament, plight, quandary, dilemma; case, instance

size · the amount of measurable space or area occupied by a thing *syn* dimensions, area, extent, magnitude, volume *rel* amplitude, expanse, spread, stretch; bulk, mass, volume

skedaddle *syn* SCUTTLE, scurry, scamper, sprint *rel* flee, fly, escape, decamp; retreat, recede; withdraw, retire, go

skeleton *syn* STRUCTURE, anatomy, framework

skepticism *syn* UNCERTAINTY, doubt, dubiety, mistrust

sketch *n* **1** · a rough drawing representing the chief features of an object or scene *syn* outline, diagram, delineation, draft, tracing, plot, blueprint *rel* design, plan, scheme, project; chart, map **2** *syn* COMPENDIUM, précis, aperçu, syllabus, digest, pandect, survey

sketch *vb* • to make a sketch, rough draft, or outline of *syn* outline, diagram, delineate, draft, trace, plot, blueprint *rel* design, plan, scheme, project; chart, map, graph

skewbald *syn* VARIEGATED, parti-colored, motley, checkered, checked, pied, piebald, dappled, freckled

skid *syn* SLIDE, slip, glide, glissade, slither, coast, toboggan

skill *syn* ART, cunning, craft, artifice *rel* proficiency, adeptness, expertness; efficiency, effectiveness; readiness, facility, dexterity, ease

skilled *syn* PROFICIENT, skillful, adept, expert, masterly *rel* apt, ready, quick, prompt; practiced, exercised, drilled; competent, qualified, able, capable *ant* unskilled

skillful *syn* PROFICIENT, adept, expert, skilled, masterly *rel* dexterous, adroit, deft; efficient, effective; conversant, versed *ant* unskillful

skim **1** *syn* FLY, float, dart, scud, shoot, sail **2** *syn* BRUSH, graze, glance, shave *rel* slide, glide, slip, slither; flit, hover

skimpy *syn* MEAGER, scrimpy, exiguous, scanty, scant, spare, sparse

skin *n* • an outer or surface layer esp. the outer limiting layer of an animal body *syn* hide, pelt, rind, bark, peel

skin *vb* • to remove the surface, skin, or thin outer covering of *syn* decorticate, peel, pare, flay

skinny *syn* LEAN, scrawny, rawboned, angular, gaunt, lank, lanky, spare *ant* fleshy

skip *vb* • to move or advance with successive springs or leaps *syn* bound, hop, curvet, lope, lollop, ricochet

skirmish *syn* ENCOUNTER, brush *rel* contest, conflict, combat, fight, affray, fray; engagement, action, battle

skit *syn* LIBEL, squib, lampoon, pasquinade

skulk *syn* LURK, couch, slink, sneak *rel* secrete, hide, conceal

skyline *syn* OUTLINE, profile, contour, silhouette

slack **1** *syn* NEGLIGENT, lax, remiss, neglectful *rel* lazy, indolent, slothful, faineant, indifferent, unconcerned, detached, aloof; sluggish, lethargic **2** *syn* LOOSE, relaxed, lax *rel* weak, feeble, infirm; inert, supine, passive, inactive; slow, leisurely, laggard

slacken *syn* DELAY, retard, slow, detain *rel* abate, reduce, lessen, decrease; restrain, curb, check, inhibit; moderate, temper, qualify *ant* quicken

slander *n, syn* DETRACTION, calumny, backbiting, scandal *rel* defamation, vilification, aspersion, traducing; abuse, vituperation, invective, obloquy, scurrility

slander *vb, syn* MALIGN, defame, libel, calumniate, traduce, asperse, vilify *rel* decry, depreciate, detract, derogate, disparage, belittle; injure, damage, hurt; attack, assail

slang *syn* DIALECT, vernacular, patois, lingo, jargon, cant, argot

slant *vb* • to set or be set at an angle *syn* slope, incline, lean *rel* veer, swerve, deviate, diverge

slant *n, syn* POINT OF VIEW, viewpoint, standpoint, angle *rel* attitude, position, stand; bias, prejudice, predilection

slap *syn* STRIKE, hit, smite, punch, slug, slog, swat, clout, cuff, box

slash *syn* CUT, slit, hew, chop, carve *rel* rive, rend, cleave, split, tear; penetrate, pierce, enter

slatternly • being habitually untidy and very dirty esp. in dress or appearance *syn* dowdy, frowzy, blowsy *rel* slovenly, unkempt, disheveled, sloppy, slipshod

slaughter *syn* MASSACRE, butchery, carnage, pogrom

slavery *syn* SERVITUDE, bondage

slavish *syn* SUBSERVIENT, servile, menial, obsequious *rel* mean, abject, ignoble, sordid; tame, subdued, submissive; miserable, wretched

slay *syn* KILL, murder, assassinate, dispatch, execute

sleazy *syn* LIMP, flimsy, floppy, flaccid, flabby *rel* thin, tenuous, slight; loose, slack

sleek • having a smooth bright surface or appearance *syn* slick, glossy, velvety, silken, silky, satiny *rel* bright, lustrous, brilliant; smooth, even, level

sleep • to take rest by a suspension of consciousness *syn* slumber, drowse, doze, nap, catnap, snooze *rel* rest, repose, relax

sleepy • affected by or inducing of a desire to sleep *syn* drowsy, somnolent, slumberous *rel* lethargic, sluggish, comatose

slender *syn* THIN, slim, slight, tenuous, rare *rel* lean, spare, lanky, skinny; flimsy, flaccid, flabby, limp; trivial, trifling, petty, paltry, puny

slick **1** *syn* SLEEK, glossy, velvety, silken, satiny, silky *rel* finished, consummate; flawless, impeccable, faultless; shallow, superficial **2** *syn* FULSOME, oily, unctuous, oleaginous, soapy *rel* bland, smooth, diplomatic, politic, suave, urbane; specious, plausible

slide • to go or progress with a smooth continuous motion *syn* slip, glide, skid, glissade, slither, coast, toboggan

slight *adj, syn* THIN, tenuous, rare, slender, slim *rel* imperceptible, imponderable, impalpable, intangible, insensible, inappreciable; trifling, trivial, puny, petty, paltry; minute, diminutive, wee, little, small

slight *vb, syn* NEGLECT, ignore, overlook, disregard, omit, forget *rel* scorn, disdain, contemn, despise; flout, scoff

slighting *syn* DEROGATORY, depreciatory, depreciative, disparaging, pejorative *rel* contemptuous, disdainful, scornful, despiteful

slim *syn* THIN, slender, slight, tenuous, rare *rel* lean, spare, skinny, scrawny; meager, exiguous, scant, scanty; lithe, lithesome, lissome *ant* chubby

sling *vb, syn* THROW, hurl, fling, pitch, toss, cast *rel* heave, hoist, lift, raise; impel, drive; propel, shove, thrust, push

sling *vb, syn* HANG, suspend, dangle

slink *syn* LURK, skulk, sneak

slip *vb, syn* SLIDE, glide, skid, glissade, slither, coast, toboggan

slip *n* **1** *syn* WHARF, dock, pier, quay, berth, jetty, levee **2** *syn* ERROR, lapse, mistake, blunder, faux pas, bull, howler, boner *rel* accident, chance; inadvertence, carelessness, heedlessness; fault, failing, foible, frailty, vice

slipshod • negligent of or marked by lack of neatness and order esp. in appearance or dress *syn* slovenly, unkempt, disheveled, sloppy *rel* negligent, neglectful, slack, lax, remiss; careless, heedless, inadvertent; indifferent, unconcerned; slatternly, dowdy, frowzy, blowsy

slit *syn* CUT, slash, hew, chop, carve

slither *syn* SLIDE, slip, glide, skid, glissade, coast, toboggan

slog *syn* STRIKE, hit, smite, punch, slug, swat, clout, slap, cuff, box

slogan *syn* CATCHWORD, byword, shibboleth *rel* phrase, expression, locution, idiom

slope *syn* SLANT, incline, lean *rel* deviate, diverge, veer, swerve

sloppy *syn* SLIPSHOD, slovenly,

unkempt, disheveled *rel* negligent, neglectful, slack, remiss, lax; mawkish, maudlin, soppy, slushy, sentimental; slatternly, dowdy, frowzy, blowsy

slothful *syn* LAZY, indolent, faineant *rel* inactive, inert, supine, passive, idle; slack, remiss, lax, negligent, neglectful; slow, leisurely, deliberate, dilatory, laggard *ant* industrious

slough *syn* DISCARD, cast, shed, molt, scrap, junk

slovenly *syn* SLIPSHOD, unkempt, disheveled, sloppy *rel* slatternly, dowdy, frowzy, blowsy; indifferent, unconcerned; negligent, neglectful, slack, lax, remiss

slow *adj* **1** *syn* STUPID, dull, dense, crass, dumb **2** • moving, flowing, or proceeding at less than the usual, desirable, or required speed *syn* dilatory, laggard, deliberate, leisurely *ant* fast

slow *vb, syn* DELAY, slacken, retard, detain *rel* moderate, temper, qualify; reduce, abate, decrease, lessen *ant* speed

slug *syn* STRIKE, hit, smite, punch, slog, swat, clout, slap, cuff, box

sluggish *syn* LETHARGIC, torpid, comatose *rel* inert, inactive; indolent, slothful, lazy; listless, languishing, languid *ant* brisk; expeditious; quick

sluice *syn* POUR, stream, gush *rel* flood, inundate, deluge; drench, soak

slumber *syn* SLEEP, drowse, doze, nap, catnap, snooze *rel* relax, rest, repose

slumberous *syn* SLEEPY, drowsy, somnolent

slump *syn* FALL, drop, sink, subside *rel* plunge, dive, pitch; sag, flag, droop

slushy *syn* SENTIMENTAL, mushy, romantic, mawkish, maudlin, soppy

sly • attaining or seeking to attain one's ends by devious means *syn* cunning, crafty, tricky, foxy, insidious, wily, guileful, artful *rel* furtive, clandestine, stealthy, covert, secret; devious, oblique, crooked; astute, shrewd

smack **1** *syn* TASTE, flavor, savor, tang, relish **2** *syn* TOUCH, suggestion, suspicion, soupçon, tincture, tinge, shade, spice, dash, vein, strain, streak

small • noticeably below average in size *syn* little, diminutive, petite, wee, tiny, teeny, weeny, minute, microscopic, miniature *rel* petty, puny, paltry, trifling, trivial *ant* large

small-town *syn* INSULAR, provincial, parochial, local *rel* narrow, narrow-minded, illiberal, intolerant, hidebound, bigoted; circumscribed, limited, confined, restricted *ant* cosmopolitan

smart **1** *syn* INTELLIGENT, bright, knowing, quick-witted, clever, alert *rel* sharp, keen, acute; quick, ready, prompt, apt; shrewd, astute, perspicacious *ant* dull (*of mind*) **2** *syn* STYLISH, modish, fashionable, chic, dashing *rel* elegant, exquisite, choice; finished, consummate *ant* dowdy, frowzy, blowsy

smash *syn* CRUSH, mash, bruise, squash, macerate *rel* shatter, burst, crack, break; press, squeeze, crowd, jam

smell • the quality that makes a thing perceptible to the olfactory sense *syn* scent, odor, aroma *rel* fragrance, redolence, perfume, bouquet, incense; savor, flavor, taste

smidgen *syn* PARTICLE, bit, mite, whit, atom, iota, jot, tittle

smile *vb* • to have, produce, or exhibit a smile *syn* grin, simper, smirk *ant* frown

smile *n* • a facial expression in which the lips curve slightly upward esp. in expression of pleasure or amusement *syn* simper, smirk, grin *ant* frown

smirch *syn* SOIL, dirty, sully, tarnish, foul, befoul, besmirch, grime, begrime

smirk *vb, syn* SMILE, simper, grin

smirk *n, syn* SMILE, simper, grin

smite *syn* STRIKE, hit, punch, slug, slog, swat, clout, slap, cuff, box *rel* beat, pummel, buffet; punish, discipline, correct

smog *syn* HAZE, fog, mist

smooth **1** *syn* LEVEL, even, plane, plain, flat, flush *rel* sleek, slick, glossy *ant* rough **2** *syn* EASY, effortless, light, simple, facile *rel* agreeable, pleasant, pleasing, gratifying, grateful; serene, tranquil, calm, placid, peaceful *ant* labored **3** *syn* SUAVE, bland, diplomatic, politic, urbane *rel* polite, courteous, courtly, civil; oily, unctuous, slick, fulsome *ant* bluff **4** *syn* SOFT, bland, mild, gentle, lenient, balmy

smother *syn* SUFFOCATE, asphyxiate, stifle, choke, strangle, throttle

smug *syn* COMPLACENT, self-complacent, self-satisfied, priggish *rel* self-respecting, self-esteeming, self-admiring; pharisaical, sanctimonious, hypocritical

smuggled • imported or exported secretly and in violation of the law *syn* bootleg, contraband

snag *syn* OBSTACLE, obstruction, impediment, bar *rel* projection, protuberance; difficulty, hardship, vicissitude; barring, blocking, block, hindering, hindrance

snap **1** *syn* JERK, twitch, yank *rel* seize, snatch, clutch, grasp, take **2** *syn* BREAK, crack, burst, bust, shatter, shiver *rel* part, separate, sever, sunder

snappish *syn* IRRITABLE, fractious, peevish, waspish, petulant, pettish, huffy, fretful, querulous *rel* testy, touchy, cranky, irascible; surly, crabbed, morose, sullen

snappy *syn* PUNGENT, piquant, poignant, racy, spicy *rel* sharp, keen, acute; vivacious, lively, animated; quick, prompt, ready; smart, dashing, chic, modish, stylish

snare *n, syn* LURE, trap, bait, decoy *rel* trickery, deception, chicanery, chicane

snare *vb, syn* CATCH, ensnare, trap, entrap, bag, capture *rel* lure, entice, inveigle, tempt, seduce, decoy

snarl *n, syn* CONFUSION, disorder, chaos, disarray, jumble, clutter, muddle *rel* complexity, complication, intricateness, intricacy; difficulty, hardship

snarl *vb, syn* BARK, bay, howl, growl, yelp, yap

snatch *syn* TAKE, grasp, grab, clutch, seize *rel* catch, capture; pull, drag, draw

sneak *syn* LURK, slink, skulk

sneer *syn* SCOFF, jeer, gird, flout, gibe, fleer *rel* deride, taunt, mock, ridicule; scout, despise, scorn, disdain

snip *syn* SHEAR, poll, clip, trim, prune, lop, crop *rel* cut, slit, slash, chop; bite

snitch *syn* STEAL, pilfer, filch, purloin, lift, pinch, swipe, cop

snoopy *syn* CURIOUS, inquisitive, prying, nosy *rel* meddlesome, officious, intrusive, impertinent, obtrusive; interfering, interposing

snooze *syn* SLEEP, slumber, drowse, doze, nap, catnap

snug **1** *syn* NEAT, trim, trig, shipshape, tidy, spick-and-span *rel* compact, close; orderly, methodical, systematic **2** *syn* COMFORTABLE, cozy, easy, restful *rel* safe, secure; familiar, intimate, close; sheltered, harbored

so *syn* THEREFORE, hence, consequently, then, accordingly

soak *vb* • to permeate or be permeated with a liquid *syn* saturate, drench, steep, impregnate, sop, waterlog *rel* dip, immerse, submerge; permeate, pervade, penetrate

soak *n, syn* DRUNKARD, inebriate, alcoholic, dipsomaniac, sot, toper, tosspot, tippler

soapy *syn* FULSOME, slick, oily, unctuous, oleaginous

soar *syn* RISE, arise, ascend, mount, tower, rocket, levitate, surge *rel* fly, dart, shoot; aspire, aim

sob *vb, syn* SIGH, moan, groan *rel* weep, wail, cry, blubber

sob *n, syn* SIGH, moan, groan *rel* weeping, wailing, crying, blubbering

sober **1** · having or exhibiting self-control and avoiding extremes of behavior *syn* temperate, continent, unimpassioned *rel* abstaining, refraining, forbearing; forgoing, eschewing, abnegating; cool, collected, composed; reasonable, rational *ant* drunk; excited **2** *syn* SERIOUS, grave, sedate, staid, solemn, somber, earnest *rel* decorous, decent, proper; calm, placid, tranquil, serene; dispassionate, impartial, fair, equitable *ant* gay

sobriety *syn* TEMPERANCE, abstinence, abstemiousness, continence *rel* moderateness, temperateness; quietness, stillness; seriousness, gravity, somberness, sedateness *ant* drunkenness; excitement

sociable *syn* GRACIOUS, cordial, affable, genial *rel* social, companionable, convivial, gregarious; intimate, familiar, close; amiable, obliging, complaisant, good-natured *ant* unsociable

social · inclined to seek or enjoy the company of others *syn* gregarious, cooperative, convivial, companionable, hospitable *rel* gracious, cordial, sociable, genial, affable; amicable, neighborly, friendly *ant* unsocial, antisocial, asocial

society **1** *syn* ARISTOCRACY, elite, nobility, gentry, county **2** *syn* ASSOCIATION, order, club

soft · free from all harshness, roughness, or intensity *syn* bland, mild, gentle, smooth, lenient, balmy *rel* moderated, tempered; smooth, effortless, easy; velvety, silken, sleek, slick; serene, tranquil, calm, placid, peaceful *ant* hard; stern

soil · to make or become unclean *syn* dirty, sully, tarnish, foul, befoul, smirch, besmirch, grime, begrime

sojourn *syn* RESIDE, lodge, stay, put up, stop, live, dwell

solace *syn* COMFORT, console *rel* relieve, assuage, mitigate, allay, alleviate, lighten; gladden, rejoice, delight, please, gratify

sole *syn* SINGLE, unique, solitary, lone, separate, particular *rel* alone, only; exclusive, picked, select

solecism *syn* BARBARISM, corruption, impropriety, vulgarism, vernacular

solemn **1** *syn* CEREMONIAL, ceremonious, formal, conventional *rel* liturgical, ritualistic; full, complete, plenary; imposing, august, majestic, magnificent, grand **2** *syn* SERIOUS, grave, somber, sedate, earnest, staid, sober *rel* impressive, moving; sublime, superb, splendid; ostentatious, showy

solemnize *syn* KEEP, celebrate, observe, commemorate

solicit **1** *syn* ASK, request *rel* resort, refer, apply, go, turn; beg, entreat, beseech, implore, supplicate **2** *syn* INVITE, bid, court, woo *rel* importune, adjure, beg; demand, claim, exact; evoke, elicit, extract, extort, educe

solicitor *syn* LAWYER, attorney, counselor, barrister, counsel, advocate

solicitous *syn* WORRIED, concerned, anxious *rel* apprehensive, fearful, afraid; agitated, disturbed, disquieted, upset; uneasy, fidgety, jittery, impatient *ant* unmindful; negligent

solicitude *syn* CARE, concern, anxiety, worry *rel* misgiving, apprehension, foreboding, presentiment; compunction, qualm, scruple; fear, alarm, consternation, dismay *ant* negligence; unmindfulness

solid *syn* FIRM, hard *rel* compact, close, dense; consolidated, concentrated, compacted *ant* fluid, liquid

solidarity *syn* UNITY, union, integrity *rel* consolidation, concentration, unification; cooperation, concurrence, combination

solidify *syn* HARDEN, indurate, petrify, cake *rel* compact, consolidate, concentrate; condense, contract, compress; congeal, coagulate, set, clot, jelly, jell

solitary **1** *syn* ALONE, lonely, lonesome, lone, forlorn, lorn, desolate *rel* isolated, secluded; retired, withdrawn; forsaken, deserted, abandoned **2** *syn* SINGLE, sole, unique, lone, separate, particular *rel* alone, only

solitude • the state of one who is alone *syn* isolation, alienation, seclusion *rel* retreat, refuge, asylum, shelter; retirement, withdrawal

solve • to find an explanation or solution for something obscure, mysterious, or incomprehensible *syn* resolve, unfold, unravel, decipher *rel* decide, determine, settle; illuminate, enlighten; interpret, elucidate, explain

somatic *syn* BODILY, physical, corporeal, corporal

somber *syn* SERIOUS, grave, solemn, sedate, staid, sober, earnest *rel* gloomy, dark, murky; dismal, bleak, cheerless; melancholy, melancholic *ant* garish

somnolent *syn* SLEEPY, drowsy, slumberous *rel* sluggish, comatose, lethargic; inert, inactive, passive, supine

sonorous *syn* RESONANT, ringing, resounding, vibrant, orotund *rel* deep, profound; rich, opulent; loud, stentorian

soon **1** *syn* PRESENTLY, shortly, directly **2** *syn* EARLY, beforehand, betimes

soothe *syn* CALM, compose, quiet, quieten, still, lull, settle, tranquilize *rel* mollify, appease, placate, pacify, propitiate, conciliate; allay, alleviate, assuage, mitigate, relieve *ant* annoy; excite

sop *syn* SOAK, saturate, drench, steep, impregnate, waterlog

sophism *syn* FALLACY, sophistry, casuistry

sophistical *syn* FALLACIOUS, casuistical *ant* valid

sophisticate *syn* ADULTERATE, load, weight, doctor

sophisticated • experienced in the ways of the world *syn* worldly-wise, worldly, blasé, disillusioned *rel* cultivated, cultured; intellectualized; knowing, brilliant, intelligent, clever, alert *ant* unsophisticated

sophistry *syn* FALLACY, sophism, casuistry *rel* plausibility, speciousness; equivocation, ambiguity, tergiversation; evading, evasion, avoiding, avoidance

soppy *syn* SENTIMENTAL, romantic, mawkish, maudlin, mushy, slushy

sorcery *syn* MAGIC, witchcraft, witchery, wizardry, alchemy, thaumaturgy

sordid *syn* MEAN, ignoble, abject *rel* mercenary, venal; squalid, foul, filthy, nasty, dirty; contemptible, despicable, sorry, scurvy, cheap, beggarly, shabby

sorrow *n* • distress of mind *syn* grief, heartache, heartbreak, anguish, woe, regret *rel* mourning, grieving; distress, suffering, misery, agony; melancholy, dejection, sadness, depression *ant* joy

sorrow *vb, syn* GRIEVE, mourn *rel* cry, weep, wail, keen; sob, moan, groan, sigh

sorry *syn* CONTEMPTIBLE, pitiable, despicable, scurvy, cheap, beggarly, shabby *rel* mean, ignoble, sordid, abject; miserable, wretched; paltry, petty, trifling, trivial

sort *n, syn* TYPE, kind, stripe, kidney, ilk, description, nature, character

sort *vb, syn* ASSORT, classify, pigeonhole *rel* arrange, methodize, systematize, order; cull, pick, choose, select

sot *syn* DRUNKARD, inebriate, alcoholic, dipsomaniac, soak, toper, tosspot, tippler

soul **1** *syn* MIND, intellect, psyche, brain, intelligence, wit *rel* powers, faculties, functions **2** • the immortal part of a human being believed to have permanent individual existence *syn* spirit *ant* body

sound *adj* **1** *syn* HEALTHY, wholesome, robust, hale, well *rel* vigorous, lusty, nervous, energetic, strenuous; strong, sturdy, stalwart, stout; intact, whole, entire, perfect **2** *syn* VALID, cogent, convincing, compelling, telling *rel* impeccable, flawless, faultless, errorless; correct, exact, precise, accurate; rational, reasonable *ant* fallacious

sound *n* • a sensation or effect produced by stimulation of the auditory receptors *syn* noise *ant* silence

sound *n, syn* STRAIT, channel, passage, narrows

sound *vb, syn* FATHOM, plumb

soupçon *syn* TOUCH, suspicion, suggestion, tincture, tinge, shade, smack, spice, dash, vein, strain, streak

sour • having a taste devoid of sweetness *syn* acid, acidulous, tart, dry *rel* bitter, acrid; sharp, keen; morose, sullen, glum, crabbed, saturnine, dour

source *syn* ORIGIN, root, inception, provenance, provenience, prime mover *rel* beginning, commencement, starting, start; cause, determinant, antecedent *ant* termination; outcome

souse *syn* DIP, immerse, submerge, duck, dunk *rel* soak, steep, saturate, impregnate

souvenir **1** *syn* REMEMBRANCE, remembrancer, reminder, memorial, memento, token, keepsake **2** *syn* MEMORY, remembrance, recollection, reminiscence, mind

sovereign **1** *syn* DOMINANT, predominant, paramount, preponderant, preponderating *rel* supreme, transcendent, surpassing; absolute, ultimate **2** *syn* FREE, independent, autonomous, autarchic, autarkic *rel* highest, loftiest; chief, principal, foremost; governing, ruling; commanding, directing

sovereignty *syn* FREEDOM, independence, autonomy, autarky, autarchy *rel* supremacy, ascendancy; command, sway, control, dominion, power, authority

sow *syn* STREW, straw, scatter, broadcast

spacious • larger in extent or capacity than the average *syn* commodious, capacious, ample *rel* vast, immense, enormous, huge; broad, wide, deep; extended, extensive

spade *syn* DIG, delve, grub, excavate

spangle *syn* SPOT, spatter, sprinkle, mottle, fleck, stipple, marble, speckle, bespangle

spangled *syn* SPOTTED, spattered, sprinkled, mottled, flecked, stippled, marbled, speckled, bespangled

spare **1** *syn* SUPERFLUOUS, extra, surplus, supernumerary *rel* excessive, immoderate, exorbitant, inordinate **2** *syn* LEAN, lank, lanky, skinny, scrawny, gaunt, rawboned, angular *rel* thin, slender, slim, slight; sinewy, athletic, muscular *ant* corpulent **3** *syn* MEAGER, exiguous, sparse, scanty, scant, skimpy, scrimpy *rel* economical, sparing, frugal, thrifty *ant* profuse

sparing · careful in the use of one's money or resources *syn* frugal, thrifty, economical *rel* meager, exiguous, spare; stingy, niggardly, parsimonious, penurious; moderate, temperate *ant* lavish

sparkle *syn* FLASH, gleam, glance, glint, glitter, glisten, scintillate, coruscate, twinkle

sparse *syn* MEAGER, spare, exiguous, scanty, scant, skimpy, scrimpy *rel* scattered, dispersed; sporadic, occasional, infrequent, uncommon; thin, slim, slender *ant* dense

spasm *syn* FIT, paroxysm, convulsion, attack, access, accession

spasmodic *syn* FITFUL, convulsive *rel* intermittent, alternate, recurrent, periodic; irregular, unnatural; abnormal, aberrant, atypical

spat *n, syn* QUARREL, bickering, squabble, wrangle, altercation, tiff *rel* dispute, controversy, argument; contention, difference, variance, discord

spat *vb, syn* QUARREL, bicker, squabble, wrangle, altercate, tiff *rel* dispute, argue, agitate, debate, discuss; differ, disagree

spate *syn* FLOOD, deluge, inundation, torrent, cataract *rel* flow, stream, current, tide; succession, progression, series

spatter *syn* SPOT, sprinkle, mottle, fleck, stipple, marble, speckle, spangle, bespangle *rel* bespatter, asperse, splash

spattered *syn* SPOTTED, sprinkled, mottled, flecked, stippled, marbled, speckled, spangled, bespangled

spay *syn* STERILIZE, castrate, emasculate, alter, mutilate, geld

speak · to articulate words so as to express thoughts *syn* talk, converse *rel* pronounce, articulate, enunciate; stammer, stutter; discourse, expatiate, dilate, descant

special · of or relating to one thing or class *syn* especial, specific, particular, individual *rel* distinctive, peculiar, characteristic; exceptional; uncommon, occasional, rare, infrequent

specie *syn* MONEY, cash, currency, legal tender, coin, coinage

specific *adj* **1** *syn* SPECIAL, especial, particular, individual *ant* generic **2** *syn* EXPLICIT, definite, express, categorical *rel* designating, naming; clear, lucid, perspicuous; precise, exact *ant* vague

specific *n, syn* REMEDY, cure, medicine, medicament, medication, physic

specify *syn* MENTION, name, instance *rel* cite, quote; stipulate

specimen *syn* INSTANCE, example, sample, illustration, case

specious *syn* PLAUSIBLE, believable, colorable, credible *rel* vain, nugatory, empty, hollow, idle; delusory, delusive, misleading, deceptive; deceitful, dishonest, untruthful, mendacious, lying

speckle *syn* SPOT, spatter, sprinkle, mottle, fleck, stipple, marble, spangle, bespangle

speckled *syn* SPOTTED, spattered, sprinkled, mottled, flecked, stippled, marbled, spangled, bespangled

spectator · one who looks on or watches *syn* observer, beholder, looker-on, onlooker, witness, eyewitness, bystander, kibitzer

specter *syn* APPARITION, spirit, ghost, phantasm, phantom, wraith, shade, revenant

speculate *syn* THINK, reason,

reflect, cogitate, deliberate *rel* ponder, meditate, muse, ruminate; consider, weigh, study, contemplate, excogitate

speculative **1** *syn* THOUGHTFUL, contemplative, meditative, reflective, pensive *rel* conjecturing, conjectural, surmising, guessing; pondering, musing, ruminating **2** *syn* THEORETICAL, academic

speech **1** *syn* LANGUAGE, tongue, dialect, idiom **2** • a usu. formal discourse delivered to an audience *syn* address, oration, harangue, lecture, talk, sermon, homily

speechless *syn* DUMB, mute, inarticulate

speed *n* **1** *syn* HASTE, hurry, expedition, dispatch *rel* celerity, legerity, alacrity; fleetness, rapidity, swiftness, quickness; velocity, pace, headway **2** • rate of motion, performance, or action *syn* velocity, momentum, impetus, pace, headway

speed *vb* • to go or make go fast or faster *syn* accelerate, quicken, hasten, hurry, precipitate *rel* advance, forward, further, promote; adjust, regulate, fix

speedy *syn* FAST, expeditious, quick, swift, fleet, rapid, hasty *rel* brisk, nimble, agile; prompt, quick, ready *ant* dilatory

spell • a limited period or amount of activity *syn* shift, tour, trick, turn, stint, bout, go *rel* period; allotment, assignment, apportionment

spend • to use up or pay out *syn* expend, disburse *rel* distribute, dispense, divide, deal, dole; allot, assign, allocate, apportion; scatter, disperse, dissipate; pay, compensate, remunerate *ant* save

spendthrift • a person who spends foolishly and wastefully *syn* prodigal, profligate, waster, wastrel

spew *syn* BELCH, burp, vomit, disgorge, regurgitate, throw up

sphere *syn* FIELD, domain, province, territory, bailiwick *rel* dominion, sway, jurisdiction, control, power; range, reach, scope, compass; function, office, duty

spice *syn* TOUCH, suggestion, suspicion, soupçon, tincture, tinge, shade, smack, dash, vein, strain, streak

spick-and-span *syn* NEAT, tidy, trim, trig, snug, shipshape *rel* clean, cleanly; fresh, new *ant* filthy

spicy *syn* PUNGENT, piquant, poignant, racy, snappy *rel* spirited, high-spirited, gingery, fiery, peppery; aromatic, redolent, balmy, odorous

spin *syn* TURN, revolve, rotate, gyrate, circle, twirl, whirl, wheel, eddy, swirl, pirouette *rel* swing, sway, oscillate, vibrate

spine • the articulated column of bones that is the central and axial feature of a vertebrate skeleton *syn* backbone, back, vertebrae, chine

spirit **1** *syn* SOUL *rel* mind, intellect, psyche **2** *syn* APPARITION, ghost, phantasm, phantom, wraith, specter, shade, revenant **3** *syn* COURAGE, mettle, resolution, tenacity *rel* fortitude, pluck, grit, backbone, sand, guts; zeal, fervor, ardor, passion, enthusiasm; energy, strength, might, power, force **4** *syn* VIGOR, vim, dash, esprit, verve, punch, élan, drive *rel* vitality, animation, aliveness; vivacity, liveliness, gaiety, sprightliness

spirited • full of energy, animation, or courage *syn* high-spirited, mettlesome, spunky, fiery, peppery, gingery *rel* courageous, intrepid, bold, audacious, valiant, brave; impetuous, precipitate; eager, avid, keen; passionate, enthusiastic, zealous, fervent, ardent *ant* spiritless

spiritless *syn* LANGUID, languishing, languorous, listless, enervated, lackadaisical *rel* lethargic, sluggish, comatose; dull, slow, stupid, dense, crass; tame, subdued, submissive *ant* spirited

spiritual **1** *syn* IMMATERIAL, incorporeal *ant* physical **2** *syn* HOLY, sacred, divine, religious, blessed *rel* supernatural, supranatural; celestial, heavenly *ant* physical; carnal; material; temporal

spite *syn* MALICE, despite, malignity, malignancy, spleen, grudge, ill will, malevolence *rel* rancor, animus, antipathy, enmity; vindictiveness, revengefulness, revenge, vengefulness, vengeance

spiteful *syn* MALICIOUS, malignant, malevolent, malign *rel* rancorous, antipathetic, antagonistic, hostile; vindictive, revengeful, vengeful

spleen *syn* MALICE, malignity, malignancy, grudge, spite, despite, malevolence, ill will *rel* animosity, antipathy, animus, rancor, antagonism, enmity; venom, poison; vindictiveness, revengefulness

splendid · extraordinarily or transcendently impressive *syn* resplendent, gorgeous, glorious, sublime, superb *rel* radiant, effulgent, luminous, brilliant, bright; illustrious, eminent, famous; excelling, excellent, surpassing, transcending, transcendent

splenetic *syn* IRASCIBLE, choleric, testy, touchy, cranky, cross *rel* morose, sullen, glum, gloomy; irritable, querulous, peevish, snappish; captious, carping, caviling, critical

split *vb, syn* TEAR, rend, cleave, rive, rip *rel* separate, part, divide, sever; cut, chop, hew

split *n, syn* BREACH, break, schism, rent, rupture, rift *rel* crack, cleft, fissure; estrangement, alienation; schism, heresy

split second *syn* INSTANT, moment, second, minute, flash, jiffy, twinkling

spoil *n* · something taken from another by force or craft *syn* plunder, booty, prize, loot, swag *rel* theft, robbery, larceny, burglary; acquisitions, acquirements

spoil *vb* **1** *syn* INJURE, harm, hurt, damage, impair, mar *rel* ruin, wreck; destroy, demolish **2** *syn* INDULGE, pamper, humor, baby, mollycoddle *rel* favor, accommodate, oblige; debase, deprave, vitiate, debauch **3** *syn* DECAY, decompose, rot, putrefy, disintegrate, crumble *rel* corrupt, vitiate, debase; ruin, wreck; impair, harm, injure

spoliate *syn* RAVAGE, despoil, devastate, waste, sack, pillage *rel* rob, plunder, rifle, loot; defraud, swindle, cheat

sponge, sponger *syn* PARASITE, sycophant, favorite, toady, lickspittle, bootlicker, hanger-on, leech

sponsor · one who assumes responsibility for some other person or thing *syn* patron, surety, guarantor, backer, angel *rel* supporter, support, upholder, champion, advocator, advocate; promoter, furtherer

spontaneity *syn* UNCONSTRAINT, abandon *rel* spontaneousness, instinctiveness, impulsiveness; extemporaneousness, offhandedness, unpremeditatedness; naturalness, simplicity, unsophistication, naïveté, ingenuousness

spontaneous · acting or activated without deliberation *syn* impulsive, instinctive, automatic, mechanical *rel* extemporaneous, extempore, impromptu, improvised, offhand, unpremeditated; natural, simple, ingenuous, unsophisticated

spoon *syn* DIP, ladle, dish, bail, scoop

sporadic *syn* INFREQUENT, occasional, rare, scarce, uncommon *rel* scattered, dispersed; sparse, exiguous, meager

sport *vb, syn* PLAY, disport, frolic, rollick, romp, gambol *rel* divert, amuse, recreate, entertain; skip, bound, hop

sport *n* **1** *syn* PLAY, disport, frolic, rollick, romp, gambol *rel* amusement, diversion, recreation, entertainment; merriment, jollity **2** *syn* FUN, jest, game, play *rel* mirth, glee, hilarity, jollity **3** *pl* **sports** *syn* ATHLETICS, games

sportive *syn* PLAYFUL, frolicsome, roguish, waggish, impish, mischievous *rel* blithe, merry, jocund, jovial, jolly; mirthful, gleeful, hilarious

spot *n, syn* PLACE, position, location, situation, site, station *rel* locality, district, neighborhood, vicinity; region, area, tract, belt, zone; section, sector, part

spot *vb* • to mark or become marked with or as if with spots or sometimes streaks *syn* spatter, sprinkle, mottle, fleck, stipple, marble, speckle, spangle, bespangle *rel* splash, bespatter, besprinkle, asperse; soil, sully, dirty, smirch, besmirch; variegate, checker, dapple, freak

spotted • marked with spots or streaks *syn* spattered, sprinkled, mottled, flecked, stippled, marbled, speckled, spangled, bespangled

sprain *n, syn* STRAIN

sprain *vb, syn* STRAIN

spread *vb* • to extend or cause to extend over an area or space *syn* circulate, disseminate, diffuse, propagate, radiate *rel* distribute, dispense, deal; scatter, dissipate

spread *n, syn* EXPANSE, amplitude, stretch *rel* extent, area, magnitude, size; range, reach, scope, compass

sprightly *syn* LIVELY, animated, vivacious, gay *rel* active, live, dynamic; agile, nimble, brisk, spry; merry, blithe, jocund

spring *vb* **1** • to come up or out of something into existence *syn* arise, rise, originate, derive, flow, issue, emanate, proceed, stem *rel* emerge, loom, appear; come, arrive; begin, commence, start **2** *syn* JUMP, leap, bound, vault *rel* frolic, rollick, gambol, disport, play

spring *n* **1** *syn* MOTIVE, impulse, incentive, inducement, spur, goad *rel* origin, source, root, inception; cause, determinant, antecedent; stimulus, stimulant, excitant, incitement, impetus **2** *syn* JUMP, leap, bound, vault

springy *syn* ELASTIC, resilient, flexible, supple *rel* yielding, submitting; recoiling, rebounding

sprinkle *syn* SPOT, spatter, mottle, fleck, stipple, marble, speckle, spangle, bespangle

sprinkled *syn* SPOTTED, spattered, mottled, flecked, stippled, marbled, speckled, spangled, bespangled

sprint *syn* SCUTTLE, scurry, scamper, skedaddle *rel* rush, dash, charge, shoot, tear; speed, hurry, hasten; dart, fly, scud

spry *syn* AGILE, brisk, nimble *rel* quick, ready, prompt; vigorous, energetic, strenuous; hale, healthy, sound, robust *ant* doddering

spume *syn* FOAM, froth, scum, lather, suds, yeast

spunky *syn* SPIRITED, high-spirited, mettlesome, fiery, peppery, gingery *rel* dauntless, undaunted, bold, brave; daring, venturesome, adventurous; restive, restless, impatient

spur *n, syn* MOTIVE, goad, spring, impulse, incentive, inducement *rel* stimulus, stimulant, excitant, incitement, impetus; activation, actuation, motivation; cause, determinant; provoking, provocation, exciting, excitement

spur *vb, syn* URGE, egg, exhort, goad, prod, prick, sic *rel* rouse, arouse, stir, awaken, rally; incite, instigate; excite, provoke, stimulate; encourage, countenance, favor *ant* curb

spurious *syn* COUNTERFEIT, bogus, fake, sham, pseudo, pinchbeck, phony *rel* false; simulated, feigned, shammed; supposititious, reputed, putative, supposed *ant* genuine

spurn *syn* DECLINE, reject, repudiate, refuse *rel* disdain, scorn, scout, despise, contemn; flout, scoff, sneer *ant* crave; embrace

squabble *n, syn* QUARREL, wrangle, altercation, bickering, spat, tiff *rel* dispute, controversy, argument; row, rumpus, scrap, brawl, broil

squabble *vb, syn* QUARREL, wrangle, altercate, bicker, spat, tiff *rel* contend, fight, battle, war; struggle, strive; dispute, agitate, argue, discuss

squalid *syn* DIRTY, nasty, filthy, foul *rel* slovenly, unkempt, disheveled, sloppy, slipshod; sordid, abject, mean; slatternly, frowzy

squander *syn* WASTE, dissipate, fritter, consume *rel* scatter, disperse, dissipate, dispel; spend, expend, disburse

square *syn* AGREE, conform, accord, harmonize, correspond, tally, jibe *rel* equal, match, approach, touch, rival; balance, offset, compensate; concur, coincide

squash *syn* CRUSH, mash, smash, bruise, macerate *rel* press, squeeze, jam, crowd; compact, concentrate, consolidate

squat *syn* STOCKY, thickset, thick, chunky, stubby, dumpy *ant* lanky

squeal *vb, syn* SHOUT, yell, shriek, scream, screech, holler, whoop *rel* cry, wail

squeal *n, syn* SHOUT, yell, shriek, scream, screech, holler, whoop

squeamish *syn* NICE, finicky, finicking, finical, particular, fussy, persnickety, pernickety, fastidious, dainty *rel* exacting, demanding, requiring; hypercritical, critical, faultfinding, caviling, captious, carping

squeeze *syn* PRESS, bear, bear down, crowd, jam *rel* compress, contract; extract, elicit, educe, extort; force, compel, constrain, coerce

squib *syn* LIBEL, skit, lampoon, pasquinade

squirm *syn* WRITHE, agonize *rel* twist, bend, curve; wince, flinch, blench, shrink, recoil

stabilize • to make or become stable, steadfast, or firm *syn* steady, poise, balance, ballast, trim *rel* regulate, adjust, fix; set, settle, establish

stable *syn* LASTING, durable, perdurable, permanent, perpetual *rel* enduring, persisting, abiding; secure, safe; steady, constant; staunch, steadfast, resolute *ant* unstable; changeable

stack *n, syn* HEAP, pile, mass, bank, shock, cock

stack *vb, syn* HEAP, pile, mass, bank, shock, cock *rel* collect, gather, assemble; amass, accumulate, hoard

stagger *syn* REEL, whirl, totter *rel* sway, waver, fluctuate, swing; stumble, lurch, blunder, flounder

staid *syn* SERIOUS, sedate, grave, somber, sober, earnest *rel* decorous, decent, seemly; cool, collected, composed; smug, priggish, self-complacent, complacent *ant* jaunty

stain *syn* STIGMA, blot, brand *rel* blemish, defect, flaw; mark, sign, token; disgrace, dishonor

stake *syn* BET, wager, pot, ante

stalemate *syn* DRAW, tie, deadlock, standoff

stalwart *syn* STRONG, stout, sturdy, tough, tenacious *rel* husky, brawny, muscular, sinewy, athletic; lusty, nervous, vigorous; robust, sound, healthy

stammer • to make involuntary stops and repetitions in speaking *syn* stutter

stamp *vb, syn* MARK, brand, label, tag, ticket *rel* impress, imprint, print; authenticate, validate, confirm, avouch, warrant, assert

stamp *n* **1** *syn* IMPRESSION, impress, imprint, print **2** *syn* MARK, brand, label, tag, ticket

stand *vb, syn* BEAR, tolerate, brook, suffer, endure, abide

stand *n, syn* POSITION, attitude *rel* point of view, standpoint, viewpoint, slant, angle

standard **1** *syn* FLAG, ensign, banner, color, streamer, pennant, pendant, pennon, jack **2** • a means of determining what a thing should be *syn* criterion, gauge, yardstick, touchstone *rel* norm, median, par, mean, average; rule, law; principle, fundamental, axiom **3** *syn* MODEL, ideal, beau ideal, pattern, exemplar, example, mirror *rel* see STANDARD 2

stand-in *syn* SUBSTITUTE, supply, understudy, double, locum tenens, alternate, pinch hitter

standoff *syn* DRAW, tie, stalemate, deadlock

standpoint *syn* POINT OF VIEW, viewpoint, angle, slant *rel* stand, position, attitude

stare *syn* GAZE, gape, glare, peer, gloat *rel* look, watch, see; glower, lower, scowl, frown

stark *syn* STIFF, rigid, inflexible, tense, wooden *rel* settled, established, fixed, set

starry • of, relating to, or suggestive of a star or group of stars *syn* stellar, astral, sidereal

start *syn* BEGIN, commence, initiate, inaugurate *rel* institute, found, establish, organize; enter, penetrate; originate, proceed, spring

startle *syn* FRIGHTEN, scare, alarm, terrify, terrorize, fright, affray, affright *rel* surprise, astonish, astound; rouse, arouse, stir; electrify, thrill

state *n* • the way in which one manifests existence or the circumstances under which one exists or by which one is given distinctive character *syn* condition, mode, situation, posture, status *rel* phase, aspect; plight, predicament, quandary, dilemma; pass, juncture, exigency, emergency, crisis

state *vb* **1** *syn* SAY, utter, tell **2** *syn* RELATE, report, rehearse, recite, recount, narrate, describe *rel* expound, explain, elucidate, interpret; assert, affirm, declare, profess

stately *syn* GRAND, magnificent, imposing, majestic, august, noble, grandiose *rel* princely, regal, royal, kingly, imperial; splendid, glorious, superb, sublime; sumptuous, opulent, luxurious

statesman *syn* POLITICIAN, politico

station **1** *syn* PLACE, position, location, situation, site, spot *rel* locality, district, vicinity, neighborhood; region, area, zone, belt, tract **2** *syn* HABITAT, biotope, range

stature *syn* QUALITY, caliber *rel* capacity, ability; competence, qualification

status *syn* STATE, situation, posture, condition, mode

statute *syn* LAW, ordinance, regulation, rule, precept, canon

staunch *syn* FAITHFUL, loyal, true, constant, steadfast, resolute *rel* trusty, trustworthy, reliable, dependable, tried; stout, strong, tough, tenacious, sturdy, stalwart

stay *vb* **1** • to continue to be in one place for a noticeable time *syn* remain, wait, abide, tarry, linger *rel* delay, procrastinate, lag, loiter; arrest, check, interrupt; continue, persist **2** *syn* RESIDE, sojourn, lodge, put up, stop, live, dwell **3** *syn* DEFER, postpone, suspend, intermit *rel* delay, retard, slow, slacken, detain; restrain, check, curb; hinder, obstruct, impede

stay *vb, syn* BASE, found, ground, bottom, rest

steadfast *syn* FAITHFUL, staunch, resolute, constant, true, loyal *rel* settled, established, set, fixed; steady; stable, durable, perdurable, lasting; enduring, persisting, abiding *ant* capricious

steady *adj* · not varying throughout a course or extent *syn* uniform, even, equable, constant *rel* stable, durable, perdurable, perpetual, lasting; enduring, persisting, continuing; staunch, steadfast, resolute, faithful; persevering, persisting *ant* unsteady; nervous, jumpy

steady *vb, syn* STABILIZE, poise, balance, ballast, trim

steal · to take from another without right or without detection *syn* pilfer, filch, purloin, lift, pinch, snitch, swipe, cop *rel* rob, plunder, rifle, loot, burglarize

stealthy *syn* SECRET, covert, furtive, clandestine, surreptitious, underhand, underhanded *rel* sly, cunning, crafty, artful, tricky, wily; sneaking, slinking, skulking

steel *syn* ENCOURAGE, inspirit, hearten, embolden, cheer, nerve *rel* fortify, reinforce, invigorate, strengthen; determine, resolve, decide

steep *adj* · having an incline approaching the perpendicular *syn* abrupt, precipitous, sheer *rel* elevated, lifted, raised; lofty, high

steep *vb, syn* SOAK, saturate, impregnate, drench, sop, waterlog *rel* infuse, imbue, ingrain; penetrate, pierce, probe

steer *syn* GUIDE, lead, pilot, engineer *rel* conduct, direct, manage, control; govern, rule

stellar *syn* STARRY, sidereal, astral

stem *syn* SPRING, proceed, issue, emanate, derive, flow, originate, arise, rise

stentorian *syn* LOUD, earsplitting, hoarse, raucous, strident, stertorous *rel* resounding, orotund, resonant; vociferous, clamorous, blatant; harsh, rough

stereotyped *syn* TRITE, hackneyed, threadbare, shopworn *rel* conventional, formal, ceremonial; obsolete, archaic, antiquated, old; used, employed, utilized, applied *ant* changeful

sterile · not able to bear fruit, crops, or offspring *syn* barren, impotent, unfruitful, infertile *rel* bare, bald, naked; arid, dry; meager, exiguous; empty, hollow, nugatory, vain *ant* fertile; exuberant

sterilize **1** · to make incapable of producing offspring *syn* castrate, spay, emasculate, alter, mutilate, geld *ant* fertilize **2** · to free from living microorganisms *syn* disinfect, sanitize, fumigate

stern *syn* SEVERE, austere, ascetic *rel* strict, rigid, rigorous, stringent; grim, implacable, unrelenting; inflexible, inexorable; disciplined, trained, schooled *ant* soft; lenient

stertorous *syn* LOUD, stentorian, earsplitting, hoarse, raucous, strident *rel* harsh, rough

stew *syn* BOIL, seethe, simmer, parboil

stick **1** · to become or cause to become closely and firmly attached *syn* adhere, cohere, cling, cleave *rel* tie, bind; attach, fasten, affix, fix; implant **2** *syn* DEMUR, stickle, balk, shy, boggle, scruple, jib, strain

stickle *syn* DEMUR, balk, shy, boggle, jib, scruple, stick, strain *rel* hesitate, vacillate, falter, waver; object, kick, protest

stick out *syn* BULGE, jut, protrude, project, overhang, beetle *rel* extend, prolong, elongate, lengthen; expand, swell, distend; obtrude

stiff • difficult to bend *syn* rigid, inflexible, tense, stark, wooden *rel* tough, tenacious, strong, stout; firm, hard, solid; formal, conventional, ceremonious, ceremonial; frigid, cold, cool; difficult, hard, arduous *ant* relaxed; supple

stiff-necked *syn* OBSTINATE, stubborn, mulish, dogged, pertinacious, pigheaded, bullheaded

stifle *syn* SUFFOCATE, asphyxiate, smother, choke, strangle, throttle

stigma • a mark of shame or discredit *syn* brand, blot, stain *rel* disgrace, dishonor, opprobrium, odium, shame; contamination, tainting, taint, defilement, pollution

still *adj* • making no stir or noise *syn* stilly, quiet, silent, noiseless *rel* calm, tranquil, serene, placid, peaceful; restful, comfortable *ant* stirring; noisy

still *vb, syn* CALM, compose, quiet, quieten, lull, soothe, settle, tranquilize *rel* allay, assuage, alleviate, relieve; pacify, placate, mollify, appease; silence *ant* agitate

stilly *syn* STILL, quiet, silent, noiseless *rel* soft, gentle, mild, bland; placid, peaceful, calm, tranquil, serene

stimulant *syn* STIMULUS, excitant, incitement, impetus *rel* provocation, excitement, stimulation, quickening, galvanizing; incentive, spur, goad, motive *ant* anesthetic; anodyne

stimulate *syn* PROVOKE, excite, quicken, pique, galvanize *rel* animate, enliven, vivify; activate, energize, vitalize; rouse, arouse, stir, rally, waken, awaken *ant* unnerve; deaden

stimulus • something that rouses or incites to activity *syn* stimulant, excitant, incitement, impetus *rel* spur, goad, incentive, motive, inducement; excitement, piquing, provocation; irritation, nettling

stingy • being unwilling or showing unwillingness to share with others *syn* close, closefisted, tight, tightfisted, niggardly, parsimonious, penurious, miserly, cheeseparing, penny-pinching *rel* mean, sordid, ignoble; scrimpy, skimpy, meager; greedy, acquisitive, avaricious, covetous, grasping; sparing, economical, frugal, thrifty *ant* generous

stinking *syn* MALODOROUS, fetid, noisome, putrid, rank, rancid, fusty, musty *rel* foul, filthy, nasty, dirty; offensive, repulsive, revolting

stint **1** *syn* TASK, duty, assignment, job, chore *rel* quantity, amount, sum; allotment, apportionment; prescribing, prescription, assigning; sharing, share, participation **2** *syn* SPELL, bout, shift, tour, trick, turn, go

stipend *syn* WAGE, wages, salary, fee, emolument, pay, hire *rel* remuneration, compensation, recompensing, recompense

stipple *syn* SPOT, spatter, sprinkle, mottle, fleck, marble, speckle, spangle, bespangle

stippled *syn* SPOTTED, spattered, sprinkled, mottled, flecked, marbled, speckled, spangled, bespangled

stipulation *syn* CONDITION, terms, provision, proviso, reservation, strings *rel* specification; restriction, circumscription

stir *vb* • to cause to shift from quiescence or torpor into activity *syn* rouse, arouse, awaken, waken, rally *rel* excite, provoke, stimulate, quicken, galvanize; incite, foment, instigate; activate, energize, vitalize; move, drive, impel, actuate

stir *n* **1** *syn* MOTION, movement, move, locomotion *rel* acting, activity, working, work, behaving, behavior, reaction; change, alteration, variation, modification **2** · signs of excited activity, hurry, or commotion *syn* bustle, flurry, pother, fuss, ado *rel* agitation, disturbance, disquieting, disquiet; excitement, stimulation; din, uproar, hubbub, pandemonium *ant* tranquillity

stitch *syn* PAIN, twinge, ache, pang, throe

stock *syn* VARIETY, subspecies, race, breed, cultivar, strain, clone

stocky · compact, sturdy, and relatively thick in build *syn* thickset, thick, chunky, stubby, squat, dumpy

stodgy *syn* DULL, humdrum, dreary, monotonous, pedestrian *rel* heavy, weighty, ponderous; irksome, tedious, wearisome, tiresome, boring; stuffy, straitlaced, prudish, prim

stoic *syn* IMPASSIVE, phlegmatic, apathetic, stolid *rel* detached, aloof, indifferent, unconcerned; imperturbable, composed, collected, cool; unassailable, indomitable, invincible; patient, long-suffering, resigned

stoicism *syn* IMPASSIVITY, impassiveness, phlegm, apathy, stolidity *rel* fortitude, grit, backbone, pluck, guts, sand; detachment, aloofness, indifference, unconcernedness, unconcern

stolid *syn* IMPASSIVE, phlegmatic, apathetic *rel* dull, blunt, obtuse; stupid, slow, dense, crass, dumb; heavy, ponderous; passive, supine, inert, inactive *ant* adroit

stolidity *syn* IMPASSIVITY, impassiveness, phlegm, apathy, stoicism

stomach *syn* ABDOMEN, belly, paunch, gut

stoop · to descend from one's real or pretended level of dignity *syn* condescend, deign *rel* abase, demean, humble; vouchsafe, accord, grant, concede; favor, accommodate, oblige

stop **1** · to suspend or cause to suspend activity *syn* cease, quit, discontinue, desist *rel* arrest, check, interrupt; intermit, suspend, stay, defer, postpone; frustrate, thwart, foil, balk, circumvent **2** *syn* RESIDE, stay, put up, lodge, sojourn, live, dwell

stopgap *syn* RESOURCE, makeshift, shift, expedient, resort, substitute, surrogate

storm *syn* ATTACK, bombard, assault, assail

story **1** *syn* ACCOUNT, report, chronicle, version *rel* history, annals; relation, rehearsing, recital, recounting **2** · a recital of happenings less elaborate than a novel *syn* narrative, tale, anecdote, yarn *rel* narration, description; fiction, fable, fabrication **3** *syn* LIE, falsehood, untruth, fib, misrepresentation

stout **1** *syn* STRONG, sturdy, stalwart, tough, tenacious *rel* brave, bold, intrepid, valiant, valorous; indomitable, invincible; resolute, staunch, steadfast, faithful; vigorous, energetic, lusty **2** *syn* FLESHY, fat, portly, corpulent, obese, plump, rotund, chubby *rel* thick, thickset, stocky; burly, brawny, husky, muscular *ant* cadaverous

straightforward · free from all that is dishonest or secretive *syn* forthright, aboveboard *rel* honest, upright, honorable, just; fair, equitable, impartial; candid, frank, open, plain *ant* devious; indirect

strain *n* **1** *syn* VARIETY, subspecies, race, breed, cultivar, clone, stock **2** *syn* TOUCH, streak, vein, suggestion, suspicion, soupçon, tincture, tinge, shade, smack, spice, dash

strain *vb* **1** · to injure (as a body part) by overuse or misuse *syn* sprain **2** *syn* DEMUR, scruple, balk, jib, shy, boggle, stickle, stick

strain *n* **1** *syn* STRESS, pressure, tension **2** · an injury to a part of the body from undue stretching *syn* sprain

strained *syn* FORCED, labored, far-fetched *rel* tense, taut, tight; artificial, factitious; unnatural, irregular; stiff, rigid, inflexible, wooden

strait **1** · a comparatively narrow stretch of water connecting two larger bodies of water *syn* sound, channel, passage, narrows **2** *syn* JUNCTURE, pass, exigency, pinch, emergency, contingency, crisis *rel* difficulty, hardship, vicissitude, rigor; perplexity, bewilderment, mystification; plight, predicament, fix, quandary

straitlaced *syn* PRIM, priggish, prissy, prudish, puritanical, stuffy *rel* narrow, narrow-minded, hidebound, intolerant, illiberal; rigid, rigorous, strict *ant* libertine

strand *syn* SHORE, coast, beach, bank, littoral, foreshore

strange · departing from what is ordinary, usual, and to be expected *syn* singular, unique, peculiar, eccentric, erratic, odd, queer, quaint, outlandish, curious *rel* abnormal, atypical, aberrant; fantastic, bizarre, grotesque; surprising, astonishing, amazing, flabbergasting *ant* familiar

stranger · a nonresident or an unknown person in a community *syn* foreigner, alien, outlander, outsider, immigrant, émigré

strangle *syn* SUFFOCATE, asphyxiate, stifle, smother, choke, throttle

stratagem *syn* TRICK, ruse, maneuver, gambit, ploy, artifice, wile, feint *rel* device, contrivance, contraption; expedient, shift, resource, resort; machination, intrigue, conspiracy, plot

strategic · of, relating to, or marked by strategy *syn* tactical, logistic

strategy · the art of devising or employing plans toward a usu. military goal *syn* tactics, logistics

straw *syn* STREW, scatter, sow, broadcast

stray *syn* WANDER, roam, ramble, rove, range, prowl, gad, gallivant, traipse, meander

streak *syn* TOUCH, strain, vein, suggestion, suspicion, soupçon, tincture, tinge, shade, smack, spice, dash

stream *n, syn* FLOW, current, flood, tide, flux

stream *vb, syn* POUR, gush, sluice *rel* flow, issue, emanate, proceed, spring; flood, deluge, inundate

streamer *syn* FLAG, pennant, pendant, pennon, banner, ensign, standard, color

strength *syn* POWER, force, might, energy, puissance *rel* stoutness, sturdiness, toughness, tenaciousness; soundness, healthiness; possessions, means, resources, assets

strengthen · to make strong or stronger *syn* invigorate, fortify, energize, reinforce *rel* embolden, steel, nerve, encourage, inspirit, hearten, cheer; vitalize, activate; galvanize, quicken, stimulate, provoke; intensify, heighten, aggravate *ant* weaken

strenuous *syn* VIGOROUS, energetic, lusty, nervous *rel* virile, manful, manly; dynamic, live, active, operative; spirited, high-spirited, mettlesome; vehement, intense, fierce, violent

stress **1** · the action or effect of force exerted within or upon a thing *syn* strain, pressure, tension **2** *syn* EMPHASIS, accent, accentuation

stretch *syn* EXPANSE, amplitude, spread *rel* area, tract, region; extent, magnitude, size

strew • to throw loosely or at intervals *syn* straw, scatter, sow, broadcast *rel* spread, disseminate; disperse, dissipate, scatter

strict *syn* RIGID, stringent, rigorous *rel* stern, severe, austere, ascetic; inflexible, inexorable; exacting, oppressive, onerous, burdensome *ant* lax; loose; lenient, indulgent

stricture *syn* ANIMADVERSION, aspersion, reflection *rel* criticism, censuring, censure, condemnation, denouncing, denunciation *ant* commendation

strident 1 *syn* LOUD, stentorian, earsplitting, hoarse, raucous, stertorous *rel* harsh, rough; resounding, resonant 2 *syn* VOCIFEROUS, blatant, clamorous, boisterous, obstreperous *rel* harsh, uneven, rough

strife *syn* DISCORD, conflict, contention, dissension, difference, variance *rel* combat, conflict, fight, affray, fray, contest; dispute, controversy, argument; brawl, broil, fracas; altercation, wrangle, quarrel, squabble *ant* peace; accord

strike 1 • to deliver (a blow) in a strong, vigorous manner *syn* hit, smite, punch, slug, slog, swat, clout, slap, cuff, box *rel* beat, pummel, buffet, pound, baste, belabor, thrash 2 *syn* AFFECT, impress, touch, influence, sway

striking *syn* NOTICEABLE, arresting, signal, salient, conspicuous, outstanding, remarkable, prominent *rel* effective, effectual, efficacious; telling, convincing, compelling, cogent, valid; forcible, forceful, powerful; impressive, moving

string 1 *syn* SUCCESSION, progression, series, sequence, chain, train 2 *pl* **strings** *syn* CONDITION, stipulation, terms, provision, proviso, reservation

stringent *syn* RIGID, strict, rigorous *rel* severe, austere, stern; limiting, restricting, circumscribing, confining; restraining, curbing; exacting, oppressive, onerous

strip *vb* • to remove what clothes, furnishes, or invests a person or thing *syn* divest, denude, bare, dismantle *rel* despoil, spoliate, devastate, waste, ravage; rifle, loot, plunder, rob *ant* furnish; invest

strip *n* • long narrow piece or area *syn* stripe, band, ribbon, fillet

stripe 1 *syn* STRIP, band, ribbon, fillet 2 *syn* TYPE, character, description, nature, kind, sort, kidney, ilk

strive *syn* ATTEMPT, struggle, endeavor, essay, try *rel* work, labor, toil, travail; contend, fight

striving *syn* ATTEMPT, struggle, endeavor, essay, try *rel* work, labor, toil, travail; contending; contest, conflict, combat, fight

stroll *syn* SAUNTER, amble

strong • showing power to resist or to endure *syn* stout, sturdy, stalwart, tough, tenacious *rel* vigorous, energetic, lusty; powerful, potent, forcible, forceful; robust, sound, healthy; vehement, intense, fierce, exquisite, violent *ant* weak

stronghold *syn* FORT, citadel, fortress, fastness

structure 1 *syn* BUILDING, edifice, pile 2 • something made up of interdependent parts in a definite pattern of organization *syn* anatomy, framework, skeleton *rel* integration, articulation, concatenation; organization, arrangement; system, organism, scheme, complex

struggle *vb, syn* ATTEMPT, strive, endeavor, essay, try *rel* contend, fight; compete, vie, rival, emulate; toil, labor, work, travail

struggle *n, syn* ATTEMPT, striving, endeavor, essay, try *rel* toil, labor, work, travail; contest, conflict, fight, affray, fray; contending

strut · to walk with an air of pomposity or affected dignity *syn* swagger, bristle, bridle *rel* expose, exhibit, flaunt, parade, show

stubborn *syn* OBSTINATE, dogged, pertinacious, mulish, stiff-necked, pigheaded, bullheaded *rel* rebellious, contumacious, insubordinate; intractable, recalcitrant, refractory; obdurate, adamant, inexorable, inflexible

stubby *syn* STOCKY, thickset, thick, chunky, squat, dumpy

studied *syn* DELIBERATE, considered, advised, premeditated, designed *rel* thoughtful, considerate, attentive; intentional, voluntary, willing, willful

study *n, syn* ATTENTION, concentration, application *rel* consideration, contemplation, weighing; reflection, thought, speculation; pondering, musing, meditation, rumination

study *vb, syn* CONSIDER, contemplate, weigh, excogitate *rel* scrutinize, examine, inspect; ponder, muse, meditate; think, reflect, reason, speculate

stuff *n, syn* MATTER, substance, material *rel* constituent, ingredient, component, element; item, detail, particular

stuff *vb, syn* PACK, crowd, cram, ram, tamp *rel* distend, expand, swell; squeeze, jam, press; gorge, glut, surfeit, sate, satiate

stuffy *syn* PRIM, priggish, prissy, prudish, puritanical, straitlaced *rel* stodgy, dull, humdrum; irksome, tedious; narrow, narrow-minded, illiberal, hidebound

stumble · to move so clumsily or unsteadily as to fall or nearly fall *syn* trip, blunder, lurch, flounder, lumber, galumph, lollop, bumble *rel* stagger, totter, reel; plunge, pitch, dive; falter, hesitate, waver, vacillate; chance, venture; encounter, meet, confront

stun *syn* DAZE, bemuse, stupefy, benumb, paralyze, petrify *rel* astound, amaze, flabbergast, surprise; bewilder, dumbfound, nonplus, confound

stupefy *syn* DAZE, stun, bemuse, benumb, paralyze, petrify *rel* confuse, muddle, addle, fuddle, befuddle, faze, rattle; dumbfound, nonplus, bewilder, mystify, puzzle

stupendous *syn* MONSTROUS, tremendous, prodigious, monumental *rel* enormous, immense, huge, vast, colossal, gigantic; astounding, amazing, astonishing

stupid · lacking in power to absorb ideas or impressions *syn* slow, dull, dense, crass, dumb *rel* foolish, silly, simple, fatuous, asinine; sluggish, comatose, lethargic; inert, idle, supine, inactive; phlegmatic, stolid, impassive *ant* intelligent

stupor *syn* LETHARGY, torpor, torpidity, lassitude, languor *rel* phlegm, impassivity, stolidity; inertness, inertia, passivity, supineness, inactivity, idleness; insensibility, anesthesia

sturdy *syn* STRONG, stout, stalwart, tough, tenacious *rel* sound, robust, healthy; vigorous, energetic, lusty; dogged, pertinacious, obstinate *ant* decrepit

stutter *syn* STAMMER

stygian *syn* INFERNAL, chthonic, chthonian, Hadean, Tartarean, hellish

style **1** *syn* LANGUAGE, diction, phraseology, phrasing, vocabulary *rel* taste, zest, gusto, relish; form, convention, usage, convenance **2** *syn* FASHION, mode, vogue, fad, rage, craze, dernier cri, cry *rel* modishness, smartness, chicness, stylishness, fashionableness **3** *syn* NAME, designation, title, denomination, appellation

stylish · conforming to current fashion *syn* fashionable, modish, smart, chic, dashing *rel* new, novel, new-fashioned, newfangled, modernistic; showy, ostentatious, pretentious

suave · pleasantly tactful and well-mannered *syn* urbane, diplomatic, bland, smooth, politic *rel* gracious, cordial, affable, genial, sociable; courteous, courtly, polite, civil; fulsome, unctuous, slick *ant* bluff

subdue *syn* CONQUER, subjugate, reduce, overcome, surmount, overthrow, rout, vanquish, defeat, beat, lick *rel* control, manage, direct; discipline, punish, correct; foil, thwart, circumvent, frustrate; suppress, repress *ant* awaken, waken

subdued *syn* TAME, submissive *rel* meek, humble, modest, lowly; timid, timorous; docile, tractable, amenable, obedient *ant* intense; barbaric (*of taste*); bizarre (*of effects*); effervescent (*of character and temperament*)

subject *n* **1** *syn* CITIZEN, national *ant* sovereign **2** · the basic idea or the principal object of attention in a discourse or artistic composition *syn* matter, subject matter, argument, topic, text, theme, motive, motif, leitmotiv

subject *adj* **1** *syn* SUBORDINATE, dependent, secondary, tributary, collateral *rel* subservient, servile, slavish; conditional, contingent, dependent, relative *ant* sovereign, dominant **2** *syn* LIABLE, open, exposed, prone, susceptible, sensitive *rel* apt, likely *ant* exempt

subject matter *syn* SUBJECT, matter, argument, topic, text, theme, motive, motif, leitmotiv

subjoin *syn* ADD, append, annex, superadd *rel* attach, affix, fasten; unite, conjoin, combine

subjugate *syn* CONQUER, subdue, reduce, overcome, surmount, overthrow, rout, vanquish, defeat, beat, lick *rel* circumvent, outwit, foil, thwart, frustrate; compel, coerce, force

sublime *syn* SPLENDID, glorious, superb, resplendent, gorgeous *rel* transcendent, transcendental, ideal, abstract; divine, spiritual, sacred, holy; majestic, august, noble, stately, grand

sublunary *syn* EARTHLY, terrestrial, earthy, mundane, worldly

submerge *syn* DIP, immerse, duck, souse, dunk *rel* soak, saturate, drench, impregnate

submission *syn* SURRENDER, capitulation *rel* yielding, submitting, succumbing, bowing, caving in; compliance, acquiescence, resignation *ant* resistance

submissive *syn* TAME, subdued *rel* docile, tractable, amenable, biddable, obedient; meek, lowly, humble; subservient, servile, slavish, menial *ant* rebellious

submit *syn* YIELD, capitulate, succumb, relent, defer, bow, cave *rel* surrender, abandon, resign, relinquish; abide, endure, suffer, bear *ant* resist, withstand

subordinate *adj* · placed in or occupying a lower class, rank, or status *syn* secondary, dependent, subject, tributary, collateral *rel* auxiliary, subsidiary, subservient, contributory, adjuvant; accidental, incidental, fortuitous *ant* chief, leading; dominant

subordinate *n, syn* INFERIOR, underling *ant* chief

subscribe *syn* ASSENT, agree, acquiesce, consent, accede *rel* concur, coincide; approve, endorse, sanction; promise, pledge, covenant *ant* boggle

subservient **1** *syn* AUXILIARY, subsidiary, contributory, ancillary, adjuvant, accessory *rel* subordinate, secondary, dependent, subject **2** · showing or characterized by extreme compliance or abject obedience *syn* servile, slavish, menial, obsequious *rel* fawning, cringing, truckling, cowering; compliant, acquiescent, resigned; mean, ignoble, abject *ant* domineering; overbearing

subside **1** *syn* FALL, drop, sink, slump *rel* sag, flag, droop, wilt; shrink, contract, constrict **2** *syn* ABATE, wane, ebb *rel* dwindle, diminish, decrease

subsidiary *syn* AUXILIARY, contributory, subservient, ancillary, adjuvant, accessory

subsidy *syn* APPROPRIATION, grant, subvention

subsist *syn* BE, exist, live

subsistence *syn* LIVING, livelihood, sustenance, maintenance, support, keep, bread, bread and butter

subspecies *syn* VARIETY, race, breed, cultivar, strain, clone, stock

substance **1** · the inner significance or central meaning of something written or said *syn* purport, gist, burden, core, pith *rel* center, nucleus, heart, focus; principle, fundamental; foundation, base, groundwork **2** *syn* MATTER, material, stuff

substantial *syn* MASSIVE, massy, bulky, monumental *ant* airy, ethereal

substantiate *syn* CONFIRM, verify, corroborate, authenticate, validate *rel* prove, demonstrate, try, test

substitute **1** *syn* RESOURCE, surrogate, resort, expedient, shift, makeshift, stopgap *rel* device, contrivance, contraption; duplicate, copy, reproduction **2** · a person who takes the place of or acts instead of another *syn* supply, locum tenens, alternate, understudy, double, stand-in, pinch hitter

subsume *syn* INCLUDE, comprehend, embrace, involve, imply

subtle *syn* LOGICAL, analytical *rel* penetrating, piercing, probing; deep, profound; abstruse, recondite *ant* dense; blunt

subtract *syn* DEDUCT *ant* add

subvention *syn* APPROPRIATION, grant, subsidy

subvert *syn* OVERTURN, overthrow, capsize, upset *rel* ruin, wreck; destroy, demolish; corrupt, pervert, deprave, debase *ant* uphold, sustain

succeed **1** *syn* FOLLOW, ensue, supervene *rel* displace, supplant, replace, supersede *ant* precede **2** · to attain or be attaining a desired end *syn* prosper, thrive, flourish *rel* attain, achieve, gain, compass, reach; effect, fulfill, perform *ant* fail; attempt

succession · a number of things that follow each other in some order *syn* progression, series, sequence, chain, train, string *rel* consecutiveness, successiveness; articulation, concatenation, integration

successive *syn* CONSECUTIVE, sequent, sequential, serial *rel* continuous, continual, constant, incessant; rotating, alternating

succinct *syn* CONCISE, terse, laconic, summary, pithy, compendious *rel* brief, short; compressed, condensed, contracted; compact, close; curt, brusque, blunt, bluff *ant* discursive

succumb *syn* YIELD, submit, capitulate, relent, defer, bow, cave *rel* surrender, abandon, resign, relinquish

sudden *syn* PRECIPITATE, hasty, headlong, abrupt, impetuous *rel* quickened, hurried, speeded, accelerated; fast, rapid, swift, fleet, expeditious

suds *syn* FOAM, froth, spume, lather, scum, yeast

sue *syn* PRAY, plead, petition *rel*

entreat, beseech, beg, importune, implore, supplicate; solicit, request, ask; demand, claim, exact, require

suffer 1 *syn* BEAR, endure, abide, tolerate, stand, brook *rel* accept, receive, admit; yield, submit, bow 2 *syn* EXPERIENCE, undergo, sustain *rel* submit, succumb, defer, yield 3 *syn* LET, permit, allow, leave

sufferance *syn* PERMISSION, leave *rel* toleration, endurance; acquiescence, resignation, compliance

suffering *syn* DISTRESS, misery, agony, dolor, passion *rel* affliction, tribulation, trial, visitation; adversity, misfortune; sorrow, grief, anguish, woe, heartache, heartbreak

sufficient • being what is necessary or desirable *syn* enough, adequate, competent

suffocate • to stop the respiration of *syn* asphyxiate, stifle, smother, choke, strangle, throttle

suffrage • the right, privilege, or power of expressing one's choice or wish (as in an election or in the determination of policy) *syn* franchise, vote, ballot

suffuse *syn* INFUSE, imbue, ingrain, inoculate, leaven *rel* introduce, interpose, interject; impregnate, penetrate, pervade, permeate

suggest 1 • to convey an idea indirectly *syn* imply, hint, intimate, insinuate *rel* present, offer; infuse, imbue, inoculate, leaven; advance, further; allude, refer, advert; connote, denote *ant* express 2 • to call to mind by thought, through close connection, or by association *syn* adumbrate, shadow *ant* manifest

suggestion *syn* TOUCH, suspicion, soupçon, tincture, tinge, shade, smack, spice, dash, vein, strain, streak

suit 1 *syn* PRAYER, plea, petition, appeal *rel* entreaty, importuning, importunity, imploring, supplication; asking, requesting, request, soliciting, solicitation 2 • a legal proceeding instituted for the sake of demanding justice or enforcing a right *syn* lawsuit, action, cause, case

suitable *syn* FIT, meet, proper, appropriate, fitting, apt, happy, felicitous *rel* decorous, decent, seemly, nice; advisable, expedient, politic; due, rightful, condign *ant* unsuitable; unbecoming

sulky *syn* SULLEN, surly, morose, glum, crabbed, saturnine, dour, gloomy *rel* cranky, cross, testy, touchy, irascible; peevish, petulant, fretful, querulous, irritable

sullen • showing a forbidding or disagreeable mood *syn* glum, morose, surly, sulky, crabbed, saturnine, dour, gloomy *rel* lowering, glowering, frowning, scowling; spiteful, malevolent, malicious, malign; cynical, pessimistic

sully *syn* SOIL, dirty, tarnish, foul, befoul, smirch, besmirch, grime, begrime *rel* spot, spatter, sprinkle; defile, pollute, taint, contaminate

sum *n* • the result of simple addition of all the numbers or particulars in a given group *syn* amount, number, aggregate, total, whole, quantity

sum *vb*, *syn* ADD, total, tot, cast, figure, foot *rel* compute, calculate, estimate, reckon; count, enumerate, number

summary *syn* CONCISE, pithy, compendious, terse, succinct, laconic *rel* brief, short; quick, prompt, ready, apt; compacted, compact, concentrated *ant* circumstantial

summative *syn* CUMULATIVE, accumulative, additive

summit • the highest point attained or attainable *syn* peak, pinnacle, climax, apex, acme, culmination, meridian, zenith, apogee

summon, summons • to demand or

request the presence or service of *syn* call, cite, convoke, convene, muster *rel* command, order, bid, enjoin; evoke, elicit, educe

sumptuous *syn* LUXURIOUS, opulent *rel* magnificent, stately, majestic, grand; splendid, resplendent, gorgeous, superb; showy, ostentatious, pretentious; lavish, prodigal, profuse

sunder *syn* SEPARATE, sever, divide, part, divorce *rel* rend, rive, cleave, split, tear *ant* link

sundry *syn* MANY, several, various, divers, numerous, multifarious *rel* different, disparate, diverse, divergent; distinct, separate; individual, distinctive, peculiar

superadd *syn* ADD, annex, append, subjoin *rel* fasten, attach, affix

superannuated *syn* AGED, old, elderly

superb *syn* SPLENDID, resplendent, glorious, gorgeous, sublime *rel* superlative, transcendent, surpassing, supreme; sumptuous, luxurious, opulent; imposing, stately, majestic, magnificent, grand

supercilious *syn* PROUD, disdainful, overbearing, arrogant, haughty, lordly, insolent *rel* vain, vainglorious; contemptuous, scornful

supererogatory · given or done without compulsion, need, or warrant *syn* gratuitous, uncalled-for, wanton *rel* free, independent, autonomous; excessive, extreme, exorbitant; superfluous, supernumerary, extra, spare

superficial · lacking in depth or solidity *syn* shallow, cursory, uncritical *ant* radical

superfluity *syn* EXCESS, surplus, surplusage, overplus *rel* overflowing, overflow, teeming, swarming; exuberance, profusion, lavishness, prodigality

superfluous · exceeding what is needed or necessary *syn* surplus, supernumerary, extra, spare *rel* supererogatory, gratuitous, uncalled-for, wanton; profuse, lavish, prodigal, exuberant; excessive, inordinate, extravagant, extreme

superhuman *syn* SUPERNATURAL, preternatural, miraculous, supranatural *rel* potent, puissant, powerful, forcible, forceful; Herculean, cyclopean, titanic, gigantic

superimpose *syn* OVERLAY, superpose, appliqué

superior *syn* BETTER, preferable *ant* inferior

superlative *syn* SUPREME, transcendent, surpassing, peerless, incomparable, preeminent *rel* consummate, finished, accomplished; splendid, glorious, sublime, superb

supernatural · of or relating to an order of existence beyond the visible observable universe *syn* supranatural, preternatural, miraculous, superhuman *rel* divine, spiritual, sacred, holy, blessed; infinite, eternal, boundless, illimitable

supernumerary *syn* SUPERFLUOUS, surplus, extra, spare

superpose *syn* OVERLAY, superimpose, appliqué

supersede *syn* REPLACE, displace, supplant *rel* repudiate, spurn, reject; abandon, desert, forsake; stay, suspend, intermit, defer

supervene *syn* FOLLOW, succeed, ensue *rel* add, append, annex, subjoin, superadd; combine, unite, conjoin, cooperate

supervision *syn* OVERSIGHT, surveillance *rel* controlling, control, management, direction, conducting, conduct; leading, guiding

supine **1** *syn* PRONE, prostrate, recumbent, couchant, dormant **2** *syn* INACTIVE, inert, passive, idle *rel* slothful, lazy, indolent, faineant; lethargic, sluggish, torpid; apathetic, impassive, phlegmatic

supplant *syn* REPLACE, displace,

supersede *rel* eject, oust, dismiss, expel; uproot, eradicate, extirpate, exterminate

supple 1 *syn* ELASTIC, flexible, resilient, springy *rel* pliable, pliant, plastic; soft, gentle, mild *ant* stiff 2 · able to bend or twist with ease and grace *syn* limber, lithe, lithesome, lissome *rel* graceful, elegant; easy, smooth, effortless, facile

supplement *n* 1 *syn* COMPLEMENT 2 *syn* APPENDIX, addendum, addenda

supplement *vb, syn* COMPLEMENT *rel* improve, better; heighten, enhance, aggravate, intensify

supplicate *syn* BEG, implore, beseech, entreat, importune, adjure *rel* pray, sue, plead, appeal, petition; ask, request, solicit

supply *vb, syn* PROVIDE, furnish *rel* replace, supplant, supersede; compensate, satisfy, recompense; fulfill, satisfy, answer; sustain, support, prop, bolster, buttress

supply *n, syn* SUBSTITUTE, locum tenens, alternate, understudy, pinch hitter, double, stand-in

supply *adj, syn* TEMPORARY, provisional, ad interim, acting

support *vb* 1 · to hold up in position by serving as a foundation or base for *syn* sustain, prop, bolster, buttress, brace *rel* carry, bear, convey; endure, suffer, stand; evidence, evince, show; indicate, attest, argue, betoken; uphold, advocate, back, champion 2 · to favor actively one that meets opposition *syn* uphold, advocate, back, champion *rel* approve, endorse, sanction; espouse, embrace, adopt; defend, protect, shield

support *n, syn* LIVING, maintenance, sustenance, livelihood, subsistence, keep, bread *ant* adversary, antagonist

supposed · accepted or advanced as true or real on the basis of less than conclusive evidence *syn* supposititious, suppositious, reputed, putative, purported, conjectural, hypothetical *rel* assumed, presumed, presupposed, postulated; tentative, provisional; doubtful, dubious, questionable; theoretical, speculative, academic; alleged *ant* certain

supposititious, suppositious *syn* SUPPOSED, reputed, putative, purported, conjectural, hypothetical *rel* pretended, simulated, feigned, shammed, counterfeited, counterfeit; questionable, dubious, doubtful; factitious, artificial

suppress 1 *syn* CRUSH, quell, extinguish, quench, quash *rel* subdue, overcome, surmount, conquer; abolish, annihilate; destroy; ruin, wreck 2 · to hold back more or less forcefully someone or something that seeks an outlet *syn* repress *rel* arrest, check, interrupt; extinguish, abolish, annihilate; forbid, prohibit, ban; subdue, overcome, surmount, conquer

supranatural *syn* SUPERNATURAL, miraculous, preternatural, superhuman

supremacy · the position of being first (as in rank, power, or influence) *syn* ascendancy *rel* preeminence, transcendence, superlativeness, peerlessness, incomparability; power, authority, dominion, control, sway

supreme · developed to the utmost and not exceeded by any other in degree, quality, or intensity *syn* superlative, transcendent, surpassing, preeminent, peerless, incomparable *rel* chief, foremost, leading, capital; predominant, dominant, paramount, sovereign

sure 1 *syn* CONFIDENT, assured, sanguine, presumptuous *rel* relying, trusting, depending, counting, banking; inerrant, unerring, infallible; safe, secure 2 · having no doubt or uncertainty *syn* certain, positive, cocksure *rel* decisive, decided; self-assured, assured, self-confident; dogmatic, doctrinaire, oracular, dictatorial *ant* unsure

surety 1 *syn* GUARANTEE, security, bond, guaranty, bail *rel* pledge, earnest, token, hostage, pawn 2 *syn* SPONSOR, guarantor, backer, patron, angel

surfeit *syn* SATIATE, sate, cloy, pall, glut, gorge *ant* whet

surge *syn* RISE, arise, ascend, mount, soar, tower, rocket, levitate

surly *syn* SULLEN, morose, glum, crabbed, sulky, saturnine, dour, gloomy *rel* rude, ungracious, ill-mannered, discourteous; boorish, churlish; snappish, waspish, fractious, irritable *ant* amiable

surmise *vb, syn* CONJECTURE, guess *rel* infer, gather, judge, deduce, conclude; think, conceive, fancy, imagine; consider, regard, deem

surmise *n, syn* CONJECTURE, guess *rel* inference, deduction, conclusion; hypothesis, theory

surmount *syn* CONQUER, overcome, overthrow, rout, vanquish, defeat, subdue, subjugate, reduce, beat, lick *rel* surpass, transcend, outdo, outstrip, excel, exceed

surpass *syn* EXCEED, transcend, excel, outdo, outstrip *rel* surmount, overcome, beat, conquer

surpassing *syn* SUPREME, transcendent, superlative, preeminent, peerless, incomparable *rel* excelling, outdoing, outstripping; consummate, finished, accomplished

surplus *n, syn* EXCESS, superfluity, surplusage, overplus *rel* remainder, residue, residuum *ant* deficiency

surplus *adj, syn* SUPERFLUOUS, supernumerary, extra, spare

surplusage *syn* EXCESS, surplus, superfluity, overplus *rel, ant* see SURPLUS *n*

surprise 1 • to attack unawares *syn* waylay, ambush *rel* catch, capture; take, seize, grasp, grab 2 • to impress forcibly through unexpectedness *syn* astonish, astound, amaze, flabbergast *rel* startle, alarm, scare, frighten; bewilder, nonplus, confound, dumbfound, puzzle, embarrass, disconcert, discomfit, rattle, faze

surrender *vb, syn* RELINQUISH, abandon, resign, yield, leave, cede, waive *rel* abdicate, renounce; forgo, forbear, sacrifice, eschew; submit, capitulate, succumb; commit, consign, confide, entrust

surrender *n* • the yielding of one's person, forces, or possessions to another *syn* submission, capitulation

surreptitious *syn* SECRET, underhand, underhanded, covert, stealthy, furtive, clandestine *rel* sneaking, slinking, skulking, lurking; hidden, concealed, screened

surrogate *syn* RESOURCE, substitute, shift, makeshift, expedient, resort, stopgap

surround • to close in or as if in a ring about something *syn* environ, encircle, circle, encompass, compass, hem, gird, girdle, ring *rel* enclose, envelop, wall, fence, cage, coop; circumscribe, confine, limit

surveillance *syn* OVERSIGHT, supervision *rel* inspection, scrutiny, examination

survey *vb, syn* SEE, view, espy, descry, behold, observe, notice, remark, note, perceive, discern *rel* scrutinize, scan, inspect, examine; look, watch

survey *n, syn* COMPENDIUM, syllabus, digest, pandect, sketch, précis, aperçu

survive *syn* OUTLIVE, outlast *rel*

endure, continue, persist, last; withstand, resist, fight

susceptible 1 *syn* LIABLE, sensitive, subject, exposed, prone, open *rel* inclined, disposed, predisposed; alive, awake, sensible, conscious, aware *ant* immune 2 *syn* SENTIENT, sensitive, impressible, impressionable, responsive *rel* affected, impressed, touched, influenced, swayed; stirred, aroused, roused

suspect *syn* DISTRUST, mistrust, doubt, misdoubt

suspend 1 *syn* EXCLUDE, disbar, shut out, eliminate, debar, blackball, rule out *rel* eject, dismiss, oust; banish, exile, ostracize 2 *syn* DEFER, stay, intermit, postpone *rel* arrest, check, interrupt; stop, cease, discontinue; delay, detain, retard 3 *syn* HANG, sling, dangle *rel* poise, balance, steady, stabilize

suspended • hanging from or remaining in place as if hanging from a support *syn* pendent, pendulous

suspicion 1 *syn* UNCERTAINTY, mistrust, doubt, dubiety, dubiosity, skepticism *rel* misgiving, foreboding, presentiment, apprehension; distrust, mistrust 2 *syn* TOUCH, suggestion, soupçon, tincture, tinge, shade, smack, spice, dash, vein, strain, streak

sustain 1 *syn* SUPPORT, prop, bolster, buttress, brace *rel* continue, persist, endure, abide; uphold, back; prove, demonstrate *ant* subvert 2 *syn* EXPERIENCE, undergo, suffer *rel* receive, accept, take; endure, bear, stand, brook; meet, encounter, face, confront

sustenance 1 *syn* FOOD, nourishment, nutriment, aliment, pabulum, pap 2 *syn* LIVING, maintenance, support, livelihood, subsistence, keep, bread

suture *syn* JOINT, articulation

swag *syn* SPOIL, plunder, loot, booty, prize

swagger *syn* STRUT, bristle, bridle *rel* flourish, brandish, shake, swing, wave; brag, boast, vaunt, crow, gasconade

swallow *syn* EAT, ingest, devour, consume *rel* receive, accept, take; believe, credit; absorb, imbibe, assimilate

swarm *syn* TEEM, abound, overflow

swat *syn* STRIKE, hit, smite, punch, slug, slog, clout, slap, cuff, box *rel* beat, pound, pummel, baste, belabor

sway *vb* 1 *syn* SWING, oscillate, fluctuate, pendulate, vibrate, waver, undulate *rel* shake, rock, agitate, convulse 2 *syn* AFFECT, influence, impress, strike, touch *rel* control, direct, manage, conduct; rule, govern; bias, incline, dispose, predispose

sway *n, syn* POWER, dominion, control, command, authority *rel* supremacy, ascendancy; range, reach, scope, sweep; spread, stretch, amplitude, expanse

swearing *syn* BLASPHEMY, profanity, cursing

sweep *syn* RANGE, gamut, reach, radius, compass, scope, orbit, horizon, ken, purview *rel* expanse, amplitude, spread

sweeping *syn* INDISCRIMINATE, wholesale *rel* promiscuous, heterogeneous, motley, miscellaneous

sweet • distinctly pleasing or charming *syn* engaging, winning, winsome, dulcet *rel* pleasant, pleasing, agreeable, gratifying, grateful, welcome; delicious, delectable, luscious, delightful; lovely, fair, beautiful; ineffable, unutterable *ant* sour; bitter

swell *syn* EXPAND, amplify, distend, inflate, dilate *rel* extend, elongate, lengthen; intensify, heighten, enhance; increase, augment, enlarge *ant* shrink

swerve • to turn aside from a straight course *syn* veer, deviate, depart, digress, diverge *rel* turn, divert, deflect, sheer, avert; curve, bend

swift *syn* FAST, rapid, fleet, quick, speedy, hasty, expeditious *rel* easy, effortless, smooth, facile; headlong, precipitate, sudden

swimming *syn* GIDDY, dizzy, vertiginous, dazzled *rel* reeling, whirling, tottering; swaying, wavering, fluctuating

swindle *syn* CHEAT, overreach, cozen, defraud *rel* dupe, gull, bamboozle, hoodwink, trick; steal, pilfer, purloin, filch

swing 1 • to wield or cause to move to and fro or up and down *syn* wave, flourish, brandish, shake, thrash *rel* parade, flaunt, display, exhibit, show 2 • to move from one direction to its opposite *syn* sway, oscillate, vibrate, fluctuate, pendulate, waver, undulate *rel* turn, spin, whirl, wheel, revolve, rotate, gyrate; shake, tremble, quiver, quaver, quake 3 *syn* HANDLE, wield, manipulate, ply *rel* control, manage, direct, conduct

swipe *syn* STEAL, pilfer, filch, purloin, lift, pinch, snitch, cop

swirl *syn* TURN, circle, spin, twirl, whirl, wheel, eddy, revolve, rotate, gyrate, pirouette

sybaritic *syn* SENSUOUS, sensual, luxurious, voluptuous, epicurean

sycophant *syn* PARASITE, favorite, toady, lickspittle, bootlicker, hanger-on, leech, sponge, sponger *rel* blandisher, cajoler, wheedler; fawner, truckler

syllabus *syn* COMPENDIUM, digest, pandect, survey, sketch, précis, aperçu *rel* conspectus, synopsis, epitome, abridgment, brief, abstract

symbol 1 • something concrete that represents or suggests another thing that cannot in itself be pictured *syn* emblem, attribute, type *rel* sign, mark, token, badge; device, motif, design, figure, pattern 2 *syn* CHARACTER, sign, mark *rel* device, contrivance; diagram, delineation, outline, sketch

symbolism *syn* ALLEGORY

symmetry • beauty of form or arrangement arising from balanced proportions *syn* proportion, balance, harmony

sympathetic 1 *syn* CONSONANT, congenial, congruous, compatible, consistent *rel* agreeing, harmonizing, harmonious, accordant, correspondent 2 *syn* TENDER, compassionate, warm, warmhearted, responsive *rel* kindly, kind, benign, benignant; understanding, appreciating, comprehending *ant* unsympathetic

sympathy 1 *syn* ATTRACTION, affinity *rel* reciprocality, correspondence; harmony, consonance, accord, concord *ant* antipathy 2 • the act or capacity for sharing in the interests and esp. in the painful experiences of another *syn* pity, compassion, commiseration, condolence, ruth, empathy *rel* tenderness, warmheartedness, warmth, responsiveness; kindliness, kindness, benignness, benignancy

symptom *syn* SIGN, mark, token, badge

synchronous *syn* CONTEMPORARY, coeval, coetaneous, contemporaneous, simultaneous, coincident, concomitant, concurrent

syndicate *syn* MONOPOLY, corner, pool, trust, cartel

syndrome *syn* DISEASE, disorder, condition, affection, ailment, malady, complaint, distemper

synopsis *syn* ABRIDGMENT, brief, conspectus, epitome, abstract

synthetic *syn* ARTIFICIAL, ersatz, factitious

system 1 • an organized integrated

whole made up of diverse but interrelated and interdependent parts *syn* scheme, network, complex, organism *ant* chaos **2** *syn* METHOD, mode, manner, way, fashion *rel* plan, project, scheme, design; procedure, process, proceeding

systematic *syn* ORDERLY, methodical, regular *rel* systematized, organized, ordered, arranged; logical, analytical

systematize *syn* ORDER, organize, methodize, arrange, marshal *rel* adjust, regulate, fix

T

table *syn* LIST, catalog, schedule, register, roll, roster, inventory

taciturn *syn* SILENT, uncommunicative, reserved, reticent, secretive, close, close-lipped, close-mouthed, tight-lipped *rel* dumb, mute, inarticulate; restrained, inhibited, curbed, checked *ant* garrulous; clamorous (*esp. of crowds*); convivial

tackle *syn* EQUIPMENT, apparatus, machinery, paraphernalia, outfit, gear, matériel

tact · skill and grace in dealing with others *syn* address, poise, savoir faire *rel* diplomacy, policy, suavity, urbanity; courtesy, amenity, gallantry *ant* awkwardness

tactical *syn* STRATEGIC, logistic

tactics *syn* STRATEGY, logistics

tag *n, syn* MARK, brand, stamp, label, ticket

tag *vb* **1** *syn* MARK, brand, stamp, label, ticket **2** *syn* FOLLOW, pursue, chase, trail, tail

tail *syn* FOLLOW, pursue, chase, trail, tag

taint *syn* CONTAMINATE, pollute, defile *rel* debase, deprave, corrupt, vitiate; spoil, decompose, rot, putrefy, decay; imbue, inoculate, infuse

take **1** · to get hold of by or as if by catching up with the hand *syn* seize, grasp, clutch, snatch, grab *rel* have, hold, own, possess; catch, capture; confiscate, appropriate, preempt, arrogate **2** *syn* RECEIVE, accept, admit *rel* acquiesce, accede, assent, consent, subscribe **3** *syn* BRING, fetch *rel* carry, convey, bear

tale *syn* STORY, narrative, anecdote, yarn *rel* fiction, fable; myth, legend, saga

talent *syn* GIFT, genius, faculty, aptitude, knack, bent, turn *rel* capacity, ability, capability; art, skill, craft, cunning; endowment

talisman *syn* FETISH, charm, amulet

talk *vb, syn* SPEAK, converse *rel* discuss, dispute, argue; discourse, expatiate, dilate, descant; chat, chatter, prate

talk *n, syn* SPEECH, address, oration, harangue, lecture, sermon, homily

talkative · given to talk or talking *syn* loquacious, garrulous, voluble, glib *rel* vocal, fluent, articulate, eloquent; vociferous, clamorous *ant* silent

talkativeness · the inclination to talk or to talking *syn* loquacity, loquaciousness, garrulity, garrulousness, volubility, glibness *rel* fluency, articulateness, eloquence *ant* silence

tall *syn* HIGH, lofty *ant* short

tally *syn* AGREE, square, accord, harmonize, correspond, conform, jibe *rel* match, equal; coincide, concur

tame *adj* · made docile and tractable *syn* subdued, submissive *rel* tractable, amenable, docile, biddable, obedient; timid, timorous; pliant, pliable *ant* fierce

tamp *syn* PACK, crowd, cram, stuff, ram *rel* press, squeeze, jam; compact, consolidate, concentrate

tamper *syn* MEDDLE, interfere, intermeddle *rel* interpose, intervene; trouble, discommode, inconvenience

tang *syn* TASTE, flavor, savor, relish, smack *rel* pungency, piquancy, raciness

tangent *syn* ADJACENT, abutting, adjoining, contiguous, conterminous, juxtaposed

tangible *syn* PERCEPTIBLE, sensible, palpable, appreciable, ponderable *rel* material, physical, corporeal, objective; actual, real, true; obvious, evident, manifest *ant* intangible

tantalize *syn* WORRY, tease, harass, harry, annoy, plague, pester *rel* vex, irk, bother; torment, torture, try, afflict; bait, badger *ant* satisfy

tantamount *syn* SAME, selfsame, very, identical, identic, equivalent, equal *rel* like, alike, uniform, similar

tap *vb* · to strike or hit audibly *syn* knock, rap, thump, thud *rel* strike, smite; beat

tap *n* · a light usu. audible blow or the sound made by such a blow *syn* rap, knock, thump, thud

tar *syn* MARINER, sailor, seaman, gob, bluejacket

tardy · not arriving, occurring, or done at the set, due, or expected time *syn* late, behindhand, overdue *rel* dilatory, laggard, slow; delayed, detained, retarded *ant* prompt

tarnish *syn* SOIL, dirty, sully, foul, befoul, smirch, besmirch, grime, begrime *rel* darken, dim, bedim, obscure; defile, pollute, taint, contaminate *ant* polish

tarry *syn* STAY, remain, wait, abide, linger *rel* delay, procrastinate, lag, loiter, dawdle

tart *syn* SOUR, acid, acidulous, dry *rel* piquant, pungent; sharp, keen; curt, brusque, blunt, bluff; irritable, snappish, waspish

Tartarean *syn* INFERNAL, chthonian, chthonic, Hadean, stygian, hellish

task · a piece of work to be done *syn* duty, assignment, job, stint, chore *rel* function, office, province; work, labor, toil; employment, occupation, business

taste **1** · the property of a substance which makes it perceptible to the gustatory sense *syn* flavor, savor, tang, relish, smack **2** · a liking for or enjoyment of something because of the pleasure it gives *syn* palate, relish, gusto, zest *rel* predilection, prepossession, partiality; appreciation, understanding, comprehension; inclination, disposition, predisposition; discernment, discrimination, penetration, insight, acumen *ant* antipathy

tasty *syn* PALATABLE, savory, sapid, appetizing, toothsome, flavorsome, relishing *ant* bland

tat *syn* WEAVE, knit, crochet, braid, plait

tattle *syn* GOSSIP, blab *rel* divulge, disclose, betray, reveal

taunt *syn* RIDICULE, mock, deride, twit, rally *rel* scoff, jeer, gibe, flout; affront, insult, offend, outrage; scorn, disdain, scout, despise; chaff, banter

taut *syn* TIGHT, tense

tautology *syn* VERBIAGE, redundancy, pleonasm, circumlocution, periphrasis

tawdry *syn* GAUDY, garish, flashy, meretricious *rel* showy, pretentious; vulgar, gross, coarse; flamboyant, ornate, florid

tax *syn* BURDEN, encumber, cumber, weigh, weight, load, lade, charge, saddle

teach · to cause to acquire knowledge or skill *syn* instruct, educate, train, discipline, school *rel* impart, communicate; practice, drill, exercise; inculcate, instill, implant

tear · to separate forcibly *syn* rip, rend, split, cleave, rive *rel* slit, slash, cut; pull, drag; damage, injure, impair **2** *syn* RUSH, dash, shoot, charge *rel* speed, hasten, hurry; dart, fly, scud

tease *syn* WORRY, tantalize, pester, plague, harass, harry, annoy *rel* bait, badger, hector, chivy; importune, adjure, beg; fret, chafe, gall

tedious *syn* IRKSOME, tiresome, wearisome, boring *rel* burdensome, onerous, oppressive; fatiguing, exhausting, fagging, jading; slow, dilatory, deliberate *ant* exciting

tedium · a state of dissatisfaction and weariness *syn* boredom, ennui, doldrums *rel* irksomeness, tediousness, tiresomeness, wearisomeness; melancholy, dumps, blues, gloom, sadness

teem · to be present in large quantity *syn* abound, swarm, overflow *rel* bear, produce, yield, turn out; generate, engender, breed, propagate; multiply, augment, increase

teeny *syn* SMALL, tiny, little, diminutive, petite, wee, weeny, minute, microscopic, miniature

teeter *syn* SHAKE, tremble, quake, totter, quiver, shiver, shudder, quaver, wobble, shimmy, dither

tell 1 *syn* COUNT, enumerate, number **2** *syn* SAY, utter, state **3** *syn* REVEAL, divulge, discover, disclose, betray *rel* impart, communicate; relate, rehearse, recite, recount; inform, acquaint, apprise

telling *syn* VALID, compelling, convincing, cogent, sound *rel* forceful, forcible, powerful, potent; effective, effectual, efficacious; conclusive, decisive, determinative, definitive

temerity · conspicuous or flagrant boldness *syn* audacity, hardihood, effrontery, nerve, cheek, gall *rel* rashness, recklessness, foolhardiness, daring, venturesomeness; precipitateness, impetuosity, abruptness; impertinence, intrusiveness, officiousness *ant* caution

temper *vb, syn* MODERATE, qualify *rel* adjust, regulate, fix; mitigate, alleviate, lighten, assuage, allay, relieve; mollify, pacify, appease *ant* intensify

temper *n* **1** *syn* MOOD, humor, vein *rel* mettle, spirit, courage; emotion, feeling, affection, passion; attitude, position, stand **2** *syn* DISPOSITION, temperament, complexion, character, personality, individuality *rel* state, condition, posture, situation; quality, property, attribute

temperament *syn* DISPOSITION, temper, complexion, character, personality, individuality *rel* mind, soul; nature, kind, type

temperance · self-restraint in the gratification of appetites or passions *syn* sobriety, abstinence, abstemiousness, continence *rel* forgoing, forbearing, forbearance, sacrificing, sacrifice, eschewal; frugality, sparingness, thriftiness; restraining, curbing, checking

temperate 1 *syn* MODERATE *rel* mild, gentle, lenient, soft; steady, even, equable, constant; restrained, curbed, checked *ant* intemperate; inordinate **2** *syn* SOBER, continent, unimpassioned *rel* sparing, frugal, economical; abstaining, refraining, forbearing; dispassionate, just, equitable, fair

temporal *syn* PROFANE, secular, lay

rel material, objective, physical, corporeal *ant* spiritual

temporary • lasting, continuing, or serving for a limited time *syn* provisional, ad interim, acting, *ant* permanent

tempt *syn* LURE, entice, inveigle, decoy, seduce *rel* allure, attract; invite, solicit, court, woo; induce, persuade, prevail, get

tenacious *syn* STRONG, tough, stout, sturdy, stalwart *rel* dogged, pertinacious, obstinate, stubborn; resolute, staunch, steadfast, true, faithful; persevering, persisting

tenacity *syn* COURAGE, resolution, spirit, mettle *rel* pluck, grit, guts, sand, fortitude, backbone; hardihood, audacity, nerve, temerity

tend • to supervise or take charge of *syn* attend, mind, watch *rel* defend, protect, shield, guard, safeguard; nurse, nurture, foster, cherish, cultivate

tendency • movement in a particular direction *syn* trend, drift, tenor *rel* leaning, propensity, penchant, proclivity; inclination, disposition, predisposition; bent, turn, genius, aptitude, gift

tender *adj* • showing or expressing interest in another *syn* compassionate, sympathetic, warm, warmhearted, responsive *rel* gentle, lenient, mild, soft; humane, benevolent, charitable, altruistic; pitiful, piteous *ant* callous; severe

tender *vb, syn* OFFER, proffer, present, prefer *rel* propose, purpose, design; suggest, intimate

tender *n, syn* OVERTURE, approach, advance, bid

tenet *syn* DOCTRINE, dogma *rel* belief, conviction, persuasion, view, opinion; principle, fundamental, axiom

tenor *syn* TENDENCY, drift, trend *rel* movement, motion, move; procedure, proceeding; meaning, significance, import

tense **1** *syn* TIGHT, taut *rel* strained; nervous, unquiet, uneasy, jittery, impatient *ant* slack **2** *syn* STIFF, rigid, inflexible, stark, wooden *rel* tough, tenacious, stout, strong; firm, hard *ant* expansive

tension **1** *syn* STRESS, strain, pressure **2** *syn* BALANCE, equilibrium, equipoise, poise

tentative *syn* PROVISIONAL *rel* temporary, ad interim, acting; testing, trying, demonstrating, proving *ant* definitive

tenuous *syn* THIN, rare, slender, slim, slight *rel* ethereal, aerial, airy *ant* dense

tergiversation *syn* AMBIGUITY, equivocation, double entendre

term **1** *syn* LIMIT, end, confine, bound **2** *syn* WORD, vocable **3** *pl* **terms** *syn* CONDITION, stipulation, provision, proviso, reservation, strings *rel* restriction, limit; requisite, prerequisite, requirement

termagant *syn* VIRAGO, scold, shrew, vixen, amazon

terminal *syn* LAST, final, concluding, latest, eventual, ultimate *rel* closing, ending, terminating, concluding *ant* initial

terminate *syn* CLOSE, end, conclude, finish, complete *rel* abolish, extinguish, abate; stop, cease, discontinue

termination *syn* END, ending, terminus *rel* result, issue, outcome; concluding, conclusion, completion, closing, close *ant* inception; source

terminus *syn* END, termination, ending *ant* starting point

terrestrial *syn* EARTHLY, earthy, mundane, worldly, sublunary *ant* celestial

terrible *syn* FEARFUL, terrific, frightful, dreadful, awful, horrible, horrific, shocking, appalling *rel* frightening, alarming, startling; agitating, upsetting, disturbing, perturbing

terrific *syn* FEARFUL, terrible, frightful, dreadful, horrible, horrific, awful, shocking, appalling *rel* frightening, alarming, terrorizing; agitating, upsetting, disquieting

terrify *syn* FRIGHTEN, fright, scare, alarm, terrorize, startle *rel* agitate, upset, perturb, disquiet, discompose; dismay, appall, horrify, daunt; cow, intimidate, browbeat, bulldoze

territory *syn* FIELD, domain, province, sphere, bailiwick *rel* region, tract, area, zone, belt; limits, confines, bounds

terror *syn* FEAR, panic, consternation, dread, fright, alarm, dismay, horror, trepidation *rel* apprehensiveness, fearfulness; agitation, disquiet, perturbation, upsetting, upset; appalling, daunting, dismaying

terrorize *syn* FRIGHTEN, terrify, fright, alarm, scare, startle, affray, affright *rel* intimidate, cow, bulldoze, browbeat; coerce, compel, force; drive, impel, move; agitate, upset, discompose

terse *syn* CONCISE, succinct, laconic, summary, pithy, compendious *rel* brief, short; compact, close; expressive, sententious, meaningful; incisive, crisp, clear-cut

test *n, syn* PROOF, trial, demonstration *rel* examination, inspection, scrutiny; verification, substantiation, corroboration, confirmation

test *vb, syn* PROVE, try, demonstrate *rel* essay, attempt; examine, inspect, scrutinize; verify, substantiate, confirm

testimonial *syn* CREDENTIAL, recommendation, character, reference *rel* commendation; approval, endorsement

testy *syn* IRASCIBLE, choleric, splenetic, touchy, cranky, cross *rel* irritable, peevish, snappish, waspish; hasty, sudden, impetuous; captious, carping, caviling, faultfinding, critical

text *syn* SUBJECT, topic, argument, theme, matter, subject matter, motive, motif, leitmotiv

thankful *syn* GRATEFUL *rel* appreciating, appreciative, valuing, prizing, cherishing, treasuring; satisfied, content *ant* thankless

thaumaturgy *syn* MAGIC, sorcery, witchcraft, witchery, wizardry, alchemy

thaw *syn* LIQUEFY, melt, deliquesce, fuse *ant* freeze

theatrical *syn* DRAMATIC, dramaturgic, melodramatic, histrionic *rel* artificial, factitious; formal, conventional, ceremonial, ceremonious; affecting, pretending, assuming, simulating, feigning; showy, pretentious, ostentatious

theft • an unlawful taking of property esp. personal property stolen from its rightful owner *syn* larceny, robbery, burglary

theme **1** *syn* SUBJECT, text, topic, argument, matter, subject matter, motive, motif, leitmotiv **2** *syn* ESSAY, composition, paper, article

then *syn* THEREFORE, hence, consequently, accordingly, so

theorem *syn* PRINCIPLE, axiom, fundamental, law

theoretical • concerned principally with abstractions and theories *syn* speculative, academic *rel* conjectural, hypothetical, supposed; postulated, premised, presupposed

therefore • for this or that reason *syn* hence, consequently, then, accordingly, so

thesis *syn* DISCOURSE, dissertation, treatise, monograph, disquisition *rel* exposition; argumentation, disputation; article, paper, essay

thespian *syn* ACTOR, player, impersonator, trouper, performer, mummer, mime, mimic

thick 1 *syn* STOCKY, thick, thickset, chunky, stubby, squat, dumpy *rel* broad, wide, deep *ant* thin 2 *syn* CLOSE, compact, dense *rel* condensed, compressed, contracted; concentrated, compacted 3 *syn* FAMILIAR, close, confidential, chummy, intimate

thickset *syn* STOCKY, thick, chunky, stubby, squat, dumpy *rel* bulky, massive, massy; fleshy, stout, portly, plump

thief · one that steals esp. stealthily or secretly *syn* robber, burglar, larcener, larcenist

thin *adj* · not thick, broad, abundant, or dense *syn* slender, slim, slight, tenuous, rare *rel* lean, spare, lank, lanky, gaunt; meager, exiguous, scanty; cadaverous, pinched, wasted, haggard; attenuated, extenuated, diluted *ant* thick

thin *vb* · to make thin or thinner or less dense *syn* attenuate, extenuate, dilute, rarefy *rel* reduce, lessen, diminish, decrease; liquefy, melt *ant* thicken

thing 1 *syn* AFFAIR, matter, concern, business 2 · whatever is apprehended as having actual, distinct, and demonstrable existence *syn* object, article *rel* item, detail, particular

think 1 · to form an idea of *syn* conceive, imagine, fancy, realize, envisage, envision *rel* consider, weigh, study, contemplate; understand, comprehend, appreciate; surmise, conjecture, guess 2 · to use one's powers of conception, judgment, or inference *syn* cogitate, reflect, reason, speculate, deliberate *rel* ponder, meditate, muse, ruminate; infer, deduce, conclude, judge

thirst *syn* LONG, hunger, pine, yearn, hanker *rel* covet, crave, desire, wish, want

though · in spite of the fact that *syn* although, albeit

thought *syn* IDEA, concept, conception, notion, impression *rel* opinion, view, sentiment, belief, conviction, persuasion

thoughtful 1 · characterized by or exhibiting the power to think *syn* reflective, speculative, contemplative, meditative, pensive *rel* serious, earnest, grave, sober; engrossed, absorbed, intent; abstracted, preoccupied 2 · mindful of others *syn* considerate, attentive *rel* solicitous, concerned, careful, anxious; courteous, polite, gallant, chivalrous, civil *ant* thoughtless

thoughtless *syn* CARELESS, heedless, inadvertent *rel* rash, reckless, foolhardy; indifferent, unconcerned, incurious, aloof; lax, remiss, negligent *ant* thoughtful

thrash 1 *syn* BEAT, pound, pummel, buffet, baste, belabor *rel* strike, smite, slug, slap 2 *syn* SWING, flourish, brandish, shake, wave *rel* wield, manipulate, ply, handle

threadbare 1 *syn* SHABBY, dilapidated, dingy, faded, seedy *rel* damaged, injured, impaired; worn, haggard 2 *syn* TRITE, shopworn, hackneyed, stereotyped *rel* antiquated, obsolete, archaic, old; exhausted, depleted, drained, impoverished

threaten · to announce or forecast impending danger or evil *syn* menace *rel* intimidate, bulldoze, cow, browbeat; forebode, portend, presage, augur, foretell; warn, forewarn, caution

thrifty *syn* SPARING, economical, frugal *rel* provident, prudent, foresighted; saving, preserving, conserving *ant* wasteful

thrill · to thrill with emotions that stir or excite or to be so excited *syn* electrify, enthuse *rel* excite, stimulate, galvanize, quicken, provoke; stir, arouse, rouse, rally; penetrate, pierce, probe, enter; quiver, tremble, shiver, shake

thrive *syn* SUCCEED, prosper, flourish *rel* increase, augment, multiply, enlarge *ant* languish

throb *vb, syn* PULSATE, beat, pulse, palpitate

throb *n, syn* PULSATION, beat, pulse, palpitation

throe *syn* PAIN, ache, pang, twinge, stitch

throng *syn* CROWD, press, crush, mob, rout, horde *rel* multitude, army, host, legion; assembly, congregation, gathering, collection

throttle *syn* SUFFOCATE, asphyxiate, stifle, smother, choke, strangle

through *syn* BY, with

throw • to cause to move swiftly through space by a propulsive movement or a propelling force *syn* cast, fling, hurl, pitch, toss, sling *rel* drive, impel; propel, thrust, shove, push; heave, raise, lift, boost

throwback *syn* REVERSION, atavism

throw up *syn* BELCH, burp, vomit, disgorge, regurgitate, spew

thrust *syn* PUSH, shove, propel *rel* throw, cast, fling; drive, impel, move; enter, penetrate, pierce

thud *vb, syn* TAP, thump, knock, rap *rel* hit, strike, smite; pound, beat

thud *n, syn* TAP, thump, knock, rap *rel* slumping, falling

thump *vb, syn* TAP, thud, knock, rap *rel* pound, beat, belabor; punch, smite, strike

thump *n, syn* TAP, thud, knock, rap *rel* pounding, beating, pummeling

thwart *syn* FRUSTRATE, foil, baffle, balk, circumvent, outwit *rel* hinder, impede, obstruct, block, bar; defeat, overcome, surmount, conquer; check, curb, restrain; prevent, forestall, anticipate

ticket *n, syn* MARK, brand, stamp, label, tag

ticket *vb, syn* MARK, brand, stamp, label, tag *rel* affix, attach, fasten; append, add

tickle *syn* PLEASE, regale, gratify, delight, rejoice, gladden *rel* divert, amuse, entertain; thrill, electrify

tide *syn* FLOW, flood, stream, current, flux

tidings *syn* NEWS, intelligence, advice

tidy *syn* NEAT, trim, trig, snug, shipshape, spick-and-span *rel* orderly, methodical, systematic *ant* untidy

tie *n* **1** *syn* BOND, band **2** *syn* DRAW, stalemate, deadlock, standoff *rel* equality, equivalence

tie *vb* • to make fast and secure *syn* bind *rel* fasten, attach; secure, rivet, anchor, moor; join, connect, link *ant* untie

tier *syn* LINE, row, rank, file, echelon

tiff *n, syn* QUARREL, bickering, spat, squabble, wrangle, altercation *rel* scrap, rumpus, row, brawl, broil; difference, variance, dissension, contention, discord

tiff *vb, syn* QUARREL, spat, bicker, squabble, wrangle, altercate *rel* dispute, argue; differ, disagree; contend, fight

tight **1** • fitting, drawn, or stretched so that there is no slackness or looseness *syn* taut, tense *rel* strict, stringent, rigid; close, compact; constricted, contracted, compressed, condensed, shrunken; snug, shipshape, neat *ant* loose **2** *also* **tightfisted** *syn* STINGY, close, closefisted, niggardly, parsimonious, penurious, miserly, cheeseparing, penny-pinching *rel* mean, ignoble, sordid, abject **3** *syn* DRUNK, tipsy, intoxicated, drunken, inebriated

tight-lipped *syn* SILENT, uncommunicative, taciturn, close, close-lipped, closemouthed, reticent, reserved, secretive

time *syn* OPPORTUNITY, occasion, chance, break *rel* juncture, contingency, emergency, exigency

timely *syn* SEASONABLE, well-timed, opportune, pat *rel* appropriate, fitting, meet, proper, suitable, fit; fortunate, lucky, happy, providential *ant* untimely

timetable *syn* PROGRAM, schedule, agenda

timid • marked by or exhibiting a lack of boldness, courage, or determination *syn* timorous *rel* fearful, apprehensive, afraid; cautious, circumspect, calculating, wary, chary

timorous *syn* TIMID *rel* fearful, apprehensive, afraid; recoiling, shrinking, quailing, blenching; trembling, quivering, shivering, shuddering *ant* assured

tincture *syn* TOUCH, suggestion, tinge, suspicion, soupçon, shade, smack, spice, dash, vein, strain, streak

tinge 1 *syn* COLOR, tint, shade, hue, tone 2 *syn* TOUCH, tincture, suggestion, shade, suspicion, soupçon, smack, spice, dash, vein, strain, streak

tint *syn* COLOR, hue, shade, tinge, tone

tiny *syn* SMALL, minute, miniature, diminutive, wee, little, teeny, weeny

tippler *syn* DRUNKARD, inebriate, alcoholic, dipsomaniac, sot, soak, toper, tosspot

tipsy *syn* DRUNK, intoxicated, inebriated, drunken, tight

tirade • a violent, often long-winded, and usu. denunciatory speech or writing *syn* diatribe, jeremiad, philippic *rel* harangue, oration, speech; invective, vituperation, abuse; denunciation, censure, condemnation *ant* eulogy

tire • to make or become unable or unwilling to continue (as from a loss of physical strength or endurance) *syn* weary, fatigue, exhaust, jade, fag, tucker *rel* irk, vex, annoy, bother; deplete, drain, exhaust, impoverish, bankrupt

tireless *syn* INDEFATIGABLE, weariless, untiring, unwearying, unwearied, unflagging *rel* assiduous, sedulous, diligent, industrious, busy; energetic, strenuous, vigorous

tiresome *syn* IRKSOME, wearisome, tedious, boring *rel* oppressive, burdensome, onerous, exacting; fatiguing, exhausting, jading, fagging; arduous, hard, difficult

titanic *syn* HUGE, vast, immense, enormous, elephantine, mammoth, giant, gigantic, gigantean, colossal, gargantuan, Herculean, cyclopean, Brobdingnagian

title 1 *syn* CLAIM, pretension, pretense *rel* right, privilege, prerogative, birthright; reason, ground, argument, proof; due, desert, merit 2 *syn* NAME, designation, denomination, appellation, style

tittle *syn* PARTICLE, bit, mite, smidgen, whit, atom, iota, jot

toady *n, syn* PARASITE, sycophant, favorite, lickspittle, bootlicker, hanger-on, leech, sponge, sponger

toady *vb, syn* FAWN, truckle, cringe, cower *rel* follow, tag, trail, tail; blandish, cajole, wheedle, coax

toboggan *syn* SLIDE, coast, slip, glide, skid, glissade, slither

tocsin *syn* ALARM, alert *rel* signal, sign

toil *syn* WORK, labor, travail, drudgery, grind *rel* effort, exertion, pains, trouble; employment, occupation, calling, pursuit, business *ant* leisure

token 1 *syn* SIGN, mark, symptom, badge, note *rel* symbol, emblem, attribute; evidence, testimony; indication, proving, proof, betokening 2 *syn* PLEDGE, pawn, hostage *rel* guarantee, guaranty, security, surety **3** *syn* REMEMBRANCE, remembrancer, reminder, memorial, memento, keepsake, souvenir *rel* gift, present, favor

tolerance *syn* FORBEARANCE, leniency, indulgence, clemency, mercifulness *rel* mercy, charity, grace, lenity; patience, long-suffering, longanimity *ant* intolerance; loathing

tolerant *syn* FORBEARING, lenient, indulgent, clement, merciful *rel* charitable, benevolent, humane; forgiving, excusing, condoning *ant* intolerant; severe

tolerantly *syn* FORBEARINGLY, clemently, mercifully, leniently, indulgently

tolerate *syn* BEAR, endure, abide, suffer, stand, brook *rel* accept, receive; submit, yield, bow, succumb

tone *syn* COLOR, hue, shade, tint, tinge

tongue *syn* LANGUAGE, dialect, speech, idiom

tongue-lash *syn* SCOLD, upbraid, rate, berate, jaw, bawl, chew out, wig, rail, revile, vituperate

too *syn* ALSO, likewise, besides, moreover, furthermore

tool *syn* IMPLEMENT, instrument, appliance, utensil *rel* device, contrivance, contraption, gadget; machine, mechanism, apparatus; mean, instrument, instrumentality, agent, agency

toothsome *syn* PALATABLE, appetizing, savory, sapid, tasty, flavorsome, relishing

toper *syn* DRUNKARD, inebriate, alcoholic, dipsomaniac, sot, soak, tosspot, tippler

topic *syn* SUBJECT, matter, subject matter, argument, text, theme, motive, motif, leitmotiv

torment *syn* AFFLICT, torture, rack, try *rel* worry, annoy, harry, harass, plague, pester; distress, trouble; bait, badger, hector; agonize, writhe

tornado • a violent whirling wind accompanied by a funnel-shaped cloud *syn* cyclone, twister *rel* whirlwind, whirly; hurricane, tropical storm, typhoon

torpid *syn* LETHARGIC, sluggish, comatose *rel* inert, inactive, idle, passive; phlegmatic, impassive, stolid *ant* agile

torpidity *syn* LETHARGY, torpor, stupor, languor, lassitude *rel* inertness, inactivity, idleness, passiveness

torpor *syn* LETHARGY, torpidity, stupor, languor, lassitude *rel* apathy, phlegm, impassivity, stolidity; inertness, inertia, passiveness, inactivity *ant* animation

torrent *syn* FLOOD, deluge, inundation, spate, cataract

tortuous *syn* WINDING, sinuous, serpentine, flexuous *rel* crooked, devious; roundabout, circuitous, indirect

torture *syn* AFFLICT, rack, torment, try *rel* writhe, agonize; persecute, oppress, wrong; distress, trouble; worry, annoy, harry, harass; maim, mutilate, mangle

toss *syn* THROW, pitch, sling, cast, fling, hurl *rel* impel, drive; thrust, propel, push

tosspot *syn* DRUNKARD, inebriate, alcoholic, dipsomaniac, sot, soak, toper, tippler

tot *syn* ADD, total, sum, cast, figure, foot

total *adj, syn* WHOLE, entire, all, gross *rel* complete, full, plenary; including, inclusive, comprehending, comprehensive

total *n, syn* SUM, aggregate, whole, amount, number, quantity

total *vb, syn* ADD, tot, sum, figure, cast, foot

totter **1** *syn* SHAKE, tremble, quake, quaver, quiver, shiver, shudder, wobble, teeter, shimmy, dither *rel* rock, agitate, convulse; sway, swing, fluctuate, oscillate, waver **2** *syn* REEL, stagger, whirl *rel* stumble, lurch, blunder, flounder, trip

touch *vb* **1** · to probe with a sensitive part of the body (as a finger) so as to get or produce a sensation often in the course of examining or exploring *syn* feel, palpate, handle, paw *rel* examine, inspect, scrutinize; investigate **2** *syn* AFFECT, influence, impress, strike, sway *rel* arouse, stir; excite, stimulate, quicken, provoke; injure, harm, damage, hurt, impair **3** *syn* MATCH, approach, rival, equal

touch *n* **1** *syn* CONTACT *rel* feeling, sense, sensation, sensibility; tangibleness, palpableness; impact, impingement, shock, clash **2** · a very small amount or perceptible trace of something added *syn* suggestion, suspicion, soupçon, tincture, tinge, shade, smack, spice, dash, vein, strain, streak *rel* trace, vestige; contamination, pollution, defilement, tainting; impression, impress, imprint, stamp, print

touching *syn* MOVING, affecting, impressive, poignant, pathetic *rel* tender, responsive, sympathetic, compassionate; pitiful, piteous, pitiable

touchstone *syn* STANDARD, criterion, gauge, yardstick *rel* test, proof, trial, demonstration

touchy *syn* IRASCIBLE, choleric, splenetic, testy, cranky, cross *rel* irritable, fractious, snappish, waspish, peevish; captious, caviling, faultfinding, carping, critical *ant* imperturbable

tough *syn* STRONG, tenacious, stout, sturdy, stalwart *rel* resisting, resistant, withstanding, opposing; firm, hard; intractable, refractory, recalcitrant, headstrong; dogged, pertinacious, obstinate, stubborn *ant* fragile

tour **1** *syn* SPELL, shift, trick, turn, stint, bout, go **2** *syn* JOURNEY, voyage, trip, cruise, expedition, jaunt, excursion, pilgrimage

tow *syn* PULL, tug, haul, hale, draw, drag

tower *syn* RISE, mount, ascend, soar, rocket, arise, levitate, surge

toxic *syn* POISONOUS, venomous, virulent, mephitic, pestilent, pestilential, miasmic, miasmatic, miasmal

toxin *syn* POISON, venom, virus, bane

toy *syn* TRIFLE, dally, flirt, coquet *rel* play, sport, disport, frolic; fondle, caress, pet, cosset, cuddle, dandle

trace *n* · a perceptible sign made by something that has passed *syn* vestige, track *rel* sign, mark, token

trace *vb, syn* SKETCH, outline, diagram, delineate, draft, plot, blueprint *rel* copy, duplicate, reproduce; map, chart, graph

tracing *syn* SKETCH, outline, diagram, delineation, draft, plot, blueprint *rel* reproduction, copy, duplicate; plan, project, scheme, design

track *syn* TRACE, vestige *rel* print, stamp, imprint, impression; sign, mark, token

tract *syn* AREA, region, zone, belt *rel* expanse, stretch, spread, amplitude; locality, district, vicinity; section, sector, part, portion

tractable *syn* OBEDIENT, amenable, biddable, docile *rel* pliant, pliable, plastic; submissive, subdued, tame; compliant, acquiescent *ant* intractable; unruly

trade **1** · a pursuit followed as an occupation or means of livelihood and requiring technical knowledge and skill *syn* craft, handicraft, art, profession *rel* work, employment, occupation, pursuit **2** *syn* BUSINESS, commerce, industry, traffic

traduce *syn* MALIGN, asperse, vilify, calumniate, defame, slander, libel *rel* decry, detract, derogate, depreciate, disparage; revile, vituperate

traffic 1 *syn* BUSINESS, commerce, trade, industry *rel* transportation, conveyance, carrying 2 *syn* INTERCOURSE, commerce, dealings, communication, communion, conversation, converse, correspondence *rel* familiarity, intimacy, closeness

trail *syn* FOLLOW, pursue, chase, tag, tail

train *n, syn* SUCCESSION, progression, series, sequence, chain, string

train *vb* 1 *syn* TEACH, discipline, school, instruct, educate *rel* practice, exercise, drill; habituate, accustom; harden, season 2 *syn* DIRECT, aim, point, level, lay *rel* turn, divert, deflect

traipse *syn* WANDER, stray, roam, ramble, rove, range, prowl, gad, gallivant, meander

trait *syn* CHARACTERISTIC, feature *rel* quality, character, property, attribute

traitorous *syn* FAITHLESS, treacherous, perfidious, false, disloyal *rel* recreant, renegade, apostate; seditious, mutinous, rebellious, insubordinate; disaffected, estranged, alienated

trammel *syn* HAMPER, fetter, shackle, clog, manacle, hog-tie *rel* hinder, impede, obstruct, block, bar; restrain, curb, check, inhibit; limit, restrict, circumscribe, confine

tramp *syn* VAGABOND, vagrant, hobo, truant, bum

tranquil *syn* CALM, serene, placid, peaceful, halcyon *rel* quiet, still, silent, noiseless; soft, gentle, mild; restful, comfortable; cool, composed, collected *ant* troubled

tranquilize *syn* CALM, compose, quiet, quieten, still, lull, soothe, settle *rel* allay, assuage, alleviate, relieve; mollify, appease, pacify *ant* agitate

transcend *syn* EXCEED, surpass, excel, outdo, outstrip *rel* surmount, overcome, conquer

transcendent 1 *syn* SUPREME, surpassing, superlative, peerless, preeminent, incomparable *rel* consummate, finished, accomplished; perfect, entire, whole, intact 2 *syn* ABSTRACT, transcendental, ideal *rel* absolute, ultimate, categorical; infinite, boundless, eternal

transcendental *syn* ABSTRACT, transcendent, ideal *rel* supernatural, supranatural; categorical, ultimate

transcript *syn* REPRODUCTION, copy, carbon copy, duplicate, facsimile, replica

transfer 1 *syn* MOVE, remove, shift *rel* carry, convey, transport, transmit; commit, consign 2 • to shift title or possession from one owner to another *syn* convey, alienate, deed

transfiguration *syn* TRANSFORMATION, metamorphosis, transmutation, conversion, transmogrification *rel* exaltation, magnification; enhancing, heightening, intensifying

transfigure *syn* TRANSFORM, metamorphose, transmute, convert, transmogrify *rel* exalt, magnify; heighten, enhance, intensify

transform • to change a thing into a different thing *syn* metamorphose, transmute, convert, transmogrify, transfigure *rel* change, alter, modify, vary

transformation • change of one thing into another different thing *syn* metamorphosis, transmutation, conversion, transmogrification, transfiguration *rel* change, alteration, modification, variation; evolution, development

transgression *syn* BREACH, trespass, violation, infraction, infringement, contravention *rel* encroachment, invasion, entrenchment;

slip, lapse, error; offense, sin, vice, crime

transient • lasting or staying only a short time *syn* transitory, passing, ephemeral, momentary, fugitive, fleeting, evanescent, short-lived *ant* perpetual

transitory *syn* TRANSIENT, passing, ephemeral, momentary, fugitive, fleeting, evanescent, short-lived *ant* everlasting; perpetual

translation • a restating often in a simpler language of something previously stated or written *syn* version, paraphrase, metaphrase

translucent *syn* CLEAR, lucid, pellucid, diaphanous, limpid, transparent *rel* luminous, radiant, brilliant, effulgent, bright; iridescent, opalescent, prismatic

transmit 1 *syn* SEND, forward, remit, route, ship, dispatch 2 *syn* CARRY, bear, convey, transport *rel* move, remove, shift, transfer; communicate, impart; propagate, breed, engender, generate

transmogrification *syn* TRANSFORMATION, metamorphosis, transmutation, conversion, transfiguration

transmogrify *syn* TRANSFORM, metamorphose, transmute, convert, transfigure

transmutation *syn* TRANSFORMATION, metamorphosis, conversion, transmogrification, transfiguration

transmute *syn* TRANSFORM, metamorphose, convert, transmogrify, transfigure

transparent *syn* CLEAR, lucid, pellucid, diaphanous, translucent, limpid *ant* opaque

transpire *syn* HAPPEN, occur, chance, befall, betide

transport *vb* 1 *syn* CARRY, bear, convey, transmit *rel* move, remove, shift, transfer; bring, fetch, take 2 • to carry away by strong and usu. pleasurable emotion *syn* ravish, enrapture, entrance *rel* quicken, stimulate, excite, provoke; agitate, upset, perturb, discompose; lift, elevate 3 *syn* BANISH, deport, exile, expatriate, ostracize, extradite *rel* expel, eject, oust

transport *n, syn* ECSTASY, rapture *rel* enthusiasm, passion, fervor, ardor; inspiration, fury, frenzy; bliss, beatitude, blessedness, felicity, happiness

transpose *syn* REVERSE, invert *rel* exchange, interchange; transfer, shift, move

trap *n, syn* LURE, bait, decoy, snare *rel* stratagem, ruse, trick, maneuver, gambit, ploy, artifice, wile, feint; ambush, ambuscade; intrigue, machination, plot, conspiracy

trap *vb, syn* CATCH, entrap, snare, ensnare, bag, capture *rel* seize, take, clutch, grasp; betray, beguile, delude, deceive

trash 1 *syn* REFUSE, waste, rubbish, debris, garbage, offal 2 *syn* NONSENSE, twaddle, drivel, bunk, balderdash, poppycock, gobbledygook, rot, bull

trauma, traumatism *syn* WOUND, lesion, bruise, contusion

travail *syn* WORK, labor, toil, drudgery, grind *rel* effort, exertion, pains, trouble

traverse *syn* DENY, gainsay, contradict, negative, impugn, contravene *rel* controvert, confute, refute, disprove, rebut *ant* allege

travesty *n, syn* CARICATURE, parody, burlesque

travesty *vb, syn* CARICATURE, parody, burlesque *rel* copy, mimic, ape, mock, imitate

treacherous *syn* FAITHLESS, perfidious, traitorous, false, disloyal *rel* betraying, deceiving, misleading, double-crossing; seditious, mutinous, rebellious, insubordinate; dangerous, perilous

treason *syn* SEDITION *rel* revolution, revolt, rebellion, uprising, insurrection; betrayal, deceiving, deception, double-crossing; overthrowing, overthrow, subverting, subversion *ant* allegiance

treasure *syn* APPRECIATE, prize, value, cherish *rel* esteem, respect, regard, admire; revere, reverence, venerate; save, preserve, conserve

treat **1** *syn* CONFER, parley, negotiate, commune, consult, advise *rel* discuss, dispute, argue, debate; consider, weigh, study; think, reason, deliberate **2** • to have to do with or behave toward (a person or thing) in a specified manner *syn* deal, handle *rel* conduct, manage; regard, respect; consider, account; estimate, appraise, evaluate, value, rate

treatise *syn* DISCOURSE, disquisition, dissertation, thesis, monograph *rel* article, paper, essay; exposition

treaty *syn* CONTRACT, bargain, compact, pact, entente, convention, cartel, concordat

tremble *syn* SHAKE, quake, quiver, shiver, shudder, quaver, totter, wobble, teeter, shimmy, dither *rel* thrill, electrify; falter, waver, hesitate; quail, shrink, wince, recoil

tremendous *syn* MONSTROUS, stupendous, monumental, prodigious *rel* enormous, immense, huge, vast, gigantic, colossal; astounding, amazing, flabbergasting; terrifying, alarming, startling, frightening

trenchant *syn* INCISIVE, clear-cut, cutting, biting, crisp *rel* piercing, penetrating, probing; sharp, keen, acute; sarcastic, satiric, ironic, sardonic; caustic, mordant, acrid, scathing; poignant, pungent, piquant

trend *syn* TENDENCY, drift, tenor *rel* movement, motion, move; inclination, disposition, predisposition; progression, progress

trepidation *syn* FEAR, horror, terror, panic, consternation, dread, fright, alarm, dismay *rel* apprehensiveness, fearfulness; anxiety, worry, concern, solicitude, care; awe, reverence

trespass *n, syn* BREACH, transgression, violation, infraction, infringement, contravention *rel* invading, invasion, entrenchment, encroachment; intrusion, obtrusion; offense, sin, vice, crime

trespass *vb* • to make inroads upon the property, territory, or rights of another *syn* encroach, entrench, infringe, invade *rel* intrude, obtrude, interlope, butt in; interfere, intervene, interpose

trial **1** *syn* PROOF, test, demonstration *rel* inspection, examination, scanning, scrutiny; process, proceeding, procedure **2** • the state or fact of being tested (as by suffering) *syn* tribulation, affliction, visitation, cross *rel* distress, suffering, misery, agony; sorrow, grief, anguish, woe, heartbreak; misfortune, adversity; difficulty, hardship, vicissitude, rigor

tribulation *syn* TRIAL, affliction, visitation, cross *rel* oppression, persecution, wronging, wrong; sorrow, grief, anguish, woe; distress, suffering, misery, agony *ant* consolation

tributary *syn* SUBORDINATE, secondary, dependent, subject, collateral *rel* conquered, vanquished, subjugated, subdued; auxiliary, subsidiary, ancillary, adjuvant, contributory

tribute *syn* ENCOMIUM, eulogy, panegyric, citation

trick *n* **1** • an indirect means to gain an end *syn* ruse, stratagem, maneuver, gambit, ploy, artifice, wile, feint *rel* imposture, deceit, deception, counterfeit, humbug, fake, cheat, fraud; fun, jest, sport, game, play **2** *syn* SPELL, turn, tour, shift, stint, bout, go

trick *vb, syn* DUPE, gull, befool,

hoax, hoodwink, bamboozle *rel* deceive, delude, beguile, mislead; outwit, circumvent; cajole, wheedle, blandish, coax

trickery *syn* DECEPTION, double-dealing, chicanery, chicane, fraud *rel* deceit, dissimulation, guile, cunning, duplicity; imposture, cheat, sham, fake, humbug, counterfeit

tricky *syn* SLY, crafty, foxy, insidious, cunning, wily, guileful, artful *rel* crooked, devious, oblique; deceptive, delusive, misleading, delusory; deceitful, dishonest

tried *syn* RELIABLE, dependable, trustworthy, trusty *rel* staunch, steadfast, constant, faithful; proved, demonstrated, tested

trifle · to deal with or act toward without serious purpose *syn* toy, dally, flirt, coquet *rel* palter, fib, equivocate, prevaricate, lie; waver, vacillate, falter, hesitate; dawdle

trifling *syn* PETTY, trivial, puny, paltry, measly, picayunish, picayune *rel* inane, wishy-washy, banal, jejune, vapid, insipid; vain, idle, otiose, nugatory, empty, hollow; venial, pardonable

trig *syn* NEAT, trim, tidy, spick-and-span, snug, shipshape *rel* orderly, methodical

trill *syn* SING, troll, carol, descant, warble, hymn, chant, intone

trim *vb* **1** *syn* SHEAR, poll, clip, prune, lop, snip, crop **2** *syn* STABILIZE, steady, poise, balance, ballast *rel* adjust, regulate, fix; counterbalance, counterpoise, offset, compensate

trim *adj, syn* NEAT, tidy, trig, snug, shipshape, spick-and-span *rel* clean, cleanly; compact, close *ant* frowzy

trip *vb, syn* STUMBLE, blunder, lurch, flounder, lumber, galumph, lollop, bumble *rel* totter, stagger, reel; fall, drop

trip *n, syn* JOURNEY, voyage, tour, excursion, cruise, expedition, jaunt, pilgrimage

trite · lacking the freshness that evokes attention or interest *syn* hackneyed, stereotyped, threadbare, shopworn *rel* old, antiquated, archaic, obsolete; banal, flat, jejune, insipid, vapid; depleted, exhausted, drained, impoverished *ant* original; fresh

triumph *syn* VICTORY, conquest *rel* vanquishing, subjugation, surmounting, overthrowing, routing

trivial *syn* PETTY, trifling, puny, paltry, measly, picayunish, picayune *rel* small, little, diminutive; futile, vain, fruitless, bootless; slight, slim, slender, thin, tenuous *ant* weighty; momentous

troll *syn* SING, carol, descant, warble, trill, hymn, chant, intone

troop *syn* COMPANY, band, troupe, party *rel* crowd, throng, press; assembly, gathering, collection; legion, host, army, multitude

troubadour *syn* POET, versifier, rhymer, rhymester; poetaster, bard, minstrel

trouble *vb* **1** · to cause to be uneasy or upset *syn* distress, ail *rel* discompose, disquiet, disturb, perturb, upset, agitate; vex, irk, annoy, bother **2** *syn* INCONVENIENCE, incommode, discommode *rel* embarrass, discomfit, disconcert, abash; worry, annoy, plague, pester; perplex, puzzle, distract

trouble *n, syn* EFFORT, exertion, pains *rel* flurry, fuss, ado, stir, bustle, pother; labor, toil, work; difficulty, rigor, vicissitude, hardship

troupe *syn* COMPANY, troop, band, party

trouper *syn* ACTOR, player, performer, mummer, mime, mimic, thespian, impersonator

truant *syn* VAGABOND, vagrant, tramp, hobo, bum

truce · a suspension of or an agreement for suspending hostilities *syn* cease-fire, armistice, peace

truckle *syn* FAWN, toady, cringe, cower *rel* defer, succumb, bow, cave, yield, submit; follow, tag, trail, tail

truculent *syn* FIERCE, ferocious, barbarous, savage, inhuman, cruel, fell *rel* intimidating, cowing, bulldozing, browbeating, bullying; terrorizing, terrifying, frightening; threatening, menacing

true 1 *syn* FAITHFUL, loyal, constant, staunch, steadfast, resolute *rel* reliable, dependable, trustworthy, tried; persevering, persisting; sincere, wholehearted, whole-souled, unfeigned *ant* false; fickle 2 *syn* REAL, actual *rel* genuine, authentic, veritable, bona fide; exact, precise, correct, right; typical, natural, regular *ant* false

truism *syn* COMMONPLACE, platitude, bromide, cliche *rel* triteness, threadbareness; banality, jejuneness, inanity

trust *n* 1 · assured reliance on the character, ability, strength, or truth of someone or something *syn* confidence, reliance, dependence, faith *rel* assurance, conviction, certitude, certainty; belief, credence, credit *ant* mistrust 2 *syn* MONOPOLY, corner, pool, syndicate, cartel

trust *vb, syn* RELY, depend, count, reckon, bank *rel* confide, entrust, commit, consign; hope, expect, look

trustworthy *syn* RELIABLE, dependable, trusty, tried *rel* safe, secure; veracious, truthful; staunch, constant, steadfast, faithful; honest, upright, scrupulous *ant* deceitful; dubious

trusty *syn* RELIABLE, trustworthy, tried, dependable *rel* faithful, staunch, steadfast, constant

truth · the quality or state of keeping close to fact and avoiding distortion or misrepresentation *syn* veracity, verity, verisimilitude *rel* exactness, precision, correctness, rightness; authenticity, genuineness, veritableness *ant* untruth; lie, falsehood

try *vb* 1 *syn* PROVE, test, demonstrate *rel* judge, adjudge, adjudicate; inspect, examine, scrutinize 2 *syn* AFFLICT, torment, torture, rack *rel* worry, harass, harry, plague, pester; trouble, distress; irk, vex, bother, annoy 3 *syn* ATTEMPT, endeavor, essay, strive, struggle *rel* aim, aspire; intend, mean, propose, purpose, design

try *n, syn* ATTEMPT, endeavor, essay, striving, struggle *rel* effort, exertion, trouble, pains; test, trial, proof

tryst *syn* ENGAGEMENT, rendezvous, assignation, appointment, date

tucker *syn* TIRE, fatigue, exhaust, jade, fag, weary *rel* deplete, drain, exhaust, impoverish, bankrupt

tug *syn* PULL, tow, hale, haul, drag, draw

tumid *syn* INFLATED, flatulent, turgid *rel* expanded, distended, swollen, dilated; pretentious, showy, ostentatious; bombastic, grandiloquent, magniloquent, rhetorical

tumult *syn* COMMOTION, agitation, turmoil, turbulence, confusion, convulsion, upheaval *rel* agitation, perturbation, disturbance; uprising, insurrection, rebellion, revolt, mutiny; disorder, unsettlement; din, uproar, pandemonium

tune *n, syn* MELODY, air

tune *vb, syn* HARMONIZE, attune *rel* adjust, regulate, fix; adapt, accommodate, reconcile, conform

turbid · not clear or translucent but clouded with or as if with sediment *syn* muddy, roily *rel* obscure, dark, murky; dirty, foul, nasty *ant* clear; limpid

turbulence *syn* COMMOTION, agitation, tumult, turmoil, confusion, convulsion, upheaval *rel* din, uproar, babel, pandemonium; agitation, perturbation, disturbance

turgid *syn* INFLATED, tumid, flatulent *rel* expanded, distended, amplified, swollen; magniloquent, grandiloquent, rhetorical, bombastic

turmoil *syn* COMMOTION, agitation, tumult, turbulence, confusion, convulsion, upheaval *rel* agitation, disquiet, disturbance, perturbation; restlessness, nervousness, uneasiness, jitteriness

turn *vb* **1** · to move or cause to move in a curved or circular path on or as if on an axis *syn* revolve, rotate, gyrate, circle, spin, twirl, whirl, wheel, eddy, swirl, pirouette *rel* swing, oscillate, vibrate, fluctuate, pendulate, undulate **2** · to change or cause to change course or direction *syn* divert, deflect, avert, sheer *rel* swerve, veer, deviate, diverge, digress, depart; move, shift **3** *syn* RESORT, refer, apply, go **4** *syn* DEPEND, hinge, hang

turn *n* **1** *syn* SPELL, trick, tour, shift, stint, bout, go **2** *syn* GIFT, bent, faculty, aptitude, genius, talent, knack *rel* inclination, disposition, predisposition, bias; propensity, proclivity, penchant, leaning, flair

turncoat *syn* RENEGADE, apostate, recreant, backslider *rel* deserter, forsaker, abandoner

turn out *syn* BEAR, produce, yield *rel* make, form, fashion, shape, manufacture, fabricate; propagate, breed, generate, engender

tussle *syn* WRESTLE, grapple, scuffle *rel* contend, fight; resist, combat, withstand, oppose; compete, vie, rival

twaddle *syn* NONSENSE, drivel, bunk, balderdash, poppycock, gobbledygook, trash, rot, bull

tweet *n, syn* CHIRP, chirrup, cheep, peep, twitter, chitter

tweet *vb, syn* CHIRP, chirrup, cheep, peep, twitter, chitter

twine *syn* WIND, coil, curl, twist, wreathe, entwine *rel* curve, bend; interweave, interplait, weave; entangle, enmesh

twinge *syn* PAIN, ache, pang, throe, stitch

twinkle *syn* FLASH, gleam, glance, glint, sparkle, glitter, glisten, scintillate, coruscate

twinkling *syn* INSTANT, moment, minute, second, flash, jiffy, split second

twirl *syn* TURN, revolve, rotate, gyrate, circle, spin, whirl, wheel, eddy, swirl, pirouette

twist **1** *syn* WIND, coil, curl, twine, wreathe, entwine *rel* combine, unite, associate, join; plait, braid, knit, weave; encircle, surround **2** *syn* CURVE, bend *rel* spin, twirl, whirl, turn; contort, distort, deform

twister *syn* TORNADO, cyclone *rel* whirlwind, whirly; hurricane, tropical storm, typhoon

twit *syn* RIDICULE, deride, mock, taunt, rally *rel* reproach, chide, reprove; reprehend, blame, censure, criticize; scoff, jeer, gibe

twitch *syn* JERK, snap, yank *rel* pull, drag, tug; clutch, snatch, grasp

twitter *vb, syn* CHIRP, chirrup, cheep, peep, tweet, chitter

twitter *n, syn* CHIRP, chirrup, cheep, peep, tweet, chitter

type **1** *syn* SYMBOL, emblem, attribute *rel* sign, mark, token; intimation, suggestion; adumbration, shadowing *ant* antitype **2** · a number of individuals thought of as a group because of a common quality or qualities *syn* kind, sort, stripe, kidney, ilk, description, nature, character *rel* exemplar, example, model, pattern

typhoon *syn* HURRICANE, tropical storm *rel* whirlwind, whirly; typhoon

typical *syn* REGULAR, natural, normal *rel* generic, general, universal, common; specific *ant* atypical; distinctive

tyrannical, tyrannous *syn* ABSOLUTE, despotic, arbitrary, autocratic *rel* dictatorial, authoritarian, magisterial; totalitarian; domineering, imperious, masterful

tyro *syn* AMATEUR, dilettante, dabbler *rel* novice, apprentice, probationer, neophyte

U

ubiquitous *syn* OMNIPRESENT

ugly · unpleasing to the sight *syn* hideous, ill-favored, unsightly *rel* plain, homely; grotesque, bizarre *ant* beautiful

ultimate **1** *syn* LAST, latest, final, terminal, concluding, eventual **2** · being so fundamental as to represent the extreme limit of actual or possible knowledge *syn* absolute, categorical

ululate *syn* ROAR, bellow, bluster, bawl, vociferate, clamor, howl *rel* wail, keen, weep, cry; bewail, lament

ululation *syn* ROAR, bellow, bluster, bawl, vociferation

umbra *syn* SHADE, penumbra, shadow, umbrage, adumbration

umbrage **1** *syn* SHADE, shadow, umbra, penumbra, adumbration **2** *syn* OFFENSE, resentment, pique, dudgeon, huff *rel* annoyance, vexation, irking; irritation, exasperation, provocation, nettling; indignation, rage, fury, wrath, anger, ire

umpire *syn* JUDGE, referee, arbiter, arbitrator

unacceptable *syn* OBJECTIONABLE, undesirable, unwanted, unwelcome

unaffected *syn* NATURAL, artless, simple, ingenuous, naïve, unsophisticated

unafraid *syn* BRAVE, fearless, dauntless, undaunted, bold, intrepid, audacious, courageous, valiant, valorous, doughty *rel* cool, composed, imperturbable; confident, assured, sure *ant* afraid

unassailable *syn* INVINCIBLE, impregnable, inexpugnable, invulnerable, unconquerable, indomitable *rel* stout, sturdy, tenacious, tough, strong, stalwart

unavoidable *syn* INEVITABLE, ineluctable, inescapable, unescapable *rel* certain, positive, sure

unbecoming *syn* INDECOROUS, improper, unseemly, indecent, indelicate *rel* unfitting, inappropriate, unsuitable, unfit; inept, awkward, maladroit, gauche, clumsy

unbelief · the attitude or state of mind of one who does not believe *syn* disbelief, incredulity *rel* uncertainty, doubt, dubiety, dubiosity, skepticism *ant* belief

unbeliever *syn* ATHEIST, freethinker, agnostic, infidel, deist

unbiased *syn* FAIR, impartial, dispassionate, just, equitable, uncolored, objective *rel* uninterested, disinterested, detached, aloof, indifferent *ant* biased

unburden *syn* RID, clear, disabuse, purge *rel* disencumber, unload, discharge; free, release, liberate *ant* burden

uncalled-for *syn* SUPEREROGATORY, gratuitous, wanton *rel* impertinent, intrusive, officious; foolish, silly, absurd, preposterous

uncanny *syn* WEIRD, eerie *rel* strange, singular, erratic, eccentric, odd, queer; mysterious, inscrutable

unceasing *syn* EVERLASTING, endless, interminable

uncertainty • lack of sureness about someone or something *syn* doubt, dubiety, dubiosity, skepticism, suspicion, mistrust *ant* certainty

uncircumscribed *syn* INFINITE, boundless, illimitable, sempiternal, eternal *ant* circumscribed

uncivil *syn* RUDE, ill-mannered, impolite, discourteous, ungracious *rel* boorish, loutish, churlish; brusque, blunt, gruff, crusty, bluff *ant* civil

uncolored **1** *syn* COLORLESS, achromatic **2** *syn* FAIR, dispassionate, impartial, objective, unbiased, just, equitable

uncommon *syn* INFREQUENT, scarce, rare, occasional, sporadic *rel* strange, singular, unique; exceptional; choice, exquisite *ant* common

uncommunicative *syn* SILENT, taciturn, reticent, reserved, secretive, close, close-lipped, closemouthed, tight-lipped *ant* communicative

unconcerned *syn* INDIFFERENT, incurious, aloof, detached, uninterested, disinterested *rel* cool, collected, composed, nonchalant; apathetic, impassive, stolid, phlegmatic *ant* concerned

uncongenial *syn* INCONSONANT, unsympathetic, incompatible, inconsistent, incongruous, discordant, discrepant *rel* antipathetic, unsympathetic, averse; repugnant, repellent, abhorrent, obnoxious *ant* congenial

unconquerable *syn* INVINCIBLE, indomitable, impregnable, inexpugnable, unassailable, invulnerable *ant* conquerable

unconstraint • freedom from constraint or pressure *syn* abandon, spontaneity *rel* spontaneousness, impulsiveness, instinctiveness; naturalness, simplicity, unsophistication, ingenuousness, naïveté

uncouth *syn* RUDE, rough, crude, raw, callow, green *rel* awkward, clumsy, gauche

uncritical *syn* SUPERFICIAL, shallow, cursory *ant* critical

unctuous *syn* FULSOME, oily, oleaginous, slick, soapy *rel* bland, politic, smooth, diplomatic, suave; obsequious, subservient *ant* brusque

undaunted *syn* BRAVE, courageous, unafraid, fearless, intrepid, valiant, valorous, dauntless, doughty, bold, audacious *rel* resolute, staunch, steadfast, faithful; confident, assured, sanguine, sure *ant* afraid

under *syn* BELOW, beneath, underneath

undergo *syn* EXPERIENCE, sustain, suffer *rel* bear, endure, abide, tolerate; accept, receive; submit, bow, yield, defer

underhand, underhanded *syn* SECRET, covert, stealthy, furtive, clandestine, surreptitious *rel* deceitful, dishonest; crooked, devious, oblique; sly, cunning, crafty, tricky, insidious, wily, guileful *ant* aboveboard

underling *syn* INFERIOR, subordinate *ant* leader, master

underlying **1** *syn* FUNDAMENTAL, basic, basal, radical *rel* essential, cardinal, vital; requisite, indispensable, necessary, needful **2** *syn* ELEMENTAL, basic, elementary, essential, fundamental, primitive

undermine *syn* WEAKEN, enfeeble, debilitate, sap, cripple, disable *rel* ruin, wreck; injure, damage, impair; thwart, foil, frustrate *ant* reinforce

underneath *syn* BELOW, under, beneath

understand · to have a clear or complete idea of *syn* comprehend, appreciate *rel* conceive, realize, envision, envisage, think; interpret, elucidate, construe, explain; penetrate, pierce, probe

understanding 1 *syn* REASON, intuition *rel* comprehension, apprehension; discernment, discrimination, insight, penetration 2 *syn* AGREEMENT, accord

understudy *syn* SUBSTITUTE, supply, locum tenens, alternate, pinch hitter, double, stand-in

undesirable *syn* OBJECTIONABLE, unacceptable, unwanted, unwelcome

undulate *syn* SWING, waver, sway, oscillate, vibrate, fluctuate, pendulate *rel* pulsate, pulse, beat, throb, palpitate

undying *syn* IMMORTAL, deathless, unfading *rel* everlasting, endless, unceasing, interminable

unearth *syn* DISCOVER, ascertain, determine, learn *rel* dig, delve; expose, exhibit, show; reveal, disclose, discover

uneasy *syn* IMPATIENT, nervous, unquiet, restless, restive, fidgety, jumpy, jittery *rel* anxious, worried, solicitous, concerned, careful; disturbed, perturbed, agitated, disquieted

uneducated *syn* IGNORANT, illiterate, unlettered, untaught, untutored, unlearned *rel* rude, crude, rough, raw, callow, green, uncouth *ant* educated

unerring *syn* INFALLIBLE, inerrable, inerrant *rel* reliable, dependable, trustworthy; exact, accurate, precise, correct

unescapable *syn* INEVITABLE, ineluctable, inescapable, unavoidable *rel, ant* see INESCAPABLE

uneven *syn* ROUGH, harsh, rugged, scabrous *ant* even

unfading *syn* IMMORTAL, deathless, undying *rel* everlasting, endless; lasting, perdurable, perpetual

unfeigned *syn* SINCERE, wholehearted, whole-souled, heartfelt, hearty *rel* genuine, veritable, bona fide, authentic; natural, simple, naïve; spontaneous, impulsive

unfit · not adapted or appropriate to a particular end or purpose *syn* unsuitable, improper, inappropriate, unfitting, inapt, unhappy, infelicitous *ant* fit

unfitting *syn* UNFIT, inappropriate, improper, unsuitable, inapt, unhappy, infelicitous *rel* unbecoming, unseemly, indecorous *ant* fitting

unflagging *syn* INDEFATIGABLE, unwearied, unwearying, tireless, untiring, weariless *rel* persevering, persisting, persistent; steady, constant

unflappable *syn* COOL, composed, collected, unruffled, imperturbable, nonchalant

unfold 1 · to disclose by degrees to the sight or understanding *syn* evolve, develop, elaborate, perfect *rel* show, manifest, evidence, evince, demonstrate; exhibit, display, expose 2 *syn* SOLVE, resolve, unravel, decipher

unformed *syn* FORMLESS, shapeless *ant* formed

unfortunate *syn* UNLUCKY, disastrous, ill-starred, ill-fated, calamitous, luckless, hapless *rel* baleful, malefic, sinister; miserable, wretched; unhappy, infelicitous *ant* fortunate

unfounded *syn* BASELESS, groundless, unwarranted *rel* false, wrong; misleading, deceptive; mendacious, dishonest, untruthful

unfruitful *syn* STERILE, barren, infertile, impotent *ant* fruitful, prolific

ungodly *syn* IRRELIGIOUS, godless,

unreligious, nonreligious *rel* wicked, evil, ill, bad; reprobate, abandoned, profligate; impious, blasphemous, profane

ungovernable *syn* UNRULY, intractable, refractory, recalcitrant, willful, headstrong *rel* contrary, perverse, froward, wayward; contumacious, insubordinate, rebellious, factious *ant* governable; docile

ungracious *syn* RUDE, ill-mannered, impolite, discourteous, uncivil *rel* churlish, boorish; brusque, gruff, blunt, curt, bluff *ant* gracious

unhappy *syn* UNFIT, infelicitous, inapt, unsuitable, improper, inappropriate, unfitting *rel* inept, maladroit, gauche, awkward *ant* happy

uniform **1** *syn* LIKE, alike, similar, analogous, comparable, akin, parallel, identical *rel* same, equivalent, equal *ant* various **2** *syn* STEADY, constant, even, equable *rel* consistent, consonant, compatible; regular, orderly *ant* multiform

unify *syn* COMPACT, consolidate, concentrate *rel* integrate, articulate, concatenate; organize, systematize, order; unite, combine, conjoin

unimpassioned *syn* SOBER, temperate, continent *rel* cool, composed, collected, imperturbable; calm, serene, placid, tranquil; impassive, stolid, stoic, phlegmatic *ant* impassioned

uninterested *syn* INDIFFERENT, unconcerned, incurious, aloof, detached, disinterested

union *syn* UNITY, solidarity, integrity *rel* integration, articulation, concatenation; harmony, consonance, accord, concord

unique **1** *syn* SINGLE, sole, lone, solitary, separate, particular *rel* only, alone **2** *syn* STRANGE, singular, peculiar, eccentric, erratic, odd, queer, quaint, outlandish, curious *rel* exceptional; uncommon, rare, infrequent

unite **1** *syn* JOIN, conjoin, combine, connect, link, associate, relate *rel* mix, blend, merge, amalgamate; weave, knit; integrate, concatenate, articulate *ant* divide; alienate **2** · to join forces or act in concert *syn* combine, conjoin, cooperate, concur *rel* mingle, commingle, coalesce, fuse, adhere, cohere, stick, cling, cleave *ant* part

unity · the character of a thing that is a whole composed of many parts *syn* solidarity, integrity, union *rel* identification, incorporation, embodiment, assimilation; cooperation, concurrence, uniting, combining; integration, concatenation, articulation

universal **1** · present or significant throughout the world *syn* cosmic, ecumenical, catholic, cosmopolitan *rel* earthly, terrestrial, worldly, mundane; whole, entire, all, total **2** · of, belonging, or relating to all or the whole *syn* general, generic, common *ant* particular

unkempt *syn* SLIPSHOD, slovenly, sloppy, disheveled *rel* frowzy, slatternly, blowsy, dowdy; negligent, neglectful, lax, slack, remiss

unlawful · contrary to or prohibited by the law *syn* illegal, illegitimate, illicit *rel* iniquitous, nefarious, flagitious *ant* lawful

unlearned *syn* IGNORANT, illiterate, unlettered, uneducated, untaught, untutored *rel* crude, rude, rough, raw, callow, green, uncouth

unlettered *syn* IGNORANT, illiterate, uneducated, untaught, untutored, unlearned

unlikeness *syn* DISSIMILARITY, difference, divergence, divergency, distinction *rel* diversity, variety; disparity, variousness; discrepancy, discordance, incongruousness, incompatibility, inconsistency, inconsonance *ant* likeness

unlucky • involving or suffering misfortune that results from chance *syn* disastrous, ill-starred, ill-fated, unfortunate, calamitous, luckless, hapless *rel* inept, awkward; distressing, troubling; sinister, malign, baleful *ant* lucky

unman *syn* UNNERVE, emasculate, enervate *rel* sap, undermine, weaken, enfeeble, debilitate; abase, degrade; deplete, drain, exhaust, impoverish, bankrupt

unmarried • being without a spouse *syn* single, celibate, virgin, maiden

unmatured *syn* IMMATURE, unripe, unmellow *ant* matured

unmellow *syn* IMMATURE, unmatured, unripe *ant* mellow, mellowed

unmindful *syn* FORGETFUL, oblivious *rel* heedless, thoughtless, careless, inadvertent; negligent, neglectful, remiss *ant* mindful; solicitous

unmitigated *syn* OUTRIGHT, out-and-out, arrant

unnatural *syn* IRREGULAR, anomalous *rel* abnormal, aberrant, atypical; monstrous, prodigious; fantastic, grotesque, bizarre *ant* natural

unnerve • to deprive of strength or vigor and the capacity for effective action *syn* enervate, unman, emasculate *rel* upset, agitate, perturb, discompose; bewilder, distract, confound, puzzle; weaken, enfeeble, sap, undermine

unoffending *syn* HARMLESS, innocuous, innocent, inoffensive

unpremeditated *syn* EXTEMPORANEOUS, extempore, extemporary, improvised, impromptu, offhand *ant* premeditated

unpretentious *syn* PLAIN, homely, simple *rel* natural, unsophisticated, simple, ingenuous, unaffected; unassuming

unpropitious *syn* OMINOUS, portentous, fateful, inauspicious *rel* sinister, baleful, malign, malefic, maleficent; threatening, menacing; adverse, antagonistic, counter *ant* propitious

unqualified *syn* INCAPABLE, incompetent *rel* disabled, crippled, weakened, debilitated; unfit, unsuitable *ant* qualified

unquiet *syn* IMPATIENT, nervous, restless, restive, uneasy, fidgety, jumpy, jittery *rel* agitated, upset, perturbed, disquieted, disturbed; worried, anxious, solicitous, concerned, careful *ant* quiet

unravel *syn* SOLVE, resolve, unfold, decipher *rel* disentangle, untangle, extricate; elucidate, explicate, interpret, explain, expound

unreasonable *syn* IRRATIONAL *rel* absurd, preposterous, foolish, silly; simple, fatuous, asinine; excessive, immoderate, inordinate *ant* reasonable

unrelenting *syn* GRIM, implacable, relentless, merciless *rel* inexorable, obdurate, inflexible, adamant; stiff, rigid; severe, stern *ant* forbearing

unreligious *syn* IRRELIGIOUS, ungodly, godless, nonreligious

unremitting *syn* CONTINUAL, constant, incessant, continuous, perpetual, perennial *rel* unceasing, interminable, endless, everlasting; assiduous, sedulous, diligent; indefatigable, untiring

unripe *syn* IMMATURE, unmatured, unmellow *rel* crude, raw, green, callow, rude; premature, untimely, forward, precocious *ant* ripe

unruffled *syn* COOL, imperturbable, unflappable, nonchalant, composed, collected *rel* calm, placid, peaceful, serene, tranquil; poised, balanced *ant* ruffled; excited

unruly • not submissive to government or control *syn* ungovernable, intractable, refractory, recalcitrant, willful, headstrong *rel* insubordinate, rebellious, contumacious; obstreperous, boisterous, strident, vociferous; contrary, perverse, froward, wayward; fractious, irritable, snappish, waspish *ant* tractable, docile

unseemly *syn* INDECOROUS, improper, unbecoming, indecent, indelicate *rel* unfitting, unsuitable, inappropriate, incongruous, incompatible, inconsistent, inconsonant *ant* seemly

unsettle *syn* DISORDER, derange, disarrange, disorganize, disturb *rel* discommode, incommode, trouble, inconvenience; upset, agitate, perturb, discompose, disquiet *ant* settle

unsightly *syn* UGLY, hideous, ill-favored *rel* distasteful, obnoxious, repellent, repugnant; hateful, odious, detestable, abominable

unsocial • disliking or avoiding the company of others *syn* asocial, antisocial, nonsocial *ant* social

unsophisticated *syn* NATURAL, simple, ingenuous, naïve, artless *rel* candid, frank, open, plain; genuine, bona fide, authentic; crude, callow, green, uncouth, rude *ant* sophisticated

unspeakable *syn* UNUTTERABLE, inexpressible, ineffable, indescribable, indefinable *rel* offensive, loathsome, repulsive, revolting; repugnant, repellent, obnoxious, distasteful; abominable, odious, hateful, detestable

unstable *syn* INCONSTANT, fickle, capricious, mercurial *rel* changeable, variable, mutable, protean; volatile, effervescent, buoyant, resilient, elastic *ant* stable

unsuitable *syn* UNFIT, improper, inappropriate, unfitting, inapt, unhappy, infelicitous *rel* unbecoming, unseemly, indecorous, indecent; inept, maladroit, awkward, clumsy, gauche *ant* suitable

unsympathetic **1** *syn* INCONSONANT, uncongenial, discordant, incongruous, incompatible, inconsistent, discrepant *ant* sympathetic **2** *syn* ANTIPATHETIC *rel* indifferent, unconcerned, incurious, aloof; hardened, callous, indurated *ant* sympathetic

untangle *syn* EXTRICATE, disentangle, disencumber, disembarrass *rel* free, release, liberate

untaught *syn* IGNORANT, illiterate, unlettered, uneducated, untutored, unlearned *ant* taught

untimely *syn* PREMATURE, forward, advanced, precocious *rel* immature, unmatured, unripe, unmellow *ant* timely

untiring *syn* INDEFATIGABLE, tireless, weariless, unwearying, unwearied, unflagging *rel* unceasing, interminable, everlasting; assiduous, sedulous, diligent; persevering, persisting

untouchable *syn* OUTCAST, castaway, derelict, reprobate, pariah

untruth *syn* LIE, falsehood, fib, misrepresentation, story *rel* mendaciousness, mendacity, dishonesty, deceitfulness; equivocation, tergiversation, ambiguity *ant* truth

untruthful *syn* DISHONEST, lying, mendacious, deceitful *rel* false, wrong; misleading, deceptive, delusive, delusory *ant* truthful

untutored *syn* IGNORANT, illiterate, unlettered, uneducated, untaught, unlearned *ant* tutored

unusual *syn* exceptional, extraordinary, phenomenal unwonted

unutterable • not capable of being put into words *syn* inexpressible, unspeakable, ineffable, indescribable, indefinable

unwanted *syn* OBJECTIONABLE, unacceptable, undesirable, unwelcome

unwarranted *syn* BASELESS, groundless, unfounded *rel* unauthorized, unaccredited; unapproved, unsanctioned *ant* warranted

unwearied *syn* INDEFATIGABLE, tireless, weariless, untiring, unwearying, unflagging *rel* persevering, persisting, persistent; unceasing, interminable, everlasting; constant, steady

unwearying *syn* INDEFATIGABLE, tireless, weariless, untiring, unwearied, unflagging *rel* see UNTIRING

unwelcome *syn* OBJECTIONABLE, unacceptable, undesirable, unwanted

unwholesome • detrimental to physical, mental, or moral well-being *syn* morbid, sickly, diseased, pathological *rel* detrimental, deleterious, noxious, pernicious, baneful; toxic, poisonous; injurious, hurtful, harmful, mischievous *ant* wholesome

unwonted *syn* EXCEPTIONAL, extraordinary, phenomenal, unusual

upbraid *syn* SCOLD, rate, berate, tongue-lash, revile, vituperate, jaw, bawl, chew out, wig, rail *rel* reprehend, reprobate, blame, censure, denounce, criticize; reproach, reprimand, rebuke, reprove

upheaval *syn* COMMOTION, agitation, tumult, turmoil, turbulence, confusion, convulsion *rel* heaving, raising, lifting; alteration, change; cataclysm, catastrophe, disaster

uphold *syn* SUPPORT, advocate, back, champion *rel* help, aid, assist; defend, vindicate, justify, maintain; sanction, approve, endorse *ant* contravene; subvert

upright • having or showing a strict regard for what is morally right *syn* honest, just, conscientious, scrupulous, honorable *rel* moral, ethical, virtuous, righteous; fair, equitable, impartial; straightforward, aboveboard

uprising *syn* REBELLION, revolution, revolt, insurrection, mutiny, putsch, coup *rel* fight, combat, conflict, fray, contest; strife, contention, dissension, discord; aggression, attack

uproar *syn* DIN, pandemonium, hullabaloo, babel, hubbub, clamor, racket *rel* strife, contention, dissension, discord, conflict, variance; confusion, disorder, chaos; fracas, brawl, broil, melee

uproot *syn* EXTERMINATE, eradicate, deracinate, extirpate, wipe *rel* abolish, extinguish, annihilate, abate; supplant, displace, replace, supersede; subvert, overthrow, overturn; destroy, demolish *ant* establish; inseminate

upset **1** *syn* OVERTURN, capsize, overthrow, subvert *rel* invert, reverse; bend, curve **2** *syn* DISCOMPOSE, agitate, perturb, disturb, disquiet, fluster, flurry *rel* bewilder, distract, confound, puzzle; discomfit, rattle, faze, embarrass; unnerve, unman

upshot *syn* EFFECT, outcome, issue, result, consequence, aftereffect, aftermath, event, sequel *rel* end, termination, ending; climax, culmination; concluding, conclusion, finishing, finish, completion

urbane *syn* SUAVE, smooth, diplomatic, bland, politic *rel* courteous, polite, courtly, civil; poised, balanced; cultured, cultivated, refined *ant* rude; clownish, bucolic

urge *vb* • to press or impel to action, effort, or speed *syn* egg, exhort, goad, spur, prod, prick, sic *rel* impel, drive, actuate, move; stimulate, excite, quicken, provoke

urge *n, syn* DESIRE, lust, passion, appetite *rel* motive, spring, spur, goad, incentive; longing, yearning, pining; craving, coveting, desiring

urgent *syn* PRESSING, imperative, crying, importunate, insistent, exigent, instant *rel* impelling, driving; constraining, compelling, obliging

usage 1 *syn* HABIT, practice, custom, use, habitude, wont *rel* method, mode, manner, way, fashion; procedure, proceeding, process; guiding, guidance, leading, lead; choice, preference 2 *syn* FORM, convention, convenance *rel* formality, ceremony

use *n* 1 • a useful or valuable end, result, or purpose *syn* service, advantage, profit, account, avail *rel* benefit; value, worth; function, office, duty; purpose, intention, object 2 • a capacity for serving an end or purpose *syn* usefulness, utility *rel* applicability, relevance, pertinence; suitability, fitness, appropriateness 3 *syn* HABIT, wont, practice, usage, custom, habitude *rel* form, usage; rite, ceremony, formality

use *vb* • to put into service esp. to attain an end *syn* employ, utilize, apply, avail *rel* handle, manipulate, ply, wield; practice, exercise

usefulness *syn* USE, utility *rel* value, worth; excellence, merit

usual • familiar through frequent or regular repetition *syn* customary, habitual, wonted, accustomed *rel* regular, natural, normal, typical; common, ordinary, familiar; prevalent, prevailing, rife, current

usurp *syn* ARROGATE, preempt, appropriate, confiscate *rel* seize, take, grab, grasp *ant* abdicate

utensil *syn* IMPLEMENT, tool, instrument, appliance *rel* device, contrivance, contraption, gadget

utility *syn* USE, usefulness *rel* suitability, fitness, appropriateness; value, worth

utilize *syn* USE, employ, apply, avail *rel* benefit, profit; handle, manipulate, ply, wield; forward, further, promote, advance

utopian *syn* AMBITIOUS, pretentious *rel* impracticable, unfeasible, impossible; visionary, quixotic, chimerical, imaginary; ideal, transcendental, abstract

utter 1 *syn* SAY, tell, state *rel* enunciate, articulate, pronounce; speak, talk 2 *syn* EXPRESS, vent, voice, broach, air, ventilate *rel* reveal, disclose, discover, divulge; declare, announce, publish, advertise

V

vacant *syn* EMPTY, blank, vacuous *rel* bare, barren; destitute, void, devoid; idiotic, imbecilic, foolish

vacate *syn* ANNUL, abrogate, void, quash

vacillate *syn* HESITATE, waver, falter *rel* fluctuate, sway, oscillate, swing; demur, scruple, boggle

vacuous *syn* EMPTY, vacant, blank, void *rel* barren, bare; inane, wishy-washy, insipid

vacuum *syn* HOLE, void, cavity, hollow, pocket

vagabond • a person who wanders at will or as a habit *syn* vagrant, truant, tramp, bum, hobo *rel* wanderer, roamer, rover

vagary *syn* CAPRICE, freak, fancy, whim, whimsy, conceit, crotchet *rel* mood, humor, temper, vein; fancy, fantasy, dream, daydream; notion, idea

vagrant *n, syn* VAGABOND, truant, tramp, hobo, bum *rel* wanderer, roamer, rover

vagrant *adj, syn* ITINERANT, peripatetic, ambulatory, ambulant, nomadic *rel* moving, shifting; wandering, roaming, roving, rambling, straying, ranging; strolling, sauntering

vague *syn* OBSCURE, dark, enigmatic, cryptic, ambiguous, equivocal *rel* formless, unformed; doubtful, dubious; abstruse, recondite *ant* definite; specific; lucid

vain **1** • being without worth or significance *syn* nugatory, otiose, idle, empty, hollow **2** *syn* FUTILE, fruitless, bootless, abortive *rel* ineffective, ineffectual, inefficacious; trivial, trifling, puny, petty, paltry; delusive, delusory, misleading **3** *syn* PROUD, vainglorious *rel* self-satisfied, self-complacent, complacent, priggish, smug; conceited, egoistic, egotistic

vainglorious *syn* PROUD, vain *rel* arrogant, haughty, supercilious, disdainful, insolent; boasting, boastful, bragging, vaunting, gasconading

vainglory *syn* PRIDE, vanity *rel* pomp, display, parade; flaunting, parading, exhibition; rhapsody, rodomontade, rant, bombast

valiant *syn* BRAVE, courageous, unafraid, fearless, intrepid, valorous, dauntless, undaunted, doughty, bold, audacious *rel* stout, sturdy, tenacious, stalwart, strong; indomitable, unconquerable, invincible *ant* timid; dastardly

valid • having such force as to compel serious attention and usu. acceptance *syn* sound, cogent, convincing, compelling, telling *rel* conclusive, determinative, definitive, decisive; effective, effectual; legal, lawful, licit; logical, analytical, subtle *ant* fallacious, sophistical

validate *syn* CONFIRM, authenticate, substantiate, verify, corroborate *rel* certify, attest, witness, vouch *ant* invalidate

valor *syn* HEROISM, prowess, gallantry *rel* courage, mettle, tenacity, spirit, resolution; indomitableness, unconquerableness, invincibility; fortitude, guts, sand, backbone

valorous *syn* BRAVE, courageous, unafraid, fearless, intrepid, valiant, dauntless, undaunted, doughty, bold, audacious *rel* venturesome, daring, adventurous; stout, sturdy, tenacious, stalwart, tough, strong

valuable *syn* COSTLY, precious, invaluable, priceless, expensive, dear *rel* estimated, appraised, evaluated; valued, appreciated, prized, treasured; esteemed, admired, respected

value *n, syn* WORTH *rel* price, charge, cost, expense; importance, consequence, significance, weight; use, usefulness, utility

value *vb* **1** *syn* ESTIMATE, appraise, evaluate, rate, assess, assay *rel* calculate, compute, reckon; judge, adjudge, adjudicate **2** *syn* APPRECIATE, prize, treasure, cherish *rel* esteem, respect, admire; love, enjoy, like; revere, reverence, venerate

vanish • to pass from view or out of existence *syn* evanesce, evaporate, disappear, fade *rel* escape, flee, fly; dispel, disperse, dissipate, scatter *ant* appear; loom

vanity *syn* PRIDE, vainglory *rel* self-esteem, self-love, conceit, egotism, egoism, amour propre; complacency, self-complacency, self-satisfaction, smugness, priggishness; show, ostentation, pretense

vanquish *syn* CONQUER, defeat, beat, lick, subdue, subjugate, reduce, overcome, surmount, overthrow, rout *rel* frustrate, foil, outwit, circumvent; overturn, subvert

vanquisher *syn* VICTOR, conqueror, winner, champion

vapid *syn* INSIPID, flat, jejune, banal, wishy-washy, inane *rel* soft, bland, gentle, mild; tame, subdued, submissive; mawkish, maudlin, soppy, slushy, mushy, sentimental

variable *syn* CHANGEABLE, protean, changeful, mutable *rel* fitful, spasmodic; fickle, mercurial, unstable, inconstant, capricious; mobile, movable *ant* constant; equable

variance *syn* DISCORD, contention, dissension, difference, strife, conflict *rel* diversity, divergency, disparateness; separation, division, severing, sundering; incongruousness, uncongeniality, incompatibility, discordance, discrepancy

variation *syn* CHANGE, alteration, modification *rel* variety, diversity; difference, divergence, divergency, dissimilarity; deviation, deflection, aberration

variegated · having a pattern involving different colors or shades of color *syn* parti-colored, motley, checkered, checked, pied, piebald, skewbald, dappled, freaked *rel* flecked, stippled, marbled, mottled, spattered, spotted

variety 1 · the quality or state of being composed of different parts, elements, or individuals *syn* diversity *rel* dissimilarity, unlikeness, difference, divergence, divergency; multifariousness, variousness; miscellaneousness, miscellany, heterogeneousness, heterogeneity, assortedness, assortment 2 · a group of related plants or animals narrower in scope than a species *syn* subspecies, race, breed, cultivar, strain, clone, stock

various 1 *syn* DIFFERENT, diverse, divergent, disparate *rel* distinct, separate; distinctive, peculiar, individual; varying, changing *ant* uniform; cognate 2 *syn* MANY, several, sundry, divers, numerous, multifarious *rel* miscellaneous, heterogeneous, assorted

vary 1 *syn* CHANGE, alter, modify *rel* transform, metamorphose, convert 2 *syn* DIFFER, disagree, dissent *rel* deviate, diverge, digress, depart; separate, divide, part

vast *syn* HUGE, immense, enormous, elephantine, mammoth, giant, gigantic, gigantean, colossal, gargantuan, Herculean, cyclopean, titanic, Brobdingnagian *rel* stupendous, tremendous, prodigious, monstrous; large, big, great; spacious, capacious

vault *vb, syn* JUMP, leap, spring, bound *rel* surmount, conquer; mount, ascend, rise, soar

vault *n, syn* JUMP, leap, spring, bound *rel* surmounting; rising, mounting, ascending, soaring

vaunt *syn* BOAST, brag, crow, gasconade *rel* parade, flaunt, exhibit, display, show; magnify, aggrandize, exalt

veer *syn* SWERVE, deviate, depart, digress, diverge *rel* shift, transfer, move; turn, divert, deflect, sheer

vehement *syn* INTENSE, fierce, exquisite, violent *rel* forcible, forceful, powerful, potent; fervid, perfervid, impassioned, passionate, ardent; furious, frantic, wild, rabid, delirious

vehicle *syn* MEAN, instrument, instrumentality, agent, agency, medium, organ, channel

veil *syn* COVER, overspread, envelop, wrap, shroud *rel* mask, cloak, camouflage, disguise; conceal, hide, secrete, screen

vein 1 *syn* MOOD, humor, temper *rel* disposition, complexion, temperament 2 *syn* TOUCH, strain, streak, suggestion, suspicion, soupçon, tincture, tinge, shade, smack, spice, dash

velocity *syn* SPEED, momentum, impetus, pace, headway *rel* celerity, legerity, alacrity; haste, hurry, expedition, dispatch

velvety *syn* SLEEK, silken, silky, satiny, glossy, slick

venal *syn* MERCENARY, hireling, hack *rel* corrupt, nefarious, iniquitous, vicious, infamous, flagitious; sordid, ignoble, mean

venerable *syn* OLD, ancient, antique, antiquated, archaic, obsolete, antediluvian *rel* venerated, revered, reverenced; aged

venerate *syn* REVERE, reverence, worship, adore *rel* esteem, respect, admire, regard; cherish, prize, treasure, value, appreciate

veneration *syn* REVERENCE, worship, adoration *rel* deference, homage, obeisance, honor

vengeance *syn* RETALIATION, revenge, retribution, reprisal *rel* punishment, disciplining, discipline, castigation; avenging, revenging; recompensing, recompense, repayment

vengeful *syn* VINDICTIVE, revengeful *rel* rancorous, inimical, hostile, antagonistic; malevolent, spiteful, malicious, malignant

venial • not warranting punishment or the imposition of a penalty *syn* pardonable *ant* heinous; mortal

venom *syn* POISON, toxin, virus, bane

venomous *syn* POISONOUS, virulent, toxic, mephitic, pestilent, pestilential, miasmic, miasmatic, miasmal *rel* malignant, malign, malevolent, malicious; baleful, malefic, maleficent, sinister; pernicious, baneful, noxious, deleterious, detrimental

vent *syn* EXPRESS, utter, voice, broach, air, ventilate *rel* reveal, disclose, discover, divulge; assert, declare, aver, avow *ant* bridle

ventilate *syn* EXPRESS, vent, air, utter, voice, broach *rel* expose, exhibit, display, show; disclose, divulge, discover, reveal; publish, advertise, broadcast, declare

venture • to expose to risk or loss *syn* hazard, risk, chance, jeopardize, endanger, imperil

venturesome *syn* ADVENTUROUS, daring, daredevil, rash, reckless, foolhardy *rel* bold, audacious, intrepid, brave; stout, sturdy, stalwart, strong

veracity *syn* TRUTH, verity, verisimilitude *rel* integrity, probity, honesty, honor

verbiage • an excess of words usu. of little or obscure content *syn* redundancy, tautology, pleonasm, circumlocution, periphrasis *rel* wordiness, verboseness, prolixity, diffuseness

verbose *syn* WORDY, prolix, diffuse, redundant *rel* grandiloquent, magniloquent, flowery, bombastic; loquacious, voluble, glib, garrulous, talkative *ant* laconic

verge *syn* BORDER, edge, rim, brim, brink, margin *rel* bound, limit, end, confine; circumference, perimeter, compass

verify *syn* CONFIRM, corroborate, substantiate, authenticate, validate *rel* prove, test, try, demonstrate; certify, attest, witness, vouch; establish, settle

verisimilitude *syn* TRUTH, veracity, verity *rel* agreement, accordance, harmonizing, harmony, correspondence; likeness, similitude, resemblance

veritable *syn* AUTHENTIC, genuine, bona fide *rel* actual, real, true *ant* factitious

verity *syn* TRUTH, veracity, verisimilitude

vernacular **1** *syn* DIALECT, patois, lingo, jargon, cant, argot, slang **2** *syn* BARBARISM, corruption, impropriety, solecism, vulgarism

versatile • having a wide range of skills or abilities or many different uses *syn* many-sided, all=

around *rel* gifted, talented; accomplished, finished, consummate; ready, apt, quick, prompt

verse *syn* PARAGRAPH, article, clause, plank, count

versed *syn* CONVERSANT *rel* learned, erudite; informed, acquainted; intimate, familiar

versifier *syn* POET, rhymer, rhymester, poetaster, bard, minstrel, troubadour

version 1 *syn* TRANSLATION, paraphrase, metaphrase 2 *syn* ACCOUNT, report, story, chronicle

vertebrae *syn* SPINE, backbone, back, chine

vertical · being at right angles to a base line *syn* perpendicular, plumb *ant* horizontal

vertiginous *syn* GIDDY, dizzy, swimming, dazzled *rel* reeling, whirling, staggering, tottering

verve *syn* VIGOR, vim, spirit, dash, esprit, punch, élan, drive *rel* vivacity, animation, liveliness; buoyancy, resiliency, elasticity

very 1 *syn* SAME, selfsame, identical, identic, equivalent, equal, tantamount 2 *syn* MERE, bare

vessel *syn* BOAT, ship, craft

vestige *syn* TRACE, track *rel* print, imprint, impression, stamp

vex *syn* ANNOY, irk, bother *rel* chafe, fret, gall, abrade; irritate, exasperate, nettle, provoke *ant* please, regale

viands *syn* FOOD, provisions, comestibles, feed, victuals, provender, fodder, forage

vibrant *syn* RESONANT, sonorous, ringing, resounding, orotund *rel* pulsating, pulsing, throbbing, beating; thrilling, electrifying

vibrate *syn* SWING, sway, oscillate, fluctuate, pendulate, waver, undulate *rel* pulsate, pulse, beat, throb, palpitate; quiver, quaver, tremble, shake

vice 1 *syn* FAULT, failing, frailty, foible *rel* defect, flaw, blemish; infirmity, weakness 2 *syn* OFFENSE, sin, crime, scandal *rel* transgression, trespass, violation, breach, infraction; immorality; evil, ill *ant* virtue

vicinity *syn* LOCALITY, neighborhood, district *rel* region, area; section, sector, part

vicious · highly reprehensible or offensive in character, nature, or conduct *syn* villainous, iniquitous, nefarious, flagitious, infamous, corrupt, degenerate *rel* debased, depraved, debauched, perverted; dissolute, profligate, abandoned, reprobate; lewd, lascivious, wanton, lecherous, libidinous, licentious *ant* virtuous

vicissitude 1 *syn* CHANGE, alteration, mutation, permutation *rel* turning, rotation, revolving, revolution; reversal, transposition; succession, progression, sequence, series; variety, diversity 2 *syn* DIFFICULTY, hardship, rigor *rel* misfortune, mischance, adversity; trial, tribulation, affliction

victim · one killed or injured for the ends of the one who kills or injures *syn* prey, quarry

victor · one that defeats an enemy or opponent *syn* winner, conqueror, champion, vanquisher

victory · a successful outcome in a contest or struggle *syn* conquest, triumph *rel* winning, gaining; ascendancy, supremacy; control, sway, dominion, command, power, authority *ant* defeat

victuals *syn* FOOD, feed, viands, provisions, comestibles, provender, fodder, forage

vie *syn* RIVAL, compete, emulate *rel* contend, fight; strive, struggle, essay, endeavor

view *n* 1 *syn* LOOK, sight, glance, glimpse, peep, peek *rel* scrutiny, scanning, inspection, examination 2 *syn* OPINION, belief, conviction, persuasion, sentiment *rel* idea, thought, concept, conception; inference, deduction, conclusion, judgment

view *vb, syn* SEE, survey, contemplate, observe, note, remark, notice, perceive, discern, behold, descry, espy *rel* scan, scrutinize, inspect, examine; consider, regard, account

viewpoint *syn* POINT OF VIEW, standpoint, angle, slant *rel* position, stand, attitude; ground, reason

vigilant *syn* WATCHFUL, alert, wide-awake *rel* anxious, agog, keen, avid, eager; circumspect, wary, chary, cautious; quick, ready, prompt; sharp, acute

vigor • a quality of force, forcefulness, or energy *syn* vim, spirit, dash, esprit, verve, punch, élan, drive *rel* strength, force, power, might, energy; soundness, healthiness; virility

vigorous • having or showing great vitality and force *syn* energetic, strenuous, lusty, nervous *rel* virile, manly, manful; muscular, athletic, sinewy, husky; stout, sturdy, stalwart, strong, tough *ant* languorous; lethargic

vile *syn* BASE, low *rel* depraved, corrupted, perverted, debased, debauched; coarse, vulgar, obscene, gross; foul, filthy, nasty, dirty; mean, abject, sordid; offensive, repulsive, revolting, loathsome

vilify *syn* MALIGN, traduce, asperse, calumniate, defame, slander, libel *rel* abuse, outrage, mistreat, misuse; assail, attack; revile, vituperate, berate *ant* eulogize

villain • a low, mean, reprehensible person utterly lacking in principles *syn* scoundrel, blackguard, knave, rascal, rogue, scamp, rapscallion, miscreant *rel* offender, sinner; criminal, malefactor

villainous *syn* VICIOUS, iniquitous, nefarious, flagitious, infamous, corrupt, degenerate *rel* debased, depraved, perverted; atrocious, outrageous, heinous; dissolute, profligate, abandoned

vim *syn* VIGOR, spirit, dash, esprit, verve, punch, élan, drive *rel* force, strength, power, energy

vindicate **1** *syn* MAINTAIN, justify, defend, assert *rel* support, uphold, advocate **2** *syn* EXCULPATE, exonerate, absolve, acquit *rel* disprove, refute, confute; defend, protect, shield, guard *ant* calumniate

vindictive • showing or motivated by a desire for vengeance *syn* revengeful, vengeful *rel* implacable, unrelenting, relentless, merciless, grim; spiteful, malicious, malignant, malign

violation *syn* BREACH, infraction, transgression, trespass, infringement, contravention *rel* offense, sin, vice, crime, scandal; desecration, profanation, sacrilege, blasphemy; invading, invasion, encroachment, entrenchment

violence *syn* FORCE, compulsion, coercion, duress, constraint, restraint *rel* vehemence, intensity, fierceness; effort, exertion, pains, trouble; attack, assault, onslaught, onset

violent *syn* INTENSE, vehement, fierce, exquisite *rel* powerful, potent, forceful, forcible; excessive, immoderate, inordinate, extreme, extravagant

virago • a loud, overbearing, ill-tempered woman *syn* amazon, termagant, scold, shrew, vixen

virgin *syn* UNMARRIED, single, celibate, maiden

virginal *syn* YOUTHFUL, maiden, boyish, juvenile, puerile *rel* chaste, pure, modest, decent; fresh, new

virile *syn* MALE, manful, manly, masculine, manlike, mannish *ant* effeminate; impotent

virtual *syn* IMPLICIT, constructive *ant* actual

virtually · not absolutely or actually, yet so nearly so that the difference is negligible *syn* practically, morally

virtue 1 *syn* GOODNESS, morality, rectitude *rel* honor, honesty, integrity, probity; fidelity, piety, fealty, loyalty; righteousness, nobility, virtuousness *ant* vice 2 *syn* EXCELLENCE, merit, perfection *rel* worth, value, effectiveness, efficacy, effectualness; strength, might, power, force

virtuoso *syn* EXPERT, adept, artist, artiste, wizard

virtuous *syn* MORAL, ethical, righteous, noble *rel* pure, chaste, modest, decent; upright, just, honorable *ant* vicious

virulent *syn* POISONOUS, venomous, toxic, mephitic, pestilent, pestilential, miasmic, miasmatic, miasmal *rel* deadly, mortal, fatal, lethal; pernicious, noxious, baneful, deleterious; malignant, malign, malicious

visage *syn* FACE, countenance, physiognomy, mug, puss

vision 1 *syn* REVELATION, prophecy, apocalypse 2 *syn* FANCY, fantasy, phantasy, phantasm, dream, daydream, nightmare *rel* illusion, delusion, hallucination, mirage; imagination

visionary *syn* IMAGINARY, fanciful, fantastic, chimerical, quixotic *rel* romantic, sentimental, maudlin; utopian, ambitious, pretentious; ideal, transcendent, transcendental; illusory, seeming, apparent

visit · a usu. brief stay with another as an act of friendship or courtesy *syn* visitation, call

visitant *syn* VISITOR, guest, caller

visitation 1 *syn* VISIT, call 2 *syn* TRIAL, tribulation, affliction, cross *rel* misfortune, mischance, adversity; calamity, catastrophe, disaster; hardship, vicissitude, difficulty

visitor · one who visits another *syn* visitant, guest, caller

vital 1 *syn* LIVING, alive, animate, animated *rel* vigorous, energetic, lusty; active, live, dynamic 2 *syn* ESSENTIAL, fundamental, cardinal *rel* important, significant, consequential, weighty, momentous; indispensable, requisite, necessary, needful

vitalize · to arouse to activity, animation, or life *syn* energize, activate *rel* animate, quicken, enliven, vivify; stimulate, galvanize, excite, provoke *ant* atrophy

vitiate *syn* DEBASE, deprave, corrupt, pervert, debauch *rel* pollute, defile, taint, contaminate; degrade, demean, abase; impair, spoil, injure, damage; annul, invalidate, nullify

vitiated *syn* DEBASED, depraved, corrupted, debauched, perverted *rel* defiled, polluted, contaminated, tainted; impaired, spoiled, injured; invalidated, annulled

vituperate *syn* SCOLD, revile, berate, rate, upbraid, tongue-lash, jaw, bawl, chew out, wig, rail *rel* condemn, denounce, censure, blame, reprehend, reprobate, criticize; vilify, asperse, traduce, malign, calumniate; execrate, objurgate

vituperation *syn* ABUSE, invective, obloquy, scurrility, billingsgate *rel* animadversion, aspersion, stricture, reflection; attack, assault, onslaught, onset; condemnation, denunciation, censuring, censure; vilifying, vilification, maligning, calumniation *ant* acclaim, praise

vituperative *syn* ABUSIVE, opprobrious, contumelious, scurrilous *rel* coarse, vulgar, gross, obscene; insulting, offending, outraging; condemning, condemnatory, denouncing, denunciatory

vivacious *syn* LIVELY, animated, gay, sprightly *rel* buoyant, effervescent, volatile; merry, blithe, jocund; frolicsome, sportive, playful *ant* languid

vivid *syn* GRAPHIC, picturesque, pictorial *rel* sharp, keen, acute; dramatic, dramaturgic, theatrical; expressive, eloquent, meaningful; nervous, lusty, vigorous; clear, lucid, perspicuous

vivify *syn* QUICKEN, animate, enliven *rel* vitalize, energize, activate; renew, restore, refresh; stir, rouse, arouse; stimulate, galvanize, excite, provoke

vixen *syn* VIRAGO, shrew, scold, termagant, amazon

vocable *syn* WORD, term

vocabulary *syn* LANGUAGE, phraseology, diction, phrasing, style

vocal **1** · uttered by the voice or having to do with such utterance *syn* articulate, oral **2** · being able to express oneself clearly or easily *syn* articulate, fluent, eloquent, voluble, glib *rel* expressing, voicing, venting; expressive, sententious, eloquent

vociferate *syn* ROAR, bellow, bluster, bawl, clamor, howl, ululate *rel* shout, yell, shriek, scream, screech, holler

vociferation *syn* ROAR, bellow, bluster, bawl, ululation

vociferous · so loud or insistent as to compel attention *syn* clamorous, blatant, strident, boisterous, obstreperous *rel* noisy, sounding; bewildering, distracting

vogue *syn* FASHION, mode, style, fad, rage, craze, dernier cri, cry

voice *syn* EXPRESS, utter, vent, broach, air, ventilate *rel* reveal, disclose, tell, discover, divulge; communicate, impart; speak, talk

void *adj* **1** *syn* EMPTY, vacant, blank, vacuous *rel* exhausted, depleted, drained; bare, barren; hollow, empty, nugatory, vain **2** *syn* DEVOID, destitute

void *n, syn* HOLE, vacuum, hollow, cavity, pocket *rel* emptiness, vacancy, vacuity; abyss, gulf, abysm

void *vb, syn* ANNUL, vacate, abrogate, quash

volatile *syn* ELASTIC, effervescent, buoyant, expansive, resilient *rel* unstable, mercurial, inconstant, fickle, capricious; light-minded, frivolous, flippant, flighty; variable, changeable, protean

volatility *syn* LIGHTNESS, light-mindedness, levity, frivolity, flippancy, flightiness *rel* vivaciousness, vivacity, gaiety, liveliness, animation, sprightliness; unstableness, instability, mercurialness, inconstancy; variability, changeableness

volcano *syn* MOUNTAIN, mount, peak, alp, mesa

volition *syn* WILL, conation *rel* choice, election, option

volubility *syn* TALKATIVENESS, glibness, garrulity, loquacity *rel* fluency, eloquence, articulateness

voluble **1** *syn* VOCAL, fluent, glib, eloquent, articulate *rel* copious, abundant, plentiful; easy, facile, effortless, smooth *ant* stuttering, stammering **2** *syn* TALKATIVE, glib, garrulous, loquacious *ant* curt

volume **1** *syn* SIZE, magnitude, extent, dimensions, area **2** *syn* BULK, mass

voluntary · done or brought about of one's own will *syn* intentional, deliberate, willful, willing *rel* chosen, elected, opted; free, independent, autonomous *ant* involuntary; instinctive

voluptuous *syn* SENSUOUS, luxurious, sybaritic, epicurean, sensual *rel* indulging, indulgent, pampering; luxurious, opulent, sumptuous *ant* ascetic

vomit *syn* BELCH, burp, disgorge, regurgitate, spew, throw up *rel* eject, expel, oust

voracious · excessively greedy *syn* gluttonous, ravenous, ravening, rapacious *rel* greedy, grasping, acquisitive, covetous; satiating, sating, surfeiting, gorging

vortex *syn* EDDY, whirlpool, maelstrom

votary *syn* ADDICT, devotee, habitué *rel* enthusiast, fanatic, zealot, bigot

vote *syn* SUFFRAGE, franchise, ballot

vouch *syn* CERTIFY, attest, witness *rel* support, uphold; confirm, substantiate, verify, corroborate

vouchsafe *syn* GRANT, accord, concede, award *rel* give, bestow, confer, present; condescend, deign, stoop; oblige, accommodate, favor

voyage *syn* JOURNEY, tour, trip, excursion, cruise, expedition, jaunt, pilgrimage

vulgar **1** *syn* COMMON, ordinary, familiar, popular *rel* universal, general; prevailing, prevalent, current, rife; usual, customary; crude, rude, rough, uncouth; sordid, ignoble, mean **2** *syn* COARSE, gross, obscene, ribald *rel* low, base, vile; offensive, loathsome, repulsive, revolting; indelicate, indecent, indecorous

vulgarism *syn* BARBARISM, corruption, impropriety, solecism, vernacular

W

wage, wages • the price paid a person for his or her labor or services *syn* salary, stipend, fee, pay, hire, emolument *rel* remuneration, recompensing, recompense

wager *syn* BET, stake, pot, ante

waggish *syn* PLAYFUL, sportive, frolicsome, impish, mischievous, roguish *rel* facetious, jocose, jocular, humorous, witty; jovial, jolly, merry; comic, comical, laughable, droll, ludicrous, funny

wail *syn* CRY, weep, whimper, blubber, keen *rel* mourn, grieve; lament, bewail, bemoan, deplore; moan, sob, sigh, groan

wait *syn* STAY, remain, abide, tarry, linger *rel* delay, loiter

waive *syn* RELINQUISH, cede, yield, resign, abandon, surrender, leave *rel* forgo, forbear, sacrifice; concede, grant, allow

waken *syn* STIR, awaken, arouse, rouse, rally *rel* excite, stimulate, quicken, galvanize, provoke; fire, kindle, light; impel, move, actuate, drive *ant* subdue

wall *syn* ENCLOSE, envelop, fence, pen, coop, corral, cage *rel* surround, environ, encircle, hem; confine, circumscribe, limit, restrict

wallow • to move clumsily and in a debased or pitable condition *syn* welter, grovel *rel* crawl, creep; defile, pollute, contaminate, taint; debase, debauch, corrupt, deprave, pervert

wan *syn* PALE, pallid, ashen, ashy, livid *rel* blanched, whitened, decolorized; languid, languishing, languorous; haggard, cadaverous, worn

wander • to move about from place to place more or less aimlessly and without a plan *syn* stray, roam, ramble, rove, range, prowl, gad, gallivant, traipse, meander

wane *syn* ABATE, subside, ebb *rel* decrease, dwindle, lessen, diminish *ant* wax

want *vb* **1** *syn* LACK, need, require *rel* demand, claim, exact **2** *syn* DESIRE, wish, crave, covet *rel* long, yearn, hanker, pine, hunger, thirst; aspire, pant, aim

want *n* **1** *syn* LACK, dearth, absence, defect, privation *rel* need, necessity, exigency; deficiency **2** *syn* POVERTY, destitution, indigence, privation, penury *rel* pinch, strait, pass, exigency, juncture; meagerness, scantiness, exiguousness

wanton **1** *syn* LICENTIOUS, libertine, lewd, lustful, lascivious, libidinous, lecherous *rel* immoral, unmoral, amoral; abandoned, profligate, dissolute, reprobate *ant* chaste **2** *syn* SUPEREROGATORY, uncalled-for, gratuitous *rel* malicious, malevolent, spiteful; wayward, contrary, perverse

war *syn* CONTEND, battle, fight *rel* resist, withstand, combat, oppose; strive, struggle, endeavor, essay, attempt

warble *syn* SING, troll, carol, descant, trill, hymn, chant, intone

ward *syn* PREVENT, avert, preclude, obviate *rel* block, bar, obstruct, impede, hinder; forestall, anticipate, prevent; frustrate, balk, thwart, foil *ant* conduce to

wariness *syn* CAUTION, chariness, circumspection, calculation *rel* alertness, watchfulness; prudence, discretion, foresight, forethought, providence *ant* foolhardiness; brashness

warlike *syn* MARTIAL, military *rel* bellicose, belligerent, pugnacious, combative, contentious; fighting, warring, contending, battling

warm *syn* TENDER, warmhearted, sympathetic, compassionate, responsive *rel* loving, affectionate; cordial, gracious, affable; ardent, fervent, passionate; sincere, heartfelt, hearty, wholehearted *ant* cool; austere

warmhearted *syn* TENDER, warm, sympathetic, compassionate, responsive *rel* loving, affectionate; kind, kindly, benign, benignant; heartfelt, hearty, wholehearted, sincere *ant* coldhearted

warn • to let one know of approaching danger or risk *syn* forewarn, caution *rel* apprise, inform, advise, notify; admonish, reprove; counsel

warp *syn* DEFORM, distort, contort *rel* twist, bend, curve; injure, damage, impair, mar

warrant **1** *syn* ASSERT, declare, profess, affirm, aver, protest, avouch, avow, predicate *rel* state, relate; maintain, assert; assure, ensure, insure **2** *syn* JUSTIFY *rel* vindicate, maintain; sanction, approve, endorse; authorize

wary *syn* CAUTIOUS, chary, circumspect, calculating *rel* alert, watchful; prudent, discreet, foresighted, forethoughtful, provident *ant* foolhardy; brash

waspish *syn* IRRITABLE, snappish, fractious, peevish, petulant, pettish, huffy, fretful, querulous *rel* testy, touchy, cranky, cross, irascible; impatient; contrary, perverse; spiteful, malicious

waste *n* **1** • an area of the earth unsuitable for cultivation or general habitation *syn* desert, badlands, wilderness **2** *syn* REFUSE, rubbish, trash, debris, garbage, offal

waste *vb* **1** *syn* RAVAGE, devastate, sack, pillage, despoil, spoliate *rel* plunder, loot, rob, rifle; destroy, demolish; ruin, wreck *ant* conserve, save **2** • to spend or expend freely and usu. foolishly or futilely *syn* squander, dissipate, fritter, consume *rel* spend, expend, disburse; distribute, dispense; scatter, disperse, dispel; deplete, drain, exhaust, impoverish *ant* save; conserve

wasted *syn* HAGGARD, pinched, cadaverous, worn, careworn *rel* gaunt, scrawny, skinny, angular, rawboned, lean

waster *syn* SPENDTHRIFT, profligate, prodigal, wastrel *rel* idler, loafer, lounger; squanderer, dissipater, fritterer

wastrel *syn* SPENDTHRIFT, profligate, prodigal, waster *rel* reprobate, outcast; loafer, idler, lounger; scoundrel, rascal, rogue, scamp, villain

watch 1 *syn* TEND, mind, attend *rel* guard, protect, shield, safeguard, defend 2 *syn* SEE, look *rel* gaze, gape, stare, glare; scrutinize, scan, inspect, examine

watchful · on the lookout esp. for danger or for opportunities *syn* vigilant, wide-awake, alert *rel* cautious, wary, chary, circumspect; quick, ready, prompt

waterlog *syn* SOAK, drench, saturate, steep, impregnate, sop

wave *syn* SWING, flourish, brandish, shake, thrash *rel* wield, swing, manipulate, handle, ply; undulate, sway, swing, fluctuate; shake, quiver, quaver

waver 1 *syn* SWING, fluctuate, oscillate, pendulate, vibrate, sway, undulate *rel* flicker, flutter, hover, flit, flitter; quiver, quaver, tremble, shake 2 *syn* HESITATE, falter, vacillate *rel* balk, boggle, stickle, scruple, demur, shy; fluctuate, oscillate, swing

way 1 · a track or path traversed in going from one place to another *syn* route, course, passage, pass, artery 2 *syn* METHOD, mode, manner, fashion, system *rel* procedure, process, proceeding; plan, design, scheme; practice, habit, habitude, custom, use, usage, wont

waylay *syn* SURPRISE, ambush *rel* attack, assault, assail; prevent, forestall

wayward *syn* CONTRARY, perverse, froward, restive, balky *rel* insubordinate, contumacious, rebellious; refractory, recalcitrant, intractable, headstrong, unruly; capricious, inconstant, fickle, unstable

weak · lacking physical, mental, or moral strength *syn* feeble, frail, fragile, infirm, decrepit *rel* debilitated, weakened, enfeebled; powerless, impotent *ant* strong

weaken · to lose or cause to lose strength, vigor, or energy *syn* enfeeble, debilitate, undermine, sap, cripple, disable *rel* enervate, emasculate, unnerve, unman; impair, injure, damage; dilute, thin, attenuate, extenuate *ant* strengthen

wealthy *syn* RICH, affluent, opulent *ant* indigent

wean *syn* ESTRANGE, alienate, disaffect *rel* separate, part, divide, sunder, sever, divorce *ant* addict

weariless *syn* INDEFATIGABLE, unwearying, unwearied, tireless, untiring, unflagging *rel* dogged, pertinacious, obstinate; assiduous, sedulous, diligent, busy

wearisome *syn* IRKSOME, tiresome, tedious, boring *rel* fatiguing, exhausting, fagging, tiring; dull, slow, stupid

weary *syn* TIRE, fatigue, exhaust, jade, fag, tucker *rel* debilitate, enfeeble, weaken; depress, oppress, weigh

weave · to make a textile or to form an article by interlacing threads or strands of material *syn* knit, crochet, braid, plait, tat

wedding *syn* MARRIAGE, matrimony, nuptial, espousal, wedlock

wedlock *syn* MARRIAGE, matrimony, nuptial, espousal, wedding

wee *syn* SMALL, diminutive, tiny, teeny, weeny, little, minute, microscopic, miniature, petite

weeny *syn* SMALL, tiny, teeny, wee, diminutive, minute, microscopic, miniature, little

weep *syn* CRY, wail, keen, whimper, blubber *rel* bewail, bemoan, lament, deplore; sob, moan, sigh, groan

weigh 1 *syn* CONSIDER, study, contemplate, excogitate *rel* ponder, meditate, ruminate, muse; think, reflect, cogitate, reason, speculate **2** *syn* BURDEN, encumber, cumber, weight, load, lade, tax, charge, saddle *rel* balance, ballast, trim, poise, stabilize; set, settle **3** *syn* DEPRESS, oppress *rel* worry, annoy, harass, harry; torment, torture, afflict, try, rack

weight *n* **1** *syn* IMPORTANCE, significance, moment, consequence, import *rel* worth, value; magnitude, size, extent; seriousness, gravity **2** *syn* INFLUENCE, authority, prestige, credit *rel* effectiveness, efficacy; emphasis, stress; powerfulness, potency, forcefulness, forcibleness

weight *vb* **1** *syn* ADULTERATE, load, sophisticate **2** *syn* BURDEN, encumber, cumber, weigh, load, lade, tax, charge, saddle *rel* see WEIGH 2

weighty *syn* HEAVY, ponderous, cumbrous, cumbersome, hefty *rel* onerous, burdensome, oppressive, exacting

weird · fearfully and mysteriously strange or fantastic *syn* eerie, uncanny *rel* mysterious, inscrutable; fearful, awful, dreadful, horrific; strange, odd, queer, curious, peculiar

welcome *syn* PLEASANT, pleasing, agreeable, grateful, gratifying *rel* satisfying, contenting; congenial, sympathetic, consonant *ant* unwelcome

well *syn* HEALTHY, sound, wholesome, robust, hale *ant* unwell, ill

well-nigh *syn* NEARLY, almost, approximately

well-timed *syn* SEASONABLE, timely, opportune, pat *rel* apt, happy, felicitous, appropriate, fitting, fit

welter *syn* WALLOW, grovel *rel* struggle, strive, attempt

wet · covered or more or less soaked with liquid *syn* damp, dank, moist, humid *rel* soaked, saturated, drenched, waterlogged *ant* dry

wharf · a structure used by boats and ships for taking on or landing cargo or passengers *syn* dock, pier, quay, slip, berth, jetty, levee

wheedle *syn* COAX, blandish, cajole *rel* entice, inveigle, lure, seduce, decoy

wheel *syn* TURN, revolve, rotate, gyrate, circle, spin, twirl, whirl, swirl, pirouette, eddy

while · to pass time, esp. leisure time, without boredom or in pleasant ways *syn* wile, beguile, fleet *rel* divert, amuse, entertain

whim *syn* CAPRICE, freak, fancy, whimsy, conceit, vagary, crotchet *rel* inclination, disposition; fancy, fantasy, vision, dream; notion, idea

whimper *syn* CRY, weep, blubber, wail, keen

whimsy *syn* CAPRICE, freak, fancy, whim, conceit, vagary, crotchet *rel* see WHIM

whirl **1** *syn* TURN, twirl, spin, wheel, swirl, revolve, rotate, gyrate, circle, pirouette, eddy **2** *syn* REEL, stagger, totter

whirlpool *syn* EDDY, maelstrom, vortex

whirlwind · a rotating windstorm of limited extent *syn* whirly *rel* cyclone, typhoon, hurricane, tornado, waterspout, twister

whirly *syn* WHIRLWIND

whit *syn* PARTICLE, mite, jot, iota, bit, smidgen, tittle, atom

whiten **1** · to change from an original color to white or almost to white *syn* blanch, bleach, decolorize, etiolate *ant* blacken **2** *syn* PALLIATE, whitewash, gloze, gloss, extenuate *rel* see WHITEWASH

whitewash *syn* PALLIATE, whiten, gloze, gloss, extenuate *rel* disguise, cloak, mask, dissemble, camouflage; condone, excuse

whole *adj* **1** *syn* PERFECT, entire,

intact *rel* sound, well, healthy, robust, wholesome; complete, plenary, full **2** · having every constituent element or individual *syn* entire, total, all, gross *ant* partial

whole *n, syn* SUM, total, aggregate, amount, number, quantity *ant* part; constituent; particular

wholehearted *syn* SINCERE, whole-souled, heartfelt, hearty, unfeigned *rel* ardent, fervent, impassioned, passionate; genuine, bona fide, authentic; earnest, serious

wholesale *syn* INDISCRIMINATE, sweeping

wholesome **1** *syn* HEALTHFUL, healthy, salubrious, salutary, hygienic, sanitary *ant* noxious **2** *syn* HEALTHY, sound, robust, hale, well *rel* strong, sturdy, stalwart, stout

whole-souled *syn* SINCERE, wholehearted, heartfelt, hearty, unfeigned *rel* see WHOLEHEARTED

whoop *vb, syn* SHOUT, yell, shriek, scream, screech, squeal, holler

whoop *n, syn* SHOUT, yell, shriek, scream, screech, squeal, holler

wicked *syn* BAD, evil, ill, naughty *rel* immoral, unmoral, amoral; iniquitous, vicious, villainous; abandoned, reprobate, profligate, dissolute

wide *syn* BROAD, deep *rel* spacious, capacious, ample; extended, extensive *ant* strait

wide-awake *syn* WATCHFUL, vigilant, alert *rel* aware, alive, awake, conscious, sensible

wield *syn* HANDLE, swing, manipulate, ply *rel* flourish, brandish, shake, wave; control, direct, manage, conduct; exercise, drill, practice

wig *syn* SCOLD, tongue-lash, jaw, bawl, chew out, berate, upbraid, rate, rail, revile, vituperate *rel* reprimand, reproach, rebuke, reprove, chide

wild *syn* FURIOUS, frantic, frenzied, frenetic, delirious, rabid *rel* distracted, bewildered, perplexed, puzzled; confused, muddled, addled; agitated, upset, perturbed, discomposed; mad, crazy, demented, deranged, insane

wilderness *syn* WASTE, desert, badlands

wile *n, syn* TRICK, artifice, feint, ruse, maneuver, stratagem, gambit, ploy *rel* deception, fraud, trickery, chicanery, chicane; cunning, deceit, duplicity, dissimulation, guile

wile *vb, syn* WHILE, beguile, fleet *rel* see WHILE

will *n* · the power or act of making or effecting a choice or decision *syn* volition, conation *rel* intention, intent, purpose, design; choice, election, preference; character, disposition, temper, temperament

will *vb* · to give to another by will *syn* bequeath, devise, leave, legate

willful **1** *syn* VOLUNTARY, deliberate, intentional, willing *rel* determined, decided, resolved; intended, purposed; obstinate, stubborn, dogged, pertinacious **2** *syn* UNRULY, headstrong, intractable, refractory, recalcitrant, ungovernable *rel* rebellious, contumacious, factious, insubordinate; obstinate, mulish, bullheaded, pigheaded *ant* biddable

willing *syn* VOLUNTARY, intentional, deliberate, willful *rel* prone, open, liable; inclined, predisposed, disposed *ant* unwilling

wilt *syn* DROOP, flag, sag *rel* slump, sink, drop, fall; languish

wily *syn* SLY, cunning, crafty, tricky, foxy, insidious, guileful, artful *rel* astute, sagacious, shrewd; deceitful, cunning

win *syn* GET, gain, acquire, obtain, procure, secure *rel* achieve, accomplish, effect, perform; attain, reach, compass; induce, persuade, prevail *ant* lose

wince *syn* RECOIL, flinch, shrink,

blench, quail *rel* cringe, cower, fawn; balk, shy, stick, stickle, demur; squirm, writhe

wind · to follow a circular, spiral, or writhing course *syn* coil, curl, twist, twine, wreathe, entwine *rel* bend, curve; surround, encircle, circle, gird, girdle; enclose, envelop

winding · curving repeatedly first one way and then another *syn* sinuous, serpentine, tortuous, flexuous *rel* curving, bending, twisting; circuitous, indirect, roundabout; crooked, devious; meandering, wandering *ant* straight

window · an opening in the wall of a building that is usu. covered with glass and serves to admit light and air *syn* casement, oriel

wing *syn* ANNEX, ell, extension

wink · to close and open one's eyelids quickly *syn* blink

winner *syn* VICTOR, conqueror, champion, vanquisher *ant* loser

winning *syn* SWEET, engaging, winsome, dulcet *rel* charming, alluring, captivating, enchanting, bewitching, attractive

winsome *syn* SWEET, engaging, winning, dulcet *rel* see WINNING

wipe *syn* EXTERMINATE, extirpate, eradicate, uproot, deracinate *rel* obliterate, erase, efface, expunge, blot out; abolish, extinguish, annihilate; destroy, demolish

wisdom *syn* SENSE, judgment, gumption *rel* discretion, prudence, foresight; judiciousness, sageness, saneness, sapience; sagacity, perspicacity, shrewdness *ant* folly; injudiciousness

wise · exercising or involving sound judgment *syn* sage, sapient, judicious, prudent, sensible, sane *rel* discreet, prudent, foresighted; cautious, circumspect, calculating; sagacious, perspicacious, shrewd, astute; knowing, intelligent, alert, bright, smart *ant* simple

wisecrack *syn* JOKE, crack, gag, jest, jape, quip, witticism

wish *syn* DESIRE, want, crave, covet *rel* long, yearn, hanker, pine, hunger, thirst; aspire, pant, aim; hope, expect

wishy-washy *syn* INSIPID, vapid, flat, jejune, banal, inane *rel* spiritless, enervated, languid, listless; weak, feeble; diluted, attenuated, thinned

wit **1** *syn* MIND, intelligence, brain, intellect, soul, psyche *rel* reason, understanding, intuition; comprehension, apprehension; sagaciousness, sagacity, perspicaciousness, perspicacity **2** · a mode of expression intended to arouse amusement *syn* humor, irony, sarcasm, satire, repartee *rel* quick-wittedness, alertness, brightness, brilliancy, cleverness, smartness, intelligence; raillery, badinage, persiflage; pungency, piquancy, poignancy

witchcraft *syn* MAGIC, wizardry, witchery, sorcery, alchemy, thaumaturgy

witchery *syn* MAGIC, sorcery, witchcraft, wizardry, alchemy, thaumaturgy

with *syn* BY, through

withdraw *syn* GO, leave, depart, quit, retire *rel* abscond, decamp, escape, flee, fly; retreat, recede

wither · to lose freshness and substance by or as if by loss of natural moisture *syn* shrivel, wizen *rel* dry, parch, desiccate; shrink, contract, constrict

withhold *syn* KEEP, detain, keep back, keep out, retain, hold, hold back, reserve *rel* restrain, curb, check, bridle, inhibit; refuse, decline

withstand *syn* RESIST, contest, oppose, fight, combat, conflict, antagonize *rel* bear, endure, stand, tolerate, suffer; thwart, baffle, balk, foil, frustrate; assail, attack, assault

witness *n, syn* SPECTATOR, observer, beholder, looker-on, onlooker, eyewitness, bystander, kibitzer

witness *vb, syn* CERTIFY, attest, vouch *rel* subscribe, assent

witticism *syn* JOKE, jest, jape, quip, wisecrack, crack, gag *rel* wit, humor, sarcasm, satire, irony, repartee

witty • provoking or intended to provoke laughter *syn* humorous, facetious, jocular, jocose *rel* amusing, diverting, entertaining; sparkling, scintillating; caustic, mordant, acrid, scathing; penetrating, piercing, probing

wizard *syn* EXPERT, adept, artist, artiste, virtuoso

wizardry *syn* MAGIC, witchcraft, witchery, sorcery, alchemy, thaumaturgy

wizen *syn* WITHER, shrivel *rel* shrink, contract; dwindle, diminish, reduce, decrease

wobble *syn* SHAKE, teeter, totter, shimmy, quiver, shiver, shudder, quaver, quake, tremble, dither

woe *syn* SORROW, grief, anguish, heartache, heartbreak, regret *rel* distress, suffering, misery, agony, dolor; lamenting, bewailing, bemoaning, deploring

woebegone *syn* DOWNCAST, disconsolate, dispirited, dejected, depressed *rel* melancholy, lugubrious, doleful; forlorn, despondent; spiritless, listless, languid

woman *syn* FEMALE, lady

womanish *syn* FEMALE, womanlike, womanly, ladylike, feminine *ant* mannish

womanlike *syn* FEMALE, womanly, womanish, ladylike, feminine

womanly *syn* FEMALE, womanlike, ladylike, womanish, feminine *rel* mature, matured, grown-up, adult *ant* unwomanly, manly

wonder **1** • something that causes astonishment or admiration *syn* marvel, prodigy, miracle, phenomenon **2** • the complex emotion aroused by the incomprehensible and esp. the awe-inspiring *syn* wonderment, amazement, admiration *rel* awe, reverence, fear; astonishment, amazement; perplexity, puzzlement, bewilderment

wonderment *syn* WONDER, amazement, admiration

wont *syn* HABIT, habitude, practice, usage, custom, use *rel* way, manner, fashion, method

wonted *syn* USUAL, accustomed, customary, habitual *rel* familiar, common, ordinary; natural, regular, normal, typical

woo *syn* INVITE, court, solicit, bid *rel* allure, attract; lure, entice, seduce; blandish, coax, cajole, wheedle; pursue, chase, follow, trail

wooden *syn* STIFF, rigid, inflexible, tense, stark *rel* firm, hard, solid; heavy, weighty, ponderous; clumsy, awkward

word • a pronounceable sound or combination of sounds that expresses and symbolizes an idea *syn* vocable, term *rel* expression, idiom, phrase, locution

wordy • using or marked by the use of more words than are necessary to express the thought *syn* verbose, prolix, diffuse, redundant *rel* inflated, turgid, tumid, flatulent; bombastic, rhetorical; loquacious, garrulous, voluble, glib, talkative

work *n* **1** • strenuous activity that involves difficulty and effort and usually affords no pleasure *syn* labor, travail, toil, drudgery, grind *rel* exertion, effort, pains, trouble; task, duty, job, chore *ant* play **2** • a sustained activity that affords one a livelihood *syn* employment, occupation, calling, pursuit, business *rel* trade, craft, handicraft, art, profession **3** • something brought into being by the exertion of effort and the exercise of skill *syn* product, production, opus, artifact *rel* article, object, thing; accomplishment, achievement, performance

work *vb, syn* ACT, operate, function, behave, react

worker • one who earns his living by labor, esp. by manual labor *syn* workman, workingman, laborer, craftsman, handicraftsman, mechanic, artisan, hand, operative, roustabout *ant* idler

workingman *syn* WORKER, workman, laborer, craftsman, handicraftsman, mechanic, artisan, operative, hand, roustabout

workman *syn* WORKER, workingman, laborer, craftsman, handicraftsman, mechanic, artisan, operative, hand, roustabout

world *syn* EARTH, globe, planet

worldly **1** *syn* EARTHLY, mundane, terrestrial, earthy, sublunary *rel* temporal, profane, secular; material, physical, corporeal; carnal, fleshly, sensual **2** *syn* SOPHISTICATED, worldly-wise, blasé, disillusioned

worldly-wise *syn* SOPHISTICATED, worldly, blasé, disillusioned

worn *syn* HAGGARD, careworn, pinched, wasted, cadaverous *rel* exhausted, tired, wearied, fatigued, fagged, jaded; gaunt, scrawny, skinny, lean

worried • distressed or troubled usu. about something anticipated *syn* anxious, concerned, careful, solicitous *rel* apprehensive, afraid, fearful; troubled, distressed; harassed, harried

worry *vb* • to disturb one or destroy one's peace of mind by repeated or persistent tormenting attacks *syn* annoy, harass, harry, plague, pester, tease, tantalize *rel* disquiet, disturb, discompose, perturb, agitate, upset; torment, try, torture, afflict; oppress, persecute, wrong, aggrieve

worry *n, syn* CARE, anxiety, concern, solicitude *rel* apprehension, foreboding, misgiving, presentiment; anguish, woe, heartache, sorrow; uncertainty, doubt, mistrust

worship *n, syn* REVERENCE, adoration, veneration *rel* honor, homage, obeisance; respect, regard, esteem, admiration

worship *vb* **1** *syn* REVERE, adore, venerate, reverence *rel* exalt, magnify; respect, esteem **2** *syn* ADORE, idolize *rel* love, dote, like; admire, regard

worth • equivalence in good qualities expressed or implied *syn* value *rel* excellence, merit, virtue, perfection; use, usefulness, utility

wound • an injury to the body *syn* trauma, traumatism, lesion, bruise, contusion *rel* injury, hurt; burning, burn

wraith *syn* APPARITION, phantasm, phantom, ghost, spirit, specter, shade, revenant

wrangle *vb, syn* QUARREL, altercate, squabble, bicker, spat, tiff *rel* argue, dispute, debate, discuss; fight, contend

wrangle *n, syn* QUARREL, altercation, squabble, bickering, spat, tiff *rel* argument, dispute, controversy; discord, contention, dissension, conflict

wrap *syn* COVER, overspread, envelop, shroud, veil *rel* enclose; surround, encompass, environ, gird, girdle; cloak, mask, camouflage, disguise

wrath *syn* ANGER, rage, indignation, ire, fury *rel* resentment, dudgeon, offense; acrimony, acerbity, asperity

wrathful *syn* ANGRY, irate, indignant, mad, wroth, acrimonious *rel* infuriated, incensed, enraged

wreathe *syn* WIND, coil, curl, twist, twine, entwine

wreck *syn* RUIN, dilapidate *rel*

destroy, demolish, raze; injure, damage, impair

wrench · to turn or twist forcibly *syn* wrest, wring *rel* twist, bend, curve; force, compel, coerce, constrain; strain, sprain

wrest *syn* WRENCH, wring *rel* twist, bend, curve; usurp, arrogate, confiscate; extort, extract, elicit, educe; distort, contort, deform

wrestle · to struggle with an opponent at close quarters *syn* tussle, grapple, scuffle *rel* contend, fight, battle, war; resist, withstand, combat, oppose; strive, endeavor, essay, attempt; labor, toil, travail

wretched *syn* MISERABLE *rel* despondent, forlorn, hopeless, despairing; doleful, dolorous, melancholy; abject, sordid, mean; pitiable, piteous, pitiful

wring *syn* WRENCH, wrest *rel* press, squeeze; crush, mash, smash, bruise; extract, extort, elicit, educe; distort, contort, deform; twist, bend, curve

writhe · to twist or turn in physical or mental distress *syn* agonize, squirm *rel* twist, bend, curve; distort, contort, deform; wince, blench, flinch, recoil

wrong *n, syn* INJUSTICE, injury, grievance *rel* damage, injury, harm, mischief; violation, infraction, breach, trespass, transgression; hardship, difficulty

wrong *adj* **1** *syn* FALSE *rel* fallacious, sophistical, misleading, deceptive, delusive, delusory *ant* right **2** *syn* BAD, poor *rel* improper, unfit, inappropriate, unfitting, unsuitable, inapt, unhappy, infelicitous; awry, askew; amiss, astray

wrong *vb* · to inflict injury without just cause or in an outrageous manner *syn* oppress, persecute, aggrieve *rel* abuse, mistreat, maltreat, ill-treat, outrage; injure, harm, hurt

wroth *syn* ANGRY, irate, indignant, wrathful, acrimonious, mad

Y

yank *syn* JERK, snap, twitch *rel* pull, drag, tug; snatch, clutch, take; wrench, wrest

yap *syn* BARK, bay, howl, growl, snarl, yelp

yardstick *syn* STANDARD, criterion, gauge, touchstone

yarn *syn* STORY, tale, narrative, anecdote

yearn *syn* LONG, pine, hanker, hunger, thirst *rel* crave, desire, wish, want, covet; aspire, pant, aim

yeast *syn* FOAM, froth, spume, scum, lather, suds

yell *vb, syn* SHOUT, shriek, scream, screech, squeal, holler, whoop *rel* vociferate, roar, clamor, bellow, bawl

yell *n, syn* SHOUT, shriek, scream, screech, squeal, holler, whoop

yelp *syn* BARK, bay, howl, growl, snarl, yap

yield **1** *syn* BEAR, produce, turn out *rel* generate, engender, breed, propagate; create, invent; form, shape, make, fabricate, fashion **2** *syn* RELINQUISH, surrender, cede, abandon, leave, resign, waive *rel* forgo, forbear, abnegate, eschew, sacrifice; abdicate, renounce, resign **3** · to give way before a force that one cannot further resist *syn* submit, capitulate, succumb, relent, defer, bow, cave *rel* surrender, cede, waive, relinquish; concede, accord, award, grant

yoke *syn* COUPLE, pair, brace

yokel *syn* BOOR, bumpkin, hick, rube, clodhopper, clown, lout, churl

young *syn* OFFSPRING, progeny, issue, descendant, posterity

youth · the period in life when one passes from childhood to maturity *syn* adolescence, puberty, pubescence *ant* age

youthful · relating to or characteristic of one who is between childhood and adulthood *syn* juvenile, puerile, boyish, virgin, virginal, maiden *rel* immature, unmatured *ant* aged

Z

zeal *syn* PASSION, enthusiasm, fervor, ardor *rel* energy, force, power; zest, gusto, taste; earnestness, seriousness; intensity, vehemence, fierceness *ant* apathy

zealot *syn* ENTHUSIAST, fanatic, bigot *rel* partisan, sectary, adherent, disciple, follower; devotee, votary, addict

zenith *syn* SUMMIT, apogee, culmination, meridian, peak, pinnacle, climax, apex, acme *ant* nadir

zest *syn* TASTE, relish, gusto, palate *rel* enthusiasm, fervor, ardor, zeal, passion; spiritedness, spirit, high-spiritedness; enjoyment, delight, delectation, pleasure

zone *syn* AREA, belt, tract, region *rel* locality, district; section, sector, segment, part